PEARSON   ALWAYS LEARNING

Kathleen T. McWhorter

Reading and Writing about Contemporary Issues

Custom Edition

Taken from:
Reading and Writing about Contemporary Issues
Kathleen T. McWhorter

Cover Art: Image courtesy of Getty/Photodisc

Taken from:

Reading and Writing about Contemporary Issues
by Kathleen T. McWhorter
Copyright © 2015 by Pearson Education, Inc.
Published by Pearson Education, Inc.

Pearson Learning Solutions, 501 Boylston Street, Suite 900, Boston, MA 02116
A Pearson Education Company
www.pearsoned.com

Printed in the United States of America

13 14 15 16 17 V011 18 17 16 15 14

000200010271769738

RM/SK

ISBN 10: 1-269-33435-2
ISBN 13: 978-1-269-33435-8

Brief Contents

Detailed Contents

Preface

PURPOSE

Reading and Writing About Contemporary Issues offers an integrated approach to reading and writing using a handbook for reference and instruction followed by readings for analysis and writing. The nonfiction readings are organized into units that focus on contemporary issues. The readings—all of which are chosen to interest and motivate students—have been selected from books, textbooks, periodicals, popular magazines, newspapers, blogs, Web sites, and Internet sources. The objective is to provide stimulating readings on contemporary issues that enable students to build schema, apply reading and critical thinking skills, and respond to the readings through writing.

FOCUS

This custom book was prepared using the curriculum guidelines created by the state of North Carolina. The content corresponds to the instructional goals and competency standards outlined in "NCCS Developmental Reading and English (DRE) Curriculum." The book is designed to be used in all three courses—DRE 096, 097, and 098—and contains material that meets the competency standards of each. This design offers instructors the flexibility of selecting content that is appropriate to the course being taught and to the needs of particular students in a class. Students who need to review specific skills may do so independently by referring to unassigned chapters or sections.

MYSKILLSLAB

MySkillsLab, Pearson's online diagnostic/instructional program, has been customized to correspond to North Carolina's competency standards and can be used to supplement content in this custom book. Students lacking particular competencies may be referred to MySkillsLab for further instruction or practice.

CONTENT OVERVIEW

Reading and Writing About Contemporary Issues guides students in developing basic vocabulary and comprehension skills, as well as inferential and critical reading and thinking skills. Writing skills are cultivated through skill review, activities, and writing prompts that require students to write in response to the articles and essays they read. Each chapter in Part Two begins with an overview of a contemporary issue, providing context and background information, tips for reading, a rubric for writing essays, and a revision and proofreading checklist. Each selection is preceded by a section that provides context for the reading, prepares students for how to read it, and helps them make connections to prior learning. Each is followed by exercises and assignments that enable students to demonstrate mastery of critical thinking and reading skills and respond to the reading through writing and collaborative exercises.

The book is organized into three parts:

Part One: A Handbook for Reading and Writing in College, presents a concise introduction to reading and writing skills. Written in handbook format (1a, 1b, etc.), this part serves as a guide and reference tool for the skills students need to read and write about the readings in Part Two.

Part Two: Reading and Writing About Contemporary Issues, consists of four chapters, each containing three reading selections on a contemporary issue for reading and response.

Part Three: A Casebook for Critical Thinking: Global Warming, contains eight sources that offer a focused, in-depth examination of a single contemporary issue—global warming and climate change. It provides tips for reading about the issue, tips for synthesizing sources, and previewing exercises. Each selection is followed by critical thinking questions that encourage students to evaluate the reliability of the source, identify the author's main points, and think about and extend upon what they have read.

PART ONE: A HANDBOOK FOR READING AND WRITING IN COLLEGE

The handbook guides students in learning the reading, critical thinking, and writing skills essential for college success.

It contains the following features:

■ **Students learn an integrated approach to reading and writing.** Reading and writing are approached as complementary processes that are best learned together. A concise overview of both the reading and writing process is followed by integrated coverage of topics such as strategies for strengthening vocabulary for reading and writing, reading and writing paragraphs and essays, organizing information, thinking critically, recognizing and using organizational patterns, and writing a documented paper.

- **Students learn the skills to meet their course's competency standards.** The handbook contains instruction on all of the skills listed in DRE 096, 097, and 098 competency standards. Students enrolled in DRE 097 or 098 may use material appropriate for 096 as a refresher or to learn a specific skill in which they are deficient.
- **Students approach reading and writing as thinking.** Reading and writing are approached as thinking processes involving interaction with textual material and sorting, evaluating, and responding to its organization and content. The apparatus preceding and following each reading focuses, guides, and shapes the students' thought processes and encourages thoughtful and reasoned responses.
- **Students develop a wide range of critical reading and thinking skills.** Because simply understanding what a writer says is seldom sufficient in college courses, this handbook teaches students to examine, interpret, analyze, and evaluate ideas. Students learn to make inferences, consider an author's techniques, and identify his or her biases in relation to the message presented.
- **Students learn to write in response to what they read.** Most college reading assignments require written responses of some sort—essay exams, papers, or research projects. This book shows students how to analyze reading and writing assignments and teaches them the important skills of annotating, paraphrasing, summarizing, outlining, and mapping which enable and prepare them to write response papers.
- **Students can refer to Part One to get help answering questions.** The activities following each reading are parallel to the topics in Part One of the book, which presents a brief skill overview in a handbook format. For example, if students have difficulty answering inferential questions, students may refer to the section in Part One that explains how to make inferences.

PART TWO: READING AND WRITING ABOUT CONTEMPORARY ISSUES

Each chapter in Part Two begins with an introduction that focuses students' attention on the issue, provides context and background information, and discusses its importance and relevance to college coursework. Tips for reading about the issue are also provided, as well as rubrics for essay writing, revision, and proofreading. Each chapter in Part Two concludes with activities that provide further options for exploring the issue, collaborating with classmates, and writing in response to the issue.

Choice of Readings: Length and Lexile Levels

Non-fiction readings were chosen to be interesting and engaging and to serve as good models of writing. These readings are taken from a variety of sources including textbooks, books, articles, and essays. Each chapter contains three readings of differing lengths: the first is short and accessible (approximately 2–3 pages long), the second is more difficult and of moderate length (4–6 pages), and the third is the longest (8–10 pages).

Lexile levels are provided for all readings: the first reading meets the range for DRE 096, the second meets the range for DRE 097, and the third the range for DRE 098. The exercises and activities for each reading are designed for application of the competencies appropriate to the course level of the reading (i.e., the exercises and activities for the first reading will relate to the DRE 096 competencies).

Organization of the Apparatus

Pre-Reading

- **Source and Context.** This brief section introduces the reading, identifies its source, provokes the students' interest, and provides a framework or context for reading.
- **A Note on the Reading.** This section is intended to introduce and interest students in the reading and help them establish a purpose for reading.
- **Previewing the Reading.** Students are directed to preview the reading using the guidelines that are provided in Part One and to answer several questions based on their preview.
- **Using Prior Knowledge.** This brief section encourages students to draw connections between the topic of the reading and their own knowledge and experience.

During Reading

- **Reading Tip.** The reading tip is intended to help students approach and work through the reading. A different reading tip is offered for each reading. For example, a reading tip might suggest how to highlight to strengthen comprehension or how to write annotations to enhance critical thinking.
- **Reading Selection/Vocabulary Annotation.** Most reading selections contain some vocabulary words, specific to the topic, that are essential to the meaning of the selection. Often these are words that students are unlikely to know and cannot figure out from context. These words are highlighted, and their meanings are given as marginal annotations. Preferable to a list of words preceding the reading, this format allows students to check meanings on an as-needed basis, within the context of the selection. Annotations are also used occasionally to provide necessary background information that students may need to grasp concepts in a reading.

Post-Reading

Note: The following exercises form the basis for skill application in each reading. They are reworked for each reading so that exercises for the first reading focus more directly and exclusively on competencies for DRE 096, the second reading for 097, and the third reading for 098.

Understanding and Analyzing the Reading

- **Building Vocabulary.** The first part of this section focuses on vocabulary in context, while the second is concerned with word parts. Using words from the reading selection, exercises are structured to encourage students to expand their vocabulary and strengthen their word-analysis skills. A brief review of the meanings of prefixes, roots, and suffixes used in the exercise is provided for ease of reference and to create a meaningful learning situation.

- **Understanding the Thesis and Other Main Ideas.** This section helps students figure out the thesis of the reading and identify the main idea of selected paragraphs.

- **Identifying Details.** This section focuses on recognizing the relationship between main ideas and details, as well as distinguishing primary from secondary details. The format of questions within this section varies to expose students to a variety of thinking strategies.

- **Recognizing Methods of Organization and Signal Words and Phrases.** This part of the apparatus guides students in identifying the overall organizational pattern of the selection and in identifying signal words and phrases within the reading. Prompts are provided that serve as teaching tips or review strategies.

- **Reading and Thinking Visually.** Since textbooks and electronic media have become increasingly visual, students need to be able to read, interpret, and analyze visuals. This section guides students in responding to visuals that accompany text.

- **Figuring Out Implied Meanings.** The ability to think inferentially is expected of college students. This section guides students in making inferences based on information presented in the reading selection.

- **Thinking Critically: Analyzing the Author's Technique.** This section encourages students to examine the techniques and strategies writers use to convey their message. Skills include distinguishing fact from opinion, identifying the author's purpose, identifying tone, and analyzing figurative language.

- **Thinking Critically: Analyzing the Author's Message.** Topics explored in this section teach students to analyze ideas presented by the author. Students learn to examine bias, consider the reliability of data and evidence, and evaluate the quantity, relevance, and timeliness of information.

Writing in Response to a Reading

Questions in this section are intended to stimulate thought, provoke discussion, and serve as a springboard to writing about the reading.

- **Writing a Summary.** Since many students are proficient at literal recall of information but have difficulty condensing and synthesizing ideas, this section offers instruction and practice in summarizing. For the DRE 096 readings, students are guided in summarizing a paragraph using a fill-in-the-blank format; for the DRE 097 readings, students are given guidelines for writing a summary of several paragraphs; and for the DRE 098 readings, students are asked to summarize the entire reading.

- **Analyzing the Issue.** These open-ended questions encourage students to think critically and formulate an oral or written response to the issues raised in the reading.
- **Writing Paragraphs and Essays.** This section contains high stakes paragraph and/or essay writing assignments that give students practice in writing in response to what they read and the opportunity to demonstrate the competencies specified in their course. They ask students to explore issues related to the chapter theme and to examine applications of the issue to their lives and the world around them.
- **Working Collaboratively.** Collaborative activities are included for each reading selection. They are designed to engage the students and encourage them to learn from each other. The activities demand a variety of thinking skills including thinking deeply, thinking critically, thinking about reading strategies, and thinking personally.

Activities: Exploring Issues

Appearing at the end of each chapter, this section asks students to synthesize what they have learned about the issue addressed in the chapter, extend their critical reading and thinking skills, and explore the issue further through discussion and writing.

PART THREE: CASEBOOK ON GLOBAL WARMING AND CLIMATE CHANGE

The casebook contains eight readings that focus on the issue of global warming and climate change. The readings represent a variety of genres, including online news, blogs, infographics, essays, and textbooks. They offer a variety of perspectives on the issue of global warming and demonstrate the far-reaching effects of a single contemporary issue so that students see the social, financial, economic, and geographic implications. Each reading is followed by critical thinking questions. The casebook concludes with synthesis and integration writing prompts that draw together two or more of the readings from the casebook.

BOOK-SPECIFIC ANCILLARIES

Annotated Instructor's Edition

The Annotated Instructor's Edition is identical to the student text but includes all the answers printed directly on the pages where questions, exercises, or activities appear. (ISBN: 1-269-33426-3)

Online Instructor's Manual

The online Instructor's Manual provides strategies for teaching integrated reading and writing courses, a pacing guide, sample syllabi, examples of how to use readings at each level to teach course competencies, and strategies for teaching several skills within an activity. (ISBN: 0-321-96052-1)

MySkillsLab® MySkillsLab

Efficiently blending the market-leading and proven practice from MyWritingLab and MyReadingLab into a single application and learning path, MySkillsLabs offers a wealth of practice opportunity and extensive progress tracking for integrated reading-writing courses:

For more than half a decade, MySkillsLab has been the most widely used online learning application for the integrated reading-writing course across two- and four-year institutions. We have published case studies demonstrating how MySkillsLab (or, individually, MyReadingLab and MyWritingLab) consistently benefits students' mastery of key reading skills, reading comprehension, writing skills, and critical thinking.

Reading MySkillsLab improves students' mastery of 26 reading skills across four levels of difficulty via mastery-based skill practice, and improves students' reading levels with the Lexile® framework (www.Lexile.com) to measure both reader ability and text difficulty on the same scale and pair students with readings within their Lexile range.

Writing MySkillsLab offers skill remediation in grammar and punctuation, paragraph development, essay development, and research, and improves students' overall writing through automatic scoring by Pearson's proven Intelligent Essay Assessor (IEA).

North Carolina Course Redesign The North Carolina DRE course competencies have been built into MySkillsLab. In Course Settings, instructors can click on View and then choose the standards for the DRE course they are teaching. When they do this, the modules, objectives and standards they see will all be customized for that course. This allows instructors to choose what content they want to cover, see how their students are performing, and report on their progress.

ACKNOWLEDGEMENTS

I would like to express my gratitude to my reviewers for their excellent ideas, suggestions, and advice on the preparation and revision of this text:

Andrea Berta, University of Texas, El Paso; Frances Boffo, St. Phillip's College; Louise Brown, Salt Lake Community College; Lyam Christopher, Palm Beach State College;

Louise Clark, Austin Community College; Yanely Cordero, Miami Dade, Homestead; Cynthia Crable, Allegany College of Maryland; Kathy Daily, Tulsa Community College; Scott Empric, Housatonic Community College; Sally Gearhart, Santa Rosa Junior College; Brent Green, Salt Lake Community College; Elizabeth Hall, RCC; Eric Hibbison, J. Sargeant Reynolds Community College; Suzanne Hughes, Florida State College at Jacksonville; Patty Kunkel, Sante Fe College; James Landers, Community College of Philadelphia; Susan Monroe, Housatonic Community College; Mary Nielson, Dalton State College; Elizabeth A O'Scanlon, Santa Barbara Community College; Adalia Reyna, South Texas College; Jason Roberts, Salt Lake Community College; Amy Rule, Collin College; Mike Sfiropoilos, Palm Beach State College; Susan Swan, Glendale Community College; Stacey Synol, Glendale Community College; Jeanine Williams, The Community College of Baltimore County.

I wish to thank Gillian Cook, my development editor, for her creative vision of the project, her helpful suggestions, her careful editing, and her overall assistance in preparing and organizing the manuscript. I also thank Eric Stano, Editor–in–Chief of Developmental Education for his support of the project.

I also appreciate the valuable feedback and suggestions from the following North Carolina instructors, especially Karen Nelson and Kelly Terzaken, who shared their expertise as course redesign committee members:

Crystal Edmonds, Robeson Community College; Wes Anthony, Cleveland Community College; Caroline Helsabeck, Forsyth Technical Community College; Jennifer Johnson, Vance-Granville Community College; Dawn Langley, Piedmont Community College; Joy Lester, Forsyth Technical Community College; Nancy Marguardt, Gaston College; Barbara Marshall, Rockingham Community College; Emily Chevalier Moore, Wake Technical Community College; Arlene Neal, Catawba Valley Community College; Karen Nelson, Craven Community College; Gloria Rabun, Caldwell Community College; Kelly Terzaken, Coastal Carolina Community College, B. J. Zamora, Cleveland Community College.

Finally, I owe a debt of gratitude to Kathy Tyndall, recently retired department head of the Pre-Curriculum Department at Wake Technical Community College, for consulting with me about the project. She was very helpful in numerous ways: interpreting and explaining North Carolina's course redesign, advising about Part One content, previewing and evaluating reading selections, and drafting apparatus to accompany readings in Part Two. This book would not have been possible without her professional review and guidance.

A Handbook for Reading and Thinking in College

PART

ONE

1 Active Reading Strategies

What does it take to do well in college? In answer to this question, many college students are likely to say:

- "Knowing how to study."
- "You have to like the course."
- "Hard work!"
- "Background in the subject area."
- "A good teacher!"

Students seldom mention reading and writing as essential skills. In a sense, reading and writing are the hidden factors in college success. When you think of college, you think of attending classes and labs, completing assignments, studying for and taking exams, doing research in the library or on the Internet, and writing papers. A closer look at these activities, however, reveals that reading and writing are important parts of each.

Throughout this handbook, you will learn numerous ways to use reading and writing as tools for college success. You will improve your basic comprehension skills and learn to think critically about the materials you read. Thinking critically is essential to analyzing and evaluating not only college reading materials (textbooks, journal articles, research papers, and so on) but also materials that are written for a wider audience (newspapers, magazines, Web sites, and so on). You will also learn to write effective paragraphs and essays and use your skills to respond to articles, essays, and textbook excerpts that you read. Finally, you will also learn to handle High Stakes Writing Assignments that involve using sources to explain and support your own ideas.

1a   ACTIVE READING: THE KEY TO ACADEMIC SUCCESS

LEARNING OBJECTIVE 1
Learn to read actively.

Reading involves much more than moving your eyes across lines of print, more than recognizing words, and more than reading sentences. Reading is *thinking*. It is an active process of identifying important ideas and comparing, evaluating, and applying them.

Have you ever gone to a ball game and watched the fans? Most do not sit and watch passively. Instead, they direct the plays, criticize the calls, encourage the players, and reprimand the coach. They care enough to get actively involved in the game. Just like interested fans, active readers get involved. They question, challenge, and criticize, as well as understand. Table 1.1 contrasts the active strategies of successful readers with the passive strategies of less successful readers. Not all strategies will work for everyone. Experiment to discover those that work particularly well for you.

TABLE 1.1 ACTIVE VERSUS PASSIVE READING

ACTIVE READERS...	PASSIVE READERS...
Tailor their reading to suit each assignment.	Read all assignments the same way.
Analyze the purpose of an assignment.	Read an assignment because it was assigned.
Adjust their speed to suit their purpose.	Read everything at the same speed.
Question ideas in the assignment.	Accept whatever is in print as true.
Compare and connect textbook material with lecture content.	Study lecture notes and the textbook separately.
Skim headings to find out what an assignment is about before beginning to read.	Check the length of an assignment and then begin reading.
Make sure they understand what they are reading as they go along.	Read until the assignment is completed.
Read with pencil in hand, highlighting, jotting notes, and marking key vocabulary.	Read.
Develop personalized strategies that are particularly effective.	Follow routine, standard methods. Read all assignments the same way.
Look for the relevance of the assignment to their own lives.	Fixate on memorizing terms and definitions solely to pass the exam or get a good grade.
Engage with the contemporary issues under discussion with an open mind.	React emotionally to reading assignments without taking the time to carefully consider the author's key points.

Consider each of the following reading assignments. Discuss ways to get actively involved in each assignment.

1. Reading two poems by Maya Angelou for an American literature class.

   _____

   _____

2. Reading the procedures for your next chemistry lab.

   _____

3. Reading an article in *Time* magazine, or on the *Time* magazine Web site, assigned by your political science instructor in preparation for a class discussion.

   _____

PRE-READING STRATEGIES

1b   PREVIEW BEFORE YOU READ

LEARNING OBJECTIVE 2
Preview before reading.

Previewing is a means of familiarizing yourself with the content and organization of an assignment *before* you read it. Think of previewing as getting a "sneak preview" of what a chapter or reading will be about. You can then read the material more easily and more rapidly.

How to Preview Reading Assignments

Use the following tips to preview an entire source, such as a complete book or magazine.

- **Books, textbooks, and essay collections:** Look at the table of contents (found at the front of the book), noting the titles of chapters or essays. These will give you an overall sense of the topics covered.
- **Magazines:** Examine the table of contents, noting the sections and the articles included in the magazine. For instance, a weekly news magazine often has articles listed under the categories of Politics, Movies and Books, Business, and People.
- **Newspapers:** Flip through the paper, noting the largest (most important) headlines and the categories covered, such as Local News, International News, and Sports. If the newspaper has sections, flip through them to look for the materials in which you are most interested. Many newspapers feature different sections on different days. For example,

there may be a special Science section on Tuesday, a Fashion section on Friday, and an Entertainment section on Saturday.

- ■ **Web sites:** Use the navigation panel (usually found at the top, bottom, left, or right of the screen) to understand how the site is organized. Click on each section and look for large headlines or any other element that stands out on the screen.

After you have previewed the full source, use the following steps to become familiar with the content and organization of a chapter, essay, or article. Many Web sites are simply collections of articles and images, so these suggestions apply to Web sites, too.

1. **Read the title and subtitle.** The title indicates the topic of the article or chapter; the subtitle suggests the specific focus of, or approach to, the topic.

2. **Check the author and source of an article and essay.** This information may provide clues about the article's content or focus. If you are reading a collection of essays, each essay may provide a **head note** before the essay. Head notes often provide concise background information about the author and the article.

3. **Read the introduction or the first paragraph.** The introduction or first paragraph serves as a lead-in, establishing the overall subject and suggesting how it will be developed.

4. **Read each boldfaced (dark black print) or color heading.** Headings label the contents of each section and announce the major topics covered. If there are no headings, read the first sentence of several paragraphs on each page.

5. **Read the first sentence under each heading.** The first sentence often states the central thought of the section. If the first sentence seems introductory, read the last sentence; often this sentence states or restates the central thought. (For more on central thoughts, see Section 3a.)

6. **If headings are not provided, read the first sentence of each paragraph.** This sentence is often the topic sentence, which states the main idea of the paragraph. By reading first sentences, you will encounter most of the key ideas in the article.

7. **Note any typographical aids and information presented in list format.** Colored print, boldfaced font, and italics are often used to emphasize important terminology and definitions, distinguishing them from the rest of a passage. Material that is numbered 1, 2, 3; lettered a, b, c; or presented in list form is also of special importance.

8. **Read the first sentence of each item presented as a list.**

9. **Note any graphic aids.** Graphs, charts, photographs, and tables often suggest what is important. As part of your preview, read the captions of photographs and the legends on graphs, charts, and tables.

10. **Read the last paragraph or summary.** This provides a condensed view of the article or chapter, often outlining the key points.

11. **Read quickly any end-of-article or end-of-chapter material.** This material might include references, study questions, discussion questions, chapter

outlines, or vocabulary lists. If study questions are included, read them through quickly because they tell you what to look for in the chapter. If a vocabulary list is included, rapidly skim through it to identify the terms you will be learning as you read.

A section of a sociology textbook chapter discussing social class is reprinted here to illustrate how previewing is done. The portions to focus on when previewing are shaded. Read only those portions. After you have finished, test how well your previewing worked by completing Exercise 1-2, "What Did You Learn from Previewing?"

Issue: Wealth and Poverty

Consequences of Social Class

1   Does social class matter? And how! Think of each social class (whether upper-class, middle-class, working-class, or poor/underclass) as a broad **subculture** with distinct approaches to life, so significant that it affects our health, family life, education, religion, politics, and even our experiences with crime and the criminal justice system. Let's look at how social class affects our lives.

Physical Health

2   The principle is simple: As you go up the social-class ladder, health increases. As you go down the ladder, health decreases (Hout 2008). Age makes no difference. Infants born to the poor are more likely to die before their first birthday, and a larger percentage of poor people in their old age—whether 75 or 95—die each year than do the elderly who are wealthy.

3   How can social class have such dramatic effects? While there are many reasons, here are three. First, social class opens and closes doors to medical care. People with good incomes or with good medical insurance are able to choose their doctors and pay for whatever treatment and medications are prescribed. The poor, in contrast, don't have the money or insurance to afford this type of medical care.

4   A second reason is lifestyle, which is shaped by social class. People in the lower classes are more likely to smoke, eat a lot of fats, be overweight, abuse drugs and alcohol, get little exercise, and practice unsafe sex (Chin et al. 2000; Dolnick 2010). This, to understate the matter, does not improve people's health.

5   There is a third reason, too. Life is hard on the poor. The persistent stresses they face cause their bodies to wear out faster (Geronimus et al. 2010). The rich find life better. They have fewer problems and more resources to deal with the ones they have. This gives them a sense of control over their lives, a source of both physical and mental health.

Mental Health

6   Sociological research from as far back as the 1930s has found that the mental health of the lower classes is worse than that of the higher classes (Faris and Dunham 1939; Srole et al. 1978; Peltham 2009). Greater mental problems are part of the higher stress that accompanies poverty. Compared with middle- and upper-class

Americans, the poor have less job security and lower wages. They are more likely to divorce, to be the victims of crime, and to have more physical illnesses. Couple these conditions with bill collectors and the threat of eviction, and you can see how they can deal severe blows to people's emotional well-being.

7   People higher up the social class ladder experience stress in daily life, of course, but their stress is generally less, and their coping resources are greater. Not only can they afford vacations, psychiatrists, and counselors, but *their class position also gives them greater control over their lives, a key to good mental health.*

Family Life

8   Social class also makes a significant difference in our choice of spouse, our chances of getting divorced, and how we rear our children.

9   **Choice of Husband or Wife.** Members of the upper class place strong emphasis on family tradition. They stress the family's history, even a sense of purpose or destiny in life (Baltzell 1979; Aldrich 1989). Children of this class learn that their choice of husband or wife affects not just them, but the entire family, that it will have an impact on the "family line." These background expectations shrink the field of "eligible" marriage partners, making it narrower than it is for the children of any other social class. As a result, parents in this class play a strong role in their children's mate selection.

10   **Divorce.** The more difficult life of the lower social classes, especially the many tensions that come from insecure jobs and inadequate incomes, leads to higher marital friction and a greater likelihood of divorce. Consequently, children of the poor are more likely to grow up in broken homes.

11   **Child Rearing.** Lower-class parents focus more on getting their children to follow rules and obey authority, while middle-class parents focus more on developing their children's creative and leadership skills (Lareau and Weininger, 1977). Sociologists have traced this difference to the parents' occupations (Kohn 1977). Lower-class parents are closely supervised at work, and they anticipate that their children will have similar jobs. Consequently, they try to teach their children to defer to authority. Middle-class parents, in contrast, enjoy greater independence at work. Anticipating similar jobs for their children, they encourage them to be more creative. Out of these contrasting orientations arise different ways of disciplining children; lower-class parents are more likely to use physical punishment, while the middle classes rely more on verbal persuasion.

Education

12   Education increases as one goes up the social class ladder. It is not just the amount of education that changes, but also the type of education. Children of the upper class bypass public schools. They attend exclusive private schools where they are trained to take a commanding role in society. These schools teach upper-class values and prepare their students for prestigious universities (Beeghley 2008; Stevens 2009).

13   Keenly aware that private schools can be a key to upward social mobility, some upper-middle-class parents make every effort to get their children into the prestigious

preschools that feed into these exclusive prep schools. Although some preschools cost $23,000 a year, they have a waiting list (Rohwedder 2007). Not able to afford this kind of tuition, some parents hire tutors to train their 4-year-olds in test-taking skills so they can get into public kindergartens for gifted students. They even hire experts to teach these preschoolers to look adults in the eye while they are being interviewed for these limited positions (Banjo 2010). You can see how such parental involvement and resources make it more likely that children from the more privileged classes go to college—and graduate.

Religion

14   One area of social life that we might think would not be affected by social class is religion. ("People are just religious, or they are not. What does social class have to do with it?"). However, the classes tend to cluster in different religious denominations. Episcopalians, for example, are more likely to attract the middle and upper classes, while Baptists draw heavily from the lower classes. Patterns of worship also follow class lines: The lower classes are attracted to more expressive worship services and louder music, while the middle and upper classes prefer more "subdued" worship.

This young woman is being "introduced" to society at a debutante ball in Laredo, Texas. Like you, she has learned from her parents, peers, and education a view of where she belongs in life. How do you think her view is different from yours? (Courtesy of Bob Daemmrich/The Image Works.)

Politics

15   The rich and poor walk different political paths. The higher that people are on the social class ladder, the more likely they are to vote for Republicans (Hout 2008). In contrast, most members of the working class believe that the government should intervene in the economy to provide jobs and to make citizens financially secure. They are more likely to vote for Democrats. Although the working class is more liberal on *economic issues* (policies that increase government spending), it is more conservative on *social issues* (such as opposing the Equal Rights Amendment) (Houtman 1995; Hout 2008). People toward the bottom of the class structure are also less likely to be politically active—to campaign for candidates or even to vote (Gilbert 2003; Beeghley 2008).

Crime and Criminal Justice

16   If justice is supposed to be blind, it certainly is not when it comes to one's chances of being arrested (Henslin 2012). Social classes commit different types of crime. The **white-collar crimes** of the more privi-

leged classes are more likely to be dealt with outside the criminal justice system, while the police and courts deal with the street crimes of the lower classes. One consequence of this class standard is that members of the lower classes are more likely to be in prison, on probation, or on parole. In addition, since those who commit street crimes tend to do so in or near their own neighborhoods, the lower classes are more likely to be robbed, burglarized, or murdered.

—Adapted from Henslin, *Sociology: A Down-to Earth Approach*, pp. 261–264

EXERCISE 1-2 WHAT DID YOU LEARN FROM PREVIEWING?

Without referring to the passage, answer each of the following true/false questions.

_____ 1. Members of the lower classes are more likely to be in prison.

_____ 2. The higher your class, the more education you are likely to have.

_____ 3. Marital friction and divorce are more common among the upper classes than the lower classes.

_____ 4. Lower-class parents tend to encourage their children's creativity.

_____ 5. The young woman in the photograph is likely a member of the upper class.

You probably were able to answer all (or most) of the questions correctly. Previewing, then, does provide you with a great deal of information. If you were to return to the passage from the textbook and read the entire section, you would find it easier to do than if you hadn't previewed it.

Why Previewing Is Effective

Pre-reading is effective for several reasons:

- **Previewing helps you make decisions about how you will approach the material.** On the basis of what you discover about the selection's organization and content, you can select the reading and study strategies that will be most effective.
- **Previewing puts your mind in gear and helps you start thinking about the subject.**
- **Previewing gives you a mental outline of the content.** It enables you to see how ideas are connected. And because you know where the author is headed, your reading will be easier than if you had not pre-read. However, previewing is never a substitute for careful, thorough reading.

Assume you are taking a health course. Your instructor has assigned the following excerpt, "A Blueprint for Better Nutrition," from a chapter in a health textbook titled Choosing Health. *Preview, but do not read, the article using the procedure described on pp. 4–6. When you have finished, answer the questions that follow.*

Issue: Health and Health Care

A Blueprint for Better Nutrition
April Lynch, Barry Elmore, and Tanya Morgan

1   The Dietary Guidelines for Americans is a set of nine strategies for maintaining or improving your health. The following is a brief summary of each. For a complete listing of dietary guidelines, visit www.health.gov/dietaryguidelines.

Obtain Adequate Nutrients Within Calorie Needs

2   Be careful that you don't take in more calories than you need each day. Choosing fresh fruits, vegetables, whole grains, and low-fat or fat-free dairy products will help you stay within your calorie allowance. That's because these foods are *nutrient-dense*, meaning they provide generous amounts of vitamins, minerals, fiber, and other health-producing substances but contain relatively few calories.

Focus on Healthful Foods

3   Build meals and vegetables around four food groups: fruits, vegetables, whole grains, and low-fat or fat-free dairy products. These foods are low in saturated and *trans* fats, cholesterol, added sugars, and salt, but rich in essential nutrients as well as fiber and phytochemicals. They are also lower in calories, so choosing them will help you stay within your calorie allowance each day.

Watch Your Intake of Fats

4   The type and amount of fat you consume can make a big difference to the health of your heart. To reduce your risk of heart disease, keep your intake of saturated and *trans* fats as low as possible. Replace these with unsaturated fats from fish, nuts, and plant oils. When selecting red meat, poultry, and dairy products, make choices that are lean, low-fat, or fat-free. Also keep your total fat intake between 20% and 35% of your total calorie intake.

Choose Carbohydrates Wisely

5   Fresh fruits, vegetables, and whole grains promote health and reduce your risk of chronic disease. Eat more of these and less of foods containing refined carbohydrates, such as pastries, white bread, white rice, crackers, and candies. Also avoid sweetened beverages, from soft drinks to flavored waters, as these contain huge

amounts of simple sugars. Drink more low-fat or non-fat milk. It contains many essential nutrients. If you're not sure whether a food or beverage has added sweeteners, look for these terms on the food label: sugars (brown, invert, raw, beet, or cane), corn sweetener, corn syrup, high fructose corn syrup, fruit juice concentrates, honey, malt syrup, molasses, glucose, fructose, maltose, sucrose, lactose, and dextrose.

Maintain Proper Levels of Sodium and Potassium

6   If you're like most Americans, you consume substantially more salt (sodium chloride) than you need. On average, as sodium intake rises, so does blood pressure, so by reducing your sodium intake, you help keep your blood pressure down. Keeping your blood pressure in the normal range, approximately 120 over 80 millimeters of mercury (120/80 mm Hg), reduces your risk of heart disease and stroke. Surprisingly, hiding the salt shaker is not the most important strategy for controlling your sodium intake. That's because most of us get far more sodium every day from the processed foods we eat. So read the Nutrition Facts panel on food labels (Figure 1-1) to check the amount of sodium in the food. Less than 140 milligrams (mg) or 5% of the Daily Value is low in salt. At the same time, make sure you're getting enough potassium, which helps blunt the effects of sodium on blood pressure. The best potassium sources are fruits and vegetables, especially apricots, bananas, broccoli, cantaloupe, carrots, dates, mushrooms, oranges, potatoes, prunes, raisins, spinach, sweet potato, watermelon, and winter squash. Other good potassium sources are milk products, legumes, peanuts, and almonds.

Manage Your Body Weight

7   Achieve and maintain a healthful body weight by balancing the calories you consume in foods and beverages with the calories you burn in physical activity.

Engage in Regular Physical Activity

8   Regular physical activity improves physical fitness, promotes psychological well-being, and helps manage weight. It also reduces the risk of many chronic diseases. Adults should be moderately actively for at least 30 minutes most days of the week.

FIGURE 1-1 READ FOOD LABELS WISELY
When reading a Nutrition Facts panel, note the serving size, calories (and calories from fat), and the nutrients contained per serving.

Use Alcohol Moderately or Not at All

9   Alcoholic beverages supply 7 calories per gram—that's 150 calories for a 12-ounce beer! No wonder drinking a lot of alcohol can make it hard to maintain a healthy weight. Moderate alcohol intake—defined as up to one drink per day for women and up to two drinks per day for men—is associated with mortality reduction in middle-aged and older adults. But among younger people, alcohol consumption provides little, if any, health benefit, and it is harmful for women who are or may become pregnant or are breastfeeding, anyone taking medications, people with certain medical conditions, and anyone who will be driving or using machinery.

Be Food Safe

10   Every year about 76 million people in the U.S. experience food borne illness. Simple measures such as washing your hands and food-contact surfaces; separating raw, cooked, and ready-to-eat foods while shopping, preparing, or storing them; cooking foods to the proper temperature; and keeping cold foods cold will reduce your risk of food borne illness.

—Adapted from Lynch/Elmore/Morgan, *Choosing Health,* pp. 77–78

1. What is the overall subject of this article?

   _____

2. What is the common name for sodium chloride?

   _____

3. List three benefits of physical activity.

   _____

   _____

4. Two of the four food groups are whole grains and fruits. What are the other two?

   _____

5. On a scale of 1 to 5 (1 = easy, 5 = very difficult), how difficult do you expect the article to be?

   _____

   _____

1c   ACTIVATING PRIOR KNOWLEDGE

LEARNING OBJECTIVE 3
Activate your prior knowledge.

After previewing your assignment, you should take a moment to think about what you already know about the topic. Whatever the topic, you probably know *something* about it: This is your **prior knowledge**. For example, a student was asked to read an article titled "Growing Urban Problems" for a government class. His first thought was that he knew very little about urban problems because he lived in a rural area. But when he thought of a recent trip to a nearby city, he remembered seeing the homeless people and crowded conditions. This recollection helped him remember reading about drug problems, drive-by shootings, and muggings.

Activating your prior knowledge aids your reading in three ways. First, it makes reading easier because you have already thought about the topic. Second, the material is easier to remember because you can connect the new information with what you already know. Third, topics become more interesting if you can link them to your own experiences. Here are some techniques to help you activate your background knowledge.

- **Ask questions and try to answer them.** If a chapter in your biology textbook titled "Human Diseases" contains headings such as "Infectious diseases," "Cancer," and "Vascular diseases," you might ask and try to answer such questions as the following: What kinds of infectious diseases have I seen? What causes them? What do I know about preventing cancer and other diseases?

- **Draw on your own experience.** If a chapter in your business textbook is titled "Advertising: Its Purpose and Design," you might think of several ads you have seen and analyze the images used in each, as well as the purpose of each ad.

- **Brainstorm.** Write down everything that comes to mind about the topic. Suppose you're about to read a chapter in your psychology textbook on domestic violence. You might list types of violence—child abuse, spousal abuse, and so on. You might write questions such as "What causes child abuse?" and "How can it be prevented?" Alternatively, you might list incidents of domestic violence you have heard or read about. Any of these approaches will help to make the topic interesting and relevant.

EXERCISE 1-4 ACTIVATING PRIOR KNOWLEDGE

Use one of the three strategies listed above to discover what you already know about dieting and exercise.

DURING-READING STRATEGIES

1d   HIGHLIGHTING TO STRENGTHEN READING AND RECALL

LEARNING OBJECTIVE 4
Highlight as you read.

Many students find that reading with a pen or a highlighter in their hand is an excellent way to continue their active-reading mindset. Highlighting key information in a reading helps you focus your attention, sort ideas, and create a document that helps you review the material at a later date. Consider the following passages. One is highlighted; the other is not.

> The major challenge facing single people through the ages has been building a satisfying life in a society highly geared toward marriage. Until recently, the general tendency in U.S. popular culture has been to portray singles as belonging in one of two stereotypical groups. On the one side is the "swinging single"—the partygoer who is carefree, uncommitted, sexually adventuresome, and the subject of envy by married friends. Poles apart from this image is the "lonely loser"—the unhappy, frustrated, depressed single who lives alone and survives on TV dinners, a fate few people would envy.

> The major challenge facing single people through the ages has been building a satisfying life in a society highly geared toward marriage. Until recently, the general tendency in U.S. popular culture has been to portray singles as belonging in one of two stereotypical groups. On the one side is the "swinging single"—the partygoer who is carefree, uncommitted, sexually adventuresome, and the subject of envy by married friends. Poles apart from this image is the "lonely loser"—the unhappy, frustrated, depressed single who lives alone and survives on TV dinners, a fate few people would envy.

> —Mary Ann Schwartz and BarBara Marliene Scott, *Marriages and Families*, p. 212

Which version would you prefer to study and why? You likely prefer the highlighted version, because it highlights the selection's key points and aids review.

To highlight effectively, read the selection completely through first, then go back and highlight during your second reading. Do not highlight too much or too little. If you highlight too much, you have not selected the reading's main points. If you highlight too little, you will miss key points during your review. Avoid highlighting complete sentences. Highlight only enough so that your highlighting makes sense when you read it. (For more information on highlighting, see section 7b.)

Highlighting is beneficial for several reasons:

- **Highlighting** forces you to sift through what you have read to identify important information. This sifting or sorting helps you weigh and evaluate what you read.
- **Highlighting** keeps you physically active while you read and improves concentration.
- **Highlighting** can help you discover the organization of facts and ideas as well as their connections and relationships.
- **Highlighting** helps you determine whether you have understood a passage you just read. If you don't know what to highlight, you don't understand it.

A word of caution: Do not assume that what is highlighted is learned. You must process the information by organizing it, expressing it in your own words, and testing yourself periodically.

Two additional active reading strategies are *annotating* (using a pen to underline key phrases, make notes in the margin, and so on) and *summarizing* (writing a brief summary of the reading's key points). Both of these strategies use writing to increase recall and engagement with the material. We discuss annotation in detail in section 7c and summarizing in section 7g.

POST-READING STRATEGIES

1e   CHECKING YOUR COMPREHENSION

LEARNING OBJECTIVE 5
Check your comprehension.

What happens when you read material you can understand easily? Does it seem that everything "clicks"? Do ideas seem to fit together and make sense? Is that "click" noticeably absent at other times?

Table 1.2 lists and compares common signals to assist you in checking your comprehension. Not all the signals appear at the same time, and not all the signals work for everyone. But becoming aware of these positive and negative signals will help you gain more control over your reading.

TABLE 1.2 COMPREHENSION SIGNALS

POSITIVE SIGNALS	NEGATIVE SIGNALS
You feel comfortable and have some knowledge about the topic.	The topic is unfamiliar, yet the author assumes you understand it.
You recognize most words or can figure them out from context.	Many words are unfamiliar.
You can express the main ideas in your own words.	You must reread the main ideas and use the author's language to explain them.
You understand why the material was assigned.	You do not know why the material was assigned and cannot explain why it is important.
You read at a regular, comfortable pace.	You often slow down or reread.
You are able to make connections between ideas.	You are unable to detect relationships; the organization is not apparent.
You are able to see where the author is leading.	You feel as if you are struggling to stay with the author and are unable to predict what will follow.
You understand what is important.	Nothing (or everything) seems important.
You read calmly and try to assess the author's points without becoming too emotionally involved.	When you encounter a controversial topic, you close your mind to alternative viewpoints or opinions.

EXERCISE 1-5 CHECKING YOUR COMPREHENSION

Read the article titled "Consequences of Social Class" that appears on page 6. Be alert for positive and negative comprehension signals as you read. After reading the article, answer the following questions.

1. On a scale of 1 to 5 (1 = very poor, 5 = excellent), how would you rate your overall comprehension? _____

2. What positive signals did you sense? List them below.

   _____

   _____

   _____

3. What negative signals did you experience, if any? List them below.

   _____

   _____

   _____

4. In which sections was your comprehension strongest? List the paragraph numbers. _____

5. Did you feel at any time that you had lost, or were about to lose, comprehension? If so, go back to that part now. What made it difficult to read?

   _____

   _____

1f   STRENGTHENING YOUR COMPREHENSION

LEARNING OBJECTIVE 6

Strengthen your comprehension.

When you have finished reading, don't just close the book. Stop and assess how well you understood what you read. Test yourself. Take a heading and turn it in to question. Cover up the text following it and see if you can answer your questions. For example, for a heading "Effects of Head Trauma" convert it to the question "What are the effects of head trauma?" and then answer your question mentally or by writing. Then check your answer by looking at the text itself. This self-testing process will also help you remember more of what you read because you are reviewing what you just read.

If you are not satisfied with your self-test, or if you experienced some or all of the negative signals mentioned in Table 1.2, be sure to take action to strengthen your comprehension. Chapter 4 presents basic comprehension strategies for reading paragraphs, including identifying main ideas, details, and signal words. Chapter 6 discusses how to read textbooks, essays, and longer works. In these chapters you strengthen your comprehension by making text to text connections. Using context clues to figure out words you don't know is covered in Chapter 2. Be sure to consult these chapters. Here are some immediate things you can do when you realize you need to strengthen your comprehension.

1. **Analyze the time and place in which you are reading.** If you've been reading or studying for several hours, mental fatigue may be the source of the problem. If you are reading in a place with distractions or interruptions, you might not be able to concentrate on what you're reading.

2. **Rephrase each paragraph in your own words.** You might need to approach complicated material sentence by sentence, expressing each sentence in your own words.

3. **Read aloud sentences or sections that are particularly difficult.** Reading out loud sometimes makes complicated material easier to understand.

4. **Reread difficult or complicated sections.** At times, several readings are appropriate and necessary.

5. **Slow down your reading rate.** On occasion, simply reading more slowly and carefully will provide you with the needed boost in comprehension.

6. **Write questions next to headings.** Refer to your questions frequently and jot down or underline answers in the reading selection.

7. **Write a brief outline of major points.** This will help you see the overall organization and progression of ideas. (For more on outlining, see Section 7e.)

8. **Annotate (make notes) in the margins.** Explain or rephrase difficult or complicated ideas or sections. (For more on annotating, see section 7c).

9. **Determine whether you lack prior knowledge.** Comprehension is difficult, and at times impossible, if you lack essential information that the writer assumes you have. Suppose you are reading a political science textbook in which the author describes implications of the balance of power in the Third World. If you do not understand the concept of balance of power, your comprehension will break down. When you lack background information, take immediate steps to correct the problem:

   ■ Consult other sections of your text, using the glossary and index.

   ■ Obtain a more basic text that reviews fundamental principles and concepts.

   ■ Consult reference materials (encyclopedias, subject or biographical dictionaries, reliable Web sources).

   ■ Ask your instructor to recommend additional sources, guidebooks, or review texts.

SUMMARY OF LEARNING OBJECTIVES

Objective 1 Learn to read actively.	**Active reading** is the process of identifying important ideas in a reading selection and comparing, evaluating, and applying them. **Active readers** determine the purpose of a reading assignment and then adjust their speed to suit the purpose.
Objective 2 Preview before reading.	**Previewing** is a means of familiarizing yourself with the content and organization of an assignment *before* you read it. Previewing involves using the title and subtitle, headings, the introductory and concluding paragraphs, key sentences, and typographical aids to get a "sneak preview" of what a reading selection will be about.
Objective 3 Activate your prior knowledge.	**Your prior knowledge** is what you already know about the topic you are reading about. Effective readers connect their existing knowledge to what they read.
Objective 4 Highlight as you read.	**Highlighting** helps focus your attention, sort ideas, and make review easier and faster. **To highlight effectively**, read the selection first, then go back and highlight key points.
Objective 5 Check your comprehension.	**Active readers use comprehension signals** (*such as the level of the vocabulary and their ability to make connections among ideas*) while they read to determine how well they understand the material. If they experience a low level of comprehension, they adjust their reading strategy.
Objective 6 Strengthen your comprehension.	To **strengthen comprehension,** use self-testing to be sure you understood what you just read. Also, be sure your reading area is free of distractions. Rephrase paragraphs and ideas in your own words, and reread complicated sections. Decrease your reading rate or read sentences aloud. Use questions, outlines, highlighting, and margin notes to engage with the reading. Assess your background knowledge and consult other sources if necessary.

2 The Writing Process

LEARNING OBJECTIVES

1 Understand the writing process

2 Use technology appropriately

Prewriting Strategies

3 Consider your audience, purpose, tone, and point of view

4 Use prewriting to generate ideas for your writing

5 Use prewriting to organize your ideas

Drafting Strategies

6 Write an effective paragraph

7 Understand the structure of an effective essay

8 Write a first draft of your essay

Revision Strategies

9 Revise a draft

10 Proofread for correctness

Like any other skill (such as playing basketball, accounting, or cooking), reading and writing require both instruction and practice. In Chapter 1, we provided an overview of the active reading process. In this chapter, we discuss the writing process. Reading and writing go hand in hand: Readers read what writers have written, and writers write for readers.

Writing involves much more than sitting down at your computer and starting to type. It involves reading about others' ideas, generating and organizing your own ideas, and expressing your ideas in sentence, paragraph, or essay form. Writing is a *process*; it involves prewriting, drafting, revising and editing/proofreading your work. Following the sample student essay in this chapter (beginning on page 37) will give you a good sense of what writing involves. The final version of this essay appears in Chapter 11, p. 313.

2a   UNDERSTANDING THE WRITING PROCESS

LEARNING OBJECTIVE 1
Understand the writing process.

Writing, like many other skills, is not a single-step process. Think of the game of football, for instance. Football players spend a great deal of time planning and developing offensive and defensive strategies, trying out new plays, improving existing plays, training, and practicing. Writing involves similar planning and preparation. It also involves testing ideas and working out the best way to express them. Writers often explore how their ideas might "play out" in several ways before settling upon one plan of action.

Writing should always be an expression of your own ideas. Be sure that you do not use ideas or wording of other authors without giving them credit through a source citation in your essay or paragraph. Using the ideas of others without giving proper acknowledgment is known as **plagiarism,** and it can result in academic penalties such as failing grades or even academic dismissal. For a more detailed explanation of plagiarism, see Chapter 10, p. 291.

All writing involves five basic steps, as outlined in Table 2.1.

TABLE 2.1 STEPS IN THE WRITING PROCESS

STEP	DESCRIPTION
1. Prewriting	Finding ideas to write about and discovering ways to arrange your ideas logically.
2. Drafting	Expressing your ideas in sentence, paragraph, or essay form.
3. Revising	Rethinking your ideas and finding ways to make your writing clearer, more complete, and more interesting. Revising involves changing, adding, deleting, and rearranging your ideas and words to improve your writing.
5. Editing/Proofreading	Checking for errors in spelling, punctuation, capitalization, and grammar.

2b   USING TECHNOLOGY FOR WRITING

LEARNING OBJECTIVE 2
Use technology effectively.

Technology has much to offer writers for each step in the writing process. Technology can help you produce a well-written correct paragraph or essay, save you time, and allow you to spend more time with the creative task of writing and less time on the mechanical details of presenting your work in a readable, visually appealing form.

Choose an Appropriate Word Processing Program

If you need assistance choosing an appropriate word processing program, check with your college's computer lab. Also pay attention to any special requests or preferences your instructor may have.

Use Technology to Generate Ideas

The methods suggested for prewriting that follow (section 2c, p. 22) can be done on the computer, often more easily than on paper. You might try dimming your computer screen so you are not distracted by what you are typing, and do not become concerned with correctness or typing errors. And, after you have finished, usable ideas can be easily moved and rearranged.

You might also use social media such as *Facebook* or blogs to generate ideas and share them with others. Think of your page as a type of journal in which you record and exchange ideas. Your posts may feel conversational, but they will work in helping you share and explore ideas and responses. Because you can post different types of media, you might include photos and videos that stimulate your thinking, spur your creativity, and help you generate ideas. Be sure to check your privacy settings so access is restricted, and never post anything on the site that you would not want everyone to see.

Using Technology for Drafting

Drafting on your computer is faster and more efficient than on paper. When drafting on a computer be sure to

- **Format your paper before you begin,** considering font, spacing, margins, page numbering, and so forth. Check to be sure you are using a format preferred by your instructor or specified by MLA or APA style (see Ch. 10).
- **Name and store each document so you can easily retrieve it.**
- **Create a new file for each new draft.** Date each draft so you can move back and forth between them. You may want to go back to an earlier draft to include things from it.
- **Save your work frequently** and every time you leave your computer so you do not lose material.
- **Use the Internet to exchange drafts with classmates.**

Using Technology for Revision and Editing

As you begin revising, be sure to save each version as a separate file and save your work frequently. Many course management systems such as *Blackboard* make it easy to share your work with your classmates for peer review. Check with your instructor or computer lab for more information.

The following box contains tips that will help you use the features in your word processing program for editing and proofreading.

Word Processing Features for Writers

- **Use a spell-checker to identify misspellings and typing mistakes**. However, do **not** rely on the program to catch all the errors. The spell-checker will not flag words that you have misused (*to*, instead of *two*, for example). It may also suggest incorrect alternatives, so be sure to evaluate each suggested alternative.
- **Use a grammar and style checker** to help you identify incorrect grammar or punctuation, repeated words, and awkward or wordy sentences. Do **not** rely on the checker to spot all your errors, and realize that the checker may flag things that are correct.
- **Use the Find command to locate and correct common problems or errors**, such as words commonly misspelled, overused words, or wordy phrases.

PREWRITING STRATEGIES

Prewriting is an important first step in the writing process. Many students mistakenly believe they can just sit down at a computer and start writing a paragraph or essay. Writing requires thinking, planning, and organizing. Although these strategies take time, they pay off in the long run by saving you time and enabling you to produce a more effective piece of writing.

2c   PREWRITING: THINKING ABOUT AUDIENCE, PURPOSE, TONE, AND POINT OF VIEW

LEARNING OBJECTIVE 3
Consider your audience, purpose, tone, and point of view.

Consider Your Audience

Considering your audience is essential to good writing. When you write, ask yourself: Who will be reading what I write? How should I express myself so that my readers will understand what I write?

What is appropriate for one audience may be inappropriate for another. For example, if you were writing about social issues that affect life in your city, you would write one way to a close friend and another way to a member of the city council. When writing for a friend, you might use casual, informal language. When writing for the city council, you would use more formal language. Study the following e-mails. What differences do you notice?

E-mail to a Friend

From: Moreno, Jasmin
Sent: Friday, 15 February 2013 2:38 PM
To: Delgado, Marie
Subject: I'm going insane!!!!!!!!!!!!!

You asked how I am—I am going insane about graffiti all over the neighbourhood. My landlord tries his best—he just painted the side of my building last week, and this morning when I left it there it was again—filled with tags from the local gangs. And not only that, the taggers painted some really nasty stuff that I don't want my kids to see. The landlord tried putting up a fence, they climb over it. He tried putting up a camera, they broke it. It's like it's a game for them. Well I am fed up with it and I am going to do something about it. Do you think a neighbourhood watch would work?? Any other ideas?

E-mail to a Member of the City Council

From: Moreno, Jasmine
Sent: Friday, 15 February 2013 4:45 PM
To: Cervantes, Isabella
Subject: Neighbourhood Graffiti

Dear Councillor Cervantes,

I think you would agree that we are experiencing a serious problem with graffiti in the third ward, where I live with my family. I have heard you speak about these problems, and I am wondering if I can help in any way. I agree with you: Tagging shows a lack of respect for people and property, and I don't want my children to think tagging is acceptable. I am willing to start a neighbourhood watch to try to discourage taggers, and I am also open to any suggestions you may have about how to tackle this problem.

Yours sincerely,

Jasmine Moreno

While the e-mail to the friend is casual, the note to the councilwoman is businesslike. The writer included details and described her feelings when telling her friend about the graffiti problem, but she focused on finding a solution to the problem in her note to the city councilwoman.

Writers make many decisions based on the audience they have in mind. As you write, consider the following:

- **How many and what kinds of details are necessary?**
- **What format is appropriate** (paragraph, essay, e-mail, etc.)?
- **What kinds of words should you use** (simple, technical, emotional, etc.)?
- **What tone should you use** (friendly, knowledgeable, formal, etc.)?

Here are four key questions you can ask to assess and write for your audience:

- Who is your audience and what is your relationship with your audience?
- How is your audience likely to respond to your message?
- What does your audience already know about your topic?
- What does your audience need to know to understand your point?

Write for a Purpose

When you call a friend on the phone, you have a reason for calling, even if it is just to stay in touch. When you ask a question in class, you have a purpose for asking. When you describe to a friend an incident you were involved in, you are relating the story to make a point or share an experience. These examples demonstrate that you use spoken communication to achieve specific purposes.

Good writing must also achieve your *intended purpose*. If you write a paragraph on how to change a flat tire, your reader should be able to change a flat tire after reading the paragraph. Likewise, if your purpose is to describe the sun rising over a misty mountaintop, your reader should be able to visualize the scene. If your purpose is to argue that the legal age for drinking alcohol should be 25, your reader should be able to follow your reasoning, even if he or she is not won over to your view.

EXERCISE 2-1 WRITING A PARAGRAPH

Think of a public event you recently attended, such as a concert or film showing. Complete two of the following activities. Make sure you adjust your writing to suit each audience.

1. Write a paragraph describing the event to a friend.

2. Write a paragraph describing the event to your English instructor.

3. Write a paragraph describing the event as the movie or music critic for your local newspaper.

Consider Your Tone

Tone refers to how you "sound" or come across to your reader. You might sound angry, or sympathetic, or excited, for instance. Tone reveals your attitudes or feelings toward the subject you are writing about. Be sure to choose a tone that is appropriate for your audience and your purpose. If your audience is a serious group of people, for example, your tone should appeal to serious-minded people. A tone that is sarcastic or cynical might not appeal to them, so you probably do not want to "sound" angry when trying to convince your readers to agree with you; a serious, thoughtful tone might be more effective. For more about tone, see Chapters 8 and 9.

Consider Your Point of View

Your **point of view** is the perspective from which you are writing. Writing in the first person (*I, me*) allows the writer to speak as him or herself directly to the reader. Writing in the second person (*you*), is more formal, but addresses the reader directly. The third person (*he, she, they, James,* etc.) is the most formal and is most commonly used in academic writing. In choosing a point of view, consider both your audience and purpose. What point of view will accomplish your purpose and suit your audience?

2d   PREWRITING: GENERATING IDEAS

LEARNING OBJECTIVE 4
Generate ideas for your writing.

Before you can write about a topic, you must generate ideas to write about. Three techniques are helpful in collecting ideas: *freewriting, brainstorming,* and *diagramming.*

Freewriting

Freewriting is writing nonstop about a topic for a specified period of time. In freewriting, you write whatever comes into your mind without worrying about punctuation, spelling, and grammatical correctness. After you have finished, you go back through your writing and pick out ideas that you might be able to use.

Here is a sample freewrite on the topic of climate change:

> It's so hard to sort out the facts about climate change. On the one hand it seems like the weather has been crazy. I'm 22 years old and I never remember summers being so hot when I was a kid. And the humidity is so bad too, it seems like summer now starts in April and goes straight

through to December. We've had hurricanes, tornadoes, and unbelievable rainfall, plus high winds that have brought trees crashing down. And I keep reading that climate change is responsible for this extreme weather. But on the other hand I know that a lot of people don't believe that climate change is really happening. From what I can figure out, they think "climate change" is not really happening and that all the talk of "global warming" is greatly exaggerated. It's so hard to know who to believe, everyone seems to have an agenda and it seems like nobody reports the facts. Even when facts and figures are reported, can I really trust them? Because as soon as they come out, people start disputing them.

Brainstorming

Brainstorming involves making a list of everything you can think of that is associated with your topic. When you brainstorm, try to stretch your imagination and think of everything related to your topic: facts, ideas, examples, questions, and feelings. When you have finished, read through what you have written and highlight usable ideas.

Imagine that you have been asked to write an essay about "identity" and how you see yourself. Here is the brainstorming list that one student, Santiago Quintana Garcia, wrote about his identity.

Identity—Mexican? White? Very arbitrary and flimsy

Easily deconstructed when seen from the edges

Not wrong to subscribe to a certain identity

Everyone has their in-betweens, not all race and nationality

Mexican stereotype: I don't look Mexican. I'm foreign in my own country/race

White: Not quite. I *am* Mexican after all.

Creates a struggle between the ideal and the reality, from this comes synthesis, movement

Feelings of not belonging as a teenager. No comfort objects. No cushion to fall back to easily, BUT growth and awareness.

I am Mexican. I still subscribe but with a lot more awareness of how that label is not representative and exhaustive. It is necessary; practical.

Living in between = energy, movement, growth.

Diagramming

Drawing diagrams or drawings is a useful way to generate ideas. Begin by drawing a 2-inch oval in the middle of a page. Write your topic in that oval. Think of the oval as a tree trunk. Next, draw lines radiating out from the trunk, as branches would. Write an idea related to your topic at the end of each branch. When you have finished, highlight the ideas you find most useful.

Here is a sample branching diagram on the topic of labor unions:

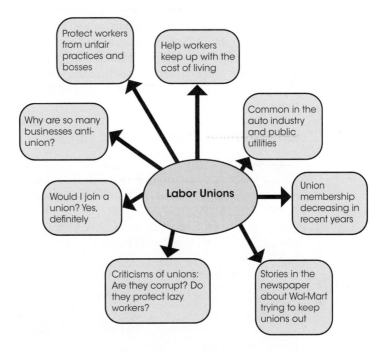

EXERCISE 2-2 THE WRITING PROCESS: GENERATING IDEAS

Select two of the following topics. Then generate ideas using two different idea-generation techniques.

1. Identity theft

2. Texting while driving

3. Legalization of marijuana

4. Advertising ploys and gimmicks

5. Airport security

2e   PREWRITING: ORGANIZING IDEAS

Two common methods of organizing ideas are outlining and idea mapping. Understanding each will help you decide how to arrange the ideas that you have identified as useful.

Outlining

When you create an **outline**, you list the main points you will cover, the details you will use to support your main points, and the order in which you will present them. To prepare an outline, list the most important ideas on separate lines on the left side of a sheet of paper, leaving space underneath each main idea. Then, in the space under each main idea, list the details that you will include to explain that main idea. Indent the list of details that fits under each of your main ideas.

Here is a sample outline for the essay that Santiago Quintana Garcia wrote about identity. His final essay appears in Chapter 11, p. 313.

I. Living in two Worlds

   A. Never completely part of either world

      1. Complicated

      2. Interesting

   B. Living in between encourages growth and maturity

      1. Nothing to hold on to

      2. Effects of culture

   C. Living in between offers a vantage point

      1. Analyze opinions and habits

      2. See virtues and faults through different eyes

   D. Live where outsider meets insider

Idea Mapping

An **idea map** shows how you will organize the content of your writing. It shows how ideas are connected and can help you identify which ideas are not relevant to your topic. Following is a sample idea map drawn for the topic of protecting your identity.

To protect your identity, take several precautions when making purchases or posting online.

Choose unique passwords that use a combination of numbers and letters.

Do not share your passwords or access codes with anyone.

Carefully examine e-mail to be sure you are not responding to scams.

Protect all your credit card and banking information.

Never give information to anyone who has called you. Get their phone number and call them back. Be sure you are talking with a legitimate representative of the company.

EXERCISE 2-3 THE WRITING PROCESS: USING OUTLINING OR MAPPING

Prepare an outline or idea map for one of the topics you chose in Exercise 2-2.

DRAFTING STRATEGIES

2f   DRAFTING AND REVISING PARAGRAPHS

LEARNING OBJECTIVE 6
Write an effective paragraph.

A **paragraph** is a group of sentences, usually at least three or four, that express one main idea. Paragraphs may stand alone to express one thought, or they may be combined into essays or longer readings. Paragraphs are one of the basic building blocks of writing.

The Structure of a Paragraph

A paragraph's one main idea is often expressed in a single sentence called the **topic sentence**. The other sentences in the paragraph, which explain or support the main idea, are called **supporting details**. (These terms are explained in more detail in Chapter 4.) You can visualize a paragraph as follows:

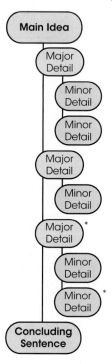

*The number of major and minor details will vary according to purpose, topic, and audience.

Here is a sample paragraph; its idea map follows.

Turkey continues to find itself strategically positioned between diverse, often contradictory geopolitical forces. Many pro-Westerners within Turkey, for example, are committed to joining the European Union (EU). To do so, the country has embarked on an active agenda of reforms designed to demonstrate its commitment to democracy. Press freedoms and multiparty elections have been permitted, the role of the military downplayed, and minority groups (particularly the Kurds) have gained greater recognition from the central government. At the same time, anti-Western Islamist political elements have been on the rise, linked to a growing number of terrorist bombings in the country since 2003. Moderate Turks are hoping that its road to the EU will not be interrupted with the violence, but Islamists and ultra-nationalists are suspicious of the EU pledge to move the country in a radically different direction. Turkey also has continuing tensions with nearby Greece and Cyprus, two countries that are both in the EU.

—Rowntree et al., *Diversity Amid Globalization*, p. 326

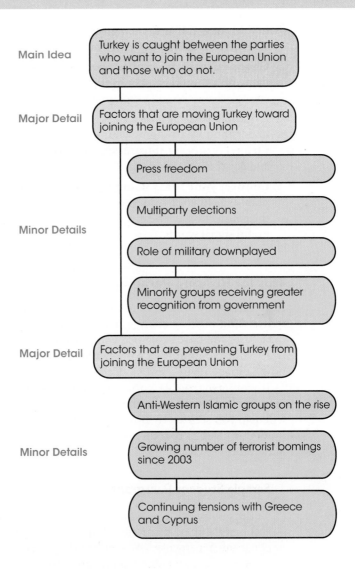

Main Idea	Turkey is caught between the parties who want to join the European Union and those who do not.
Major Detail	Factors that are moving Turkey toward joining the European Union
Minor Details	Press freedom
	Multiparty elections
	Role of military downplayed
	Minority groups receiving greater recognition from government
Major Detail	Factors that are preventing Turkey from joining the European Union
Minor Details	Anti-Western Islamic groups on the rise
	Growing number of terrorist bomings since 2003
	Continuing tensions with Greece and Cyprus

Tips for Writing Effective Paragraphs

You can write an effective paragraph if you follow the organization shown in the diagram above. Use the following suggestions to make sure your paragraph is clear and understandable.

1. **Choose a manageable topic.** Your topic should be broad enough to allow you to add interesting and relevant details, but specific enough to allow you to adequately cover it in approximately 5 to 10 sentences.

2. **Write a clear topic sentence.** Your topic sentence should state the main point of your paragraph. Often it works well to place your topic sentence first

in the paragraph and then go on to explain and support it in the remaining sentences. Avoid announcing your topic ("This paragraph is about …").

3. **Choose details to support your topic sentence.** Each sentence in your paragraph should explain or support your topic sentence. Be sure to include enough details to fully explain it.

4. **Organize your details in a logical manner.** Make your paragraph easy to understand by arranging your details using one of the patterns described in Chapter 5: process, illustration, definition, cause and effect, and comparison and contrast.

5. **Connect your ideas using signal words and phrases.** Signal words and phrases help your reader move from one detail to the next and understand the connection between and among them. See Chapters 5 and 9 for lists of useful signal words.

Tips for Revising Paragraphs

Revision involves examining your ideas by rereading all the sentences you have written and making changes to them. Your goal is to examine your ideas to make sure you have explained your ideas clearly and correctly. It is usually best to let your paragraph sit for a while before you revise it. Turn to p. 39 to see how Santiago revised several draft paragraphs within his essay.

If you have trouble knowing what to revise, try drawing an idea map of your ideas. Construct a map similar to the one shown on page 29. A map will help you see exactly how much support you have for your topic sentence, how your ideas fit together, and whether a detail is off-topic. Here is a sample paragraph.

Sample Student Paragraph

The disposal of toxic waste has caused serious health hazards. Love Canal is one of the toxic dump sites that has caused serious health problems. This dump site in particular was used by a large number of nearby industries. The canal was named after a man named Love. Love Canal, in my opinion, was an eye-opener on the subject of toxic dump sites. It took about ten years to clean the dump site up to a livable condition. Many people living near Love Canal developed cancers. There were many miscarriages and birth defects. This dump site might have caused irreversible damage to our environment, so I am glad it has been cleaned up.

The following idea map shows the topic sentence of the paragraph and, underneath it, the supporting details that directly relate to the topic sentence. All the unrelated details are in a list to the right of the map. Note that the concluding sentence is also included in the map, since it is an important part of the paragraph.

Idea Map

Disposal of toxic wastes causes health hazards.	Unrelated details

> Chemicals in Love Canal caused health problems.

1. Love Canal was used by many industries.

> Many people developed cancer.

2. It was named after a man named Love.

> There were many miscarriages and birth defects.

3. It was an eye-opener.

4. It took ten years to clean up.

> I am glad it has been cleaned up.

In this paragraph the author began by supporting her topic sentence with the example of Love Canal. However, she began to drift when she explained how Love Canal was named. To revise this paragraph, the author could include more detailed information about Love Canal health hazards or examples of other disposal sites and their health hazards.

You can use an idea map to spot where you begin to drift away from your topic. You might also ask a classmate to read and comment on your paragraph. For suggestions on finding grammatical errors in your paragraph, see section 2j on proofreading later in this chapter (p. 41).

Below is a Revision Checklist that you can use to make sure you have done a careful and thorough revision.

Paragraph Revision Checklist

Paragraph Development

1. Is the topic manageable (neither too broad nor too narrow)?
2. Is the paragraph written with the reader in mind?
3. Does the topic sentence identify the topic?
4. Does the topic sentence make a point about the topic?
5. Does each sentence support the topic sentence?
6. Is there sufficient detail?
7. Is there a sentence at the end that brings the paragraph to a close?

Sentence Development

8. Are there any sentence fragments, run-on sentences, or comma splices?
9. Are ideas combined to produce more effective sentences?
10. Are adjectives and adverbs used to make the sentences vivid and interesting?

11. Are relative clauses and prepositional phrases like *-ing* phrases used to add detail?

12. Are pronouns used correctly and consistently?

EXERCISE 2-4 THE WRITING PROCESS: DRAFTING A PARAGRAPH

Using one or more of the ideas you generated and organized in Exercises 2-2 and 2-3, write and revise a paragraph about the topic you chose.

EXERCISE 2-5 DRAFTING A PARAGRAPH

Following all the steps of the writing process, write and revise a well-developed paragraph on one of the following topics.

1. Women in the military

2. Animal rights

3. The cost of college

2g   UNDERSTANDING THE STRUCTURE OF ESSAYS

LEARNING OBJECTIVE 7
Understand the structure of an effective essay.

An **essay** is a group of paragraphs about one subject. It contains one key idea about the subject. This key idea is called the **thesis statement**. Each paragraph in the essay supports or explains some aspect of the thesis statement.

An essay follows a logical and direct plan. It introduces an idea (the thesis statement), explains it, and draws a conclusion. Therefore, an essay usually has at least three paragraphs:

1. Introductory paragraph
2. Body (one or more paragraphs)
3. Concluding paragraph

The Introductory Paragraph

Your introductory paragraph should accomplish three goals:

- It should establish the topic of the essay.
- It should present your essay's thesis statement in a manner that is appropriate for your intended audience.
- It should stimulate your audience's interest. That is, it should make readers want to read your essay.

The Body

The body of your essay should accomplish three goals:

- It should provide information that supports and explains your thesis statement.
- It should present each main supporting point in a separate paragraph.
- It should contain enough detailed information to make the main point of each paragraph (that is, the topic sentence) understandable and believable.

The Concluding Paragraph

Your concluding paragraph should accomplish two goals:

- It should reemphasize but not restate your thesis statement.
- It should draw your essay to a close.

The following idea map shows the ideal organization of an essay.

Idea Map

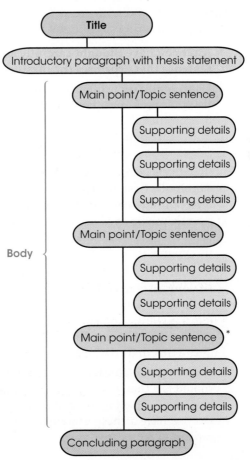

* Number of main points may vary. Each main point should contain a sufficient number of details.

2h   WRITING THE FIRST DRAFT OF AN ESSAY

LEARNING OBJECTIVE 8
Write a first draft of
your essay.

To understand what drafting involves, consider the following comparison. Suppose you need to buy a car. You have decided that you can afford a used car and you have in mind the basic features you need. You visit a used car lot and look at various cars that fit your requirements. After narrowing down your choices, you test drive several cars, then go home to think about how each one might suit you. You revisit the used car lot, go for another test drive, and finally decide which car to buy.

Writing a draft of an essay is similar to buying a car. Once you have used prewriting to develop and organize your ideas, you are ready to write a first draft of the essay. You have to try out different ideas through prewriting, see how they work together as you organize them, express them in different ways, and, after writing several drafts, settle on what you will include. **Drafting** is a way of trying out ideas to see if and how they work.

A first draft expresses your ideas in sentence form. Work from your list of ideas (see section 2d), and don't be concerned with grammar, spelling, or punctuation at this point. Instead, focus on expressing and developing each idea fully. The following suggestions will help you write effective first drafts.

1. **After you have thought carefully about the ideas on your list, write one sentence that expresses the thesis statement (main point) of your essay.**

2. **Concentrate on explaining your thesis statement using ideas from your list.** Devote one paragraph to each main idea that supports your thesis. Focus first on the ideas that you think express your main point particularly well. The main point of each paragraph is the topic sentence. It usually appears first in the paragraph, but it can appear anywhere in the paragraph. Later in the writing process, you may find you need to add other ideas from your list.

3. **Think of a first draft as a chance to experiment with different ideas and different ways of organizing them.** While you are drafting, if you think of a better way to organize or express your ideas, or if you think of new ideas, make changes. Be flexible. Do not worry about getting your wording exact at this point.

4. **As your draft develops, feel free to change your focus or even your topic (if your instructor has not assigned a specific topic).** If your draft is not working out, don't hesitate to start over completely. Go back to generating ideas. It is always all right to go back and forth among the steps in the writing process. Many writers make a number of "false starts" before they produce a first draft that satisfies them.

5. **Don't expect immediate success.** When you finish your first draft, you should feel that you have the beginnings of a paper you will be happy with. Now ask yourself if you have a sense of the direction your paper will take. Do you have a thesis statement for your essay? Do the paragraphs each explain or support your thesis? Does each paragraph have sufficient sup-

porting details? Is the organization logical? If you can answer "yes" to these questions, you have something good to work with and revise.

The following first draft evolved from Santiago's brainstorming list on page 26 and outline on page 28. The highlighting indicates the main points he developed as he wrote.

First Draft of Santiago's Essay

Introductory paragraph	1	There are around twenty million people living in Mexico City, and this number is constantly increasing. Mexico is where I was born and grew up, before I moved to Beloit, Wisconsin to attend Beloit College. The town of Beloit has roughly thirty thousand people. This means that about seven hundred towns the size of Beloit would fit inside Mexico City. In Mexico City, I was no more than a speck of dust in a dirty room. In Beloit, if I go have breakfast in one of three downtown cafés, I can be sure that there will be at least one person I know, probably around five
Working thesis statement		or more. Beloit and Mexico City are two completely different worlds that I have come to call home.
Topic sentence	2	I am Mexican. I probably have beautiful cinnamon skin, hair black as night and falling straight like a waterfall to frame two glowing brown eyes. Many people think this is what a "true Mexican" looks like. Drawing a line between what is a true Mexican and what isn't based on looks is not a simple task. I myself think it is impossible. This stereotype has played a role in my life both in Mexico and Beloit. I have white skin, the only blue eyes in my family of brown eyes, and curly light brown hair. When I go to the market to buy vegetables for the week, people don't bother to ask my name. They call me *güerito*, blonde. I get asked if I am from the United States or from another country. I was never completely a part of the nation I was born and grew up in. In Beloit though, people are fascinated by my cultural background and ask about my customs and daily life back home. Inevitably, at some point in the conversation they tell me that I don't look Mexican. I live between two worlds; being racially "foreign" in Mexico, and being culturally "foreign" in Beloit.
Topic sentence	3	Living a life in-between two worlds, never completely a part of any, is a very complicated and extremely interesting place to be. Living in-between encourages growth and maturity. On one hand, in my teenage years, when I desperately wanted to feel I was a part of something, there wasn't anything to take refuge in and feel strongly about. On the other, though, this made me see the effects of the culture I grew up with on my way of thinking. Standing in this middle ground was a vantage point where I could analyze the opinions I held and the habits I developed and see the virtues and faults through different eyes. The hardiest weeds live where the pavement meets the prairie. I live where outsider meets insider.
Topic sentence	4	I became used to being in the middle. I discovered that most questions can have more than one answer, or no answer at all. I realized that people are a lot more complex than I thought, and you really can't stick a label to them that

won't become old and fall off. I had thought that people who fit snugly into the stereotype would never experience being an outsider. But I soon found out otherwise. Some had to choose between going to the cinema with their friends and going to church with their family. Some loved playing soccer in the mornings, and then go ballroom dancing in the afternoon. Everyone had their own experience of being in-between two places they sometimes love and sometimes hate.

Topic sentence | 5

Concluding paragraph

It is the places in-between where the most potential for growth lives. Everyone has their own place where they feel like outsiders, or not completely insiders. Realizing that this is where you are standing, and that it is perfectly fine to have one foot inside and one foot outside, will let the unique reveal itself through you. Being in-between can be difficult, but it is there that the most unexpected and wonderful things happen.

EXERCISE 2-6 THE WRITING PROCESS: WRITING THE FIRST DRAFT OF AN ESSAY

Choosing one of the topics you did not use in Exercise 2-2, generate ideas about it using freewriting, brainstorming, or diagramming . Then create an outline or idea map to organize the ideas that best support your topic, and write a short essay.

REVISION STRATEGIES

2i   REVISING THE FIRST DRAFT OF AN ESSAY

LEARNING OBJECTIVE 9
Revise a draft.

Think again about the process of buying a car. At first you may think you have considered everything you need and are ready to make a decision. Then, a while later, you think of other features that would be good to have in your car; in fact, these features are at least as important as the ones you have already thought of. Now you have to rethink your requirements and perhaps reorganize your thoughts about what features are most important to you. You might eliminate some features, add others, and rearrange the importance of others.

A similar thing often happens as you revise your first draft. When you finish a first draft, you are more or less satisfied with it. Then you reread it later and see you have more work to do. When you revise, you have to rethink your entire paper, re-examining every part and idea.

Revising is more than changing a word or rearranging a few sentences, and it is not concerned with correcting punctuation, spelling, or grammar. (You make these proofreading changes later, after you are satisfied that you have presented your ideas in the best way. See section 2j.) Revision is your chance to make significant improvements to your first draft. It might mean changing, adding, deleting, or rearranging whole sections of your essay.

Here is an excerpt from a later draft of Santiago Quintana Garcia's essay. In this revised draft of the second and third paragraphs, you can see how Santiago expands his ideas, adding words and details (underlined), and deleting others. You can read his final essay in Chapter 11, p. 313.

Santiago's Revision of Paragraphs 2 and 3

Santiago adds details to explain living in-between

3   Living a life in-between two worlds, never completely a part of any, is a very complicated and extremely interesting place to be. Living in-between encourages growth and maturity. As a teenager, I struggled with feelings of belonging and wanting to be a part of a group. I did not play soccer, or the guitar, and suffered from bullying. The impact this had in my life was emotionally wrecking. Often when people find themselves in similar situations, they turn to familiar things for comfort. Things like a group you belong to, like a culture, or a race, or a religious group. This was not accessible to me in the same way as it was to others. ~~On one hand, in my teenage years, when I desperately wanted to feel I was part of something, there wasn't anything to take refuge in and feel strongly about.~~ On the other

Santiago adds mentions of college

hand, though, standing on no man's land let ~~this made~~ me observe ~~see~~ the effects of the culture I grew up with on my way of thinking, and has greatly influenced my area of focus in my college studies. Standing in this middle ground was a vantage point from which I could analyze the opinions I held and the habits I developed and see my virtues and faults through different eyes. The hardiest weeds live where the pavement meets the prairie. I live where outsider meets insider.

Santiago revises to add specifics about his conflict

4   ~~I became used to being in the middle. I discovered that most questions can have more than one answer, or no answer at all. I realized that people are a lot more complex that I thought, and you really can't stick a label to them that won't become old and fall off.~~ What happens in this middle ground is that concepts such as gender, race, nationality, and other identities seem held up by pins. They are extremely volatile and impermanent, constantly changing and molding. This knowledge is present with me every time I say "I am Mexican" or "I am white." I had thought that people who fit snugly into a stereotype would never experience being an outsider. But I soon found out otherwise.

Essay Revision Checklist

Use these suggestions to revise an essay effectively.

1. **Reread the sentence that expresses your main point, the thesis statement of your essay.** It must be clear, direct, and complete. Experiment with ways to improve it.

2. **Make sure each paragraph supports your thesis statement.** Do all the paragraphs relate directly to the thesis? If not, cross out or rewrite those that do not to clarify their connection to the main point.

3. **Make sure your essay has a beginning and an end.** An essay should have introductory and concluding paragraphs.

4. **Replace words that are vague or unclear with more specific or more descriptive words.**

5. **Seek advice.** If you are unsure about how to revise, visit your writing instructor during office hours and ask for advice, or try peer review (discussed below).

6. **When you have finished revising, you should feel satisfied with what you have said and with the way you have said it.** If you do not feel satisfied, revise your draft again. Once you are satisfied, you are ready to edit and proofread.

The Revision Process: Peer Review

Peer review entails asking one or more of your classmates to read and comment on your writing. It is an excellent way to discover what is good in your draft and what needs improvement. Here are some suggestions for making peer review as valuable as possible.

When You Are the Writer . . .

1. Prepare your draft in readable form. Double-space your work and print it on standard 8.5″ × 11″ paper.

2. When you receive your peers' comments, weigh them carefully. Keep an open mind, but do not feel that you must accept every suggestion.

3. If you have questions or are uncertain about your peers' advice, talk with your instructor.

When You Are the Reviewer . . .

1. Read the draft through at least once before making any suggestions.

2. Use the revision checklist on p. 33 as a guide.

3. As you read, keep the writer's intended audience in mind (see section 2c). The draft should be appropriate for that audience.

4. Offer positive comments first. Say what the writer did well.

5. Be specific in your review and offer suggestions for improvement.

6. Be supportive; put yourself in the place of the person whose work you are reviewing. Phrase your feedback in the way you would want to hear it!

EXERCISE 2-7 THE WRITING PROCESS: REVISING A DRAFT

Revise the first draft you wrote for Exercise 2-6.

EXERCISE 2-8 USING PEER REVIEW

Pair with a classmate for this exercise. Read and evaluate each other's drafts written for Exercise 2-6, using the peer review guidelines provided in this section.

2j   EDITING AND PROOFREADING YOUR WORK

LEARNING OBJECTIVE 10
Proofread for correctness.

Editing and proofreading require a final reading of your paper to check for errors. In this final polishing of your work, the focus is on correctness, so don't proofread until you have completed your drafting and revising. When you are ready to edit and proofread, you should check your writing for errors in

- sentences (run-ons or fragments)
- grammar
- spelling
- punctuation
- capitalization

Editing and Proofreading Checklist

The following tips will help you as you edit and proofread.

1. **Review your paper once for each type of error.** First, read it for run-on sentences or fragments. Take a short break, and then read it four more times, each time paying attention to one of the following: *grammar, spelling, punctuation,* and *capitalization.* Don't do this when you are tired; you might miss some mistakes or introduce new ones.

2. **To find spelling errors and identify fragments, read your paper from the last sentence to the first sentence and from the last word to the first word.** By reading this way, you will not get distracted by the flow of ideas, so you can focus on finding spelling errors. Also use the spell-checker on your computer, but be sure to proofread for the types of errors it cannot catch: missing words, errors that are themselves words (such as *of* for *or*), and homonyms (for example, using *it's* for *its*).

3. **Read each sentence, slowly and deliberately.** This technique will help you catch endings that you have left off verbs or missing plurals.

4. **Check for errors one final time after you print out your paper.** Ask a classmate or friend to read your paper to catch any mistakes you missed.

Here is a paragraph that shows the errors that a student corrected during editing and proofreading. Notice that errors in grammar, spelling, and punctuation were corrected.

> ~~The~~ Robert Burns, said that the dog is man's best friend. To a large extent, this statement may be ~~more true~~ *truer* than we thinks. What makes dogs so special to humans is ~~they're~~ *their* unending loyalty and their unconditional love. Dogs have been known to cross the entire United states to return home. *They* ~~Never~~ make fun of you or criticize you, ~~Or~~ throw fits, and they are always happy to see you. Dogs never ~~lye~~ *lie* to you, never betray your confidences, and never stays angry with you for more than five minutes. *The* ~~World~~ would be a better place if only people could be more like dogs.

To view Santiago Quintana Garcia's final, proofread essay, see Reading Selection 1, "The Space In-Between," on pages 313–314.

EXERCISE 2-9 WRITING IN PROCESS: EDITING AND PROOFREADING

Prepare a final version of your essay by editing and proofreading the revised draft you created in Exercise 2-6.

SUMMARY OF LEARNING OBJECTIVES

Objective 1 Understand the writing process.	The writing process consists of four basic steps: prew... ideas and organize ideas, writing a first draft, revising, proofreading.
Objective 2 Use technology appropriately.	Drafting on a computer is faster and more efficient than o... your paper before you begin, name and save different versi... quently, and use the Internet to obtain peer review. Use spel... ...rs and grammar and style checkers when revising and editing, but do not rely on them to catch all errors.
Objective 3 Consider your audience, purpose, tone, and point of view.	To consider your *audience*, ask yourself who will be reading what you write. To consider your *purpose*, think about what you are trying to achieve through your writing. Choose a *point of view* and *tone* appropriate to your audience and purpose.
Objective 4 Use prewriting to generate ideas for your writing.	Three techniques for generating ideas are *freewriting*, *brainstorming*, and *diagramming*.
Objective 5 Use prewriting to organize your ideas.	Two common methods of organizing ideas are *outlining* (listing main points and details in the order in which you will present them) and *idea mapping* (creating a drawing that shows the content and organization of your writing).
Objective 6 Write an effective paragraph	A *paragraph* is a group of sentences that expresses one main idea. It may stand alone to express one thought or be combined with others to form an essay. An effective paragraph contains a clear topic sentence and details that explain and illustrate it.
Objective 7 Understand the structure of an effective essay.	An *essay* is a group of at least three paragraphs about one subject. Essays should include an introductory paragraph, a body, and a concluding paragraph. (See the idea map for essays on page 35.)
Objective 8 Write a first draft of an essay.	To *draft* an essay, think carefully about the ideas you have generated and write a thesis statement that expresses your main point; devote one paragraph to each idea that supports your thesis; be flexible and reorganize and change your ideas; and do not expect immediate success.
Objective 9 Revise an essay draft.	*Revision* allows you to make significant improvements to your draft by changing, adding, deleting, or rearranging words, parts, and ideas.
Objective 10 Edit and proofread for correctness.	*Edit* and *proofread* by checking for errors in sentences, grammar, spelling, punctuation, and capitalization. Read your paper once for each type of error, read your paper from the end to the beginning, read aloud, and check for errors again after you print your paper.

3 Vocabulary Building

LEARNING OBJECTIVES

1 Use resources for vocabulary building
2 Use context clues
3 Use affixes: prefixes, roots, and suffixes
4 Use language effectively

Your vocabulary can be one of your strongest assets or one of your greatest liabilities. It defines and describes you by revealing a great deal about your level of education and your experience. Your vocabulary contributes to that all-important first impression people form when they meet you. A strong vocabulary provides both immediate academic benefits and long-term career effects, increasing your comprehension and critical-thinking skills. This chapter helps you to strengthen your vocabulary and use language effectively when you write.

3a RESOURCES FOR READERS AND WRITERS

LEARNING OBJECTIVE 1
Use resources.

To read and write effectively, you need resources to help find meanings of unfamiliar words as you read and to locate exact and precise words that convey your intended meaning when you write.

Using a Dictionary

There are several types of dictionaries, each with its own purpose and use:

1. **Online dictionaries** are readily available. Two of the most widely used are *Merriam-Webster* (http://www.m-w.com) and *American Heritage* (http://yourdictionary.com/index.shtml). Online dictionaries have several important advantages over print dictionaries.

   ■ **Audio component.** Some online dictionaries such as *Merriam-Webster Online* and *The American Heritage Dictionary of the English Language* feature an audio component that allows you to hear how words are pronounced.

- **Multiple dictionary entries.** Some sites, such as Dictionary.com, display entries from several dictionaries for each word you look up.
- **Misspellings.** If you aren't sure of how a word is spelled or you mistype it, several possible words and their meanings will be provided.

2. **A pocket or paperback dictionary** is an inexpensive, easy-to-carry, shortened version of a standard desk dictionary. It is small enough to carry to classes and costs around $7.

3. **A desk dictionary** is a more complete and extensive dictionary. Although a pocket dictionary is convenient, it is also limited in use. A pocket edition lists about 50,000 to 60,000 words; a standard desk edition lists up to 150,000 words. Also, the desk edition provides more complete information about each word. Several standard dictionaries are available in both desk and paperback editions. These include:

   The Random House Dictionary of the English Language

   Merriam-Webster's Collegiate Dictionary

   The American Heritage Dictionary of the English Language

4. **An unabridged dictionary** is found in the reference section of the library. The unabridged edition provides the most complete information for each word in the English language.

EXERCISE 3-1 USING A DICTIONARY

Use a dictionary to answer each of the following items. Write your answer in the space provided.

1. What does the abbreviation *e.g.* stand for?

   _____

2. How is the word *deleterious* pronounced? (Record its phonetic spelling.)

   _____

3. From what languages is the word *delicatessen* taken?

   _____

4. Locate one restricted meaning for the word *configuration*.

   _____

   _____

5. What is the history of the word *mascot*?

   _____

   _____

   _____

   _____

6. What is the plural spelling of *addendum*?

_____

7. What type of punctuation is a virgule?

_____

8. List a few words that contain the following sound: ī.

_____

9. Who or what is a *Semite*?

_____

10. Can the word *phrase* be used other than as a noun? If so, how?

_____

A dictionary lists all the common meanings of a word, but usually you are looking for only one definition. Meanings in an entry are grouped and numbered consecutively according to part of speech. If you are able to identify the part of speech of the word you are looking up, you can skip over all parts of the entry that do not pertain to that part of speech. If you cannot identify the part of speech of a word you are looking up, begin with the first meaning listed. Generally, the most common meaning appears first, and more specialized meanings appear toward the end of the entry. When you find a meaning that could fit into the sentence you are working with, replace the word with its definition and then read the entire sentence. If the definition makes sense in the sentence, you can be fairly certain that you have selected the appropriate meaning.

EXERCISE 3-2 FINDING MEANINGS

Write an appropriate meaning for the underlined word in each of the following sentences. Use the dictionary to help you find the meaning that makes sense in the sentence.

1. He affected a French accent.

_____

2. The amphibian took us to our destination in less than an hour.

_____

3. The plane stalled on the apron.

_____

4. We circumvented the problem by calculating in metrics.

_____

5. Many consumers have become embroiled in the debate over the rising inflation rate.

_____

Using a Thesaurus

A **thesaurus,** or dictionary of synonyms, is a valuable reference for locating a
precise, accurate, or descriptive word to fit a particular situation. Suppose you
are searching for a more precise term for the expression _looked over,_ as used in
the following sentence:

> My instructor _looked over_ my essay exam.

The thesaurus lists the synonyms of the phrase, and you can choose from
the list the word that most closely suggests the meaning you want to convey.
Choices include _scrutinize, examine, skimmed,_ and so forth. The easiest way to do
this is to test out, or substitute, various choices in your sentence to see which
one is most appropriate; check the dictionary if you are not sure of a word's
exact meaning.

Many students misuse the thesaurus by choosing words that do not fit the
context. _Be sure to use words only when you are familiar with all their shades of mean-
ing._ Remember, a misused word is often a more serious error than a wordy or
imprecise expression.

The most widely used print thesaurus is _Roget's Thesaurus;_ it is readily available in an inexpensive paperback edition. Online thesauruses are available at

- Roget's Thesaurus   http://www.bartleby.com/62/
- Merriam-Webster   http://merriam-webster.com/

You can also pick a thesaurus from search choices.

EXERCISE 3-3 USING A THESAURUS

_Replace the underlined word or phrase in each sentence with a more descriptive
word or phrase. Use a thesaurus to locate your replacement._

1. When Sara learned that her sister had committed a crime, she was sad.

2. Compared with earlier chapters, the last two chapters in my chemistry text
are hard.

3. The instructor spent the entire class <u>talking about</u> the causes of inflation and deflation.

4. The main character in the film was a <u>thin</u>, talkative British soldier.

5. We went to see a <u>great</u> film that won the Academy Award for best picture.

3b   USING CONTEXT CLUES

LEARNING OBJECTIVE 2
Use context clues.

Read the following brief paragraph in which several words are missing. Try to figure out the missing words and write them in the blanks.

> Rate refers to the _____ at which you read. If you read too
> _____, your comprehension may suffer. If you read too
> _____, you are not likely to complete your assignments
> on time.

Did you insert the word *speed* in the first blank, *fast* in the second blank, and *slowly* in the third blank? Most likely you correctly identified all three missing words. You could tell from the sentence which word to put in. The words around the missing words—the sentence **context**—provided clues as to which word would fit and make sense; such clues are called **context clues.**

While you probably won't find missing words on a printed page, you will often find words whose meaning you do not know. Context clues can help you figure out the meanings of unfamiliar words.

Example

> A **neurosis,** such as short-term depression, mild anxiety, or hypochondria, can make it difficult for a person to live a fully healthy life.

From the sentence, you can tell that *neurosis* means "a relatively mild mental illness." Here's another example:

> The couple finally **secured** a reservation at the wildly popular new ski lodge.

You can figure out that *secured* means "got" or "succeeded in getting" a reservation.

There are four types of context clues to look for: (1) definition, (2) example, (3) contrast, and (4) logic of the passage. Study the chart below to learn how to use each type.

TYPES OF CONTEXT CLUES

CONTEXT CLUE	HOW TO FIND MEANING	EXAMPLE
Definition	1. Look for words that announce that meanings will follow (*is, are, refers to, means*).	Broad, flat noodles that are served with sauce or butter are called **fettuccine.**
	2. Look for parentheses, dashes, or commas that set apart synonyms or brief definitions.	Psychologists often wonder whether **stereotypes**—the assumptions we make about what people are like—might be self-fulfilling.
Example	Figure out what the examples have in common. (For example, both peas and beans are vegetables and grow in pods.)	Most **condiments**, such as pepper, mustard, and ketchup, are used to improve the flavor of foods.
Contrast	Look for a word or phrase that is the opposite of a word whose meaning you don't know.	Before their classes in manners, the children were disorderly; after graduation, they acted with more **decorum.**
Logic of the Passage	Use the rest of the sentence to help you. Pretend the word is a blank line and fill in the blank with a word that makes sense.	On hot, humid afternoons, I often feel **languid.**

EXERCISE 3-4 USING DEFINITION CLUES

Read the following paragraphs and use definition clues to help you determine the meaning of each boldfaced word or phrase.

Issue: Cultural Similarities and Differences

Within every culture, there is an overall sense of what is beautiful and what is not beautiful, what represents good taste as opposed to tastelessness or even obscenity. Such considerations are matters of **aesthetics**. Global marketers must understand the importance of visual aesthetics embodied in the color or shape of a product, label, or package. Aesthetic elements that are attractive, appealing, and in good taste in one country may be perceived differently in another. In some cases, a **standardized color** can be used in all countries; an example is the distinctive yellow color on Caterpillar's earth-moving equipment and its licensed outdoor gear.

Music is an aesthetic component of all cultures and is accepted as a form of artistic expression and a source of entertainment. In one sense, music represents a **transculture** that is not identified with any particular nation. However, sociologists have noted that national identity derives in part from a country's **indigenous**, or native, music; a unique musical style can represent the uniqueness of the culture and the community.

—Adapted from Keegan and Green, *Global Marketing*, p. 104

1. aesthetics _____

_____

2. standardized color _____

_____

3. transculture _____

_____

4. indigenous _____

EXERCISE 3-5 USING EXAMPLE CLUES

Read the following paragraphs and use definition and example clues to help you determine the meaning of each boldfaced word or phrase.

Issue: Terrorism

Terrorism is the systematic use of violence by a group in order to **intimidate** a population or **coerce** a government into granting its demands. Terrorists attempt to achieve their **objectives** through organized acts that spread fear and anxiety among the population, such as bombing, kidnapping, hijacking, taking of hostages, and **assassination**. They consider violence necessary as a mean of bringing widespread publicity to goals and **grievances** that are not being addressed through peaceful means. Belief in their cause is so strong that terrorists do not hesitate to strike despite knowing they will probably die in the act.

Distinguishing terrorism from other acts of political violence can be difficult. For example, if a Palestinian suicide bomber kills several dozen Israeli teenagers in a Jerusalem restaurant, is that an act of terrorism or wartime **retaliation** against Israeli government policies and army actions? Competing arguments are made: Israel's **sympathizers** denounce the act as a terrorist threat to the country's existence, whereas **advocates** of the Palestinian cause argue that long-standing injustices and Israeli army attacks on Palestinian civilians provoked the act.

—James M. Rubinstein, *Contemporary Human Geography*, p. 190

1. terrorism _____

   _____

2. intimidate _____

3. coerce _____

4. objectives _____

5. assassination _____

6. grievances _____

7. retaliation _____

8. sympathizers _____

9. advocates _____

EXERCISE 3-6 USING CONTRAST CLUES

Read the following paragraph and use contrast clues to help you determine the meaning of each boldfaced word. Consult a dictionary, if necessary.

Issue: "Dirty" Political Campaigns

The Whigs chose General William Henry Harrison to run against President Martin Van Buren in 1840, using a **specious** but effective argument: General Harrison is a plain man of the people who lives in a log cabin. Contrast him with the suave Van Buren, **luxuriating** amid "the Regal Splendor of the President's Palace." Harrison drinks ordinary hard cider with his hog meat and grits, while Van Buren **eschews** plain food in favor of expensive foreign wines and fancy French cuisine. The general's furniture is **unpretentious** and sturdy; the president dines off gold plates and treads on carpets that cost the people $5 a yard. In a country where all are equal, the people will reject an **aristocrat** like Van Buren and put their trust in General Harrison, a simple, brave, honest, public-spirited common man. (In fact, Harrison came from a distinguished family, was well educated and financially comfortable, and certainly did not live in a log cabin.)

—Adapted from Carnes and Garraty, *The American Nation,* p. 267

1. specious _____

2. luxuriating _____

3. eschews _____

4. unpretentious _____

5. aristocrat _____

EXERCISE 3-7 USING LOGIC OF THE PASSAGE CLUES

Read the following paragraph and use the logic of the passage clues to help you select the correct meaning of each boldfaced word or phrase.

Issue: Cultural Similarities and Differences

In 2005, while writing a children's book on the life of the **prophet** Mohammed, Danish author Klare Bluitgen searched unsuccessfully for an **illustrator**. The problem: Many of the world's Muslims believe that it is **blasphemy** to **depict** images of the prophet. Denmark's conservative *Jyllands-Posten* newspaper picked up the story; concerned that this was a case of **self-censorship**, the paper's cultural editor challenged dozens of well-known illustrators to "draw Mohammed in the way they see him." In September 2005, *Jyllands-Posten* printed submissions from 12 illustrators **in conjunction with** articles on freedom of speech; one of the images depicted Mohammed with a bomb in his turban.

—Keegan and Green, *Global Marketing*, p. 105

1. prophet _____

2. illustrator _____

3. blasphemy _____

4. depict _____

5. self-censorship _____

6. in conjunction with _____

3c   LEARNING AFFIXES: PREFIXES, ROOTS, AND SUFFIXES

LEARNING OBJECTIVE 3
Use prefixes, roots, and suffixes.

Suppose you come across the following sentence in a human anatomy textbook:

> Trichromatic plates are used frequently in the text to illustrate the position of body organs.

If you did not know the meaning of *trichromatic,* how could you determine it? There are no context clues in the sentence. One solution is to look up the word in a dictionary. An easier and faster way is to break the word into parts and analyze the meaning of each part. Many words in the English language are made up of affixes called **prefixes, roots,** and **suffixes.** These affixes have specific meanings that, when added together, can help you determine the meaning of the word as a whole.

The word *trichromatic* can be divided into three parts: prefix, root, and suffix.

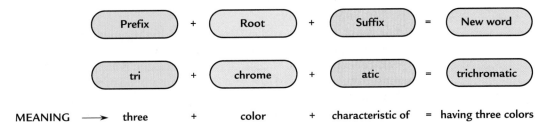

You can see from this analysis that *trichromatic* means "having three colors." Here are two other examples of words that you can figure out by using prefixes, roots, and suffixes:

> The student found the philosophy textbook completely **incomprehensible.**
>
> **in-** = not
>
> **comprehend** = understand
>
> **-ible** = able to do something
>
> **incomprehensible** = not able to be understood

> I wanted to run the marathon, but after suffering from the flu for two weeks, I was a **nonstarter.**
>
> **non-** = not
>
> **start** = begin
>
> **-er** = one who does something
>
> **nonstarter** = someone who fails to take part in (or begin) a race

The first step in using the prefix-root-suffix method is to become familiar with the most commonly used affixes. The prefixes and roots listed in Tables 3.1 and 3.2 (pages 55 and 57) will give you a good start in determining the meanings of thousands of words without having to look them up in the dictionary. Before you begin to use affixes to figure out new words, there are a few things you need to know:

1. **In most cases, a word is built upon at least one root.**
2. **Words can have more than one prefix, root, or suffix.**
   a. Words can be made up of two or more roots (*geo/logy*).
   b. Some words have two prefixes (*in/sub/ordination*).
   c. Some words have two suffixes (*beauti/ful/ly*).
3. **Words do not always have a prefix and a suffix.**
   a. Some words have neither a prefix nor a suffix (*read*).
   b. Others have a suffix but no prefix (*read/ing*).
   c. Others have a prefix but no suffix (*pre/read*).
4. **The spelling of roots may change as they are combined with suffixes.**
   Some common variations are included in Table 3.2.

5. **Different prefixes, roots, or suffixes may have the same meaning.** For example, the prefixes *bi-*, *di-*, and *duo-* all mean "two." The prefixes *un-*, *in-*, and *non-* all mean "not."

6. **Some roots, prefixes, and suffixes have different meanings in different words.** The meaning is based on whether the word part comes from Latin or Greek. For example, the biological term for mankind is *homo sapiens*. Here, *homo* means "man." In the word *homogenous*, which means "all of the same kind," *homo* means "same." Other words that use the Greek meaning of homo are *homogenize* (to make uniform or similar) and *homonyms* (two words that sound the same).

7. **Sometimes you may identify a group of letters as a prefix or root but find that it does not carry the meaning of that prefix or root.** For example, the letters *mis* in the word *missile* are part of the root and are not the prefix *mis-*, which means "wrong; bad."

Prefixes

Prefixes appear at the beginning of many English words, and they alter the meaning of the root to which are connected. For example, if you add the prefix *re-* to the word *read,* the word *reread* is formed, meaning "to read again." If *pre-* is added to the word *reading,* the word *prereading* is formed, meaning "before reading." If the prefix *post-* is added, the word *postreading* is formed, meaning "after reading." Table 3.1 lists common prefixes grouped according to meaning.

EXERCISE 3-8   USING PREFIXES

Read the following paragraph and choose the correct prefix from the box below to fill in the blank next to each boldfaced word part. One prefix will not be used.

multi	uni	in
eu	bi	dis

Issue: Mental Health Disorders

Major depression is sometimes referred to as a (1) _____ **polar** disorder because the emotional problems exist at only one end, or "pole," of the emotional range. When a person suffers from severe mood swings that go all the way from depression to manic episodes (excessive excitement, energy, and elation), that person is said to suffer from a (2) _____ **polar** disorder, meaning that emotions cycle between the two poles of possible emotions (American Psychiatric Association, 2000). Unlike mild or moderate mood (3) _____ **orders**, there is usually no external cause for the extreme ups and downs of the bipolar person. The depressive phases of a bipolar person are (4) _____ **distinguishable** from major depression but give way to manic episodes that may last from a few weeks to a few months. In these manic episodes, the person is extremely happy or (5) _____ **phoric** without any real cause to be so happy.

—Ciccarelli and White, *Psychology,* 3rd edition, Pearson Prentice Hall, p. 547

TABLE 3.1 COMMON PREFIXES

PREFIX	MEANING	SAMPLE WORD
Prefixes referring to amount or number		
mono-/uni-	one	monocle/unicycle
bi-/di-/du-	two	bimonthly/divorce/duet
tri-	three	triangle
quad-	four	quadrant
quint-/pent-	five	quintet/pentagon
dec-/deci-	ten	decimal
centi-	hundred	centigrade
homo-	same	homogenized
mega-	large	megaphone
milli-	thousand	milligram
micro-	small	microscope
multi-/poly-	many	multipurpose/polygon
nano-	extremely small	nanoplankton
semi-	half	semicircle
equi	equal	equidistant
Prefixes meaning "not" (negative)		
a-	not	asymmetrical
anti-	against	antiwar
contra-/counter-	against, opposite	contradict
dis-	apart, away, not	disagree
in-/il-/ir-/im-	not	incorrect/illogical/irreversible/impossible
mal-	poorly, wrongly	malnourished
mis-	wrongly	misunderstand
non-	not	nonfiction
un-	not	unpopular
pseudo-	false	pseudoscientific
Prefixes giving direction, location, or placement		
ab-	away	absent
ad-	toward	adhesive
ante-/pre-	before	antecedent/premarital

(continued on next page)

(continued from preceding page)

PREFIX	MEANING	SAMPLE WORD
circum-/peri-	around	circumference/perimeter
com-/col-/con-	with, together	compile/collide/convene
de-	away, from	depart
dia-	through	diameter
ex-/extra-	from, out of, former	ex-wife/extramarital
hyper-	over, excessive	hyperactive
hypo-	below, beneath	hypodermic
inter-	between	interpersonal
intro-/intra-/in-	within, into, in	introduction
post-	after	posttest
pre-	before	preview
re-	back, again	review
retro-	backward	retrospect
sub-	under, below	submarine
super-	above, extra	supercharge
tele-	far	telescope
trans-	cross, over	transcontinental

Roots

Roots carry the basic or core meaning of a word. Hundreds of root words are used to build words in the English language. Some of the most common and most useful are listed in Table 3.2. Knowing the meanings of these roots will help you unlock the meanings of many words. For example, if you know that the root *dic/dict* means "tell or say," then you have a clue to the meanings of such words as *dictate* (to speak for someone to write down), *diction* (wording or manner of speaking), and *dictionary* (book that "tells" what words mean).

TABLE 3.2 COMMON ROOTS

COMMON ROOT	MEANING	SAMPLE WORD
anthropo	human being	anthropology
archaeo	ancient or past	archeology
aster/astro	star	astronaut
aud/audit	hear	audible
bene	good, well	benefit
bio	life	biology
cap	take, seize	captive
cardi	heart	cardiology
chron(o)	time	chronology
corp	body	corpse
cred	believe	incredible
dict/dic	tell, say	predict
duc/duct	lead	introduce
eco	earth	ecological
fact/fac	make, do	factory
fem	female	feminine
gen	create	generate
geo	earth	geophysics
graph	write	telegraph
gyneco	woman	gynecology
log/logo/logy	study, thought	psychology
mit/miss	send	permit/dismiss
mort/mor	die, death	immortal
neuro	nerve	neurology
path	feeling	sympathy
phono	sound, voice	telephone
photo	light	photosensitive
port	carry	transport
pulmo	lungs	pulmonary
scop	see	microscope
scrib/script	write	inscription

(continued on next page)

(continued from preceding page)

COMMON ROOT	MEANING	SAMPLE WORD
sen/sent	feel	insensitive
spec/spic/spect	look, see	retrospect
tend/tent/tens	stretch or strain	tension
terr/terre	land, earth	territory
theo	god	theology
ven/vent	come	convention
vert/vers	turn	invert
vis/vid	see	invisible/video
voc	call	vocation

EXERCISE 3-9 USING ROOTS

Read the following paragraph and choose the correct root from the box below to fill in the blank next to each boldfaced word part. One root will not be used.

osteo	phys	mort
vasc	cardio	dic

Issue: Health and Fitness

(1) _____ **respiratory** fitness reflects the heart and lungs' ability to perform exercise using large-muscle groups at moderate to high intensity for prolonged periods. Because it requires the blood vessels of the (2) **cardio** _____ **ular** system as well as respiratory systems to supply oxygen to the body during sustained physical activity, it is a good (3) **in** _____ **ator** of overall health. Low levels of fitness are associated with increased risk of premature death and disease.

A common affliction among older adults is (4) _____ **porosis**, a disease characterized by low bone mass and deterioration of bone tissue, which increase facture risk. Bone, like other human tissues, responds to the demands placed on it. Women (and men) have much to gain by remaining (5) _____ **ically** active as they age—bone mass levels are significantly higher among active than among sedentary women. Regular weight-bearing exercise, when combined with a healthy diet containing adequate calcium, helps keeps bones healthy.

—Adapted from Donatelle, *Health: The Basics, Green Edition,* pp. 329–330

Suffixes

Suffixes are word endings that often change the word's tense and/or part of speech. For example, adding the suffix -*y* to the noun *cloud* forms the adjective *cloudy*. Accompanying the change in part of speech is a shift in meaning (*cloudy* means "resembling clouds; overcast with clouds; dimmed or dulled as if by clouds").

Often, several different words can be formed from a single root word with different suffixes. If you know the meaning of the root word and the ways in which different suffixes affect the meaning of the root word, you will be able to figure out a word's meaning when a suffix is added.

Example

Root	+	Suffix	=	New word
class	+	ify	=	classify
class	+	ification	=	classification
class	+	ic	=	classic
right	+	ly	=	rightly
right	+	ful	=	rightful
right	+	eous	=	righteous

A list of common suffixes and their meanings appears in Table 3.3 on page 60.

You can expand your vocabulary by learning the variations in meaning that occur when suffixes are added to words you already know. When you find a word whose meaning you do not know, look for the root. Then, using context, figure out what the word means with the suffix added. Occasionally you may find that the spelling of the root word has changed. For instance, a final *e* may be dropped, a final consonant may be doubled, or a final *y* may be changed to *i*. Consider the possibility of such changes when trying to identify the root word.

Examples

The article was a **compilation** of facts.

    root + suffix

compil(e) + -ation = something that has been compiled, or put together into an orderly form

I was concerned with the **morality** of my decision.

    root + suffix

moral + -ity = pertaining to moral matters

Our college is one of the most **prestigious** in the state.

    root + suffix

prestig(e) + -ous = having prestige or distinction

TABLE 3.3 COMMON SUFFIXES

SUFFIX	MEANING	SAMPLE WORD	MEANING OF SAMPLE WORD
Suffixes that refer to a state, condition, or quality			
-able	capable of	touchable	capable of being touched
-ance	characterized by	assistance	the action of helping
-ation	action or process	confrontation	an act of confronting or meeting face to face
-ence	state or condition	reference	an act or instance of referring or mentioning
-ible	capable of	tangible	capable of being felt, having substance
-ion	action or process	discussion	
-ity	state or quality	superiority	the quality or condition of being higher in rank or status
-ive	performing action	permissive	characterized by freedom of behavior
-ment	action or process	amazement	a state of overwhelming surprise or astonishment
-ness	state, quality, condition	kindness	the quality of being kind
-ous	possessing, full of	jealous	envious or resentful of another
-ty	condition, quality characterized by	loyalty	the state of being loyal or faithful
-y		creamy	resembling or containing cream

(continued on next page)

(continued from preceding page)

SUFFIX	MEANING	SAMPLE WORD	MEANING OF SAMPLE WORD
Suffixes that mean "one who"			
-an		Italian	one who is from Italy
-ant		participant	one who participates
-ee		referee	one who enforces the rules of a game or sport
-eer		engineer	one who is trained in engineering
-ent		resident	one who lives in a place
-er		teacher	one who teaches
-ist		activist	one who takes action to promote or advocate a cause
-or		advisor	one who advises
Suffixes that mean "pertaining to or referring to"			
-al		autumnal	occurring in or pertaining to autumn
-ship		friendship	the state of being friends
-hood		brotherhood	the relationship between brothers
-ward		homeward	leading towards home

EXERCISE 3-10 USING SUFFIXES

Read the following paragraph. For each pair of words in parentheses, underline the word that correctly completes the sentence.

Issue: Business Ethics

Oil companies aren't usually known for their (environmentalism / environmentally) responsible reputations. Global energy giant BP, however, has made an effort to market an image that is Earth-friendly. For the most part, this strategy has (worked / working)—leading many to overlook the facts (suggesting / suggestion) that BP's claims are exaggerated or even completely false.

For the past several years, BP has (commitment / committed) environmental offenses almost (annually / annual). In 2000, the company was convicted of a felony for failing to report that its subcontractor was dumping (hazardously / hazardous) waste in Alaska. In 2005, BP allegedly ignored knowledge that its Texas City refinery was unsafe in a cost-cutting effort that led to an (explosive / explosion), 15 deaths, and even more injuries. The following year, BP's negligence at its Prudhoe Bay oil field (caused / causes) a 200,000-gallon oil spill and violation of the Clean Water Act. Then, in 2007, BP lobbied Indiana regulators for an (exemption / exemptive) allowing it to increase its daily release of ammonia and sludge into Lake Michigan.

—Adapted from Ebert and Griffin, *Business Essentials*, p. 21

3d   USING LANGUAGE EFFECTIVELY

LEARNING OBJECTIVE 4
Use language effectively when you read and write.

Words have incredible power. On the positive side, words can inspire, comfort, and educate. At the other end of the spectrum, words can inflame, annoy, or deceive. Good writers understand that word choices greatly influence the reader, and they choose words that will help them achieve their goals. Careful readers understand the nuances of words and pay attention to how writers use them. This section describes numerous language features important to both readers and writers.

Denotation and Connotation

To understand the nuances (shades of meaning) of words, it is important to understand the difference between denotation and connotation. Which of the following would you like to be a part of: *a crowd, mob, gang, audience, congregation,* or *class?* Each of these words has the same basic meaning: "an assembled group of people." But each has a different *shade* of meaning. *Crowd* suggests a large, disorganized group. *Audience,* on the other hand, suggests a quiet, controlled group. Try to decide the meanings suggested by each of the other words in the list.

This example shows that words have two levels of meanings—a literal meaning and an additional shade of meaning. A word's **denotation** is the meaning stated in the dictionary—its literal meaning. A word's **connotation** is the set of additional implied meanings, or nuances, that a word may take on. Often the connotation carries either a positive or negative association. The words *mob* and *gang* have a negative connotation because they imply a disorderly, disorganized group. *Congregation, audience,* and *class* have a positive connotation because they suggest an orderly, organized group.

Here are a few more examples. Would you prefer to be described as "slim" or "skinny"? As "intelligent" or "brainy"? As "heavy" or "fat"? As "frugal" or "cheap"? Notice that the words in each pair have a similar literal meaning, but that each word has a different connotation.

Depending on the words they choose, writers can suggest favorable or unfavorable impressions of the person, object, or event they are describing. For example, through the writer's choice of words, the two sentences below create two entirely different impressions. As you read them, notice the italicized words and their positive or negative connotations.

Examples

> The *unruly* crowd *forced* its way through the restraint barriers and *ruthlessly attacked* the rock star.
>
> The *enthusiastic* group of fans *burst* through the fence and *rushed* toward the rock star.

Connotations can help writers paint a picture to influence the reader's opinion. Thus a writer who wishes to be kind to an overweight politician might describe him as "pleasingly plump" (which carries an almost pleasant connotation) or even "quite overweight" (which is a statement of fact that remains mostly neutral). However, a writer who wishes to be negative about the same politician might describe him as "morbidly obese."

When reading, pay attention to the writer's choice of words and their connotations. Ask yourself: What words does the writer use, and how do they affect me?

EXERCISE 3-11 USING CONNOTATIVE LANGUAGE

For each of the following pairs of word or phrases, write two sentences. One sentence should use the word with the more positive connotation; the second should use the word with a less positive connotation.

1. request   demand

_____

_____

2. overlook   neglect

_____

_____

3. ridicule   tease

_____

_____

4. display   expose

_____

_____

5. garment   gown

_____

_____

6. gaudy   showy

_____

_____

7. artificial   fake

_____

_____

8. cheap   cost effective

_____

_____

9. choosy   picky

_____

_____

10. seize   take

_____

_____

EXERCISE 3-12 USING CONNOTATIVE LANGUAGE

For each of the following sentences, underline the word in parentheses that has the more appropriate connotative meaning. Consult a dictionary, if necessary.

1. The new superintendent spoke (extensively / enormously) about the issues facing the school system.

2. The day after we hiked ten miles, my legs felt extremely (rigid / stiff).

3. Carlos thought he could be more (productive / fruitful) if he had a home office.

4. The (stubborn / persistent) ringing of my cell phone finally woke me up.

5. The investment seemed too (perilous / risky), so we decided against it.

Synonyms and Antonyms

Synonyms are words with similar meanings; **antonyms** are words with opposite meanings. Both categories of words are useful to expand and diversify your reading and writing vocabulary. When writing, you may want to find a synonym, a word with a more exact, descriptive, or specific meaning than the one that first comes to mind. For example, you might want to explain how a person walks. There are many words that mean *walk*, although each may have a different connotation: *strut, meander, stroll, hike, saunter,* and *march.* A thesaurus can help you choose the word with the exact meaning you intend.

Antonyms are useful when making a contrast or explaining differences. You might be describing two different types of communication styles of friends. One style is decisive. Finding antonyms for the word *decisive* may suggest a way to describe differing styles. Antonyms include *faltering, waivering,* or *hesitant.*

Slang

Most of what you read in textbooks, magazines, newspapers, and a variety of online sources is written in Standard written English. This means it is written using a set of conventions and rules that make language clear, correct, and easy to understand by anyone who reads it. **Slang** is an informal, nonstandard form of expression used by a particular group. It is used by people who want to give themselves a unique identity, and it can be useful in some social situations, in informal writing, and in some forms of creative writing. It is *not* appropriate to use in academic writing, so be sure to avoid using it in papers, essays, and exams.

Slang She and her mom are so tight.
Standard written English She and her mom have a close relationship.

Slang On Saturday I plan to chill by the pool.
Standard written English On Saturday I plan to relax by the pool.

Colloquial Language

Colloquial language refers to casual, everyday spoken language. Be sure to avoid it in most formal writing assignments. Words that fall into this category are labeled *informal* or *colloquial* in a dictionary.

Colloquial I almost flunked bio last sem.
Standard written English I almost failed biology last semester.

Colloquial Janice go to the store.
Standard written English Janice goes to the store.

Idioms

An **idiom** is a phrase with a meaning different than the phrase's individual words. Sometimes you can figure out an idiom's meaning from context within the sentence or paragraph, but more commonly you must simply know the idiom to understand it.

Examples

> The $10,000 he embezzled was just the **tip of the iceberg** (a small, observable part of something much larger).
>
> While the company's sales are excellent, its **bottom line** (total profit) is awful. ("Bottom line" refers to the last line of a financial statement, showing the company's overall profit or loss.)
>
> The only **sure-fire** (guaranteed to work) method of losing weight is diet and exercise.
>
> We have **buried our head in the sand** (denied reality) about our nation's deficit for far too long.

As you read, be on the lookout for phrases that use common words but do not make sense no matter how many times you reread them. When you find such a phrase, you have likely encountered an idiom. (It is estimated that the English language has almost 25,000 idiomatic expressions.)

EXERCISE 3-13 UNDERSTANDING IDIOMS

For each sentence, write the meaning of the idiomatic expression in boldface.

1. The kidnapping of the twins from Utah in 1985 has turned into a **cold case**.

   _____

2. Jake decided to **zero in on** his goal of becoming a firefighter.

   _____

3. I am trying to make an appointment with my academic advisor, but she's been hard to **pin down**.

   _____

4. The mystery novels of P.D. James **blur the line** between popular fiction and literature.

   _____

5. Milton **saw red** when someone rear-ended his car.

   _____

Analogies

Analogies are abbreviated statements that express similarities between two pairs of items. You will find them on a variety of entrance and competency tests and exams. They are tests of both your thinking skills and your word knowledge. Analogies are often written in the following format:

> black : white :: dark : light

This can be read in either of two ways:

1. Black is to white as dark is to light.
2. White has the same relationship to black as light does to dark. (White is the opposite of black and light is the opposite of dark.)

In analogies the relationship between the words or phrases is critically important. Analogies become test items when one of the four items is left blank, and you are asked to supply or select the missing item.

> Celery : vegetable :: orange: _____
>
> video : watch :: audio : _____

A variety of relationships are expressed in analogies. These include

- Opposites yes: no :: stop : start
- Whole/part year : month :: week : day
- Synonyms moist: damp :: happy : glad
- Categories dessert : cake :: meat : beef
- Similarities lemon : orange :: broccoli : cabbage
- Association or action train : conductor :: airplane : pilot
- Knowledge Picasso : painter :: Shakespeare : writer

EXERCISE 3-14 WORKING WITH ANALOGIES

Complete each of the following analogies by supplying a word or phrase that completes it.

1. sculptor: statue :: musician : _____

2. Allah : Islam :: God : _____

3. fresh : rancid :: unique : _____

4. hasten : speed up :: outdated : _____

5. old age : geriatrics :: infancy : _____

Technical and Academic Language

One of the first tasks you face in a new college course is to learn its specialized language. This is particularly true of introductory courses in which a new discipline or field of study is explained.

Have you noticed that each sport and hobby has its own language—a specialized set of words and phrases with very specific meanings? Baseball players and fans talk about slides, home runs, errors, and runs batted in, for example. Each academic discipline also has its own language. For each course you take, you will encounter an extensive set of words and terms that have a particular, specialized meaning in that subject area. It is important to learn to understand the language of a course when reading and to use the language of a course when speaking and writing. In this reading and writing course, you will learn terms such as *topic sentence, supporting details, signal words, idea map,* and *transitions.*

A sample of the words introduced in economics and chemistry are given below. Some of the terms are common, everyday words that take on a specialized meaning; others are technical terms used only in that subject area.

New Terms: Economics Text	New Terms: Chemistry Text
capital	matter
ownership	element
opportunity cost	halogen
distribution	isotope

Recognition of academic and technical terminology is only the first step in learning the language of a course. More important is the development of a systematic way of identifying, marking, recording, and learning these terms. Because new terminology is introduced in both class lectures and course textbooks, be sure to develop a procedure for handling the specialized terms in each. You might highlight them, annotate, or create a vocabulary log using a computer file or notebook, for example.

SUMMARY OF LEARNING OBJECTIVES

Objective 1 Use resources for vocabulary building.	Online, pocket, desk and unabridged *dictionaries* are useful resources for locating the meanings of unfamiliar words. Meanings in an entry are grouped and numbered consecutively according to part of speech. If you know the part of speech of a word, skip to that section; if not, look for a meaning that fits the context of the word. A *thesaurus*, a dictionary of synonyms, is useful for selecting the most accurate and precise word to fit a particular situation.
Objective 2 Use context clues.	Context clues help readers figure out the meaning of unfamiliar words. Context clues fall into four categories: (1) *definition clues*, (2) *example clues*, (3) *contrast clues*, and (4) *logic of the passage clues*.
Objective 3 Use affixes: prefixes, roots, and suffixes.	Many words are composed of some combination of prefix, root, and suffix. The *prefix* precedes the main part of the word; the *root* is the key part of the word that carries its core meaning; and the *suffix* appears at the end of the word. In the word *unteachable*, *un-* is the prefix, *teach* is the root, and *–able* is the suffix. Knowing the meanings of key prefixes, roots, and suffixes will help you unlock the meaning of many unfamiliar words.
Objective 4 Use language effectively.	The *denotative meaning* of a word is its stated dictionary meaning; a word's *connotation* is a set of implied meanings a word may take on. *Synonyms* are words of similar meaning; *antonyms* are words of opposite meaning. *Slang* refers to nonstandard or everyday informal language used by a particular group. *Colloquial language* refers to casual, everyday spoken language. An *idiom* is a phrase with a meaning different than the phrase's individual words. *Analogies* are abbreviated statements that express a relationship between two pairs of items. *Technical and academic language* refers to specialized use of terms in particular academic disciplines.

4 Reading Paragraphs: Main Ideas, Supporting Details, and Signal Words

LEARNING OBJECTIVES

1 Understand the structure of a paragraph

2 Find stated main ideas

3 Recognize supporting details

4 Find implied main ideas

5 Recognize signal words

Most articles, essays, and textbook chapters contain numerous ideas expressed in paragraph form. As you read, your job is to sort out the important ideas from those that are less important. As you write, you are expected to express your ideas clearly and correctly in paragraph form. In this chapter, you will learn to identify main ideas and supporting details. You will also learn how to find implied main ideas and learn how signal words link ideas together.

4a WHAT IS A PARAGRAPH?

LEARNING OBJECTIVE 1
Structure of a paragraph.

A **paragraph** is a group of related sentences that develop a main thought, or idea, about a single topic. The structure of a paragraph is not complex. There are usually four basic elements: (1) a topic, (2) a main idea, or topic sentence, (3) supporting details, and (4) signal words.

A **topic** is the one thing a paragraph is about. The **topic sentence** expresses an idea about that topic. The topic sentence states the main point or controlling idea. The sentences that explain this main point are called **supporting details**. Words and phrases that connect and show relationships between and among ideas are called **signal words**. Stand-alone paragraphs (those not part of an essay) often include a concluding sentence that wraps up the paragraph and brings it to a close. These elements help you know what to look for and ensure that you will understand and remember what you read.

Now read the following paragraph, and notice how all the details relate to one point and explain the topic sentence, which is highlighted and labeled.

Detail 1

Detail 2

Detail 3

> There is some evidence that colors affect you physiologically. For example, when subjects are exposed to red light, respiratory movements increase; exposure to blue decreases respiratory movements. Similarly, eye blinks increase in frequency when eyes are exposed to red light and decrease when exposed to blue. This seems consistent with the intuitive feelings about blue being more soothing and red being more arousing. After changing a school's walls from orange and white to blue, the blood pressure of the students decreased while their academic performance improved.
>
> —DeVito, *Human Communication: The Basic Course*, p. 182

In this paragraph, look at the highlighted topic sentence. It identifies the topic as *color* and states that *colors affect people physiologically*. The remaining sentences provide further information about the effects of color. Since this paragraph first appeared in a textbook chapter, it does not have a concluding sentence.

You can think about and visualize a paragraph this way:

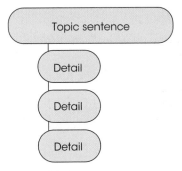

Here's how you might visualize the paragraph on color:

Colors affect people physiologically.

Respiratory movements increase in red light and decrease in blue light.

Eye blinks increase in red light and decrease in blue light.

A change in a school's walls from orange and white to blue decreased students' blood pressure and improved academic performance.

Findings are consistent with the idea that blue is soothing and red is arousing.

4b   FINDING STATED MAIN IDEAS

LEARNING OBJECTIVE 2
Find stated main ideas.

In most paragraphs the main idea is expressed in a single sentence called the **topic sentence**. Occasionally, you will find a paragraph in which the main idea is not expressed in any single sentence. The main idea is **implied**; that is, it is suggested but not directly stated in the paragraph. (For more on implied main ideas, see section 4d.)

You can visualize a paragraph as shown in the accompanying diagram.

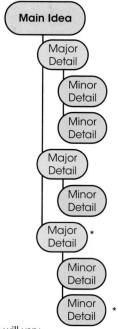

*Number of major and minor details will vary.

Distinguishing Between General and Specific Ideas

A **general idea** applies to a large number of individual items. The term *television programs* is general because it refers to a large collection of shows—soap operas, sports specials, sitcoms, and so on. A **specific idea** or term is more detailed or particular. It refers to an individual item. The term *reality TV*, for example, is more specific than the word *program*. The title *The Real Housewives of Atlanta* is even more specific.

Examples

General:	Continents	*General:*	U.S. Presidents
Specific:	Asia	*Specific:*	John F. Kennedy
	Africa		Barack Obama
	Australia		Thomas Jefferson

EXERCISE 4-1 IDENTIFYING GENERAL IDEAS

For each list of items, write a word or phrase that best describes that grouping.

1. sadness, joy, anger, bereavement

   _____

2. Capricorn, Aquarius, Taurus, Libra

   _____

3. U.S. Constitution, Bill of Rights, Federalist Papers, First Amendment

   _____

4. Mars, Saturn, Jupiter, Mercury

   _____

Now that you are familiar with the difference between general and specific, you will be able to use these concepts in the rest of the chapter.

Finding the Topic

We have defined a paragraph as a group of related ideas. The sentences are related to one another, and all are about the same person, place, thing, or idea. The common subject or idea is called the *topic*—what the entire paragraph is about. As you read the following paragraph, you will see that its topic is unemployment and inflation.

Issue: The Economy

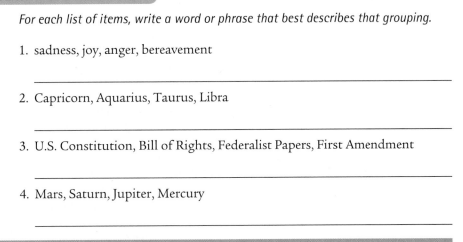

Unemployment and inflation are the economic problems that are most often discussed in the media and during political campaigns. For many people, the state of the economy can be summarized in just two measures: the unemployment rate and the inflation rate. In the 1960s, Arthur Okun, who was chairman of the Council of Economic Advisors during President Lyndon Johnson's administration, coined the term *misery index*, which adds together the inflation rate and the unemployment rate to give a rough measure of the state of the economy. Although unemployment and inflation are important problems in the short run, the long-run success of an economy is best judged by its ability to generate high levels of real GDP (gross domestic product) per person.

—Adapted from Hubbard and O'Brien, *Essentials of Economics*, p. 408

Each sentence of this paragraph discusses or describes unemployment and inflation. To identify the topic of a paragraph, ask yourself: *"What or whom is the paragraph about?"*

EXERCISE 4-2 IDENTIFYING THE TOPIC

After reading each of the following paragraphs, select the choice that best represents the topic of the selection.

Issue: Prejudice and Stereotypes

_____ 1.   Everyone is familiar with the legacy of racial prejudice in the United States. Arguments over the legitimacy of slavery are 150 years in the past and it has been decades since public schools were integrated, yet racial prejudice remains a major concern among all demographic groups in this country. The emphasis on race has also increased our awareness of other forms of stereotyping. For example, psychologists have researched stereotypes and prejudice related to weight and body size, sexual orientation, and religious affiliation. Racial, ethnic, and other out-group stereotypes are pervasive and, unfortunately, seem to thrive in times of hardship. For example, during economic slumps, an out-group (a collection of people who are perceived as different) is often targeted for taking jobs from the in-group or for draining resources from the local economy.

—Adapted from Krause and Corts, *Psychological Science*, p. 569

    a. racial prejudice and forms of stereotyping

    b. U.S. history

    c. in-groups and out-groups

    d. the results of economic hardship

Issue: Personal Relationships

_____ 2.   According to Bella DePaulo and Wendy Morris (2006), one of the major disadvantages of not being married is that single adults are the targets of *singlism*, the negative stereotypes and discrimination faced by singles. Their research found that single people were viewed more negatively than married people. Compared to married or coupled people, who are often described in very positive terms, singles are assumed to be immature, maladjusted, and self-centered. Loneliness, lack of companionship, being excluded from couples' events, or feeling uncomfortable in social settings involving mostly couples, not having children, and social disapproval of their lifestyle are among the other frequently reported disadvantages of being single. Another disadvantage of living alone is more gender-specific. Women living alone confront safety issues in deciding where to live, what mode of transportation to use, and which leisure activities to attend.

—Schwartz and Scott, *Marriages and Families*, p. 211

a. singlism

b. gender-specific perceptions

c. disadvantages of being single

d. societal perceptions of married people

Issue: Environmental Conservation

_____   3.   Our planet is called the "Blue Marble," and for good reason: Over 70% of Earth's surface is covered with water. Solar energy and gravity drive the hydrologic cycle, moving water between the oceans, the atmosphere, and the land. Precipitation that falls on land may evaporate back into the atmosphere, percolate down into aquifers in the ground, or flow back to the sea in one of the thousands of streams and rivers that course across every continent. Lakes and inland seas store water and slow its movement. Wetlands store and filter water. Human use of water affects every part of Earth's hydrologic cycle, including the distribution of water in streams, lakes, and groundwater and the kinds and amounts of chemicals and sediments that water carries.

—Norm Christensen, *The Environment and You*, p. 336

a. Earth

b. precipitation

c. water

d. lakes and rivers

Stated Main Ideas

The **main idea** of a paragraph is what the author wants you to know about the topic. It is the broadest, most important idea that the writer develops throughout the paragraph. The entire paragraph explains, develops, and supports this main idea. A question that will guide you in finding the main idea is *"What key point is the author making about the topic?"* In the paragraph about unemployment and inflation on page 73, the writer's main idea is that unemployment and inflation are two important measures of the economy's overall health.

Often, but not always, one sentence expresses the main idea. This sentence is called the **topic sentence**.

Finding the Topic Sentence

To find the topic sentence, search for the one general sentence that explains what the writer wants you to know about the topic. A topic sentence is a broad, general statement; the remaining sentences of the paragraph provide details about or explain the topic sentence.

In the following paragraph, the topic is practical learning in the United States. Read the paragraph to find out what the writer wants you to know about this topic. Look for the one sentence that states this.

Issue: Education

> In the United States, the educational system stresses the value of *practical learning,* knowledge that prepares people for their future jobs. This is in line with what the educational philosopher John Dewey (1859–1952) called *progressive education,* having the schools make learning relevant to people's lives. Students seek out subjects of study that they believe will give them an advantage when they are ready to compete in the job market. For example, as concerns about international terrorism have risen in recent years, so have the number of students choosing to study geography, international conflict, and Middle Eastern history and culture (M. Lord, 2001).
>
> —Macionis, *Society: The Basics,* 12th Edition, p. 376

The paragraph opens with a statement and then proceeds to explain it with supporting evidence. The first sentence is the topic sentence, and it states the paragraph's main point: The U.S. educational system stresses practical learning.

Here are some tips that will help you find the topic sentence.

TIPS FOR LOCATING TOPIC SENTENCES

1. **Identify the topic.** Figure out the general subject of the entire paragraph. In the preceding sample paragraph, "practical learning" is the topic.
2. **Locate the most general sentence (the topic sentence).** This sentence must be broad enough to include all of the other ideas in the paragraph. The topic sentence in the sample paragraph ("In the United States, the educational system stresses the value of *practical learning,* knowledge that prepares people for their future jobs") covers all of the other details in the paragraph.

Common Positions for the Topic Sentence

The topic sentence can be located anywhere in the paragraph. However, there are several positions where it is most likely to be found.

Topic Sentence First

Most often the topic sentence is placed first in the paragraph. In this type of paragraph, the writer first states his or her main point and then explains it.

Issue: Popular Psychology

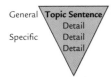

General
Specific

> Color influences perceptions and behaviors. People's acceptance of a product, for example, is largely determined by its packaging—especially its color. In one study the very same coffee taken from a yellow can was described as weak, from a dark brown can as too strong, from a red can as rich, and from a blue can as mild. Even your acceptance of a person may depend on the color he or she wears. Consider, for example, the comments of one color expert: "If you have to pick the wardrobe for your defense lawyer heading into court and choose anything but blue, you deserve to lose the case." Black is so powerful it could work against the lawyer with the jury. Brown lacks sufficient authority. Green would probably elicit a negative response.
>
> —DeVito, *Human Communication: The Basic Course*, c. 2012, pp. 127–128

Here the writer first states that color influences perceptions and behaviors. The rest of the paragraph presents evidence and examples to support the topic sentence.

Topic Sentence Last

The second most likely place for a topic sentence to appear is last in the paragraph. When using this arrangement, a writer leads up to the main point and then directly states it at the end.

Issue: Parents and Children

> To spank or not to spank has been a controversial issue for many years now. Child development experts have typically advised parents to use other methods of disciplining their children, citing the possibility of encouraging child abuse as well as the role played by spanking in the modeling of aggression. Now the results of a new study suggest there is a significantly increased risk of higher levels of aggression at age 5 when spanking is used at age 3. While older studies have found similar results, the study by Dr. Catherine Taylor and her colleagues differs from those earlier studies in that possible maternal risk factors such as neglect, the mother's use of drugs, and maternal psychological problems were measured and controlled. The Taylor study found that when mothers stated that they spanked their 3-year-olds more than twice in the previous month, those same children at 5 years of age were much more likely to be aggressive. The conclusion seems to be that sparing the rod may spare the child (and those around the child) from an unpleasant personality trait.
>
> —Adapted from Ciccarelli and White, *Psychology*, p. 191

Specific
General

In this paragraph, the author ponders the relationship between spanking and aggression and concludes with the paragraph's main point: that children who are spanked are more likely to become aggressive.

Topic Sentence in the Middle

If it is placed neither first nor last, then the topic sentence appears somewhere in the middle of the paragraph. In this arrangement, the sentences before the topic sentence lead up to or introduce the main idea. Those that follow the main idea explain or describe it.

Issue: Wildlife Conservation

> In colonial days, huge flocks of snowy egrets inhabited the coastal wetlands and marshes of the southeastern United States. In the 1800s, when fashion dictated fancy hats adorned with feathers, egrets and other birds were hunted for their plumage. By the late 1800s, egrets were almost extinct. In 1886, the newly formed National Audubon Society began a press campaign to shame "feather wearers" and end the practice. The campaign caught on, and gradually, attitudes changed; new laws followed. Government policies that protect animals from overharvesting are essential to keep species from the brink of extinction. Even when cultural standards change due to the efforts of individual groups (such as the National Audubon Society), laws and policy measures must follow to ensure that endangered populations remain protected. Since the 1800s, several important laws have been passed to protect a wide variety of species.
>
> —Wright and Boorse, *Environmental Science: Toward a Sustainable Future,* p. 150

In this paragraph, the writers first give an example of a species that nearly became extinct. Then they state their main point: Government policies are needed to protect species nearing extinction. The remainder of the paragraph explains why laws are needed and mentions that several laws protecting a wide range of species have been passed.

Topic Sentence First and Last

Occasionally the main idea is stated at the beginning of a paragraph and again at the end, or elsewhere in the paragraph. Writers may use this organization to emphasize an important idea or to explain an idea that needs clarification. At other times, the first and last sentences together express the paragraph's main idea.

Issue: Government and Politics

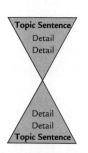

> A key instrument of a state's [country's] power against its enemies is its security forces, which include official groups such as the regular military and the secret police, as well as unofficial armed groups. In some countries, such as Libya, Syria, and Yemen, the secret police have a record of using violence against anti-government demonstrators. In Columbia, paramilitary forces, which are not officially part of the Columbian military, have been held respon-

sible for 70 to 80% of political murders in recent years. Another form of state power is judicial systems and prison systems, which punish those whose behaviors displease the state.

—Adapted from Danzinger, *Understanding the Political World*, p. 320

The first and last sentences together explain the key forms of a country's powers against the people it perceives as its enemies.

EXERCISE 4-3 FINDING TOPIC SENTENCES 1

Underline the topic sentence of each of the following paragraphs.

Paragraph 1
Issue: Poverty

Sociologists have several different ways of defining poverty. *Transitional poverty* is a temporary state that occurs when someone loses a job for a short time. *Marginal poverty* occurs when a person lacks stable employment (for example, if your job is lifeguarding at a pool during the summer season, you might experience marginal poverty when the season ends). The next, more serious level, *residual poverty*, is chronic and multigenerational. A person who experiences *absolute poverty* is so poor that he or she doesn't have resources to survive. *Relative poverty* is a state that occurs when we compare ourselves with those around us.

—Adapted from Carl, *Think Sociology*, p. 122

Paragraph 2
Issue: Medical Liability and the Law

In the past, exposure to liability made many doctors, nurses, and other medical professionals reluctant to stop and render aid to victims in emergency situations, such as highway accidents. Almost all states have enacted a Good Samaritan law that relieves medical professionals from liability for injury caused by their ordinary negligence in each set of circumstances. Good Samaritan laws protect medical professionals only from liability for their *ordinary negligence*, not for injuries caused by their gross negligence or reckless or intentional conduct. Many Good Samaritan laws have protected licensed doctors and nurses and laypersons who have been certified in CPR. Good Samaritan statutes generally do not protect laypersons who are not trained in CPR—that is, they are liable for injuries caused by their ordinary negligence in rendering aid.

—Goldman and Cheeseman, *Paralegal Professional*, p. 459

Paragraph 3
Issue: Fashion

One of the best ways to analyze your wardrobe is to determine which items you already own. This requires a thorough closet cleaning, purging items that no longer fit, are out of fashion, are not appropriate for your career or leisure time, or have not been worn in a year. Trying on everything gives you the opportunity to categorize clothing into piles labeled: keepers, "iffy," resells, and purge. After this exercise, organize the garments that remain by category and color, starting with neutrals and moving to brights in this order: shirts/tops, bottoms, jackets/coats/ sweaters, and for women dresses. Put out-of-season in another storage area. After wearing, always replace garments in their original location.

—Adapted from Marshall, Jackson, and Stanley, *Individuality in Clothing Selection and Personal Appearance*, p. 293

Paragraph 4
Issue: Electronic Communication and Social Media

With so many people participating in social networking sites and keeping personal blogs, it's increasingly common for a single disgruntled customer to wage war online against a company for poor service or faulty products. Unhappy customers have taken to the Web to complain about broken computers or poor customer service. Individuals may post negative reviews of products on blogs, upload angry videos outlining complaints on YouTube, or join public discussion forums where they can voice their opinion about the good and the bad. In the same way that companies celebrate the viral spread of good news, they must also be on guard for online backlash that can damage a reputation.

—Adapted from Ebert and Griffin, *Business Essentials*, p. 161

Paragraph 5
Issue: Cultural Similarities and Differences

In Japan, it's called *kuroi kiri* (black mist); in Germany, it's *schmiergeld* (grease money), whereas Mexicans refer to *la mordida* (the bite), the French say *pot-de-vin* (jug of wine), and Italians speak of the *bustarella* (little envelope). They're all talking about *bakshseesh*, the Middle Eastern term for a "tip" to grease the wheels of a transaction. Giving "gifts" in exchange for getting business is common and acceptable in many countries, even though this may be frowned on elsewhere.

—Adapted from Solomon, *Consumer Behavior*, p. 21

EXERCISE 4-4　FINDING TOPIC SENTENCES

Underline the topic sentence of each of the following paragraphs.

Issue: Popular Psychology

Introspection

The process of **introspection**, or thinking about your own thoughts, is not as helpful as conventional wisdom would lead us to believe. In fact, some research suggests the process can lead us astray more often than not. In a number of studies, when people were asked to analyze their reasons for holding particular attitudes, their stated attitudes were *less* likely to match up with their actual behaviors. This shows that we are not always good at predicting or understanding our feelings. This is also why we are likely to make better decisions based on instinct than when we engage in analysis.

We are also less in touch with our "inner selves" when it comes to predicting the impacts that certain events will have on our feelings and attitudes. Think about your dream job, car, and house. If someone suddenly handed you all those things today, how do you think you would feel five years from now? Chances are pretty high that you wouldn't feel as happy then as you might guess right now. This is because our attempts at **affective forecasting**, predicting the impact future events will have on our overall emotional states, are usually inaccurate.

We tend to overestimate the intensity and duration of our emotional responses. For instance, Daniel Gilbert and his colleagues asked college students to predict how they would feel two months into the future if their girlfriends or boyfriends broke up with them. Participants guessed that they would be unhappy for a long time, but in reality, students who had been through a breakup two months earlier did *not* report being as unhappy as they had predicted; in fact, they were generally just as happy as students who had not been through the same experience.

—Adapted from Kimberley J. Duff, *Think Social Psychology*, pp. 61–62

EXERCISE 4-5 FINDING MAIN IDEAS

After reading the following passage, select the choice that best completes each of the statements that follow.

Issue: Health and Nutrition

What Makes Eating So Enjoyable?

1   As much fun as it is to eat, you're not just taking in food for fun. Food satisfies a genuine physical need. Eating food and drinking fluids often begins with the sensation of either **hunger** or **thirst**. The amount of food that we eat and the timing of our meals are driven by physical needs. **Appetite** is another powerful drive, but it is often unreliable. Appetite is influenced by our food preferences and the psychological stimulation to eat. In other words, you can become interested in food, pursue food, and experience the desire to eat too much food without actually needing nourishment or being hungry.

We Develop a Taste for Certain Foods

2   Everyone enjoys eating food that tastes delicious, but what exactly *is* taste? There are five basic categories of taste: sweet, salty, sour, bitter, and savory ("umami"). Most taste buds are located on the tongue, but additional taste buds are found in the throat and elsewhere in the mouth. Food scientists estimate that each of us has at least 10,000 taste buds.

3   Even though we each have our own favorite foods, we share some taste traits. In general, we all have an innate preference for sweet, salty, and fatty foods. There is a scientific explanation for these preferences. Sugar seems to elicit universal pleasure (even among infants), and the brain seeks pleasure. Salt provides two important **electrolytes** (sodium and chloride) that are essential to your body and can stimulate the appetite. Your liking of both sugar and salt makes carbohydrate-rich foods appealing to you. Foods rich in carbohydrates provides the fuel that your body needs daily. High-fat foods not only have rich textures and aromas that round out the flavors of food, but also provide essential nutrients that are critical to your health. Thus, while we tend to enjoy rich sauces, gravies, and salad dressings, we are, at the same time, meeting our nutritional needs.

4   Sometimes, our food preferences and our nutritional needs conflict. We may eat too much because the food is so pleasurable. When there is a reason to change our food habits, such as a need to lose weight or reduce salt or fat intake, we realize how challenging it can be to control our food choices.

5   How does the brain recognize taste? When food is consumed, portions of the food are dissolved in saliva. These fluids then make contact with the tongue's surface. The taste (gustatory) cells send a message to the brain. The brain then translates the nerve impulses into taste sensations that you recognize.

Aromas and Flavors Enhance the Pleasure of Eating

6   The sensing structures in the nose are also important to the ability to taste foods. The average person is capable of distinguishing 2,000 to 4,000 aromas. We detect food aroma through the nose when we smell food and, as we eat, when food odors enter the mouth and migrate to the back of the throat and into the nasal cavities. The average person has about 10 million to 20 million olfactory cells (odor cells) in the nasal cavity. Therefore, both your mouth and your nose contribute to the tasting of foods. This explains why you lose interest in eating when you have a cold or other forms of nasal congestion. Food loses some of it appeal when you can't smell it.

7   Both the taste and the aroma of a food contribute to it flavor. The term *flavor* also refers to the complete food experience. For example, when you eat a candy bar, you sense a sweet taste, but the flavor is chocolate.

8   The presence of fat tends to enhance the flavor of foods. When the fat content increases, the intensity of the flavor also increases, as many aromatic compounds are soluble in fat. Increased fat content causes the flavor of food to last longer compared with flavor compounds dissolved in water. Flavors dissolved in water are quickly detected, but also quickly dissipated. This explains why most people prefer premium ice cream over frozen popsicles. It also explains why several low-fat foods have an acceptable flavor, but they are not as delicious as their high-fat counterparts.

—Blake, *Nutrition and You: My Plate Edition*, pp. 66–67

_____ 1. The topic sentence of the first paragraph begins with the words
   a. "As much fun."
   b. "Food satisfies."
   c. "Eating food and drinking fluids."
   d. "In other words."

_____ 2. The topic of the second paragraph is
   a. taste.
   b. sweetness.
   c. umami.
   d. food science.

_____ 3. The topic of the sixth paragraph is
   a. odors and aromas.
   b. the effects of sickness on the sense of taste.
   c. olfactory cells.
   d. sensing structures in the nose and throat.

_____ 4. In the eighth paragraph, the topic sentence begins with the words
   a. "The presence of fat."
   b. "Flavors dissolved in water."
   c. "This explains why."
   d. "It also explains."

4c   RECOGNIZING SUPPORTING DETAILS

LEARNING OBJECTIVE 3
Recognize supporting details.

Supporting details are those facts and ideas that prove or explain the main idea of a paragraph. While all the details in a paragraph support the main idea, not all details are equally important. As you read, try to identify and pay attention to the most important details. Pay less attention to details of lesser importance. The key details directly explain the main idea. Other details may provide additional information, offer an example, or further explain one of the key details.

Figure A on the next page shows how details relate to the main idea and how details range in degree of importance. In the diagram, more important details are placed toward the left; less important details are closer to the right.

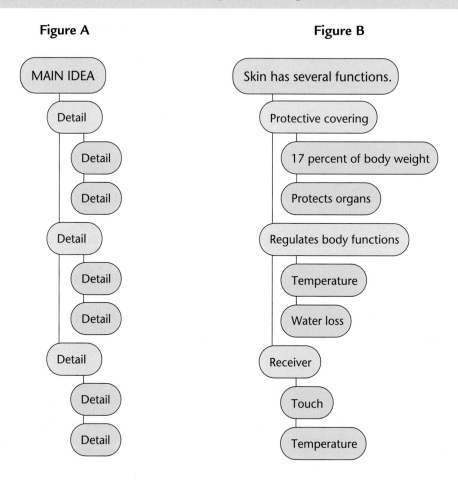

Figure A   Figure B

Read the following paragraph and study Figure B.

Issue: Health and Wellness

> The skin of the human body has several functions. First, it serves as a protective covering. In doing so, it accounts for 17 percent of the body weight. Skin also protects the organs within the body from damage or harm. The skin serves as a regulator of body functions. It controls body temperature and water loss. Finally, the skin serves as a receiver. It is sensitive to touch and temperature.

From the diagram you can see that the details stating the three functions of skin are the key details. Other details, such as "protects the organs," provide further information and are less important.

Read the following paragraph and try to pick out the more important details.

Issue: Cultural Similarities and Differences

Many cultures have different rules for men and women engaging in conflict. Asian cultures are more strongly prohibitive of women's conflict strategies. Asian women are expected to be exceptionally polite; this is even more important when women are in conflict with men and when the conflict is public. In the United States, there is a verbalized equality; men and women have equal rights when it comes to permissible conflict strategies. In reality, there are many who expect women to be more polite, to pursue conflict in a non-argumentative way, while men are expected to argue forcefully and logically.

This paragraph could be diagrammed as follows (key details only):

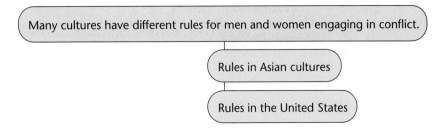

Many cultures have different rules for men and women engaging in conflict.

Rules in Asian cultures

Rules in the United States

EXERCISE 4-6 RECOGNIZING SUPPORTING DETAILS 1

Each of the following topic sentences states the main idea of a paragraph. After each topic sentence are five sentences containing details that may or may not support the topic sentence. Read each sentence and put an "S" beside those that contain details that support the topic sentence.

1. **Topic Sentence:** A monopoly is a company that controls the sale of a certain good and therefore is able to set high prices.

   _____ a. The automobile industry is a good example of an oligopoly, because none of the large companies (such as Ford, Toyota, and Honda) controls the industry.

   _____ b. Markets for agricultural products like cotton and wheat are considered very competitive, and farmers are often unable to set high prices for their goods.

   _____ c. Many critics have accused monopolies of unfair pricing.

   _____ d. The DeBeers Company, which mines diamonds in Africa and elsewhere, holds a monopoly in the world market for diamonds.

   _____ e. Some common examples of monopolies are public utility companies and the sports franchises in major U.S. cities.

2. **Topic Sentence:** *Mens rea*, a term that refers to a person's criminal intent when committing a crime, or his or her state of mind, can be evaluated in several ways.

_____ a. Confessions by criminals are direct evidence of their criminal intent.

_____ b. Circumstantial evidence can be used to suggest mental intent.

_____ c. *Actus rea* is the set of a person's actions that make up a crime.

_____ d. People who commit crimes are often repeat offenders.

_____ e. Expert witnesses may offer an opinion about a person's criminal intent.

3. **Topic Sentence:** Food irradiation is a process in which food is treated with radiation to kill bacteria.

_____ a. Many consumers are concerned about the increasing number of genetically modified foods.

_____ b. The radioactive rays pass through the food without damaging it or changing it.

_____ c. One form of irradiation uses electricity as the energy source for irradiation.

_____ d. Irradiation increases the shelf life of food because it kills all bacteria present in the food.

_____ e. *E. coli*, salmonella, and listeria cause many illnesses each year.

4. **Topic Sentence:** The television and film industries promote unhealthy body images for both women and men.

_____ a. Many Hollywood films feature unacceptable levels of violence.

_____ b. Many TV and film stars have undergone extensive plastic surgery that make them look not quite human.

_____ c. Movies and television programs portray the ideal female body type as slender and curvaceous.

_____ d. Television relies on advertisements to fund its programming.

_____ e. Many teenage boys are injecting themselves with illegal steroids to achieve muscular bodies like those they see on television and in the movies.

Underline only the most important details in each of the following paragraphs.

Paragraph 1
Issue: Drugs and Addiction

Physiological dependence, the adaptive state that occurs with regular addictive behavior and results in withdrawal syndrome, is only one indicator of addiction. Chemicals are responsible for the most profound addictions because they cause cellular changes to which the body adapts so well that it eventually requires the chemical to function normally. Psychological dynamics, though, also play an important role. Psychological and physiological dependence are intertwined and nearly impossible to separate; all forms of addiction probably reflect dysfunction of certain biochemical systems in the brain.

—Donatelle, *My Health: An Outcomes Approach*, p. 122

Paragraph 2
Issue: Globalization and Cultural Diversity

The Abkhasians (an agricultural people who live in a mountainous region of Georgia, a republic of the former Soviet Union) may be the longest-lived people on earth. Many claim to live past 100—some beyond 120 and even 130. Although it is difficult to document the accuracy of these claims, government records indicate that an extraordinary number of Abkhasians do live to a very old age. Three main factors appear to account for their long lives. The first is their diet, which consists of little meat, much fresh fruit, vegetables, garlic, goat cheese, cornmeal, buttermilk, and wine. The second is their lifelong physical activity. They do slow down after age 80, but even after the age of 100 they still work about four hours a day. The third factor—a highly developed sense of community—goes to the very heart of the Abkhasian culture. From childhood, each individual is integrated into a primary group, and remains so throughout life. There is no such thing as a nursing home, nor do the elderly live alone.

—Adapted from Henslin, *Sociology: A Down-to-Earth Approach*, pp. 380–381

Paragraph 3
Issue: Crime and Communities

There are four different dimensions of an arrest: legal, behavioral, subjective, and official. In legal terms, an arrest is made when someone lawfully deprives another person of liberty; in other words, that person is not free to go. The actual word *arrest* need not be uttered, but the other person must be brought under the control of the arresting individual. The behavioral element in arrests is often nothing more than the phrase "You're under arrest." However, that statement is usually backed up by a tight grip on the arm or collar, or the drawing of an officer's handgun, or the use of handcuffs. The subjective dimension of arrest refers to whenever people believe they are not free to leave; to all intents and purposes, they are under arrest. In any case, the arrest lasts only as long as the person is in custody, which might be a matter of a few minutes or many hours. Many people are briefly detained on the street and then released. Official arrests are those detentions that the police record in an administrative record. When a suspect is "booked" at the police station, a record is made of the arrest.

—Barlow, *Criminal Justice in America*, p. 238

Paragraph 4
Issue: Crime and Criminals

Mental illness can play a role in a criminal case in two ways. First, it must be asked whether the defendant is sane enough to be placed on trial. Second, it must be established whether the defendant was sane at the time of the act. Defendants must be mentally competent to stand trial so as to understand the legal proceedings against them. The legal standard for determining competency to stand trial was established back in 1960, when the U.S. Supreme Court held that a person is incompetent to stand trial if he or she lacks the ability to consult with a lawyer with a reasonable degree of understanding *and* lacks a rational and factual understanding of the legal proceedings.

—Albanese, *Criminal Justice*, p. 98.

Paragraph 5
Issue: Health and Appearance

The use of cosmetics has a long and interesting history, but past usage doesn't even come close to the amounts and varieties of cosmetics used by people in the modern industrial world. Each year, we spend billions of dollars on everything from hair sprays to nail polishes, from mouthwashes to foot powders. Combined sales of the world's 100 largest cosmetics companies were more than $125 billion in 2008. What is a cosmetic? The U.S. Food, Drug, and Cosmetic Act of 1938 defined cosmetics as "articles intended to be rubbed, poured, sprinkled, or sprayed on, introduced into, or otherwise applied to the human body or any part thereof, for cleansing, beautifying, promoting attractiveness or altering the appearance." Soap, although obviously used for cleansing, is specifically excluded from coverage by the law. Also excluded are substances that affect the body's structure or functions. Antiperspirants, products that reduce perspiration, are legally classified as drugs, as are antidandruff shampoos.

—Hill, McCreary, and Kolb, *Chemistry for Changing Times*, c. 2013, p. 663

EXERCISE 4-8 RECOGNIZING SUPPORTING DETAILS 3

Reread the article "Consequences of Social Class" on page 6 and underline the most important supporting details in each paragraph.

4d   UNDERSTANDING IMPLIED MAIN IDEAS

LEARNING OBJECTIVE 4
Find implied main ideas.

Study the cartoon below. What main point is it making? Although the cartoonist's message is not directly stated, you were able to figure it out by looking at the details in the cartoon. Just as you figured out the cartoonist's main point, you often have to figure out the implied main ideas of speakers and writers. When an idea is **implied**, it is suggested but not stated outright. Suppose your favorite shirt is missing from your closet and you know that your roommate often borrows your clothes. You might say to your roommate, "If my blue plaid shirt is back in my closet by noon, I'll forget it was missing." This statement does not directly accuse your roommate of borrowing the shirt, but your message is clear—Return my shirt! Your statement implies or suggests to your roommate that he has borrowed the shirt and should return it.

Roadkill

Courtesy of Chris Madden.

EXERCISE 4-9 UNDERSTANDING IMPLIED MAIN IDEAS

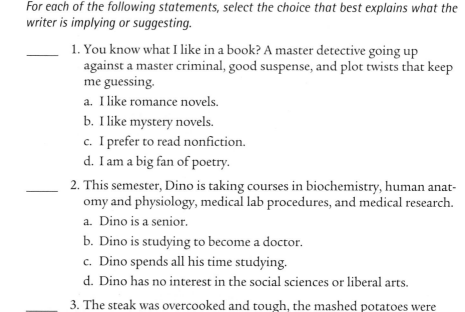

For each of the following statements, select the choice that best explains what the writer is implying or suggesting.

_____ 1. You know what I like in a book? A master detective going up against a master criminal, good suspense, and plot twists that keep me guessing.

    a. I like romance novels.

    b. I like mystery novels.

    c. I prefer to read nonfiction.

    d. I am a big fan of poetry.

_____ 2. This semester, Dino is taking courses in biochemistry, human anatomy and physiology, medical lab procedures, and medical research.

    a. Dino is a senior.

    b. Dino is studying to become a doctor.

    c. Dino spends all his time studying.

    d. Dino has no interest in the social sciences or liberal arts.

_____ 3. The steak was overcooked and tough, the mashed potatoes were cold, the green beans were withered, and the chocolate pie was mushy.

    a. The dinner was tasty.

    b. The dinner was nutritious.

    c. The dinner was prepared poorly.

    d. The dinner was served carelessly.

When trying to figure out the implied main idea in a paragraph, it is important to remember the distinction between general and specific ideas (see p. 72). You know that a *general* idea refers to many items or ideas, while a *specific* idea refers to a particular item. The word *color*, for instance, is general because it refers to many other specific colors—purple, yellow, red, and so forth. The word *shoe* is general because it can apply to many types, such as running shoes, high heels, loafers, and slippers.

You also know that the main idea of a paragraph is not only its most important point but also its most *general* idea. *Specific* details back up or support the main idea. Although most paragraphs have a topic sentence, some do not. Instead, they contain only details or specifics that, taken together, point to the main idea. The main idea, then, is implied but not directly stated. In such paragraphs you must **infer**, or reason out, the main idea. **Inference** is a process of adding up the details and deciding what they mean together or what main idea they all support or explain.

What general idea do the following specific sentences suggest?

The plumber made appointments he did not keep.

The plumber exaggerated the extent of the needed repairs in order to overcharge his customers.

The plumber did not return phone calls when people complained about his work.

You probably determined that the plumber is inconsiderate, incompetent, and unethical.

What larger, more general idea do the specific details and the accompanying photograph point to?

The wind began to howl at over 90 mph.

A dark gray funnel cloud was visible in the sky.

Severe storms had been predicted by the weather service.

Courtesy of Samuel Acosta/Shutterstock.

Together these three details and the photograph suggest that a tornado has devastated the area.

EXERCISE 4-10 WRITING GENERAL IDEAS

For each item, read the specific details. Then select the word or phrase from the box below that best completes the general idea in the sentence that follows. Make sure that each general idea fits all of its specific details. Not all words or phrases in the box will be used.

different factors	genetic	contributes	nonverbal messages
store's image	advertisers	characteristics	techniques
process	problems	dangerous effects	

1. a. Celebrity endorsements catch consumers' attention.

   b. Fear emphasizes negative consequences unless a particular product or service is purchased.

   c. "Sex sells" is a common motto among those who write commercials.

   General idea: _____ use a variety of appeals to sell products.

2. a. Children who are abused are more likely to be abusers when they become parents.

   b. Abused children often suffer from low self-esteem.

   c. Those who have been abused as children often find it difficult to develop healthy romantic relationships.

   General idea: Child abuse has _____.

3. a. Many immigrants come to the United States because they cannot make enough money to feed their families in their home country.

   b. Immigrants often come to the United States in order to be closer to their families.

   c. Sometimes immigrants are forced to flee their home countries due to warfare or persecution.

   General idea: A number of different _____ contribute to people leaving their country in search of a better life.

How to Find Implied Main Ideas in Paragraphs

When a writer leaves his or her main idea unstated, it is up to you to look at the details in the paragraph and figure out the writer's main point. The details, when taken together, will all point to a general and more important idea. Use the following steps as a guide to find implied main ideas:

1. **Find the topic.** As you know from earlier sections in this chapter, the *topic* is the general subject of the entire paragraph. Ask yourself: "What *one thing* is the author discussing throughout the paragraph?"

2. **Figure out the most important idea the writer wants you to know about that topic.** Look at each detail and decide what larger idea is being explained.

3. **Express the main idea in your own words.** Make sure that the main idea is a reasonable one. Ask yourself: "Does it apply to all of the details in the paragraph?"

Here is a sample passage; identify the main idea.

Issue: Health and Appearance

> The Romans, with their great public baths, probably did not use any sort of soap. They covered their bodies with oil, worked up a sweat in a steam bath, and then wiped off the oil. A dip in a pool of fresh water completed the "cleansing."
>
> During the Middle Ages, bodily cleanliness was prized in some cultures, but not in others. For example, twelfth-century Paris, with a population of about 100,000, had many public bathhouses. In contrast, the Renaissance, a revival of learning and art that lasted from the fourteenth to the seventeenth centuries, was not noted for cleanliness. Queen Elizabeth I of England (1533–1603) bathed once a month, a habit that caused many to think her overly fastidious. A common remedy for unpleasant body odor back then was the liberal use of perfume.
>
> And today? With soap, detergent, body wash, shampoo, conditioner, deodorant, antiperspirant, aftershave, cologne, and perfume, we may add more during and after a shower than we remove in the shower.
>
> —Adapted from John W. Hill et al., *Chemistry for Changing Times*, 13th edition, p. 644

The topic of this passage is personal cleanliness. The author's main point is that standards for bodily cleanliness have fluctuated over human history. You can figure out this writer's main idea even though no single sentence states this directly. You can visualize this paragraph as follows:

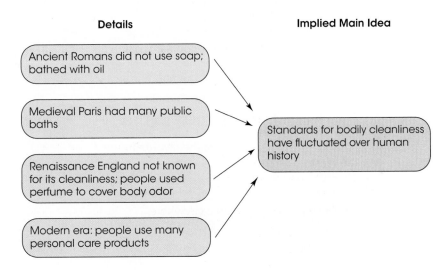

EXERCISE 4-11 FINDING IMPLIED MAIN IDEAS 1

After reading each of the paragraphs, complete the diagram that follows by filling in the missing information.

Paragraph A
Issue: Health and Diet

The average American consumer eats 21 pounds of snack foods in a year, but people in the West Central part of the country consume the most (24 pounds per person) whereas those in the Pacific and Southeast regions eat "only" 19 pounds per person. Pretzels are the most popular snack in the mid-Atlantic area, pork rinds are most likely to be eaten in the South, and multigrain chips turn up as a favorite in the West. Not surprisingly, the Hispanic influence in the Southwest has influenced snacking preferences—consumers in that part of the United States eat about 50 percent more tortilla chips than do people elsewhere.

—Adapted from Solomon, *Consumer Behavior*, p. 184

Topic:_____

Details

The average consumer eats _____ of snack food in a year.

People in _____ part of the country consume the most.

People in _____ regions consume the least.

_____ are the most popular snack in the mid-Atlantic area.

Pork rinds are most likely to be eaten in _____.

_____ are the favorite in the West.

Consumers in _____ eat more tortilla chips than do people elsewhere.

Implied Main Idea

_____ differ in their preferences for

_____

according to where they live.

Paragraph B
Issue: Alternative Medicine

By now, most people know that the herb echinacea may help conquer the common cold. Herbal remedies that are less well known include flaxseed, for treating constipation, and fennel, for soothing an upset stomach. In addition, the herb chamomile may be brewed into a hot cup of tea for a good night's sleep.

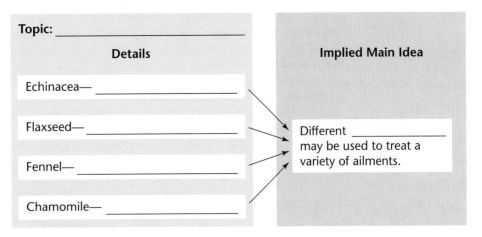

Topic: _____

Details	Implied Main Idea
Echinacea— _____	
Flaxseed— _____	Different _____ may be used to treat a variety of ailments.
Fennel— _____	
Chamomile— _____	

Paragraph C
Issue: Personal Relationships

Men's friendships are often built around shared activities—attending a ball game, playing cards, working on a project at the office. Women's friendships, on the other hand, are built more around a sharing of feelings, support, and "personalism." One study found that similarity in status, in willingness to protect one's friend in uncomfortable situations, in academic major, and even in proficiency in playing Password were significantly related to the relationship closeness of male-male friends but not of female-female or female-male friends.

—DeVito, *Messages: Building Interpersonal Communication Skills*, p. 290

Details	Implied Main Idea
Men's friendships are based on _____.	
Women's friendships are based on _____.	Men and women have _____ criteria for building _____.
Similarity is important in _____ friendships but not in _____.	

EXERCISE 4-12 FINDING IMPLIED MAIN IDEAS 2

Write a sentence that states the main idea for each of the following paragraphs.

Paragraph 1
Issue: Homelessness

The true causes of homelessness are not what most people expect. Deinstitutionalization of mentally ill people, released from hospitals without adequate care and community support, accounts for some recent gains in homelessness. The exodus of manufacturing firms, chronic unemployment, and decline in real wages in many American cities have pushed many others into the streets. At the same time, real estate speculation and high rents have made it impossible for large segments of the poor to find housing. Today, the majority of the poor pay more than half of their incomes for housing, and many single moms pay almost three-fourths of their meager earnings just to keep a roof over their family's heads.

—Adapted from Thompson and Hickey, *Society in Focus*, p. 216

Main idea: _____

_____

Paragraph 2
Issue: Wars and Warfare

Most African states [countries] have not achieved peace and prosperity. Some bloody conflicts or simply unbridled violence—most notably in eastern Congo and the Darfur region of Sudan—are still ongoing, their human consequences catastrophic and ultimate resolution still unclear. Economic problems remain extremely threatening, but progress is being made after decades of failures. The heavy burdens of the past—be they regional rivalries, religious and linguistic divisions, major economic and social-policy mistakes in early independence, the corruption and violence that feed the outside world's demands for diamonds or critical metals, or the crippling experience of apartheid—still present formidable hurdles. Probably even more serious are the newer problems of public health, environmental degradation, social instability, and development with which almost all African nations have to contend as they strive to build better societies.

—Adapted from Albert M. Craig et al., *The Heritage of World Civilizations: Combined Volume*, pp. 1036–1037

Main idea: _____

_____

Paragraph 3
Issue: Women's Issues

In 1985, an anonymous group of women that called themselves the Guerrilla Girls began hanging posters in New York City. They listed the specific galleries who represented less than 1 woman out of every 10 men [artists]. Another poster asked: "How Many Women Had One-Person Exhibitions at NYC Museums Last Year?" The answer:

Guggenheim 0
Metropolitan 0
Modern 1
Whitney 1

One of the Guerrilla Girls' most daring posters was distributed in 1989. It asked, "When racism & sexism are no longer fashionable, what will your art collection be worth?" It listed 67 women artists and pointed out that a collection of works by all of them would be worth less than the art auction value of any *one* painting by a famous male artist. Its suggestion that the value of the male artists' work might be drastically inflated struck a chord with many.

—Adapted from Sayre, *Discovering the Humanities*, pp. 490–491

Main idea: _____

_____

Paragraph 4
Issue: Health and Wellness

Have you ever noticed that you feel better after a belly laugh or a good cry? Humans have long recognized that smiling, laughing, singing, dancing, and other actions can elevate our moods, relieve stress, make us feel good, and help us improve our relationships. Crying can have similar positive physiological effects. Several recent articles have indicated that laughter and joy may increase endorphin levels, increase oxygen levels in the blood, decrease stress levels, relieve pain, enhance productivity, and reduce risks of chronic disease; however, the long-term effects on immune functioning and protective effects for chronic diseases is only just starting to be understood.

—Donatelle, *Health: The Basics*, pp. 92–93

Main idea: _____

_____

EXERCISE 4-13 FINDING IMPLIED MAIN IDEAS 3

After reading each of the following paragraphs or passages, select the choice that best answers each of the questions that follow.

Paragraph A
Issue: Politics and Public Relations

Presidents are not passive followers of public opinion. The White House is a virtual whirlwind of public relations activity. John Kennedy, the first "television president," held considerably more public appearances than did his predecessors. Kennedy's successors, with the notable exception of Richard Nixon, have been even more active in making public appearances. Indeed, they have averaged more than one appearance every weekday of the year. Bill Clinton and George W. Bush invested enormous time and energy in attempting to sell their programs to the public.

—Edwards, Wattenberg, and Lineberry, *Government in America*, p. 392

_____ 1. What is the topic?

a. the presidency

b. the effects of television

c. President Kennedy

d. public appearances of the president

_____ 2. What main idea is the writer implying?

a. U.S. presidents all enjoy being in the public eye.

b. The successors of President Kennedy have tried to imitate him.

c. Presidents have placed increasing importance on making public appearances.

d. Presidents spend too much time making public appearances.

Paragraph B
Issue: Social Networking and Privacy

When registering for online services under a screen name, it can be tempting to think your identity is a secret to other users. Many people will say or do things on the Internet that they would never do in real life because they believe that they are acting anonymously. However, most blogs, e-mail and instant messenger services, and social networking sites are tied to your real identity in some way. While your identity may be superficially concealed by a screen name, it often takes little more than a quick Google search to uncover your name, address, and other personal and possibly sensitive information.

—Ebert and Griffin, *Business Essentials*, p. 188

_____ 3. What is the topic?

    a. online identity

    b. screen names

    c. online services

    d. Google searches

_____ 4. What is the writer saying about the topic?

    a. Google searches offer clues to your identity.

    b. People write things on the Internet they would never say face-to-face.

    c. Your identity is not secret on the Internet.

    d. Screen names help conceal your identity.

Paragraph C
Issue: Business Ethics

"Frugal engineering." "Indovation." "Reverse innovation." These are some of the terms that GE, Procter & Gamble, Siemens, and Unilever are using to describe efforts to penetrate more deeply into emerging markets. As growth in mature markets slows, executives and managers at many global companies are realizing that the ability to serve the needs of the world's poorest consumers will be a critical source of competitive advantage in the decades to come. Procter & Gamble CEO Robert McDonald has set a strategic goal of introducing 800 million new consumers to the company's brands by 2015. This will require a better understanding of what daily life is like in, say, hundreds of thousands of rural villages in Africa, South America, and China.

Consider, for example, that two-thirds of the world's population—more than 4 billion people—live on less than $2 per day. This segment is sometimes referred to as the "bottom of the pyramid" and includes an estimated 1.5 billion people who live "off the grid"; that is, they have no access to electricity to provide light or to charge their cell phones. Often, a villager must walk several miles to hire a taxi for the trip to the nearest city with electricity. Such trips are costly in terms of both time and money.

—Keegan and Green, *Global Marketing*, p. 192

_____ 5. What is the topic?

    a. global branding and income inequality

    b. life off the grid

    c. marketing strategies aimed at the poor

    d. supply and demand in developing countries

_____ 6. What main idea is the writer implying?

    a. The poor people of the world do not have access to transportation.

    b. Companies are looking for ways to make money by selling their products to the world's poor people.

    c. Procter & Gamble is the world leader in supplying inexpensive products to developing nations.

    d. Cell phones offer developing nations many opportunities for increasing the standard of living.

_____ 7. Which one of the following conclusions does not logically follow from the passage?

    a. Reverse innovation is aimed at getting more products into the hands of wealthy consumers.

    b. "Emerging markets" are home to huge numbers of poor people.

    c. The majority of the world's people live on less than $2 per day.

    d. In the world's developing countries, many residents of the countryside are poor.

Paragraph D
Issue: Family

In all societies, people have ways of organizing their relationships with other people, especially their primary relationships with kin. As children, our earliest and most influential interactions are with our parents, siblings, and other relatives. We rely on our families for all of our survival needs. Our families feed us, clothe us, and provide our shelter. They also help us adjust to the world around us, teaching us the behavior and attitudes that our culture expects, and they provide emotional support in both good times and bad.

Many of our relatives continue as important economic and emotional supports throughout our lives. Even as adults, we can turn to our kin in networks of reciprocity, asking for aid in times of need. In turn, we may be asked to respond to their requests when they are in need. We may align ourselves with our relatives when they are engaged in disputes with others. We may expect loyalty from our kin when we are in conflict with neighbors or other community members. During personal or family crises, we may expect emotional support from our relatives. Together we celebrate happy occasions such as births and marriages, and we mourn the deaths of our kin.

—Nancy Bonvillain, *Cultural Anthropology*, pp. 186–187

_____ 8. What is the topic?

    a. parents

    b. siblings

    c. family

    d. culture

_____ 9. What is the writer saying about the topic?

    a. Family is more important in some societies than in others.

    b. Regardless of culture, family is one of the most important and constant influences in our lives.

    c. Most people see their family members as their "safety net" in times of difficulty.

    d. It is impossible to define the terms *kinship* and *family* with any accuracy.

EXERCISE 4-14 FINDING STATED AND IMPLIED MAIN IDEAS

Turn to the article titled "Consequences of Social Class" on page 6. Using your own paper, number the lines from 1 to 16, to correspond to the sixteen paragraphs in the article. For each paragraph number, if the main idea is stated, record the sentence number in which it appears (first, second, etc.). If the main idea is unstated and implied, write a sentence that expresses the main idea.

4e RECOGNIZING SIGNAL WORDS

LEARNING OBJECTIVE 5
Recognize signal words.

Signal words are linking words or phrases used to lead the reader from one idea to another. If you get in the habit of recognizing signal words, you will see that they often guide you through a paragraph, helping you to read it more easily. When writing, be sure to use these words to help your reader follow your train of thought and to see connections between and among your ideas.

In the following paragraph, notice how the underlined signal words lead you from one important detail to the next.

Example

Kevin works as a forensic scientist. When he examines a crime scene, he follows a certain procedure. <u>First of all</u>, he puts on special gear to avoid contaminating the crime scene. <u>For example</u>, he wears gloves (so that he doesn't leave fingerprints) and a special hat (so that he does not leave hair samples). <u>Next</u>, he prepares his camera and other forensic equipment, <u>such as</u> plastic bags and glass slides. <u>Then</u>, he presses "record" on his tape recorder so that he can describe the crime scene as he examines it. <u>Finally</u>, he goes over the crime scene one square foot at a time, very slowly, so that he does not miss any evidence.

Not all paragraphs contain such obvious signal words, and not all signal words serve as such clear markers of major details. Often, however, signal words are used to alert you to what will come next in the paragraph. If you see the phrase *for instance* at the beginning of a sentence, then you know that an example will follow. When you see the phrase *on the other hand*, you can predict that a different, opposing idea will follow. Table 4.1 lists some of the most common signal words used within a paragraph and indicates what they tell you.

TABLE 4.1 COMMON SIGNAL WORDS

TYPES OF SIGNAL WORDS	EXAMPLES	WHAT THEY TELL THE READER
Time or Sequence	first, later, next, finally	The author is arranging ideas in the order in which they happened.
Example	for example, for instance, to illustrate, such as	An example will follow.
Enumeration or Listing	first, second, third, last, another, next	The author is marking or identifying each major point (sometimes these may be used to suggest order of importance).
Continuation	also, in addition, and, further, another	The author is continuing with the same idea and is going to provide additional information.
Contrast	on the other hand, in contrast, however	The author is switching to a different, opposite, or contrasting idea than previously discussed.
Comparison	like, likewise, similarly	The writer will show how the previous idea is similar to what follows.
Cause and Effect	because, thus, therefore, since, consequently	The writer will show a connection between two or more things, how one thing caused another, or how something happened as a result of something else.

EXERCISE 4-15 RECOGNIZING SIGNAL WORDS

Select the signal word or phrase from the box below that best completes each of the following sentences. Two of the signal words in the box may be used more than once.

on the other hand	for example	because	in addition
similarly	after	next	however
also			

1. Typically, those suffering from post-traumatic stress disorder (PTSD) are soldiers after combat. Civilians who witnessed or lived through events such as the World Trade Center destruction can _____ experience PTSD.

2. Columbus was determined to find an oceanic passage to China _____ finding a direct route would mean increased trading and huge profits.

3. In the event of a heart attack, it is first important to identify the symptoms. _____, call 911 or drive the victim to the nearest hospital.

4. In the 1920s, courtship between men and women changed dramatically. _____, instead of visiting the woman's home with her parents present, men began to invite women out on dates.

5. Direct exposure to sunlight is dangerous because the sun's ultraviolet rays can lead to skin cancer. _____, tanning booths emit ultraviolet rays and are as dangerous as, if not more dangerous than, exposure to sunlight.

6. Lie detector tests are often used by law enforcement to help determine guilt or innocence. _____, because these tests often have an accuracy rate of only 60 to 80 percent, the results are not admissible in court.

7. The temporal lobes of the brain process sound and comprehend language. _____, the temporal lobes are responsible for storing visual memories.

8. The theory of multiple intelligences holds that there are many different kinds of intelligence, or abilities. _____, musical ability, control of bodily movements (athletics), spatial understanding, and observational abilities are all classified as different types of intelligence.

9. During World War II, Japanese Americans were held in relocation camps. _____ the war was over, the United States paid reparations and issued an apology to those who were wrongfully detained.

10. Many believe that the United States should adopt a flat tax in which every person pays the same tax rate. _____, it is unlikely that the tax code will be overhauled any time soon.

EXERCISE 4-16   RECOGNIZING SIGNAL WORDS

Each of the following beginnings of paragraphs uses a signal word or phrase to tell the reader what will follow. Read each, paying particular attention to the underlined word or phrase. Then, in the space provided, specifically describe what you would expect to find immediately after the signal word or phrase.

1. Proximity should not be the only factor to consider in choosing a doctor or health-care provider. Many other factors should be considered. For instance,...

   _____

   _____

2. There are a number of things you can do to manage your stress level. First,...

   _____

3. Many banks have privacy policies. However,...

   _____

   _____

4. One advantage of taking online courses is all the time you will save by not having to travel to and from campus. Another...

   _____

5. To select the classes you will take next term, first consult with your faculty advisor about the courses you are required to take. Next...

   _____

EXERCISE 4-17 IDENTIFYING SIGNAL WORDS AND THEIR FUNCTION

For each paragraph in Exercise 4-13, highlight each signal word and indicate what each tells the reader.

SUMMARY OF LEARNING OBJECTIVES	
Objective 1 Understand the structure of a paragraph.	A *paragraph* is composed of a topic, a main idea, or topic sentence, details that support that main idea, and signal words that connect the ideas.
Objective 2 Find stated main ideas.	A *main idea* expresses a single idea about the topic of a paragraph. Main ideas are often expressed directly in a topic sentence. The *topic sentence* is the most general sentence in the paragraph. The topic sentence often appears first in a paragraph, but it may also appear in the middle or at the end of the paragraph. Sometimes it appears both at the beginning and at the end of the paragraph.
Objective 3 Recognize supporting details.	*Supporting details* are facts and ideas that prove or explain a paragraph's main idea. Not all details are equally important.
Objective 4 Find implied main ideas.	When a main idea is *implied*, it is not stated outright. To identify an implied main idea, look at the details in the paragraph and figure out the writer's main point. The details, when taken together, will point to a general and more important idea. This is the implied main idea.
Objective 5 Recognize signal words.	*Signal words or phrases* lead the reader from one idea to another. They are often used to alert the reader to what is coming next.

5 Writing and Revising Paragraphs: Main Ideas, Supporting Details, and Signal Words

> **LEARNING OBJECTIVES**
>
> **1** Write effective topic sentences
> **2** Select and organize details to support the topic sentence
> **3** Use signal words and phrases to connect details
> **4** Revise paragraphs

A **paragraph** is a group of related sentences. The sentences are all about one thing, called the **topic.** A paragraph expresses a single idea about that topic. This idea is called the **main idea.** All the other sentences in the paragraph support this main idea. These sentences are called **supporting details.** Not all details in a paragraph are equally important. Ideas are connected using **signal words.**

5a   WRITE EFFECTIVE TOPIC SENTENCES

LEARNING OBJECTIVE 1
Write effective topic sentences.

As a writer, it is important to develop clear and concise topic sentences that help your readers understand your main ideas and guide them through your paragraphs.

The Function of Topic Sentences

A good topic sentence does two things:

- It makes clear what the paragraph is about—the topic.
- It expresses a view or makes a point about the topic.

In the following examples, the topic is IN BOLD and the point about the topic is underlined.

1. **The first week of college** is a frustrating experience.
2. **State-operated lotteries** are growing in popularity.
3. **Time management** is a vital skill in college and on the job.

EXERCISE 5-1 EXPRESSING VIEWPOINTS ABOUT A TOPIC

Working with a classmate, create two topic sentences that offer differing or opposing points of view about each of the following topics.

1. Shopping malls are often appealing to teenagers.

   _____

   _____

2. Most fast-food restaurants are not concerned with their customers' health or nutrition.

   _____

   _____

3. Monday morning is a time to get organized for the week.

   _____

   _____

4. Violence on television may promote physical aggressiveness among young children.

   _____

   _____

5. College professors make sincere efforts to understand their students' needs.

   _____

   _____

Narrowing Your Focus

To write a good paragraph, you need to narrow your focus to a manageable topic, one that is neither too broad nor too narrow. Your topic must be general enough to allow you to add interesting details that will engage your reader. It must also be specific or narrow enough that you can cover it adequately in a few sentences. If your topic is too general, you'll end up with a few unrelated details that do not add up to a specific point. If your topic is too narrow, you will not have enough to say.

Suppose you have decided to write a paragraph about sports. You write the following topic sentence:

Sports are a favorite activity for many people.

This topic is much too broad to cover in one paragraph. Think of all the different aspects you could write about. Which sports would you consider? Would you write about both playing sports and watching them? Would you write about both professional and amateur sports? Would you write about the reasons people enjoy sports? The topic sentence must be more specific:

> My whole family likes to watch professional football on Sunday afternoons.

Here you have limited your topic to a specific sport (football), a specific time (Sunday afternoon), and some specific fans (your family).

Here are other examples of sentences that are too general. Each has been revised to be more specific.

> **Too General** My parents have greatly influenced my life.
> **Revised** My parents helped me make the decision to attend college.

> **Too General** Sex education is worthwhile.
> **Revised** Sex-education courses in high school allow students to discuss sex openly.

If your topic is too specific (narrow), you will not have enough details to use in the paragraph, or you may end up including details that do not relate directly to the topic. Suppose you decide to write a paragraph about the Internet and come up with this topic sentence:

> The Internet allows me to stay in touch with friends in other parts of the country.

What else would your paragraph say? You might name some specific friends and where they are, but this list wouldn't be very interesting. This topic sentence is too specific. It might work as a detail, but not as a main idea. To correct the problem, ask, "What else does the Internet allow me to do?" You might say that it allows you to stay in touch with friends by e-mail, that it makes doing research for college papers easier, and that the World Wide Web has information on careers and even specific job openings. Here is a possible revised topic sentence:

> The Internet is an important part of my personal, college, and work life.

Here are a few other examples of topic sentences that are too narrow, along with revisions for each one:

> **Too Narrow** Only 36 percent of Americans voted in the last election.
> **Revised** Many Americans do not exercise their right to vote.

Too Narrow Markel Carpet Company offers child-care leave to both men and women.

Revised The child-care leave policy at Markel Carpet Company is very flexible.

Too Narrow A yearly subscription to *Appalachian Voice* costs $25.

Revised *Appalachian Voice*, a magazine devoted to environmental issues, is a bargain, considering the information it provides.

How can you tell if your topic sentence is too general or too specific? Try brainstorming or branching to generate ideas. If you find you can develop the topic in many different directions, or if you have trouble choosing details from a wide range of choices, your topic is probably too general. If you cannot think of anything to explain or support it, your topic sentence is too specific.

EXERCISE 5-2 EVALUATING TOPIC SENTENCES

Evaluate the following topic sentences. Label each "G" for too general or "S" for too specific. Then rewrite each to create an effective topic sentence.

_____   1. Learning a new sport is challenging.

_____   2. Dinner for two at my favorite Italian restaurant costs $25.

_____   3. The new day-care center opens earlier than most.

_____   4. Many rules of etiquette have changed over the past 25 years.

_____   5. Passive cigarette smoke makes me feel sick.

Tips for Writing Effective Topic Sentences

Use the following suggestions to write clear topic sentences.

1. **Your topic sentence should state the main point of your paragraph.** Be sure your topic sentence has two parts. It should identify your topic and express a view toward it.
2. **Be sure to choose a manageable topic.** It should be neither too general nor too specific.
3. **Make sure your topic sentence is a complete thought.** Be sure your topic sentence is not a fragment or run-on sentence.

4. **Place your topic sentence first in the paragraph.** Topic sentences often appear in other places in paragraphs, as described earlier, or their controlling idea is implied, not stated. For now, it will be easier for you to put yours at the beginning. That way, as you write, you can make sure you stick to your point, and your readers will immediately be alerted to that point.

5. **Avoid announcing your topic.** Sentences that sound like announcements are usually unnecessary. Avoid such sentences as "This paragraph will discuss how to change a flat tire," or "I will explain why I object to legalized abortion." Instead, directly state your main point:

"Changing a flat tire involves many steps," or "I object to abortion on religious grounds."

Not all expert or professional writers follow all of these suggestions. Sometimes, a writer may use one-sentence paragraphs or include topic sentences that are fragments to achieve a special effect. You will find these paragraphs in news and magazine articles and other sources. Although professional writers can use these variations effectively, you probably should not experiment with them too early. It is best while you are polishing your skills to use a more standard style of writing.

EXERCISE 5-3 EVALUATING TOPIC SENTENCES

Evaluate each of the following topic sentences and mark them as follows:

E = effective; G = too general; A = announcement; N = not complete thought; S = too specific

_____ 1. This paper will discuss the life and politics of Simón Bolívar.

_____ 2. Japanese culture is fascinating to study because its family traditions are so different from American traditions.

_____ 3. The admission test for the police academy includes vocabulary questions.

_____ 4. The discovery of penicillin was a great step in the advancement of modern medicine.

_____ 5. I will talk about the reasons for the popularity of reality television shows.

_____ 6. A habit leading to weight gain.

_____ 7. Each year Americans are the victims of more than 1 million auto thefts.

_____ 8. The White House has many famous rooms and an exciting history.

_____ 9. There are three factors to consider when buying a flat screen TV.

_____ 10. Iraq has a long and interesting history.

EXERCISE 5-4 REVISING TOPIC SENTENCES

Analyze the following topic sentences. If a sentence is too general or too specific, or if it makes a direct announcement or is not a complete thought, revise it to make it more effective.

1. World hunger is a crime.

   Revised: _____

2. E-mail is used by a great many people.

   Revised: _____

3. I will point out the many ways energy can be saved in the home.

   Revised: _____

4. Because Congress is very important in the United States.

   Revised: _____

5. In 2010, over 10,000 people died in alcohol-related driving crashes.

   Revised: _____

5b SELECT AND ORGANIZE DETAILS TO SUPPORT YOUR TOPIC SENTENCE

LEARNING OBJECTIVE 2
Select and organize your details to support your topic sentence.

A paragraph must have **unity,** that is, it must identify and explain a single idea. It must also have **coherence,** meaning that all the sentences make sense together. The following section will show you how to achieve both unity and coherence.

   The details you choose to support your topic sentence must be both relevant and sufficient. **Relevant** means that the details directly explain and support your topic sentence. For example, if you were to write a paragraph for your employer explaining why you deserve a raise, it would not be relevant to mention that you plan to use the money to go to Florida next spring. A vacation has nothing to do with—is not relevant to—your job performance.

Sufficient means that you must provide enough information to make your topic sentence understandable and convincing. In your paragraph explaining why you deserve a raise, it would probably not be sufficient to say that you are always on time. You would need to provide more information about your job performance: for example, that you always volunteer to work holidays, that you've offered good suggestions for displaying new products, and that several customers have written letters praising your work.

In addition to choosing relevant and sufficient details, be sure to select a variety of details, use specific words, and organize your paragraph effectively.

Selecting Relevant Details

Relevant details directly support your topic sentence. They help clarify and strengthen your ideas, whereas irrelevant details make your ideas unclear and confusing. Here is the first draft of a paragraph written by a student named Alex to explain why he decided to attend college. Can you locate the detail that is not relevant?

> [1]I decided to attend college to further my education and achieve my goals in life. [2]I am attempting to build a future for myself. [3]When I get married and have kids, I want to be able to offer them the same opportunities my parents gave me. [4]I want to have a comfortable style of living and a good job. [5]As for my wife, I don't want her to work because I believe a married woman should not work. [6]I believe college is the way to begin a successful life.

Sentence 5 does not belong in the paragraph. The fact that Alex does not want his wife to work is not a reason for attending college. Use the following simple test to be sure each detail you include belongs in your paragraph.

Test for Relevant Details

1. **Read your topic sentence in combination with each of the other sentences in your paragraph.** For example,
   - read the topic sentence + the last sentence.
   - read the topic sentence + the second-to-last sentence.
   - read the topic sentence + the third-to-last sentence.
2. **For each pair of sentences, ask yourself, "Do these two ideas fit together?"** If your answer is "No," then you have found a detail that is not relevant to your topic. Delete it from your paragraph.

Another student wrote the following paragraph on the subject of the legal drinking age. As you read it, cross out the details that are not relevant.

> [1]The legal drinking age should be raised to 25. [2]Anyone who drinks should be old enough to determine whether or not it is safe to drive after drinking.

> [3]Bartenders and others who serve drinks should also have to be 25. [4]In general, teenagers and young adults are not responsible enough to limit how much they drink. [5]The party atmosphere enjoyed by so many young people encourages crazy acts, so we should limit who can drink. [6]Younger people think drinking is a game, but it is a dangerous game that affects the lives of others.

Which sentence did you delete? Why did you delete it? The third sentence does not belong in the paragraph because the age of those who bartend or serve drinks is not relevant to the topic. Sentence 5, about partying, should also be eliminated or explained because the connection between partying and drinking is not clear.

EXERCISE 5-5 IDENTIFYING RELEVANT DETAILS

Place a check mark by those statements that provide relevant supporting details.

1. Sales representatives need good interpersonal skills.
   a. They need to be good listeners.
   b. They should like helping people.
   c. They should know their products well.

2. Water can exist in three forms, which vary with temperature.
   a. At a high temperature, water becomes steam; it is a gas.
   b. Drinking water often contains mineral traces.
   c. At cold temperatures, water becomes ice, a solid state.

3. Outlining is one of the easiest ways to organize facts.
   a. Formal outlines use Roman numerals and letters and Arabic numerals to show different levels of importance.
   b. Outlining emphasizes the relationships among facts.
   c. Outlines make it easier to focus on important points.

Including Sufficient Detail

Including sufficient detail means that your paragraph contains an adequate amount of specific information for your readers to understand your main idea. Your supporting details must thoroughly and clearly explain why you believe your topic sentence is true. Be sure that your details are specific; do not provide summaries or unsupported statements of opinion.

Let's look at a paragraph a student wrote on the topic of billboard advertising.

> There is a national movement to oppose billboard advertising. Many people don't like billboards and are taking action to change what products are advertised on them and which companies use them. Community activists are destroying billboard advertisements at an increasing rate. As a result of their actions, numerous changes have been made.

This paragraph is filled with general statements. It does not explain who dislikes billboards or why they dislike them. It does not say what products are advertised or name the companies that make them. No detail is given about how the billboards are destroyed, and the resulting changes are not described. There is not sufficient support for the topic sentence. Here is the revised version:

> Among residents of inner-city neighborhoods, a national movement is growing to oppose billboard advertising. Residents oppose billboards that glamorize alcohol and target people of color as its consumers. Community activists have organized and are taking action. They carry paint, rollers, shovels, and brooms to an offending billboard. Within a few minutes the billboard is painted over, covering the damaging advertisement. Results have been dramatic. Many liquor companies have reduced their inner-city billboard advertising. In place of these ads, some billboard companies have placed public-service announcements and ads to improve community health.

If you have trouble thinking of enough details to include in a paragraph, try brainstorming or one of the other techniques for generating ideas described in Chapter 2. Write your topic sentence at the top of a sheet of paper. Then list everything that comes to mind about that topic. Include examples, events, incidents, facts, and reasons. You will be surprised at how many useful details you think of. When you finish, read over your list and cross out details that are not relevant. (If you still don't have enough, your topic may be too specific. See p. 108.) The section "Arranging Details Logically" on the next page will help you decide in what order you will write about the details on your list.

Types of Supporting Details

There are many types of details that you can use to explain or support a topic sentence. The most common types of supporting details are (1) examples, (2) facts or statistics, (3) reasons, (4) descriptions, and (5) steps or procedures. It is advisable to vary the types of details you use, and to choose those appropriate to your topic.

EXERCISE 5- 6   WRITING SUPPORTING DETAILS

Working with a classmate, for each topic sentence, write at least three different types of details that could be used to support it. Label each detail as example, fact or statistic, reason, description, or steps or procedure.

1. People make inferences about you based on the way you dress.

2. Many retailers with traditional stores have decided to market their products through Web sites as well.

3. Many Americans are obsessed with losing weight.

4. Historical and cultural attractions can be found in a variety of shapes, sizes, and locations throughout the world.

5. Using a search engine is an effective, though not perfect, method of searching the Internet.

Arranging Details Logically

Nan had an assignment to write a paragraph about travel. She drafted the paragraph and then revised it. As you read each version, pay particular attention to the order in which she arranged the details.

First Draft

This summer I had the opportunity to travel extensively. Over Labor Day weekend I backpacked with a group of friends in the Allegheny Mountains. When spring semester was over, I visited my seven cousins in Florida. My friends and I went to New York City over the Fourth of July to see fireworks and explore the city. During June I worked as a wildlife-preservation volunteer in a Colorado state park. On July 15 I celebrated my twenty-fifth birthday by visiting my parents in Syracuse.

Revision

This summer I had the opportunity to travel extensively in the United States. When the spring semester ended, I went to my cousins' home in Florida to relax. When I returned, I worked during the month of June as a wildlife-preservation volunteer in a Colorado state park. Then my friends and I went to New York City to see the fireworks and look around the city over the Fourth of July weekend. On July 15th, I celebrated my twenty-fifth birthday by visiting my parents in Syracuse. Finally, over Labor Day weekend, my friends and I backpacked in the Allegheny Mountains.

Did you find Nan's revision easier to read? In the first draft, Nan recorded details as she thought of them. There is no logical arrangement to them. In the second version, she arranged the details in the order in which they happened. Nan chose this arrangement because it fit her details logically.

The three common methods for arranging details are as follows:

1. Time sequence
2. Spatial arrangement
3. Least/most arrangement

Time Sequence

Time sequence means the order in which something happens. For example, if you were to write about a particularly bad day, you could describe the day in the order in which everything went wrong. You might begin with waking up in the morning and end with going to bed that night. If you were describing a busy or an exciting weekend, you might begin with what you did on Friday night and end with the last activity on Sunday. Here is an example of a time sequence paragraph:

> When Su-ling gets ready to study at home, she follows a set routine. First of all, she tries to find a quiet place, far away from her kid sisters. This place might be her bedroom or the porch, or the basement, depending on the noise levels in her household. Next, she finds a snack to eat while she is studying, perhaps potato chips or a candy bar. If she is on a diet, she tries to find some healthy fruit. Finally, Su-ling tackles the most difficult assignment first because she knows her level of concentration is higher at the beginning of study sessions.

Spatial Arrangement

Suppose you are asked to describe the room in which you are sitting. You want your reader, who has never been in the room, to visualize it. You need to describe it in an orderly way, noting where items are positioned. You could describe the room from left to right, from ceiling to floor, or from door to window. In other situations, your choices might include front to back, inside to outside, near to far, east to west, and so on. This method of presentation is called **spatial arrangement.** How are the details arranged in the following paragraph?

> Keith's antique car was gloriously decorated for the Fourth of July parade. Red, white, and blue streamers hung in front from the headlights and bumper. The hood was covered with small American flags. The windshield had gold stars pasted on it, arranged to form an outline of our state. On the sides, the doors displayed red plastic-tape stripes. The convertible top was down, and Mary sat on the trunk dressed up like the Statue of Liberty. In the rear, a neon sign blinked "God Bless America." His car was not only a show-stopper but the highlight of the parade.

The details are arranged from front to back in the example paragraph. The topic you are writing about will often determine the arrangement you choose. In writing about a town, you might choose to begin with the center and then move to each surrounding area. In describing a building, you might go from bottom to top.

EXERCISE 5-7 USING SPATIAL ARRANGEMENT

Indicate which spatial arrangement you would use to describe the following topics. Then write a paragraph on one of the topics.

1. A local market or favorite store

2. A photograph you value

3. A prized possession

4. A building in which you work

5. Your campus cafeteria, bookstore, or lounge

The Least/Most Arrangement

Another method of arranging details is to present them in order from least to most or most to least, according to some quality or characteristic. For example, you might arrange details from least to most *expensive*, least to most *serious*, or least to most *important*. The writer of the following paragraph uses a least-to-most arrangement.

> The entry level job in many industries today is administrative assistant. Just because it's a lower-level job, don't think it's an easy job. A good administrative assistant must have good computer skills. If you aren't proficient on a computer you won't be able to handle your supervisor's correspondence and other paperwork. Even more important, an administrative assistant must be well organized. Every little task—from answering the phone to setting up meetings to making travel arrangements—lands on the administrative assistant's desk. If you can't juggle lots of loose ends, this is not the job for you. Most important of all, though, an administrative assistant needs a sense of humor. On the busiest days, when the office is in total chaos, the only way to keep your sanity—and your temper—is to take a deep breath, smile, and say "When all this is over, I'm going to have a well-earned nervous breakdown!"

Notice that this writer wrote about a basic requirement for the job—computer skills—and then worked up to the most important requirement.

You can also arrange details from most to least. This structure allows you to present your strongest point first. Many writers use this method to construct a case or an argument. For example, if you were writing a business letter requesting a refund for damaged mail-order merchandise, you would want to begin with the most serious damage and put the minor complaints at the end, as follows:

> I am returning this merchandise because it is damaged. The white sneakers have dark streaks across both toes. One of the shoes has a red mark on the heel. The laces also have some specks of dirt on them. I trust you will refund my money promptly.

5c   USE SIGNAL WORDS AND PHRASES TO CONNECT DETAILS

LEARNING OBJECTIVE 3
Use signal words and phrases to connect details.

Signal words allow readers to move easily from one detail to another; they show how details relate to one another. You might think of them as words that guide and signal. They guide the reader through the paragraph and signal what is to follow. As you read the following paragraph, notice the signal words and phrases (highlighted) that this student used.

> I have so many things to do when I get home today. First, I have to take my dog, Othello, for a walk. Next, I should do my homework for history and study the chapter on franchises for business. After that I should do some laundry, since my drawers are empty. Then my brother is coming over to fix the tailpipe on my car. Afterward, we will probably order a pizza for a speedy dinner.

Table 5.1 shows some commonly used signal words and phrases for each method of arranging details discussed on pages 116–118. To understand how these signal words and phrases work, review the sample paragraph for each of these arrangements. Underline each signal word or phrase.

TABLE 5.1 FREQUENTLY USED SIGNAL WORDS AND PHRASES

ARRANGEMENT	SIGNAL WORDS AND PHRASES
Time Sequence	*first, next, during, eventually, finally, later, meanwhile, soon, when, then, suddenly, currently, after, afterward, before, now, until*
Spatial	*above, below, behind, in front of, beside, next to, inside, outside, to the west (north, etc.) of, beneath, nearby, on the other side of*
Least/Most Important	*most, above all, especially, even more*

5d   USE SPECIFIC LANGUAGE

When you are writing a paragraph, use specific words to give your reader as much information as possible. You can think of words the way an artist thinks of colors on a palette. Vague words are brown and muddy; specific words are brightly colored and lively. Try to paint pictures for your reader with specific, vivid words. Here are a few examples of vague words along with more specific words or phrases for the same idea:

Vague fun
Specific thrilling, relaxing, enjoyable, pleasurable

Vague dark
Specific hidden in gray-green shadows

Vague experienced
Specific five years in the job

Vague tree
Specific red maple

Ways to Develop Details

The following suggestions will help you develop your details using specific language:

1. **Use specific verbs.** Choose verbs (action words) that help your reader picture the action.

   Vague The woman left the restaurant.

   Specific The woman stormed out of the restaurant.

2. **Give exact names.** Include the names of people, places, objects, and brands.

   Vague A man was eating outside.

   Specific Anthony Hargeaves lounged on the deck of his yacht *Penelope*, spearing Heinz dill pickles out of a jar.

3. **Use adjectives before nouns to convey details.**

   Vague Juanita had a dog on a leash.

   Specific A short, bushy-tailed dog strained at the end of the leash in Juanita's hand.

4. **Use words that appeal to the senses**. Choose words that suggest touch, taste, smell, sound, and sight.

   Vague The florist shop was lovely.

   Specific Brilliant red, pink, and yellow roses filled the florist shop with their heady fragrance.

   To summarize, use words that help your readers create mental pictures.

   Vague Al was handsome.

   Specific Al had a slim frame, curly brown hair, deep brown almond-shaped eyes, and perfectly straight, gleaming white teeth.

EXERCISE 5-8 USING SPECIFIC WORDS

Rewrite these vague sentences, using specific words.

1. The hair stylist used a gel on my hair.

2. Dress properly for an interview.

3. I found an interesting Web site on the Internet.

4. The job fair was well attended.

5. I'm going to barbecue something for dinner.

EXERCISE 5-9 WRITING A PARAGRAPH

Using the process described in this chapter, write a paragraph on one of the following topics, or a topic assigned by your instructor.

1. Hunting is (is not) a cruel sport.

2. My hometown (city) has (has not) changed in the past five years.

3. Religion is (is not) important in my life.

4. White parents should (should not) be allowed to adopt African American children.

5. Most doctors are (are not) sensitive to their patients' feelings.

5e   HOW AND WHEN TO REVISE

LEARNING OBJECTIVE 4
Revise paragraphs.

It is usually best after writing a draft to wait a day before beginning to revise it. You will have a fresh outlook on your topic and will find that it is easier to see what you need to change, add, or delete.

Even after giving yourself some distance from your work, it may be difficult to know how to improve your own writing. Simply rereading may not help you discover flaws, weaknesses, or needed changes. The remainder of this section offers guidelines to follow and questions to ask to help you spot problems. It also shows you how to use a revision map and includes a revision checklist to guide your revision.

Revise Ineffective Paragraphs

To revise a paragraph, begin by examining your topic sentence and then, once you are satisfied with it, determine whether you have provided adequate details to support it.

Revise Ineffective Topic Sentences

Your topic sentence is the sentence around which your paragraph is built, so be sure it is strong and effective. The most common problems with topic sentences include

- The topic sentence lacks a point of view.
- The topic sentence is too broad.
- The topic sentence is too narrow.

For suggestions on how to revise ineffective topic sentences, see Tips for Writing Effective Topic Sentences on page 109.

Revise Paragraphs to Add Supporting Details

The details in a paragraph should give your reader sufficient information to make your topic sentence believable. Paragraphs that lack necessary detail are called *underdeveloped paragraphs*. **Underdeveloped paragraphs** lack supporting sentences to prove or explain the point made in the topic sentence. As you read the following student paragraph, keep the topic sentence in mind and consider whether the rest of the sentences support it.

Sample Student Paragraph

> I am a very impatient person, and my impatience interferes with how easily I can get through a day. If I ask for something, I want it immediately. If I'm going somewhere and I'm ready and somebody else isn't, I get very upset. I hate driving behind someone who drives slowly when I cannot pass. I think that annoys me the most, and it never happens unless I am in a hurry. If I were less impatient, I would probably feel more relaxed and less pressured.

This paragraph begins with a topic sentence that is focused (it is neither too broad nor too narrow) and that includes a point of view. It promises to explain how the writer's impatience makes it difficult for him to get through a day. However, the rest of the paragraph does not fulfill this promise. Instead, the writer gives two very general examples of his impatience: (1) wanting something and (2) waiting for someone. The third example, driving behind a slow driver, is a little more specific, but it is not developed well. The last sentence suggests, but does not explain, that the writer's impatience makes him feel tense and pressured.

Taking into account the need for more supporting detail, the author revised his paragraph as follows:

Revised Paragraph

> I am a very impatient person, and my impatience interferes with how easily I can get through a day. For example, when I decide to buy something, such as a new phone, I *have* to have it right away—that day. I usually drop everything and run to the store. Of course, I shortchange myself on studying, and that hurts my grades. My impatience hurts me, too, when I am waiting for someone, which I hate to do. If my friend Alex and I agree to meet at noon to work on his car, I get annoyed if he is even five minutes late. Then I usually end up saying something nasty or sarcastic like "What a surprise, you're actually here!" which I regret later. Perhaps I am most impatient when I am behind the steering wheel. If I get behind a slow driver, I get annoyed and start honking and beeping my horn. I know this might fluster the other driver, and afterwards I feel guilty. I have tried talking to myself to calm down; sometimes it works, so I hope I'm overcoming this bad trait.

Did you notice that the writer became much more specific in the revised version? He gave an example of something he wanted—a phone—and he described his actions and their consequences. The example of waiting for someone was provided by the incident involving his friend Alex. Finally, the writer explained the driving example in more detail and stated its consequences. With the extra details and supporting examples, the paragraph is more interesting and effective.

The following suggestions will help you revise an underdeveloped paragraph.

Ways to Revise Underdeveloped Paragraphs

■ **Analyze your paragraph sentence by sentence.** If a sentence does not add new, specific information to your paragraph, delete it or add to it so that it becomes relevant.

■ **Think of specific situations, facts, or examples that illustrate or support your topic.** Often you can make a general sentence more specific.

■ **Brainstorm, freewrite, or branch.** To come up with additional details or examples to use in your paragraph, try some prewriting techniques. If necessary, start fresh with a new approach and new set of ideas.

■ **Reexamine your topic sentence.** If you are having trouble generating details, your topic sentence may be the problem. Consider changing the approach.

　　Example Rainy days make me feel depressed.

　　Revised Rainy days, although depressing, give me a chance to catch up on household chores.

■ **Consider changing your topic.** If a paragraph remains troublesome, look for a new topic and start over.

EXERCISE 5-10 REVISING A PARAGRAPH

The following paragraph is poorly developed. What suggestions would you make to the writer to improve the paragraph? Write them in the space provided. Be specific. Which sentences are weak? How could each be improved?

　　I am attending college to improve myself. By attending college, I am getting an education to improve the skills that I'll need for a good career in broadcasting. Then, after a successful career, I'll be able to get the things that I need to be happy in my life. People will also respect me more.

_____

_____

_____

_____

_____

EXERCISE 5-11 EVALUATING A PARAGRAPH

Evaluate the following paragraph by answering the questions that follow it.

One of the best ways to keep people happy and occupied is to entertain them. Every day people are being entertained, whether it is by a friend for a split second or by a Broadway play for several hours. Entertainment is probably one of the nation's biggest businesses. Entertainment has come a long way from the past; it has gone from plays in the park to films in eight-screen movie theaters.

1. Evaluate the topic sentence. What is wrong with it? How could it be revised?

   _____

   _____

2. Write a more effective topic sentence about entertainment.

   _____

3. Evaluate the supporting details. What is wrong with them?

   _____

4. What should the writer do to develop her paragraph?

   _____

5. Use the topic sentence you wrote in question 2 above to develop a paragraph about entertainment.

Use Idea Maps to Find Revision Problems

Some students find revision a troublesome step because it is difficult for them to see what is wrong with their own work. After working hard on a first draft, it is tempting to say to yourself that you've done a great job and to think, "This is fine." Other times, you may think you have explained and supported an idea clearly when actually you have not. In other words, you may be blind to your own paper's weaknesses. Almost all writing, however, needs and benefits from revision. An idea map can help you spot weaknesses and discover what you may not have done as well as you thought.

An idea map will show how each of your ideas fits with and relates to all of the other ideas in a paragraph or essay. When you draw an idea map, you reduce your ideas to a skeleton form that allows you to see and analyze them more easily. You can use an idea map to (1) discover problems in a paragraph and (2) guide your revision. Here are four questions to ask that will help you identify weaknesses in your writing with suggestions for ways to revise your paragraphs to correct each weakness.

- Does the paragraph stray from the topic?
- Does every detail belong?
- Are the details arranged and developed logically?
- Is the paragraph repetitious?

Does the Paragraph Stray from the Topic?

When you are writing a first draft of a paragraph, it is easy to drift away from the topic. As you write, one idea triggers another and that idea another, and eventually you end up with ideas that have little or nothing to do with your original topic, as in the following first-draft student paragraph.

Sample Student Paragraph

A Checklist for Leaving Home on Time

If you are not a naturally well-organized person, you may need to compensate by being super organized in the morning so you can leave on time. A detailed checklist can help you achieve the seemingly impossible goal of leaving home exactly when you are supposed to. It is especially difficult to leave on time if you are tired or feeling lazy. When making such a checklist, most people find it helpful to make plans the previous evening. Check if you have clean clothes for the next day or need to do a load of laundry. Are materials for school or work neatly assembled, or is there a landslide of papers covering your desk? Do you need to pack lunch? You get the picture. In your checklist, include tasks to complete the night before as well as a precise sequence of morning tasks with realistic estimates of the time required for each task. If you have children, help them make checklists to keep track of homework assignments. Child development experts stress the importance of predictable structure in children's lives. If you live with a friend or spouse, make sure to divide all the chores in an equitable way. Often one person tends to be neater than the other, so you may need to make compromises, but having an explicit agreement can help prevent resentment and conflicts at home. As you can see, it is important to be organized in the morning in order to get a timely start to the day.

The following idea map shows the topic sentence of the paragraph and, underneath it, the supporting details that directly relate to the topic sentence. All the unrelated details are in a list to the right of the map. Note that the concluding sentence is also included in the map, since it is an important part of the paragraph.

Idea Map for a Checklist for Leaving Home

If you are not organized, you may need to be super organized in order to leave on time in the morning.

A detailed checklist can help.

In your checklist, include tasks to complete the night before.

If you have children, help them make checklists to keep track of homework assignments.

It is important to be organized in order to get a timely start in the morning.

Unrelated details

1. It is especially difficult to leave on time if you are tired or feeling lazy.

2. Child development experts stress the importance of predictable structure.

3. If you live with a friend or spouse, make sure to divide chores equitably.

4. Explicit agreements about household responsibilities and a willingness to compromise helps prevent resentment and conflict.

In this paragraph the author began by supporting her topic sentence with examples of what needs to be included in a checklist to help with leaving home on time in the mornings. However, she began to drift when she started talking about how to negotiate about chores with a spouse or roommate. To revise this paragraph, the author could delete irrelevant details and include more information about the tasks that need to be completed in the morning.

You can use an idea map to spot where you begin to drift away from your topic. To do this, take the last idea in the map and compare it with your topic sentence. Does the last idea directly support your topic sentence? If not, you may have drifted from your topic. Check the second-to-last detail, going through the same comparison process. Working backward, you'll see where you started to drift. This is the point at which to begin revising.

What to Do If You Stray Off Topic

Use the following suggestions to revise your paragraph if it strays from your topic:

- **Locate the last sentence that does relate to your topic, and begin your revision there.** What could you say next that *would* relate to the topic?

- **Consider expanding your existing ideas.** If, after two or three details, you have strayed from your topic, consider expanding the details you have, rather than searching for additional details.

- **Reread your brainstorming, freewriting, or branching to find more details.** Look for additional ideas that support your topic. Do more brainstorming, if necessary.
- **Consider changing your topic.** Drifting from your topic is not always a loss. Sometimes by drifting you discover a more interesting topic than your original one. If you decide to change topics, revise your entire paragraph. Begin by rewriting your topic sentence.

EXERCISE 5-12 DRAWING AN IDEA MAP

Read the following first-draft paragraph. Then draw an idea map that includes the topic sentence, only those details that support the topic sentence, and the concluding sentence. List the unrelated details to the side of the map, as in the example on page 126. Identify where the writer began to stray from the topic, and make specific suggestions for revising this paragraph.

Junk food lacks nutrition and is high in calories. Junk food can be anything from candy and potato chips to ice cream and desserts. All of these are high in calories. But they are so tasty that they are addictive. Once a person is addicted to junk food, it is very hard to break the addiction. To break the habit, one must give up any form of sugar. And I have not gone back to my old lifestyle in over two weeks. So it is possible to break an addiction, but I still have the craving.

Does Every Detail Belong?

Every detail in a paragraph must directly support the topic sentence or one of the other details. Unrelated information should not be included, a mistake one student made in the following first-draft paragraph.

Sample Student Paragraph

In a world where stress is an everyday occurrence, many people relieve stress through entertainment. There are many ways to entertain ourselves and relieve stress. Many people watch movies to take their minds off day-to-day problems. However, going to the movies costs a lot of money. Due to the cost, some people rent or stream movies. Playing sports is another stress reliever. Exercise always helps to give people a positive attitude and keeps them in shape. Racquetball really keeps you in shape because it is such a fast game. A third form of entertainment is going out with friends. With friends, people can talk about their problems and feel better about them. But some friends always talk and never listen, and such conversation creates stress instead of relieving it. So if you are under stress, be sure to reserve some time for entertainment.

The following idea map shows that this writer included four unrelated details:

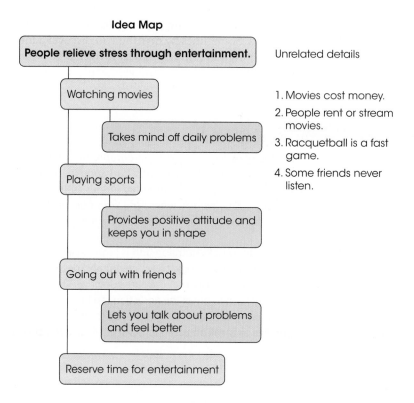

Idea Map

People relieve stress through entertainment.   Unrelated details

Watching movies

Takes mind off daily problems

Playing sports

Provides positive attitude and keeps you in shape

Going out with friends

Lets you talk about problems and feel better

Reserve time for entertainment

1. Movies cost money.
2. People rent or stream movies.
3. Racquetball is a fast game.
4. Some friends never listen.

To spot unrelated details, draw an idea map. To decide whether a detail is unrelated, ask, "Does this detail directly explain the topic sentence or one of the other details?" If you are not sure, ask, "What happens if I take this out?" If meaning is lost or if confusion occurs, the detail is important. Include it in your map. If you can make your point just as well without the detail, mark it "unrelated."

In the sample student paragraph, the high cost of movies and the low-cost alternatives of renting or streaming them do not directly explain how or why movies are entertaining. The racquetball detail does not explain how exercise relieves stress. The detail about friends not listening does not explain how talking to friends is helpful in reducing stress.

Making Sure Every Detail Belongs

The following suggestions will help you use supporting details more effectively:

- **Add explanations to make the connections between your ideas clearer.** Often a detail may not seem to relate to the topic because you have not explained *how* it relates. For example, health-care insurance may seem to have little to do with the prevention of breast cancer deaths until you explain that mammograms, which are paid for by some health-care plans, can prevent deaths.

- **Add signal words.** Signal words make it clearer to your reader how one detail relates to another.
- **Add new details.** If you've deleted several nonessential details, your paragraph may be too sketchy. Return to the prewriting step to generate more details you can include.

EXERCISE 5-13 IDENTIFYING UNRELATED DETAILS

Read the following paragraph and draw an idea map of it. Underline any unrelated details and list them to the side of your map. Compare your results with those of a classmate and then decide what steps the writer should take to revise this paragraph.

Your credit rating is a valuable thing that you should protect and watch over. A credit rating is a record of your loans, credit card charges, and repayment history. If you pay a bill late or miss a payment, that information becomes part of your credit rating. It is, therefore, important to pay bills promptly. Some people just don't keep track of dates; some don't even know what date it is today. Errors can occur in your credit rating. Someone else's mistakes can be put on your record, for example. Why these credit-rating companies can't take more time and become more accurate is beyond my understanding. It is worthwhile to get a copy of your credit report and check it for errors. Time spent caring for your credit rating will be time well spent.

Are the Details Arranged and Developed Logically?

Details in a paragraph should follow some logical order. As you write a first draft, you are often more concerned with expressing your ideas than with presenting them in the correct order. As you revise, however, you should make sure you have followed a logical arrangement. The following boxes review possible arrangements:

METHODS OF ARRANGING AND DEVELOPING DETAILS

METHOD	DESCRIPTION
Time sequence	Arranges details in the order in which they happen
Spatial	Arranges details according to their physical location
Least/Most	Arranges details from least to most or from most to least, according to some quality or characteristic

The methods of organization discussed in Chapter 6 offer ways to organize ideas. They are summarized below.

METHODS OF ORGANIZING USING PATTERNS

METHOD	DESCRIPTION
Process	Arranges steps in order in which they are completed
Definition	Explains a term by giving its general class and specific characteristics
Illustration	Explains by giving situations that illustrate a general idea or statement
Cause and effect	Explains why something happened or what happened as a result of a particular action
Comparison and contrast	Explains an idea by comparing or contrasting it with another, usually more familiar, idea

Your ideas need a logical arrangement to make them easy to follow. Poor organization creates misunderstanding and confusion. After drafting the following paragraph, a student drew an idea map that showed her organization was haphazard.

Sample Student Paragraph

When I was pregnant with my son, I wondered if life would ever be normal again. There were the nights I couldn't sleep because of all the kicking and the baby moving up to my lungs so I couldn't breathe. That was when I really had it! Each month I got bigger and bigger, and after a while I was so big I couldn't bend over or see my feet. Then there was the morning sickness. I don't know why they call it that because you're sick all the time for the first two months. Then there were all those doctor visits during which she told me, "Not for another week or two." Of course, when I realized my clothes didn't fit, I broke down and cried. But all of a sudden everything started up, and I was at the hospital delivering the baby two weeks early, and it's like it happened so fast and it was all over, and I had the most beautiful baby in my arms and I knew it was worth all that pain and suffering.

An idea map lets you see quickly when a paragraph has no organization or when an idea is out of order. This student's map (next page), showed that her paragraph did not present the events of her pregnancy in the most logical arrangement: time sequence.

Idea Map

When I was pregnant, I wondered if life would ever be normal.

Couldn't sleep—baby kicking, breathing difficult

Got bigger and bigger

Morning sickness

Doctor: "Not for another week"

Clothes didn't fit

Birth

She therefore reorganized the events in the order in which they happened and revised her paragraph as follows:

Revised Paragraph

When I was pregnant with my son, I wondered if life would ever be normal again. First there was the morning sickness. I don't know why they call it that because I was sick all the time for the first two months. Of course, when I realized my clothes didn't fit, I broke down and cried. Each month I got bigger and bigger, and finally I was so big I couldn't bend over or see my feet. Then there were the nights I couldn't sleep because of all the kicking and the baby moving up to my lungs so I couldn't breathe. That was when I really had it. Finally, there were all those doctor visits during which she told me, "Not for another week or two." But all of a sudden everything started to happen, and I was at the hospital delivering the baby two weeks early. Everything happened so fast. It was all over, and I had the most beautiful baby in my arms. Then I knew it was worth all that pain and suffering.

Arranging and Developing Details Logically

The following suggestions will help you revise your paragraph if it lacks organization:

- **Review the methods of arranging and developing details and of organizing and presenting material** (see the boxes on pp. 129–130).

Will one of those arrangements work? If so, number the ideas in your idea map according to the arrangement you choose. Then begin revising your paragraph.

If you find one or more details out of logical order in your paragraph, do the following:

1. **Number the details in your idea map to indicate the correct order, and revise your paragraph accordingly.**
2. **Reread your revised paragraph and draw another idea map.**
3. **Look to see if you've omitted necessary details.** After you have placed your details in a logical order, you are more likely to recognize gaps.

■ **Look at your topic sentence again.** If you are working with a revised arrangement of supporting details, you may need to revise your topic sentence to reflect that arrangement.

■ **Check whether additional details are needed.** Suppose, for example, you are writing about an exciting experience, and you decide to use the time-sequence arrangement. Once you make that decision, you may need to add details to enable your reader to understand exactly how the experience happened.

■ **Add signal words.** Signal words and phrases help make your organization obvious and easy to follow.

EXERCISE 5-14 EVALUATING ARRANGEMENT OF IDEAS

Read the following student paragraph, and draw an idea map of it. Evaluate the arrangement of ideas. What revisions would you suggest?

The minimum wage is not an easily resolved problem; it has both advantages and disadvantages. Its primary advantage is that it does guarantee workers a minimum wage. It prevents the economic abuse of workers. Employers cannot take advantage of workers by paying them less than the minimum. Its primary disadvantage is that the minimum wage is not sufficient for older workers with families to support. For younger workers, such as teenagers, however, this minimum is fine. It provides them with spending money and some economic freedom from their parents. Another disadvantage is that as long as people, such as a teenagers, are willing to work for the minimum, employers don't need to pay a higher wage. Thus, the minimum wage prevents experienced workers from getting more money. But the minimum wage does help our economy by requiring a certain level of income per worker.

Is the Paragraph Repetitious?

In a first draft, you may express the same idea more than once, each time in a slightly different way. As you are writing a first draft, repetitive statements may help you stay on track. They keep you writing and help generate new ideas. However, it is important to eliminate repetition at the revision stage. Repetitive statements add nothing to your paragraph. They detract from its clarity. An idea map will bring repetition to your attention quickly because it is then easier to spot two or more very similar items.

As you read the following first-draft student paragraph, see if you can spot the repetitive statements. Then notice how the idea map below it clearly identifies the repetition.

Sample Student Paragraph

Chemical waste dumping is an environmental concern that must be dealt with, not ignored. The big companies care nothing about the environment. They would just as soon dump waste in our backyards as not. This has finally become a big issue and is being dealt with by forcing the companies to clean up their own messes. It is incredible that large companies have the nerve to dump just about anywhere. The penalty should be steep. When the companies are caught, they should be forced to clean up their messes.

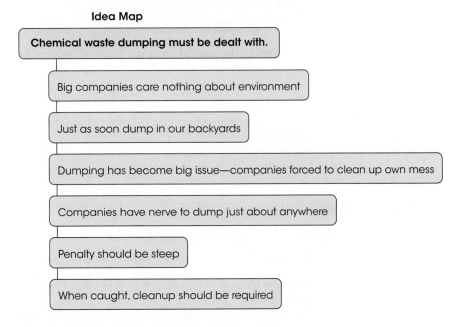

Idea Map

Chemical waste dumping must be dealt with.

Big companies care nothing about environment

Just as soon dump in our backyards

Dumping has become big issue—companies forced to clean up own mess

Companies have nerve to dump just about anywhere

Penalty should be steep

When caught, cleanup should be required

The idea map shows that points 1, 2, and 5 say nearly the same thing—that big companies don't care about the environment and dump waste nearly anywhere. Because there is so much repetition, the paragraph lacks development. To revise, the writer first needs to eliminate the repetitious statements. Then she needs to generate more ideas that support her topic sentence and explain why or how chemical waste dumping must be dealt with.

How to Avoid Repetition

The following suggestions will help you revise a paragraph with repetitive ideas:

- **Try to combine ideas.** Select the best elements and wording of each idea and use them to produce a revised sentence. Add more detail if needed.

- **Review places where you make deletions.** When you delete a repetitious statement, check to see whether the sentence before and the sentence after the deletion connect. Often a transition will be needed to help the paragraph flow easily.

- **Decide whether additional details are needed.** Often we write repetitious statements when we don't know what else to say. Thus, repetition often signals lack of development. Refer to page 123 for specific suggestions on revising underdeveloped paragraphs.

- **Watch for statements that are only slightly more general or specific than one another.** For example, although the first sentence below is general and the second is more specific, they repeat the same idea.

> Ringing telephones can be distracting. The telephone that rang constantly throughout the evening distracted me.

To make the second sentence a specific example of the idea in the first sentence, rather than just a repetition of it, the writer would need to add specific details about how the telephone ringing throughout the evening was a distraction.

> The telephone that rang continuously in my neighbor's apartment yesterday woke my baby and made it impossible to get her back to sleep.

EXERCISE 5-15 IDENTIFYING AND REVISING REPETITIVE STATEMENTS

Read the following paragraph and delete all repetitive statements. Make suggestions for revision.

Children misbehaving is an annoying problem in our society. I used to work as a waiter at Denny's, and I have seen many incidences in which parents allow their children to misbehave. I have seen many situations that you would just not believe. Once I served a table at which the parents allowed their four-year-old to make his toy spider crawl up and down my pants as I tried to serve the food. The parents just laughed. Children have grown up being rewarded for their actions, regardless of whether they are good or bad. Whether the child does something the parents approve of or whether it is something they disapprove of, they react in similar ways. This is why a lot of toddlers and children continue to misbehave. Being rewarded will cause the child to act in the same way to get the same reward.

Refer to the following Revision Checklist to help you revise paragraphs.

Revision Checklist
Paragraph Development

1. Is the topic manageable (neither too broad nor too narrow)?

2. Is the paragraph written with the reader in mind?

3. Does the topic sentence identify the topic?

4. Does the topic sentence make a point about the topic?

5. Does each sentence support the topic sentence?

6. Is there sufficient detail?

7. Are the details arranged and developed logically?

8. Is the paragraph repetitious?

9. Is there a sentence at the end that brings the paragraph to a close?

Sentence Development

10. Are there any sentence fragments, run-on sentences, or comma splices?

11. Are ideas combined to produce more effective sentences?

12. Are adjectives and adverbs used to make the sentences vivid and interesting?

13. Are relative clauses and prepositional phrases like -*ing* phrases used to add detail?

14. Are pronouns used correctly and consistently?

EXERCISE 5-16 REVISING A PARAGRAPH

Review the paragraph your wrote for Exercise 5-9. Use the Revision Checklist to guide your revision.

SUMMARY OF LEARNING OBJECTIVES

Objective 1 Write effective topic sentences.	An *effective topic* sentence identifies the topic and expresses a view or makes a point about the topic. Choose a manageable topic and be sure the sentence expresses a complete thought.
Objective 2 Select and organize details to support the topic sentence.	Use *relevant details* that directly explain and support the topic sentence. Use *sufficient details* to make your topic sentence understandable and convincing. Use a *variety of details* to develop the topic sentence: examples, facts or statistics, reasons, descriptions, and steps or procedures. To paint a vivid picture for readers, use *specific words and phrases,* choose action words, give exact names, include adjectives, and select words that appeal to the senses. *Organize details logically* based on the topic of the paragraph using time sequence, spatial, or least-to-most arrangements.
Objective 3 Use signal words and phrases to connect details.	*Signal words and phrases* show how details are related to one another and guide readers through paragraphs by signaling what is to come. They also indicate the method by which details have been arranged. See Table 5.1 (p. 119) for a list of common signal words.
Objective 4 Revise paragraphs.	*Revise paragraphs* by evaluating your topic sentence, adding supporting details, and using a revision map. A *map* will help you discover whether you have *strayed from your topic,* be sure that *every detail belongs,* that the *details are arranged and developed logically,* and that you have *avoided repetition.* Use the Revision Checklist on page 135 to help you revise.

6 Organizational Patterns

Most college students take courses in several different disciplines each semester. They may study psychology, anatomy and physiology, mathematics, and English composition all in one semester. In the course of one day, they may read a poem, solve math problems, study early developments in psychology, and learn about controversial issues in politics and government.

What few students realize is that biologists and psychologists, for example, think about and approach their subject matter in similar ways. Both carefully define terms, examine causes and effects, study similarities and differences, explain processes, and illustrate ideas. They may study different subject matter and use different language, but their approaches to their studies are basically the same. Researchers, textbook authors, your professors, and professional writers use standard approaches, or **organizational patterns**, to express their ideas. In English composition, they are sometimes called the **rhetorical modes** or simply **modes**.

To learn what patterns of organization are and why they are useful for reading and writing, consider the following lists.

Lists A and B each contain five facts. Which would be easier to learn?

List A

1. Cheeseburgers contain more calories than hamburgers.

2. Christmas cactus plants bloom once a year.

3. Many herbs have medicinal uses.

4. Many ethnic groups live in Toronto.

5. Fiction books are arranged alphabetically by author.

List B

1. Effective advertising has several characteristics.
2. An ad must be unique.
3. An ad must be believable.
4. An ad must make a lasting impression.
5. An ad must substantiate a claim.

Most likely, you chose list B. There is no connection between the facts in list A; the facts in list B, however, are related. The first sentence makes a general statement, and each remaining sentence gives a particular characteristic of effective advertising. Together they fit into a *pattern*.

The details of a paragraph, paragraphs within an essay, events within a short story, or sections within a textbook often fit a *pattern*. If you can recognize the pattern, you will find it easier to understand and remember the content. You will be able to comprehend the work as a unified whole rather than independent pieces of information.

Patterns are useful when you write, as well. They provide a framework within which to organize and develop your ideas and help you present them in a clear, logical manner. Sections of this chapter are devoted to reading and writing each of the following patterns: *illustration, process, definition, cause and effect*, and *comparison and contrast*. Each of these patterns can work alone or with other patterns.

The organizational patterns can work for you in several ways:

- Patterns help you anticipate the author's thought development and thus focus your reading.
- Patterns help you remember and recall what you read.
- Patterns are useful in your own writing; they help you organize and express your ideas in a coherent, comprehensible form.

Each section of this chapter describes a common pattern and provides examples of its use.

6a   READING AND WRITING ILLUSTRATION

LEARNING OBJECTIVE 1
Recognize and use illustration.

Illustration uses examples—specific instances or situations—to explain a general idea or statement. Peaches and plums are examples of fruit. Presidents' Day and Veterans Day are examples of national holidays. Here are a few sample general statements along with specific examples that illustrate them.

General Statement	Examples
I had an exhausting day.	■ I had two exams.
	■ I worked four hours.
	■ I swam 20 laps in the pool.
	■ I did three loads of laundry.

General Statement	Examples
Research studies demonstrate that reading aloud to children improves their reading skills.	■ Whitehurst (2011) found that reading picture books to children improved their vocabulary. ■ Crain-Thompson and Dale (2012) reported that reading aloud to language-delayed children improved their reading ability.

General Statement	Examples
You can improve your efficiency at work by working smarter, not harder.	■ An efficient day begins the night before: get a good night's sleep. ■ Every morning, make a list of your priorities for the day and stick to it. ■ Handle each piece of mail once; either respond to it, forward it to your assistant to handle, or throw it away.

In each case, the examples make the general statement clear, understandable, and believable by giving specific illustrations or supporting details.

EXERCISE 6-1 BRAINSTORMING USE OF EXAMPLES

Working with another student, brainstorm a list of examples to illustrate one of the following statements:

1. Effective teaching involves caring about students.

2. Dogs (or cats) make good companions.

3. Volunteerism has many benefits.

Example paragraphs consist of examples that support the topic sentence. You can visualize an example paragraph as shown below:

**Example Paragraph
Idea Map**

Topic sentence

Example 1

Example 2

Example 3

Reading Illustration

The **illustration pattern** uses specific instances or detailed situations or examples to explain an idea or concept. One of the clearest ways to explain something is to give an example. This is especially true when a subject is unfamiliar. Suppose, for instance, that your younger brother asks you to explain what anthropology is. You might give him examples of the topics you study, such as apes and early humans, and the development of modern humans. Through examples, your brother would get a fairly good idea of what anthropology is all about.

When organizing a paragraph, a writer often states the main idea first and then follows it with one or more examples. In a longer piece of writing, a separate paragraph may be used for each example. Notice how the illustration pattern is developed in the following paragraph.

> Static electricity is all around us. We see it in lightning. We receive electric shocks when we walk on a nylon rug on a dry day and then touch something (or someone). We can see sparks fly from a cat's fur when we pet it in the dark. We can rub a balloon on a sweater and make the balloon stick to the wall or the ceiling. Our clothes cling together when we take them from the dryer.
>
> —Newell, *Chemistry: An Introduction,* p. 11

In the preceding paragraph, the writer explains static electricity through the use of everyday examples. You could visualize the paragraph as follows:

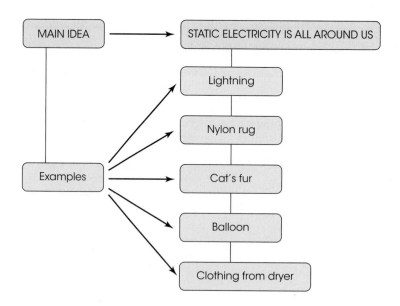

Writers often use signal words—*for example, for instance,* or *such as*—to signal the reader that an example is to follow.

Charlie agrees with the old saying that "a dog is a man's best friend." When he comes home from work, <u>for instance</u>, his dog Shadow is always happy to see him. He wags his tail, licks Charlie's hand, and leaps joyously around the room. Shadow is also good company for him. The dog is always there, <u>for example</u>, when Charlie is sick or lonely or just needs a pal to take for a walk. Many pets, <u>such as</u> cats and parakeets, provide companionship for their owners. But Charlie would put his dog Shadow at the top of any "best friend" list.

By using examples and signal words, the writer explains why Shadow is Charlie's best friend.

EXERCISE 6-2 ANALYZING THE ILLUSTRATION PATTERN

The following paragraphs, all of which are about stress, use the example pattern. Read each of them and answer the questions that follow.

A.   Any single event or situation by itself may not cause stress. But, if you experience several mildly disturbing situations at the same time, you may find yourself under stress. For instance, getting a low grade on a biology lab report by itself may not be stressful, but if it occurred the same week during which your car "died," you argued with a close friend, and you discovered your checking account was overdrawn, then it may contribute to stress.

1. What signal word or phrase does the writer use to introduce the examples?

_____

2. List the four examples the writer provides as possible causes of stress.

a. _____

b. _____

c. _____

d. _____

B.   Every time you make a major change in your life, you are susceptible to stress. Major changes include a new job or career, marriage, divorce, the birth of a child, or the death of someone close. Beginning college is a major life change. Try not to create multiple simultaneous life changes, which multiply the potential for stress.

3. Does the topic sentence occur first, second, or last?

_____

4. The writer gives six examples of major changes. List them briefly.

a. _____   d. _____

b. _____   e. _____

c. _____   f. _____

C.   Because you probably depend on your job to pay part or all of your college expenses, your job is important to you and you feel pressure to perform well in order to keep it. Some jobs are more stressful than others. Those, for example, in which you work under constant time pressure tend to be stressful. Jobs that must be performed in loud, noisy, crowded, or unpleasant conditions—a hot kitchen, a noisy machine shop, with co-workers who don't do their share—can be stressful. Consider changing jobs if you are working in very stressful conditions.

5. Does the topic sentence occur first, second, or last?

_____

6. What transition does the writer use to introduce the first type of job?

_____

7. To help you understand "jobs that must be performed in loud, noisy, crowded, or unpleasant conditions," the writer provides three examples. List these examples in the diagram below.

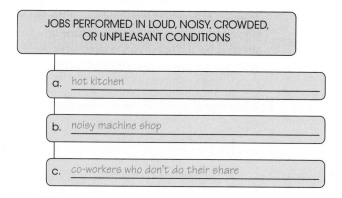

JOBS PERFORMED IN LOUD, NOISY, CROWDED, OR UNPLEASANT CONDITIONS

a. hot kitchen

b. noisy machine shop

c. co-workers who don't do their share

Writing Illustration

Writing paragraphs using examples involves writing a clear topic sentence, selecting appropriate and sufficient examples, arranging your details, and using transitions. When writing illustration paragraphs, be sure to use the third person in most situations (see "point of view," Ch. 2, p. 25).

Write Your Topic Sentence

You must create a topic sentence before you can generate examples to support it. Consider what you want to say about your topic and what your main point or fresh insight is. From this main idea, compose a first draft of a topic sentence. Be sure it states your topic and the point you want to make about it. (See Chapter 5, p. 109, if necessary, for a review of developing your point.) You will probably want to revise your topic sentence once you've written the paragraph, but for now, use it as the basis for gathering examples.

Select Appropriate and Sufficient Examples

Use brainstorming to create a list of as many examples as you can think of to support your topic sentence. Suppose your topic is dog training. Your tentative topic sentence is, "You must be firm and consistent when training dogs; otherwise, they will not respond to your commands." You might produce the following list of examples:

> My sister's dog jumps on people; sometimes she disciplines him and sometimes she doesn't.
>
> Every time I want my dog to heel, I give the same command and use a firm tone of voice.
>
> If my dog does not obey the command to sit, I repeat it, this time saying it firmly while pushing down on his back.
>
> The dog trainer at obedience class used a set of hand signals to give commands to his dogs.

Then you would review your list and select between two and four examples to support your topic sentence. Here is an example of a paragraph you might have written:

> When training dogs, you must be firm and consistent; otherwise, they will not respond to your commands. The dog trainer at my obedience class has a perfectly trained dog. She uses a set of hand signals to give commands to her dog, Belle. The same signal always means the same thing, it is always enforced, and Belle has learned to obey each command. On the other hand, my sister's dog is a good example of what not to do. Her dog Maggie jumps on people; sometimes she disciplines Maggie, and sometimes she doesn't. When she asks Maggie to sit, sometimes she insists Maggie obey; other times she gets discouraged and gives up. Consequently, the dog has not learned to stop jumping on people or to obey the command to sit.

Idea Map

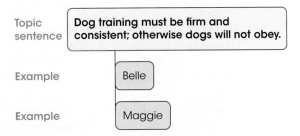

In the example paragraph, you probably noticed that some of the brainstormed examples were used; others were not. New examples were also added. Use the following guidelines when selecting details to include:

Guidelines for Selecting Details

- **Each example should illustrate the idea stated in your topic sentence.** Sometimes you may find that your examples do not clarify your main point or that each example you think of seems to illustrate something slightly different. If your topic is too broad, narrow your topic using the suggestions in Chapter 5.

- **Each example should be as specific and vivid as possible, accurately describing an incident or situation.** Suppose your topic sentence is, "Celebrities are not reliable sources of information about a product because they are getting paid to praise it." For your first example you write: "Many sports stars are paid to appear in TV commercials." "Many sports stars" is too general. To be convincing, your example has to name specific athletes and products or sponsors: "Tom Brady, star quarterback for the Patriots, endorses UGG Boots and Under Armour; LeBron James, basketball superstar, endorses Nike products."

- **Choose a sufficient number of examples to make your point understandable.** The number you need depends on the complexity of the topic and your reader's familiarity with it. One example is sufficient only if it is well developed. The more difficult and unfamiliar the topic, the more examples you will need. For instance, if you are writing about how poor service at a restaurant can be viewed as an exercise in patience, two examples may be sufficient. Your paragraph could describe your long wait and your rude waiter and make its point quite powerfully. However, if you are writing about test anxiety as a symptom of poor study habits, you probably would need more than two examples. In this case, you might discuss the need to organize one's time, set realistic goals, practice relaxation techniques, and work on self-esteem.

- **Draw the connection for your reader between your example and your main point.** The following is a presentation by a social worker during a closed staff meeting at Carroll County Mental Health Services:

> We are continuing to see the aftereffects of last spring's tornado on our clients. In some cases, we have had to make referrals to meet our clients' needs. Several children have suffered PTSD (post traumatic stress disorder). Natoya Johns, for example, has nightmares and panic attacks. Natoya and the other children have been referred to Dr. Browntree at the Children's Clinic. We are also seeing increased occurrences of domestic violence that seem to be due to economic problems caused by the tornado. The worst case was Betsy Coster, who came to her counseling session with broken ribs, a black eye, and bruises. Betsy was referred to Safe Harbor, where she will receive legal and medical assistance while in protected housing. Several cases of substance abuse appeared to be aggravated by the stress of the situation. We put four clients in touch with AA, and Ken Lacoutez was referred to City Hospital for the inpatient program.
>
> (*Note:* Names have been changed to protect client privacy.)

Use the guidelines in the box below when choosing examples.

CHOOSING APPROPRIATE EXAMPLES

- **Make sure your example illustrates your topic sentence clearly.** Do not choose an example that is complicated or has too many parts; your readers may not be able to see the connection to your topic sentence clearly.
- **Choose examples that your readers are familiar with and understand.** If you choose an example that is out of the realm of your readers' experience, the example will not help them understand your main point.
- **Choose interesting, original examples.** Your readers are more likely to pay attention to them.
- **Vary your examples.** If you are giving several examples, choose a wide range from different times, places, people, and so on.
- **Choose typical examples.** Avoid outrageous or exaggerated examples that do not accurately represent the situation.

Arrange Your Details

Once you have selected examples to include, arrange your ideas in a logical sequence. Here are a few possibilities:

- **Arrange the examples chronologically.** If some examples are old and others more recent, you might begin with the older examples and then move to the more current ones.

- **Arrange the examples from most to least familiar.** If some examples are more detailed or technical, and therefore likely to be unfamiliar to your reader, place them after more familiar examples.

- **Arrange the examples from least to most important.** You may want to begin with less convincing examples and finish with the strongest, most convincing example, thereby leaving your reader with a strong final impression.

- **Arrange the examples in the order suggested by the topic sentence.** In the earlier sample paragraph about dog training, being firm and consistent is mentioned first in the topic sentence, so an example of firm and consistent training is given first.

Use Signal Words

Signal words and phrases are needed in illustration paragraphs, both to signal your reader that you are offering an example and to signal that you are moving from one example to another. Notice in the following paragraph how the signal words connect the examples and make them easy to follow.

> Electricity is all around us, often in the form of static electricity. For example, when we walk on a nylon rug and then touch something or someone, we receive a mild electrical shock. This shock occurs because accumulated

electrical energy is being discharged. <u>Similarly</u>, when we rub a balloon on a sweater and make the balloon stick to the wall or ceiling, energy is again discharged. <u>Another</u> instance of electrical discharge occurs when clothes cling together after removal from a dryer.

COMMON ILLUSTRATION SIGNAL WORDS

for example	for instance	such as	in particular
to illustrate	an example is	also	when

EXERCISE 6-3 WRITING A PARAGRAPH

Select one of the topics listed below and write a paragraph that follows the guidelines given above.

1. Slang language

2. Daily hassles or aggravations

3. The needs of infants or young children

4. Overcommercialization of holidays

5. Irresponsible behavior of crowds or individuals at public events

---

6b   READING AND WRITING PROCESS

LEARNING OBJECTIVE 2
Recognize and use process.

The term *process* refers to the order in which something occurs or the order in which it is done. When textbook authors explain how to do something or how something works, they use a pattern called **process**, presenting ideas in sequence. **Chronological order** is a variation of process. When a writer describes historical events, for example, he or she uses chronological order—describing the events in the order in which they happened. Another variation is *narration*. When writers tell a story, they often describe the events in order, creating a narrative. While this section focuses on process, you can use many of the same guidelines for reading and writing chronological order and narration, as well.

When writing process paragraphs, it is sometimes acceptable to write in the second person (you), but it is not acceptable to use the second person when writing in other patterns.

Reading Process Paragraphs

Disciplines and careers that focus on procedures, steps, or stages use the process pattern. In some cases, however, certain steps may happen at the same time or in no particular order. Using bulleted and numbered lists allows writers to provide clear, step-by-step explanations of processes. Note that the following selection uses numbered points to walk the reader through the process of performing mouth-to-mask ventilation in the correct, step-by-step manner. Notice that all of the steps are parallel: they begin with verbs. This paragraph does not have a concluding sentence because it appeared as part of a longer piece of writing.

Mouth-to-mask ventilation is performed using a pocket face mask, which is made of soft, collapsible material and can be carried in your pocket, jacket, or purse. Many emergency medical technicians (EMTs) purchase their own pocket face masks for workplace or auto first aid kits.

To provide mouth-to-mask ventilation, follow these steps:

1. Position yourself at the patient's head and open the airway. It may be necessary to clear the airway of obstructions. If appropriate, insert an oropharyngeal airway to help keep the patient's airway open.

2. Connect oxygen to the inlet on the mask and run at 16 liters per minute. If oxygen is not immediately available, do not delay mouth-to-mask ventilations.

3. Position the mask on the patient's face so that the apex (top of the triangle) is over the bridge of the nose and the base is between the lower lip and prominence of the chin. (Center the ventilation port of the patient's mouth.)

4. Hold the mask firmly in place while maintaining head tilt.

5. Take a breath and exhale into the mask port or one-way valve at the top of the mask port. Each ventilation should be delivered over 1 second in adults, infants, and children and be of just enough volume to make the chest rise. Full expansion of the chest is undesirable; the ventilation should cease as soon as you notice the chest moving.

6. Remove your mouth from the port and allow for passive exhalation. Continue as you would for mouth-to-mouth ventilation or CPR.

—Adapted from Limmer and O'Keefe, *Emergency Care*, pp. 211–212

You can visualize the process pattern as follows:

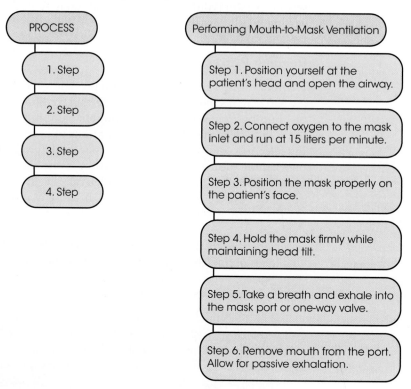

EXERCISE 6-4 USING PROCESS

Read the following selection and answer the questions that follow.

Issue: Organ Donation

The young motorcyclist was a good candidate for organ donation because he died from a brain injury. People who die from cardiac death can be tissue donors, but the lack of oxygen experienced during cardiac death causes organs to deteriorate, making such people less suitable organ donors. Since many more people will die of cardiac death than brain injury, tissues can be banked for future use, but there is a shortage of organs for use in transplant operations.

If the family agrees, the young man will be kept on a ventilator so that his organs continue to be nourished with oxygen and blood until the organs can be surgically removed. While the organs are being removed, medical personnel will attempt to find the best recipient. To select the recipient, a search of a computerized database is performed. Starting at the top of the list, medical staff will narrow down possible recipients, based in part on how long the recipient has been waiting. People at the top of the waiting list for a given organ tend to be very ill and will die if a transplant does not become available in a matter of days or weeks. These people are often hospitalized or waiting at home or in hotels near the hospital, hoping to receive a call telling them that an organ has become available. Recipients must be located close to the hospital since donor organs cannot be preserved indefinitely; they must be transplanted as soon as possible. Lungs, for instance, can be preserved for around 6 hours before the transplant operation must begin.

Organ donors and recipients must have the same blood type so that the recipient's immune system does not react against the organ. Likewise, donors and recipients are matched for the presence of certain markers on the surface of their tissues. When it has been determined that blood and marker types of donor and recipient are a close enough match, a transplant may occur. The most commonly transplanted organs are the liver, kidney, heart, and lungs. Around 10% of people on waiting lists for replacement organs will die before one becomes available.

If you would like to be an organ donor, discuss your plans with your family. Even if you carry a signed organ donor card and indicate your preference to be a donor on your driver's license, your family will need to agree to donate your tissues and organs. If you should suffer an accidental death, like the young motorcyclist, your family will be forced to make many difficult decisions quickly. Having a discussion about organ donation now will relieve them of the burden of trying to make this decision for you.

—Belk and Maier, *Biology: Science for Life with Physiology*, pp. 436–436

1. Which processes does this passage explain?

   _____

   _____

2. Highlight each topic sentence.

3. What is the best way to ensure that someone who needs your organs receives them after you die?

   _____

   _____

4. How many steps are involved in the process? List them on your own paper.

5. Highlight each of the signal words used in the passage.

Writing Process Paragraphs

There are two types of process paragraphs—a "how-to" paragraph and a "how-it-works" paragraph.

- **"How-to" paragraphs explain how something is done.** For example, they may explain how to change a flat tire, aid a choking victim, or locate a reference source in the library.

- **"How-it-works" paragraphs explain how something operates or happens.** For example, they may explain the operation of a pump, how the human body regulates temperature, or how children acquire speech.

Here are examples of both types of paragraphs. The first explains how to wash your hands in a medical environment. The second describes the process of hibernation. Be sure to study the idea map for each.

"How-to" Paragraph

Washing your hands may seem a simple task, but in a medical environment it is your first defense against the spread of disease and infection, and must be done properly. Begin by removing all jewelry. Turn on the water using a paper towel, thus avoiding contact with contaminated faucets. Next, wet your hands under running water and squirt a dollop of liquid soap in the palm of your hand. Lather the soap, and work it over your hands for two minutes. Use a circular motion, since it creates friction that removes dirt and organisms. Keep your hands pointed downward, so water will not run onto your arms, creating further contamination. Use a brush to clean under your fingernails. Then rinse your hands, reapply soap, scrub for one minute, and rinse again thoroughly. Dry your hands using a paper towel. Finally, use a new dry paper towel to turn off the faucet, protecting your hands from contamination.

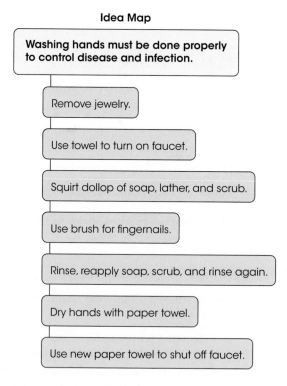

Idea Map

Washing hands must be done properly to control disease and infection.

Remove jewelry.

Use towel to turn on faucet.

Squirt dollop of soap, lather, and scrub.

Use brush for fingernails.

Rinse, reapply soap, scrub, and rinse again.

Dry hands with paper towel.

Use new paper towel to shut off faucet.

"How-It-Works" Paragraph

Hibernation is a biological process that occurs most frequently in small animals. The process enables animals to adjust to a diminishing food supply. When the outdoor temperature drops, the animal's internal thermostat senses the change. Then bodily changes begin to occur. First, the animal's heartbeat slows, and oxygen intake is reduced by slowed breathing. Metabolism is then reduced. Food intake becomes minimal. Finally, the animal falls into a sleeplike state during which it relies on stored body fat to support life functions.

Idea Map

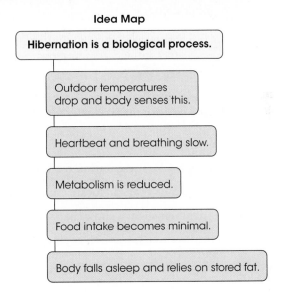

Hibernation is a biological process.

Outdoor temperatures drop and body senses this.

Heartbeat and breathing slow.

Metabolism is reduced.

Food intake becomes minimal.

Body falls asleep and relies on stored fat.

Select a Topic and Generate Ideas

Before you can describe a process, you must be very familiar with it. You should have done it often or have a complete understanding of how it works. Both how-to and how-it-works paragraphs describe steps that occur in a specified order. Begin developing your paragraph by listing these steps in the order in which they must occur. It is helpful to visualize the process.

For how-to paragraphs, imagine yourself actually performing the task. For complicated how-it-works descriptions, draw diagrams and use them as guides in identifying the steps and putting them in the proper order.

Write Your Topic Sentence

For a process paragraph, your topic sentence should accomplish two things:

- It should identify the process or procedure.
- It should explain to your reader why familiarity with the process is useful or important (*why* he or she should learn about the process). Your topic sentence should state a goal, offer a reason, or indicate what can be accomplished by using the process.

Here are a few examples of topic sentences that contain both of these important elements.

> Reading maps, a vital skill if you are orienteering, is a simple process, except for the final refolding.
>
> Because leisure reading encourages a positive attitude toward reading in general, every parent should know how to select worthwhile children's books.
>
> To locate books in the library, you must know how to use the computerized catalog.

EXERCISE 6-5 REVISING TOPIC SENTENCES

Working with a classmate, revise these topic sentences to make clear why the reader should learn the process.

1. Making pizza at home involves five steps.

2. Making a sales presentation requires good listening and speaking skills.

3. Bloodhounds that can locate criminals are remarkable creatures.

4. The dental hygienist shows patients how to use dental floss.

5. Here's how to use a search engine.

Develop and Sequence Your Ideas

Because your readers may be unfamiliar with your topic, try to include helpful information that will enable them to understand (for how-it-works paragraphs) and follow or complete the process (for how-to paragraphs). Consider including the following:

- **Definitions** Explain terms that may be unfamiliar. For example, explain the term *bindings* when writing about skiing.

- **Needed equipment** For how-to paragraphs, tell your readers what tools or supplies they will need to complete the process. For example, for a how-to paragraph on making chili, list the ingredients.

- **Pitfalls and problems** Alert your reader about potential problems and places where confusion or error may occur. For example, warn your chili-making readers to add chili peppers gradually and to taste along the way so the chili doesn't get too spicy.

Use the following tips to develop an effective process paragraph.

DEVELOPING A PROCESS PARAGRAPH

1. Place your topic sentence first. This position provides your reader with a purpose for reading.
2. Present the steps in a process in the order in which they happen.
3. Include only essential, necessary steps. Avoid comments, opinions, or unnecessary information because they may confuse your reader.
4. Assume that your reader is unfamiliar with your topic (unless you know otherwise). Be sure to define unfamiliar terms and describe clearly any technical or specialized tools, procedures, or objects.
5. Use a consistent point of view. Use either the first person ("I") or the second person ("you") throughout. Don't switch between them. (Note: Process is the *only* pattern in which it is acceptable to use the second person.)

Use Signal Words

Signal words are particularly important in process paragraphs because they lead your reader from one step to the next. Specifically, they signal to your reader that the next step is about to begin. In the following paragraph, notice how each of the highlighted signal words announce that a new step is to follow:

Do you want to teach your children something about their background, help develop their language skills, *and* have fun at the same time? Make a family album together! First, gather the necessary supplies: family photos, sheets of colored construction paper, yarn, and glue. Next, fold four sheets of paper in half; this will give you an eight-page album. Unfold the pages and lay them flat, one on top of the other. After you've evened them up, punch holes at the top and bottom of the fold, making sure you get through all four sheets. Next, thread the yarn through the holes. Now tie the yarn securely and crease the paper along the fold. Finally, glue a photo to each page. After the glue has dried, have your child write the names of the people in the pictures on each page and decorate the cover. Remember to talk to your children about the people you are including in your album. Not only will they learn about their extended family, but they also will have great memories of doing this creative project with you.

Refer to page 119 for a list of commonly used signal words and phrases that are useful in process paragraphs.

EXERCISE 6-6 WRITING A PROCESS PARAGRAPH

Think of a process or procedure you are familiar with, or select one from the following list. Use the guidelines presented in this section to write a process paragraph on the topic.

1. How to find a worthwhile part-time job

2. How to waste time

3. How to learn to like _____

4. How the NFL football draft works

5. How to win at _____

6. How to make a marriage or relationship work

7. How to protect your right to privacy

8. How to improve your skill at _____

9. How to make your boss want to promote you

READING AND WRITING DEFINITION

Each academic discipline, field of study, and business has its own specialized vocabulary. One of the primary purposes of introductory textbooks is to introduce students to this new language. Consequently, definition is a commonly used pattern throughout most introductory-level texts. **Definition** is also used in general-interest magazines to help readers become familiar with new ideas and concepts; for example, if *Time* publishes an article about gerrymandering (the process of changing boundaries of voting districts to favor a particular candidate or political party), you can expect the author to define the term early in the article.

Reading Definition Paragraphs

Suppose you are asked to define the word *actuary* for someone unfamiliar with the term. First, you would probably say that an actuary is a person who works with numbers. Then you might distinguish an actuary from other people who work with numbers by saying that an actuary compiles and works with statistics. Finally, you might mention, by way of further explanation, that many actuaries work with insurance companies to help them understand risks and calculate insurance premiums. Although you may have presented it informally, your definition would have followed the standard, classic pattern. The first part of your definition tells what general class or group the term belongs to (people who work with numbers). The second part tells what distinguishes the term from other items in the same class or category (such as accountants). The third part includes further explanation, characteristics, examples, or applications.

See how the term *squatter settlement* is defined in the following paragraph, and notice how the term and the general class are presented. The remainder of the paragraph presents the distinguishing characteristics of squatter settlements. Sometimes writers use typographical aids, such as *italics*, **boldface**, or color to emphasize the term being defined. Here is an example.

> Overurbanization, or the too-rapid growth of cities, often results in **squatter settlements**, illegal developments of makeshift housing on land neither owned nor rented by their inhabitants. Such settlements are often built on steep hillsides or even on river floodplains that expose the occupants to the dangers of landslide and floods. Squatter settlements also are often found in the open space of public parks or along roadways, where they are regularly destroyed by government authorities, usually to be quickly rebuilt by migrants who have no other alternatives.
>
> —Rowntree et al., *Diversity Amid Globalization*, p. 26

You can visualize the definition pattern as follows:

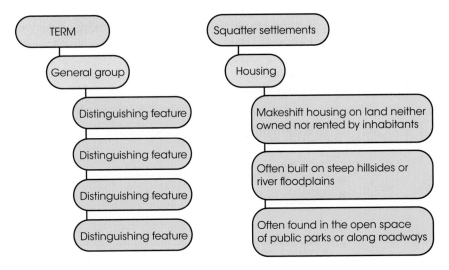

Writers often provide clues called **signal words** that signal the organizational pattern being used. These signals may occur within single sentences or as connections between sentences. (Signal words that occur in phrases are italicized in the box below to help you spot them.)

SIGNAL WORDS FOR THE DEFINITION PATTERN

Genetics *is* . . .
Bureaucracy *means* . . .
Patronage *refers to* . . .
Aggression *can be defined* as . . .
Deficit is *another term* that . . .
Balance of power *also means* . . .

EXERCISE 6-7 USING DEFINITION

Read each of the following passages and answer the questions that follow.

A. Issue: Globalization and Cultural Diversity

A **pidgin** is a language that blends elements of at least two parent languages and that emerges when two different cultures with different languages come in contact and must communicate. All speakers of pidgin have their own native language(s) but learn to speak pidgin as a second, rudimentary language. Pidgins are typically limited to specific functional domains, such as trade and basic social interactions. Many pidgins of the Western Hemisphere were the result of the Atlantic slave trade and plantation slavery. Owners needed to communicate with their slaves, and slaves in various parts of Africa needed to communicate with each other. Pidgins are common throughout the South Pacific.

A pidgin often evolves into a **creole**, a language descended from a pidgin which subsequently has its own native speakers, with a richer vocabulary than a pidgin has and a more developed grammar. Throughout the Western Hemisphere, many localized creoles have developed in areas such as Louisiana, the Caribbean, Ecuador, and Suriname. Though a living reminder of the heritage of slavery, Creole languages and associated literature and music are also evidence of resilience and creativity in the African diaspora.

—Miller, *Cultural Anthropology in a Globalizing World*, pp. 196–196

1. What terms are being defined?

   _____

2. Explain the meaning of the terms in your own words.

   _____

   _____

   _____

3. Where will you find pidgin and creole languages spoken?

   _____

   _____

B. Issue: Health and Wellness

Stress can be associated with most daily activities. Generally, positive stress—stress that presents the opportunity for personal growth and satisfaction—is termed **eustress**. Getting married, successfully kayaking Class II rapids, beginning a career, and developing new friends may all give rise to eustress. **Distress**, or negative stress, is caused by events that result in debilitative stress and strain, such as financial problems, the death of a loved one, academic difficulties, and the breakup of a relationship. Prolonged distress can have negative effects on health.

—Donatelle, *Health: The Basics, Green Edition*, p. 68

4. What terms are being defined, and what are the definitions?

_____

_____

_____

5. List at least three activities that the author provides to help readers understand the definition of each term.

_____

_____

_____

Writing Definition Paragraphs

Developing a definition paragraph involves writing a topic sentence and adding explanatory details. Be sure to write using the third person (*he, they, Samantha*).

Write Your Topic Sentence

The topic sentence of a definition paragraph should accomplish two things:

1. **It should identify the term you are explaining.**
2. **It should place the term in a general group.** It may also provide one or more distinguishing characteristics.

In the topic sentence below, the term being defined is *psychiatry*, the general group is "a branch of medicine," and its distinguishing feature is that it "deals with mental and emotional disorders."

> Psychiatry is a branch of medicine that deals with mental and emotional disorders.

Add Explanatory Details

Your topic sentence will usually *not* be sufficient to give your reader a complete understanding of the term you are defining. You will need to explain it further in one or more of the following ways:

1. **Give examples.** Examples can make a definition more vivid and interesting to your reader.
2. **Break the term into subcategories.** Breaking your subject down into subcategories helps to organize your definition. For example, you might explain the term *discrimination* by listing some of its types: racial, gender, and age.
3. **Explain what the term is not.** To bring the meaning of a term into focus for your reader, it is sometimes helpful to give counterexamples, or to discuss in what ways the term means something different from what

one might expect. Notice that student Ted Sawchuck does this in the following paragraph on sushi.

> Sushi is a Japanese food consisting of small cakes of cooked rice wrapped in seaweed. While it is commonly thought of as raw fish on rice, it is actually any preparation of vinegared rice. Sushi can also take the form of conical hand rolls and the more popular sushi roll. The roll is topped or stuffed with slices of raw or cooked fish, egg, or vegetables. Slices of raw fish served by themselves are commonly mistaken for sushi but are properly referred to as *sashimi*.

4. **Trace the term's meaning over time.** If the term has changed or expanded in meaning over time, it may be useful to trace this development as a way of explaining the term's current meaning.

5. **Compare an unfamiliar term to one that is familiar to your readers.** If you are writing about rugby, you might compare it to football, a more familiar sport. Be sure to make the connection clear to your readers by pointing out characteristics that the two sports share.

How to Organize a Definition Paragraph

You should logically arrange the distinguishing characteristics of a term. You might arrange them from most to least familiar or from more to less obvious, for example. Be sure to use strong transitional words and phrases to help your readers follow your presentation of ideas, guiding them from one distinguishing characteristic to another. Useful transitional words and phrases are shown on p. 155.

EXERCISE 6-8 WRITING A DEFINITION PARAGRAPH

Write a paragraph defining one of the following terms. Be sure to include a group and distinguishing characteristics.

1. shirt

2. horror

3. hip-hop

4. age discrimination

5. ballroom dancing

6d   READING AND WRITING CAUSE AND EFFECT

LEARNING OBJECTIVE 4
Recognize and use cause and effect.

The **cause-and-effect** pattern expresses a relationship between two or more actions, events, or occurrences that are connected in time. The relationship differs, however, from chronological order. In the cause-and-effect pattern, one event leads to another by *causing* it. Information organized with the cause-and-effect pattern may

- explain causes, sources, reasons, motives, and actions.
- explain the effect, result, or consequence of a particular action.
- explain both causes and effects.

Reading Cause-and-Effect Paragraphs

Cause and effect are clearly illustrated by the following paragraph, which gives the sources of fashions or the reasons why fashions occur.

> Why do fashions occur in the first place? One reason is that some cultures, like that of the United States, *value change:* What is new is good. And so, in many modern societies, clothing styles change yearly, while people in traditional societies may wear the same style for generations. A second reason is that many industries *promote* quick changes in fashion to increase sales. A third reason is that fashions usually *trickle down from the top*. A new style may occasionally originate from lower-status groups, as blue jeans did. But most fashions come from upper-class people, who like to adopt some style or artifact as a badge of their status. They cannot monopolize most status symbols for long, however. Their style is adopted by the middle class and may be copied or modified for use by lower-status groups, offering many people the prestige of possessing a high-status symbol.
>
> —Thio, *Sociology: A Brief Introduction*, p. 409

You can visualize the cause and effect pattern as follows:

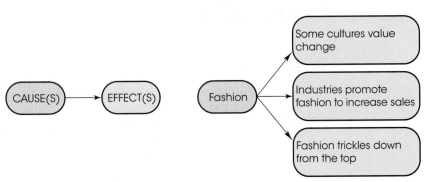

The cause-and-effect pattern is used extensively in many academic fields. All disciplines that ask the question "Why?" employ the cause-and-effect thought pattern. It is widely used in careers in the sciences, technologies, and social sciences.

Many statements expressing cause-and-effect relationships appear in direct order, with the cause stated first and the effect stated second: "When demand for a product increases, prices rise." However, reverse order is sometimes used, as in the following statement: "Prices rise when a product's demand increases."

The cause-and-effect pattern is not limited to an expression of a simple one-cause, one-effect relationship. There may be multiple causes, or multiple effects, or both multiple causes and multiple effects. For example, both slippery road conditions and your failure to buy snow tires (causes) may contribute to your car sliding into the ditch or into another car (effects).

In other instances, a chain of causes or effects may occur. For instance, failing to set your alarm clock may force you to miss your 8:00 A.M. class, which in turn may cause you not to submit your term paper on time, which may result in a penalty grade. This is sequence is known as a causal chain.

SIGNAL WORDS FOR THE CAUSE-AND-EFFECT PATTERN

Stress *causes* . . .
Aggression *creates* . . .
Depression *leads to* . . .
Forethought *yields* . . .
Low self-esteem *stems from* . . .
Good hygiene *helps to* . . .
Life changes *produce* . . .
Hostility *breeds* . . .
Avoidance *results in* . . .
Other cause-and-effect signal words are *therefore, consequently, hence, thus, for this reason,* and *since.*

EXERCISE 6–9 USING CAUSE AND EFFECT

Read each of the following selections and answer the questions that follow.

A. Issue: Health and Fitness

Physical activity is one of the best things you can do for yourself. It benefits every aspect of your health, at every stage of your life. Some of these benefits are purely physical, such as producing a stronger heart and healthier lungs. But physical activity can also put you in a better mood and help you manage stress. Physical activity results in a lower risk of premature death, and as you age it will help postpone physical decline and many of the diseases that can reduce quality of life in your later years.

—Adapted from Lynch, Elmore, and Morgan, *Choosing Health,* p. 92

1. What are the purely physical effects of exercise?

   _____

   _____

2. What are the nonphysical effects of exercise?

   _____

3. Underline the signal words used in the paragraph.

B. Issue: Health and Wellness

It's the end of the term and you have finished the last of several papers. After hours of nonstop typing, your hands are numb and you feel an intense, burning pain that makes the thought of typing one more word almost unbearable. If this happens, you may be suffering from one of several **repetitive motion disorders** (RMDs), sometimes called *overuse syndrome, cumulative trauma disorders,* or *repetitive stress injuries.* These refer to a family of painful soft tissue injuries that begin with inflammation and gradually become disabling.

Repetitive motion disorders include carpal tunnel syndrome, bursitis, tendonitis, and ganglion cysts, among others. Twisting of the arm or wrist, overexertion, and incorrect posture or position are usually contributors. The areas most likely to be affected are the hands, wrists, elbows, and shoulders, but the neck, back, hips, knees, feet, ankles, and legs can be affected, too. Usually, RMDs are associated with repeating the same task in an occupational setting and gradually irritating the area in question. However, certain sports (tennis, golf, and others), gripping the wheel while driving, keyboarding or texting, and a number of newer technology-driven activities can also result in RMDs.

—Donatelle, *Access to Health*, p. 646–647

4. What is the cause of RMDs?

_____

5. What do students often do that can cause RMDs?

_____

6. Underline the signal words used in the passage.

Writing Cause-and-Effect Paragraphs

Writing a cause-and-effect paragraph involves writing a clear topic sentence that indicates whether you are talking about causes, effects, or both; organizing supporting details; and using signal words.

Write Your Topic Sentence

To write effective topic sentences for cause-and-effect paragraphs, do the following:

1. **Clarify the cause-and-effect relationship.** Before you write, carefully identify the causes and the effects. If you are uncertain, divide a sheet of paper into two columns. Label one column "Causes" and the other "Effects." Brainstorm about your topic, placing your ideas in the appropriate column.

2. **Decide whether to emphasize causes or effects.** In a single paragraph, it is best to focus on either causes or effects—not both. For example, suppose you are writing about students who drop out of college. You need to decide whether to discuss why they drop out (causes) or what happens to students who drop out (effects). Your topic sentence should indicate whether you

are going to emphasize causes or effects. (In essays, you may consider both causes and effects.)

3. **Determine whether the events are related or independent.** Analyze the causes or effects to discover if they occurred as part of a chain reaction or if they are not related to one another. Your topic sentence should suggest the type of relationship about which you are writing. If you are writing about a chain of events, your topic sentence should reflect this—for example, "A series of events led up to my sister's decision to drop out of college." If the causes or effects are not related to one another, then your sentence should indicate that—for example, "Students drop out of college for a number of different reasons."

Now read the following paragraph that a sales representative wrote to her regional manager to explain why she had failed to meet a monthly quota. Then study the diagram that accompanies it. Notice that the topic sentence makes it clear that she is focusing on the causes (circumstances) that led to her failure to make her sales quota for the month.

In the past, I have always met or exceeded my monthly sales quota at Thompson's Office Furniture. This January I was $20,000 short, due to a set of unusual and uncontrollable circumstances in my territory. The month began with a severe snowstorm that closed most businesses in the area for most of the first week. Travel continued to be a problem the remainder of the week, and many purchasing agents did not report to work. Once they were back at their desks, they were not eager to meet with sales reps; instead, they wanted to catch up on their backlog of paperwork. Later that month, an ice storm resulted in power losses, again closing most plants for almost two days. Finally, some of our clients took extended weekends over the Martin Luther King holiday. Overall, my client contact days were reduced by more than 26%, yet my sales were only 16% below the quota.

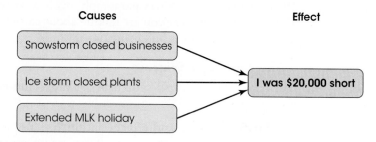

EXERCISE 6-10 WRITING TOPIC SENTENCES

Select one of the topics below, and write a topic sentence for a paragraph that will explain either its causes or effects.

1. Watching too much TV

2. Children who misbehave

3. The popularity of horror films

4. Rising cost of attending college

5. Eating junk food

Provide Supporting Details

Providing supporting details for cause-and-effect paragraphs requires careful thought and planning. Details must be relevant, sufficient, and effectively organized.

Provide Relevant and Sufficient Details   Each cause or effect you describe must be relevant to the situation introduced in your topic sentence. Suppose you are writing a paragraph explaining why you are attending college. Each sentence must explain this topic. You should not include ideas, for example, about how college is different from what you expected.

If, while writing, you discover you have more ideas about how college is different from what you expected than you do about your reasons for attending college, you need to revise your topic sentence in order to refocus your paragraph.

Each cause or reason requires explanation, particularly if it is *not* obvious. For example, it is not sufficient to write, "One reason I decided to attend college was to advance my position in life." This sentence needs further explanation. For example, you could discuss the types of advancement (financial, job security, job satisfaction) you hope to attain.

Jot down a list of the causes or reasons you plan to include. This process may help you think of additional causes and will give you a chance to consider how to explain or support each one. You might decide to eliminate one or to combine several. Here is one student's list of reasons for attending college.

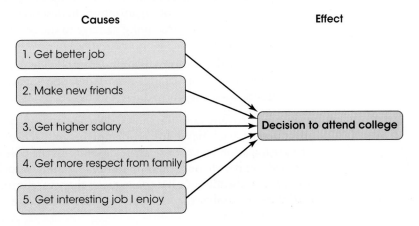

By listing his reasons, this student realized that the first one—to get a better job—was too general and was covered more specifically later in the list, so he eliminated it. He also realized that "get higher salary" and "get interesting job" could be combined. He then wrote the following paragraph:

> There are three main reasons I decided to attend Ambrose Community College. First, and most important to me, I want to get a high-paying, interesting job that I will enjoy. Right now, the only jobs I can get pay minimum wage, and as a result, I'm working in a fast-food restaurant. This kind of job doesn't make me proud of myself, and I get bored with routine tasks. Second, my parents have always wanted me to have a better job than they do, and I know my father will not respect me until I do. A college degree would make them proud of me. A third reason for attending college is to make new friends. It is hard to meet people, and everyone in my neighborhood seems stuck in a rut. I want to meet other people who are interested in improving themselves like I am.

Organize Your Details   There are several ways to arrange the details in a cause-and-effect paragraph. The method you choose depends on your purpose in writing, as well as your topic. Suppose you are writing a paragraph about the effects of a hurricane on a coastal town. Several different arrangements of details are possible:

- **Chronological** A chronological organization arranges your details in the order in which situations or events happened. The order in which the hurricane damage occurred becomes the order for your details.

- **Order of importance** In an order-of-importance organization, the details are arranged from least to most important or from most to least important. In describing the effects of the hurricane, you could discuss the most severe damage first and then describe lesser damage. Alternatively, you could build up from the least to the most important damage for dramatic effect.

- **Spatial** Spatial arrangement of details uses physical or geographical position as a means of organization. In describing the hurricane damage, you could start by describing damage to the beach and work toward the center of town.

- **Categorical** This form of arrangement divides the topic into parts or categories. Using this arrangement to describe hurricane damage, you could recount what the storm did to businesses, roads, city services, and homes.

As the hurricane example shows, there are many ways to organize cause and effect details. Each has a different emphasis and achieves a different purpose. The organization you choose, then, depends on the point you want to make.

Once you decide on a method of organization, return to your preliminary list of effects. Study your list again, make changes, eliminate, or combine. Then rearrange or number the items on your list to indicate the order in which you will include them.

Use Signal Words

To blend your details smoothly, use signal words and phrases. Some common signal words for the cause-and-effect pattern are listed on page 160.

The student paragraph on page 164 is a good example of how signal words and phrases are used. Notice how these signal words function as markers and help you to locate each separate reason.

EXERCISE 6-11 WRITING A PARAGRAPH

Choose one of the following topic sentences and develop a paragraph using it. Organize your paragraph by using one of the methods described above.

1. Exercise has several positive (or negative) effects on the body.

2. Professional athletes deserve (or do not deserve) the high salaries they are paid.

3. There are several reasons why parents should reserve time each day to spend with their children.

4. Many students work two or even three part-time jobs; the results are often disastrous.

6e READING AND WRITING COMPARISON AND CONTRAST

LEARNING OBJECTIVE 5
Recognize comparison and contrast.

The **comparison organizational pattern** emphasizes or discusses similarities between or among ideas, theories, concepts, or events. The **contrast pattern** emphasizes differences. When a speaker or writer is concerned with both similarities and differences, a combination pattern called **comparison-contrast** is used. You can visualize these three variations of the pattern as follows:

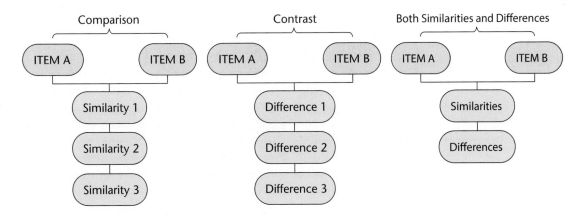

Reading Comparison-Contrast Paragraphs

The comparison-contrast pattern is widely used in the social sciences, which study different groups, societies, cultures, and behaviors. Literature courses may require comparisons among poets, among several literary works, or among stylistic features. A business course may examine various management styles, compare organizational structures, or contrast retailing plans.

A contrast is shown in the following selection, which outlines the differences among felonies, misdemeanors, and violations.

> The sources of local criminal laws are city or county charters, municipal or county ordinances or violations, common law, and decisions of municipal judges interpreting codes and common law. Nearly all local laws are misdemeanors, or violations. Serious criminal conduct is called a **felony**, and less-serious criminal conduct is called a **misdemeanor**. The difference between a felony and a misdemeanor is usually defined by the amount of time in prison or jail that the offender can receive as punishment for violation of a statute. Felonies commonly are crimes for which an offender can receive a punishment of 1 year or more in a state prison, whereas misdemeanors are crimes for which an offender can receive a punishment of 1 year or less in a state prison or county jail.
>
> Violations, a relatively new classification of prohibited behaviors, commonly regulate traffic offenses. A **violation** is less than a misdemeanor and might carry the punishment of only a fine or suspension of privilege, such as losing one's driver's license temporarily. Many states have redefined misdemeanor traffic offenses as violations. The advantage of this is that violations free up the resources of the criminal courts for more serious cases and allow for speedier processing of cases through the system.
>
> —Fagin, *CJ2012*, p. 43

A map of this passage might look like this:

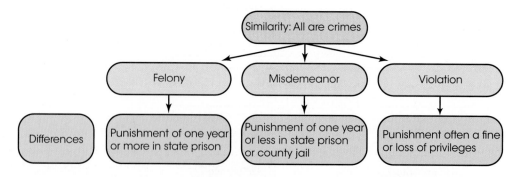

Depending on whether the speaker or writer is concerned with similarities, differences, or both similarities and differences, the pattern might be organized in different ways. Suppose a professor of American literature asks you to compare the work of two English poets, William Wordsworth and John Keats. Each of the following assignments is possible:

1. **Compare and then contrast the two.** That is, first discuss how Wordsworth's poetry and Keats's poetry are similar, and then discuss how they are different.

2. **Discuss by author.** Discuss the characteristics of Wordsworth's poetry, then discuss the characteristics of Keats's poetry, and then summarize their similarities and differences.

3. **Discuss by characteristic.** First discuss the two poets' use of metaphor, next discuss their use of rhyme, and then discuss their common themes.

SIGNAL WORDS THAT SHOW CONTRAST

Unlike Whitman, Frost . . .
Less wordy *than* Whitman . . .
Contrasted with Whitman, Frost . . .
Frost *differs from* . . .
Other signal words of contrast are *in contrast, however, on the other hand, as opposed to,* and *whereas.*

SIGNAL WORDS THAT SHOW COMPARISON

Similarities between Frost and Whitman . . .
Frost is *as* powerful *as* . . .
Like Frost, Whitman . . .
Both Frost and Whitman . . .
Frost *resembles* Whitman in that . . .
Other signal words of comparison are *in a like manner, similarly, similar to, likewise, correspondingly,* and *in the same way.*

EXERCISE 6-12 USING COMPARISON AND CONTRAST

Read each of the following selections and answer the questions that follow.

A. **Issue: Business Structures**

Supermarkets are the most frequently visited type of retail store. Today, however, they are facing slow sales growth because of slower population growth and an increase in competition from discounters (Walmart, Costco, Dollar General) on the one hand and specialty food stores (Whole Foods Market, Trader Joe's, Sprouts) on the other. Supermarkets also have been hit hard by the rapid growth of out-of-home eating over the past two decades. In fact, supermarkets' share of the groceries and food market plunged from 66 percent in 2002 to less than 62 percent in

2009. Meanwhile, during the same time period, supercenters boosted their market share from 16.6 percent to 20.6 percent.

Superstores are much larger than regular supermarkets and offer a large assortment of routinely purchased food products, nonfood items, and services. Walmart, Target, Meijer, and other discount retailers offer supercenters, very large combination food and discount stores. While a traditional grocery store brings in about $486,000 a week in sales, a supercenter brings in about $1.6 million a week. Walmart, which opened its first supercenter in 1988, has almost 3,000 supercenters in North America and is opening new ones at a rate of about 140 per year.

—Armstrong and Kotler, *Marketing: An Introduction*, pp. 327–328

1. What three types of stores are discussed?

_____

2. Does this passage mainly use comparison, contrast, or both?

_____

3. Explain how the three types of stores are similar and different.

_____

_____

_____

_____

4. What type of store is Trader Joe's?

_____

5. Underline the signal words in the paragraph, regardless of the type of organizational pattern they signal.

B. **Issue: Environmental Issues and Conservation**

Local and regional variation in temperatures produces weather and climate. **Climate** refers to atmospheric conditions such as temperature, humidity, and rainfall that exist over large regions and relatively long periods of time. In contrast, **weather** refers to short-term variations in local atmospheric conditions. When we say that Los Angeles will experience a cool, foggy morning and hot afternoon, we're talking about weather. When we say that Southern California has mild, moist winters and hot, dry summers, we are describing the climate of this region.

—Christensen, *The Environment and You*, p. 86

6. What two things are being compared or contrasted?

_____

7. Which two factors are used to define the difference between weather and climate?

_____

8. Which signal phrase signals the paragraph's primary organizational pattern?

_____

9. Which term would be used to describe a snowstorm that occurred in Chicago in November, 2013?

_____

10. Which term would be used to describe the high level of heat but relatively low level of humidity found in Arizona and New Mexico?

_____

Writing Comparison-Contrast Paragraphs

Writing a comparison-contrast paragraph involves identifying similarities and differences between two items, writing a topic sentence that indicates the item you will be comparing and contrasting and your point, organizing your paragraph, developing your points, and using signal words.

Identify Similarities and Differences

If you have two items to compare or contrast, the first step is to figure out how they are similar and how they are different. Be sure to select subjects that are neither too similar nor too different. If they are, you will have either too little or too much to say. Follow this effective two-step approach:

1. Brainstorm to produce a two-column list of characteristics.
2. Match up the items and identify points of comparison and contrast.

Brainstorm to Produce a Two-Column List Let's say you want to write about two friends—Maria and Vanessa. Here is how to identify their similarities and differences:

1. **Brainstorm and list the characteristics of each person.**

MARIA	VANESSA
Reserved, quiet	Age 27
Age 22	Single parent, two children
Private person	Outgoing person
Friends since childhood	Loves to be center of attention
Married, no children	Loves sports and competition
Hates parties	Plays softball and tennis
Fun to shop with	
Tells me everything about her life	

2. **When you finish your list, match up items that share the same point of comparison or contrast—age, personality type, marital status—as shown below.**

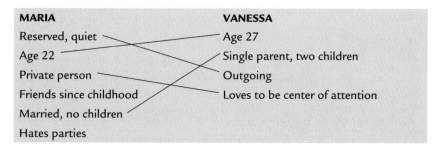

MARIA	VANESSA
Reserved, quiet	Age 27
Age 22	Single parent, two children
Private person	Outgoing
Friends since childhood	Loves to be center of attention
Married, no children	
Hates parties	

3. **When you have listed an item in a certain category for one person but not for the other, think of a corresponding detail that will balance the lists.** For instance, you listed "friends since childhood" for Maria, so you could indicate how long you have known Vanessa. This will give you additional points of comparison and contrast.

Identify Points of Comparison and Contrast The next step is to reorganize the lists so that the items you matched up appear next to each other. Now, in a new column to the left of your lists, write the term that describes or categorizes each set of items in the lists. These are general categories we will call "Points of Comparison/Contrast." Points of comparison and contrast are the characteristics you use to examine your two subjects. As you reorganize, you may find it easier to group several items together. For example, you might group some details about Maria and Vanessa together under the category of personality. Study the following list, noticing the points of comparison and contrast in the left-hand column.

POINTS OF COMPARISON/ CONTRAST	MARIA	VANESSA
Personality	Quiet, reserved, private person	Outgoing, loves to be center of attention
Marital status	Married, no children	Single parent, two children
Length of friendship	Friends since childhood	Met at work last year
Shared activities	Go shopping	Play softball together, go to parties

This two-step process can work in reverse order as well. You can decide points of comparison/contrast first and then brainstorm characteristics for each point. For example, suppose you are comparing and contrasting two restaurants. Points of comparison/contrast might be location, price, speed of service, menu variety, and quality of food. If you are comparing or contrasting two professors, Rodriguez and Meyer, you might do so using the following points:

POINTS OF COMPARISON/ CONTRAST	PROFESSOR MEYER	PROFESSOR RODRIGUEZ
Amount of homework		
Type of exams		
Class organization		
How easy to talk to		
Grading system		
Style of teaching		

You could then fill in columns 2 and 3 with appropriate details, as shown below.

POINTS OF COMPARISON/ CONTRAST	PROFESSOR MEYER	PROFESSOR RODRIGUEZ
Amount of homework	Assignment due for every class	Hardly any
Type of exams	Essay	Multiple choice and essay
Class organization	Well organized	Free and easy
How easy to talk to	Always around, approachable	Approachable but talks a lot
Grading system	50 percent class participation, 50 percent essay exams	100 percent exams
Style of teaching	Lecture	Class discussion, questions

Once you have completed your three-column list, the next step is to study your list and decide whether to write about similarities or differences, or both. It is usually easier to concentrate on one or the other. If you see similarities as more significant, you might need to omit or de-emphasize differences—and vice-versa if you decide to write about differences.

EXERCISE 6-13 SELECTING A TOPIC AND LISTING POINTS OF COMPARISON/CONTRAST

List at least three points of comparison/contrast for each of the following topics. Then choose one topic and make a three-column list on a separate sheet of paper.

1. Two films you have seen recently
   Points of comparison/contrast: _____

2. Two jobs you have held
   Points of comparison/contrast: _____

3. Baseball and football players
   Points of comparison/contrast: _____

Write Your Topic Sentence

Your topic sentence should do two things:

- It should identify the two subjects that you will compare or contrast.
- It should state whether you will focus on similarities, differences, or both.

It may also indicate what points you will compare or contrast. Suppose you are comparing two world religions—Judaism and Hinduism. Obviously, you could not cover every aspect of these religions in a single paragraph. Instead, you could limit your comparison to their size, place of worship, or the type of divine being(s) worshipped.

Here are a few sample topic sentences that meet the above requirements:

1. Judaism is one of the smallest of the world's religions; Hinduism is one of the largest.
2. Neither Judaism nor Hinduism limits worship to a single location, although both hold services in temples.
3. Unlike Hinduism, Judaism teaches belief in only one god.

Be sure to avoid topic sentences that announce what you plan to do. For example: "I'll compare network news and local news and show why I prefer local news."

Organize Your Paragraph

Once you have identified similarities and differences and drafted a topic sentence, you are ready to organize your paragraph. There are two ways you can organize a comparison or contrast paragraph:

- subject by subject
- point by point

Subject-by-Subject Organization In the subject-by-subject method, you write first about one of your subjects, covering it completely, and then about the other, covering it completely.

Ideally, you cover the same points of comparison/contrast for both, and in the same order. Let's return to the comparison between Professors Meyer and Rodriguez. With subject-by-subject organization, you first discuss Professor Meyer—his class organization, exams, and grading system; you then discuss Professor Rodriguez—her class organization, exams, and grading system. You can visualize the arrangement this way:

Subject-by-Subject Organization Map

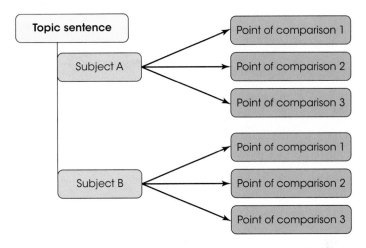

To develop each subject, focus on the same kinds of details and discuss the same points of comparison in the same order. If you are discussing only similarities or only differences, organize your points within each topic, using a most-to-least or least-to-most arrangement. If you are discussing both similarities and differences, you might discuss points of similarity first and then points of difference, or vice versa.

Here is a sample paragraph using the subject-by-subject method and a map showing its organization:

Two excellent teachers, Professor Meyer and Professor Rodriguez, present a study in contrasting teaching styles. Professor Meyer is extremely organized. He conducts every class the same way. He reviews the assignment, lectures on the new chapter, and explains the next assignment. He gives essay exams and they are always based on important lecture topics. Because the topics are predictable, you know you are not wasting your time when you study. Professor Meyer's grading depends half on class participation and half on the essay exams. Professor Rodriguez, on the other hand, has an easy going style. Each class is different and emphasizes whatever she thinks will help us better understand the material. Her classes are fun because you never know what to expect. Professor Rodriguez gives both multiple-choice and essay exams. These are difficult to study for because they are unpredictable. Our final grade is based entirely on the exams, so each exam requires a lot of studying beforehand. Although each professor teaches very differently, I am figuring out how to learn from each particular style.

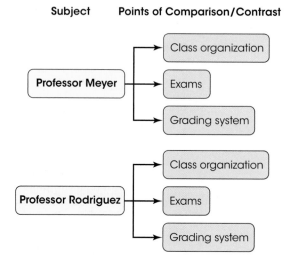

Subject   Points of Comparison/Contrast

Using Point-by-Point Organization In the **point-by-point method of organization,** you discuss both of your subjects together for each point of comparison/contrast. You can visualize this organization as follows:

Point-by-Point Organization Map

Topic sentence

Point of comparison 1 — Subject A, Subject B

Point of comparison 2 — Subject A, Subject B

Point of comparison 3 — Subject A, Subject B

When using this organization, maintain consistency by discussing the same subject first for each point. (That is, always discuss Professor Meyer first and Professor Rodriguez second for each point.)

If your paragraph focuses only on similarities or only on differences, arrange your points in a least-to-most or most-to-least pattern.

Here is a sample paragraph using the point-by-point method and a map showing its organization:

> Professor Meyer and Professor Rodriguez demonstrate very different teaching styles in how they operate their classes, how they give exams, and how they grade us. Professor Meyer's classes are highly organized; we work through the lesson every day in the same order. Professor Rodriguez uses an opposite approach. She creates a lesson to fit the material, which enables us to learn the most. Their exams differ too. Professor Meyer gives standard, predictable essay exams that are based on his lectures. Professor Rodriguez gives both multiple-choice and essay exams, so we never know what to expect. In addition, each professor grades differently. Professor Meyer counts class participation as half of our grade, so if you talk in class and do reasonably well on the exams, you will probably pass the course. Professor Rodriguez, on the other hand, counts the exams 100 percent, so you *have* to do well on them to pass the course. Each professor has a unique, enjoyable teaching style, and I am learning a great deal from each.

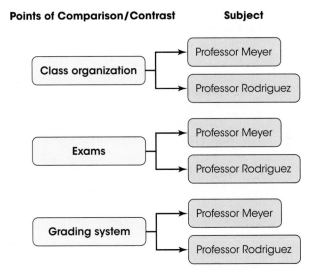

Develop Your Points of Comparison/Contrast As you discuss each point, don't feel as if you must compare or contrast in every sentence. Your paragraph should not just list similarities and/or differences. For every point, provide explanation, descriptive details, and examples.

Try to maintain a balance in your treatment of each subject and each point of comparison and contrast. Give equal attention to each point and each subject. If you give an example for one subject, try to do so for the other as well.

Use Signal Words

Signal words are particularly important in comparison-contrast writing. Because you are discussing two subjects and covering similar points for each, your readers can easily become confused. The following box lists commonly used signal words and phrases.

COMPARISON		CONTRAST	
also	likewise	although	in contrast
both	similarly	as opposed to	instead
in comparison	to compare	but	on the contrary
in the same way	too	differs from	on the other hand
		however	unlike

Each method of organization uses different signal words in different places. If you choose a subject-by-subject organization, you'll need the strongest transition in the middle of the paragraph, when you switch from one subject to another. You will also need a transition each time you move from one point to another while still on the same subject. In the following paragraph written by a paralegal comparing recent court cases, notice the transitional sentence highlighted in pink.

> *Green v. Lipscomb* and *Walker v. Walker* are the two most recent cases that deal with the custody of siblings. *Green* holds that siblings have a right to live together. It says that when a court decides custody, putting siblings together is the controlling concern. In this case, custody was given to the father because it was in the best interest of the oldest child to live with him. The other children were to live there as well because it was more important that they live together. *Walker* presents a more subjective position. *Walker* says that while the sibling relationship is an important factor in deciding custody, it alone is not controlling. The best interest of each child must be evaluated. The sibling relationship must be considered in this evaluation.

This paragraph uses a subject-by-subject organization. A strong transition emphasizes the switch from one case to another.

If you choose point-by-point organization, use transitions as you move from one subject to the other. On each point, your reader needs to know quickly whether the two subjects are similar or different. Here is an example:

> Although colds and hay fever are both annoying, their symptoms and causes differ. Hay fever causes my eyes to itch and water. I sneeze excessively, bothering those around me. Colds, on the other hand, make me feel stuffy, with a runny nose and a cough. For me, hay fever arrives in the summer, but colds linger on through late fall, winter, and early spring. Their causes differ, too. Pollens produce hay fever. I am most sensitive to pollen from wildflowers

> and corn tassels. Unlike hay fever, viruses, which are passed from person to person by air or body contact, cause colds.

Notice that each time the writer switched from hay fever to colds, a transition was used.

Organize Your Details

Regardless of the method of organization you choose, it is important to organize the details in each method so that your paragraph or essay is easy to follow. Use the following suggestions:

ORGANIZING DETAILS

For subject-by-subject organization:

- Be sure to cover the same points of comparison for each subject.
- Cover the points of comparison in the same order in each half of your paragraph or essay.
- Make sure you include a strong transition that signals you are moving from one subject to another.

For point-by-point organization:

- As you work back and forth between your subjects, try to mention the subjects in the same order.
- Decide how to organize your points of comparison. You could move from the simplest to the most complex similarity, or from the most obvious to least obvious difference, for example.

EXERCISE 6-14 WRITING A COMPARISON-CONTRAST PARAGRAPH

Choose one of the following topics. Using the guidelines presented in the section, write a comparison-contrast paragraph.

1. Two courses you are taking

2. Two tasks (one difficult, one easy)

3. Two forms of communication

4. Two decisions you made recently

5. Two businesses

6. Two types of entertainment

6f   READING AND WRITING MIXED PATTERNS

LEARNING OBJECTIVE 6
Recognize and use
mixed patterns.
Organizational patterns are often combined. In describing a process, a writer may also give reasons why each step must be followed in the prescribed order. An instructor may define a concept by comparing it with something similar or familiar. Suppose a chapter in your political science textbook opens by stating, "The distinction between 'power' and 'power potential' is an important one in considering the balance of power." You might expect a definition pattern (where the two terms are defined), but you also might anticipate that the chapter would discuss the difference between the two terms (contrast pattern). The longer the reading selection, the more likely it combines multiple patterns of organization.

Reading Mixed-Pattern Paragraphs

In the following paragraph, notice how the author combines two patterns: definition and contrast.

Definition #1 →

Contrast →
Definition #2 →

A city's central business district, or CBD, grows around the city's most accessible point, and it typically contains a dense concentration of offices and stores. CBDs grow with the needs of the community; they expand and contract organically as the city grows and changes. In contrast, a master-planned community is a residential suburban development. In master-planned developments, houses are designed to look alike and "match," and the community also offers private recreational facilities (such as tennis courts and swimming pools) for its residents. Often, the community is gated to prevent non-residents from entering.

Look back over the examples provided in this chapter and notice that many of them combine more than one organizational pattern. The paragraph on dog training (p. 143) uses comparison and contrast in addition to illustration, for example.

EXERCISE 6-15 USING MIXED PATTERNS 1

For each of the following topic sentences, anticipate what organizational pattern(s) the paragraph is likely to exhibit.

1. Narcissistic personality disorder—in which the sufferer is excessively occupied with himself or herself—usually results from a number of factors working together.

   Pattern: _____

2. GDP, or gross domestic product, is the total value of goods and services produced in a country during a given year.

   Pattern: _____

3. To migrate to the United States legally, an immigrant must follow a strict set of rules.

   Pattern: _____

4. A poor diet and lack of exercises are the leading causes of obesity in the world today.

   Pattern: _____

5. Many of the contestants on *American Idol* share a number of characteristics. They are all fairly young, they are all amateurs, they all cultivate a certain image, and they all believe they are talented.

   Pattern: _____

Writing Mixed-Pattern Paragraphs

Individual patterns of organization provide a clear method for organizing and presenting your thoughts. Each of these patterns allows you to focus on one important aspect of the topic. When combining patterns, your paragraph should always have one primary pattern. The main pattern provides the framework for the paragraph. Additional patterns can be used for further details and information but should not distract your reader from the main pattern.

Choose a Primary Pattern of Organization for Your Paragraph

There are four main factors to consider when choosing a primary pattern of organization:

- The assignment
- Your purpose
- Your audience
- The complexity of your topic

The Assignment

In some cases, your instructor will ask you to choose a topic and write about it. However, instructors often provide specific writing assignments or writing prompts. Analyzing the assignment will help you determine the primary pattern of organization. Look in the assignment for key words and phrases that offer clues. Suppose, for example, you receive the following assignment in your hotel and restaurant management class:

> Choose one of the following beverages and write an essay describing how
> it is made: espresso, beer, or soda.

The assignment makes it clear that process is required. The key phrase "how it
is made" is your clue. The key word *describing* also appears in the assignment, so
be sure to include some description. Suppose you choose to write about soda.
Your goal, then, is to organize your essay to focus on the *process* of soda making. Your essay might also include examples of specific types of soda (cola, gin-
ger ale) or a narrative about John Pemberton, who created Coca-Cola.

Your Purpose

When an instructor gives you a specific writing assignment, your purpose for writing is quite clear: to answer the question that has been raised. You simply need to
follow the directions, write a good essay, and collect a good grade! However, when
you must choose your own topic, you need to determine your purpose for writing.
You can clarify your purpose by asking yourself the following questions.

- What am I trying to accomplish?
- What do I want my readers to understand?

Your Audience

All good writing takes the audience into account. To determine the primary
pattern of organization for your essay, ask these questions.

- How much do my readers know about the topic?
- What can I assume about my readers' backgrounds and experiences?
- Who is most likely to read what I've written?

The Complexity of Your Topic

Some topics are simply more complex or more multifaceted than others. Consider the following topics:

- The range of human emotions
- The three branches of the U.S. government: executive, legislative, judicial
- Your bedroom

Which of these topics is the simplest? Which is the most complicated? Most
likely you would agree that your bedroom is the simplest topic, and the range
of human emotions is the most complicated. For an essay about your bedroom,
you could write effectively using one of the less complicated patterns, such as
description or *example*, because your bedroom is most likely a fairly small room
with limited contents: a bed, a television, a bookshelf, a closet. However, for an
essay on the much more complicated topic of human emotions, you will want
to choose a pattern that allows for greater depth of analysis, such as *comparison and contrast* (How do conscious feelings differ from subconscious feelings?),
classification (What are the different kinds of emotions?), or *cause and effect* (What
causes depression? What are effects of depression?).

EXERCISE 6-16 CHOOSING MULTIPLE PATTERNS OF ORGANIZATION

Choose a primary pattern of organization for each of the following writing assignments. Indicate what other patterns you might use and why.

1. Mystery novels are a popular genre and people read them for a variety of reasons. Define mystery novels and give reasons for their popularity.

   _____

   _____

2. Those who don't travel on airplanes are often unprepared for the demands of air travel. What steps can an inexperienced traveler take to ensure a comfortable airline flight?

   _____

   _____

3. Two of the most famous American poets are Emily Dickinson and T.S. Eliot. How did each poet approach the writing of poetry? In what ways are the poems of Dickinson and Eliot similar? In what ways are they different?

   _____

   _____

   _____

EXERCISE 6-17 WRITING A MIXED-PATTERN PARAGRAPH

Analyze the following writing assignment and answer the questions that follow.

Writing assignment: You are a volunteer for a charitable foundation that "rescues" golden retrievers. People who can no longer take care of their pets contact your foundation, and volunteers provide foster homes for the animals until a permanent home can be found. The president of the foundation has asked you to write a paragraph urging people to donate $10 to the organization.

1. Describe your intended audience.

2. What is your purpose for writing?

3. Brainstorm a list of ideas your readers might find helpful or illuminating.

4. Determine a primary pattern of organization for the assignment. Which secondary patterns will you use?

5. Write the paragraph, and then share it with a classmate. Revise and finalize.

SUMMARY OF LEARNING OBJECTIVES

Objective 1 Read and write illustration.	*Illustration* uses examples—specific instances or situations—to explain a general idea or statement. *As you read,* look for signal words—*for example, for instance,* or *such as*—that signal examples are to follow. *As you write,* use vivid, accurate, examples that are typical and familiar to readers, drawing connections between them and your main point, and organizing them logically.
Objective 2 Read and write process.	*Process* focuses on the procedures, steps, or stages by which actions are accomplished and is used to explain how things work and how to perform specific actions. *As you read,* look for numbered or bulleted lists and transitions that indicate a process is being described. *As you write,* identify the process you are describing and why it is important, provide necessary definitions, identify required equipment, provide only the essential steps in a logical order, and note possible problems.
Objective 3 Read and write definition.	In the *definition pattern*, a key word, phrase, or concept is defined and explained. *As you read,* ask what is being defined and what makes it different from other items or ideas. *As you write,* place the term in a general group, break it into categories, explain it with examples, trace its meaning over time, explain what it is not, and compare it to a familiar term.
Objective 4 Read and write classification.	The *classification pattern* explains a topic by dividing it into parts or categories. *As you read,* be sure you understand *how* and *why* the topic was divided as it was. *As you write,* decide on a basis for breaking your topic into subgroups, or categories, that is uncomplicated and with which you are familiar, and consider your audience.
Objective 5 Read and write cause and effect.	The *cause-and-effect pattern* expresses a relationship between two or more actions, events, or occurrences that are connected in time. One event leads to another by causing it. There may be multiple causes and/or effects. *As you read,* look for explanations of why events occurred and their effects and cause and effect transitional words. *As you write,* identify the relationship you are discussing, decide on your emphasis (causes or effects), and determine if causes and/or effects are related or independent. Provide explanations of your reasons.
Objective 6 Read and write comparison and contrast.	The *comparison pattern* emphasizes or discusses similarities among ideas, theories, concepts, or events. The *contrast pattern* emphasizes differences. Both patterns can be used together, creating the comparison-contrast pattern. *As you read,* identify whether the writer is comparing or contrasting items or doing both, and look for signal words that indicate which pattern is being used. *As you write,* identify the subjects you will compare and/or contrast; decide on what bases you will compare or contrast them; and determine your purpose for writing about them.
Objective 7 Read and write mixed patterns.	*Organizational patterns are often combined* in paragraphs, essays, and longer readings. *As you read,* look for indications (signal words, formatting, type of topic) to identify the overall pattern of a piece of writing and the additional pattern used to support it. *As you write,* use a primary pattern as a framework for your paragraph, using additional patterns to provide further details and information.

7 Reading Non-Fiction Text

LEARNING OBJECTIVES

1 Read textbooks

2 Read essays

3 Read longer works

4 Read visuals

5 Think critically about source materials

7a READING TEXTBOOKS

LEARNING OBJECTIVE 1
Read textbooks.

In most college courses, textbooks are the primary source of reading. In general, students are expected to read the assignment before class. Each textbook reading will present key terms and information that you will explore in more depth in classroom lectures and discussions. Students who do not read assignments before class put themselves at a disadvantage. They are always playing catch-up.

Textbooks are almost always written by college teachers. Because of their experience in the classroom, they know what you are likely to need help understanding. They know when you need, for example, a diagram to help you visualize a concept. Consequently, they build valuable learning aids into each chapter.

Guidelines for Getting the Most Out of Textbooks

Use the following guidelines to get the most from your textbooks.

1. **Use the textbook's pedagogical aids to help you learn.** Textbooks provide many features designed to help you learn and remember the content. Some common textbook features include:

   - **Learning objectives.** These appear at the beginning of the chapter and outline specific learning goals, clearly stating what you should know (or what you should be able to do) when you have finished reading the chapter. After you've completed the assignment, review the learning objectives.

If you cannot accomplish all of the goals, reread the relevant parts of the reading selection until you can.

- **Headings.** Each chapter in a textbook provides headings that serve as an outline of the chapter. Before you begin reading, preview all the headings, formulating guide questions as you go along. (You may have noticed that this handbook is divided into numbered sections, or headings, to help you find what you need quickly.)

- **Opening stories or examples.** Many textbook chapters begin with a story that introduces the subject matter in a way designed to capture students' attention and interest. For example, a chapter on social class may begin with a story about the "Untouchables" of India, while a chapter on abnormal psychology may provide a case study about a person suffering from multiple-personality disorder.

- **Marginal vocabulary and definitions.** Each academic discipline has its own special vocabulary. (For instance, in common English, *affect* is a verb that means "to have an effect on." But in psychology, *affect* is pronounced differently and is a synonym for the display of emotions.) To learn the chapter material, you must learn and memorize many new words and definitions. Often, key terms frequently appear in **boldface** or *italics* in the text; these terms and their definitions may then be repeated in the margin as a way of reinforcing their importance and helping you learn them.

- **Visual aids.** Visual aids are designed to work with the text, so examine the visual aid (whether table, diagram, infographic, photo, or any other type) when the text tells you to. For example, the textbook may say: "As Figure 8-2 shows. . . ." or "As Table 4.1 shows. . . ." Moving back and forth between the text and the visual aid helps you learn the material. Don't rush through the visual aids; many of them summarize important information or processes. For more on reading and interpreting visual aids, see section 7d.

- **Boxes.** Some textbooks include boxes, which are set off from the main text. Boxes often feature discussions of interesting or relevant topics related to chapter content, and they usually highlight key or controversial issues in the discipline. For example, a psychology textbook may include "Brain and Behavior" boxes in each chapter because brain studies have become extremely important in psychological research.

- **End-of-chapter material.** Most textbook chapters end with a summary of key points (sometimes tied to the chapter's learning objectives), a vocabulary list, and exercises or problems. Exercises come in many varieties. For example, a geography textbook will have map-based exercises, while a business textbook might offer case studies of real-world companies for you to analyze. If your instructor assigns exercises from the end of the chapter, read them *before* you start the chapter. Doing so will tell you what to look for as you read.

- **Answers or solutions.** Some, but not all, textbooks include an answer section at the end of the book. Use the answer section judiciously to check your work *after* you have completed it. Do not use the answer key as a shortcut; doing so will not help you prepare for exams!

- **Glossary and index.** Most textbooks include a glossary at the end of the book. A *glossary* lists all the key vocabulary in the book (along with definitions) in alphabetical order. Think of the glossary as a mini-dictionary for the subject you are studying. An *index* is an alphabetical listing of all the topics, terms, people, and places in the textbook. A page reference is included with each item, allowing you to find the discussion quickly and easily.

2. **Pay close attention to the examples.** Many students find that they learn concepts and ideas best by way of examples. For this reason, textbook authors work hard to provide many relevant, interesting, real-world examples in every chapter. If your textbook does not provide an example of an important concept, ask your instructor for one.

3. **Be patient, and reward yourself when you have reached key milestones in the assignment.** It is unlikely that you will find every discipline and every reading assignment equally interesting. Try to keep an open mind, if only because you know that you'll be tested on the material later. Take occasional breaks from reading (a 10-minute break after an hour of reading is a good guideline), and reward yourself with a healthy snack (or something else that motivates you to complete the assignment with a high level of comprehension).

4. **Look for relevance to your own life.** When you actively think about how a textbook discussion relates to your own life, it is much easier to learn new concepts. For instance, a business textbook might discuss the fact that some expensive brand names have generic equivalents that are a fraction of the price. How might these concepts help you the next time you need to buy aspirin or orange juice?

5. **Use additional print-based or online resources.** Many textbooks offer a printed study guide or workbook to help you work through the textbook. A study guide can be an excellent investment, especially in more challenging courses like economics. In addition, a book's Web site can feature chapter quizzes, electronic flashcards, self-tests, tutorials, videos, and additional exercises. Use the Web site for review and exam preparation. (If the Web site does not provide electronic flashcards, you can make your own using standard index cards.)

6. **Read with a highlighter or pen in hand.** Highlighting (see section 6e) can be a particularly helpful way of marking key points in the textbook. Annotating (see section 8b) is also a useful study aid. Many studies have proven that students learn better when they write, annotate, and take notes as they read.

EXERCISE 7-1 READING COLLEGE TEXTBOOKS

Using a textbook from one of your other courses, check to see which of the following features it contains. Place a checkmark in front of each item you find. (Not all textbooks will have all features.) Then briefly indicate how you can use it to study.

Textbook Title: _____

Author: _____

Textbook Web site or URL: _____

Feature   **How to Use It**

___ Chapter objectives   _____

___ Chapter outline   _____

___ Boxes in each chapter   _____

___ Timelines   _____

___ Charts, graphics, and photos   _____

___ Tables   _____

___ Section summaries   _____

___ Review sections within the chapter   _____

___ Marginal vocabulary terms   _____

___ Problems or exercises   _____

___ Highlighted or worked examples   _____

___ Chapter summary   _____

___ Key terms list   _____

___ Discussion or critical
    thinking questions   _____

___ Internet exercises   _____

___ Suggested readings   _____

___ Appendixes   _____

___ Other (list):   _____

7b   READING ESSAYS

LEARNING OBJECTIVE 2
Read essays.

Unlike many textbook readings, an *essay* presents information on a specific topic from the writer's point of view. While textbooks are often neutral presentations of facts, essays are often quite personal and reflect writers' perspectives.

An essay can be as short as a few paragraphs or as long as twenty pages (sometimes longer, depending on the topic). Here are some sample essay titles:

- "Beyond the Burqa"
- "The Touch Screen Generation"
- "Ending a Relationship"
- "Extreme Health"
- "The Mad Potter of Biloxi"
- "Climate Change and Extinction"

Here are some specific suggestions for reading essays:

1. **Closely examine the title and subtitle.** The title of an essay often announces the topic and may reveal the author's point of view. In some cases, though, the meaning or the significance of the title becomes clear only as you read the essay, or after you have finished reading. When included, subtitles can provide additional clues regarding the author's beliefs or viewpoint. For example, the essay titled "The Mad Potter of Biloxi" suggests the topic relates to a mad potter, but it is not until you read it that you realize that George Ohr, for all his eccentricities, was a great artist.

2. **Read the head note.** Many essays, especially those in college textbooks and anthologies (collections of writing), provide background information about the essay, the author, or the topic in a **head note** preceding the essay. The contents of head notes vary widely. Some provide context for the essay, while others talk about the writer and his or her qualifications. Some head notes point to key aspects of the essay, while others provide a list of questions for the reader to consider while reading. For example, the head notes to "The Mad Potter of Biloxi" (Source and Context and A Note on the Reading) provide information about the author, the magazine he wrote the article for, and a concise overview of the main point of the piece.

3. **Carefully read the introduction to the essay.** The essay's opening paragraph often provides background information to grab the reader's attention and/or announces the topic and the writer's point of view. Some introductory paragraphs carefully define words, ideas, and issues; be sure you understand these definitions before you read the entire essay. The opening paragraph of "The Mad Potter of Biloxi" reads as follows:

> Riding the train south through the deep pine woods of Mississippi, tourists to the Gulf Coast came to Biloxi for sunshine and surf. Along with its beaches, the little town had its own opera house, white streets paved with crushed oyster shells, and fine seafood. Yet back in the 1880s, there were no casinos in Biloxi as there are now, and not much to do besides swim, stroll, and eat shrimp. Then the town added a new tourist attraction, one based on genius or madness, depending on your point of view.
>
> —Watson, "The Mad Potter of Biloxi," from *The Smithsonian*

Notice that the introductory paragraph describes the setting for the story about to be told and includes the thesis statement.

4. **Find the thesis statement.** The **thesis** is the main point of an entire reading selection. In many essays, writers place their thesis in a single **thesis sentence** or **thesis statement** in the first or second paragraph. However, the thesis statement may sometimes appear in the middle of or at the end of the essay instead. Test your understanding of the thesis statement by rewriting it in your own words.

   Occasionally, the writer will imply or suggest a thesis statement rather than state it directly. When you cannot find a clear thesis statement, ask yourself: "What is the one main point the author is making?" Your answer is the implied thesis statement. In "The Mad Potter of Biloxi," the thesis statement appears at the end of the first paragraph: "Then the town added a new tourist attraction, one based on genius or madness, depending on your point of view."

5. **Within the essay, identify main ideas (topic sentences), supporting details, and other evidence used by the author to support his or her thesis statement.** Keep track of the essay's main ideas, as well as its major supporting details (review section 4c if necessary). Supporting details fall into many categories: *personal experiences and observations, examples, descriptions, statistics, facts, anecdotes (stories that illustrate a point), expert opinions,* and *quotations from recognized authorities.* Highlight main ideas as you read, then review your highlighting as soon as you've completed the reading assignment. (For specific highlighting guidelines, see p. 185). Here are some of the topic sentences in "The Mad Potter of Biloxi":

   - Today, the mad pottery of George Ohr sells for a small fortune.
   - Potters say that fire adds devilish details to their work.
   - Ohr also stepped up his own self-promotion.

6. **Closely read the essay's concluding paragraph.** An essay's final paragraph or paragraphs frequently revisit the author's thesis. They may also offer possible solutions, ideas for further thought or discussion, additional sources of information, or ways to get involved in the cause. This is the closing paragraph of "The Mad Potter of Biloxi":

   No longer dismissed as mad, Ohr has been hailed as "the **Picasso** of art pottery" and a "clay prophet." His resurrection proves that madness, like beauty, is in the eye of the beholder. But then, he always knew that, and so did any visitors to his shop who were paying strict attention. On their way out of the cluttered, crowded studio, they passed one final hand-lettered sign. It suggested neither madness nor genius but the self-confidence that helped a mad potter endure decades of rejection. Translated for its Latin, the sign read: "A Masterpiece, second to none, The Best; Therefore, I am!"

   —Watson, "The Mad Potter of Biloxi," from *The Smithsonian*

7. **Respond to the essay by writing.** Writing about a reading helps you better engage with and understand the essay. See Chapter 8 for specific writing techniques, such as outlining, summarizing, and drawing a graphic organizer.

EXERCISE 7-2 READING AN ESSAY

Read the following essay and answer the questions that follow.

Issue: Wildlife Conservation

Can the World's Disappearing Species Be Saved from Poachers?

Barun S. Mitra

In this essay, Barun S. Mitra argues that bans and restrictions on wildlife trade are actually more helpful than harmful. What experiences have you had with wildlife? How have those experiences formed your outlook of the natural environment? Should people benefit economically from the wildlife around them?

1   Despite trade bans and restrictions, many wildlife species today are more threatened than ever before. So we have the paradox of extremely valuable wildlife, such as tigers or rhinos, threatened with extinction while economically less valued farm animals, like chickens and cows, are thriving.

2   By banning the wildlife trade, it is driven underground, often with the aid of corrupt officials. This gives us the second paradox: Trade restrictions increase the prospect of illicit profit, which attracts the worst elements to take the risk and reap huge benefits.

3   For decades, efforts have focused on saving wildlife such as tigers, elephants, rhinos and others, yet these animals remain on the edge of extinction. On the other hand, commercially bred and traded animals, such as crocodiles, thrive. More than a million crocodiles are harvested and traded for their skins each year across the world, from Australia to the United States. The availability of freely traded crocodile skins has virtually wiped out crocodile poaching in a country like India, where the animal still remains endangered and may not be farmed or traded. Poachers stop poaching because they can simply not compete, in terms of price and quality, with legally traded animals.

4   Today, a dead tiger could fetch from $30,000 to $70,000, for its skin, bones and other organs, which are used in traditional Chinese medicinal products. Similarly, rhino horn powder is said to be more valuable than gold to Chinese consumers.

5   Yet wildlife in its natural environment can be a very valuable resource for the surrounding community and the country. In the United States, environmental recreation—including nature trails, bird watching, camping, etc.—generates more than

$100 billion a year. Fishing and hunting contribute another $20 billion. With proper ownership and management, the potential economic benefit from the wildlife and natural environment could be immense for Africa and Asia.

6   Unfortunately, it is fashionable today to preach the non-economic values of nature, while some of the poorest people in the world languish in abject poverty amidst amazing environmental wealth. This is clearly unsustainable. When people do not gain from the wildlife around them, they have little interest in managing those resources properly. Thus, the single biggest threat to wildlife is the conflict between man and animal.

7   Commerce can easily save our wildlife by eliminating that conflict. Commerce and conservation are not mortal enemies as often portrayed; they can easily complement each other, if only we allow it.

—Mitra, "Can the World's Disappearing Species Be Saved from Poachers?"

1. What has eliminated poaching in India?

_____

2. How much is a dead tiger worth?

_____

3. How much money does environmental recreation generate in the United States each year?

_____

4. What is this essay's implied thesis statement?

_____

_____

5. What is your opinion on the issue discussed in this essay? Do you agree or disagree with the author? Why?

_____

7c   READING LONGER WORKS

LEARNING OBJECTIVE 3
Read longer works.

Most college textbooks are designed to be read one chapter at a time. That is, students rarely sit down and read a textbook straight through. Many essays and articles are also fairly short, allowing you to finish them in one or two sittings. However, in your college studies and beyond, you will often be asked to read longer works.

Suppose, for example, you are taking an ethics course in which you study various viewpoints about contemporary issues. Your textbook may include chapters on various topics: decriminalization of drug possession, amnesty for illegal/ undocumented immigrants, business ethics, government involvement in the economy and people's lives, and animal rights. For the class sessions that focus on animal rights, your instructor may require you to read more than the textbook chapter on animal rights. You may also have to read opinion essays, articles from scholarly journals, and even sections from complete books on the topic.

Longer works such as full-length books and anthologies provide much more information, and much more detail, than briefer works. For this reason, they are often assigned in college courses that closely examine specific topics. In addition, many people who are interested in contemporary issues seek out longer works as a way of learning more about the issue.

The following are some suggestions for reading longer works.

1. **Preview the selection using the guidelines in section 1b.** This will give you an overview of the book as well as a framework on which to build your knowledge. Identify portions that pertain to the particular topic or issue that you are concerned with.

2. **Read relevant portions, starting at the beginning of the book and read through to the end.** Many times, college instructors change the order of textbook chapters, so in your psychology class you may end up reading Chapter 15 before Chapter 7. Textbook authors know that instructors like to customize textbooks to meet their teaching needs (and their students' needs), so they often write each chapter in a *modular* fashion that keeps all related subject matter in one chapter. In contrast, books on a single topic gradually build the reader's knowledge base, so you must read earlier chapters before you will be able to understand later chapters.

3. **Write summary notes at the end of each section or chapter.** Each time you complete a chapter, jot down that chapter's two or three main points. By the time you are done reading the book, you will have a summary of the entire work to use for review, study, and discussion.

4. **Plan to read in concentrated periods.** Most readers benefit from reading books or longer works in a somewhat concentrated period—over the course of a week rather than a month. So, even though you may have a month to finish the assignment, it's better to plan to read a good chunk of it each night for a week. This is particularly helpful when you are reading novels. Reading in a concentrated period will help you remember key details about character, plot, and sequences of events. If you put down a novel and come back to it two weeks later, you may find that you remember very little of what you've read!

5. **Divide the reading task into manageable chunks.** Suppose you have two weeks to read six chapters from Paul Waldau's *Animal Rights: What Everyone Needs to Know*. You might plan to read three chapters. Try not to stop reading in the middle of a chapter; schedule your time so that you can concentrate on a solid, identifiable chunk of the assignment with each reading. In the case of Waldau's book, each chapter is a manageable chunk.

EXERCISE 7-3 THINKING CRITICALLY ABOUT LONGER WORKS

Complete the following matching exercise about animal rights books. Use the books' titles and your inference skills to complete the exercise.

_____ 1. *Animal Rights: Current Debates and New Directions*

_____ 2. *Animal Rights: What Everyone Needs to Know*

_____ 3. *Dominion: The Power of Man, the Suffering of Animals, and the Call to Mercy*

_____ 4. *Animal Liberation: The Definitive Classic of the Animal Movement*

a. Likely to emphasize the pain that humans cause animals

b. Likely to be a good introductory book for people who do not know much about the issues involved in animal rights

c. Likely to present multiple viewpoints and perspectives on the animal rights controversy

d. Likely a book that has been widely read and serves as a "manifesto" of the animal rights movement

---

7d   READING AND INTERPRETING VISUALS

LEARNING OBJECTIVE 4
Read visuals.

In many of your textbooks and other reading materials, you probably noticed the large number of graphics and photographs. All **visual aids** share one goal: to illustrate concepts and help you understand them better. As a reader, your key goal is to extract important information from them. Visual aids work best when you read them *in addition to* the text, not *instead of* the text. As a writer, you need to be able to use, interpret, and condense information from visual aids as you make text-to-text and text-to-world connections.

Keep in mind that the author chose the visual aid, or **graphic**, for a specific purpose. To fully understand the graphic, be sure you can explain its purpose.

A General Approach to Reading Graphics

You will encounter many types of graphics in your reading materials. These include

- photos
- charts
- graphs
- diagrams

Here is a step-by-step approach to reading any type of graphic effectively. As you read, apply each step to Figure 7-1.

1. Make connections between written text and graphics. Look for the reference in the text. The author will usually refer you to each specific graphic.

FIGURE 7-1 THE GENDER PAY GAP, BY EDUCATION[1]

The gender pay gap—that is, the difference in average salary between men and women doing the same job—shows up at all levels of education.

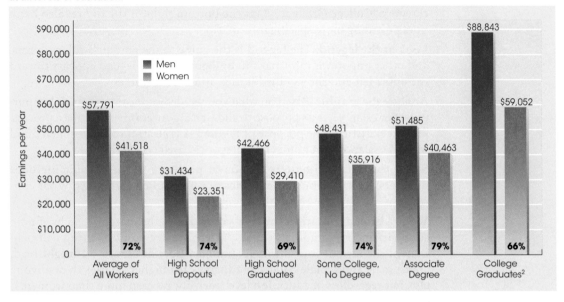

[1]Full-time workers in all fields. The percentages at the bottom of each red bar indicates the women's average percentage of men's incomes.
[2]Bachelor's and all higher degrees, including professional degrees.

Henslin, *Sociology: A Down-to-Earth Approach*, 10th Edition, p. 317

When you see the reference, finish reading the sentence, then look at the graphic. In some cases, you will need to go back and forth between the text and the graphic, making text-to-text connections, especially if the graphic has multiple parts. Here is the reference in which Figure 7-1 originally appeared:

> I'm going to reveal how you can make an extra $1,357 per month between the ages of 25 and 75. Is this hard to do? Actually, it is simple for some, and impossible for others. As Figure 7-1 shows, all you have to do is be born a male.

2. **Read the title and caption.** The **title** will identify the subject, and the **caption** will provide important information. In some cases, the caption will specify the graphic's key take-away point. The title of Figure 7-1 makes the graph's subject clear: the differences between men's salaries and women's salaries. The caption summarizes one of the graphic's important points.

3. **Examine how the graphic is organized and labeled.** Read all headings, labels, and notes. Labels tell you what topics or categories are being

discussed. Sometimes a label is turned sideways, like the words "Earnings per year" in Figure 7-1. Note that the title has a note (found at the bottom of the graphic) that provides information on how to read the graphic. The category "College Graduates" (at the bottom right of the figure) also has a note providing more specific information.

4. **Look at the legend.** The **legend** is the guide to the graphic's colors, terms, and other important information. In Figure 7-1, the legend appears toward the upper left and shows blue for men and red for women.

5. **Analyze the graphic.** Based on what you see, determine the graphic's key purpose. For example, is its purpose to show change over time, describe a process, present statistics? The purpose of Figure 7-1 is clear: It compares men's and women's salaries for a number of categories based on education level.

6. **Study the data to identify trends or patterns.** If the graphic includes numbers, look for unusual statistics or unexplained variations. What conclusions can you draw from the data?

7. **Write a brief annotation (note to yourself).** In the margin, jot a brief note summarizing the graphic's trend, pattern, or key point. Writing will help cement the idea in your mind. A summary note of Figure 7-1 might read, "Both male and female college graduates earn higher salaries than anyone else, but regardless of education level, men always earn more than women."

Reading and Analyzing Photographs

An old saying goes, "A picture is worth a thousand words." Photographs can help writers achieve many different goals. For example, writers can use photos to spark interest, provide perspective, or offer examples. Let's look at the photo in Figure 7-2 and use a step-by-step process to analyze it.

1. **First read the text that refers to the photo.** Photos are not a substitute for the reading. They should be read *along with* the text. For this reason, many readings include specific references to each photo, usually directly after a key point. For example:

> To counter our own tendency to use our own culture as the standard by which we judge other cultures, we can practice cultural relativism; that is, we can try to understand a culture on its own terms. With our own culture so deeply embedded within us, however, practicing cultural relativism can challenge our orientations to life. For example, most U.S. citizens appear to have strong feelings against raising bulls for the purpose of stabbing them to death in front of crowds that shout "Olé!" According to cultural relativism, however, bullfighting must be viewed from the perspective of the culture in which it takes place—*its* history, *its* folklore, *its* ideas of bravery, and *its* ideas of sex roles (Figure 7-2).
>
> —Henslin, *Sociology*, p. 39

Look at the photo as soon as you see the reference. The photo will help you visualize the concept under discussion, making it easier to remember.

FIGURE 7–2 THE BULLFIGHT: CULTURAL EXPERIENCE OR ANIMAL CRUELTY?

Courtesy of Felipe Rodriguez/Superstock.

Many Americans perceive bullfighting as a cruel activity that should be illegal everywhere. To most Spaniards, bullfighting is a sport that pits matador and bull in a unifying image of power, courage, and glory. *Cultural relativism* requires that we suspend our own perspectives in order to grasp the perspectives of others, something easier said than done.

—Henslin, *Sociology*, p. 39

2. **Read the photo's title and/or caption.** The caption is usually placed above, below, or to the side of the photo and explains how the photo fits into the discussion.

3. **Ask: What is my first overall impression? Why has the author included this photo?** Because photos can be so powerful, they are often chosen to elicit a strong reaction. Analyze your response to the photo. For example, Figure 7-2 is quite violent; note the blood running down the bull. What purpose is the author trying to achieve by including this photo?

4. **Examine the details.** Look closely at the picture, examining both the foreground and the background. Details can provide clues regarding the date and location of the photograph. For example, people's hairstyles and clothing often give hints to the year or decade. Landmarks and buildings help point to location. In Figure 7-2, you can see that bullfighting takes place in front of an audience. What point is the author making about the audience's cultural experiences and beliefs regarding bullfighting?

5. **Look for connections to society or your life.** Ask yourself how the photo relates to what you are reading or to your own experiences. For example, what are your own thoughts about bullfighting? Do you know anyone who feels differently? What are the sources of your disagreement?

> **EXERCISE 7-4 ANALYZING A PHOTOGRAPH**
>
> *Flip through one of your textbooks and choose a photo of interest to you. Analyze it according to the five-step process outlined above.*

7e   THINKING CRITICALLY ABOUT SOURCE MATERIALS

LEARNING OBJECTIVE 5
Think critically about source materials.

A recent study noted that college students tend to focus on the first page of results generated by a Google search. Many mistakenly believe that the first page of "hits" on a Google search contains the "best" links, but the best, most valuable information may be found on (for example) the tenth page of results. Google allows paid advertisers to buy placement for their links on the first page of results, and various companies offer what they call "search engine optimization" that will make a business's Web site one of the first to appear on the Google results page.

The lesson here is simple: Just as you think critically about materials you are reading, you should think critically about the *sources* of these materials. Who wrote the material, and why? Is it trustworthy? For example, do you think you can expect *High Times*, a magazine devoted to legalizing marijuana usage, to present fair evidence regarding the effects of smoking marijuana? Can you trust the Web site of the National Rifle Association (NRA), which is strictly opposed to gun control, to offer full information about the impacts of guns on American society? Most likely you cannot. These sources are one-sided and biased. Although the NRA's Web site (www.nra.org) uses the .org extension to indicate that it is a nonprofit organization, the association is an advocacy group with a strong agenda. You cannot expect its Web site to be impartial regarding a controversial issue like gun control.

To evaluate source materials, consider their content, accuracy and reliability, authority, timeliness, and objectivity.

Evaluate Content

When evaluating a source's content, examine its appropriateness, its level of technical detail, and its completeness.

- **Appropriateness.** To be worthwhile, the source should contain the information you need. It should answer one or more of the questions you need answered. If the source does not answer your questions in detail, check other sources for more information. Some Web sites will provide additional links to more detailed sites with more complete information. Many books will provide a list of references at the end; these references may contain the information you're searching for.

- **Level of technical detail.** A usable source should contain the level of technical detail that suits your purpose. Some sources may provide information that is too sketchy or incomplete; others assume a level of background knowledge or technical sophistication that you may lack. For example, if you are writing a short, introductory-level paper on ecological threats to marine animals, information on the Scripps Institution of Oceanography Web site may be too technical and contain more information than you need. Unless you already have some background knowledge in that field, you may want to search for a different Web site.

- **Completeness.** Determine whether the source provides complete information on the topic. Does it address all aspects of the topic that you feel it should? For example, if a book about important twentieth-century American poets does not mention Emily Dickinson, then it is incomplete. If you discover a source that is incomplete (and many are), search for sources that provide a more thorough treatment of the topic.

Evaluate Accuracy and Reliability

When using a source to research or write an academic paper, be sure that it contains accurate and reliable information. The source itself will also provide clues about the accuracy of the information it contains, so ask the following questions:

1. **Is the source professionally edited and presented? Has it been published by a professional organization or reputable publisher?** Check the copyright page to see whether the source has been professionally edited and published, or whether it has been "self-published" by someone with few credentials. Errors such as misspellings, grammatical mistakes, a messy or cluttered layout, unclear graphics, and a lot of typographical errors usually signal an unreliable source.

2. **Is the information presented in the source verifiable?** Compare the information you find with the information in other sources (periodicals, books, Web sites) on the same topic. If you find a discrepancy, conduct further research to determine which sources are trustworthy and which are not.

3. **Does the source provide a list of works cited?** In all serious research, the sources of information and the techniques used to collect and analyze data are fully documented. If the source does not contain a References or Works Cited section, you should question its accuracy and reliability.

4. **Is the information complete or in summary form?** If it is a summary, use the Works Cited or References section to locate the original source. Original information is less likely to contain errors.

5. **Could the information be a spoof or parody?** Some publications and Web sites that appear serious are actually spoofs, hoaxes, or satires designed to poke fun at topics and issues. An example is *The Onion* newspaper and its Web site at www.theonion.com. *The Onion* appears to offer legitimate information but actually provides political and social commentary through made-up stories.

Evaluate Authority

Before using information from a source, use the following questions to evaluate the authority of the person or group presenting the information.

1. **Who is the publisher or sponsor?** Is the publisher or sponsor a university press, a respected publisher, a private individual, an institution, a corporation, a government agency, or a nonprofit organization? Identifying the publisher or sponsor is often the key to evaluating the source's authority and expertise. For example, a Web site sponsored by Nike is designed to promote its athletic products, while a site sponsored by a university library is designed to help students learn to use its resources. A book published by the Sierra Club (a well-respected environmental organization) will likely provide authoritative, but biased, information about environmental issues. Material published by the U.S. government either in print form (for example, *The Statistical Abstract of the United States*) or on the Web (any URL ending in .gov) is highly authoritative and reliable. In general, if the author, business, publisher, or sponsoring agency is not identified, the source lacks authority and reliability.

2. **Who wrote the material?** Is the author's name provided, and are his or her professional credentials listed? If the author's name is not given, the source lacks authority. If the author's name is given, is the author an expert in his or her field? If not, the information may not be trustworthy.

3. **Is the author's contact information provided?** Often, authors provide an e-mail address or other address at which they can be reached. If no contact information is provided, the source may not be reliable.

When working with Web sites, it is sometimes useful to trace a particular Webpage back to its source. For example, suppose you found a paper about Berlin during World War II and want to track its source. Suppose the URL is http://hti.math.uh.edu/curriculum/units/2004/01/04.01.09.php. If you shorten the URL to http://hti.math.uh.edu, you will be taken to the University of Houston Teachers Institute, where this paper was submitted as a curriculum unit.

Evaluate Timeliness

Many books that represented the most current thinking or research in an area when they were published can become dated or even obsolete as new information is uncovered. Such books may be useful for historical information, but in most areas—whether business disciplines, the sciences, or the latest in medical advances—you will generally want to consult recently published materials.

The same holds true for Web sites. Although the Web often provides up-to-the-minute information, not all Web sites are current. Evaluate a Web site's timeliness by checking:

- the date on which the materials were posted to the Web site.
- the date when the site was last revised or updated.
- the date when the links were last checked.

Evaluate Objectivity

Reliable sources fall into two categories:

(1) sources that treat the subject in a fair, unbiased manner (see Chapter 11, section 11c, for more about bias); and

(2) sources that support a particular viewpoint.

A source with a specific viewpoint is not necessarily unreliable. In fact, many people who write about contemporary issues strongly argue in favor of or against a particular policy, practice, or government action. Such sources often cite supporting studies or examples, and they are often written by educated authorities and experts whose experiences can be trusted. You can use these sources as a way of opening up your mind to alternative viewpoints, but in the end you must evaluate the competing viewpoints and decide your own opinions.

Still, you must carefully evaluate each source's objectivity. An **objective** source is not influenced by personal prejudices or emotions; instead, it seeks to present all the facts in an even, unbiased way. To assess the source's objectivity, ask yourself the following questions:

1. **What is the author's goal?** Is it to present information objectively or to persuade you to accept a particular point of view or to take a specific action? If it is not to present balanced information, you can justifiably question the author's objectivity.

2. **Are opinions clearly identified?** An author is free to express opinions, but these should be clearly identified as such. Look for words and phrases that identify ideas as opinions. (See Chapter 9, section 9b, for a list of these words and phrases.) If a source presents opinions as facts or does not distinguish between facts and opinions, the source is most likely unreliable.

3. **Is the source a mask for advertising?** Be cautious of sources that present information to persuade you to purchase a product or service. If a magazine, newspaper, letter, or Web site resembles an infomercial you might see on television, be just as suspicious of it as you would be of an infomercial.

EXERCISE 7-5 EVALUATING ONLINE MATERIALS

Conduct a Google search on a contemporary issue that you find interesting. Choose two Web sites to examine. Evaluate the content, accuracy, reliability, authority, timeliness, and objectivity of each.

SUMMARY OF LEARNING OBJECTIVES

Objective 1 Read textbooks.	To *read a textbook selection*, use the textbook's pedagogical aids (learning objectives, headings, marginal terms, etc.) to help you learn. Pay close attention to the examples, and be patient as you make your way through the assignment. Look for relevance to your own life and use additional print-based or online resources if necessary to improve your comprehension. Read with a highlighter or pen in hand.
Objective 2 Read essays.	An *essay* presents information on a specific topic from the writer's point of view. To *read an essay*, first examine the title and subtitle. Read the head note (if one is provided) as well as the introduction to the essay. Find the thesis statement and identify main ideas, supporting details, and other evidence used to support the thesis statement. Closely read the essay's concluding paragraph, and respond to the essay by writing.
Objective 3 Read longer works.	To *read a longer work*, first preview it. Start at the beginning of the book and read through to the end. Write summary notes at the end of each chapter. Plan to read in concentrated periods, and divide the reading task into manageable chunks.
Objective 4 Read visuals.	To *read visuals effectively*, make connections between the text and graphics, examine the title and caption and legend, study its organization, determine its purpose, identify trends and patterns, and write annotations. When analyzing photographs, read the accompanying text, study the title and/or caption, consider your first impression, examine the details, and connect to society or your own life.
Objective 5 Think critically about source materials.	To *think critically* about source materials, first evaluate their content. Then consider their accuracy and reliability, as well as the author's authority, the timeliness of the source, and the objectivity of the content.

8 Organizing Information in Response to Reading

Have you ever wondered how you will learn all the facts and ideas from your instructors, textbooks, and other source materials? How will you keep track of the multiple opinions on various aspects of contemporary issues? Reading and learning a large amount of information is a two-step process. First, you must reduce the amount to be learned by deciding what is most important, less important, and unimportant to learn. Then you must organize the information to make it more meaningful and easier to learn. This chapter describes how to analyze your reading and writing tasks. It then offers two strategies for reducing the information to be learned—*annotating* and *paraphrasing*. It also offers three means of organizing information—*outlining, mapping,* and *summarizing*—and concludes with tips for writing in response to what you've read.

8a PREPARING TO READ AND WRITE: ANALYZE THE TASK

LEARNING OBJECTIVE 1
Analyze the reading and writing task.

In most college assignments, reading is only the first step in the learning process. Very rarely will instructors give you a reading assignment without another task, or set of tasks, to complete when you are done reading. At the most basic level, you may need to read a textbook chapter so that you can take part in classroom discussions the following day. Then, at various times in the term, you will be tested on the material you've read. Exams will test your comprehension of basic terms and concepts as well as your ability to analyze and evaluate what you've read. Many times, instructors will provide specific assignments to be completed after you've finished reading a selection. Perhaps you will have to answer a series of end-of-chapter questions or prepare a summary to submit for a grade.

To get the most from your reading assignment, you must analyze the task before you begin. Here are some tips for doing so.

Tips for Getting the Most Out of Reading Assignments

1. **Determine what you must do after you have finished the reading.** If you must answer a series of questions at the end of a chapter, read those questions before you begin the assignment. Doing so will provide you with clues regarding what to look for as you read. If you must write a paper or a journal entry in response to the reading, use annotation (section 8b) and paraphrasing (section 8c) to help you keep track of ideas as you read.

2. **Read the assignment several times before you begin.** Express in your own words what the assignment requires. If you have a choice of assignments, take a fair amount of time to choose. It is worth taking a few minutes to think about your choices so that you choose the assignment that you will find most worthwhile (and on which you will get the best grade).

3. **Look for key words in the assignment.** Take apart the assignment word by word so that you know exactly what is required. Many assignments have two specific parts: limiting words and topic. Consider the following example:

Trace the history of legalized gambling in Atlantic City, New Jersey.

       ↑   ↑   ↑

  limiting word   topic   limiting word

Here the topic, legalized gambling, is clearly defined, and it is limited or restricted in two ways: (1) you are concerned only with its history—not its status today, or its effects; and (2) you are concerned only with the city of Atlantic City, New Jersey, not with any other gambling venues, such as Las Vegas or casinos on Indian reservations. Also notice the word "trace." It suggests that you must track something through time in chronological order. Table 8.1 summarizes some common words found in assignments. Note that these words often correspond to the patterns of organization you studied in Chapter 4. Understanding these words will also be very useful when you are taking essay exams.

EXERCISE 8-1 ANALYZING ASSIGNMENTS

Read each of the following assignments. Discuss the meaning of the first word of each assignment and how it affects your preparation for reading. Be aware that each assignment may contain more than one part.

1. Discuss the long-term effects of the trend toward a smaller, more self-contained family structure.

2. List four factors that influence memory or recall ability, and explain how each can be used to make study more efficient.

TABLE 8.1 COMMON WORDS FOUND IN ASSIGNMENTS

WORD	INFORMATION TO INCLUDE	EXAMPLE
Argue	Make the case for a particular idea or course of action, providing convincing, reliable, valid evidence that supports your argument.	Argue that the United States should decrease its deficit by stopping foreign aid to all other countries.
Compare	Show how items are similar as well as different; include details or examples.	Compare the causes of air pollution with those of water pollution.
Contrast	Show how the items are different; include details and examples	Contrast the health care system in the United States with that in Canada.
Criticize	Make judgments about quality of worth; include both positive and negative aspects, explaining or giving reasons for your judgments.	Criticize the current environmental controls in place to combat noise pollution.
Define	Give an accurate meaning of the term with enough detail to show that you really understand it.	Define welfare as the term is used in the United States.
Describe	Tell how something happened, including how, who, where, and why.	Describe the effects of social media on today's adolescents.
Diagram	Make a drawing and label its parts.	Diagram the stamen and pistil of the lily.
Discuss	Consider important characteristics and main points.	Discuss the effectiveness of drug rehabilitation programs.
Enumerate	List or discuss one by one.	Enumerate the reasons for U.S. involvement in Afghanistan and Iraq.
Evaluate	React to the topic in a logical way. Discuss the merits, strengths, weaknesses, advantages, or limitations of the topic, explaining your reasons.	Evaluate the strategies our society has used to treat mental illness.
Justify	Give reasons that support an action, event, or policy.	Justify the decision to place economic sanctions on Iran.
Prove	Give reasons or evidence, or establish that a concept or theory is correct, logical, or valid.	Prove that ice is a better cooling agent than air when both are at the same temperature.
State	Explain using examples that demonstrate or clarify a point or idea.	State Boyle's Law and illustrate its use.
Summarize	Cover the major points in brief form; use a sentence and paragraph form.	Summarize the arguments for and against offering sex education in public schools.
Trace	Describe the development or progress of a particular trend, event, or process in chronological order.	Trace the history of the U.S. stock exchange.

3. Trace the development of monopolies in the late nineteenth and early twentieth centuries in the United States.

4. Describe the events leading up to the U.S. invasion of Iraq.

5. Evaluate the evidence that concludes day care has serious negative effects on infants, toddlers, and young children.

8b   ANNOTATING

LEARNING OBJECTIVE 2
Use annotation to record your thinking.

In many situations, highlighting (see section 6e) is not a sufficient means of identifying what to learn. It does not give you any opportunity to comment on or react to the material. **Annotating** text as you read is an interactive process that allows you to keep track of your comprehension as well as react and respond to the ideas of the writer. You might underline important ideas, number supporting details, write comments to the author, indicate important information with an asterisk, or write questions that you want to follow up on later.

Figure 8-1 suggests various types of annotation that you can use and provides examples of each in relation to a political science textbook chapter. However, you should feel free to develop your own system of annotations, symbols, and abbreviations. Annotating is a very personal process; you should annotate using whatever system helps you study best.

Here is an example of the annotations one student made on an excerpt from a reading on how the media treat images of men and women differently.

All media?

Who selected them? Were they selected randomly?

Aren't men's faces larger?

Stereotyping ------->

Stereotyping ------->

Why?

Media images of men and women also differ in other subtle ways. In any visual representation of a person—such as a photograph, drawing, or painting—you can measure the relative prominence of the face by calculating the percentage of the vertical dimension occupied by the model's head. When Dane Archer and his colleagues (1983) inspected 1,750 photographs from *Time, Newsweek,* and other magazines, they found what they called "face-ism," a bias toward greater facial prominence in pictures of men than of women. This phenomenon is so prevalent that it appeared in analyses of 3,500 photographs from different countries, classic portraits painted in the seventeenth century, and the amateur drawings of college students.

Why is the face more prominent in pictures of men than of women? One possible interpretation is that face-ism reflects historical conceptions of the sexes. The face and head symbolize the mind and *intellect*—which are traditionally associated with men. With respect to women, more importance is attached to the heart, emotions, or perhaps just the body. Indeed, when people evaluate models from photographs, those pictured with high facial prominence are seen as smarter and more assertive, active, and ambitious—regardless of their gender (Schwarz & Kurz, 1989). Another interpretation is that facial prominence signals power and *dominance.*

—Brehm, Kassin, and Fein, *Social Psychology*

FIGURE 8-1 SAMPLE MARGINAL ANNOTATIONS

TYPES OF ANNOTATION	EXAMPLE
Circling unknown words	...redressing the apparent (asymmetry) of their relationship
Marking definitions	*def* ⌐To say that the balance of power favors one party over another is to introduce a ⌐disequilibrium.
Marking examples	*ex* ...concessions may include negative sanctions, trade agreements ...
Numbering lists of ideas, causes, reasons, or events	components of power include ① ② ③ self-image, population, natural resources, and geography ④
Placing asterisks next to important passages	⸰ ⌐Power comes from three ⌐primary sources ...
Putting question marks next to confusing passages	? ⟶ war prevention occurs through institutionalization of mediation ...
Making notes to yourself	Check def in soc text	power is the ability of an actor on the international stage to ...
Marking possible test items	T There are several key features in the relationship ...
Drawing arrows to show relationships	...natural resources ... , ...control of industrial manufacture capacity
Writing comments, noting disagreements and similarities	Can terrorism be prevented through similar balance?	war prevention through balance of power is ...
Marking summary statements	Sum	the greater the degree of conflict, the more intricate will be ...

EXERCISE 8-2 ANNOTATING 1

Review Figure 8-1 and then annotate the reading "A Blueprint for Better Nutrition" on pages 10-12.

8c   PARAPHRASING

LEARNING OBJECTIVE 3
Paraphrase ideas.

A **paraphrase** is a restatement of a reading selection's ideas in your own words. A paraphrase retains the author's meaning. However, your wording, *not the author's,* is used. We use paraphrasing frequently in everyday speech. For example, when you relay a message from one person to another you convey the meaning but generally do not use the person's exact wording.

A paraphrase can be used to make a reading selection more concise. For this reason, it is an effective learning and review strategy. Specifically, paraphrasing is useful for portions of a text for which exact, detailed comprehension is required. For example, you might paraphrase the steps in solving a math problem, the process by which a blood transfusion is administered, or the levels of jurisdiction of the Supreme Court.

Paraphrasing is also a useful way to be certain you understand difficult or complicated material. If you can express the author's ideas in your own words, you can be certain you understand it. If you find yourself at a loss for words—except for those of the author—you will know your understanding is incomplete.

Paraphrasing is also a useful strategy when working with material that is stylistically complex, poorly written, or overly formal, awkward, or biased. Figure 8-2 is a paraphrase of a paragraph from "A Blueprint for Better Nutrition" (pp. 10–12).

FIGURE 8-2 A SAMPLE PARAPHRASE

PARAGRAPH	PARAPHRASE
Fresh fruits, vegetables, and whole grains promote health and reduce your risk of chronic disease. Eat more of these and less of foods containing refined carbohydrates, such as pastries, white bread, white rice, crackers, and candies. Also avoid sweetened beverages, from soft drinks to flavored waters, as these contain huge amounts of simple sugars. Drink more low-fat or non-fat milk. It contains many essential nutrients. If you're not sure whether a food or beverage has added sweeteners, look for these terms on the food label: sugars (brown, invert, raw, beet, or cane), corn sweetener, corn syrup, high fructose corn syrup, fruit juice concentrates, honey, malt syrup, molasses, glucose, fructose, maltose, sucrose, lactose, and dextrose.	It is important to eat healthy carbohydrates. Fruits, vegetables, and whole grains are healthy because they can reduce the risk of chronic diseases. Refined carbohydrates, contained in foods such as pastries, bread, rice, crackers and candy, are less healthy because they contain a lot of simple sugar. Be sure to stay away from sweetened beverages. Instead, drink nutritious low-fat or non-fat milk. Check food labels to find out if food and beverage items have added sweeteners. Avoid items that contain any type of sugar, syrups, concentrates, honey, glucose, maltose, lactose, or dextrose (Lynch and Morgan 77).

Use the following suggestions to paraphrase effectively.

Tips for Effective Paraphrasing

1. Read slowly and carefully.
2. Read the selection through in its entirety before writing anything.
3. As you read, pay attention to exact meanings and relationships among ideas.
4. Paraphrase sentence by sentence.
5. Read each sentence and express the key idea in your own words. Reread the original sentence; then look away and write your own sentence. Then reread the original and add anything you missed.
6. Don't try to paraphrase word by word. Instead, work with ideas.
7. For words or phrases you are unsure of or words you feel uncomfortable with, check a dictionary to locate a more familiar meaning.
8. You may combine several original sentences into a more concise paraphrase.
9. Do not plagiarize; your paraphrase should use your own words as much as possible and cite the source you are paraphrasing.

EXERCISE 8-3 PARAPHRASING 1

Read each paragraph and the paraphrases following them. Then answer the questions about the paraphrases.

Paragraph A
Issue: Alternative Medicine

Leaves of the coca plant have for centuries been a key part of the health system of the Andean region of South America. Coca is important in rituals, in masking hunger pains, and in combating the cold. In terms of health, Andean people use coca to treat gastrointestinal problems, sprains, swellings, and colds. The leaf may be chewed or combined with herbs or roots and water to make a *maté (mah-tay)*, a medicinal beverage. Trained herbalists have specialized knowledge about preparing *matés*. One *maté*, for example, is for treating asthma. The patient drinks the beverage, made of ground root and coca leaves, three to four times a day until cured.

—Miller, *Cultural Anthropology*, p. 166

Paraphrase 1

A *maté* is a medicinal drink made from coca. Coca is an important plant in South America. It has a wide variety of uses, both ritualistic and medicinal.

Paraphrase 2

The coca plant is an important part of health care in the Andes Mountains of South America. The leaves of this plant are used not only in rituals but also to hide hunger pangs and to fight the common cold. It is also used to help digestive problems as well as swollen or twisted joints. Sometimes the patient chews the coca leaf, and sometimes the patient drinks a coca-based medicinal beverage called a *maté*. People who are trained in herbs and their effects generally also have knowledge about how to prepare *matés* to cure such problems as asthma (Miller 166).

Paraphrase 3

The coca plant is found only in the Andes of South America, where people use it not only for rituals but also for its medicinal properties. A *maté* is a medicinal drink made from coca leaves, and it is used primarily to treat asthma, though it can also help lessen the pain of twisted or swollen joints (Miller 166).

1. Which is the best paraphrase of Paragraph A? _____

2. Why are the other paraphrases not as good?

_____

_____

_____

_____

_____

Paragraph B
Issue: Family Trends

Today, the dominant family form in the United States is the child-free family, where a couple resides together and there are no children present in the household. With the aging of the baby boomer cohort, this family type is expected to increase over time. If current trends continue, nearly three out of four U.S. households will be childless in another decade or so.

—Thompson and Hickey, *Society in Focus, 8th Edition, 2010 Census Update*, p. 383

Paraphrase 1

A child-free family is one where two adults live together and have no children. It is the dominant family form.

Paraphrase 2

The child-free family is dominant in the United States. Baby boomers are having fewer children. Three out of four homes do not have children in them.

Paraphrase 3

> The child-free family is dominant in the United States. As baby boomers get older, there will be even more of these families. If this trend continues, three-quarters of all U.S. homes will be childless ten years from now (Thompson and Hickey 383).

3. Which is the best paraphrase of Paragraph B? _____

4. Why are the other paraphrases not as good?

_____

_____

8d   OUTLINING

LEARNING OBJECTIVE 4
Outline text.

Outlining is a writing strategy that can assist you in organizing information and pulling ideas together. It is also an effective way to pull together information from two or more sources—your textbook and class lectures, for example. Finally, outlining is a way to assess your comprehension and strengthen your recall. Use the following tips to write an effective outline.

Tips for Writing an Effective Outline

1. **Read an entire section and then jot down notes.** Do not try to outline while you are reading the material for the first time.

2. **As you read, be alert for organizational patterns** (see Chapter 6). These patterns will help you organize your notes.

3. **Record all the most important ideas in the briefest possible form.**

4. **Think of your outline as a list of the selection's main ideas and supporting details.** Organize your outline to show how the ideas are related or to reflect the organization of the selection.

5. **Write in your own words; do not copy sentences or parts of sentences from the selection.** Use words and short phrases to summarize ideas. Do not write in complete sentences.

6. **Keep entries parallel.** Each entry in your outline should use the same grammatical form. Express all of your ideas in words or all of them in phrases or all in full sentences.

7. **Use an indentation system to separate main ideas and details.** As a general rule, the more important the idea, the closer it is placed to the left margin. Ideas of lesser importance are indented and appear closer to the center of the page. Your outline should follow the format pictured here:

Outline Format

TOPIC
Main Idea
    Supporting detail
        fact
        fact
    Supporting detail
Main Idea
    Supporting detail
    Supporting detail
        fact
        fact

Now study the following sample outline. It is based on a portion (the first seven paragraphs) of the textbook excerpt "Consequences of Social Class" on pages 6–9.

I. Consequences of Social Class
  A. Physical Health
    1. Higher social class = better health; lower social class = worse health
    2. Three main reasons
      a. access to medical care
      b. lifestyle: diet, drugs, alcohol, exercise, sexual practices
      c. persistent stresses faced by poor (not faced by rich)
  B. Mental Health
    1. Higher social class = better mental health; lower social class = worse mental health
      a. poor: more stress, less job security, lower wages, more likely to divorce, be victims of crime
      b. higher social class: lower stress, better coping skills, afford vacations and doctors

EXERCISE 8-4 OUTLINING 1

Read the following passage and complete the outline.

Issue: Business Issues and Practices

Behavior segmentation focuses on whether people buy and use a product, as well as how often and how much they use or consume. Consumers can be categorized in terms of **usage rates**: heavy, medium, light, or nonusers. Consumers can also be segmented according to **user status**: potential, users, nonusers, ex-users, regulars, first-timers, or users of competitors' products. Marketers sometimes refer to the **80/20 rule** when assessing usage rates. This rule (also known as the *law of* *disproportionality* or *Pareto's Law*) suggests that 80 percent of a company's revenues or profits are accounted for by 20 percent of a firm's products or customers. Nine country markets generate about 80 percent of McDonald's revenues. This situation presents McDonald's executive with strategy alternatives: Should the company pursue growth in the handful of countries where it is already well-known and popular? Or, should it focus on expansion and growth opportunities in the scores of countries that, as yet, contribute little to revenues and profits?

—Keegan and Green, *Global Marketing*, pp. 202, 204

Behavior Segmentation

A. User status: _____

   1. potential

   2. _____

   3. _____

   4. ex-users

   5. regulars

   6. _____

   7. users of competitive products

B. _____ : how much of how often people use or consume the product

   1. _____

   2. medium

   3. _____

   4. non-users

C. 80/20 rule

   1. also known as _____ or _____

   2. ____% of customers or products account for ____% of revenue or profit

   3. McDonald's strategy

      a. _____

      b. option 1: pursue growth where the company is already well-known and popular

      c. option 2: _____

      _____

8e   MAPPING AND GRAPHIC ORGANIZERS

Mapping involves drawing a diagram to describe how a topic and its related ideas are connected. Mapping is a visual means of learning by writing; it organizes and consolidates information. This section discusses four types of maps: *conceptual maps, process diagrams, time lines,* and *part and function diagrams.* Maps are sometimes called **graphic organizers** because they organize text material visually or graphically.

Conceptual Maps

A **conceptual map** is a diagram that presents ideas spatially rather than in list form. It is a "picture" of how ideas are related. Use the following steps to construct a conceptual map.

1. **Identify the topic and write it in the center of the page.**
2. **Identify ideas, aspects, parts, and definitions that are related to the topic.** Draw each one on a line radiating from the topic.
3. **As you discover details that further explain an idea already recorded, draw new lines branching from the idea and add the details to them.**

A conceptual map of this handbook is shown in Figure 8-3. This figure shows only the major topics included in the handbook. Maps can be much more detailed and include more information than the one shown.

FIGURE 8-3 A CONCEPTUAL MAP OF THIS HANDBOOK

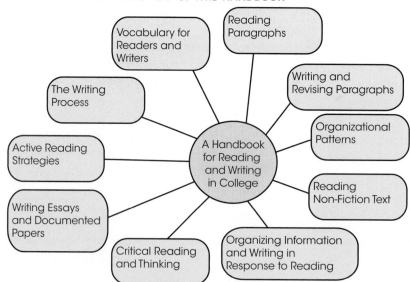

EXERCISE 8-5 DRAWING A CONCEPTUAL MAP 1

Create a conceptual map of the following paragraph about social institutions.

Issue: Social Institutions

Society cannot survive without social institutions. A **social institution** is a set of widely shared beliefs, norms, and procedures necessary for meeting the basic needs of society. The most important institutions are family, education, religion, economy, and politics. They have stood the test of time, serving society well. The family institution leads countless people to produce and raise children to ensure that they can eventually take over from the older generation the task of keeping society going. The educational institution teaches the young to become effective contributors to the welfare—such as the order, stability, or prosperity—of society. The religious institution fulfills spiritual needs, making earthly lives seem more meaningful and therefore more bearable or satisfying. The economic institution provides food, clothing, shelter, employment, banking, and other goods and services that we need to live. The political institution makes and enforces laws to prevent criminals and other similar forces from destabilizing society.

—Thio, *Sociology: A Brief Introduction*, pp. 35–36

Process Diagrams

In the technologies and the natural sciences, as well as in many other courses and careers, *processes* are an important part of the course content or job. A diagram that visually describes the steps, variables, or parts of a process will make learning easier. For example, the diagram in Figure 8-4 visually describes the steps that businesses follow in selecting a brand name for a new product.

FIGURE 8-4 A PROCESS DIAGRAM: SELECTING A BRAND NAME FOR A NEW PRODUCT

Process: Selecting a Brand Name for a New Product

Identify objectives → Brainstorm possible names → Evaluate and select better names → Field test on consumers → Select brand name

EXERCISE 8-6 DRAWING A PROCESS DIAGRAM

The following paragraph describes how emergency medical technicians (EMTs) should "size up" the scene of an automobile accident. Read the paragraph and then create a process diagram that illustrates this procedure.

The following are scene size-up considerations you should keep in mind when you approach a crash or hazardous material emergency:

As you near the collision scene:

- Look and listen for other emergency service units approaching from side streets.
- Look for signs of a collision-related power outage, such as darkened areas which suggest that wires are down at the collision scene.
- Observe traffic flow. If there is no opposing traffic, suspect a blockade at the collision scene.
- Look for smoke in the direction of the collision scene—a sign that fire has resulted from the collision.

When you are within sight of the scene:

- Look for clues indicating escaped hazardous materials, such as placards, a damaged truck, escaping liquids, fumes, or vapor clouds. If you see anything suspicious, stop the ambulance immediately and consult your hazardous-materials reference book or hazardous-materials team, if one is available. (See more information under "Establishing the Danger Zone.")
- Look for collision victims on or near the road. A person may have been thrown from a vehicle as it careened out of control, or an injured person may have walked away from the wreckage and collapsed on or near the roadway.
- Look for smoke not seen at a distance.
- Look for broken utility poles and downed wires. At night, direct the beam of a spotlight or handlight on poles and wire spans as you approach the scene. Keep in mind that wires may be down several hundred feet from the crash vehicles.
- Be alert for persons walking along the side of the road toward the collision scene. Curious onlookers (excited children in particular) are often oblivious to vehicles approaching from behind.
- Watch for the signals of police officers and other emergency service personnel. They may have information about hazards or the location of injured persons.

As you reach the scene:

- If personnel are at the scene and using the incident command/management system, follow the instructions of the person in charge. This may involve the positioning of the ambulance, wearing protective equipment and apparel, determining where to find the patients, or being aware of specific hazards. The Incident Commander may be able to provide you with lifesaving information regarding unstable conditions such as the stability of a building and the possibility of structural collapse.

Don appropriate protective apparel, including head protection, a bunker coat (or similar clothing that will protect you from sharp edges), and a reflective vest that goes over your coat and meets the requirements of OSHA. You should have extrication gloves easily available in a pocket. When temperature and weather are significant factors, be sure to protect yourself with clothing that will keep you dry and at the appropriate temperature.

Sniff for odors such as gasoline or diesel fuel or any unusual odor that may signal a hazardous material release.

—Limmer and O'Keefe, *Emergency Care*, pp. 248–249

Time Lines

When you are reading a selection focused on sequence or chronological order, a time line is a helpful way to organize the information. Time lines are especially useful in history courses. To map a sequence of events, draw a single line and mark it off in year intervals, just as a ruler is marked off in inches. Then write events next to the correct year. The time line shown in Figure 8-5 shows an effective way to organize historical events.

FIGURE 8-5 SAMPLE TIME LINE

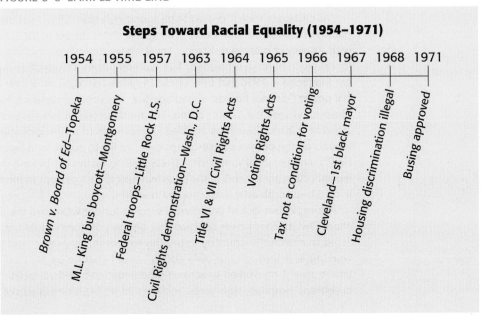

Steps Toward Racial Equality (1954–1971)

1954 — Brown v. Board of Ed–Topeka
1955 — M.L. King bus boycott–Montgomery
1957 — Federal troops–Little Rock H.S.
1963 — Civil Rights demonstration–Wash., D.C.
1964 — Title VI & VII Civil Rights Acts
1965 — Voting Rights Acts
1966 — Tax not a condition for voting
1967 — Cleveland–1st black mayor
1968 — Housing discrimination illegal
1971 — Busing approved

The following passage reviews the chronology of events in public school desegregation. Read the selection and then draw a time line that will help you visualize these historical events.

Issue: Segregation and Civil Rights

The nation's schools soon became the primary target of civil-rights advocates. The NAACP concentrated first on universities, successfully waging an intensive legal battle to win admission for qualified African Americans to graduate schools and professional programs. Led by Thurgood Marshall, NAACP lawyers then took on the broader issue of segregation in the country's public schools. Challenging the 1896 Supreme Court decision that upheld the constitutionality of separate but equal public facilities, Marshall argued that even substantially equal but separate schools did profound psychological damage to African American children and thus violated the Fourteenth Amendment.

The Supreme Court was unanimous in its 1954 decision in the case of *Brown v. Board of Education of Topeka*. Chief Justice Earl Warren, recently appointed by President Eisenhower, wrote the landmark opinion flatly declaring that "separate educational facilities are inherently unequal." To divide grade school children "solely because of their race," Warren argued, "generates a feeling of inferiority as to their status in the community that may affect their hearts and minds in a way unlikely ever to be undone." Despite this sweeping language, Warren realized that it would be difficult to change historic patterns of segregation quickly. Accordingly, in 1955, the Court ruled that desegregation of the schools should proceed "with all deliberate speed" and left the details to the lower federal courts.

"All deliberate speed" proved to be agonizingly slow. Officials in the border states quickly complied with the Court's ruling, but states deeper in the South responded with a policy of massive resistance. Local white citizens' councils organized to fight for retention of racial separation; 101 representatives and senators signed a Southern Manifesto in 1956 that denounced the *Brown* decision as "a clear abuse of judicial power." School boards, encouraged by this show of defiance, found a variety of ways to evade the Court's ruling. The most successful was the passage of pupil-placement laws. These laws enabled local officials to assign individual students to schools on the basis of scholastic aptitude, ability to adjust, and "morals, conduct, health, and personal standards." These stalling tactics led to long disputes in the federal courts; by the end of the decade, fewer than 1 percent of the black children in the Deep South attended school with whites.

A conspicuous lack of presidential support further weakened the desegregation effort. Dwight Eisenhower believed that people's attitudes could not be altered by "cold lawmaking"—only "by appealing to reason, by prayer, and by constantly working at it through our own efforts" could change be enacted. Quickly and unobtrusively, he worked to achieve desegregation in federal facilities, particularly in veterans' hospitals, navy yards, and the District of Columbia school system.

Southern leaders mistook President Eisenhower's silence for tacit support of segregation. In 1958, Governor Orville Faubus of Arkansas called out the national guard to prevent the integration of Little Rock's Central High School on grounds of a threat to public order. . . .

Despite the snail's pace of school desegregation, the *Brown* decision led to other advances. In 1958, the Eisenhower administration proposed the first general civil rights legislation since Reconstruction. Senate Majority Leader Lyndon B. Johnson overcame strong southern resistance to avoid a filibuster, but at the expense of weakening the measure considerably. The final act, however, did create a permanent Commission for Civil Rights, one of President Truman's original goals. It also provided for federal efforts aimed at "securing and protecting the right to vote." A second civil-rights act in 1960 slightly strengthened the voting rights section.

—Divine et al., *America: Past and Present, Combined Edition*, pp. 800–801

Part-and-Function Diagrams

In college courses that deal with the use and description or classification of physical objects, labeled drawings are an important learning tool. In a human anatomy and physiology course, for example, the easiest way to learn the parts and functions of the brain is to draw it. To study it, you would sketch the brain and test your recall of each part and its function. Figure 8-6 shows a part-and-function diagram of the human ear.

FIGURE 8-6 A PART-AND-FUNCTION DIAGRAM

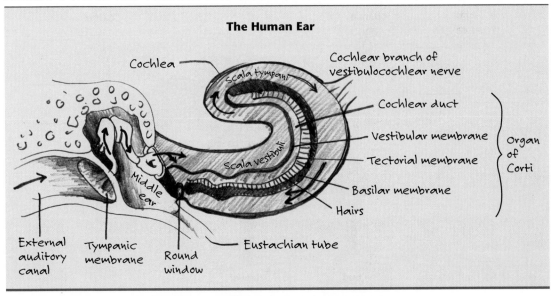

EXERCISE 8-8 DRAWING A PART-AND-FUNCTION DIAGRAM

The following passage describes the parts of a flower. Read the passage and then fill in the blanks in Figure 8-7.

Issue: Biodiversity

If you look at Figure 8-7, you can see the components of a typical flower. Taking things from the bottom, there is a modified stem, called a **pedicel**, which widens into a base called a **receptacle**, from which the flowers emerge. Flowers themselves can be thought of as consisting of four parts: sepals, petals, stamens, and a carpel. The **sepals** are the leaflike structures that protect the flower before it opens. (Drying out is a problem, as are hungry animals.) The function of the color of **petals** is to announce "food here" to pollinating animals.

The heart of the flower's reproductive structures consists of the stamens and the carpel. If you look at Figure 8-7, you can see that the **stamens** consist of a longer, slender **filament** topped by an **anther**. These anthers contain cells that ultimately will yield sperm-bearing pollen grains. Thus, the anthers are the place where *male* reproductive cells are produced. Pollen grains ultimately will be released from the anther and then carried—perhaps by a pollinating bee or bird—to the carpel of another plant. As Figure 8-7 shows, a **carpel** is a composite structure composed of three main parts: the **stigma**, which is the tip end of the carpel, on which pollen grains are deposited; the **style**, a slender tube that raises the stigma to such a prominent height that it can easily catch the pollen; and the **ovary**, the area in which fertilization of the female egg and then early development of the plant embryo take

FIGURE 8-7 THE PARTS OF A FLOWER

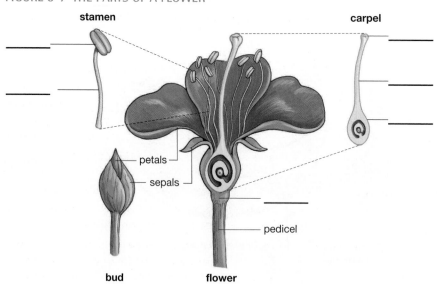

stamen   carpel

petals
sepals

pedicel

bud   flower

—Krogh, *Biology: A Guide to the Natural World*, p. 464

place. Thus, the ovary is the structure in the flower that houses the *female* reproductive cells, and it is the structure in which the male and female reproductive cells come together.

—Adapted from Krogh, *Biology: A Guide to the Natural World*, pp. 464–465

8f   SUMMARIZING

LEARNING OBJECTIVE 6
Summarize text.

Like outlining, summarizing is an excellent way to learn from your reading and to increase recall. A **summary** is a brief statement that reviews the key points of what you have read. It condenses an author's ideas or arguments into sentences written in your own words. A summary contains only the gist of the text, with limited explanation, background information, or supporting detail. Writing a summary is a step beyond recording the author's ideas; a summary pulls together the writer's ideas by condensing and grouping them. Before writing a summary, be sure you understand the material and have identified the writer's major points. Then use the following suggestions to write a summary:

1. **Highlight or write brief notes on (annotate) the material.**

2. **Write one sentence that states the author's overall concern or most important idea.** To do this, ask yourself what one topic the material is about. Then ask what point the author is trying to make about that topic. This sentence will be the topic sentence of your summary. (You may find that the author has provided this sentence for you in the form of a thesis sentence. **But you must rewrite that thesis sentence in your own words.**)

3. **Throughout the summary, be sure to paraphrase, using your own words rather than the author's.**

4. **Review the major supporting information that the author provides to explain the major idea or thesis.**

5. **The amount of detail you include, if any, depends on your purpose for writing the summary.** For example, a summary of a television documentary for a research paper might be more detailed than a summary of the same program you write to jog your memory for a class discussion.

6. **Present ideas in the summary in the same order in which they appear in the original material. Begin your summary by noting the title and author of the original material.**

7. **If the author presents a clear opinion or expresses a particular attitude toward the subject, include it in your summary.**

8. **If the summary is for your own use only and will not be submitted as an assignment, do not worry about sentence structure.** Some students prefer to write summaries using words and phrases rather than complete sentences.

Figure 8-8 (p. 220) is a sample summary of the article "Consequences of Social Class," which appears on pages 6–9.

FIGURE 8-8 A SAMPLE SUMMARY

In his article "The Consequences of Social Class," James Henslin explains that social class plays an important role in most aspects of a person's life. In terms of both physical and mental health, people of the higher social classes are healthier than those of the lower classes. In terms of family life, social class affects the choice of spouse, with upper-class parents playing a larger role in maintaining the sense of family and helping choose their children's mates. Divorce is more common among the lower classes, who are more likely than the middle and upper classes to orient their children toward following the rules. The upper classes are more educated than the lower classes, and people of different classes are even drawn to different religious denominations. Politically, the upper classes tend to vote Republican, the lower classes Democrat. Members of the lower classes are more likely to be arrested and imprisoned, while the white-collar crimes committed by the upper classes don't often land the criminals in jail.

EXERCISE 8-9 SUMMARIZING

Write a summary of the selection titled "Maintain Proper Levels of Sodium and Potassium" (paragraph 6) of the article "A Blueprint for Better Nutrition" on pages 10–12.

8g WRITING A RESPONSE PAPER

LEARNING OBJECTIVE 7
Write a response paper.

At first, reading and writing may seem like very different, even opposite, processes. A writer starts with a blank page or computer screen and creates and develops ideas, while a reader starts with a full page and reads someone else's ideas. Although reading and writing may seem very different, they are actually parts of the same communication process. Because reading and writing work together, improving one set of skills often improves the other.

Some instructors assign a response to the reading, which requires you to read a selection, analyze it, and then write about it. The response may be somewhat informal (for example, adding an entry in your writing journal or posting a response to an electronic bulletin board), or it may be more formal (for example, a standard essay that should be drafted, revised, and proofread before being handed in).

Before responding to any reading, make sure you understand the response assignment. If you are unclear about your instructor's expectations or the specifics of the assignment, ask for clarification. For example, you may want to ask:

- How long should this response be?
- Do you want my opinion on the topic, a summary of the author's ideas, or both?
- Would it be acceptable to include a map or graphic organizer as part of my response?

Writing an Informal Response

In an informal response, you simply write and respond without worrying about grammar, punctuation, and the other requirements of a formal paper. Suppose you have been assigned a reading titled "Adoption by Single People: Bad for the Parent, Bad for the Child." Your instructor asks you to write a journal entry responding to the reading. Here are some ways you might respond.

- **Write about your opinion on the topic.** Do you think single people should be allowed to adopt? Why or why not? It is acceptable to write about your emotional response to the topic in your journal. (In more formal response assignments, emotion is discouraged and convincing evidence and examples are encouraged.)
- **Talk about your personal experiences with the subject.** Do you know any single people who have adopted children? What have their experiences been? Would they agree or disagree with the author, and why?
- **Speculate why the author is so opposed to single people adopting children.** Is he basing his conclusions on his own experiences or on good, solid research?
- **Think about alternate scenarios.** Is a child better left in an orphanage than adopted by an unmarried person? Suppose you were an orphan. Would you rather be adopted by an unmarried person or left in a foster home or orphanage?

Here is a sample journal entry by a student writing in response to "Adoption by Single People: Bad for the Parent, Bad for the Child":

> I can see the writer's point even if I don't agree with it. Of course we all want to have both a mother and a father. I think that's true whether you're male or female—you always want both. But that's just not always possible, and I personally would rather be adopted by a loving unmarried woman, or man, than have to live in a group home or be out there in the world fending for myself. People who want to adopt have a lot of love in their hearts, otherwise why would they want someone else's child? I don't think it should matter if the person is unmarried, but I do think it's important that the person has the financial means to support the kid they adopt.

EXERCISE 8-10   WRITING AN INFORMAL RESPONSE

Write an informal response (in the form of a journal entry) to "A Blueprint for Better Nutrition" on pages 10–12.

Writing a Formal Response

In a formal response, you may decide to include a brief summary, but you should focus on analyzing and evaluating the reading selection. Do not discuss all of your reactions, however. Rather, select one key idea, one question the reading raises, or one issue it tackles. Then respond to that one idea, question, or issue.

For example, suppose your instructor asks you to read an article titled "Facebook: Many Friends, Few Relationships," which argues that Facebook encourages surface friendships at the expense of deeper, more lasting relationships. Your instructor asks you to write a formal one-page response paper about the article, allowing you to choose your own topic. In writing your response, you might take one of the following approaches:

- Discuss your own experiences with Facebook, as a way of confirming or refuting the author's main points.
- Evaluate the author's claim, evidence, and overall argument, either agreeing or disagreeing with her conclusions.
- Discuss some interesting aspects of Facebook that the author has not considered.
- List and discuss the author's assumptions or omissions.

Use the following suggestions when writing a formal response. Before you sit down to write, devise critical questions about the reading. Use the suggestions in Chapter 1 of this handbook to identify the author's opinions, her purpose for writing, her tone, her use of figurative language, her possible bias, and the reliability, relevance, and timeliness of her examples. Examining these aspects of the reading will likely generate many ideas to which you can choose to respond. (Of course, you will have to narrow your list and choose just one topic to write about.)

Because you will likely be graded or otherwise evaluated on your formal response, be sure to use good writing practices before you submit your formal response paper. Ask a classmate to read your first draft and offer ideas for improvement. Revise your paper to ensure it reads clearly and presents valid arguments and evidence. Before turning it in, proofread it for grammar, spelling, and punctuation.

EXERCISE 8-11   WRITING A FORMAL RESPONSE

Write a one-page formal response to "Can the World's Species Be Saved from Poachers?" on pages 189–190.

SUMMARY OF LEARNING OBJECTIVES

Objective 1 **Analyze the reading and writing task.**	To *analyze* the reading and writing task, first determine what you must do after you have finished the reading. Reread the assignment several times before you begin, looking for key words that will help you define your task.
Objective 2 **Use annotation to record your thinking.**	To *annotate* a reading, develop your own system of annotations, symbols, and abbreviations to help you react to the material as you read it.
Objective 3 **Paraphrase ideas.**	To *paraphrase* a reading selection, rewrite the selection, keeping the author's meaning but using your own words. Paraphrase sentence by sentence, but work with ideas rather than individual words. Paraphrasing can help you make a reading selection more concise (by combining several original sentences into one paraphrased sentence) and can help you check your understanding. Be sure that you credit the source that you are paraphrasing.
Objective 4 **Outline text.**	*Outlining* is a listing strategy that helps you organize information and pull ideas together. To outline a reading selection, read the entire reading selection and jot down notes, being alert for organizational patterns. Record the most important ideas and supporting details in the briefest possible form. Use your own words, and use an indentation system to separate main ideas from details. For the ideal outline format, see page 209.
Objective 5 **Draw maps and graphic organizers to show relationships.**	*Drawing maps and graphic organizers* involves drawing a diagram to show how a topic and its related ideas are connected. Four common types of maps/graphic organizers are conceptual maps, process diagrams, time lines, and part-and-function diagrams.
Objective 6 **Summarize text.**	A *text summary* reviews the key points of what you have read. It condenses the author's ideas into sentences written in your own words and contains only the gist of the text, with limited explanation, background information, or supporting detail. To write a summary, first highlight or annotate the material. Then write one sentence that states the author's overall concern or most important idea. Throughout the summary, use your own words rather than the author's. Include the amount of detail required by the assignment, and present ideas in the same order in which they appear in the original. If the author presents a clear opinion or expresses a particular attitude toward the subject, include it in your summary. Be sure to indicate clearly the source of the material you are summarizing.
Objective 7 **Write a response paper.**	Written responses to a reading may be either formal or informal. To *write an informal response* (for example, a journal entry) you might write about your opinion on the topic, discuss your personal experience, speculate about the author's purpose, or think about other aspects of the topic. To write a *formal response* (for example, an essay) select one key idea, one question raised by the reading, or one issue discussed in the reading. Then respond to that one idea, question, or issue in a piece of writing that you edit, improve, and proofread before you submit it to your instructor.

9 Critical Reading and Thinking

LEARNING OBJECTIVES

1 Make inferences and draw conclusions

2 Distinguish fact from opinion

3 Identify the author's purpose

4 Evaluate tone

5 Interpret figurative language and irony

6 Identify bias

7 Evaluate data and evidence

8 Recognize propaganda techniques

9a   MAKING ACCURATE INFERENCES AND DRAWING CONCLUSIONS

LEARNING OBJECTIVE 1
Make inferences and draw conclusions.

Look at the photograph below, which appeared in a psychology textbook. What do you think is happening here? What are the feelings of the participants?

Courtesy of Ronald Sumners/Shutterstock.

To answer these questions, you had to use information you could get from the photo and make decisions based on it. The facial expressions, body language, clothing, and musical instruments presented in this photo provide clues. This reasoning process is called "**making an inference**." You also had to use your prior knowledge about concerts, performers, musicians, and so forth. When you use both your prior knowledge and information from a text or image, you "**draw a conclusion**."

Inferences and **conclusions** are reasoned guesses about what you don't know made on the basis of what you do know. They are common in our everyday lives. When you get on a highway and see a long, slow-moving line of traffic, you might predict that there is an accident or roadwork ahead. When you see a puddle of water under the kitchen sink, you can infer that you have a plumbing problem. The inferences you make may not always be correct, even though you base them on the available information. The water under the sink might have been the result of a spill. The traffic you encountered on the highway might be normal for that time of day, but you didn't know it because you aren't normally on the road at that time. An inference is only the best guess you can make in a situation, given the information you have.

How to Make Accurate Inferences and Conclusions

When you read the material associated with your college courses, you need to make inferences and draw conclusions frequently. Writers do not always present their ideas directly. Instead, they often leave it to you—the reader—to add up and think beyond the facts they present, and to use your prior knowledge about the topic. You are expected to reason out the meaning an author intended (but did not say) on the basis of what he or she did say. Each inference and conclusion you make depends on the situation, the facts provided, and your own knowledge and experience. Here are a few guidelines to help you see beyond the factual level and make accurate inferences from your reading materials.

Understand the Literal Meaning

Be sure you have a firm grasp of the literal meaning. You must understand the stated ideas and facts before you can move to higher levels of thinking, which include inference making and drawing conclusions. You should recognize the topic, main idea, key details, and organizational pattern of each paragraph you have read.

Notice Details

As you are reading, pay particular attention to details that are unusual or stand out. Often, such details will offer you clues to help you make inferences. Ask yourself:

- What is unusual or striking about this piece of information?
- Why is it included here?

Read the following excerpt, which is taken from an essay about a young Polish immigrant to the United Kingdom, and mark any details that seem unusual or striking.

Issue: Immigration

An Immigration Plan Gone Awry

Due to her own hardship, Katja was not thrilled when her younger brother called her from Warsaw and said that he was going to join her in the United Kingdom (U.K.). Katja warned him that opportunities were scarce in London for a Polish immigrant. "Don't worry," he said in an effort to soothe her anxiety. "I already have a job in a factory." An advertisement in a Warsaw paper had promised good pay for Polish workers in Birmingham. A broker's fee of $500 and airfare were required, so her brother borrowed the money from their mother. He made the trip with a dozen other young Polish men.

The "broker" picked the young men up at Heathrow [airport] and piled them in a van. They drove directly to Birmingham, and at nightfall the broker dropped the whole crew off at a ramshackle house inside the city. He ordered them to be ready to be picked up in the morning for their first day of work. A bit dazed by the pace, they stretched out on the floor to sleep.

Their rest was brief. In the wee hours of the night, the broker returned with a gang of 10 or so thugs armed with cricket [similar to baseball] bats. They beat the young Polish boys to a pulp and robbed them of all their valuables. Katja's brother took some heavy kicks to the ribs and head, then stumbled out of the house. Once outside, he saw two police cars parked across the street. The officers in the cars obviously chose to ignore the mayhem playing out in front of their eyes. Katja's brother knew better than try to convince them otherwise; the police in Poland would act no differently. Who knows, maybe they were part of the broker's scam. Or maybe they just didn't care about a bunch of poor Polish immigrants "invading" their town.

—Batstone, "Katja's Story," from *Sojourner's*

Reprinted from *Sojourners* (June 2006).

Did you mark details such as the $500 broker's fee, the promise of a well-paying job despite scarce job opportunities for Polish immigrants, and the terrible sleeping conditions?

Add Up the Facts

Consider all of the facts taken together. To do this, ask yourself the following questions:

- What is the writer trying to suggest with this set of facts?
- What do all these facts and ideas seem to point toward or add up to?
- Why did the author include these facts and details?

Making an inference is somewhat like assembling a complicated jigsaw puzzle; you try to make all the pieces fit together to form a recognizable picture. Answering these questions requires you to add together all the individual pieces of information, which will help you arrive at an inference.

When you add up the facts in the article "An Immigration Plan Gone Awry," you realize that Katja's brother is the victim of a scam.

Be Alert to Clues

Writers often provide you with numerous hints that can point you toward accurate inferences. An awareness of word choices, details included (and omitted), ideas emphasized, and direct commentary can help you determine a writer's attitude toward the topic at hand. In "An Immigration Plan Gone Awry," the "ramshackle" house, the men "piled" into a van, and the immigrants sleeping on the floor are all clues that something is amiss.

Consider the Author's Purpose

Also study the author's purpose for writing. What does he or she hope to accomplish? In "An Immigration Plan Gone Awry" the writer is critical of immigrant brokers and of the police.

Verify Your Inference

Once you have made an inference, check to make sure that it is accurate. Look back at the stated facts to be sure you have sufficient evidence to support the inference. Also be certain you have not overlooked other equally plausible or more plausible inferences that could be drawn from the same set of facts.

EXERCISE 9-1 MAKING INFERENCES AND DRAWING CONCLUSIONS

Study the cartoon below and place a check mark in front of each statement that is a reasonable inference or conclusion that can be made from the cartoon.

Courtesy of the Cartoon Bank.

"We get it, Tom—you're management now."

_____ 1. The cartoonist thinks workers are physically abused.

_____ 2. The cartoonist is critical of those in management.

_____ 3. Many conflicts exist between workers and supervisors.

_____ 4. The cartoonist believes that people change when they become managers.

_____ 5. The cartoonist is a labor relations specialist.

EXERCISE 9-2 MAKING INFERENCES AND DRAWING CONCLUSIONS

Read each of the following statements. Place a check mark in front of each sentence that follows that is a reasonable inference or conclusion that can be made from the statement.

1. Many job applicants have found that their postings on Facebook or their tweets on Twitter have had negative effects on their getting jobs.

   _____ a. Job recruiters look up candidates' online histories.

   _____ b. Young people should be careful about what they post online.

   _____ c. The majority of people over age 23 now have Facebook accounts.

   _____ d. Tweeting has become an accepted method of staying in touch with friends.

2. Reality TV may look spontaneous and unscripted, but reality TV shows are carefully edited before they are televised.

   _____ a. In truth, reality TV is not particularly realistic.

   _____ b. The directors and producers of reality TV may distort facts and events.

   _____ c. Reality TV shows are cheaper to produce because there is no need for writers to write the dialogue.

   _____ d. Most people now prefer to watch reality TV rather than sitcoms or dramas.

3. The goal of health care reform in the United States is to ensure that as many people as possible have medical insurance and decent medical care, as in Canada and Europe.

   _____ a. The cost of medical care is likely to decrease.

   _____ b. Under the old medical care system, many people in the United States had no access to medical care.

   _____ c. As a result of health care reform, there is likely to be a shortage of doctors.

   _____ d. Canada and Europe currently do a better job of providing health care to their citizens than the United States does.

EXERCISE 9-3   MAKING INFERENCES AND DRAWING CONCLUSIONS

Read each of the following passages. Determine whether the statements following each passage are likely to be true or false. Place a T next to each true statement and an F next to each false statement.

A.   **Issue: Literacy**

On the surface, development statistics show impressive gains in education among developing countries. By the early twenty-first century, more than 80 percent of children were enrolled in primary school, and five out of six of the world's adults were literate, according to the United Nations Development Report in 2008. Yet the same report notes that only slightly over one-half of children attend school in sub-Saharan Africa and in many developing countries few children even graduate from primary school. Illiteracy rates in most middle-income nations are much lower, typically less than 20 percent. However, millions of rural and urban children receive no education whatsoever.

—Adapted from Thompson and Hickey, *Society in Focus,* p. 239

_____   1. In middle-income nations, urban children are more likely to be denied an education than rural children.

_____   2. Today, the great majority of the world's population is literate.

_____   3. Literacy rates are generally higher in middle-income nations than they are in developing nations.

_____   4. More than half the children in sub-Saharan Africa will graduate from primary school.

_____   5. The United Nations Development Report describes social and economic trends in developing (poor) nations.

B.   **Issue: Food Safety**

Building a healthy eating pattern involves following food safety recommendations to reduce your risk of foodborne illnesses, such as those caused by microorganisms and their toxins. The four food safety principles emphasized in the Dietary Guidelines are

- Clean your hands, food contact surfaces, and vegetables and fruits;
- Separate raw, cooked, and ready-to-eat foods while shopping, storing, and preparing foods;
- Cook foods to a safe temperature;
- Chill (refrigerate) perishable foods promptly.

Another important tip is to avoid unpasteurized juices and milk products and raw or undercooked meats, seafood, poultry, eggs, and raw sprouts.

—Adapted from Thompson and Manore, *Nutrition for Life,* pp. 14–15

_____ 6. To reduce risk of illness, shoppers should not purchase raw foods.

_____ 7. Vegetables should not be eaten raw.

_____ 8. Toxins are poisonous substances.

_____ 9. Countertops and stoves can transfer germs to foods.

_____ 10. The pasteurization process makes juices and milk safe to drink.

C. Issue: Family and Family Trends

Many of you have probably grown up on tales of men running from marriage, going to great lengths to avoid being "trapped." This folklore actually runs counter to the reality of women's and men's lives. In reality, men seem to prefer marriage to being single. For example, when asked if they would marry the same person again, they respond in the affirmative twice as often as their wives. In addition, most divorced and widowed men remarry, and the rate of marriage for these men at every age level is higher than the rate for single men. Furthermore, when compared with single men, married men live longer, have better mental and physical health, are less depressed, have a lower rate of suicide, are less likely to be incarcerated for a crime, earn higher incomes, and are more likely to define themselves as happy.

—Schwartz and Scott, *Marriage and Families: Diversity and Change,* p. 255

_____ 11. Marriage has a number of beneficial effects on men.

_____ 12. Marriage is more beneficial to men than to women.

_____ 13. Married men are less likely to be in jail than married women are.

_____ 14. More men than women are happy in their current marriage.

_____ 15. A man who has been married is not likely to marry again.

EXERCISE 9-4 MAKING INFERENCES AND DRAWING CONCLUSIONS

Read the following passage and the statements that follow. Place a check mark next to the statements that are reasonable inferences or conclusions.

Issue: Police Techniques

August Vollmer was the chief of police of Berkeley, California, from 1905 to 1932. Vollmer's vision of policing was quite different from most of his contemporaries. He believed the police should be a "dedicated body of educated persons comprising a distinctive corporate entity with a prescribed code of behavior." He was critical of his contemporaries and they of him. San Francisco police administrator Charley Dullea, who later became president of the International Association of Chiefs of Police, refused to drive through Berkeley in protest against Vollmer. Fellow California police chiefs may have felt their opposition to Vollmer was justified, given his vocal and strong criticism of other California police departments. For example, Vollmer publicly referred to San Francisco cops as "morons," and in an interview with a newspaper reporter, he called Los Angeles cops "low grade mental defectives."

Because of his emphasis on education, professionalism, and administrative reform, Vollmer often is seen as the counterpart of London's Sir Robert Peel and is sometimes called the "father of modern American policing." Vollmer was decades ahead of his contemporaries, but he was not able to implement significant change in policing during his lifetime. It remained for Vollmer's students to implement change. For example, O.W. Wilson, who became chief of police of Chicago, promoted college education for police officers and wrote a book on police administration that reflected many of Vollmer's philosophies. It was adopted widely by police executives and used as a college textbook well into the 1960s.

Vollmer is credited with a number of innovations. He was an early adopter of the automobile for patrol and the use of radios in police cars. He recruited college-educated police officers. He developed and implemented a 3-year training curriculum for police officers, including classes in physics, chemistry, biology, physiology, anatomy, psychology, psychiatry, anthropology, and criminology. He developed a system of signal boxes for hailing police officers. He adopted the use of typewriters to fill out police reports and records, and officers received training in typing. He surveyed other police departments to gather information about their practices. Many of his initiatives have become common practice within contemporary police departments.

—Fagin, *Criminal Justice*, pp. 245–246

_____   1. Vollmer did not have a college degree.

_____   2. Most police officers of Vollmer's time had a limited education.

_____   3. Vollmer believed police should be held accountable for their actions.

_____   4. Sir Robert Peel dramatically changed policing procedures in England.

_____   5. Vollmer received support from most police officers on the street.

_____   6. Vollmer would support recent technological advances in policing.

_____   7. Police departments of Vollmer's time were run with a careful eye toward accuracy and fairness.

_____   8. Vollmer outlawed billy clubs.

9b   FACT AND OPINION

LEARNING OBJECTIVE 2

Distinguish fact from opinion.

When working with any source, readers and writers should try to determine whether the material is factual or an expression of opinion. **Facts** are statements that are true and can be verified. **Opinions** are statements that express feelings, attitudes, or beliefs and are neither true nor false. Following are examples of each:

Facts

1. Canada, the United States, and Mexico are all members of the North American Free Trade Agreement.
2. Facebook has become the world's most popular social networking site.

Opinions

1. Employers should be banned from spying on employees and reading their e-mail.
2. All immigration into the United States must be halted for a ten-year period.

Facts, when verified or taken from a reputable source, can be accepted and regarded as reliable information. Opinions, on the other hand, are not reliable sources of information and should be questioned and carefully evaluated. Look for evidence that supports the opinion and indicates that it is reasonable. For example, opinion 2 is written to sound like a fact, but look closely. Would everyone agree with this statement? Can it be disputed?

Some writers signal the reader when they are presenting an opinion. Watch for the following words and phrases:

according to	it is believed that	presumably
apparently	it is likely that	seemingly
in my opinion	one explanation is	this suggests
in my view	possibly	

In the following excerpt from a business textbook, notice how the author uses qualifying words and phrases (underlined), as well as direct quotations from social critics, to indicate opinions on the topic, "Are advertising and marketing necessary?"

Issue: Advertising and Ethics

Are Advertising and Marketing Necessary?

More than 50 years ago, the social critic Vance Packard wrote, "Large-scale efforts are being made, often with impressive success, to channel our unthinking habits, our purchasing decisions, and our thought processes by the use of insights gleaned from psychiatry and the social sciences." The economist John Kenneth Galbraith charged that radio and television are important tools to accomplish this manipulation of the masses. Because consumers don't need to be literate to use these media, repetitive and compelling communications can reach almost everyone. This criticism may be even more relevant to online communications, where a simple click delivers a world of information to us.

Many feel that marketers arbitrarily link products to desirable social attributes, fostering a materialistic society in which we are measured by what we own. One influential critic even argued that the problem is that we are not materialistic enough—that is, we do not sufficiently value goods for the utilitarian functions they deliver but instead focus on the irrational value of goods for what they symbolize. According to this view, for example, "Beer would be enough for us, without the additional promise that in drinking it we show ourselves to be manly, young at heart, or neighborly. A washing machine would be a useful machine to wash clothes rather than an indication that we are forward-looking or an object of envy to our neighbors."

—Michael R. Solomon, *Consumer Behavior*, p. 23

Other authors do just the opposite; they try to make opinions sound like facts, or they mix fact and opinion without making clear distinctions. This is particularly true in the case of **expert opinion**, which is the opinion of a recognized authority on a topic. Political commentators on Sunday news programs (sometimes called "pundits") represent expert opinion on politics, for example. Textbook authors, too, often offer expert opinion, as in the following statement from an American government text.

Ours is a complex system of justice. Sitting at the pinnacle of the judicial system is the Supreme Court, but its importance is often exaggerated.

—Lineberry, *Government in America*, p. 540

The author of this statement has reviewed the available evidence and is providing his expert opinion regarding what the evidence indicates about the Supreme Court. The reader is free to disagree and offer evidence to support an opposing view.

The essay "Can the World's Disappearing Species Be Saved from Poachers?", on page 189, uses expert opinion, as well: "Similarly, rhino horn powder is said to be more valuable than gold to Chinese consumers."

EXERCISE 9-5 DISTINGUISHING FACT AND OPINION

Read each of the following statements and identify whether it is fact (F), opinion (O), or expert opinion (EO).

_____ 1. Toyota is the world's largest automaker.

_____ 2. Apple Computers, already one of the world's most successful companies, will continue to be successful because of its history of innovation and product design.

_____ 3. Americans spend approximately $40 billion per year on diet aids, diet books, and diet foods.

_____ 4. The best way to read a book is on the Kindle Fire.

_____ 5. A capital good, as defined by economists, is a good bought by businesses to increase their productive resources.

_____ 6. The U.S. government is comprised of three branches: executive, legislative, and judicial.

_____ 7. Anthropologists believe that some native communities in the Americas practiced human sacrifice.

_____ 8. According to Dr. Elaine Feldman, a psychologist who specializes in anxiety management, deep breathing can greatly help people reduce their stress levels.

_____ 9. The finest novels in English history were written by Jane Austen.

_____ 10. The hammer and sickle are found on Russia's national flag.

EXERCISE 9-6 DISTINGUISHING FACT AND OPINION

Each of the following paragraphs contains both facts and opinions. Read each paragraph and label each sentence as fact (F), opinion (O), or expert opinion (EO).

A. Issue: Slavery and Freedom

[1]Harriet Tubman was born a slave in Maryland in 1820 and escaped to Philadelphia in 1849. [2]Her own escape presumably required tremendous courage, but that was just the beginning. [3]Through her work on the Underground Railroad, Harriet Tubman led more than 300 slaves to freedom. [4]During the Civil War, Tubman continued her efforts toward the abolition of slavery by working as a nurse and a spy for the Union forces. [5]Today, Americans of all races consider Harriet Tubman one of the most heroic figures in our country's history.

Sentences: 1. _____   2. _____   3. _____   4. _____   5. _____

B. Issue: Drugs and Addiction

[1]Those big stogies that we see celebrities and government figures smoking are nothing more than tobacco fillers wrapped in more tobacco. [2]Since 1993, cigar sales in the United States have increased dramatically, up nearly 124 percent between 1993 and 2007. [3]The fad, especially popular among young men and women, is fueled in part by the willingness of celebrities to be photographed puffing on a cigar. [4]It's also fueled by the fact that cigars cost much less than cigarettes

in most states. [5]Also, among some women, cigar smoking symbolizes being slightly outrageous and liberated. [6]According to a recent national survey, about 11 percent of Americans aged 18 to 25 had smoked a cigar in the past month.

—Donatelle, *Access to Health*, p. 386

Sentences: 1. ____ 2. ____ 3. ____ 4. ____ 5. ____ 6. ____

C. Issue: Cultural Similarities and Differences

[1]Some sociologists believe that if any nation deserves the "pro-family" label, it is Sweden. [2]In the past century, the Swedish state, in cooperation with labor, industry, and the feminist and other social movements, has provided money and services to support family life and the employment of women. [3]And, to a lesser degree, it has sought to eliminate gender inequality and laws and customs that reinforce women's secondary place in society. [4]As a result, wrote sociologist Joan Acker, "Swedish women enjoy public programs and economic guarantees that have made Sweden a model for women in other countries."

—Adapted from Thompson and Hickey, *Society in Focus: An Introduction to Sociology, 2010 Census Update.* Boston: Pearson Allyn & Bacon, c. 2012, p. 383. ISBN 0-205-18101-5

Sentences: 1. ____ 2. ____ 3. ____ 4. ____

9c   AUTHOR'S PURPOSE

**LEARNING OBJECTIVE 3
Identify the author's purpose.**

Writers have many different reasons or purposes for writing. Read the following statements and try to decide why each was written.

1. In 2011, about 17.5 million people traveled through the Chunnel, the tunnel that connects France and England. This averages to about 48,000 people per day.

2. *New Vegetable Sticks in Sensible Portions.* Finally, a snack made from real vegetables with no added sugar or fats. We lightly sauté the vegetables until they're crispy and crunchy, and then we package them in 100-calorie packets. Buy a box this week.

3. I don't like when people repeat themselves. I also do not like when they are redundant or repetitive, or when they repeat themselves.

4. To prevent yourself from being attacked by mosquitoes or ticks on a hike, be sure to use an insect repellent made with Deet.

Statement 1 was written to give information, 2 to persuade you to buy vegetable sticks, 3 to amuse you and make a comment on human behavior, and 4 to give advice.

In each of the examples, the writer's purpose is fairly clear, as it is in most textbooks (to present information), newspaper articles (to communicate local, national, or world events), and reference books (to compile facts). However, in many other types of writing—especially materials concerning controversial contemporary issues—writers have varied, sometimes less obvious, purposes. In these cases, the writer's purpose must be inferred.

Often a writer's purpose is to express an opinion directly or indirectly. The writer may also want to encourage the reader to think about a particular issue or problem. Writers achieve their purposes by manipulating and controlling what they say and how they say it.

EXERCISE 9-7 IDENTIFYING THE AUTHOR'S PURPOSE

Read each of the following statements. Then find the author's purpose for each statement in the box and write it in the space provided.

to persuade	to entertain	to inform
to advise	to criticize	

_____　1. When choosing your courses for next year, try to find a balance between required courses and electives that you will enjoy.

_____　2. I don't want to belong to any club that will accept me as a member. (Groucho Marx)

_____　3. Travelers to Saudi Arabia should be aware that non-Muslims are not permitted in the cities of Mecca and Medina.

_____　4. Now is the time to support gun-control legislation, before more innocent lives are lost to illegal firearms.

_____　5. The mayor's plan to limit the sizes of sugary soft drinks to a maximum of 16 ounces is simply ridiculous. It is an example of intrusive government at its worst.

9d　TONE

LEARNING OBJECTIVE 4
Evaluate tone.

The tone of a speaker's voice helps you interpret what he or she is saying. If the following sentence were spoken, the speaker's voice would tell you how to interpret it: "Would you mind closing the door?" In print you cannot tell whether the speaker is polite, insistent, or angry.

Just as a speaker's tone of voice tells how the speaker feels, a writer conveys a tone, or feeling, through his or her writing. **Tone** refers to the attitude or feeling a writer expresses about his or her subject. The tone of the article "Consequences of Social Class" (page 6) is informative. The author presents facts, research, and other evidence to support his thesis.

A writer may adopt a sentimental tone, an angry tone, a humorous tone, a sympathetic tone, an instructive tone, a persuasive tone, and so forth. Here are some examples of different tones. How does each make you feel?

- **Instructive**

  When purchasing a used car, let the buyer beware. Get a CarFax report that shows the vehicle's history, and ask the seller for a copy of the maintenance records, which will tell you how closely the owner has followed the recommended maintenance schedule.

- **Sympathetic**

  Each year, millions of women have miscarriages. My heart goes out to these strong women, who often suffer in silence.

- **Persuasive**

  For just 40 cents a day, you can sponsor a poor child in a developing country. Yes, you can make a difference in a child's life for only $12 per month. The question is: How can you afford *not* to contribute?

- **Humorous**

  There are two kinds of people in the world: Italians, and those who wish they were Italian.

- **Nostalgic**

  Oh, how I long for the simplicity of the 1980s: before everyone was glued to their computers or cell phones every minute of the day; before cable television offered hundreds of channels I cannot possibly watch; before everyone decided to become a singer, celebrity, or reality TV star.

In the first example, the writer offers advice in a straightforward, informative style. In the second, the writer wants you to feel sympathy for women who have miscarried; she encourages this sympathy by describing what these women go through. In the third example, the writer tries to convince the reader to donate to a worthy cause. In the fourth example, the writer charms with a witty observation, and in the fifth example, the writer fondly reminisces about a simpler time before technology played such a prominent role in society.

To identify an author's tone, pay particular attention to descriptive language and connotations (see section 2c). Ask yourself: "How does the author feel about the subject, and how are these feelings revealed?" It is sometimes difficult to find the right word to describe the author's tone. Table 9.1 on the next page lists words that are often used to describe tone. Use this list to help you identify tone. If any of these words are unfamiliar, check their meanings in a dictionary.

TABLE 9.1 WORDS FREQUENTLY USED TO DESCRIBE TONE

abstract	condemning	formal	joyful	reverent
absurd	condescending	frustrated	loving	righteous
amused	cynical	gentle	malicious	sarcastic
angry	depressing	grim	melancholic	satiric
apathetic	detached	hateful	mocking	sensational
arrogant	disapproving	humorous	nostalgic	serious
assertive	distressed	impassioned	objective	solemn
awestruck	docile	incredulous	obsequious	sympathetic
bitter	earnest	indignant	optimistic	tragic
caustic	excited	indirect	outraged	uncomfortable
celebratory	fanciful	informative	pathetic	vindictive
cheerful	farcical	intimate	persuasive	worried
comic	flippant	ironic	pessimistic	
compassionate	forgiving	irreverent	playful	

EXERCISE 9-8 RECOGNIZING TONE

Read each of the following statements. Then choose a word from the box that describes the statement's tone, and write it in the space provided.

optimistic	angry	admiring	cynical/bitter
excited	humorous	nostalgic	disapproving
formal	informative	sarcastic	

_____ 1. Cecelia lets her young children stay awake until all hours of the night. Doesn't she realize that growing children need sleep and a predictable schedule?

_____ 2. The ostrich is the world's largest bird, the capybara is the world's largest rodent, and the tarantula is the world's largest spider.

_____ 3. Sir Walter Scott was not only a gifted novelist; he was also a kind, generous man who was widely respected and loved.

_____ 4. Every time I see figs, I think about the fig tree in my grandfather's garden.

_____ 5. I avoid clichés like the plague, and I eschew obfuscation.

_____ 6. What selfless civil servants politicians are! While everyone else struggles in a difficult economy, they vote themselves large pay raises and extended vacations.

_____ 7. The success of a newly launched news magazine, The Week, is proof that print magazines can survive and flourish in the Internet era.

_____ 8. Every time a woman asks me what I do for a living, I wonder if she is trying to figure out how much money I make.

_____ 9. Finally, after years of waiting, I am taking a cruise to Alaska!

_____ 10. Mr. and Mrs. Dane LeFever request the honor of your presence at the wedding celebration of their daughter, Sandra Anne, on Wednesday, December 5. Kindly RSVP at your earliest convenience.

EXERCISE 9-9 RECOGNIZING TONE

Read each of the following statements, paying particular attention to the tone. Then write a sentence that describes the tone. Prove your point by listing some of the words that reveal the author's feelings.

1. No one says that wind power is risk-free. There are dangers involved in all methods of producing energy. It is true that wind turbines can harm or kill birds. But science and experience have shown us the wind power can be generated cleanly and efficiently. Nuclear power is at least as safe, or safer than, many other means of generating power.

   _____

   _____

2. The state of our schools is shocking. Their hallways are littered with paper and other garbage. Their restrooms are dirty and unsafe for children. The playgrounds are frequented by drug dealers and other unsavory people. Don't we pay school taxes to give our children a safe place to learn and grow?

   _____

   _____

3. I am a tired homeowner. I am tired of mowing the lawn. I'm sick of raking leaves. I'm thoroughly worn out by cleaning and dusting. I am exhausted by leaky faucets, unpainted rooms, and messy basements.

   _____

   _____

4. Cross-country skis have heel plates of different shapes and materials. They may be made of metal, plastic, or rubber. Be sure that they are tacked on the ski right where the heel of your boot will fall. They will keep snow from collecting under your foot and offer some stability.

_____

_____

9e FIGURATIVE LANGUAGE AND IRONY

LEARNING OBJECTIVE 5
Interpret figurative language and irony.

Figurative language and irony are both ways of using words to suggest senses beyond their strict meaning.

Understanding Figurative Language

Figurative language is a way of describing something that makes sense on an imaginative level but not on a literal or factual level. Many common expressions are figurative:

> It was raining cats and dogs.
>
> His head is as hard as a rock.
>
> I was so nervous, I was sweating like a pig.

In each of these expressions, two unlike objects are compared on the basis of some quality they have in common. Take, for example, Hamlet's statement "I will speak daggers to her, but use none." Here the poet (William Shakespeare) is comparing the features of daggers (sharp, pointed, dangerous, harmful) with something that can be used like daggers—words.

Figurative language is striking, often surprising, sometimes shocking. These reactions are created by the dissimilarity of the two objects being compared. To find the similarity and understand the figurative expression, focus on connotative (the feelings and emotions that a word suggests) rather than literal meanings. For example, in reading the lines

> A sea
> Harsher than granite
>
> —Ezra Pound

from an Ezra Pound poem, you must think about the characteristics of granite, which is a type of stone: hardness, toughness, impermeability. Then you can see that the lines mean that the sea is rough and resistant.

Figurative expressions, sometimes called **figures of speech**, communicate and emphasize relationships that cannot be communicated through literal meaning. For example, Jonathan Swift's statement, "She wears her clothes as if they were thrown on by a pitchfork," creates a stronger image and conveys a more meaningful description than the statement "She dressed sloppily."

The four most common types of figurative expressions are similes, metaphors, personification, and symbols. **Similes** make a comparison explicit by using the word *like* or *as*. **Metaphors** directly equate two objects without using the word like or as. **Personification** is a technique in which human characteristics are given to objects or ideas. For instance, to say "My old computer moans and groans each morning when I turn it on" gives the computer human characteristics of moaning and groaning. A **symbol** is something that stands for something else. For instance, the eagle is often considered a symbol of the United States.

- **Similes**
  She dressed like a rag doll.
  Sam was as happy as a clam.
- **Metaphors**
  Jane wears her heart on her sleeve.
  My life is a junkyard of broken dreams.
- **Personification**
  The earthquake hath swallowed all my future plans.
  Nature abhors a peaceful man.

EXERCISE 9-10 USING FIGURATIVE LANGUAGE

Study the figurative expression in each of the following statements. Then, in the space provided, explain the meaning of each.

1. Hope is like a feather, ready to blow away.

   _____

   _____

2. Once Alma realized she had made an embarrassing error, the blush spread across her face like spilled paint.

   _____

   _____

3. A powerboat, or any other sports vehicle, devours money.

   _____

4. Sally's skin was like a smooth, highly polished apple.

   _____

5. Upon hearing the news, I took shears and shredded my dreams.

   _____

Understanding Irony

Irony is the use of language to suggest or imply a difference between the appearance of things and how they really are. Irony often refers to the use of words to express an idea that is unexpected, unintended, or opposite of the words' literal meaning. There are two common types of irony: situational and verbal.

Situational irony refers to an incongruence (or lack of fit) between what is expected or intended and what occurred. For example, if an ambulance driver has a heart attack while driving a patient to the hospital, it is said to be ironic. Or if you laugh as someone who spills a drink and while doing so, you spill your own drink, it is ironic.

Verbal irony occurs when what a speaker or writers says is different from what he or she means. For example, if someone says, "I am so glad my computer crashed; it will make my life so much easier" you know that the speaker really means the opposite. Or if your instructor says, "I hope no one will mind that I am postponing the quiz for today," you know that she really meant she knows everyone will be pleased the quiz is postponed.

EXERCISE 9-11 CREATING EXAMPLES OF IRONY

Working with a classmate, create several examples of both verbal and situational irony. Share your findings with the class.

The critical-thinking skills discussed thus far in this chapter (*making inferences and drawing conclusions, distinguishing fact and opinion, identifying purpose, understanding tone,* and *making sense of figurative language and irony*) are all essential to understanding the basic meaning of a reading selection. Beyond these skills is another set of critical-thinking tools that will help you analyze and evaluate what you read, whether textbooks, Web sites, or magazine articles about contemporary issues. These advanced critical-thinking skills include detecting bias; evaluating data and evidence; examining the quantity, relevance, and timeliness of information; and identifying propaganda.

9f   BIAS

LEARNING OBJECTIVE 6
Identify bias.

Bias refers to an author's partiality, inclination toward a particular viewpoint, or prejudice. A writer is *biased* if he or she takes one side of a controversial issue and does not recognize opposing viewpoints. Perhaps the best example of bias can be found in advertising. A magazine advertisement for a new car, for instance, describes only positive, marketable features—the ad does not recognize the car's limitations or faults.

Sometimes writers are direct and forthright in expressing their bias; other times a writer's bias might be hidden and discovered only through careful analysis. Read the following comparison of organic farming and conventional farming. The authors express a favorable attitude toward organic farming and a negative one toward conventional farming while also recognizing reality that they find frustrating. Notice, in particular, the underlined words and phrases.

Issue: Environmental Issues

Organic Farming vs. Conventional Farming

Organic farming is carried out without the use of synthetic fertilizers or pesticides. Organic farmers (and gardeners) use manure from farm animals for fertilizer, and they rotate other crops with legumes to restore nitrogen to the soil. They control insects by planting a variety of crops, alternating the use of fields. (A corn pest has a hard time surviving during the year that its home field is planted in soybeans.) Organic farming is also less energy intensive. According to a study by the Center for the Biology of Natural Systems at Washington University, comparable conventional farms used 2.3 times as much energy as organic farms. Production on organic farms was 10% lower, but costs were comparably lower. Organic farms require 12% more labor than conventional ones. Human labor is a renewable resource, though, whereas petroleum is not. Compared with conventional methods, organic farming uses less energy and leads to healthier soils.

In addition to organic practices, sustainable agriculture involves buying local products and using local services when possible, thus avoiding the cost of transportation while getting fresher goods and strengthening the economy of the local community. Sustainable agriculture promotes independent farmers and ranchers producing good food and making a good living while protecting the environment.

Conventional agriculture can result in severe soil erosion and is the source of considerable water pollution. No doubt we should practice organic farming to the limits of our ability to do so. But we should not delude ourselves. Abrupt banning of synthetic fertilizers and pesticides would likely lead to a drastic drop in food production.

—Hill, McCreary, and Kolb, *Chemistry for Changing Times*, p. 634

To identify bias, use the following suggestions:

1. **Analyze connotative meanings.** Do you encounter a large number of positive or negative terms in the reading selection?

2. **Notice descriptive language.** What impression is created?

3. **Analyze the tone.** The author's tone often provides important clues.

4. **Look for opposing viewpoints.**

EXERCISE 9-12 DETECTING BIAS

Read each of the following statements and place a check mark in front of each one that reveals bias.

_____ 1. Killing innocent animals so that wealthy women can wear fur coats is a crime against life.

_____ 2. Organic chemistry studies substances that contain carbon, the element essential to life.

_____ 3. While most Americans identify themselves as either Republicans or Democrats, an increasing number of U.S. citizens are defining themselves as Independent.

_____ 4. There's no better way to teach responsibility to a children than giving them daily chores to complete.

_____ 5. Without a doubt, the islands of the Caribbean are the most beautiful in the world.

EXERCISE 9-13 DETECTING BIAS

Read the following passages and underline words and/or phrases that reveal the author's bias.

Issue: Advertising and Ethics

The only essential ingredient in shampoo is a detergent of some sort. What, then, is all the advertising about? You can buy shampoos that are fruit or herb scented, protein enriched, and pH balanced or made especially for oily or dry hair. Shampoos for oily, normal, and dry hair seem to differ primarily in the concentration of the detergent. Shampoo for oily hair is more concentrated; shampoo for dry hair is more dilute.

—Hill, McCreary, and Kolb, *Chemistry for Changing Times*, p. 671

Issue: Environmental Issues

From its extraction to its various end uses, coal presents more environmental challenges than any other energy sources. Underground coal mining is a very hazardous occupation due to the potential for cave-ins, flooding, dust, and gas explosions. In 2010, mining accidents in the United States killed 48 coal miners, and accidents in China killed more than 2,400 miners. Even without accidents, thousands of underground coal miners suffer from respiratory diseases caused by inhaling coal dust.

Mining activities also have a direct effect on the environment. Mine tailings, the rock and debris from mining operations, often contain high concentrations of sulfide. When exposed to oxygen, these sulfides are transformed to sulfuric acid, which runs off into nearby streams, where it harms fish and other aquatic organisms.

Surface mining destroys the terrestrial ecosystems above the coal seams. The coal-mining industry in the United States has received especially harsh criticism for the environmental impact of mountaintop removal. In West Virginia and Kentucky, overburden from mountaintop removal has permanently buried more than 700 miles of mountain streams, thereby affecting wildlife, flooding nearby communities, and degrading water quality far downstream.

The exhaust and fly ash from coal fires contain a number of toxic chemicals that are harmful to many organisms, including humans. Fine particulate soot from coal fires can cause respiratory distress. In addition, coal usually contains mercury, which accumulated in the wetlands where it was formed. When coal is burned, this mercury is released into the atmosphere. Concentrations of mercury in streams and lakes near coal-fired power plants are often several times higher than normal. Eventually, this mercury accumulates in the tissues of animals, including humans, where it can cause a number of serious health problems, including neurological disorders. Fly ash also contains high concentrations of mercury, which makes it complicated to dispose of.

—Adapted from Christensen, *The Environment and You*, pp. 463–464

9g   EVALUATING THE RELIABILITY OF DATA AND EVIDENCE

LEARNING OBJECTIVE 7
Evaluate data and evidence.

Many writers who express opinions or state viewpoints provide readers with data or evidence to support their ideas. Your task as a critical reader is to weigh and evaluate the quality of this evidence. You must examine the evidence and assess its adequacy. You should be concerned with two factors: (1) the type of evidence being presented, and (2) the relevance of that evidence.

Types of Evidence

Various types of evidence include:

- personal experience or observation
- expert opinion
- research citation
- statistical data
- examples, descriptions of particular events, or illustrative situations
- analogies (comparisons with similar situations)
- historical documentation
- quotations
- description

Each type of evidence must be weighed in relation to the statement it supports. Acceptable evidence should directly, clearly, and indisputably support the case or issue in question.

EXERCISE 9-14 EVALUATING TYPES OF EVIDENCE

Refer to the article "Consequences of Social Class," on pages 6-9. For each of the following paragraphs, identify the type(s) of evidence the author provides.

1. Paragraph 2 _____

2. Paragraph 7 _____

3. Paragraph 11 _____

4. Paragraph 13 _____

EXERCISE 9-15 IDENTIFYING TYPES OF EVIDENCE

For each of the following statements, discuss the type or types of evidence that you would need in order to support and evaluate the statement. Answers will vary.

1. Individuals must accept primary responsibility for the health and safety of their babies.

2. Apologizing is often seen as a sign of weakness, especially among men.

3. There has been a steady increase in illegal immigration over the past 50 years.

4. More college women than college men agree that marijuana should be legalized.

5. Car advertisements sell fantasy experiences, not the means of transportation.

Evaluating Reliability

Three overall factors point to reliable, trustworthy writing:

- Quantity of information
- Relevance of the information
- Timeliness of the information

Quantity of Information

As a general rule, the more evidence writers provide to support the thesis statement and main ideas of the selection, the more convincing their writing is likely to be. Suppose an article includes the following thesis statement:

> Married people lead healthier, happier lives than unmarried people.

Now suppose the writer includes just one fact to support this statement: "Research shows that most married people report higher levels of happiness than unmarried people do." Does this one piece of evidence provide full support for the thesis statement? Most likely, you would argue that it does not. You may know plenty of single people who are very happy and many married people who are miserable.

Now consider an article that supports the thesis statement with the following evidence:

- Married people have a larger support network that helps them stay healthy.
- Both married women and married men earn more money than their single co-workers.
- Research has shown that married people live longer.
- Married people report lower levels of stress and depression than single people do.

Each of these supporting pieces of evidence on its own may not be enough to help the writer prove his or her thesis statement, but as a whole they greatly strengthen the argument.

Relevance of Information

Supporting evidence must be relevant to be convincing. That is, it must be closely connected to the thesis statement and to the subject under discussion. It is easy to be distracted by interesting pieces of information that are not relevant to the writer's thesis statement.

Consider the discussion of marriage and happiness above. For example, it is interesting that 48% of Americans are married, but this fact is not relevant to the thesis statement "Married people live healthier, happier lives than those who are single." When you encounter irrelevant information, ask yourself: "Why has the writer included this? Is it intended to steer my thinking in a specific direction, away from the topic at hand?"

Timeliness of Information

When evaluating the information provided by the writer, check how recent the examples, statistics, data, and research are. In general, more current facts, figures, and research are better and more reliable. In the computer age, new information and knowledge are being generated at an astonishing rate, so articles published as recently as two years ago may be out of date, and the information they contain may be obsolete. Think about it this way: Look at how quickly technology becomes outdated. This year's smart phone will be replaced next year by an even faster, even better smart phone. In the same way, advances in many areas of study leave older information in the dust.

Keep in mind, though, that some things do not change. The components of the human body are the same today as they were 200 years ago. The principles of mathematics have not changed and are not likely to change. The U.S. Constitution, great works of literature, and other important documents are as valid today as when they were written.

EXERCISE 9-16 EVALUATING QUALITY AND RELEVANCE OF INFORMATION

A magazine article has the following thesis statement: "It has been proven that animal companions, sometimes known as pets, have many benefits for their owners." A list of possible statements to support this thesis sentence follows. Place a check mark next to each statement that is relevant to the thesis statement.

_____ 1. The U.S. Center for Disease Control, an important source of medical information in the United States, has stated that owning a pet can decrease your blood pressure and cholesterol levels.

_____ 2. Men tend to prefer having dogs as pets, while women seem to prefer owning cats.

_____ 3. Sadly, many animal shelters in the United States are underfunded and desperately in need of donations.

_____ 4. The National Institute of Health has reported widespread benefits of pet ownership for older people.

_____ 5. More than half of all U.S. households have a companion animal.

_____ 6. A growing number of studies have suggested that children who grow up in a home with a "furred animal" are less likely to develop allergies or asthma.

_____ 7. On the dating scene, many singles have reported that their pets have helped them strike up conversations with the opposite sex.

_____ 8. In general, people who own pets report less depression than people who do not own pets.

_____ 9. There are more than 51 million dogs, 56 million cats, and 45 million birds in U.S. households.

_____ 10. One study showed that stockbrokers with high blood pressure who adopted a cat or dog had lower blood pressure readings in stressful situations than people without pets.

EXERCISE 9-17 EVALUATING TIMELINESS OF INFORMATION

Several types of information are provided below. Place a check mark next to each type of information that is not likely to change (that is, cases in which it is acceptable to use an older source of information).

_____ 1. A mathematics textbook teaching students how to add and subtract

_____ 2. A manual teaching you how to use a computer

_____ 3. A diagram of the parts of the human brain

_____ 4. A history textbook explaining the pilgrims' reasons for leaving England

_____ 5. A medical book that suggests the use of leeches to reduce a fever

9h   PROPAGANDA TECHNIQUES

LEARNING OBJECTIVE 9
Recognize propaganda techniques.

Propaganda is the expression of ideas and information deliberately intended to persuade or influence the reader's opinion. It is intended to help or damage the reader's view toward a person, group, idea, cause, or movement. Propaganda often appeals to a reader's emotions and is common in many sources, including advertising. There are seven types of propaganda that are commonly used.

Commonly Used Types of Propaganda

- **Name-calling.** This technique uses negative words to create an unfavorable impression of the subject. For example, if one candidate for a political office calls his competitor an uncaring, money-grabbing opportunist, the candidate is attempting to discredit the opponent using negative language. It is often a substitute for or an evasion of presenting factual evidence. The candidate, to be fair and believable, needs to present reasons and evidence to support his or her name-calling.

- **Glittering generalities.** A generality is a broad, sweeping statement not supported by facts or evidence. A product may be advertised as the "best, most effective over-the-counter pain control." These general terms do not say why or for whom it is best, how it was determined to be the best, and for what types of pain it is the best. Critical thinkers look beyond the statement for details, proof and evidence.

- **Bandwagon.** Often called "join the crowd," this technique appeals to people's desire to do what is popular and follow the crowd—to conform and do what everyone else is doing. A commercial that advertises that

Brand X is the most popular brand of toothpaste is using this technique, arguing that if most people are using this brand, they couldn't all be wrong. Critical readers must go beyond the claim and search for evidence that this brand truly meets their needs and performs to their expectations.

- **Plain folks.** Also called the "common man appeal," this technique attempts to convince the audience that common, everyday people hold the view or take a particular action. A political figure may adjust his style of dress to suit the part of the country in which he or she is campaigning so as look like and fit in with common citizens.

- **Transfer.** Also known as association, this method links something readers are expected to value or respect, such as a flag, or dislike and hate, such as a Swastika symbol, with another item to which the writer hopes to convince the reader to either accept or reject. For example, a politician often stands in front of an American flag, hoping the audience's respect for the flag will transfer to him or her.

- **Testimonial.** A respected person is used in this method to endorse a product, policy, or point of view. You may see a well-known sports star endorsing drinking milk, for example. Critical thinkers should ask whether the well-known person is an expert or authority on the product or issue at hand.

- **Card stacking.** Card stacking involves making an argument by presenting only the facts that support a viewpoint and omitting facts that do not support it. A writer arguing for stronger gun control laws may present only information about deaths resulting from handguns, but fail to discuss citizens' needs to protect themselves, for example.

SUMMARY OF LEARNING OBJECTIVES

Objective 1 Make inferences and draw conclusions.	An *inference* is a reasoned guess about what you don't know based on what you do know from the facts and information presented in a text or image. Combining inference and prior knowledge allows you to draw conclusions. To make accurate inferences and conclusions, understand the literal meaning of the reading selection, pay attention to details (ask what is unusual or striking about them and why they have been included), add up the facts, be alert to clues, and consider the writer's purpose. Once you have made an inference, verify that it is accurate.
Objective 2 Distinguish fact from opinion.	A *fact* is a statement that can be verified (proven to be true or false). An *opinion* expresses feelings, attitudes, and beliefs, and it is neither true nor false. Look for evidence that supports an opinion and indicates that it is reasonable. By distinguishing statements of fact from opinions, you will know which ideas to accept and which to verify or question.

SUMMARY OF LEARNING OBJECTIVES *continued*

Objective 3 Identify the author's purpose.	Writers have different *purposes* for writing (for example, to inform, to persuade, to entertain, or to provide an opinion). Recognizing a writer's purpose will help you grasp meaning more quickly and evaluate his or her work.
Objective 4 Evaluate tone.	*Tone* refers to the attitude or feeling a writer expresses about his or subject. To determine tone, pay particular attention to descriptive language and connotations (see Table 9.1, p. 238, for a summary of tone words). Recognizing tone will help you evaluate what a writer is attempting to accomplish through his or her writing.
Objective 5 Interpret figurative language and irony.	*Figurative language* is a way of describing something that makes sense on an imaginative level but not a literal or factual level. Recognizing and understanding figurative language helps you better understand how a writer views his or her subject. *Similes* make comparisons by using the words *like* or *as*. *Metaphors* make a comparison without using the word *like* or *as*. *Personification* attributes human characteristics to ideas and objects. A *symbol* is something that stands for something else. *Irony* is the use of language to suggest or imply a difference between the appearance of things and how they really are.
Objective 6 Identify bias.	*Bias* refers to a writer's partiality, inclination toward or against a particular viewpoint, or prejudice. A writer is biased when he or she takes one side of a controversial issue and does not recognize opposing viewpoints. Sometimes bias is overt; other times, it is subtle. To identify bias, analyze connotations and notice descriptive language. Analyze tone and look for opposing viewpoints, especially in readings that discuss controversial issues. Recognizing tone will help you evaluate whether the author is providing objective, complete information or selectively presenting information that furthers his or her purpose.
Objective 7 Evaluate data and evidence.	Types of *evidence* include personal experience or observation, expert opinion, research citations, statistical data, examples, particular events, illustrative situations, analogies, historical documentation, quotations, and descriptions. Acceptable evidence should directly, clearly, and indisputably support the case or issue in question. Three factors point to reliable, trustworthy writing: 1. the author provides sufficient support for his or her point. 2. the author provides relevant information. 3. the author provides timely information (recent examples, statistics, data, and research). By evaluating the quantity, relevance, and timeliness of information, you can determine how reliable a source is.
Objective 8 Recognize propaganda techniques.	*Propaganda techniques* include name-calling, glittering generalities, bandwagon, plain folks, transfer, testimonial, and card stacking.

10 Writing Essays and Documented Papers

If you can write paragraphs, you can write an essay. An essay is simply a group of paragraphs about a common subject and a main point. Essay writing does not require high levels of creativity or special talent. If you can write single paragraphs, then you can group several paragraphs together to form an essay. An essay need not be long or complicated; it can have as few as three or four paragraphs. However, writing an essay does take time, planning, and organization. Some essays, especially those required in a variety of academic disciplines, are longer and require that you consult sources and integrate information from them into your essay. The purpose of this chapter is to help you plan and organize an essay and to show you how to use and document sources you may consult while writing.

WRITING ESSAYS

10a THE STRUCTURE OF AN ESSAY

LEARNING OBJECTIVE 1
Understand the structure of essays.

An **essay** is a group of paragraphs that are all about one subject. Writing an essay allows you the opportunity to expand your ideas beyond the scope of a single paragraph. It allows you to connect and develop ideas in order to explain and support a larger point. Like a paragraph, an essay contains one key point. This is called a **thesis statement**, and it is similar to the topic sentence in a paragraph but addresses a broader, more complex subject. Just as the supporting details in a paragraph relate to the topic sentence, the paragraphs in an essay explain and support the thesis statement. Signal words and sentences are used in an essay to connect the ideas in the paragraphs.

An essay, then, introduces an idea, states it, explains it, and draws a conclusion about it. Most essays begin with an **introductory paragraph** that states the subject of the essay. It also states the key point the essay will make in the thesis statement. **Supporting paragraphs** contain ideas that explain the when, where, and how of the key point. An essay usually has two or more of these paragraphs, which are linked by signal words and sentences. The **concluding paragraph** ties all the ideas in the essay together in relation to the thesis statement. The chart on the next page shows the organization of an essay.

The following essay shows where each of these essential elements appears; read it and study the annotations.

When a Home Is Not a Home

The good news is that mobile homes offer affordable housing for people who want to own their own house but cannot afford the substantial down payment a free-standing house requires. The bad news is that America discriminates against mobile homes and their owners. Despite its advantages, numerous barriers stand in the way of mobile home ownership.

Did you know that if you purchase a piece of property and purchase a mobile home, your local government may not let you place your home on your property? Local zoning laws severely restrict placement of mobile homes. Why this happens leads to the issue of discrimination. People associate mobile homes with unruly children, beer cans on the lawn, and rusted-out, abandoned cars. The fact that many solid citizens live in mobile homes and more would if laws didn't prohibit them does not enter the picture.

A second type of discrimination is financial. Home buyers need every break they can get. But loans for mobile homes are treated differently from those for permanent homes. The loan rates are usually two or three points higher, and government agency financing is still difficult to obtain as well. Unfortunately, all these disadvantages are tied to the image of mobile home buyers. They are unfairly thought of as unreliable people who are poor financial risks.

What does America have against mobile homes? The answer is rooted in discriminatory attitudes toward mobile home owners.

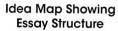

Idea Map Showing Essay Structure

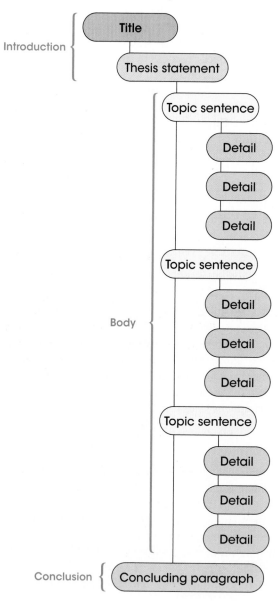

Introduction
- Title
- Thesis statement

Body
- Topic sentence
  - Detail
  - Detail
  - Detail
- Topic sentence
  - Detail
  - Detail
  - Detail
- Topic sentence
  - Detail
  - Detail
  - Detail

Conclusion
- Concluding paragraph

Note: Number of paragraphs will vary.

10b   PREWRITING: GENERATING AND ORGANIZING IDEAS AND PLANNING YOUR ESSAY

LEARNING OBJECTIVE 2
Prewrite to generate and organize ideas and plan your essay.

Writing an effective essay requires thought and planning. Use the following prewriting strategies to help you produce a well-written essay.

Choosing Your Topic

When your instructor gives you an assignment, you may not like the topic, but at least a good part of topic selection and narrowing has been done for you. When your instructor allows you to choose your own topic, you have to brainstorm for ideas and explore possible topics using prewriting. Use the following suggestions to help you choose an appropriate, effective, and workable topic.

Tips for Choosing an Appropriate, Effective, and Workable Topic

- **Take time to think about your choice.** Don't grab the first topic you come upon. Instead, think it through and weigh its pros and cons. It is often helpful to think of several topics and then choose the one you feel you are best prepared to write about.
- **Choose a topic that interests you.** You will feel more like writing about it and will find you have more to say.
- **Write about something familiar.** Select a topic you know a fair amount about. Otherwise, you will have to research your topic in the library or online. Your experience and knowledge of a familiar topic will provide the content of your essay.
- **Use your writing journal as a source for ideas.**
- **Discuss possible topics with a friend or classmate.** These conversations may help you discover worthwhile topics.

Table 10.1 on page 256 lists additional sources of ideas for essay topics.

EXERCISE 10-1   BRAINSTORMING TOPICS

Make a list of five possible topics you could use to write a two- to three-page, double-spaced essay.

Generating Ideas

Once you have chosen a working topic, the next step is to prewrite to generate ideas about it. This step will help you determine whether the topic you have selected is usable. It will also provide you with a list of ideas you can use in

TABLE 10.1 SOURCES OF IDEAS FOR TOPICS

SOURCES OF IDEAS	EXAMPLES
Your daily life. Pay attention to events you attend, activities you participate in, and routines you follow.	*Attending a sporting event may suggest topics about professional athletes' salaries, sports injuries, or violence in sports.*
Your college classes. Class lectures and discussions as well as reading assignments may give you ideas for topics.	*A class discussion in sociology about prejudice and discrimination may suggest you write about racial or ethnic identities, stereotypes, or types of discrimination (age, gender, weight, etc.).*
Your job. Your responsibilities, your boss, your co-workers, and your customers are all sources of ideas.	*Watching a family with wild, misbehaving children throwing food and annoying other customers in a restaurant may prompt you to write about restaurant policies, child rearing, or rude and annoying behavior.*
The media. Radio, television, movies, newspapers, magazines, and online sources all contain hundreds of ideas for a topic each day.	*A commercial for a weight-loss product may suggest an essay on society's emphasis on thinness or the unrealistic expectations for body image presented in commercials.*

planning and developing your essay. If you have trouble generating ideas about a topic, consider changing topics. Here are four methods for generating ideas. (See pp. 25–27 in Chapter 2 for a detailed review of each.)

1. **Freewriting.** Write nonstop for a specified time, recording all the ideas that come to mind on the topic.
2. **Brainstorming.** Write a list of all ideas that come to mind about a specific topic.
3. **Questioning.** Write a list of questions about a given topic.
4. **Diagraming.** Draw a diagram showing possible subtopics into which your topic could be divided.

When a student, Ted Sawchuck, was assigned a two-page paper on a topic of his choice, he decided to write about online social networking sites. In this chapter, we will follow Ted as he works through the various stages of the writing process, and we will see his final essay on p. 288. To generate ideas, Ted used brainstorming and wrote the following list of ideas:

Sample Student Brainstorming

Social Networking Sites

Keep tabs on and connect with friends
Create your own profile—describe yourself as you like
Profiles aren't necessarily true or accurate

Receive requests from people who want to friend you
People date online
People cheat on spouses through online relationships
Employers check applicants' Facebook sites
Unless blocked, private information can be seen by strangers
High school students use them too
Facebook and MySpace are popular ones
What did people do before these sites were available?

EXERCISE 10-2 PREWRITING

Select one of the topics you listed in Exercise 10-1. Use freewriting, brainstorming, questioning, or branching to generate ideas about the topic.

Narrowing Your Topic

Avoid working with a topic that is either too broad or too narrow. If your topic is *too narrow*, you will find you don't have enough to write about. If it is *too broad*, you will have too much to say, which will create several related problems:

- You will tend to write in generalities.
- You will not be able to explore each idea in detail.
- You will probably wander from topic to topic.
- You will become unfocused.

It is difficult to know if your topic is too broad, but here are a few warning signals:

- You feel overwhelmed when you try to think about the topic.
- You don't know where to start.
- You feel as if you are going in circles with ideas.
- You don't know where to stop.

You can use the ideas you generate during brainstorming, freewriting, questioning, or branching to help narrow your topic. One or more of those ideas may be a more manageable topic.

Often, more than one round of narrowing is necessary. You may need to reduce a topic several times by dividing it into smaller and smaller subtopics. You can do this by using one of the prewriting techniques again, or you can use a simple diagram to help you. After studying his brainstorming, Ted decided to write about online relationships. The following diagram shows how he further narrowed the topic of online relationships.

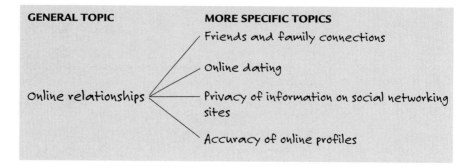

In this way, he wound up with several manageable topics related to online relationships to choose from. Finally, he decided to write about online dating relationships.

A question many students ask is, "How do I know when to stop narrowing?" For an essay, you will need at least three or four main points to support your thesis. Make sure that you have at least this number and that you can support each one with adequate detail. If you cannot do this, you'll know you have narrowed too far.

EXERCISE 10-3   NARROWING TOPICS

Working with a classmate, generate ideas and then narrow one topic you chose for Exercises 10-1 and 10-2. Continue narrowing each one until you find a topic about which you could write a five- to seven-paragraph essay.

Grouping Ideas to Discover a Thesis Statement

Some students think they should be able to sit down and write a thesis statement. But a thesis statement very rarely just springs into a writer's mind: it evolves and, in fact, may change during the process of prewriting, grouping ideas, drafting, and revising. This section will show you how to draft a thesis statement and how to polish it into a focused statement.

Once you have narrowed your topic and you know what you want to write about, the next step is to group or connect your ideas to form a thesis. Let's see how Ted produced a thesis following these steps. First, he chose to do freewriting about his topic of online dating to discover more ideas about it. His freewriting is shown below. Read his freewriting now before you continue with this section. As you will see, he wrote many ideas, far more than he needed, but that gave him choices.

Sample Student Freewriting

I use Facebook, a popular social networking site, to keep tabs on what my friends do, buy, and feel. Facebook showed me when my friend who'd launched a Facebook crusade to get back his girlfriend left her for good, that my sociology of gender prof is still up at 3 a.m. and the journalism student I'm still crushing on is also a fan of Green Day. I upload videos and post links. It's become an essential part of my life and an essential part of my relationships.

Facebook owns the college crowd because from its September 2004 launch in a Harvard dorm room until September 2006, you needed a .edu address to join. College students made the site their own community, and there was a sense that this was our world even though there's no real way to prevent nonstudents with .edu addresses from joining. The first sign of nonstudents entering what was increasingly seen as a walled community occurred in May 2006 when employers were added as available networks, followed by Facebook opening to the public in September that year.

At the University of Maryland, the dating process goes like this:

1. Get someone's name.
2. Look the person up on Facebook.
3. Use that information to decide how to proceed.

A Facebook search is the first thing I do when I meet someone and she sets off those neurons that make me hum "Maybe it's love." A Facebook page will tell me her age, indicate whether or not she's taken, and give me a decent idea (if the profile is not locked) of what image she's trying to present. Note that I don't trust Facebook to tell me who people are—merely who they want to show people they are. I look through photos and see what they value enough to show me. I check posted links, because what someone thinks is worth sharing is another window into who she is.

My first high school girlfriend couldn't even type when we started dating. She eventually got used to instant messaging, but was really slow for a year or two. After that, every relationship I had was conducted at least partially over instant messaging and e-mail at first, and then via text message later.

I e-mailed and instant messaged with romantic interests, eventually meeting a girl named Sunshine in a public chat room, which then were full of actual people instead of the ad-bots that populate them today. We talked via instant messaging for five years with the complete truthfulness you save for someone you're never going to meet in person, and fell in love. We tried to do distance, which is like feeding your heart a subsistence diet, and managed to hold it together with phone calls, instant messages, webcam chats and the occasional bus trip—17 hours one way. The relationship didn't work out, but technology made it possible. Although for most of our relationship Sunshine was pixels on a screen, she's still the standard by which I judge everyone I date.

I met Maggie at a campus newspaper meeting. After we took a liking to each other, we had a nice moment in her living room, sitting side-by-side in matching black armchairs with our laptops, as I updated my relationship status and she confirmed that we were in a relationship—although it was clear, there's something to be said for your partner being eager to share it with her friends. When we broke up, I defriended her on Facebook because I couldn't bear to read her status updates (or honestly, even realize she existed—the first week is tough), blocked her on my instant messenger, and took her e-mail address out of my contacts list. I deleted her LiveJournal from my bookmarks and finished by updating my relationship status to single. The next day, ten people asked how I was doing before I told anyone about it. Breaking up was hard to do before the Internet. Now my list after leaving someone includes blocking her on instant messaging, taking her e-mail address out of my quick contacts list and out of my e-mail's autocomplete list, avoiding her blog, and defriending her on Facebook.

Once he completed his freewriting, Ted reviewed what he had written and decided to limit his essay to one social network—Facebook. He highlighted usable ideas and tried to group or organize them logically. In his freewriting Ted saw three main groups of ideas: (1) finding someone to date, (2) dating, and (3) breaking up, so he sorted his ideas into those categories. Once had grouped his ideas into these three categories, he wrote a working thesis statement:

Working Thesis Statement: The dating process using Facebook involves screening, dating, and breaking up.

This working thesis statement identifies his topic—dating online using Facebook—and suggests that he will examine how the dating process works. You can see that this thesis statement grew out of his idea groupings. Furthermore, this thesis statement gives readers clues as to how the essay will be organized. A reader knows from this preview the order in which steps in the dating process will be discussed.

How do you know which ideas to group? Look for connections and relationships among the ideas that you generate during prewriting. Here are some suggestions:

Ways to Make Connections Between Ideas

1. **Look for categories.** Try to discover ways your ideas can be classified or subdivided. Think of categories as titles or slots in which ideas can be placed. Look for a general term that is broad enough to cover several of your ideas. For example, suppose you are writing a paper on where sexual discrimination occurs. You could break down the topic by location.

   Sample Thesis Statement Sexual discrimination exists in the workplace, in social situations, and in politics.

2. **Try organizing your ideas chronologically.** Group your ideas according to the clock or calendar. Ted organized the dating process in the order in which it happens, from start to finish.

> **Sample Thesis Statement** Tracing metal working from its early beginnings in history to modern times reveals certain social and economic patterns.

3. **Look for similarities and differences.** When working with two or more topics, see if they can be approached by looking at how similar or different they are.

> **Sample Thesis Statement** Two early biologists, Darwin and Mendel, held similar views about evolution.

4. **Separate your ideas into causes and effects or problems and solutions.** Events and issues can often be analyzed in this way.

> **Sample Thesis Statement** Both employer and employees must work together to improve low morale in an office.

5. **Divide your ideas into advantages and disadvantages or pros and cons.** When you are evaluating a proposal, product, or service, this approach may work.

> **Sample Thesis Statement** Playing on a college sports team has many advantages but also several serious drawbacks.

6. **Consider several different ways to approach your topic or organize and develop your ideas.** As you consider what your thesis statement is going to be, push yourself to see your topic from a number of different angles or a fresh perspective.

   For example, Ted could have considered how online dating differs from traditional dating, or he could have examined his freewriting and decided to focus on his personal history using Facebook to date.

Writing an Effective Thesis Statement

Think of your thesis statement as a promise; it promises your reader what your paper will deliver. Here are some guidelines to follow for writing an effective thesis statement:

Guidelines for Writing an Effective Thesis Statement

1. **It should state the main point of your essay.** It should not focus on details; it should give an overview of your approach to your topic.

> **Too Detailed** A well-written business letter has no errors in spelling.
>
> **Revised** To write a grammatically correct business letter, follow three simple rules.

2. **It should assert an idea about your topic.** Your thesis should express a viewpoint or state an approach to the topic.

> **Lacks An Assertion** Advertising contains images of both men and women.
>
> **Revised** In general, advertising presents men more favorably than women.

3. **It should be as specific and detailed as possible.** For this reason, it is important to review and rework your thesis *after* you have written and revised drafts.

> **Too General** Advertisers can influence readers' attitudes toward competing products.
>
> **Revised** Athletic-shoe advertisers focus more on attitude and image than on the actual physical differences between their product and those of their competitors.

4. **It may suggest the organization of your essay.** Mentioning key points that will be discussed in the essay is one way to do this. The order in which you mention them should be the order in which you discuss them in your essay.

> **Does Not Suggest Organization** Public-school budget cuts will negatively affect education.
>
> **Revised** Public-school budget cuts will negatively affect academic achievement, student motivation, and the drop-out rate.

5. **It should not be a direct announcement.** Do not begin with phrases such as "In this paper I will" or "My assignment was to discuss."

> **Direct Announcement** The purpose of my paper is to show that businesses lose money due to inefficiency, competition, and inflated labor costs.
>
> **Revised** Businesses lose money due to inefficiency, competition, and inflated labor costs.

6. **It should offer a fresh, interesting, and original perspective on the topic.** A thesis statement can follow the guidelines above, but if it seems dull or predictable, it needs more work.

> **Predictable** Circus acts fall into three categories: animal, clown, and acrobatic.
>
> **Revised** Each of the three categories of circus acts—animal, clown, and acrobatic—is exciting because of the risks it involves.

EXERCISE 10-4 WRITING A WORKING THESIS STATEMENT

For the topic you narrowed in Exercise 10-3, write a working thesis statement.

Audience, Purpose, Point of View, and Tone

Before you begin a draft, there are four important factors to consider: audience, purpose, point of view, and tone.

Considering Your Audience

A student wrote the following paragraph as part of an essay for a class assignment. His audience was his classmates.

> When the small, long-iron clubhead is behind the ball, it's hard to stop tension from creeping into your arms. When this happens, your takeaway becomes fast and jerky. Your backswing becomes shorter and you lose your rhythm. Even worse, this tension causes your right hand to uncock too early. One result is that the clubhead reaches its peak speed before it hits the ball. Another result is the clubhead goes outside the line of play and cuts across the ball steeply from outside to in. A slice or pull results.

His classmates found the paragraph confusing. Why? This writer made a serious error: he failed to analyze his audience. He assumed they knew as much about golf as he did. Readers who do not play golf would need more background information. Terms specific to golf should have been defined.

Analyzing your audience is always a first step when writing any essay. It will help you decide what to say and what type of detail to include. Here are some key questions to begin your analysis:

- Is my reader familiar with the topic?
- How much background or history does my reader need to understand the information?
- Do I need to define any unfamiliar terms?
- Do I need to explain any unfamiliar people, places, events, parts, or processes?

Suppose you are writing an essay on how to find an apartment to rent. As you plan your essay, you need to decide how much information to present.

This decision involves analyzing both your audience and your purpose. First, consider how much your audience already knows about the topic. If you think your readers know a lot about renting apartments, briefly review in your essay what they already know and then move on to a more detailed explanation of new information.

On the other hand, if your topic is probably brand new to your readers, capture their interest without intimidating them. Try to relate the topic to their own experiences. Show them how renting an apartment resembles something they already know how to do. For example, you might compare renting an apartment to other types of shopping for something with certain desired features and an established price range.

If you are uncertain about your audience's background, it is safer to include information they may already know rather than to assume that they know it. Readers can skim or skip over information they know, but they cannot fill in gaps in their understanding without your help.

Once you have identified your audience and decided what they will need to know, you will want to identify your purpose for writing.

Considering Your Purpose

A well-written essay should have a **purpose**, or goal; it should be written to accomplish something. Is your purpose to give your readers an overview of a topic or do you want to give your readers specific, practical information about it? You would need much more detail for the second purpose than you would for the first.

The three main purposes for writing are

- **to express yourself.** In expressive essays, you focus on your feelings and experiences. You might, for example, write an expressive essay about the value of friendship.

- **to inform.** Informative essays are written to present information. An essay on how to cook chili is an informative essay.

- **to persuade.** Persuasive essays attempt to convince readers to accept a particular viewpoint or take a particular action. A persuasive essay might attempt to convince you that zoos are inhumane.

When planning your essay, keep your essay focused on its purpose. Decide what you want your essay to accomplish, and focus on how to meet that goal.

Considering Point of View

Point of view refers to the perspective you take on your topic. Your point of view may be expressed using first, second, or third person. If you write in the first person (using words like *I* and *me*), then you are speaking personally to your reader. If you write in the second person (using words like *you* and *your*), you address your reader directly. If you write in the third person, you use nouns or pronouns to refer to a person or thing spoken about (using words like *he, she, Jody,* or *children*).

Your choice of person determines how formal or informal your essay becomes and also creates closeness or distance between the reader and writer.

Most academic writing uses the third person. The second person is rarely used. Whatever person you choose to use, stay with it throughout your essay.

EXERCISE 10-5 DEFINING AUDIENCE AND PURPOSE AND GENERATING IDEAS

For two of the following topics, define your audience and purpose and generate a list of ideas to include in an essay.

1. The lack of privacy in our society

2. The value of sports

3. Balancing job and school

4. Choosing a career

5. How to make new friends

Considering Tone

Since the purpose of an essay is to communicate ideas, your tone should reflect your seriousness about the topic. **Tone** means how you sound to your readers and how you feel about your topic. An essay can have a serious, argumentative, or informative tone, for example. A humorous, sarcastic, flip, or very informal tone can detract from your essay and suggest that what you say should not be taken seriously.

As a general rule, your tone should reflect your relationship to your audience. The less familiar you are with your audience, the more formal your tone should be. Here are a few examples of sentences in which the tone is inappropriate for most academic and career writing, showing how they could be revised to be appropriate for an academic audience.

> **Inappropriate** Making jump shots is a mean task, but I'm gonna keep tossing 'em till I'm the best there is.
>
> **Revised** Learning to make jump shots is difficult, but I'm going to practice until I'm the best on the team.
>
> **Inappropriate** I just couldn't believe that my best friend was a druggie.
>
> **Revised** I was shocked to learn that my best friend uses drugs.
>
> **Inappropriate** I busted a gut trying to make that sale and I got zilch.
>
> **Revised** I tried very hard to make the sale but didn't succeed.

Keep Your Tone Appropriate

Follow these suggestions to help keep your tone appropriate:

1. Avoid slang expressions.
2. Use first-person pronouns (*I, me*) sparingly.

3. Make your writing sound more formal than casual conversation or a letter to a close friend.

4. To achieve a more formal tone, avoid informal or everyday words. For example:

Use *met* instead of *ran into*.

Use *children* instead of *kids*.

Use *annoying* instead of *bugging*.

EXERCISE 10-6 REVISING TONE

Revise each of the following statements to give it a more formal tone.

1. I used to be a goof-off when I was in high school, but now I am trying to get with education.

2. Sam is the kind of guy every woman would like to sink her claws into.

3. Because Marco is one of those easygoing types, people think they can walk all over him.

4. In my talk to the group, I hit on why scanners are a big money saver.

5. Emily Dickinson is a fabulous poet; some of her poems are really dope.

Tone, or how you "sound" to your reader, is an important factor to consider when planning your essay. For more about tone, see Chapter 2, p. 25 and Chapter 9, p. 236.

EXERCISE 10-7 DEFINING AUDIENCE, PURPOSE, POINT OF VIEW, AND TONE

For the topic you worked with in Exercise 10-3, define your purpose and audience and select a point of view. Also decide how you want to "sound" to your reader.

Organizing Ideas Using Outlining and Mapping

Outlining is one good way to organize your ideas, discover the relationships and connections between them, and show their relative importance. Generally, an outline follows a format like the one that follows.

> I.   First major idea
>   A. First supporting detail
>   1. Detail
>   2. Detail
>   B. Second supporting detail
>   1. Detail
>   a. Minor detail or example
>   b. Minor detail or example
> II. Second major idea
>   A. First supporting detail

Notice that the most important ideas are closer to the left margin. Less important ideas are indented toward the middle of the page. A quick glance at an outline shows what is most important, what is less important, and how ideas support or explain one another.

How to Use an Outline Format

Here are a few suggestions for using the outline format:

- **Do not be overly concerned with following the outline format exactly.** As long as your outline shows the organization of your ideas, it will work for you.
- **Write complete sentences whenever possible.** Complete sentences allow for fuller expression of ideas.
- **Pay attention to headings.** Be sure that all the information you place underneath a heading explains or supports that heading. Every heading indented the same amount on the page should be of equal importance.

Now read the following outline of the essay, "When a Home Is Not a Home," on page 253.

> I.   Numerous barriers block mobile home ownership
>   A. Local zoning laws may restrict mobile home placement
>   1. People make false assumptions about occupants
>   a. unruly children
>   b. beer cans on lawn
>   c. rusted-out cars
>   2. Solid citizens would live in mobile homes if laws were not so restrictive.

continued on next page

II. Financial discrimination also exists.

    1. Loans for mobile homes are treated differently.

        a. loan rates are higher

        b. government financing is difficult

        c. mobile home owners are regarded as poor financial risks

Another way to write a solid, effective essay is to plan its development using an **idea map**, a list of the ideas you will discuss in the order you will present them. Here is a sample idea map for Ted's essay on online dating.

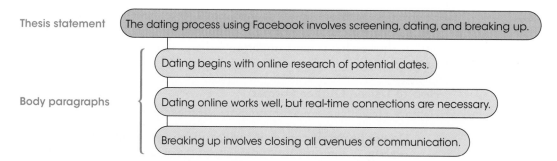

Map of Ted's Essay on Online Dating

Thesis statement — The dating process using Facebook involves screening, dating, and breaking up.

Body paragraphs
- Dating begins with online research of potential dates.
- Dating online works well, but real-time connections are necessary.
- Breaking up involves closing all avenues of communication.

EXERCISE 10-8 DRAWING A MAP OR OUTLINE

For the topic you worked with in Exercise 10-3, draw a map or outline of your ideas.

Choosing a Method of Development

Analyzing your audience and purpose will also help you choose which method or methods of development to use. Essays use the methods of development that you learned in Chapter 5, *process, example, classification, definition, comparison and contrast, and cause and effect.* You can select the one that suits your audience and purpose best.

The draft essay on online dating uses the chronological method of development. Your method of development depends on your purpose. See Table 10.2 for a few examples. You may also use more than one of these methods of development. You might define a behavior and then offer examples to explain it. Or you might explain how a group of people are classified and argue that the classification is unfair and discriminatory.

TABLE 10.2 CHOOSING A METHOD OF DEVELOPMENT

IF YOUR PURPOSE IS TO . . .	USE . . .
Explain how something works or how to perform a specific task	Process
Explain a topic, using specific examples	Example
Explain how something can be divided or grouped	Classification
Explain what something is	Definition
Emphasize similarities or differences between two topics or explain something by comparing it to something already familiar	Comparison and Contrast
Explain why something happened	Cause and Effect

EXERCISE 10-9 CHOOSING A METHOD OF DEVELOPMENT

For the topic you worked with in Exercise 10-3, choose a method of development that will best present your point.

10c   DRAFTING AN ESSAY

LEARNING OBJECTIVE 3
Draft an essay.

A **draft** is a tentative or preliminary version of an essay. You should plan to write several drafts before you end up with an essay you are satisfied with. Use the following general suggestions for getting started; then work on drafting each paragraph as described on the following pages.

Tips for Writing Essay Drafts

Here are some tips for writing essay drafts:

- **Leave time between your drafts.** If you try to write too many drafts in one sitting, you may find it difficult to sort them all out and see the strengths and weaknesses of each one.
- **Think of drafting as a chance to experiment.** Find out what works and what does not. You might want to write your essay several different ways, trying out different approaches, different content, and different ways of organizing the information.
- **Focus on ideas, not correctness.** Especially for the first few drafts, concentrate on recording your ideas. Do not worry yet about grammatical errors or sentence structure, for example.

- **Be prepared to make major changes.** As your essay develops, you may realize that you want to change direction or that you should further limit your topic. Do not hesitate to do so.
- **Have a friend or classmate read your drafts.** Ask your reviewer to identify and evaluate your thesis statement. Also ask him or her to evaluate how clearly and effectively your essay supports your thesis statement.

Drafting Body Paragraphs

Drafting is a process of composing and revising drafts. It involves adding, deleting, and reorganizing content to be sure the essay has a narrow focus, a clear main idea, and adequate supporting details. When drafting it is often best to start with the body of the essay, those paragraphs that provide the support for your thesis statement. There are a number of different ways you can begin drafting the body of your essay. Some students write an outline, others draw a map, still others write a list of topic sentences that support the thesis. Don't worry too much about the order of the items in your draft. At this point it is more important to get your ideas down in writing. In later drafts you can rearrange your ideas.

Once you have identified topics or topic sentences that support your thesis, you are ready to write first-draft paragraphs. These, too, may change, so concentrate primarily on making sure that each topic sentence supports the thesis and that each paragraph has a clear topic sentence (see Chapter 3), supporting details (see Chapter 3), and transitions (see Chapter 3).

Sample Topic Sentences for an Essay

Here is a list of topic sentences Ted wrote for his online dating essay.

> Facebook owns the college crowd and is widely popular for dating.
> Here's how the dating process works at the U. of Maryland.
> On Facebook everyone is reduced to a set of bullets.
> I use Facebook to stalk a potential date.
> When dating begins it is nice to change our status on Facebook together.
> Facebook can encourage infidelity.
> Breaking up was hard to do before the Internet.

You will see that he changed, added, and expanded these topic sentences as he wrote his first draft, which appears on p. 273.

Evaluating and Revising Your Thesis Statement

At various stages in the drafting process, you may decide to rewrite, revise, or completely change your thesis statement. Remember, a thesis statement should explain what your essay is about and also give your readers clues about its organization. You may not know, for example, how your essay will be organized until you have written one or more drafts. Use the following suggestions for making sure your thesis statement is clear and effective.

How to Revise Your Thesis Statement

The best time to evaluate and, if necessary, revise your thesis statement is after you have written a first draft. When evaluating your thesis statement, ask the following questions:

1. **Does my essay develop and explain my thesis statement?** As you write an essay, its focus and direction may change. Revise your thesis statement to reflect any changes. If you discover that you drifted away from your original thesis and want to maintain it, work on revising so that your paper delivers what your thesis promises.

2. **Is my thesis statement broad enough to cover all the points made in the essay?** As you develop your first draft, you may find that one idea leads naturally to another. Both must be covered by the thesis statement. For example, suppose your thesis statement is "Media coverage of national political events shapes public attitudes toward politicians." If, in your essay, you discuss media coverage of international events as well as national ones, then you need to broaden your thesis statement.

3. **Does my thesis statement use vague or unclear words that do not clearly focus the topic?** For example, in the thesis statement "The possibility of animal-organ transplants for humans is interesting," the word *interesting* is vague and does not suggest how your essay will approach the topic. Instead, if your paper discusses both the risks and benefits of these transplants, this approach should be reflected in your thesis: "Animal-organ transplants for humans offer both risks and potential benefits."

EXERCISE 10-10 EVALUATING THESIS STATEMENTS

Working with a classmate, identify what is wrong with the following thesis statements, and revise each one to make it more effective.

1. Jogging has a lot of benefits.

2. Counseling can help people with problems.

3. Getting involved in campus activities has really helped me.

4. Budgeting your time is important.

5. Commuting to college presents problems.

6. The movie is about parenting.

7. Violence on television must be brought to an end.

8. Divorce laws are unfair and favor women.

9. Fad diets are losing their appeal.

10. Automobile air bags save lives.

EXERCISE 10-11 DRAFTING A THESIS STATEMENT

For the topic you worked on in Exercise 10-3, draft a thesis statement.

Supporting Your Thesis with Substantial Evidence

Every essay you write should offer substantial evidence in support of your thesis statement. This evidence makes up the body of your essay. **Evidence** can consist of personal experience, anecdotes (stories that illustrate a point), examples, reasons, descriptions, facts, statistics, and quotations (taken from sources).

Many students have trouble locating concrete, specific evidence to support their thesis. Though prewriting yields plenty of good ideas and helps you focus your thesis, prewriting ideas may not always provide sufficient evidence. Often you need to brainstorm again for additional ideas. At other times, you may need to consult one or more sources to obtain further information on your topic (see section 10f).

Ted realized that he did not have enough ideas for his essay on online dating. Table 10.3 lists ways to explain a thesis statement and gives an example of how Ted could use each in his essay.

Ted does not need to use all of them; instead, he should choose the ones that are most appropriate for his audience and purpose. He could also use different types of evidence in combination. For example, he could *tell a story* that illustrates the *effects* of misleading online profiles.

Guidelines for Selecting Evidence

Use the following guidelines in selecting evidence to support your thesis:

1. **Be sure your evidence is relevant.** That is, it must directly support or explain your thesis.

2. **Make your evidence as specific as possible.** Help your readers see the point you are making by offering detailed, concrete information. For example, if you are explaining the effects of right-to-privacy violations on indi-

TABLE 10.3 WAYS TO ADD EVIDENCE

TOPIC: ONLINE DATING

EXPLAIN YOUR THESIS BY . . .	EXAMPLE
Telling a story	*Relate a story about an online dating experience.*
Adding descriptive detail	*Add a description of a social network profile.*
Explaining how something works	*Explain how a person can change his or her relationship status on Facebook.*
Giving an example	*Discuss specific instances of prescreening a potential date using Google.*
Giving a definition	*Explain the meaning of terms such as profile or defriending.*
Making distinctions	*Contrast prescreening a date online and without the use of a computer.*
Making comparisons	*Compare two social networking sites.*
Giving reasons	*Explain why breaking up is difficult when so many online connections exist.*
Analyzing effects	*Explain how online profiles can be misleading.*

viduals, include details that make the situation come alive: names of people and places, types of violations, and so forth.

3. **Be sure your information is accurate.** It may be necessary to check facts, verify stories you have heard, and ask questions of individuals who have provided information.

4. **Locate sources that provide evidence.** Because you may not know enough about your topic and lack personal experience, you may be unable to provide strong evidence. When this happens, locate several sources on your topic.

5. **Be sure to document any information that you borrow from other sources.** See section 10f for further information on crediting sources.

Now let's take a look at how Ted developed his essay on online dating. As you read notice in particular the types of evidence he uses and how his thesis statement promises what his essay delivers. In this first draft he uses his freewriting from p. 259 and his list of topic sentences on p. 270.

Sample First Draft Essay

Facebook is a social networking Internet site. It allows a user to connect with people, make friends, and join interest groups using the convenience of their own computer. It also allows a user to learn more information about said friends, as well as post text, photos, video, links, and information.

Facebook owns the college crowd, because from its September 2004 launch in a Harvard dorm room until September 2006, a user needed a .edu e-mail address to join. College students made the site their own community, and there was a sense that this was our world even though there's no real way to prevent non-students with .edu addresses from joining. The first sign of non-students entering what was our walled community occurred in May 2006 when employers were admitted, followed by Facebook opening to the public in September of that year.

Facebook has become widely popular. Much has been written about it in my student newspaper, but no one has yet dug into what the site has done to change our relationships, and specifically the dating process. The dating process has changed dramatically since Facebook came on the scene. Not all the changes have been positive.

I know when Facebook friends break up, fail tests, and hate their parents, but I don't really know them as people, just infobits on an LCD. The dating process works well initially over this medium, but real connections are only formed with substantial time-spending, preferably in person. Online talks, even via Skype or webcam, are still only a fraction of the experience and do not convey as high a percentage of the information one can glean during an in-person encounter.

At the University of Maryland, the dating process begins like this: get someone's name; look him or her up on Facebook; use that information to decide how to proceed. When I meet someone and she sets off those neurons that make me hum "Maybe it's love," I do a Facebook search. A profile page will tell me her age, indicate whether or not she's taken, and give me a decent idea (if the profile is not privacy protected) of what image she's trying to present. Note that I don't trust Facebook to tell me who people are—merely who they want to show people they are. I look through photos and see what they value enough to show me. I check posted links because what someone thinks is worth sharing is another window into who she is.

On Facebook, everyone seems reduced to a set of bullet points—"goth, tall, cat person"—that we rely on before even meeting someone. In real life, careful observation can reveal truths about people they won't discuss, especially things they don't want known.

However, a fidgety, nervous guy who sweats when he sees a pretty girl may have a better chance sending a Facebook message, which can be drafted and redrafted and edited and rewritten and shown to friends before sending, than approaching her in real life, so it does have its benefits.

After using Facebook to research the person, I have a decent idea of whether she's a probable friend or romantic interest. Next I hit Google—first searching with her e-mail address, then with her name, then with her nickname if I have reason to believe the person I'm into uses the Internet for more than e-mail. This turns up message boards, possibly her blog, both worth plumbing for details about my new fascination.

I have serious doubts as to whether being able to download someone's self with a little searching on Facebook and Google is actually a good thing for beginning relationships. For one, online searches result in tons of information with absolutely no context. Judging what you learn without cross-referencing it with the person him- or herself is a recipe for misinterpretative disaster, yet checking means admitting you've been snooping. I snoop anyway.

When I start dating someone new, it's usually a nice moment to change our relationship status on Facebook. After the last time I did that, we communicated more via messages on Facebook, posted on each other's walls, and even updated our statuses at the same time. I'm glad we never committed the ultimate act of Facebook couplehood, however.

I knew my housemate was in deep when her profile picture changed from just her to her being held by her girlfriend. I knew it was even worse when her girlfriend's photo changed the same way. The face they'd chosen to show couldn't be just theirs—it was sweet but creeped me out.

Internet access means access to your romantic interest, even during work in many cases. E-mail replaces IM for quick messages because many jobs require e-mail use. The Internet lets you do couples things like play Scrabble or check up on each other regardless of distance.

Time spent communicating with someone, especially just one person, can build connections that lead to relationships or strengthen current ones. Although Skyping someone is about as emotionally satisfying as being courteously deferential, you still get to hear his or her voice. Tone, pauses, nuance, and volume are all stripped from instant messages—at least Skype gives you those back. Human laughter beats "LOL" in pixels any day, but holding her while she tells you about her day wins whenever possible.

Facebook can also provoke new frontiers of infidelity. One way is through chatting online. It's very poor form to chat up someone else's girlfriend in a bar, but when chatting online there's no boyfriend looming over you to enforce her morality. Combine that freedom with the very personal qualities of online relationships and the large amount of time most people spend online and you've got a formula anyone who's dating anyone who gets online should worry about.

Breaking up is hard to do, but the Internet makes it easier. You don't want to get a continually updated feed of information about that person. Knowing someone's getting over you and trying to date is one thing; knowing they're doing it at seven-thirty at Club Kozmo with someone they met last weekend is another.

After I leave someone, he or she disappears from instant messaging, my e-mail contacts, Facebook friends, and my web bookmarks. Forget one step and the "getting over her" process becomes that much harder. There's a measure of comfort to be found in thinking someone's fallen off the face of the earth romantically, especially if your return to dating hasn't been as successful. After the relationship ends, I like the flood of data the Internet provides much less than in my prescreening stage.

That level of cutting someone off requires an amount of effort commonly reserved for reporters on deadline or college students who fell asleep before they got to the all-nighter. You become like a recovering alcoholic, not just avoiding them in person. Certain sites take on new meaning. Any bit of forgotten information is another barb, another pang, another realization. Invariably, you'll miss something and see a status update or a text message or a voice mail. It helps at times, when missing someone so badly means wishing the person were dead. Once you get over it, refriend the person if you can do it without going crazy. Sometimes a little bit of ignorance can be blissful indeed, but most connections are worth preserving.

EXERCISE 10-12 WRITING A FIRST DRAFT

Write a first draft of an essay for the working thesis statement you wrote in Exercise 10-11 (p. 272). Support your thesis statement with at least three types of evidence.

Using Transitions to Make Connections Among Your Ideas Clear

To produce a well-written essay, be sure to make it clear how your ideas relate to one another. There are several ways to do this:

1. **Use signal words and phrases.** Signal words and phrases are helpful for making your essay flow smoothly and communicate clearly. Table 10.4 lists useful signal words for each method of organization. Notice the use of these signal words and phrases in Ted's first draft: *however, next, for one, although, another, after.*

2. **Write a transitional sentence.** This sentence is usually the first sentence in the paragraph. It might come before the topic sentence or it might *be* the topic sentence. Its purpose is to link the paragraph in which it appears with the paragraph before it.

3. **Repeat key words.** Repeating key words also enables your reader to stay on track. Key words often appear in your thesis statement, and, by repeating some of them, you remind your reader of your thesis and how each new idea is connected to it.

    You need not repeat the word or phrase exactly as long as the meaning stays the same. You could substitute "keeps your audience on target" for "enables your reader to stay on track," for example. The following excerpt from an essay on clothing illustrates the use of key-word repetition.

The Real Functions of Clothing

Just as a product's packaging tells us a lot about the product, so does a person's clothing reveal a lot about the person. Clothing reflects the way we choose to present ourselves and reveals how we feel about ourselves.

What we wear reveals our emotions. We tend to dress according to how we feel. If we feel relaxed and comfortable, we tend to dress in comfortable, casual clothing. For instance, some people wear sweatshirts and sweatpants for a leisurely evening at home. If we feel happy and carefree, our clothing often reflects it. Think of how fans dress at a football game, for example. Their gear reflects casual comfort, and their team-supporting hats, T-shirts, etc., reveal their emotional support for the team.

Clothing also reveals our expectations and perceptions.

EXERCISE 10-13 ANALYZING A DRAFT

Review the draft you wrote for Exercise 10-12. Analyze how effectively you have connected your ideas. Add key words or transitional words, phrases, or sentences, as needed.

TABLE 10.4 USEFUL SIGNAL WORDS AND PHRASES

TYPE OF CONNECTION	SIGNAL WORDS AND PHRASES
Importance	*most important, above all, especially, particularly important*
Spatial relationships	*above, below, behind, beside, next to, inside, outside, to the west (north, etc.), beneath, near, nearby, next to, under, over*
Time sequences	*first, next, now, before, during, after, eventually, finally, at last, later, meanwhile, soon, then, suddenly, currently, after, afterward, after a while, as soon as, until*
Recounting events or steps	*first, second, then, later, in the beginning, when, while, after, following, next, during, again, after that, at last, finally*
Examples	*for example, for instance, to illustrate, in one case*
Types	*one, another, second, third*
Definitions	*means, can be defined as, refers to, is*
Similarities	*likewise, similarly, in the same way, too, also*
Differences	*however, on the contrary, unlike, on the other hand, although, even though, but, in contrast, yet*
Causes or results	*because, consequently, since, as a result, for this reason, therefore, thus*
Restatement	*in other words, that is*
Summary or conclusion	*finally, to sum up, all in all, evidently, in conclusion*

Writing the Introduction, Conclusion, and Title

The introduction, conclusion, and title each serve a specific function. Each strengthens your essay and helps your reader understand your ideas.

Writing the Introduction

An **introductory paragraph** has three main purposes:

- It presents your thesis statement.
- It interests your reader in your topic.
- It provides any necessary background information.

Although your introductory paragraph appears first in your essay, it does *not* need to be written first. In fact, it is sometimes best to write it last, after you have developed your ideas, written your thesis statement, and drafted your essay.

We have already discussed writing thesis statements earlier in the chapter (see p. 261). Here are some suggestions on how to interest your readers in your topic.

TECHNIQUES FOR WRITING INTRODUCTIONS

TECHNIQUE	EXAMPLE
Ask a provocative or controversial question.	*What would you do if you were sound asleep and woke to find a burglar in your bedroom?*
State a startling fact or statistic.	*Did you know that the federal government recently spent $687,000 on a research project that studied the influence of Valium on monkeys?*
Begin with a story or an anecdote.	*Mark Brown, a social worker, has spent several evenings riding in a police cruiser to learn about neighborhood problems.*
Use a quotation.	*As Junot Díaz wrote in* The Brief Wondrous Life of Oscar Wao, *"It's never the changes we want that change everything."*
State a little-known fact, a myth, or a misconception.	*It's hard to lose weight and even harder to keep it off. Right? Wrong! A sensible eating program will help you lose weight.*

A straightforward, dramatic thesis statement can also capture your reader's interest, as in the following example:

The dream job that I'd wanted all my life turned out to be a complete disaster.

An introduction should also provide the reader with any necessary background information. Consider what information your reader needs to understand your essay. You may, for example, need to define the term *genetic engineering* for a paper on that topic. At other times, you might need to provide a brief history or give an overview of a controversial issue.

EXERCISE 10-14 WRITING/REVISING THE INTRODUCTION

Write or revise your introduction to the essay you drafted in Exercise 10-12.

Writing the Conclusion

The final, **concluding paragraph** of your essay has two functions: It should reemphasize your thesis statement and draw the essay to a close. It should not be a direct announcement, such as "This essay has been about" or "In this paper I hoped to show that . . ."

It's usually best to revise your essay *at least once* before working on the conclusion. During your first or second revision, you often make numerous changes in both content and organization, which may, in turn, affect your conclusion.

WAYS TO WRITE AN EFFECTIVE CONCLUSION

Here are a few effective ways to write a conclusion. Choose one that will work for your essay:

1. **Suggest a direction for further thought.** Raise a related issue that you did not address in your essay, or ask a series of questions.
2. **Look ahead.** Project into the future and consider outcomes or effects.
3. **Return to your thesis.** If your essay is written to prove a point or convince your reader of the need for action, it may be effective to end with a sentence that recalls your main point or calls for action. If you choose this way to conclude, don't merely repeat your first paragraph. Be sure to reflect on the thoughts you developed in the body of your essay.
4. **Summarize key points.** Especially for longer essays, briefly review your key supporting ideas. In shorter essays, this tends to be unnecessary.
5. **Make sure your conclusion does not contain new supporting details.** If you have trouble writing your conclusion, you may need to work further on your thesis or organization.

EXERCISE 10-15 WRITING/REVISING THE CONCLUSION

Write or revise a conclusion for the essay you wrote for Exercise 10-12.

Selecting a Title

Although the title appears first in your essay, it is often the last thing you should write. The **title** should identify the topic in an interesting way, and it may also suggest the focus of the paper. To select a title, reread your final draft, paying particular attention to your thesis statement and your overall method of development. Here are a few examples of effective titles:

"Surprise in the Vegetable Bin" (for an essay on vegetables and their effects on cholesterol and cancer)

"Denim Goes High Fashion" (for an essay describing the uses of denim for clothing other than jeans)

"Babies Go to Work" (for an essay on corporate-sponsored day-care centers)

TIPS FOR WRITING ACCURATE AND INTERESTING TITLES

To write accurate and interesting titles, try the following tips:

1. **Write a question that your essay answers.** For example: "Why Change the Minimum Wage?"
2. **Use key words that appear in your thesis statement.** If your thesis state-ment is "The new international trade ruling threatens the safety of the dol-phin, one of our most intelligent mammals," your title could be "New Threat to Dolphins."
3. **Use brainstorming techniques to generate options.** Don't necessarily use the first title that pops into your mind. If in doubt, try out some options on friends to see which is most effective.

EXERCISE 10-16 SELECTING A TITLE

Come up with a good title for the essay you wrote for Exercise 10-12.

10d   REVISING: EXAMINING YOUR IDEAS

LEARNING OBJECTIVE 4
Revise an essay.

Revising is a process of closely evaluating your draft to determine if it accom-plishes what you want it to. This is the time to be sure the essay says what you want it to say and that it does so in a clear and effective way. Later, once you are confident that your ideas are expressed clearly, you can move to editing, in which you make sure your essay is error free.

General Essay Revision Strategies

Here are some general suggestions for revising your final essay draft. Also refer to the Essay Revision Checklist in Chapter 2 (p. 40) and the strategies for revising paragraphs presented in Chapter 5 (p. 121).

- **Allow time between finishing your last draft and revising until the next day if possible.** When you return to the draft, you will have a clear mind and a new perspective.
- **Look for common problems.** If you usually have trouble, for example, with writing thesis statements or with using signal words, then evaluate these features closely each time you revise.
- **Read the draft aloud.** You may hear ideas that are unclear or realize they are not fully explained.
- **Ask a friend to read your paper aloud to you.** If the person hesitates or seems confused or misreads, he or she may be having trouble grasping your ideas. Reread and revise any trouble spots.
- **Read a print copy.** Although you may be used to writing on a computer, your essay may read differently when you see a paper copy.

Using Revision Maps to Revise

A revision map will help you evaluate the overall flow of ideas as well as the effectiveness of individual paragraphs. To draw an essay revision map, work through each paragraph, recording your ideas in abbreviated form, as shown on the next page. Then write the key words of your conclusion. If you find details that do not support the topic sentence, record those details to the right of the map.

When you've completed your revision map, conduct the following tests:

1. **Read your thesis statement along with your first topic sentence.** Does the topic sentence clearly support your thesis? If not, revise to make the relationship clearer. Repeat this step for each topic sentence.
2. **Read your topic sentences, one after the other, without corresponding details.** Is there a logical connection between them? Are they arranged in the most effective way? If not, revise to make the connection clearer or to improve your organization.
3. **Examine each individual paragraph.** Are there enough relevant, specific details to support the topic sentence?
4. **Read your introduction and then look at your topic sentences.** Does the essay deliver what the introduction promises?
5. **Read your thesis statement and then your conclusion.** Are they compatible and consistent? Does the conclusion agree with and support the thesis statement?

Model Revision Map

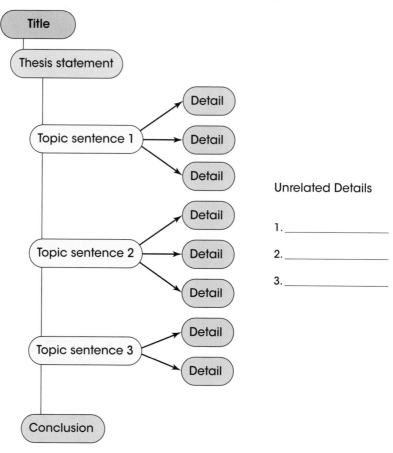

EXERCISE 10-17 DRAWING A REVISION MAP

Draw a revision map of the essay you wrote in Exercise 10-12 and make necessary revisions.

Revising Essay Content and Structure

When you have completed your revision map, you are ready to evaluate your essay's content and organization. If you do not ask yourself the right questions when evaluating your draft, you won't discover how to improve it. Each of the following questions and corresponding revision strategies will guide you in producing a clear and effective final essay.

1. **Does your essay accomplish your purpose?**

   If you are writing in response to an assignment, reread it and make sure you have covered all aspects of it. Delete any sentences or paragraphs that do not fulfill your assignment or stated purpose. Do you have enough ideas left? If not, do additional freewriting to discover new ideas.

2. **Is your essay appropriate for your audience?**

   Visualize your audience reading your essay. How will they respond? If you are not sure, ask a classmate or a person who is part of your audience to read your essay. Then, revise your essay with your audience in mind. Add examples that may appeal to them; delete those that would not. Examine your word choice. Have you used language that is understandable and will not either confuse them or create a negative impression?

3. **Is your thesis statement clearly expressed?**

   Highlight your thesis statement. Does it state the main point of your essay and make an assertion about your topic? If not, write one sentence stating what your essay is intended to explain or show. Use this sentence to help you revise your thesis statement. If you revise your thesis statement, be sure to revise the remainder of your essay to reflect your changes.

4. **Does each paragraph support your thesis?**

   Reread each topic sentence. Does each clearly and specifically explain some aspect of your thesis statement? If not, revise or drop the paragraph. Does the essay contain enough information to fully explain your thesis and make it understandable to your reader? If not, do additional prewriting to help you discover more ideas. If you are stuck, your thesis statement may be too narrow or you may need to read more about your topic. Be sure to give credit for any ideas you borrow from print or online sources. (Refer to section 10h.)

5. **Is your essay logically organized?**

   Examine your revision map to be sure your paragraphs are in the right order. If not, rearrange them. Be sure to add sentences or transitions to connect your ideas and show your new organization. Use Table 10.2, "Choosing a Method of Development" (p. 269) to consider different ways you might rearrange your ideas.

6. **Have you used signal words to connect your ideas?**

   Circle all signal words and phrases and transitional sentences. Do you use signal words to move from each main point to another? If, not, add signal words, referring to Table 10.3 (p. 273) as needed.

7. **Are your introduction, conclusion, and title effective?**

   Reread your introduction. If it does not lead your reader into the essay and/ or does not offer needed background information, it needs revision. Revise by assuming your reader knows little about the topic and has shown little interest. Decide what to add to help this uninterested reader get involved with your essay. *Next, reread your conclusion.* Does it draw the essay to a close and remind the reader of your thesis statement? If not, revise it using the suggestions on p. 279. *Finally, reconsider your title.* Is it an appropriate label for your essay? If it does not draw your reader into the essay, try to think of a snappier, more interesting title.

Revising Paragraphs

Once you are satisfied with the overall content and structure of your essay, evaluate each paragraph. Ask yourself the following questions about each paragraph. For any items for which you answer *no*, refer to the pages listed for revision help.

- Is the topic of the paragraph specific enough so that it can be adequately covered in a single paragraph? (Chapter 4, p. 72)
- Does the topic sentence clearly identify the topic and express a point of view about it? (Chapter 4, p. 72)
- Are there enough relevant details to support the topic sentence? (Chapter 4, p. 72)
- Are the details arranged in a logical order? (Chapter 4, p. 83)
- Have I used signal words and phrases to connect my ideas? (Chapter 4, p. 101)

Revising Sentences and Words

Once you are satisfied with your paragraphs, examine each sentence by asking the following questions:

- **Are your sentences wordy?** Do they express your meaning in as few words as possible? Here is an example of a wordy sentence, along with a possible revision. Notice that the first sentence contains empty words that do not contribute to its meaning.

> **Wordy** In light of the fact that cell phone technology changes every year or so, upgrading your cell phone is what everybody has to do.
>
> **Revised** Cell phone technology changes yearly, so regular upgrades are necessary.

- **Do your sentences repeat the same idea in slightly different words?** Here is an example of a sentence that says the same thing twice and a revised, more concise version of it.

> **Redundant** My decision to choose to attend college was the best decision I have made in a long time.
>
> **Revised** Choosing to attend college was one of my best decisions.

- **Do all of your sentences follow the same pattern?** That is, are they all short, or do they all start the same way? Do they seem choppy or monotonous? Sentences that are too similar make your writing seem mechanical and uninteresting.

- **Do you use strong active verbs?** These make your writing seem lively and interesting. Which of the following sentences is more interesting?

> The puppy was afraid of a laundry basket.
>
> The puppy <u>whimpered</u>, <u>quivered</u>, and <u>scampered</u> away when my sister carried a laundry basket into the room.

The second sentence helps you visualize the situation, while the first is simply factual. Reread your essay looking for verbs that seem dull or convey very little meaning. Replace them, using a dictionary or thesaurus, as needed.

- **Have you used concrete, specific language?** Your words should convey as much meaning as possible. Which phrase in each of the following pairs provides more meaning?

a fun vacation	*white-water rafting trip*
many flowers	*lavender petunias and white begonias*

Reread your essay and highlight words that seem dull and ordinary. Use a dictionary or thesaurus to help you find more concrete and specific replacements.

- **Have you used words with appropriate connotations?** A word's connotative meaning is the collection of feelings and attitudes that come along with it. The words *strolled*, *swaggered*, and *lumbered* all mean walking in a forward direction, but only *swaggered* would be appropriate when describing someone walking in a bold and arrogant manner. To be sure you have used words with appropriate connotations, check any you are unsure of in a dictionary.

- **Have you avoided clichés?** A cliché is a tired, overused expression that carries little meaning. Here are a few examples.

better late than never	shoulder to cry on
ladder of success	hard as a rock
green with envy	bite the bullet

Reread your essay and replace clichés with more exact and descriptive information. You could, for example, replace *shoulder to cry on* with *sympathetic and understanding best friend* or *bite the bullet* with *accept responsibility*.

- **Have you avoided sexist language?** Sexist language expresses narrow or unfair assumptions about men's and women's roles, positions, or value. Here are a few examples of sexist language:

  > **Sexist** A compassionate <u>nurse</u> reassures <u>her</u> patients before surgery.
  > **Revised** Compassionate <u>nurses</u> reassure <u>their</u> patients before surgery.
  >
  > **Sexist** Many <u>policemen</u> hold college degrees.
  > **Revised** Many <u>police officers</u> hold college degrees.

- **Have you used standard American English and avoided using non-standard dialect?** While dialects such as Black English, Spanglish, and Creole are acceptable in many situations, they are not acceptable when writing essays for college classes. If you speak a dialect of English in addition to standard American English, be sure to reread your essay and replace any dialect words or expressions.

EXERCISE 10-18 EVALUATING AND REVISING A DRAFT

Evaluate the draft of the essay you revised in Exercise 10-17, using the questions in the preceding section. Make revisions as needed.

10e   EDITING AND PROOFREADING: FOCUSING ON CLARITY AND CORRECTNESS

LEARNING OBJECTIVE 5
Edit and proofread essays.

Once you are satisfied that your essay expresses your ideas as you intended and is organized in a logical way, you are ready to make sure your essay is clear, error free, and presented in acceptable manuscript form. At this stage, you should try to correct errors in spelling, punctuation, and grammar, as well as typographical errors. Here are some general editing and proofreading suggestions:

General Suggestions for Effective Editing and Proofreading

- **Work with a double-spaced print copy of your essay.** You are likely to see more errors when working with a print copy than you do with an electronic version.

- **Create a log of common errors.** Read your paper once looking for each type of error and note them in your log.

- **Read your essay backward, starting with the last sentence and working toward the first.** Reading this way will help you focus on errors without the distraction of the flow of ideas.
- **Read your essay aloud.** You may catch errors in agreement, use of dialect, or punctuation.
- **Ask a classmate to proofread your paper.**

Using a Proofreading Checklist

Use the following proofreading checklist to remind you of the types of errors to look for when proofreading.

1. Does each sentence end with an appropriate punctuation mark (period, question mark, exclamation point, or quotation mark)?
2. Is all punctuation within each sentence correct (commas, colons, semicolons, apostrophes, dashes, and quotation marks)?
3. Is each word spelled correctly?
4. Are capital letters used where needed?
5. Are numbers and abbreviations used correctly?
6. Are any words left out?
7. Have all typographical errors been corrected?
8. Are the pages in the correct order and numbered?

Presenting Your Essay

Before your instructor even begins to read your essay, he or she forms a first impression of it. A paper that is carelessly assembled, rumpled, or has handwritten corrections creates a negative first impression. Always follow carefully any guidelines or requests that your instructor makes on format, method of submission, and so forth. Many instructors require you to use MLA format. See 10h. for more about MLA format. Use the following suggestions to present your paper positively.

Tips for Presenting Your Essay

- Make sure your name, course and section number, and date appear at the top of your essay (unless otherwise specified by your instructor).
- Type and double-space your essay.
- Number the pages and staple or paperclip them together.
- Present a neat, clean copy. (Carry it in a manila folder or envelope until you turn it in so it does not get rumpled or dirty.)
- If you need to make last-minute corrections, reprint your essay; do not make handwritten corrections.

- Avoid adjusting the margins to meet a page-length limit.
- If submitting your paper online, be sure to use an appropriate subject line identifying the submission.

In order to prepare his essay for publication, Ted made extensive revisions to his first draft (shown on p. 273) and produced the final version shown below.

Sample Final Essay

Ted Sawchuck   Sawchuck 1

Professor Marley

English 090

29 May 2013

Relationships 2.0: Dating and Relating in the Internet Age

Ted Sawchuck

Facebook is a social networking Internet site. It allows a user to conveniently connect online with people, make friends, and join interest groups via his or her computer. It also allows a user to learn more about his or her friends, as well as post text, photos, video links, and information. Facebook has become widely popular. Much has been written about it in my student newspaper, but no one has yet dug into how the site affects relationships on our campus, and specifically the dating process. Each stage of the dating process is influenced by Facebook; on our campus, not all the changes have been positive.

At the University of Maryland, the dating process begins like this: get someone's name; look him or her up on Facebook; then use that information to decide how to proceed. When I meet someone and she sets off those neurons that make me hum "Maybe it's love," I do a Facebook search. A profile page will tell me her age, indicate whether or not she is taken, and give me a decent idea (if the profile is not privacy protected) of what image she is trying to present. Note that I do not trust Facebook to tell me who people are—merely who they want to show other people they are. I look through photos and see what the person values enough to show me. I check posted links because what someone thinks is worth sharing is another window into who she is.

Sawchuck 2

After using Facebook to check out someone, I have a decent idea of whether she is a probable friend or possible romantic interest. Next I hit Google—searching first with her e-mail address, then with her name, and next with her nickname. This search turns up message boards, possibly her blog, and maybe even a Flickr site, all worth plumbing for details about my new fascination.

I have serious doubts as to whether being able to download someone's self with a little searching on Facebook and Google is actually a good thing for beginning a relationship. For one thing, online searches result in tons of information with absolutely no context. Judging what you learn without cross-referencing it with the person is a recipe for misinterpretative disaster, yet checking means admitting you have been snooping. I snoop anyway.

Also, on Facebook, everyone seems reduced to a set of bullet points—"goth, tall, cat person"—that you rely on before even meeting the person. In real life, careful observation can reveal truths about people they will not discuss online, especially things they do not want generally known. However, a fidgety, nervous guy who sweats when he sees a pretty girl may have a better chance sending a Facebook message, which can be drafted and redrafted and edited and rewritten and shown to friends before sending, than approaching her in real life, so it does have its benefits.

The dating process works well online initially, but real connections are only formed by spending substantial time together in person. Online talks, even via Skype or webcam, are still only a fraction of the real experience and convey only a fraction of the information one can glean during an in-person encounter. Time spent online communicating with someone can build connections that lead to a relationship or strengthen a current one. However, tone, pauses, nuance, and volume are all stripped from instant messages. Human laughter beats "LOL" any day, and holding her while she tells you about her day wins whenever possible.

Facebook can also provide new avenues for infidelity. One way is through chatting online. It is very poor form to chat up someone else's girlfriend in

Sawchuck 3

a bar, but when chatting online there is no boyfriend looming over you to enforce boundaries. Combine that freedom with the very personal qualities of online relationships and the large amount of time most people spend online and you have a situation that anyone who's dating anyone who goes online a lot should worry about.

Breaking up is hard to do but the Internet makes it easier. Once a relationship ends, you do not want to get a continually updated feed of information about the other person from any source. Knowing someone is getting over you and trying to date is one thing; knowing she is doing it at seven-thirty at Club Kozmo with someone she met last weekend is another. So now my list for after leaving someone includes blocking her on instant messaging, taking her e-mail address out of my quick contacts list and out of my e-mail's autocomplete list, avoiding her blog and defriending her on Facebook. Forget one step and the "getting over her" process becomes that much harder. There is a measure of comfort to be found in thinking someone has fallen off the face of the earth romantically, especially if your return to dating has not been as successful as hers.

Cutting someone off requires effort. Any bit of forgotten information is another barb, another pang, another realization of what you have lost. Invariably, you will miss something and see a status update or a text message or a voice mail. It helps at times, when missing someone so badly means wishing she were dead. Once you get over it yourself, refriend the person if you can do it without going crazy. Sometimes a little bit of ignorance can be blissful indeed, but most connections are worth preserving.

EXERCISE 10-19 PROOFREADING AND PRESENTING YOUR PAPER

For the draft you have revised in Exercise 10-18, use the Checklist on page 287 to prepare your essay for final presentation.

WRITING DOCUMENTED PAPERS

10f USING SOURCES AND AVOIDING PLAGIARISM

LEARNING OBJECTIVE 6
Use sources and avoid plagiarism.

Using sources in an essay involves building the information into your paper correctly so as to give credit to the authors from whom you borrowed the ideas. You can incorporate researched information into your paper in one of two ways: (1) summarize or paraphrase the information or (2) quote directly from it. In both cases, you must give credit to the authors from whom you borrowed the information by documenting your sources in a list of references so your reader can locate it easily. Failure to provide documentation of a source is called plagiarism.

What Is Plagiarism and How Can You Avoid It?

Plagiarism entails borrowing someone else's ideas or exact words *without giving that person credit.* Plagiarism can be intentional (submitting an essay written by someone else) or unintentional (failing to enclose another writer's words in quotation marks). Either way, it is considered a serious offense. If you plagiarize, you can fail the assignment or even the course.

Cyberplagiarism is a specific type of plagiarism. It takes two forms: (1) using information from the Internet without giving credit to the Web site that posted it, or (2) buying prewritten papers from the Internet and submitting them as your own work. For example, if you take information about Frank Lloyd Wright's architecture from a reference source (such as an encyclopedia or Web site) but do not specifically indicate where you found it, you have plagiarized. If you take the six-word phrase "Peterson, the vengeful, despicable drug czar" from a news article on the war on drugs, you have plagiarized.

Here are some guidelines to help you understand exactly what constitutes plagiarism.

Guidelines for Understanding Plagiarism

Plagiarism occurs when you . . .

- use another person's words without crediting that person.
- use another person's theory, opinion, or idea without listing the source of that information.

- do not place another person's exact words in quotation marks.
- do not provide a citation (reference) to the original source that you are quoting.
- paraphrase (reword) another person's ideas or words without credit.
- use facts, data, graphs, and charts without stating their source(s).

Using commonly known facts or information is not plagiarism, and you need not provide a source for such information. For example, the fact that Neil Armstrong set foot on the moon in 1969 is widely known and does not require documentation.

To avoid plagiarism, do the following . . .

- When you take notes from any published or Internet source, place anything you copy directly in quotation marks.
- As you read and take notes, separate your ideas from ideas taken from the sources you are consulting. You might use different colors of ink or different sections of a notebook page for each.
- Keep track of all the sources you use, clearly identifying where each idea comes from.
- When paraphrasing someone else's words, change as many words as possible and try to organize them differently. Credit the original source of the information.
- Write paraphrases without looking at the original text so that you rephrase information in your own words. (For more information on writing a paraphrase, see Chapter 8, p. 206.)
- Use citations to indicate the source of quotations and all information and ideas that are not your own. A citation is a notation, set off in parentheses, referring to a complete list of sources provided at the end of the essay. (For more information on citation, see page 297).

As you start researching new areas, you may ask yourself, "How can I possibly write a paper without using someone else's ideas? I don't know enough about the subject!" The good news is that it is *perfectly acceptable* to use other people's ideas in your research and writing. The key things to remember are (1) you must credit all information taken from any published or Internet sources, and (2) you must provide specific information regarding the publication from which the information is taken, as described in the following sections.

EXERCISE 10–20 IDENTIFYING PLAGIARISM

Read the following passage. Place a checkmark next to each statement in the list that follows that is an example of plagiarism.

Mexican Americans. Currently, Mexican Americans are the second-largest racial or ethnic minority group in the United States, but within two decades they will be the largest group. Their numbers will swell as a result of continual immigration from Mexico and the relatively high Mexican birth rate. Mexican Americans are one of the oldest racial-ethnic groups in the United States. Under the terms of the treaty ending the Mexican-American War in 1848, Mexicans living in territories acquired by the United States could remain there and be treated as American citizens. Those who did stay became known as "Californios," "Tejanos," or "Hispanos."

—Curry, Jiobu, and Schwirian, *Sociology for the Twenty-First Century*, p. 207

_____ 1. Mexican Americans are the second-largest minority in the United States. Their number grows as more people immigrate from Mexico.

_____ 2. After the Mexican-American War, those Mexicans living in territories owned by the United States became American citizens and were known as Californios, Tejanos, or Hispanos (Curry, Jiobu, and Schwirian, 207).

_____ 3. "Mexican Americans are one of the oldest racial-ethnic groups in the United States."

_____ 4. The Mexican-American War ended in 1848.

Recording Information from Sources

As you use sources to research a topic, you will need to record usable information that you find. One option is to photocopy the pages from print sources and download and print information from print sources. This is useful if you plan to directly quote the source. Remember, you will need complete source information so you can cite your sources (see p. 297). However, a good essay does not string together a series of quotations. Instead it uses and combines information to come up with new ideas, perspectives, and responses to what is found in the sources. There are several options for keeping track of information—*annotating*, *paraphrasing*, and *summarizing*. Each of these important skills was covered in Chapter 7.

EXERCISE 10-21 WRITING A FIRST DRAFT

Write a first draft of a paper on a topic of your choice. To support your ideas, locate and use three sources. If any of these sources are dated or not focused enough for your thesis, you may need to locate additional ones.

10g SYNTHESIZING SOURCES

LEARNING OBJECTIVE 7
Synthesize sources.

In daily life, we often consult several sources before drawing a conclusion or making a decision. For example, you might talk with several students who have taken the course American Labor History before deciding if you want to register for it. You might talk to several friends who own pickup trucks before buying one. Suppose you are debating whether or not to see a particular film. You talk with three friends who have seen it. Each liked the movie and describes different scenes. However, from their various descriptions, you may conclude that the film contains too much violence and that you do not want to see it.

In each case, you draw together several sources of information and come to your own conclusion: the course is good; the Ford pickup is best; the film is too violent for you. In these situations you are synthesizing information. **Synthesis** is a process of using information from two or more sources in order to develop new ideas about a topic or to draw conclusions about it.

Many college assignments require you to synthesize material—that is, to locate and read several sources on a topic and use them to produce a paper. Synthesizing in the college setting, then, is a process of putting ideas together to create new ideas or insights based on what you have learned from the sources you consulted. For example, in a sociology course, you may be asked to consult several sources on the topic of organized crime and then write a paper describing the relationship between organized crime and illegal drug sales. In a marketing class, your instructor may direct you to consult several sources on advertising strategies and on the gullibility of young children and write a paper weighing the effects of television commercials on young children. Both of these assignments involve synthesizing ideas from sources.

Did you notice that, in each of the above examples, you were asked to come up with a new idea, one that did not appear in any of the sources but was *based* on *all* the sources? Creating something new from what you read is one of the most basic, important, and satisfying skills you will learn in college.

Synthesis is also often required in the workplace:

- As a sales executive for an Internet service provider company, you may be asked to synthesize what you have learned about customer hardware problems.

- As a medical office assistant, you have extensive problems with a new computer system. The office manager asks you to write a memo to the company that installed the system, categorizing the types of problems you have experienced.

- As an environmental engineer, you must synthesize years of research in order to make a proposal for local river and stream cleanup.

How to Compare Sources to Synthesize

Comparing sources is part of synthesizing. Comparing involves placing them side by side and examining how they are the same and how they are different.

However, before you begin to compare two or more sources, be sure you understand each fully. Depending on how detailed and difficult each source is, use annotating, paraphrasing, and summarizing or underline, outline, or draw idea maps to make sure that you have a good grasp of your source material.

Let's assume you are taking a speech course in which you are studying nonverbal communication, or body language. You have chosen to study one aspect of body language: eye contact. Among your sources are the following excerpts.

Source A

Eye contact, or *gaze*, is also a common form of nonverbal communication. Eyes have been called the "windows of the soul." In many cultures, people tend to assume that someone who avoids eye contact is evasive, cold, fearful, shy, or indifferent; that frequent gazing signals intimacy, sincerity, self-confidence, and respect; and that the person who stares is tense, angry, and unfriendly. Typically, however, eye contact is interpreted in light of a preexisting relationship. If a relationship is friendly, frequent eye contact elicits a positive impression. If a relationship is not friendly, eye contact is seen in negative terms. It has been said that if two people lock eyes for more than a few seconds, they are either going to make love or kill each other (Kleinke, 1986; Patterson, 1983).

—Brehm and Kassin, *Social Psychology*

Source B

Eye contact often indicates the nature of the relationship between two people. One research study showed that eye contact is moderate when one is addressing a very high-status person, maximized when addressing a moderately high-status person, and only minimal when talking to a low-status person. There are also predictable differences in eye contact when one person likes another or when there may be rewards involved.

Increased eye contact is also associated with increased liking between the people who are communicating. In an interview, for example, you are likely to make judgments about the interviewer's friendliness according to the amount of eye contact shown. The less eye contact, the less friendliness. In a courtship relationship, more eye contact can be observed among those seeking to develop a more intimate relationship. One research study (Saperston, 2003) suggests that the intimacy is a function of the amount of eye gazing, physical proximity, intimacy of topic, and amount of smiling. This model best relates to established relationships.

—Weaver, *Understanding Interpersonal Communication*

To compare these sources, ask the following questions:

1. **On what do the sources agree?** Sources A and B recognize eye contact as an important communication tool. Both agree that there is a connection between eye contact and the relationship between the people involved. Both

also agree that more frequent eye contact occurs among people who are friendly or intimate.

2. **On what do the sources disagree?** Sources A and B do not disagree, though they do present different information about eye contact (see the next item).

3. **How do they differ?** Sources A and B differ on the information they present. Source A states that in some cultures the frequency of eye contact suggests certain personality traits (someone who avoids eye contact is considered to be cold, for example), but Source B does not discuss cultural interpretations. Source B discusses how eye contact is related to status—the level of importance of the person being addressed—while Source A does not.

4. **Are the viewpoints toward the subject similar or different?** Both Sources A and B take a serious approach to the subject of eye contact.

5. **Does each source provide supporting evidence for major points?** Source A cites two references. Source B cites a research study.

After comparing your sources, the next step is to form your own ideas based on what you have discovered.

EXERCISE 10-22 SYNTHESIZING SOURCES

Read each of the following excerpts from sources on the topic of lost and endangered species. Synthesize these two sources, using the steps listed above, and develop a thesis statement about the causes of the decline and loss of plant and animal species.

Source A

Habitat loss threatens the greatest number of species, but other factors are also important. Overhunting has eliminated many species and continues to threaten others. Whales, for example, have been hunted to near extinction, and a few countries continue to kill these huge mammals despite a nearly worldwide ban on whaling. Many animals and plants have also succumbed to competition from foreign species that humans have introduced. In East Africa, hundreds of species of tropical fishes in Lake Victoria are currently threatened by the Nile perch, a large species (up to 200 lbs.) that was introduced as a sport and food fish.

Often, as for the key deer, a combination of killing and habitat destruction has driven a species over the edge. In the past century, for instance, the Hawaiian Islands have lost half their bird species, mainly to overhunting, deforestation, and diseases carried by foreign bird species introduced into the islands. In Africa, elephants and rhinoceroses are being pushed toward extinction by habitat loss and by poachers catering to a black market for ivory and horns.

—Campbell, Mitchell, and Reece, *Biology*

Source B

The driving force behind today's alarming decline in species is the destruction, degradation and fragmentation of habitat due to our increasing human population and wasteful consumption of resources. Human populations virtually all around the globe are on the rise. . . . Because Americans consume so much more energy, food and raw material than our counterparts in other developed countries, our impact on our environment is proportionally much greater. As a result, wildlife and wild places in the United States are being pushed to the brink of extinction.

While the United States does not currently face as significant an increase in population as other countries, the movement of our population to new areas and the ensuing development has resulted in the destruction of species and their habitat. Thus, not surprisingly, there is a high correlation between human population and economic development trends in the United States and species decline and ecosystem destruction.

—http://www.sierraclub.org/habitat/habitatloss.asp

Reprinted courtesy of the Sierra Club.

EXERCISE 10-23 RECORDING SOURCES

List source information for the paper you drafted in Exercise 10-18 for your Works Cited list. See page 299 for tips on what information to include.

10h   DOCUMENTING SOURCES USING MLA

LEARNING OBJECTIVE 8
Document sources using MLA.

There are a number of different documentation formats (these are often called *styles*) that are used by scholars and researchers. Members of a particular academic discipline usually use the same format. For example, biologists follow a format described in *Scientific Style and Format: A Manual for Authors, Editors, and Publishers.*

Two of the most common methods of documenting and citing sources are those of the Modern Language Association (MLA), typically used in English and humanities papers, and the American Psychological Association (APA), commonly used for social science papers. Both use a system of in-text citation: a brief note in the body of the text that refers to a source that is fully described in the Works Cited list (MLA) or References (APA) at the end of the paper, where sources are listed in alphabetical order.

Use the following guidelines for providing correct in-text citations using the MLA documentation style. For a comprehensive review of MLA style, consult the *MLA Handbook for Writers of Research Papers,* 7th edition, by Joseph Gibaldi or go to the MLA Web site at www.mla.org.

MLA In-Text Citations

When you refer to, summarize, paraphrase, quote, or in any other way use another author's words or ideas, you must indicate the source from which you took them by inserting an **in-text citation** that refers your reader to your "Works Cited" list. Place your citation at the end of the sentence in which you refer to, summarize, paraphrase, or quote a source. It should follow a quotation mark, but come before punctuation that ends the sentence. If a question mark ends the sentence, place the question mark before the citation and a period after the citation.

Here are some guidelines about what to include in your in-text citations and how to incorporate quotations into your paper:

1. **If the source is introduced by a phrase that names the author, the citation need only include the page number.**

   Miller poses the idea that if a good story is supposed to be a condensed version of life, then life should be lived like a good story in the first place (310).

2. **If the author is not named in the sentence, then include both the author's name and the page number in the citation.**

   If a good story is supposed to be a condensed version of life, then life should be lived like a good story in the first place (Miller 310).

3. **If there are two or three authors, include the last names of all of them.**

   Business ethics are important: "Many companies also have codes of ethics that guide buyers and sellers" (Lamb, Hair, and McDaniel 105).

4. **If there are four or more, include only the first author's last name and follow it with "et al.," which means "and others."**

   Therefore, impalas "illustrate the connections between animal behavior, evolution, and ecology" (Campbell et al. 703).

5. **If you have used two or more works by the same author, either include the relevant title in your sentence or include the title, if brief, or an abbreviated version in your citation.**

   In *Stealing MySpace: The Battle to Control the Most Popular Website in America*, Angwin concludes . . . (126).

   Or

   Angwin concludes . . . (*MySpace* 120).

6. **When you include a quotation in your paper, you should signal your reader that one is to follow.** For example, use such introductory phrases as the following:

> According to Miller, "[quotation]."
> As Miller notes, "[quotation]."
> In the words of Miller, "[quotation]."

7. **To use a direct quotation, copy the author's words exactly and put them in quotation marks.** You do not always have to quote the full sentences; you can borrow phrases or clauses as long as they fit into your sentence, both logically and grammatically.

> Miller comments that he "wondered whether a person could plan a story for his life and live it intentionally" (310).

8. **If the quotation is lengthy (four sentences or longer), set it apart from the rest of your paper.** Indent the entire quotation one inch from the margin, double-space the lines, and do not use quotation marks. Include an in-text citation after the final punctuation mark at the end of the quotation.

> When discussing adapting a screenplay from his memoir, Miller noted the following:
>
> > It didn't occur to me at the time, but it's obvious now that in creating the fictional Don, I was creating the person I wanted to be, the person worth telling stories about. It never occurred to me that I could re-create my own story, my real life story, but in an evolution. I had moved toward a better me. I was creating someone I could live through, the person I'd be if I redrew the world, a character that was me but flesh and soul other. And flesh and soul better too. (210)

MLA Works Cited List

Your list of works cited should include all the sources you referred to, summarized, paraphrased, or quoted in your paper. Start the list on a separate page at the end of your paper and title it "Works Cited." Arrange these entries alphabetically by each author's last name. If an author is not named (as in an editorial), then alphabetize the item by title. Double-space between and within entries. Start entries flush left, and if they run more than one line, indent subsequent lines half an inch.

1. **The basic format for a book can be illustrated as follows:**

Lin, Marvin. *Kid A*. New York: Continuum, 2011. Print.

Special cases are handled as follows:

a. **Two or more authors** If there are two or three authors, include all their names in the order in which they appear in the source. If there are four or more, give the first author's name only and follow it with "et al."

Authors   Article Title

Spicer, Mark S., and John R. Covach. *Sounding Out Pop: Analytical Essays in Popular Music*. Ann Arbor: Michigan UP, 2010. Print.

Place of Publication   Publisher   Date   Medium of Publication

b. **Two or more works by the same author** If your list contains two or more works by the same author, list the author's name only once. For additional entries, substitute three hyphens followed by a period in place of the name.

Miller, Donald. *A Million Miles in a Thousand Years: What I Learned while Editing My Life*. Nashville: Nelson, 2010. Print.

———. *Searching for God Knows What*. Nashville: Nelson, 2004. Print.

c. **Editor** If the book has an editor instead of an author, list the editor's name at the beginning of the entry and follow it with "ed."

McDannell, Colleen, ed. *Catholics in the Movies*. Oxford: Oxford UP, 2008. Print.

d. **Edition** If the book has an edition number, include it after the title.

DeVito, Joseph A. *Human Communication: The Basic Course*. 11th ed. Boston: Pearson, 2010. Print.

e. **Publisher** The entire name of the publisher is not used. For example, the Houghton Mifflin Company is listed as "Houghton."

2. **What format is used for articles?** The basic format for a periodical can be illustrated as follows:

Author   Article Title   Name of Periodical Volume/Issue No.

Wilentz, Sean. "Bob Dylan in America." *The New York Review of Books* 57.18 (2010): 34. Print.

Date Page no.   Medium of Publication

Special cases are handled as follows:

a. **Newspaper articles** Include the author, article title, name of the newspaper, date, section letter or number, page(s), and medium of publication. Abbreviate all months except May, June, and July, and place the day before the month.

> Weiner, Jonah. "Shaggy, Yes, but Finessed Just So." *New York Times* 25 Oct. 2010, New York ed.: AR20. Print.

b. **An article in a weekly magazine** List the author, article title, name of the magazine, date, page(s), and medium of publication. Abbreviate months as indicated above.

> Lilla, Mark. "The President and the Passions." *New York Times Magazine* 110 Dec. 2010: MM13. Print.

Internet Sources

Information on the Internet comes from a wide variety of sources. For example, there are journals that are online versions of print publications, but there are also journals that are published only online. There are online books, articles from online databases, government publications, government Web sites, and more. Therefore, it is not sufficient merely to state that you got something from the Web. Citations for Internet resources must adequately reflect the exact type of document or publication that was used.

Include enough information to allow your readers to locate your sources. For some Internet sources, it may not be possible to locate all the required information; provide the information that is available. For sources that appear only online, include the following information: the name(s) of the author, editor, translator, narrator, compiler, performer, or producer of the material; the title of the work; the title of the Web site (if different); the version or edition used; the publisher or sponsor of the site (if unknown write n.p.); the date of publication (day, month, year), write n.d. if not known; the medium of publication (Web); and the date of access (day, month, year). *Do not* include the URL unless the site cannot be found without using it.

1. **The basic format for an Internet source is as follows:**

   > Breihan, Tom. "My Morning Jacket Ready New Album." *Pitchfork*. Pitchfork Media Inc. 3 Mar. 2011. Web. 6 Mar. 2011.

2. **The basic format for an Internet source that originally appeared in print is as follows:** Start your entry with the same information you would for a print source. Then add the title of the Web site or database (in italics) followed by a period, the medium of publication (Web) followed by a period, and the date you accessed the source (day, month, year) followed by a period. DO NOT include the URL unless the site cannot be found without using it.

   > Wald, Mathew L. "Study Details How U.S. Could Cut 28% of Greenhouse Gases." *New York Times* 30 Nov. 2007: Business. *nytimes.com*. Web. 12 Aug. 2008.

   a. **Online book** If you consulted an entire online book, use this format:

   > Woolf, Virginia. *Monday or Tuesday*. New York: Harcourt, 1921. *Bartleby.com*. Web. 6 Aug. 2008.

b. **Online book** If you consulted part of an online book, use this format:

> Seifert, Kelvin, and David Zinger. "Effective Nonverbal Communication." *Educational Psychology*. Boston: Houghton, 2010. *The Online Books Page*. Web. 6 Feb. 2011.

c. **Article from an online periodical** If you accessed the article *directly* from an online journal, magazine, or newspaper, use this format:

> Sommers, Jeffrey. "Historical Arabesques: Patterns of History." *World History Connected* 5.3. University of Illinois at Urbana-Champaign, June 2008. Web. 15 May 2011.

d. **Article from an online database** If you accessed an article using an online database, and a Digital Object Locator (DOI) was provided for the article, include it. If not, include the name of the database and the document number, if available.

> Barnard, Neal D., et al. "Vegetarian and Vegan Diets in Type 2 Diabetes Management." *Nutrition Reviews*, 67(5), 255–263. Web. 21 Apr. 2011. doi:10.1111/j.1753-4887.20010.001108.x

> Bivins, Corey. "A Soy-free, Nut-free Vegan Meal Plan." *Vegetarian Journal*, 30(1), 14–17. *AltHealth Watch*. Web. 21 Apr. 2011. (20101018153)

e. **Online government publication** If you consulted a document published by a government entity:

> United States. Financial Crisis Inquiry Commission. *The Financial Crisis Inquiry Report: Final Report of the National Commission on the Causes of the Financial and Economic Crisis in the United States*. Washington: Financial Crisis Inquiry Commission, 2010. *FDLP Desktop*. Web. 20 Mar. 2011.

Other Electronic Sources

1. **CD-ROM nonperiodical publication**

> Beck, Mark. F. *Theory & Practice of Therapeutic Massage: Student CD-ROM*. Clifton Park, NY: Milady, 2011. CD-ROM.

2. **Interview from a radio Web site**

> Merritt, Stephin. Interview. *The Strange Powers of Stephin Merritt & the Magnetic Fields*. KEXP, 10 Dec. 2011. Web. 13 Apr. 2011.

3. **Television documentary viewed on the Internet**

> Lacy, Susan, prod. "Troubadours." *American Masters*. PBS, 2 Mar. 2011. Web. 16 Apr. 2011.

4. **Photograph viewed on the Internet**

> Warhol, Andy. *Self-Portrait*. 1963–1964. Photograph. *The Warhol*. The Andy Warhol Museum. Web. 17 Aug. 2011.

Using MLA style, add two quotations to the paper you drafted in Exercise 10-17. Add in-text citations and write a Works Cited list for your paper including entries for all your sources.

Sample Documented Paper

Adam Simmons   Simmons 1

Professor Garcia

Sociology 101

20 February 2013

Weighing the Consequences of Censorship in Media

There are different opinions about censorship in the media. Each side has good intentions; one side is saying censorship is protecting people or the country and the other is saying censorship limits the Constitutional right to freedom of speech.

People in favor of censorship of the media often talk about the morality of the content. A common argument is that some media contain inappropriate material that could unintentionally be seen by young children. In this case, inappropriate material is defined as pornographic, violent, vulgar, or sexual in any way. The argument is that it could lead kids to try and repeat what they are seeing on the television or what they are hearing about in music (Prabhakar). By censoring such materials, children would hypothetically be less likely to repeat the behavior and would not be exposed to things that might not be appropriate for their age, so censorship would protect children.

Some people also believe that censorship is important when it is used to protect military information and "helps preserve the secrets of a nation being revealed" ("Pros of Censorship"). With the government monitoring what information the media offers, it is less likely that information the government does not want leaked out will be made public. This could mean keeping troops safe and protecting domestic and foreign policy, especially in wartime when enemies can track news sources to find out about U.S. strategy. It can also help keep dangerous information, such as details about weaponry, from getting into the wrong hands.

Censorship has some dangers though. It can be viewed as directly violating the First Amendment of the Constitution and taking away freedom of speech. The amendment states "Congress shall make no law . . . abridging the freedom of speech, or of the press . . ." There are some who say the First Amendment acts as a "complete barrier to government censorship" (Pember 43); since the Constitution creates this ban, censorship is in effect unlawful. However, there are Supreme Court cases that have modified the interpretation of this amendment, such as the Smith Act which makes it "a crime to advocate the violent overthrow of the government" (Pember 52).

There are other reasons that people object to censorship. Some people argue that censorship can also be abused by the government and in the wrong hands it can lead to a loss of freedom of speech and halt a flow of ideas in a society, as seen under various dictatorships (Neuharth). It can also be said that censorship stifles creativity. Saying that some works are immoral or unsuitable is making a legal statement that some art is good and some art is bad ("What Is Censorship?"). Art, in itself, is subjective and cannot really be labeled that way. If art has to be made to meet the requirements of the censors, then it will never be able to be completely creative and free.

Both viewpoints about censorship approach the topic with the hope of doing what is best for society, but come at it from completely different angles. One hopes to make things better by removing immoral or dangerous speech and the other seeks to let every person have the ability to say what they want regardless of whether it is seen moral by others.

Works Cited

Neuharth, Al. "Google Is Gutsy to Spit in China's Eye." *USA Today* 26 Mar. 2010: 15a. Print.

Pember, Don R., and Clay Calvert. *Mass Media Law*. Boston: McGraw-Hill, 2010. Print.

Pillai, Prabhakar. "Pros and Cons of Censorship." *Buzzle Web Portal: Intelligent Life on the Web*. Buzzle.com, n.d. Web. 8 Apr. 2011.

"Pros of Censorship." *Laws.com*. n.d. Web. 8 Apr. 2011.

"What Is Censorship?" American Civil Liberties Union. 30 Aug. 2006. Web. 08 Apr. 2011.

SUMMARY OF LEARNING OBJECTIVES

Objective 1 Under-stand the structure of an essay.	An *essay* is a group of paragraphs about one subject. It contains three parts—an introductory paragraph that includes the thesis statement, sup-porting paragraphs (body), and conclusion.
Objective 2 Prewrite to generate and orga-nize ideas and plan your essay.	*Prewriting* involves choosing and narrowing your topic; generating ideas; grouping ideas to discover a thesis; writing a preliminary thesis; considering audience, purpose, and point of view; organizing ideas; choosing an appro-priate tone; and choosing a method of development.
Objective 3 Draft an essay.	*Drafting* involves writing and rewriting your essay. It includes evaluating and revising your thesis statement; supporting your thesis with substantial evi-dence; using signal words to connect your ideas; drafting body paragraphs and writing an introduction, conclusion, and title.
Objective 4 Revise your essay.	*Revision* involves examining your ideas and how effectively you have expressed them. Allow time after drafting before you revise; print a copy; look for common problems; read the draft aloud; and use peer review. Use revision idea maps to revise and evaluate your essay's content and structure, paragraphs, sentences, and words.
Objective 5 Edit and proofread for clarity and correctness.	*Editing and proofreading* involve making certain your essay is clear, error free, and presented in acceptable manuscript form. Correct errors in spelling, punctuation, and grammar, as well as typographical errors.
Objective 6 Use sources and avoid plagiarism.	Writing a paper *using sources* involves keeping track of exactly where you found information; separating your own ideas from those of sources; plac-ing direct quotes in quotation marks; and providing citation information for paraphrases. Keeping complete records will ensure you avoid plagiarism (using another person's words or ideas as though they are your own).
Objective 7 Synthesize sources.	*Synthesizing* means locating several sources on a topic, comparing how they are similar and different, and putting together the ideas you discover to cre-ate new ideas and insights about the topic.
Objective 8 Document sources using MLA.	The *Modern Language Association (MLA)* style is typically used for document-ing sources in English and the humanities. It consists of in-text citations that refer readers to a Works Cited list of all sources used in a paper that is organized alphabetically by authors' last names.

Reading and Writing About Contemporary Issues

PART

TWO

11 Defining Ourselves: Our Multiple Identities

Who are you?

Some people might answer that question by stating their name. But many people would pause because they can't give a simple answer. Consider Pang Xu, a student at San Francisco City College. Thinking about the many roles she plays, Pang might see herself in many ways. She might say:

- I am a woman.
- I am a daughter.
- I am the mother of a two-year old boy.
- I am a wife.
- I am an immigrant.
- I am Chinese-American.
- I am a student.
- I am an employee at The Gap.
- I am a lover of animals.

And the list could go on and on.

The readings in this chapter focus on *identity*: how we define ourselves, not only in our own heads but also in relationship to other people, groups, and society. Each reading in this chapter focuses on at least one type of identity, but sometimes multiple identities.

WHY IS IDENTITY SUCH AN IMPORTANT CONTEMPORARY ISSUE?

Much of what you read in the contemporary press revolves around identity politics—groups' definitions of themselves and how others perceive them. These perceptions color individuals' experiences, expectations, and even the set of choices they face or the challenges they encounter. For example, government policies may offer assistance to people belonging to certain groups (e.g., people with disabilities, elderly people, sick people). But to offer help, the government must clearly define these terms. What exactly does *disabled* mean? At what age does a person become *old*? Should people with the flu be considered as sick as those with cancer?

How Does the Concept of Identity Tie to My College Courses?

Identity is a core theme running through most humanities and social science courses. In a sociology course, for example, you might study ethnic groups in the United States and how some of them came to be considered ethnic minorities. Literature often focuses on self-expression and the quest for identity. In history and government courses, you will learn about the U.S. Census, which in recent years has struggled with defining racial and ethnic groups due to the huge diversity of the U.S. population. Abraham Maslow, a famous psychologist, defined a strong sense of self-identity as the ultimate achievement for any human being.

Tips for Reading about Identity

Here are some tips for reading not only the selections in this chapter, but any reading about identity.

- **Consider the author's background.** Check the "Source and Context" section before each reading to learn more about the author. Doing so may give you perspective on his or her viewpoints. (Outside this book, check for any biographical information provided about the author.)
- **Keep an open mind.** Some of these readings may challenge your ideas or preconceptions about a topic. You may have an emotional response because some of the readings discuss difficult topics like obesity or the treatment of women. Once you have experienced the emotion, re-read the article more objectively, with a more critical eye, to better analyze and evaluate the author's thesis.
- **Look for similarities to your own life.** As you read, ask yourself if the author's perceptions match yours. Have you had personal experiences with the topic; and if so, do your opinions match the author's? Why or why not?

Rubric for Writing Essays

In this chapter you will read articles about identity and write essays in response to them. To be sure that you write clear and correct essays use the following rubric. Think of a rubric as a set of guidelines to follow in prewriting, writing, and revising an essay. Check the rubric often, especially as you begin each stage of the writing process.

I. Planning Use of prewriting strategy is evident

II. Organization Writing is unified and coherent

- Essay effectively accomplishes your purpose
- Essay is appropriate for your audience
- Thesis statement is clear and focused
- Sentences do not stray off topic
- Body paragraphs support the thesis statement
- Essay has an appealing introduction/conclusion
- Signal words and phrases are used appropriately

III. Content/Support

- Topic sentences are clear and focused
- Details are specific and adequate
- Details are logical and supportive of topic sentences
- Details are organized appropriately

IV. Grammar and Mechanics Use of language reflects Standard written English

V. Use of Technology MLA/APA format is used correctly

Comments/Suggestions for Improvement: _____

_____

_____

_____

_____

Revision and Proofreading Checklist

Revising, or editing, involves looking again at and often making major changes to every idea and sentence you have written. Proofreading is the part of the revision process that involves adding or deleting words and sentences, as well as correcting your grammar, spelling, and punctuation.

REVISION AND PROOFREADING LIST

Revision
- Does your essay accomplish your purpose?
- Is your essay appropriate for your audience?
- Is your thesis statement clearly expressed?
- Does each paragraph support your thesis?
- Is your essay logically organized?
- Have you used transitions to connect your ideas?
- Are your introduction, conclusion, and title effective?

Proofreading
- Each sentence ends with appropriate punctuation (period, question mark, exclamation point, and/or quotation mark)
- All punctuation within each sentence is correct (commas, colons, semi-colons, apostrophes, dashes, and quotation marks)
- Every word is spelled correctly
- Capital letters are used where needed
- Numbers and abbreviations are used correctly
- No words have been omitted
- All typographical errors have been corrected
- All pages are numbered and in the correct order

SELECTION

1

Student Essay

The Space In-Between

Santiago Quintana Garcia

DRE 096   Note: This is the final draft of Santiago's essay; his prewriting, drafting and revision are shown in Chapter 2.

PRE-READING

Source and Context

Santiago Quintana Garcia is a student at Beloit College in Wisconsin, where he majors in Biochemistry and Literature. He wrote this personal essay for his freshman composition class.

A Note on the Reading

Read the selection to understand how one young man grapples with his multiple identities and his interactions with others who've had similar experiences.

Previewing the Reading

Using the steps listed on page 4, preview the reading selection. When you have finished, answer the following questions.

1. In what city and country was the author born? _____

2. In what city and state does the author live now? _____

3. Determine whether each statement is true or false.

    _____   a. The author is likely to mention issues of race, gender, and nationality.

    _____   b. The author is unhappy with his current life.

Using Prior Knowledge

Most people feel that they are part of at least one minority group. What exactly is a minority group? To which minority group(s) do you belong, if any?

Reading Tip

Although this selection is fairly short, it contains some abstract language and sophisticated concepts. Adjust your reading rate to ensure you are achieving full comprehension. Highlight and annotate key information as you read.

The Space In-Between

Santiago Quintana Garcia

1   There are around twenty million people living in Mexico City, and this number is constantly increasing. Mexico is where I was born and grew up, before I moved to Beloit, Wisconsin to attend Beloit College. The town of Beloit has roughly thirty thousand people. This means that about seven hundred towns the size of Beloit would fit inside Mexico City. In Mexico City, I was no more than a speck of dust in a dirty room. In Beloit, if I go have breakfast in one of three downtown cafés, I can be sure that there will be at least one person I know, probably around five or more. Beloit and Mexico City are two completely different worlds that I have come to call home.

2   I am Mexican. I should probably have beautiful cinnamon skin, hair black as night and falling straight like a waterfall to frame two glowing brown eyes. Many people think this is what a "true Mexican" looks like. Drawing a line between what is a true Mexican and what isn't based on looks is not a simple task. I myself think it is impossible. This stereotype has played a role in my life both in Mexico and Beloit. I have white skin, the only blue eyes in my family of brown eyes, and curly light brown hair. In Mexico City, when I went to the market to buy vegetables for the week, people didn't bother to ask my name. They called me *güerito*, blond. I got asked if I am from the United States or from another country. I was never completely a part of the nation I was born and grew up in. In Beloit though, people are fascinated by my cultural background and ask about my customs and daily life back home. Inevitably, at some point in the conversation they tell me that I don't look Mexican. I live between two worlds: being racially "foreign" in Mexico, and being culturally "foreign" in Beloit.

3   Living a life in between two worlds, never completely a part of either, is a very complicated and extremely interesting place to be. Living in-between encourages growth and maturity. As a teenager, I struggled with feelings of not belonging and wanting to be a part of a group. I did not play soccer, or the guitar, and I suffered from bullying. The impact this had on my life was emotionally wrecking. Often when people find themselves in similar situations, they turn to familiar things for comfort. Things like a group they belong to, like a culture, or a race, or a religious group. This was not accessible to me in the same way as it was to others. On the other hand,

virtues
good qualities

though, standing on no man's land let me observe the effects of the culture I grew up with on my way of thinking, and has greatly influenced my area of focus in my college studies. Standing in this middle ground was a vantage point from which I could analyze the opinions I held and the habits I developed and see my **virtues** and faults through different eyes. The hardiest weeds live where the pavement meets the prairie. I live where outsider meets insider.

4   What happens in this middle ground is that concepts such as gender, race, nationality, and other identities seem held up by pins. They are extremely volatile and impermanent, constantly changing and molding. This knowledge is present with me every time I say "I am Mexican" or "I am white." I had thought that people who fit snugly into a stereotype would never experience being an outsider. But I soon found out otherwise.

5   The first time I touched on this subject with a friend of mine, he said that he saw what I meant. I was convinced he didn't. He was the perfect example of the "Mexican" racial stereotype. He explained that he couldn't know about my situation, but that he was having a similar problem with his family. His mom had recently mentioned that he should be going to church more, instead of hanging out with his friends on Sunday mornings. That was his middle place. He identified with these two seemingly separate identities that he had created: his Catholic self, and his social self. He was having trouble negotiating between the two. He stood in a place in the middle, where his church community was not understanding about his absences, and his friends made fun of his religious background. At the edges of these groups, he had thought about these two in much greater depth than I ever had, and he shared some incredible insights about the baggage associated with both identities, and how they weren't as solid as he thought; they had blurry edges and a lot of holes subject to interpretation.

6   It is the places in-between where the most potential for growth lives. All people have a place where they feel like outsiders, or not completely insiders. Realizing that this is where you are standing, and that it is perfectly fine to have one foot inside and one foot outside, will let the unique reveal itself through you. Being in-between can be difficult, but it is there that the most unexpected and wonderful things happen.

POST-READING

UNDERSTANDING AND ANALYZING THE READING

A. Building Vocabulary

Context

Using context and a dictionary if necessary, determine the meaning of each word as it is used in the selection.

_____ 1. stereotype (paragraph 2)
    a. racial background
    b. ethnic group

     c. dual identity

     d. oversimplified idea

_____ 2. vantage point (paragraph 3)

     a. advantage

     b. intermediate location

     c. high score

     d. position

_____ 3. hardiest (paragraph 3)

     a. most difficult

     b. strongest

     c. most stubborn

     d. most beautiful

_____ 4. volatile (paragraph 4)

     a. hot

     b. unpredictable

     c. weak

     d. personal

_____ 5. baggage (paragraph 5)

     a. emotional issues

     b. suitcases

     c. happiness

     d. reasons

Word Parts

A REVIEW OF PREFIXES AND SUFFIXES

IM- means not.
-ER means one who.

Use your knowledge of word parts and the review above to fill in the blanks in the following sentences.

1. **Impermanent** (paragraph 4) means _____ permanent or _____ lasting.

2. An **outsider** (paragraph 4) is _____ sits outside the mainstream of a society or culture.

B. Understanding Main Ideas

Select the best answer.

_____ 1. Which of the following best states the main idea of the entire piece of writing?

    a. Outsiders face serious challenges in almost all aspects of their lives.

    b. People of Mexican origin generally have difficulty adjusting to life as immigrants in the United States.

    c. Not fully belonging to specific groups can be difficult, but it offers many opportunities for growth.

    d. Most adolescents have difficulty "fitting in" when they go to college or take their first full-time job.

_____ 2. The topic of paragraph 2 is

    a. the differences between Mexico City and Beloit.

    b. Mexican stereotypes of Americans.

    c. the author's personal appearance.

    d. differences in ethnic groups in North America and South America.

_____ 3. In which sentence of paragraph 5 does the main idea appear?

    a. first

    b. third

    c. sixth

    d. last

C. Identifying Details

Select the best answer.

_____ 1. Which type of identity does the author *not* discuss in "The Place In-Between"?

    a. religious identity

    b. racial identity

    c. sexual identity

    d. national identity

_____ 2. The word that Mexicans use to describe the author's hair color is

    a. *güerito.*

    b. *rubio.*

c. *peloso.*

d. *rojo.*

_____ 3. The author's friend is struggling with two sides of himself: his
_____ self and his _____ self.

a. old, new

b. social, Catholic

c. angry, friendly

d. American, Latino

_____ 4. Which of the following physical features is not described as typical
of Mexicans?

a. brown eyes

b. black, straight hair

c. cinnamon skin

d. a prominent nose

D. Recognizing Methods of Organization and Signal Words

Select the best answer.

_____ 1. The organizational pattern of paragraph 1 is

a. chronological order.

b. comparison and contrast.

c. summary.

d. order of importance.

_____ 2. The signal word or phrase in paragraph 1 that signals its pattern of
organization is

a. born.

b. no more than.

c. speck of dust.

d. different.

_____ 3. The organizational pattern of paragraph 3 is

a process.

b. classification.

c. cause and effect.

d. definition.

E. Making Inferences

Based on what is stated in the reading, indicate whether each statement is true (T) or false (F).

_____ 1. The author is an illegal immigrant in the United States.

_____ 2. The author suggests that the definitions of race, gender, and nationality are quite complicated.

_____ 3. The author has not yet accepted his position as an "outsider" in America.

_____ 4. The author suggests that most Americans hold racist views of Mexicans.

_____ 5. The author feels more popular and well-known in Beloit than he ever did in Mexico City.

_____ 6. The author was probably a "loner" as a younger man.

F. Thinking Critically: Analyzing the Author's Technique

Select the best answer.

_____ 1. When the author says that identities have "blurry edges and a lot of holes" (paragraph 5), he means that identities
   a. are primarily dictated by one's country of birth.
   b. can be clearly defined.
   c. is purely an academic term used by sociology instructors and nobody else.
   d. have many sides that don't always fit together easily.

_____ 2. To support his argument, the author uses primarily
   a. personal experience.
   b. statistics.
   c. quotations from experts.
   d. academic research.

_____ 3. The author's purpose in "The Space In-Between" is to
   a. encourage legislators to pass immigration reform so that Mexicans can more easily emigrate to the United States.
   b. describe the customs and daily life of a Mexican teenager.
   c. compare life in Mexico to life in the United States.
   d. present the challenges of one who has struggled with multiple identities.

_____ 4. The point of view of this article is

    a. first person

    b. second person

    c. third person

    d. a combination of first person and third person

_____ 5. Which one of the following sentences contains an example of **informal** language?

    a. It is the places in-between where the most potential for growth lies.

    b. I was never completely a part of the nation I grew up in.

    c. His mom had recently mentioned that he should be going to church more, instead of hanging out with friends on Sunday morning.

    d. In Mexico City, I was no more than a speck of dust in a dirty room.

_____ 6. Which of the following is a fact, not an opinion?

    a. Living a life in between two worlds, never completely a part of either, is a very complicated and extremely interesting place to be. (paragraph 3)

    b. I had thought that people who fit snugly into a stereotype would never experience being an outsider. (paragraph 4)

    c. Mexico is where I was born and grew up, before I moved to Beloit, Wisconsin to attend Beloit College. (paragraph 1)

    d. I should probably have beautiful cinnamon skin, hair black as night and falling straight like a waterfall to frame two glowing brown eyes. (paragraph 2)

G. Thinking Critically: Analyzing the Author's Message

Select the best answer.

_____ 1. According to the author, all of the following can help those people standing in-between different groups to grow and mature, *except*

    a. recognizing and admitting that they are outsiders.

    b. understanding that it is perfectly fine to exist between two groups.

    c. viewing personal opinions and habits with a critical eye.

    d. choosing one primary group with which to identify themselves.

_____ 2. The author summarizes his *current* outsider status in one sentence when he says

    a. "There are around twenty million people living in Mexico City, and this number is constantly increasing." (paragraph 1)

    b. "I live between two worlds: being racially 'foreign' in Mexico, and being culturally 'foreign' in Beloit.'" (paragraph 2)

    c. "Inevitably, at some point in the conversation, they tell me I don't look Mexican." (paragraph 2)

    d. "As a teenager, I struggled with feelings of not belonging and wanting to be a part of a group." (paragraph 3)

_____ 3. When the author says, "The hardiest weeds live where the pavement meets the prairie" (paragraph 3), he means that

    a. he considers himself as worthless as a weed.

    b. it is easier to be an outsider in an urban setting than in a rural setting.

    c. his outsider status has given him great strength.

    d. he is succeeding in overcoming the discrimination he faces every day.

WRITING IN RESPONSE TO THE READING

H. Writing a Summary

Complete the following summary of paragraph 2 by filling in the missing words. Remember that a summary should cover all of the author's main points.

The author is from _____, but his _____ does not fit the stereotype of _____. Unlike many Mexicans, the author has white skin, _____ eyes. For this reason, he never truly felt like part _____ he was born in. At _____ in Wisconsin, people ask him about life in Mexico and usually mention that he doesn't look like _____. As a result, he doesn't feel quite at home in either place. He feels racially foreign in _____ and _____ in Beloit.

I. Writing Paragraphs

Write a well-developed paragraph in response to one of the following writing prompts. As part of this assignment you will need to follow the writing process:

- Use a prewriting strategy to generate ideas
- Complete a guided outline
- Write a rough draft
- Complete a peer revision guide
- Write a final draft using proper MLA format

1. In paragraph 3, the author says that standing on no man's land "has greatly influenced my area of focus in my college studies." Write a paragraph in which you explore one factor that influenced your choice of major and or your approach to college.

2. Write a paragraph in which you summarize the author's feelings about Mexico City.

3. "The Space In-Between" is an emotional exploration of one man's feelings of being an outsider. Write a paragraph in which you suggest a few images that could effectively convey a visual sense of an outsider standing out from the crowd. For example, one image might be a punk rocker at a classical music concert.

4. This essay talks about the way a person is composed of multiple identities. What are your identities? How do they complement one another, or how do they conflict? Is one of your identities dominant over all the others? Write a paragraph exploring one of these questions.

5. Have you ever felt like an outsider looking in? Write a paragraph about one situation in which you felt this way. Do you feel that you learned anything from the experience, or matured as a result of it?

6. Santiago Garcia refers to the places in-between as the places "where the most potential for growth lies" (paragraph 6). However, he does not provide many specific examples of the ways he has grown or of what he has learned. Assume that you can step out of yourself and observe yourself for a day, just like you would observe another person. Write a paragraph about what you'd learn about yourself and the conclusions you might reach.

J. Working Collaboratively

1. **Thinking Personally** Create your own list of multiple identities like the one on page 308. Then pair up with a classmate who you do not know. Share your identities list, ask questions about the individual points on the list to get more information about your partner, and discuss your similarities and differences. Be prepared to introduce your partner to the class without reading his or her list.

2. **Thinking Deeply** After reading the selection by Santiago Quintana Garcia, break into groups and discuss the following questions:

   - What is stereotyping?
   - What examples of stereotyping can you think of in our society today?
   - What are the dangers associated with stereotyping?
   - How do you think Santiago was affected by stereotyping in both Mexico and the U.S.?

   Be prepared to report out to the class on your discussion.

3. **Thinking Visually** Working with a partner, create an acrostic for the word *stereotype* **or** the words *in between*. Each letter will be the beginning of a word or phrase that relates to the essay by Santiago Quintana Garcia. Record your acrostic on the chart paper supplied by your instructor. Here is an example for you:

Light skinned	L	i	g	h	t		s	k	i	n	n	e	d	
In between	I	n		b	e	t	w	e	e	n				
Foreign	F	o	r	e	i	g	n							
Experiences	E	x	p	e	r	i	e	n	c	e	s			

4. **Thinking Globally** Using the Internet, compile a list of facts about Mexico City and Beloit, Wisconsin. In class, break into groups of four and share your facts with each other. Using the paper supplied by your instructor, design a chart that shows the similarities and the differences in the two cities. The design of your chart may be as creative as you want it to be.

SELECTION
2
Magazine Article

Beyond the Burqa

Zuhra Bahman

DRE 097

PRE-READING

Source and Context

This article originally appeared in *The New Internationalist,* a magazine with a worldwide subscription base. According to the magazine's mission statement, *The New Internationalist* exists "to report on the issues of world poverty and inequality; to focus attention on the unjust relationship between the powerful and powerless worldwide; to debate and campaign for the radical changes necessary to meet the basic needs of all; and to bring to life the people, the ideas, and the action in the fight for global justice."

A Note on the Reading

What challenges do women face in conservative societies in the Middle East? Read "Beyond the Burqa" for some answers.

Previewing the Reading

Using the steps listed on page 4, preview the reading selection. When you have finished, complete the following items.

1. The article of women's clothing that the author sees as symbolic of conservative Muslim culture is the _____.

2. Indicate whether each statement is true (T) or false (F).

   _____ a. When this article was written, Hamid Karzai was the president of Afghanistan.

   _____ b. The author believes that rebels will always face challenges from traditionalists.

Using Prior Knowledge

Think about the society in which you live. How do traditional values sometimes come into conflict with societal changes?

Reading Tip

As you read, think carefully about the author's background and her experiences with the society she describes. How do these factors affect her credibility and her argument? Be sure to highlight and annotate as you read.

Beyond the Burqa

Zuhra Bahman

Zhura Bahman looks at how her fellow Afghans are managing the struggle between modernity and tradition. She is an Afghan writer and law researcher currently living in London. She visits Afghanistan several times a year.

Two Afghani photographers, Farzana Wahidy and Freshta Kohistany, present contrasting images of contemporary Afghan womanhood. Behind them is the Kabul River Bazaar.

Credit: Fardin Waezi / AINA PHOTO AGENCY / AFGHANISTAN www.ainaphoto.org

Taliban
Islamic fundamentalist (extremely conservative) political movement in Afghanistan

burqa
a long loose garment covering the entire body

1   During the **Taliban** era, many in the liberal world saw the **burqa** as the symbol of Taliban oppression. Now the Taliban are ousted from power, yet the burqa remains firmly on the heads of all sorts of Afghan women.

2   Why? Because the burqa is a symbol of traditionally conservative Afghan society which pre-dates the Taliban, in which women are viewed as men's possessions, to be kept hidden from other men. Freeing Afghan women from the burqa can only be

Reprinted by permission from *New Internationalist*, no. 417 (November 1, 2008).

achieved if the mindset of the nation changes. Removing the Taliban does not solve the problem.

3   The same applies to a range of other issues—such as inequality between men and women and underage marriages—which are embedded in the traditions of Afghan society. These customs are extremely hard to change, as most Afghan people and institutions either passively endorse or actively follow them.

4   At a local level, traditional conservatism is kept alive though the *jirga* (assembly of elders) and *shuras* (councils or consultations). These largely democratic, but old and male, institutions decide on a wide range of issues from family matters to land disputes.

5   They are useful for dispensing swift justice in a country which, after decades of conflict, has very little in the way of a formal legal system. However, they punish those who break with tradition in ways that are inconsistent with human rights standards—as I found on hearing the story of Homaira, a mother of five children living in the Parwan province of Afghanistan.

On the Run

6   While high on drugs, Homaira's husband, her brother-in-law, and her brother got into a scuffle. Homaira's brother-in-law shot her brother, who died instantly. Homaira's brother-in-law and husband went into hiding.

7   Following tradition, Homaira was taken back to her parents' home, whereas her children, including her two-year-old son, were given to her in-laws. Homaira stayed in her parents' house while another of her brothers sought her husband and brother-in-law to exact revenge.

8   When the search didn't bear fruit, Homaira requested that her parents and brothers allow her to go back to her in-laws so that she could be with her young children. The parents and brothers did not agree, but Homaira left anyway to join her kids.

9   Leaving the house against her brothers' wishes was a big mistake. Homaira was disowned in a gathering attended by hundreds of people in a local **mosque**, where her brothers swore to kill her for her disobedience. Fearing for her life, Homaira is still on the run with her five children. And popular support remains with her brothers.

mosque
Muslim house of worship

10   Afghanistan's national Western-style justice system has little impact on this type of traditional conservatism, where women who are raped are imprisoned rather than the men who rape them, and women who try to escape hardship are punished for setting foot outside their homes.

11   Although Western **NGO**s are working to strengthen the central justice system, its institutions are ill-equipped and often inaccessible to those who need it. How can a village woman, suffering from domestic violence, be expected to travel by donkey for two days to get to a city court and start legal proceedings that might take months to complete?

NGO
nongovernmental organization

12   The reality is that more than 80 percent of Afghan people prefer the traditional justice system because it is fast and local, albeit unjust and not human rights-friendly. It is futile to demonize the traditional system and expect people to subscribe to an alternative that is unknown to them.

What about Mrs Karzai?

13   Even people who do know about alternatives and who wield considerable influence openly endorse some of the customs that lead to human rights violations. Take the example of segregation—a tradition rigidly imposed on most women. The country's President, Hamid Karzai, has so far kept his wife behind closed doors and out of the public eye. Mrs. Karzai, who is a medical doctor, does not even attend state visits or other official engagements with her husband.

bigamous
having more than
one spouse

14   One prominent female parliamentarian and human rights activist has decided to remain in a **bigamous** and violent marriage in exchange for kudos within a traditional community that frowns upon divorcees. This personal moral sacrifice is winning her the political support of the traditionalists. However, she is setting a very bad example for ordinary people who want change.

15   Some officials use their office to impose traditional values. For instance, the Minister of Culture, Abdul Kareem Khuram, banned the broadcasting of Indian soap operas on Afghan TV channels because, he said, they challenged Afghan traditional values. The dramas showed bare arms and midriffs, and depicted social issues such as children born out of wedlock—and were massively popular with viewers.

16   The Government presents itself as a liberal force for change. But, at a personal and local level, it endorses ideas that are outright violations of human rights and freedoms.

17   This contradiction is reflected in society. When I asked a 28-year-old NGO worker, Zabi, about women's segregation, he said: "I respect and am friends with women I went to university with and work with. But when it comes to my sisters, I am a bit strict. I don't want people to talk about them behind their backs. They can go to university but can't be friends with men. When they get married they can change, depending on their husband's thinking on these matters. Afghan society is not a good place for free women."

18   Perhaps it is not the personal wish of Zabi or Mr. Karzai to keep their female relatives segregated, but they and millions of ordinary Afghan men feel compelled to follow Afghan tradition, which provides them with a collective security but leaves little room for personal opinions, freedoms and rights.

Ways of Rebelling

19   There are many, however, who rebel and fight for modernity, choice, freedom, and human rights. Everyone who attempts to rebel will face challenges from the traditionalists. Any success they have depends on their strategy towards these traditionalists.

grassroots
local and personal

20   For instance, I met a young woman, Wazhma Frogh, who is challenging the practice of child marriages and child abuse at a **grassroots** level. But she is using traditional means and methods to change tradition. For example, she uses Islamic scripture to defend women's rights. When I met her she was busy organizing a mass prayer in a mosque for victims of child abuse, in order to raise awareness of the issue.

21   I also met a local *shura* or council leader from Parwan province who told me about his attempts to bring women into the local governance system—something

that he said was "unthinkable" a few years ago. He did this by creating a separate women's shura first, so that segregation was maintained; then he slowly incorporated the men's and women's groups to form a big shura. He then introduced a quota system for the leadership of the shura so that women got a chance to lead. He was delighted at how the conservative locals had accepted change that was introduced gradually.

22   Those who attempt to bring about change through outright rebellion suffer the most. However, it is sometimes hard to gauge what is deemed acceptable and what is not. TV presenter Shaima Razayee found out the hard way. She was shot dead, two months after being dismissed from her job presenting a pop music show, for acting in a way that a council of scholars considered too "un-Islamic." Her sins were laughing and joking with her male co-presenter and wearing a scarf that was deemed too small.

23   Some people just negotiate and agree to lose some aspect of their freedom in order to gain another. The burqa and marriage are two negotiating tools that most women use to keep traditions alive, while gaining some personal freedom in exchange.

24   Friba, a high school student, wears a burqa on her way to school. She says: "My father didn't like people seeing my face in the street and he wanted me to stay at home. I begged him to let me go to school and he agreed, only on condition that I wore a burqa, and I agreed. I am very happy now."

25   Her friend Mursal has just struck a deal with her parents over going to university. She has agreed to get engaged to a man of her parents' choice in exchange for being allowed to go to university. "I really wanted to go to university, but I'm not sure if I have done the right thing. I am hoping that I will fall in love with him by the time I finish university."

26   Most people who, to an untrained Western eye, appear liberated and educated may have had to choose a severe injustice in order to gain and practice the freedom that we see. Women usually lose out in these negotiations, while older men, the representatives of the conservative traditional society, have the upper hand—which they use to their advantage.

Sex in the City

27   Waheed, a privileged young man, had befriended a young woman. He told me: "I saw her on her way home from school. I gave her my business card with my number on it. That evening she called me. We spoke for hours. We met for a burger twice. And once I took her for a drive."

28   When I asked him whether he intended taking any further the relationship with his mobile-phone girlfriend, he laughed and said: "I don't want to marry her. Today she is my girlfriend, tomorrow she might become someone else's. I can't trust her. Girls like her are not trustworthy."

29   The relationship between Waheed and his girlfriend was uncomplicated. However, I met Dr. Suhaila, a gynecologist from one of Kabul's middle-class residential areas, who claimed to be dealing with cases of abortion in unmarried girls. She also gets enquiries about reconstructive surgery of the hymen to hide the signs of

a sexual relationship before marriage. She said: "I used to deal with similar requests before and during the Taliban times too. However, at that time these issues remained hidden. Nowadays people talk about them and write about them, which gives the impression that things are getting worse, that there's more immorality."

expatriate
person who
lives outside
his or her
native country

30   The urban centers of Afghanistan now have huge **expatriate** communities where prostitution, alcoholism, and drugs are rife. But there is also education, women with small scarves, male-female relationships, and employment in such areas.

31   Traditionalists link all these vices and virtues and so instill in people fear of change; this makes it harder for those who want to promote education and greater freedom for women.

32   The people of Afghanistan have gone from living in one of the most highly regulated societies during the Taliban era to one that is now very much exposed to new ideas and practices. It is hard to achieve a balance between maintaining tradition and accepting change, especially during a time of war. The first step is for Afghans to recognize the practices within their culture which are against human rights and then find ways of dealing with them that are not too much of a threat to traditional institutions and customs.

33   The international community, too, must recognize that Afghanistan's traditional systems have survived for hundreds of years and they cannot suddenly be swapped for Western ones. Only working within the existing systems, with patience and understanding, bringing about change slowly, and with subtlety, will succeed.

"I CANNOT BELIEVE HOW LUCKY I AM"—SHOGOFA

34   I hate being 23 years old and still in year 11 of school—everyone is at least five years younger than me! But it's not my fault. I was born and brought up in Kandahar in Southern Afghanistan. Women's lives are very hard there.

35   When I was young I was engaged to a boy who was related to me. I never really spoke with him or met him but I waited to be married to him.

36   One day we got the news that the Taliban had killed my aunt's husband. We all went to see. They had left his body in front of their house. His head and hands had been chopped off and placed on his chest with some letters and leaflets. The Taliban said that he was dead because he was a teacher and he sent his daughters to school. I was extremely upset; he was a good man, very kind.

37   I was in year eight at the time. My father was very scared, so he took me out of school. I stayed at home doing housework. I got ill, and my engagement was broken off. I had nothing to look forward to. I was a sick girl with a broken engagement and no education.

38   My father refused to send us back to school because he was scared of the Taliban killing him; but he was also scared of us being caught up in a suicide bombing in the city. He said that he was scared of seeing my dead body lying bloodied and exposed on the street.

39   I knew he would never let me study in Kandahar, so when I came to Kabul to attend my cousin's wedding I refused to go home and begged my father to let me stay here. My uncle's wife took my side and promised to look after me.

40   I am now extremely happy in Kabul; I cannot believe how lucky I am to be here. I am studying hard, although I can't concentrate because I keep thinking of how unlucky I have been in life. I am also worried that my uncle's family are planning to move abroad and the time will come when they won't be able to look after me any more.

41   If all goes well I will study business and start a business of my own. At the moment I am not sure if I want to get married, because all men have created problems for me. But, since I am living in Afghanistan, and life here is hard for a single woman, I will have to get married. But I do want children; I think I will be a good mother. I will not restrict my children and make sure they have the best education and are kept away from people's superstitions.

Shogofa was interviewed by Zuhra Bahman.

POST-READING

UNDERSTANDING AND ANALYZING THE READING

A. Building Vocabulary

Context

Using context and a dictionary if necessary, determine the meaning of each word as it is used in the selection.

_____ 1. oppression (paragraph 1)

    a. mistreatment

    b. terrorism

    c. power

    d. tradition

_____ 2. scuffle (paragraph 6)

    a. crime

    b. discussion

    c. fight

    d. addiction

_____ 3. futile (paragraph 12)

    a. moving

    b. time-consuming

    c. useless

    d. medieval

—— 4. gauge (paragraph 22)

    a. dial

    b. determine

    c. lift

    d. push

—— 5. restrict (paragraph 41)

    a. adopt

    b. nurture

    c. limit

    d. anger

Word Parts

> ### A REVIEW OF PREFIXES AND SUFFIXES
>
> **DIS-** means apart, away, or not.
> **-IZE** means to make or become.

Use your knowledge of word parts and the review above to fill in the blanks in the following sentences.

1. **Disobedience** (paragraph 9) refers to a refusal to _____ rules or someone in authority.

2. To **demonize** (paragraph 12) a practice or custom is to portray it as _____ (wicked and threatening).

B. Understanding the Thesis and Other Main Ideas

Select the best answer.

—— 1. Which of the following best states the thesis statement or central thought of "Beyond the Burqa"?

    a. The United States and other Western nations must continue to offer support for women's rights in the Muslim world.

    b. Traditional systems of social structure and justice in Muslim communities must be dismantled and replaced with democratic institutions.

c. In the struggle for women's rights, Afghanistan remains far behind the progress of such nations as Saudi Arabia and Pakistan.

d. Afghanistan remains a traditional culture in which women face many challenges; the fight for women's rights has made some small advances but is far from complete.

_____ 2. The author chose to include the box titled "I Cannot Believe How Lucky I Am" (paragraphs 34–41) in order to

a. show support for Taliban policies toward Muslim women.

b. provide a case study of a young Muslim woman who is trying to determine the course of her life in a traditional society.

c. suggest that Europe and the United States should allow greater immigration of Muslim women from oppressive societies.

d. offer specific advice to abused women who are seeking to divorce their husbands.

_____ 3. Which paragraphs summarize the author's main argument in "Beyond the Burqa"?

a. paragraphs 4–5

b. paragraph 19–20

c. paragraphs 25–26

d. paragraphs 32–33

_____ 4. The topic of paragraph 21 is

a. *shura*.

b. the religious and political institutions of Parwan province.

c. segregation of males and females.

d. an attempt to change a traditional system gradually.

_____ 5. The main idea of paragraph 29 is found in the

a. first sentence.

b. third sentence.

c. fifth sentence.

d. last sentence.

C. Identifying Details

Match the aspect of Muslim society and culture in column A with its definition in column B.

Column A	Column B
_____ 1. shura	a. assembly of elders
_____ 2. jirga	b. socially conservative political movement
_____ 3. burqa	c. Muslim house of worship
_____ 4. mosque	d. city in Afghanistan
_____ 5. Taliban	e. garment worn by Muslim women
_____ 6. Kabul	f. council or council leader

D. Recognizing Methods of Organization and Signal Words

Select the best answer.

_____ 1. The two signal words that point to the use of the cause-effect pattern in paragraph 2 are
   a. *why* and *because.*
   b. *symbol* and *viewed.*
   c. *freeing* and *achieved.*
   d. *mindset* and *problem.*

_____ 2. The pattern of organization used in paragraphs 5–9 is
   a. summary.
   b. statement and clarification.
   c. generalization and example.
   d. cause and effect.

_____ 3. The pattern of organization used in the material under the heading "What About Mrs. Karzai?" (paragraphs 13–18) is
   a. order of importance.
   b. listing or enumeration.
   c. comparison and contrast.
   d. chronological order.

E. Reading and Thinking Visually

Select the best answer.

_____ 1. Sometimes a photo or a visual aid implies a certain pattern of organization. Which pattern does the photo on page 324 support?

    a. definition

    b. comparison and contrast

    c. cause and effect

    d. classification

F. Figuring Out Implied Meanings

Indicate whether each statement is true (T) or false (F).

_____ 1. The author of the article is from Pakistan.

_____ 2. Parwan is located in Afghanistan.

_____ 3. The vast majority of Afghani people prefer the traditional system of justice.

_____ 4. The author believes that Western nations should support rapid change in traditional Muslim societies.

_____ 5. Waheed (whose experiences and opinions are described in paragraphs 27–28) believes that modern, educated women cannot be trusted.

_____ 6. The author implies that a smaller head scarf is the sign of a more educated or progressive Muslim woman.

_____ 7. Traditional Muslim beliefs require women to cover their bodies and to refrain from informal relationships with men.

G. Thinking Critically: Analyzing the Author's Technique

Select the best answer.

_____ 1. The author's purpose in "Beyond the Burqa" is to

    a. argue for a complete ban on the burqa in conservative Muslim countries.

    b. encourage rapid social change in the Middle East and spur foreign investment in countries with large Muslim populations.

    c. outline the challenges faced by Muslim women in conservative societies and describe the ways in which slow progress is being made.

    d. provide an in-depth look at the life of one Muslim woman who is trying to get an education and plan her life.

_____ 2. The tone of this article is best described as

    a. impersonal.

    b. concerned.

    c. tired.

    d. humorous.

_____ 3. Which of the following is a fact, not an opinion?

    a. "Now the Taliban are ousted from power, yet the burqa remains firmly on the heads of all sorts of Afghan women." (paragraph 1)

    b. "Perhaps it is not the personal wish of Kabi or Mr. Karzai to keep their female relatives segregated, but they and millions of ordinary Afghan men feel compelled to follow Afghan tradition." (paragraph 18)

    c. "Girls like her are not trustworthy." (paragraph 28)

    d. "It is hard to achieve a balance between maintaining tradition and accepting change, especially during a time of war." (paragraph 32)

_____ 4. To support her thesis, the author uses all of the following _except_

    a. statistics.

    b. examples from Afghani women's lives.

    c. direct quotations from people she has interviewed.

    d. excerpts from the Koran (the holy book of Islam).

H. Thinking Critically: Analyzing the Author's Message

Select the best answer.

_____ 1. In paragraph 3, the author states that most Afghan people and institutions "passively endorse" traditional customs. She means that

    a. the local population has voted to maintain these traditions.

    b. each person in society has signed an agreement to abide by these rules.

    c. people in these communities accept these customs by not arguing with them.

    d. religious authorities require close adherence to these practices.

_____ 2. In paragraph 9, the phrase "popular support" means

    a. the support of the government.

    b. the support of popular religious authorities.

    c. the support of younger (school-aged) people.

    d. the support of the majority of people in the society.

_____ 3. According to the author, the chief benefit of traditional justice systems is

    a. their ability to dispense justice swiftly.

    b. their willingness to go against established customs.

    c. the quota system that allows women to take part in making important decisions.

    d. their compatibility with internationally agreed-upon standards for human rights.

_____ 4. "Beyond the Burqa" can be interpreted as

    a. propaganda.

    b. biased.

    c. name calling.

    d. objective.

_____ 5. The intended audience for "Beyond the Burqa" is

    a. Muslim women.

    b. foreign investors.

    c. the Taliban government.

    d. persons concerned about worldwide human rights.

_____ 6. Which of the following statements is an example of irony?

    a. "The country's President, Hamid Karzai, has so far kept his wife behind closed doors and out of the public eye." (paragraph 13)

    b. Wazhma Frogh, a young Afghan woman, uses Islamic scripture to defend women's rights as she challenges the practice of child marriages and child abuse. (paragraph 20)

    c. "The people of Afghanistan have gone from living in one of the most highly regulated societies during the Taliban era to one that is now very much exposed to new ideas and practices." (paragraph 32)

    d. "At the moment, I am not sure if I want to get married, because all men have created problems for me." (paragraph 41)

_____ 7. Select the sentence that best explains the figurative expression "_When the search didn't bear fruit . . ._" (paragraph 8)

    a. The search took so long that the murderers were able to escape.

    b. The search did not produce results in time to help Homaira.

    c. The search did not result in Homaira's brother finding the murderers.

    d. The search only uncovered fruit that had rotted on the vine.

_____ 8. Which of the following sentences contains an example of **informal** language?

    a. "The parents and brothers did not agree, but Homaira left anyway to join her kids." (paragraph 6)

    b. "The Taliban said he was dead because he was a teacher and he sent his daughters to school." (paragraph 36)

    c. "My father refused to send us back to school because he was scared of the Taliban killing him." (paragraph 38)

    d. "But I do want children; I think I will be a good mother." (paragraph 41)

WRITING IN RESPONSE TO THE READING

I. Writing a Summary

Write a summary of the reading (paragraphs 1–33) using the following guidelines:

- Be sure to use your own words, not those of the author
- Write an opening statement that states the author's main point.
- Include the author's most important supporting ideas.
- Include key terms, important concepts and principles.
- Present the ideas in the order in which they appear in the reading.
- Indicate the source of the material you summarized (See Chapter 10 for information on documenting sources)

J. Analyzing the Issue

1. List at least three contemporary issues discussed in "Beyond the Burqa." Phrase each issue in the form of a question.

    Example _Issue:_ U.S. involvement in the Middle East

        Question: What is the proper role for the United States in the Middle East?

2. What is the author's background? Is she qualified to write about the topic? Why or why not?

4. Does the source from which this reading is taken help you determine the credibility of the information presented? Do you find any bias in the selection?

5. Evaluate the reading on the following criteria:

    a. Is the reading timely?

    b. Has the author provided sufficient evidence to support her main ideas? What other types of evidence might she provide to strengthen her arguments?

c. Does the author offer opposing viewpoints? Overall, how would you summarize the author's viewpoints on the issues discussed in the reading?

d. What assumptions (either stated or implied) do you find in the reading?

e. Does the article offer any emotional appeals? If so, identify them and evaluate their fairness.

K. Writing Paragraphs and Essays

*Write a **well-developed** paragraph or essay in response to one of the following writing prompts. As part of this assignment you will need to follow the writing process outlined here:*

- Use a prewriting strategy to generate ideas
- Complete a guided outline
- Write a rough draft
- Complete a peer revision guide
- Write a final draft using proper MLA format

1. What is the role of the woman's head scarf in Islam? Conduct research on the Internet and write a paragraph answering this question.

2. The reading provides examples of young women who sacrifice in some areas of their lives so that they can benefit in others. For example, Friba wears a burqa so that she can attend school. What sacrifices have you made to further your education or career? Write an essay explaining this question.

3. Write a new caption to accompany the photo on page 324. The caption should summarize the article's key argument.

4. Every culture contains traditions. Write an essay in which you describe at least two traditions from your culture. These traditions may be family traditions, religious traditions, or any other type of tradition you would like to write about.

5. Conduct a Web search for nongovernmental organizations (NGOs) and choose one in which you are interested. Write an essay in which you describe the NGO's mission and activities. (One popular NGO is Doctors Without Borders.)

6. The reading discusses human rights. Write an essay in which you define the term and describe some basic human rights.

L. Working Collaboratively

1. **Thinking Deeply** After reading "Beyond the Burqa," break into groups and discuss the following questions:

   - How do the rights of U.S. women contrast with those of Afghan women?
   - What similarities exist?
   - What lessons about human rights can you take away from this reading selection?

   Be sure to use textual evidence to support your answers. You will need someone in your group to record the major points of your discussion so that you will be well prepared to report to the class.

2. **Thinking Visually** Assume that the author of "Beyond the Burqa" created a graphic organizer to organize her thoughts before she wrote the article. What information did she include in that graphic organizer and what did it look like? Your task is to work with a partner to create a graphic organizer (a web) for "Beyond the Burqa."

3. **Thinking Concisely** Using the summary of "Beyond the Burqa" that you have already written, analyze the contents and consolidate your thoughts to **one word** that summarizes the article. After you have settled on one word, join a small group of your peers and share your word. You must be prepared to explain why you chose the word. Your group must ultimately settle on the best one word summary to share with the class.

4. **Thinking Currently** Scan a current newspaper, magazine, or online news source for an example of a violation of human rights. In a small group setting, share a short oral summary of the article with your peers and explain what right has been violated. Note: the information you share must be current.

SELECTION
3
Textbook Excerpt

Enhancing Your Body Image

Rebecca J. Donatelle

DRE 098   PRE-READING

Source and Context

The following reading was taken from the textbook *Access to Health,* by Rebecca J. Donatelle. Professor Donatelle teaches at Oregon State University in the College of Public Health and Human Sciences. In the introduction to her textbook, the author says her goal is "to empower students to identify their health risks, create plans for change, and make healthy lifestyle changes part of their daily routines." She also states that her book is based on scientifically valid information in order to help students "be smarter in their health decision making, more involved in their personal health, and more active as advocates for healthy changes in their community."

A Note on the Reading

Read the selection to understand how people perceive their own bodies, their varying levels of acceptance of their physical appearance, and the problems that can result from negative body image. Which parts of the reading focus on the steps you can take to achieve a positive body image?

Previewing the Reading

Using the steps listed on page 4, preview the reading selection. When you have finished, complete the following items.

1. The topic of the reading is _____.

2. List three factors that influence body image.

   a. _____

   b. _____

   c. _____

3. List three common eating disorders.

   a. anorexia nervosa

   b. _____

   c. _____

4. Indicate whether each statement is true (T) or false (F).

_____ a. Extreme dieting is an effective weight-loss strategy.

_____ b. Some people cannot become slender no matter how hard they try.

_____ c. Very few Americans have a true body image disorder.

_____ d. A person suffering from anorexia nervosa regularly binges on food.

Using Prior Knowledge

Based on the magazines you read, the TV shows and movies you watch, and the advertisements you see all around you, what is the "ideal" body type for the American woman? For the American man?

DURING READING

Reading Tip

As you read, highlight and annotate the author's main points.

Enhancing Your Body Image
Rebecca J. Donatelle

1   As he began his arm curls, Ali checked his form in the full-length mirror on the weight-room wall. His biceps were bulking up, but after 6 months of regular weight training, he expected more. His pecs, too, still lacked definition, and his abdomen wasn't the washboard he envisioned. So after a 45-minute upper-body workout, he added 200 sit-ups. Then he left the gym to shower back at his apartment: No way was he going to risk any of the gym regulars seeing his flabby torso unclothed. But by the time Ali got home and looked in the mirror, frustration had turned to anger. He was just too fat! To punish himself for his slow progress, instead of taking a shower, he put on his Nikes and went for a 4-mile run.

Dissatisfaction with one's appearance and shape is an all-too-common feeling in today's society that can foster unhealthy attitudes and thought patterns, as well as disordered eating and exercising patterns. Courtesy of Fuse/Getty Images, Inc.

2   When you look in the mirror, do you like what you see? If you feel disappointed, frustrated, or even angry like Ali, you're not alone. A spate of recent studies is revealing that a majority of adults are dissatisfied with their bodies. For instance, a study of men in the United States, Austria, and France found that the ideal bodies they envisioned for themselves were an average of 28 pounds more muscular than their actual bodies. Most adult women—80 percent in one study—are also dissatisfied with their appearance, but for a different reason: Most want to lose weight. Tragically, negative feelings about one's body can contribute to disordered eating, excessive exercise, and other behaviors that can threaten your health—and your life. Having a healthy body image is a key indicator of self-esteem, and can contribute to reduced stress, an increased sense of personal empowerment, and more joyful living.

What Is Body Image?

3   Body image is fundamental to our sense of who we are. Consider the fact that mirrors made from polished stone have been found at archaeological sites dating from before 6000 **BCE**; humans have been viewing themselves for millennia. But the term body image refers to more than just what you see when you look in a mirror. The National Eating Disorders Association (NEDA) identifies several additional components of body image:

BCE
"Before the Common Era"; a synonym for B.C. (Before Christ)

- How you see yourself in your mind
- What you believe about your own appearance (including your memories, assumptions, and generalizations)
- How you feel about your body, including your height, shape, and weight
- How you sense and control your body as you move

4   NEDA identifies a *negative body image* as either a distorted perception of your shape, or feelings of discomfort, shame, or anxiety about your body. You may be convinced that only other people are attractive, whereas your own body is a sign of personal failure. Does this attitude remind you of Ali? It should, because he clearly exhibits signs of a negative body image. In contrast, NEDA describes a *positive body image* as a true perception of your appearance: You see yourself as you really are. You understand that everyone is different, and you celebrate your uniqueness—including your "flaws," which you know have nothing to do with your value as a person.

5   Is your body image negative or positive—or is it somewhere in between? Researchers at the University of Arizona have developed a body image continuum that may help you decide (see Figure 1, below). Like a spectrum of light, a continuum represents a series of stages that aren't entirely distinct. Notice that the continuum identifies behaviors associated with particular states, from total dissociation with one's body to body acceptance and body ownership.

FIGURE 1 BODY IMAGE CONTINUUM

This is part of a two-part continuum. Individuals whose responses fall to the far left side of the continuum have a highly negative body image, whereas responses to the right indicate a positive body image.

Courtesy of Ted Foxx/Alamy.

Courtesy of Dmitriy Shironosov/Alamy.

Body hate/ dissociation	Distorted body image	Body preoccupied obsessed	Body acceptance	Body ownership
I often feel separated and distant from my body—as if it belongs to someone else.	I spend a significant amount of time exercising and dieting to change my body.	I spend a significant amount of time viewing my body in the mirror.	I base my body image equally on social norms and my own self-concept.	My body is beautiful to me.
I don't see anything positive or even neutral about my body shape and size.	My body shape and size keep me from dating or finding someone who will treat me the way I want to be treated.	I spend a significant amount of time comparing my body to others.	I pay attention to my body and my appearance because it is important to me, but it only occupies a small part of my day.	My feelings about my body are not influenced by society's concept of an ideal body shape.
I don't believe others when they tell me I look ok.	I have considered changing or have changed my body shape and size through surgical means so I can accept myself.	I have days when I feel fat.	I nourish my body so it has strength and energy to achieve my physical goals.	I know that the significant others in my life will always find me attractive.
I hate the way I look in the mirror and often isolate myself from others.		I am preoccupied with my body.		
		I accept society's ideal body shape and size as the best body shape and size.		

Source: Adapted from Smiley/King/Avery, Campus Health Service. Original continuum, C. Schislak, Preventive medicine and Public Health, © 1997 Arizona Board of Regents. Used with permission.

Many Factors Influence Body Image

6   You're not born with a body image, but you do begin to develop one at an early age as you compare yourself against images you see in the world around you, and interpret the responses of family members and peers to your appearance. Let's look more closely at the factors that probably played a role in the development of your body image.

The Media and Popular Culture

7   Today images of six-pack loaded actors such as Taylor Lautner send young women to the movies in hoards and snapshots of emaciated celebrities such as Lindsay Lohan and Paris Hilton dominate the tabloids and sell magazines. The images and celebrities in the media set the standard for what we find attractive, leading some people to go to dangerous extremes to have the biggest biceps or fit into size 2 jeans. Most of us think of this obsession with appearance as a recent phenomenon. The truth is, it has long been part of American culture. During the early twentieth century, while men idolized the hearty outdoorsman President Teddy Roosevelt, women pulled their corsets ever tighter to achieve unrealistically tiny waists. In the 1920s and 1930s, men emulated the **burly** cops and robbers in gangster films, while women dieted and bound their breasts to achieve the boyish "flapper" look. After World War II, both men and women strove for a healthy, wholesome appearance, but by the 1960s, tough-guys like Clint Eastwood and Marlon Brando were the male ideal, whereas rail-thin supermodel Twiggy embodied the nation's standard of female beauty.

burly
heavily built

8   Today, more than 66 percent of Americans are overweight or obese; thus, a significant disconnect exists between the media's idealized images of male and female bodies and the typical American body. At the same time, the media—in the form of television, the Internet, movies, and print publications—is a more powerful and pervasive presence than ever before. In fact, one study of more than 4,000 television commercials revealed that approximately one out of every four sends some sort of "attractiveness message." Thus, Americans are bombarded daily with messages telling us that we just don't measure up.

Family, Community, and Cultural Groups

9   The members of society with whom we most often interact—our family members, friends, and others—strongly influence the way we see ourselves. Parents are especially influential in body image development. For instance, it's common and natural for fathers of adolescent girls to experience feelings of discomfort related to their daughters' changing bodies. If they are able to navigate these feelings successfully, and validate the acceptability of their daughters' appearance throughout puberty, it's likely that they'll help their daughters maintain a positive body image. In contrast, if they verbalize or indicate even subtle judgments about their daughters' changing bodies, girls may begin to question how members of the opposite sex view their bodies in general. In addition, mothers who model body acceptance or body ownership may be more likely to foster a similar positive body image in their

Courtesy of CBS Photo Archive/Getty Images, Inc.   Courtesy of Paul Popper/Getty Images, Inc.

Is the media's obsession with appearance a new phenomenon?
Although the exact nature of the "in" look may change from generation to generation, unrealistic images of both male and female celebrities are nothing new. For example, in the 1960s, images of brawny film stars such as Clint Eastwood and ultrathin models such as Twiggy dominated the media.

daughters, whereas mothers who are frustrated with or ashamed of their bodies may have a greater chance of fostering these attitudes in their daughters.

10   Interactions with siblings and other relatives, peers, teachers, coworkers, and other community members can also influence body image development. For instance, peer harassment (teasing and bullying) is widely acknowledged to contribute to a negative body image. Moreover, associations within one's cultural group appear to influence body image. For example, studies have found that European American females experience the highest rates of body dissatisfaction, and as a minority group become more **acculturated** into the mainstream, the body dissatisfaction levels of women in that group increase.

acculturate
to become
a part of   11
dominant culture

Body image also reflects the larger culture in which you live. In parts of Africa, for example, obesity has been associated with abundance, erotic desirability, and fertility. Girls in Mauritania traditionally were force-fed to increase their body size in order to signal a family's wealth, although the practice has become much less common in recent years.

physiological
related to the
functioning of   12
the body

Physiological and Psychological Factors

Recent neurological research has suggested that people who have been diagnosed with a body image disorder show differences in the brain's ability to regulate chemicals called *neurotransmitters*, which are linked to mood. Poor regulation of neurotransmitters is also involved in depression and in anxiety disorders, including obsessive-compulsive disorder. One study linked distortions in body image to a malfunctioning in the brain's visual processing region that was revealed by **MRI scanning**.

MRI scanning
magnetic resonance imaging; technology that creates images of the interior of the body, often for medical diagnosis

How Can I Build a More Positive Body Image?

13   If you want to develop a more positive body image, your first step might be to bust some toxic myths and challenge some commonly held attitudes in contemporary society. Have you been accepting these four myths? How would you answer the questions that accompany them?

14   **Myth 1: How you look is more important than who you are.** Do you think your weight is important in defining who you are? How much does your weight matter to your success? How much does it matter to you to have friends who are thin and attractive? How important do you think being thin is in trying to attract your ideal partner?

15   **Myth 2: Anyone can be slender and attractive if they work at it.** When you see someone who is extremely thin, what assumptions do you make about that person? When you see someone who is overweight or obese, what assumptions do you make? Have you ever berated yourself for not having the "willpower" to change some aspect of your body?

16   **Myth 3: Extreme dieting is an effective weight-loss strategy.** Do you believe in trying fad diets or "quick-weight-loss" products? How far would you be willing to go to attain the "perfect" body?

17   **Myth 4: Appearance is more important than health.** How do you evaluate whether a person is healthy? Do you believe it's possible for overweight people to be healthy? Is your desire to change some aspect of your body motivated by health reasons or by concerns about your appearance?

18   To learn ways to bust these toxic myths and attitudes, and to build a more positive body image, check out the **Ten Steps to a Positive Body Image** in the box below.

Ten Steps to a Positive Body Image

One list cannot automatically tell you how to turn negative body thoughts into a positive body image, but it can help you think about new ways of looking more healthfully and happily at yourself and your body. The more you do that, the more likely you are to feel good about who you are and the body you naturally have.

- **Step 1.** Appreciate all your body can do. Every day your body carries you closer to your dreams. Celebrate all of the amazing things your body does for you—running, laughing, dreaming.
- **Step 2.** Keep a list of things you like about yourself—things that aren't related to how much you weigh or how you look. Read your list often. Add to it as you become aware of more things to like about yourself.

- **Step 3.** Remind yourself that true beauty is not simply skin deep. When you feel good about yourself and who you are, you carry yourself with a sense of confidence, self-acceptance, and openness that makes you beautiful. Beauty is a state of mind, not a state of your body.
- **Step 4.** Look at yourself as a whole person. When you see yourself in a mirror or in your mind, choose not to focus on specific body parts. See yourself as you want others to see you—as a whole person.
- **Step 5.** Surround yourself with positive people. It is easier to feel good about yourself and your body when you are around others who are supportive and who recognize the importance of liking yourself just as you naturally are.
- **Step 6.** Shut down those voices in your head that tell you your body is not "right" or that you are a "bad" person. You can overpower those negative thoughts with positive ones.
- **Step 7.** Wear clothes that are comfortable and that make you feel good about your body. Work with your body, not against it.
- **Step 8.** Become a critical viewer of social and media messages. Pay attention to images, slogans, or attitudes that make you feel bad about your body. Protest these messages: Write a letter to the advertiser or talk back to the image or message.
- **Step 9.** Do something nice for yourself—something that lets your body know you appreciate it. Take a bubble bath, make time for a nap, or find a peaceful place outside to relax.
- **Step 10.** Use the time and energy that you might have spent worrying about food, calories, and your weight to do something to help others. Sometimes reaching out to other people can help you feel better about yourself and can make a positive change in our world.

Source: Reprinted with permission from the National Eating Disorders Association, www. NationalEatingDisorders.org.

Some People Develop Body Image Disorders

19   Although most Americans are dissatisfied with some aspect of their appearance, very few have a true body image disorder. However, several diagnosable body image disorders affect a small percentage of the population. Let's look at two of the most common.

Body Dysmorphic Disorder (BDD)

20   Approximately 1 percent of people in the United States suffer from **body dysmorphic disorder (BDD)**. Persons with BDD are obsessively concerned with their appearance, and have a distorted view of their own body shape, body size, weight, perceived lack of muscles, facial blemishes, size of body parts, and so on. Although the precise cause of the disorder isn't known, an anxiety disorder such as obsessive-compulsive disorder is often present as well. Contributing factors may include genetic susceptibility, childhood teasing, physical or sexual abuse, low self-esteem, and rigid sociocultural expectations of beauty.

21 People with BDD may try to fix their perceived flaws through abuse of steroids, excessive bodybuilding, repeated cosmetic surgeries, extreme tattooing, or other appearance-altering behaviors. It is estimated that 10 percent of people seeking **dermatology** or cosmetic treatments have BDD. Not only do such actions fail to address the underlying problem, but they are actually considered diagnostic signs of BDD. In contrast, psychiatric treatment, including psychotherapy and/or antidepressant medication, is often successful.

dermatology
branch of
medicine that
treats skin
disorders

Social Physique Anxiety

22 An emerging problem, seen in both young men and women, is **social physique anxiety (SPA)**. Consider this a concern about your appearance taken to the extreme: The desire to "look good" is so strong that it has destructive and sometimes a disabling effect on the person's ability to function effectively in relationships and interactions with others. People suffering from SPA may spend a disproportionate amount of time fixating on their bodies, working out, and performing tasks that are ego centered and self-directed, rather than focusing on interpersonal relationships and general tasks. Experts speculate that this anxiety may contribute to disordered eating behaviors.

What Is Disordered Eating?

23 As we've seen, people with a negative body image can fixate on a wide range of physical "flaws," from thinning hair to flat feet. Still, the "flaw" that causes distress to the majority of people with negative body image is being overweight.

24 Some people channel their anxiety about their weight into self-defeating thoughts and harmful behaviors. **Disordered eating** behaviors can include chronic dieting, abuse of diet pills and laxatives, self-induced vomiting, and many others.

Some People Develop Eating Disorders

25 Only some people who exhibit disordered eating patterns progress to a clinical **eating disorder**. The diagnosis of an eating disorder can be applied only by a physician to a patient who exhibits severe disturbances in thoughts, behavior, and body functioning—disturbances that can prove fatal. These diagnostic criteria are defined by the American Psychiatric Association (APA), which in 2010 revised its categories of eating disorders to include binge-eating disorder. The APA-defined eating disorders are *anorexia nervosa*, *bulimia nervosa*, *binge-eating disorder*, and a cluster of less distinct conditions collectively referred to as *eating disorders not otherwise specified* (EDNOS).

26 In the United States, as many as 24 million people of all ages meet the established criteria for an eating disorder. Although anorexia nervosa and bulimia nervosa affect people primarily in their teens and twenties, increasing numbers of children as young as 6 have been diagnosed, as have women as old as 76. In 2009, 3.2 percent of college students reported that they were dealing with either anorexia or bulimia. Disordered eating and eating disorders are also common among athletes, affecting

up to 62 percent of college athletes in sports such as gymnastics, wrestling, swimming, and figure skating.

27   Eating disorders are on the rise among men, who currently represent up to 25 percent of anorexia and bulimia patients and almost 40 percent of binge eaters (a category within EDNOS). Many men suffering from eating disorders fail to seek treatment, because these illnesses are traditionally thought of as being a women's problem, and treatment centers are often geared toward women.

28   What factors put individuals at risk? Eating disorders are very complex, and despite scientific research to try to understand them, their biological, behavioral, and social underpinnings remain elusive. Many people with these disorders feel **disenfranchised** in other aspects of their lives, and try to gain a sense of control through food. Many are clinically depressed, suffer from obsessive-compulsive disorder, or have other psychiatric problems. In addition, studies have shown that individuals with low self-esteem, negative body image, and high tendency for perfectionism are at risk. Figure 2 shows how individual and social factors can interact to increase the risk of an eating disorder.

disenfranchised deprived or left out

FIGURE **2** FACTORS THAT CONTRIBUTE TO EATING DISORDERS

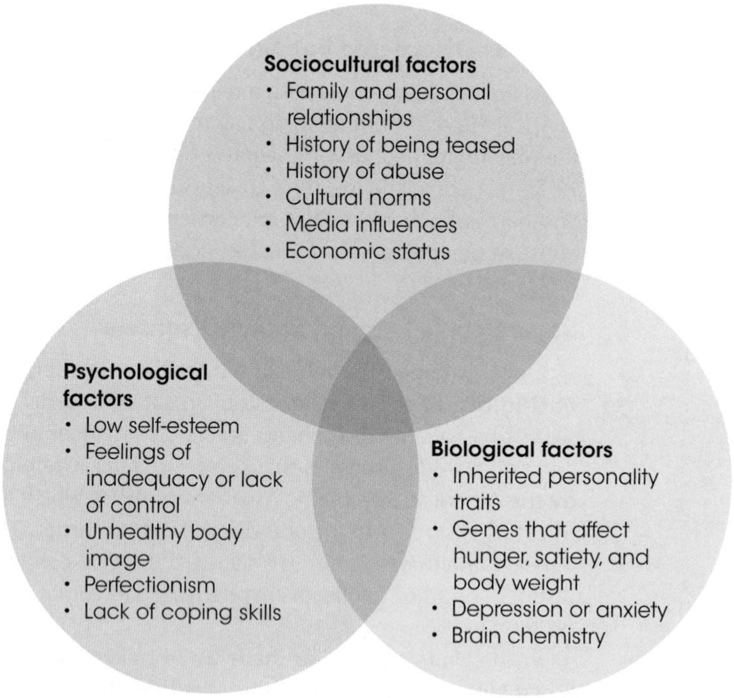

Sociocultural factors
- Family and personal relationships
- History of being teased
- History of abuse
- Cultural norms
- Media influences
- Economic status

Psychological factors
- Low self-esteem
- Feelings of inadequacy or lack of control
- Unhealthy body image
- Perfectionism
- Lack of coping skills

Biological factors
- Inherited personality traits
- Genes that affect hunger, satiety, and body weight
- Depression or anxiety
- Brain chemistry

Anorexia Nervosa

29   **Anorexia nervosa** is a persistent, chronic eating disorder characterized by deliberate food restriction and severe, life-threatening weight loss. It involves self-

starvation motivated by an intense fear of gaining weight along with an extremely distorted body image. Initially, most people with anorexia nervosa lose weight by reducing calorie foods. Eventually, they progress to restricting their intake of almost all foods. The little they do eat, they may purge through vomiting or using laxatives. Although they lose weight, people with anorexia nervosa never seem to feel thin enough and constantly identify parts that are "too fat."

30   It is estimated that between 0.5 and 3.7 percent of females suffer from anorexia nervosa in their lifetime. The revised APA criteria for anorexia nervosa are as follows:

- Refusal to maintain body weight at or above a minimally normal weight for age and height
- Intense fear of gaining weight or becoming fat, even though considered underweight by all medical criteria
- Disturbance in the way in which one's body weight or shape is experienced, undue influence of body weight or shape on self-evaluation, or denial of the seriousness of the current low body weight.

31   Because it involves starvation and can lead to heart attacks and seizures, anorexia nervosa has the highest death rate (20%) of any psychological illness.

32   The causes of anorexia nervosa are complex and variable. Many people with anorexia have other coexisting psychiatric problems, including low self-esteem, depression, an anxiety disorder such as obsessive-compulsive disorder, and substance abuse. Some people have a history of being physically or sexually abused, and others have troubled interpersonal relationships with family members. Cultural norms that value people on the basis of their appearance and glorify thinness are of course a factor, as is weight-based teasing and weight bias. Physical factors are thought to include an imbalance of neurotransmitters and genetic susceptibility.

Bulimia Nervosa

33   Individuals with **bulimia nervosa** often binge on huge amounts of food and then engage in some kind of purging, or "compensatory behavior," such as vomiting, taking laxatives, or exercising excessively, to lose the calories they have just consumed. People with bulimia are obsessed with their bodies, weight gain, and appearance, but unlike those with anorexia, their problem is often "hidden" from the public eye because their weight may fall within a normal range or they may be overweight.

34   Up to 3 percent of adolescents and young women are bulimic; rates among men are about 10 percent of the rate among women. The revised APA diagnostic criteria for bulimia nervosa are as follows:

- Recurrent episodes of binge eating (defined as eating, in a discrete period of time, an amount of food that is larger than most people would eat during a similar period of time and under similar circumstances, and experiencing a sense of lack of control over eating during the episode)

diuretic
a substance that increases urine production

- Recurrent inappropriate compensatory behavior to prevent weight gain, such as self-induced vomiting; misuse of laxatives, **diuretics**, and other medications; fasting; or excessive exercise

- Binge eating and inappropriate compensatory behavior occurs on average at least once a week for 3 months
- Body shape and weight unduly influence self-evaluation
- The disturbance does not occur exclusively during episodes of anorexia nervosa

35   One of the more common symptoms of bulimia is tooth erosion, which results from the excessive vomiting associated with this disorder. Bulimics who vomit are also at risk for electrolyte imbalances and dehydration, both of which can contribute to heart attack and sudden death.

36   A combination of genetic and environmental factors is thought to cause bulimia nervosa. A family history of obesity, an underlying anxiety disorder, and an imbalance in neurotransmitters are all possible contributing factors. In support of the role of neurotransmitters, a recent study showed that brain circuitry involved in regulating impulsive behavior seems to be less active in women with bulimia than in normal women. However, it is impossible at this point to determine whether such differences exist before bulimia develops or arise as a consequence of the disorder.

Binge-Eating Disorder

gorge
eat greedily and excessively

37   Individuals with **binge-eating disorder gorge** like their bulimic counterparts but do not take excessive measures to lose the weight that they gain. Thus, they are often clinically obese. As in bulimia, binge-eating episodes are typically characterized by eating large amounts of food rapidly, even when not feeling hungry, and feeling guilty or depressed after overeating.

38   A national survey on eating disorders conducted by Harvard-affiliated McLean Hospital reported that binge-eating disorder is more prevalent than either anorexia or bulimia nervosa. The survey showed that 3.5 percent of women and 2 percent of men experience binge-eating disorder at some point in their lives. The revised APA criteria for binge-eating disorder are as follows:

- Recurrent episodes of binge eating (defined as eating, in a discrete period of time, an amount of food that is larger than most people would eat during a similar period of time and under similar circumstances, and experiencing a sense of lack of control over eating during the episode)
- The binge-eating episodes are associated with three (or more) of the following: (1) eating much more rapidly than normal; (2) eating until feeling uncomfortably full; (3) eating large amounts of food when not feeling physically hungry; (4) eating alone because of embarrassment over how much one is eating; (5) feeling disgusted with oneself, depressed, or very guilty after overeating
- Marked distress regarding binge eating is present
- The binge eating occurs, on average, at least once a week for 3 months
- The binge eating is not associated with the recurrent use of inappropriate compensatory behavior (i.e. purging) and does not occur exclusively during the course of bulimia nervosa or anorexia nervosa

Some Eating Disorders Are Not Easily Classified

39   The APA recognizes that some patterns of disordered eating qualify as a legitimate psychiatric illness but don't fit into the strict criteria for either anorexia, bulimia, or

binge-eating disorder. These are the **eating disorders not otherwise specified (EDNOS)**. This group of disorders can include night eating syndrome and recurrent purging in the absence of binge eating.

Treatment for Eating Disorders

40   Because eating disorders are caused by a combination of many factors, spanning many years of development, there are no quick or simple solutions. The bad news is that without treatment, approximately 20 percent of people with a serious disorder will die from it; with treatment, long-term full recovery rates range from 44 to 76 percent for anorexia nervosa and from 50 to 70 percent for bulimia nervosa.

41   Treatment often focuses first on reducing the threat to life; once the patient is stabilized, long-term therapy focuses on the psychological factors that have led to the problem. Therapy allows the patient to work on adopting new eating behaviors, building self-confidence, and finding other ways to deal with life's problems. Support groups can help the family and the individual learn to foster positive actions and interactions. Treatment of an underlying anxiety disorder or depression may also be a focus.

How Can You Help Someone with Disordered Eating?

42   Although every situation is different, there are several things you can do if you suspect someone you know is struggling with disordered eating:

- **Learn** as much as you can about disordered eating through books, articles, brochures, and trustworthy websites.
- **Know the differences between facts and myths about weight, nutrition, and exercise.** Being armed with this information can help you reason against any inaccurate ideas that your friend may be using as excuses to maintain a disordered eating pattern.
- **Be honest.** Talk openly and honestly about your concerns with your friend who is struggling with eating problems. Avoiding it or ignoring it is not the solution.
- **Be caring, but be firm.** Caring about your friend does not mean allowing him or her to manipulate you. Your friend must be responsible for his or her actions and the consequences of those actions. Avoid making rules or promises that you cannot or will not uphold, such as, "I promise not to tell anyone," or "If you do this one more time, I'll never talk to you again."
- **Be a good role model** in regard to healthy eating, exercise, and self-acceptance.
- **Tell someone.** It may seem difficult to know when, if at all, to tell someone else about your concerns. Your friend needs as much support as possible, the sooner the better. Don't wait until the situation is so severe that your friend's life is in danger. Addressing disordered eating patters in their beginning stages offers your friend the best chance for working through these issues and becoming healthy again.

Can Eating Disorders Be Prevented?

43   As you've learned, eating disorders arise from a variety of physical, emotional, social and familial issues, all of which need to be addressed for effective prevention and treatment. Effective prevention must not only warn the public about the signs, symptoms, and dangers of eating disorders, but must also address the following:

- Our cultural obsession with slenderness as a physical, psychological, and moral issue
- The role of men and women in our society
- The development of people's self-esteem and self-respect in a variety of areas (school, work, community service, hobbies) that transcend physical appearance

44   Eating disorders-prevention programs are offered on many college campuses, and typically involve professionals with expertise in the field of eating disorders. Ideally, these provide opportunities for students to meet confidentially with mental health care providers.

POST-READING

UNDERSTANDING AND ANALYZING THE READING

A. Building Vocabulary

Context

Using context and a dictionary if necessary, determine the meaning of each word as it is used in the selection.

_____ 1. spate (paragraph 2)
  a. large number in quick succession
  b. type of malice
  c. unscientific research study
  d. set of possible answers

_____ 2. emaciated (paragraph 7)
  a. attacked
  b. world-famous
  c. overpaid
  d. extremely thin

_____ 3. toxic (paragraph 13)
  a. poisonous
  b. common
  c. unrealistic
  d. silly

_____ 4. chronic (paragraph 24)
  a. tiring
  b. slow
  c. harmful
  d. constant

_____ 5. elusive (paragraph 28)
  a. difficult to find
  b. numerous
  c. unexplored
  d. age-based

_____ 6. prevalent (paragraph 38)
  a. mysterious
  b. researched
  c. widespread
  d. dangerous

Word Parts

```
A REVIEW OF PREFIXES AND ROOTS

DIS- means apart, away, or not.
NEURO- means nerve.
```

Use your knowledge of word parts and the review above to fill in the blanks in the following sentences.

1. A person who is **dissatisfied** (paragraph 2) with his body is _____ satisfied with his or her appearance.

2. **Neurotransmitters** (paragraph 12) transmit electrical impulses between _____, while **neurology** is the study of _____.

B. Understanding the Thesis and Other Main Ideas

Select the best answer.

_____ 1. Which of the following is the best statement of the selection's thesis or central thought?

    a. Understanding four common myths regarding weight loss can help people set more realistic goals when they begin a diet, and most people can take ten specific steps to build a more positive body image.

    b. Many people suffer from a negative body image that is reinforced by Hollywood celebrities, media, and companies that are trying to sell products; people from all walks of life need to fight back against the unrealistic images presented by Hollywood.

    c. Body image is important to emotional well-being, and people vary greatly in their acceptance of their bodies; in some cases, preoccupation with body image and weight can lead to a variety of serious illnesses.

    d. Ideal body images change over time; women used to want voluptuous bodies but now want to be thin, while men used to prefer thinness but now want to be muscular.

_____ 2. Which of the following sentences states the main idea of paragraph 9?

    a. "The members of society with whom we most often interact—our family members, friends, and others—strongly influence the way we see ourselves."

b. "Parents are especially influential in body image development."

c. "For instance, it's common and natural for fathers of adolescent girls to experience feelings of discomfort related to their daughters' changing bodies."

d. "In addition, mothers who model body acceptance or body ownership may be more likely to foster a similar positive image in their daughters, whereas mothers who are frustrated with or ashamed of their bodies may have a greater chance of fostering these attitudes in their daughters."

_____ 3. The topic of paragraph 32 is

a. the causes of anorexia nervosa.

b. types of obsessive-compulsive disorder.

c. cultural norms and the "cult of thinness."

d. substance abuse.

C. Identifying Details

Select the best answer.

_____ 1. On which continent has obesity been associated with abundance, desirability, and fertility?

a. North America

b. Europe

c. Asia

d. Africa

_____ 2. Which of the following is *not* a component of your body image, as defined by the National Eating Disorders Association (NEDA)?

a. how you feel about the shape and weight of your body

b. how others perceive your physical appearance

c. what you believe about your own appearance

d. how you control your body as you move

_____ 3. A woman with binge-eating disorder is likely to be

a. very fat.

b. starving herself to death.

c. eating only low-fat, low-cholesterol foods.

d. purging after each meal.

_____ 4. A man who is obsessively concerned with his perceived lack of muscles, and who lifts weights constantly in order to compensate for what he sees as his physical shortcomings, is likely suffering from

    a. anorexia nervosa.

    b. bulimia nervosa.

    c. body dysmorphic disorder.

    d. EDNOS.

D. Recognizing Methods of Organization and Transitions

Select the best answer.

_____ 1. The pattern of organization used in paragraph 3 is

    a. classification.

    b. definition.

    c. cause and effect.

    d. process.

_____ 2. The overall pattern of organization used for paragraphs 6–12 (under the heading "Many Factors Influence Body Image") is

    a. classification.

    b. order of importance.

    c. chronological order.

    d. definition.

_____ 3. The organizational pattern used in paragraphs 29, 33, and 37 is

    a. comparison.

    b. contrast.

    c. chronological order.

    d. definition.

E. Reading and Thinking Visually

Select the best answer.

_____ 1. The author likely chose to include the photos on page 344 to

    a. demonstrate the ideal body type for both women and men.

    b. illustrate how unrealistic images of both men and women have permeated the media for decades.

    c. provide role models for adolescents and young adults trying to develop a more positive body image.

    d. help readers understand the obesity epidemic in America by picturing celebrities who have healthier body types.

_____ 2. Mariah looks in a mirror and thinks, "No matter how hard I exercise, my hips are too wide and I have too much belly flab. If I'm ever going to find anyone who's interested in dating me or marrying me, I'll need to have plastic surgery first." In which category of the body image continuum does Mariah fall?

    a. body preoccupied/obsessed

    b. distorted body image

    c. body hate/dissociation

    d. body acceptance

F. Figuring Out Implied Meanings

Indicate whether each statement is true (T) or false (F).

_____ 1. Emphasis on body image in America is mostly a twenty-first-century phenomenon.

_____ 2. A person who is bullied is more likely to develop a negative body image than one who is not bullied.

_____ 3. Almost all people fit perfectly into one of the five categories of the body image continuum.

_____ 4. Sam suffers from social physique anxiety. Therefore, it is likely that Sam prefers spending time at the gym over having a girlfriend.

_____ 5. Men who suffer from eating disorders may not seek treatment because society views illnesses like anorexia and bulimia as "women's problems."

_____ 6. A person whose teeth are rotting may be suffering from bulimia.

G. Thinking Critically: Analyzing the Author's Technique

Select the best answer.

_____ 1. The author begins the selection with Ali's story in order to

    a. criticize people who are obsessed with their bodies.

    b. imply that Ali needs to change his diet to achieve his fitness goals.

    c. provide a common example of a person with a negative body image.

    d. offer a role model for those who are trying to "bulk up."

_____ 2. The author's primary purpose in "Enhancing Your Body Image" is to

    a. motivate overweight readers to begin a stricter exercise regimen and a healthier diet.

    b. outline the causes and effects of three main types of disordered eating: anorexia, bulimia, and binge-eating.

      c. make readers aware of the importance of a healthy body image, the factors that affect it, and the illnesses that can result from negative body image.

      d. emphasize the role of body chemistry, personal physiology, family history, and social factors in determining a person's weight and overall health.

_____ 3. The author's tone is best described as

      a. informative.

      b. irreverent.

      c. self-righteous.

      d. abstract.

_____ 4. Three of the following sentences from the reading are facts. One is an opinion. Which one is the opinion?

      a. "Consider the fact that mirrors made from polished stone have been found at archaeological sites dating from before 6000 BCE; humans have been viewing themselves for millennia." (paragraph 3)

      b. "The images and celebrities in the media set the standard for what we find attractive, leading some people to go to dangerous extremes to have the biggest biceps or fit into size 2 jeans." (paragraph 7)

      c. "In 2009, 3.2 percent of college students reported that they were dealing with either anorexia or bulimia." (paragraph 26)

      d. "Because it involves starvation and can lead to heart attacks and seizures, anorexia nervosa has the highest death rate (20%) of any psychological illness." (paragraph 31)

H. Thinking Critically: Analyzing the Author's Message

Select the best answer.

_____ 1. In which of the following paragraphs can you find the author's key assumption about the benefits of a healthy body image?

      a. paragraph 2

      b. paragraph 6

      c. paragraph 22

      d. paragraph 40

_____ 2. What does the phrase "attractiveness message" mean in paragraph 8?

    a. a component of a TV commercial that implies what is attractive and what isn't

    b. a TV commercial that features only young people

    c. a hidden message that only younger, hipper people will understand

    d. a product endorsement made by an attractive celebrity or popular sports figure

_____ 3. The author puts quotation marks around "quick-weight-loss" and "perfect" in paragraph 16 in order to

    a. use the same terminology that many dieters use.

    b. imply her skepticism regarding those terms.

    c. signal the reader that these are key concepts in the reading.

    d. suggest that fad diets are sometimes the most effective means of weight loss.

_____ 4. In paragraphs 30, 34, and 38, the author provides bulleted lists outlining the APA (American Psychological Association) criteria for anorexia, bulimia, and binge eating. Why does the author provide these lists?

    a. She believes it is important for readers to understand every detail about these illnesses.

    b. She thinks that these lists will make it easier for students to remember the similarities and differences among these illnesses.

    c. She wants to emphasize that these eating disorders have very specific definitions, and that these illnesses can be accurately diagnosed only by a professional psychologist (or other professional health-care worker).

    d. She wants readers to consider whether they agree or disagree with the APA's definition of each disorder.

WRITING IN RESPONSE TO THE READING

I. Reviewing and Organizing Ideas with a Map

Complete the following map of paragraphs 1–17 by filling in the missing words or phrases.

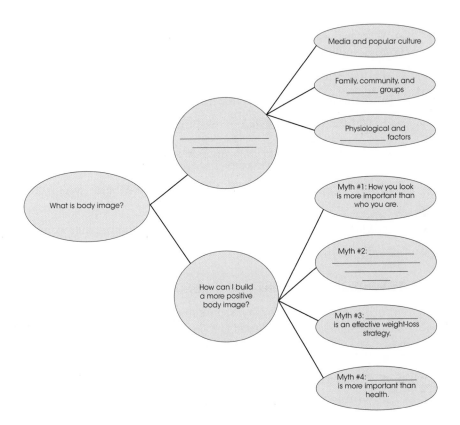

J. Writing a Summary

Write a summary of the section "What Is Body Image?" (paragraphs 3-12).

K. Analyzing the Issue and Argument

1. Identify at least three contemporary issues discussed in this reading. Then phrase each as a question that the author raises, discusses, or answers.

    Example *Issue:* America's obsession with appearance

                    Question: Why are 80% of American women dissatisfied with their appearance?

2. Write a statement that briefly summarizes the author's argument. Is the author's argument inductive or deductive?

3. Identify at least one claim of fact and one claim of value in the reading.

4. What is the author's background, and is she qualified to write about the topic? Why or why not? Do you find any bias in the selection?

5. Evaluate the argument on the following criteria:

   a. Is the argument timely? When was it published?

   b. Has the author clearly and carefully defined her terms?

   c. Has the author provided ample and relevant evidence to support her argument? Provide examples to support your answer.

   d. Does the selection include a stated or implied value system? If so, describe it.

   e. Does the author provide any opposing viewpoints that would refute her argument?

L. Writing Paragraphs and Essays

Write a paragraph or essay in response to the following writing prompts. As part of this assignment you will need to follow the writing process:

- Using a prewriting strategy to generate ideas
- Completing a guided outline
- Writing a rough draft
- Completing a peer revision guide
- Writing a final draft using proper MLA format

1. The author discusses body image in detail and talks about how to develop a positive body image as a way of living a "more joyful" life. Write a paragraph in which you explain some other factors that will help you lead a happy, healthy life.

2. The author mentions celebrities who embody the current "body ideal" for women and men, but can you think of any popular figures who do not match this ideal? Write a paragraph describing one such figure, explaining how he or she does not match the image that the media portray as the ideal.

3. On page 344, the author provides photos of two celebrities of a previous generation: Clint Eastwood and Twiggy. Which celebrities would you suggest to the author as the embodiment of what is considered the "ideal" body type for men and women today? Write a paragraph outlining your recommendations to the author.

4. The author talks about obesity, but she doesn't explore the reasons why so many Americans are overweight. Write an essay in which you explore the reasons for Americans' obesity and outline some possible solutions to the problem.

5. Write an essay about someone you know (you do not have to provide his or her real name). Where do you think he or she falls on the body image continuum? Based on this reading, what recommendations would you give this person?

6. The author claims that the media send strong signals regarding what is attractive in our society. These signals are reinforced by advertisements. Write an essay exploring some ways you can affect or help change the practices of the media and advertisers who contribute to the high levels of negative body image in U.S. society.

M. Working Collaboratively

1. **Thinking Deeply** In a small group of your peers, brainstorm a list about what the media presents as the ideal male and female body. Focus on both physical looks and dress. Next, brainstorm a list of what the typical American male and female body actually look like. Within your group, discuss the similarities and differences in the ideal body and the real body. Be prepared to share your findings with the class.

2. **Thinking Critically** In an attempt to help people combat obesity, several cities have proposed legislation relating to foods that can/cannot be sold. In New York City, the mayor has proposed limiting the sale of sugary beverages to 16 ounces or less. In another city, school officials have recommended that "junk" food not be sold at athletic events. In place of popcorn, candy, and soft drinks, officials have recommended fruit, carrot sticks, and juice. Should city and school officials be involved in decisions about healthy eating? Will the aforementioned proposals have any effect on the problem of obesity? Do you have a better idea? Working with a partner, draft a letter to the editor of the local newspaper in one of the cities above. Be sure to explain your position and offer a solution. Finally, be prepared to share your letter with the class.

3. **Thinking Visually** In a small group of your peers, examine the print ads in a magazine that your instructor will give you. Cut out at least five ads that relate to body image. Discuss the following questions about each ad: What ideal is being presented in the ad? What is the intended message of the ad? Is the ad effective in communicating the message? If so, why is it effective? How could the ad possibly be dangerous to readers?

4. **Thinking Personally** This activity will give you a chance to focus on what really counts—the inward person. Working with a partner, interview each other and talk about the qualities that lie beneath the skin—those that make a person who he or she really is. Following this brief activity, generate a list of ten adjectives/nouns that describe you—the real person. You will not have to share this list with anyone.

ACTIVITIES: EXPLORING IDENTITY

On your own or with a group of classmates, complete one of the three following activities.

1. List at least five aspects of your identity. Are any of these aspects in conflict with each other? If so, how do you negotiate the space in-between?

2. Collect at least five advertisements (from newspapers, magazines, Web sites, or any other sources) that signal the "ideal" body type for men and women in the United States. What features do the women share? What features do the men share? How closely do these images reflect the faces and body types you see in your classroom?

3. The topic of identity is so broad that entire encyclopedias have been written about it. This chapter discussed just a few aspects of the topic. Other types of identity include (but are not limited to):

- *family identity* (for example, being a mother, father, brother, sister, child, or grandchild)

- *sexual and gender identity* (for example, being male, female, straight, gay, or transgendered)

- *participation in a subculture* (for example, bikers, hip-hop, Goth, tattoo culture)

- *religious identity* (for example, affiliation with a particular religion or style of worship)

Write an essay or prepare a class presentation about an aspect of one of these identities and how it affects other parts of a person's identity. You may, of course, draw on personal experience. For instance, you might think about the grandmother's role in Latino families. How does a woman's life change when she goes from being a mother to being both a mother and a grandmother? What social expectations does she face in her new role?

This is a very broad assignment, so you should feel free to make it your own and write or present on any aspect of the topic that you find interesting.

12 Communication and Technology: Life Online and Offline

Are you wired?

If you are like most people, you use technology every day, from the technologies that provide electricity to your home, to desktop or laptop computers, to hand-held gadgets like smartphones. The strict denotation (dictionary meaning) of *technology* is "the application of scientific knowledge for practical purposes." By its very definition, then, the term applies to a wide variety of products and services that are intended to make life easier.

For most of human history, technological advance occurred slowly, as the result of many years of research and trial-and-error. But the last decade has seen an explosion in technology as a result of the computer revolution. It is not an exaggeration to say that technology now saturates every aspect of our lives.

The most visible and popular technologies today are those that facilitate communication—between people, between businesses, between groups. And these technologies are creating major changes in society. Consider just a few examples:

- Ten years ago, before everyone had an Internet connection, you had to go to stores to buy what you wanted or needed. Now you can order just about anything over the Internet. As a result, retail stores across the nation are going out of business.

- Before the explosion in popularity of Facebook and smartphones, people stayed in touched with friends by calling them on the telephone or getting together in person. Now people are increasingly communicating in very short sentences through text messages and spending time in front of a computer (often on Facebook) instead of spending "real time" in the company of friends.

All the readings in this chapter focus on communications technology and how it affects people. For example, how do criminals use the Internet and what types of scams should you be aware of? Do wireless communications technologies (such as cell phones) pose threats to human health? Do new types of mass entertainment made possible by satellite and cable technology, such as reality TV, somehow dehumanize those who are entertained by it?

WHY IS TECHNOLOGY SUCH AN IMPORTANT CONTEMPORARY ISSUE?

Some might argue that technology is *the* key factor affecting people and businesses today. Advances in technology, which are aimed at increasing efficiency and productivity, often have the effect of eliminating jobs. What becomes of people who aren't trained on the latest technologies—do they remain unemployed?

And what of the Internet? Are we becoming too reliant on it? What happens when the power goes down or technology stops working? Just as importantly, does the rise of the Internet mean fundamental changes in the way we conduct our friendships and relationships? Are these changes positive or negative (or both)?

How Does Technology Tie to My College Courses?

Almost all of your college courses will require you to use technology. Because most books, journals, newspapers, and magazines are now online, you will likely conduct research on your computer without ever going to the library. Each discipline has its own specialized software packages that are an important part of working in that field. For example, accountants use Microsoft Excel (a spreadsheet program), while social scientists such as sociologists and psychologists use SPSS, which helps them collect and analyze data. Business courses are increasingly focusing on how companies are using social media, such as Twitter and Facebook, to promote their products, and of course you'll compose many of your college papers on a computer (which may have software that will correctly format all your references for you). But beware! Instructors also have access to software that will tell them if you have plagiarized any materials from Internet sources.

Tips for Reading about Communications Technology

Here are some tips for reading not only the selections in this chapter, but any reading about communications technology.

- **Look for the pros and the cons.** Most technology is developed with a specific purpose, and it often helps people greatly improve their efficiency. Many of the current controversies over technology come from the *unexpected* effects of technology use. So, as you read, keep track of the pros as well as the cons of the subject under discussion.

- **Analyze your use of technology.** For example, how has your life changed since you bought a smartphone? Do you feel more connected to friends and family? How is technology helping you in your college studies? For example, as a result of technological advances, many students can now take courses exclusively online. What are the benefits of online courses? What are the drawbacks?

- **Think critically about technologies and their large-scale effects.**
  Because technology is developing so rapidly, you can witness changes as they happen. Think critically about these changes. Are they good for people? Are they good for society as a whole? How do all these technologies make the world both "smaller" and "larger"? What types of job opportunities are becoming available as a result of the computer revolution, and how will technological change affect the job market and the career you wish to pursue?

Rubric for Writing Essays

In this chapter you will read articles about communication and technology and write essays in response to them. To be sure that you write clear and correct essays use the following rubric. Think of a rubric as a set of guidelines to follow in prewriting, writing, and revising an essay. Check the rubric often, especially as you begin each stage of the writing process.

I. Planning Use of prewriting strategy is evident

II. Organization Writing is unified and coherent
- Essay effectively accomplishes your purpose
- Essay is appropriate for your audience
- Thesis statement is clear and focused
- Sentences do not stray off topic
- Body paragraphs support the thesis statement
- Essay has an appealing introduction/conclusion
- Signal words and phrases are used appropriately

III. Content/Support
- Topic sentences are clear and focused
- Details are specific and adequate
- Details are logical and supportive of topic sentences
- Details are organized appropriately

IV. Grammar and Mechanics Use of language reflects Standard written English

V. Use of Technology MLA/APA format is used correctly

Comments/Suggestions for Improvement: _____

_____

_____

_____

_____

Revision and Proofreading Checklist

Revising, or editing, involves looking again at and often making major changes to every idea and sentence you have written. Proofreading is the part of the revision process that involves adding or deleting words and sentences, as well as correcting your grammar, spelling, and punctuation.

REVISION AND PROOFREADING LIST

Revision

- Does your essay accomplish your purpose?
- Is your essay appropriate for your audience?
- Is your thesis statement clearly expressed?
- Does each paragraph support your thesis?
- Is your essay logically organized?
- Have you used transitions to connect your ideas?
- Are your introduction, conclusion, and title effective?

Proofreading

- Each sentence ends with appropriate punctuation (period, question mark, exclamation point, and/or quotation mark)
- All punctuation within each sentence is correct (commas, colons, semicolons, apostrophes, dashes, and quotation marks)
- Every word is spelled correctly
- Capital letters are used where needed
- Numbers and abbreviations are used correctly
- No words have been omitted
- All typographical errors have been corrected
- All pages are numbered and in the correct order

SELECTION
4
Textbook excerpt

Blogs and Democratization
John Vivian

DRE 096   PRE-READING

Source and Context

John Vivian is the author of a textbook entitled *The Media of Mass Communication*. The selection that follows is an excerpt from a chapter in Vivian's book.

A Note on the Reading

Read the selection to understand how blogs are providing mass audiences with easy access to unedited and often controversial information.

Previewing the Reading

Using the steps listed on page 4, preview the reading selection. When you have finished, answer the following questions.

1. What word does the author use to indicate the promise that blogs hold for the masses? _____

2. What do critics consider the polluting element of blogs?

   _____

3. Determine whether each statement is true or false.

   _____   a. Accuracy and truth are issues associated with blogs.

   _____   b. Newsrooms across the country have chosen not to print any information that has its origin in blogs.

Using Prior Knowledge

Blogs have become a popular tool of mass communication. There are blogs on almost any subject you can imagine, from cooking to politics. There are even Web sites that provide instructions on how to create and maintain a blog. What exactly is a blog? What blogs do you follow?

Reading Tip

Although this selection is fairly short, it contains some abstract language and sophisticated concepts. Adjust your reading rate to ensure you are achieving full comprehension. Highlight and annotate key information as you read.

Blogs and Democratization

John Vivian

1   Blogs hold promise for democratizing mass communication with affordable and technologically easy access. Critics note, however, that there is a polluting element. Blogging has no codes of conduct that require readers to be on guard against irresponsible postings. There are no gatekeepers.

2   As a mass communication tool, the Internet has outpaced older media in democratizing mass communication. This has become an era in which the price of entry to media ownership precludes most mortals. But the Internet, although young as a mass medium, is already democratizing mass communication. The rules are new. The most powerful member of the U.S. Senate, Trent Lott, never figured that his career would be sidelined under pressure created by a pip-squeak citizen in the hinterlands. It happened.

People Power

3   Joshua Marshall, creator of his own Web site, talkingpointsmemo.com, picked up on a speech by Lott that, depending on your view, was either racist or racially insensitive. Lott uttered his comment at the 100th birthday party of Senator Strom Thurmond, once a strong segregationist. Mainstream news media missed the possible implications of Lott's comments. Not Joshua Marshall. In his blog on talkingpointsmemo.com, he hammered away at Lott day after day. Other bloggers, also outraged, joined in. Three days later the story hit NBC. Four days later Lott apologized. Two weeks later his Senate colleagues voted him out as majority leader.

4   As a blogger who made a difference, Joshua Marshall is hardly alone. Best known is Matt Drudge, whose revelations propelled the Bill Clinton–Monica Lewinsky dalliances in the Oval Office into a national scandal. Another blogger, college student Russ Kirk, at his computer in Arizona, looked for information on government refusals to release photographs of caskets of fallen U.S. soldiers in Iraq and Afghanistan, which he regarded as documents to which the public, himself included, had legal access. Kirk filed a request for the documents under the Freedom of Information Act. Then on his Web site thememoryhole.org, he posted the photographs of the flag-draped coffins and also of the astronauts who had died in the Columbia disaster. The photos became front-page news. At one point Kirk's blog was receiving 4 million hits a day—almost twice the circulation of *USA Today*.

Accuracy, Truth

5   Both the beauty and the bane of blogs is their free-for-all nature. On the upside, the Web gives ordinary citizens access to mass audiences. It can be a loud and effective megaphone that is outside traditional news media, which have resulted from institutionalized practices and traditions. Joshua Marshall's work on Trent Lott is an example of outside-the-box news reporting.

6   The easy access that bloggers have to mass audiences is also a problem. Most bloggers are amateurs at news, and their lack of experience with journalistic traditions has a downside. It was bloggers, for example, who kept alive a story that presidential candidate John Kerry and an office intern had carried on an affair. So persistent were the bloggers that neither the mainstream news media nor Kerry could ignore it, although Kerry and the intern denied the allegations and there was no evidence that there was anything to it.

Glenn Reynolds
Blogger whose Instapundit.com has attracted a large audience

MEDIA PEOPLE

Glenn Reynolds

Blogmeister. He never aspired to a major media career, but his blog site Instapundit attracts more hits a day than the average U.S. newspaper's circulation. Photograph reproduced under Creative Commons Attribution-ShareAlike 3.0 Unported license.

Never had Glenn Reynolds thought of himself as a media mogul. Although a young man of strong views, he saw his future as a college prof, not a media star. As a side line lark in 2001, he set up a Web site, Instapundit.com, and tapped out libertarian opinions for anybody who might be interested. At first nobody was.

Then, a month later, came the September 11 terrorism. People by the thousands turned to the Internet, found Reynolds' impassioned commentaries from Knoxville, Tennessee, and made Instapundit a daily routine. *Wired* magazine has declared Reynolds' site the world's most popular blog—a shortened word for "Web log" or diary.

At 120,000 visits a day, Reynolds has a larger audience than the average U.S. daily newspaper and more than most cable television pundits. He's prolific, writing 20 to 30 opinion items a day, some fairly long, mostly political. He's also gotten the attention of the traditional media. *Fox News* has posted his stuff on its site. MSNBC gave him a separate blog on its site.

Reynolds' blog is not alone in its success. Thousands exist, created by individuals who have something to say. Blogs fulfill a promise of the Internet to give people of ordinary means a printing press to reach the world, enriching the dialogue in a free society to an extent once possible only to media moguls and those relatively few whom they chose to print and air.

The Internet is transforming the structure of mass communication.

What Do You Think?

■ How are blogs democratizing mass communication?

■ What does this democratization mean for existing mass media industries?

■ What does this democratization mean for society as a whole?

7   Kevin Drum, of calpundit.com, calls himself "unedited and unplugged." Although Drum never touched the Kerry intern story and is respected by his followers, his point that bloggers are "unedited and unplugged" is both the good news and the bad news about the democratizing impact of the Internet.

New Gatekeeping

8   So-called mainstream media are introducing an element of old fashioned, journalisitically valued gatekeeping into blogging. The *New York Times*, for example, picks up news generated by bloggers when it meets the paper's standards for what's worth reporting. The imprimatur of being cited in the *Times*, which involves fact-checking and news judgment, lends credibility to a blogger. When mainstream media are silent on blog content, their silence speaks volumes.

9   Increasingly common are mainstream-media summaries of blog content as a barometer of what's on the minds of participants in this emerging forum. Several times daily, CNN, as an example, reports what's new from the blogs.

10   Newsrooms everywhere keep an eye on YouTube and other selfpost sites. Oddities worth reporting such as man-bites-dog items are picked up every day. YouTube attained a special status in the 2008 presidential elections when people were invited to upload questions for candidates. Questions were put to the candidates in CNN-hosted debates. Real issues by real people on video was undeniable as a new kind of vehicle for voters to assess candidates. The videos cut through carefully manipulated campaign tactics that had come to mark U.S. elections—staged photo-ops, town-hall meetings with only prescreened participants, and politically calibrated 30-second spots. Not all YouTube-posted questions made the debates, though. As a gatekeeper, CNN used journalistic standards to winnow the chaff.

Learning Check

- Has blogging added a common person's voice to public dialogue on important issues?
- How is blogging being integrated into mainstream-media news reporting?

UNDERSTANDING AND ANALYZING THE READING

A. Building Vocabulary

Context

Using context and a dictionary if necessary, determine the meaning of each word as it is used in the selection.

_____ 1. precludes (paragraph 2)

    a. comes after

    b. rules out

    c. copies

    d. adds to

_____ 2. propelled (paragraph 4)

    a. prevented

    b. revealed

    c. refused

    d. moved

_____ 3. bane (paragraph 5)

    a. beauty

    b. curse

    c. benefit

    d. argument

_____ 4. allegations (paragraph 6)

    a. claims or assertions

    b. illegal statements

    c. conversations

    d. demands

_____ 5. barometer (paragraph 9)

    a. a summary

    b. an introduction

    c. a measuring device

    d. an important announcement

Word Parts

> ## A REVIEW OF PREFIXES AND SUFFIXES
>
> **IN-** means not.
> **-ER** means one who.

Use your knowledge of word parts and review above to fill in the blanks in the following sentences.

1. **insensitive** (paragraph 3) means _____ or caring about the feelings of others.

2. **blogger** (paragraph 4) means _____ writes a blog.

B. Understanding Main Ideas

Select the best answer.

_____ 1. Which of the following best states the main idea of the entire piece of writing?

    a. The government should do more to enforce journalistic standards on the Internet.

    b. The type of information typically found on blogs is unreliable and misleading.

    c. Mainstream media must start adapting its standards to compete with the Internet.

    d. Blogs offer easy access to mass audiences but they lack codes of conduct or standards of quality.

_____ 2. The topic of paragraph 3 is

    a. racially insensitive blogs.

    b. the blog that negatively affected Senator Trent Lott.

    c. the creation of the Web site, talkingpointsmemo.com.

    d. Senator Strom Thurmond's reaction to an insulting blog.

_____ 3. The main idea of paragraph 8 is that bloggers

    a. rely on mainstreaming media for fact-checking.

    b. gain credibility when they are cited by mainstream media.

    c. influence the quality of mainstream news reporting.

    d. have high standards for what is considered newsworthy.

C. Identifying Details

Select the best answer.

_____ 1. In this selection, the term *democratization* refers to how the Internet has made mass communication

    a. politically oriented.

    b. more modern.

    c. accessible to many.

    d. free from censorship.

_____ 2. The blogger who made public the Clinton–Lewinsky scandal was

    a. Matt Drudge.

    b. Joshua Marshall.

    c. Russ Kirk.

    d. Kevin Drum.

_____ 3. Which of the following Web sites is considered by *Wired* magazine to be the most popular blog?

    a. talkingpointsmemo.com

    b. thememoryhole.com

    c. calpundit.com

    d. instapundit.com

_____ 4. Which of the following is **NOT** an issue associated with blogs?

    a. accuracy of information

    b. easy access of bloggers to mass audiences

    c. truthfulness of information

    d. entertainment value of information

D. Recognizing Methods of Organization and Signal Words

Select the best answer.

_____ 1. The organizational pattern of paragraph 3 is

    a. chronological order.

    b. comparison and contrast.

    c. summary.

    d. order of importance.

_____ 2. A signal word or phrase in paragraph 3 that signals its pattern of organization is

    a. In his blog.

    b. Three days later.

    c. Also

    d. Other bloggers.

_____ 3. The organizational pattern of paragraph 6 is

    a. process.

    b. classification.

    c. definition.

    d. illustration.

E. Making Inferences

Based on what is stated in the reading, indicate whether each statement is true (T) or false (F).

_____ 1. The author suggests that bloggers have the capability of ruining a person's reputation.

_____ 2. The author is a well respected blogger.

_____ 3. The author believes that blogs have both good and bad qualities.

_____ 4. The author suggests that the mainstream media sees some value in blog content.

_____ 5. The author believes that the ordinary citizen does not have the capability to judge the truth of most blogs.

F. Thinking Critically: Analyzing the Author's Technique

Select the best answer.

_____ 1. When Kevin Drum calls himself "unedited and unplugged" (paragraph 6), he means that he is

a. not in touch with the mainstream opinion.

b. refusing to let others use his blogging material.

c. not copyrighting his blogging material.

d. freely writing whatever he wants to write without censorship.

_____ 2. To support his points, the author uses primarily

a. academic research about popular blogs/bloggers.

b. examples of popular blogs/bloggers.

c. quotations from bloggers.

d. statistics related to blog readership.

_____ 3. The author's purpose in writing "Blogs and Democratization" is to describe

a. different modes of communication on the Internet.

b. the effects of the widespread use of blogs.

c. advertising and marketing on the Internet.

d. the latest technology for wireless networks.

_____ 4. The point of view of this article is

a. first person.

b. second person.

c. third person.

d. a combination of first person and third person.

_____ 5. Which one of the following sentences contains an example of **informal** language?

    a. It can be a loud and effective megaphone that is outside traditional news media, which have resulted from institutionalized practices and traditions.

    b. Other bloggers, also outraged, joined in.

    c. This has become an era in which the price of entry to media ownership precludes most mortals.

    d. The most powerful member of the U.S. Senate, Trent Lott, never figured that his career would be sidelined under pressure created by a pip-squeak citizen in the hinterlands.

_____ 6. Which of the following is a fact, not an opinion?

    a. "Several times daily, CNN, as an example, reports what's new from the blogs." (paragraph 8)

    b. "Both the beauty and the bane of blogs is their free-for-all nature." (paragraph 4)

    c. "The easy access that bloggers have to mass audiences is also a problem." (paragraph 5)

    d. "The Internet is transforming the structure of mass communication." (Glenn Reynold's box)

_____ 7. The boxed feature about Glenn Reynolds deepens our understanding of

    a. what it takes to become famous by writing a blog.

    b. the amount of time it takes to write a blog each day.

    c. how easy it is to spread inaccurate stories with a blog.

    d. how blogging allows for the democratization of the news media.

G. Thinking Critically: Analyzing the Author's Message

Select the best answer.

_____ 1. According to the author, all of the following are positive effects of blogs, _except_:

    a. removing a Congressman from a position of power because of his racially insensitive remarks.

    b. propelling an Oval Office affair into a national scandal.

    c. proving the truth of a scandalous affair between a presidential candidate and an intern.

    d. bringing to light the government's refusal to release photos of caskets of fallen U.S. soldiers in Iraq and Afghanistan.

_____ 2. When the author says that blogs can be "a loud and effective mega-phone" (paragraph 5), he means that

    a. the messages that bloggers send tend to create a lot of noise.

    b. blogs have a widespread audience.

    c. blogs are intended for a diverse audience.

    d. blogs are very effective in getting the attention of the general public.

_____ 3. The author suggests that blogging is being integrated into main-stream-media news reporting in all of the following ways, *except*:

    a. newsrooms read blogs and watch YouTube videos for newswor-thy subject matter.

    b. nationwide newspapers rely on blogs for most of their human interest stories.

    c. most newspapers carefully screen blogs to make sure that they meet the required standards of news that is worth reporting.

    d. sometimes the mainstream media sends a clear message about the credibility of a blog by refusing to comment on it or print it.

WRITING IN RESPONSE TO THE READING

H. Writing a Summary

Complete the following summary of paragraph 3 by filling in the missing words. Remember that a summary should cover all of the author's main points.

Joshua Marshall is the _____ of the web site named

_____. He heard about a speech by _____ that
was given at the 100th birthday celebration of Senator _____.
Some people thought the speech was racially _____. For several days,
_____ made this speech the subject of his _____, and then
his comments got the attention of _____, a major news network.
Although Lott _____, his colleagues in the _____ removed
him from his position as _____.

I. Writing Paragraphs

Write a well-developed paragraph in response to one of the following writing prompts. As part of this assignment, you will need to follow the writing process outlined below:

- Use a prewriting strategy to generate ideas
- Complete a guided outline

- Write a rough draft
- Complete a peer revision guide
- Write a final draft using proper MLA format

1. Write a paragraph in which you discuss the effects of blogging on society as a whole.

2. Read some of Joshua Marshall's blogs at **talkingpointsmemo.com** and some of Russ Kirk's blogs at **thememoryhole.org**. After reading some of the blogs, decide on a controversial issue that you would like to address. Then write a paragraph length blog of your own on the issue you have chosen. You may use any issue that you have strong feelings about. You do not necessarily have to use one of Marshall's or Kirk's issues.

3. In one of the aforementioned blogs, find a blog that expresses a view contrary to yours. Write a well-developed paragraph that contrasts your view with that of the blogger.

4. Write a paragraph in which you discuss the **"beauty and the bane of blogs."** (paragraph 5)

5. Have you ever had something written about you that was not true? Write a paragraph in which you describe what happened and how it made you feel.

J. Working Collaboratively

1. **Thinking Deeply** After reading the selection by John Vivian, break into groups and discuss the following questions:

   - What is a blog?
   - What does democratization mean?
   - How are blogs democratizing mass communication?
   - What does this democratization mean for society as a whole?

   Be prepared to report to the class on your discussion.

2. **Thinking about Issues** Have you ever considered writing a campus blog? Maybe your school has one. As a class, brainstorm a list of campus issues that could be potential blogging material for your campus blog. Record this list on the board. Before the next class, choose an issue that interests you and write a short blog. When you return to class, break into groups and share your blog with your group members. Allow some time for group

members to discuss each blog. As you discuss each blog, be sure to consider both the truth and the accuracy of the blog and the purpose for which it was written. Finally, be prepared to report to the class on the different blogs and the discussions about them. As a follow up to this activity, you might even decide to create a campus blog if your school does not have one. On the Internet, you can find instructions on the creation and maintenance of a blog.

3. **Thinking Visually** Working with a partner, create a graphic organizer that summarizes the pros and cons of blogs. Your instructor will provide the paper for your chart. You may design your graphic organizer in any way you choose. Be creative.

SELECTION
5
Web Article

Ethics and Reality TV: Should We Really Watch?

Austin Cline

DRE 097 **PRE-READING**

Source and Context

This reading was taken from About.com, which is owned by and part of The New York Times Company. (*The New York Times* is a well-respected newspaper based in New York City.) About.com is an encyclopedic Web site that provides information on a large range of topics. According to the Web site's mission statement, "About.com covers more than 88,000 topics and adds more than 1,600 pieces of new content each week. For more than 15 years, About.com has been a trusted source for our users to solve the large and small needs of everyday life." The author of this selection, Austin Cline, was a Publicity Coordinator for the Campus Freethought Alliance. According to his biography, he has also lectured on religion, religious violence, science, and skepticism.

A Note on the Reading

Reality TV rules the airwaves, with shows ranging from the somewhat realistic (shows about people's quirky careers, such as lion tamers and ice truckers) to the outrageous (for example, supposedly true stories of wealthy "housewives") to the downright odd (for example, *My Strange Addiction*, which profiles people who are addicted to strange behaviors, such as eating a dead person's ashes). Read "Ethics and Reality TV: Should We Really Watch?" to help you think critically about the ethics of producing and watching these programs.

Previewing the Reading

Using the steps listed on page 4, preview the reading selection. When you have finished, complete the following items.

1. This reading selection is about _____ .

2. The German word used to describe people's delight in the suffering of others is _____ .

3. The author believes that producers who try to make money from the humiliation of others are _____ .

4. The key question the author is asking is: _____

Using Prior Knowledge

Do you watch reality TV? If so, which shows do you watch and how often? Why do you think those shows appeal to you? If you don't watch these shows, think about why they do not appeal to you.

DURING READING

Reading Tip

This reading contains a very strong "con" argument outlining the many problems with reality TV. As you read, carefully distinguish facts from the author's opinions. Think critically about the author's opinions and whether you agree with them or not.

Ethics and Reality TV: Should We Really Watch?

Austin Cline

1   Media both in America and around the world seem to have "discovered" that so-called "reality" shows are very profitable, resulting in a growing string of such shows in recent years. Although not all are successful, many do achieve significant popularity and cultural prominence. That does not mean, however, that they are good for society or that they should be aired.

2   The first thing to keep in mind is that "Reality TV" is nothing new. One of the most popular examples of this sort of entertainment is also one of the oldest, *Candid Camera*. Originally created by Allen Funt, it showcased hidden video of people in all manner of unusual and strange situations and was popular for many years. Even game shows, long a standard on television, are a sort of "Reality TV."

3   Today's programming, including a new version of *Candid Camera* produced by Funt's son, goes quite a bit further. The primary basis for many of these shows (but not all) seems to be to put people in painful, embarrassing, and humiliating situations for the rest of us to watch. And, presumably, we should laugh at and be entertained by them.

4   These reality TV shows wouldn't be made if we didn't watch them. So why do we watch them? Either we find them entertaining or we find them so shocking that we are simply unable to turn away. I'm not sure that the latter is an entirely defensible reason for supporting such programming. Turning away is as easy as hitting a button on the remote control. The former, however, is a bit more interesting.

Humiliation as Entertainment

5   What we are looking at here is, I think, an extension of *Schadenfreude*, a German word used to describe people's delight and entertainment at the failings and problems of others. If you laugh at someone slipping on the ice, that's Schadenfreude.

Reprinted from *About.com*.

If you take pleasure in the downfall of a company you dislike, that is also Schadenfreude. The latter example is certainly understandable. However, I don't think that's what we're seeing here. After all, we don't know the people on reality shows.

catharsis
the process of releasing, and thereby providing relief from, strong or repressed emotions

6   So what causes us to derive entertainment from the suffering of others? Certainly there may be **catharsis** involved. However, that is also achieved through fiction. We don't need to see a real person suffer in order to have a cathartic experience. Perhaps we are simply happy that these things aren't happening to us, but that seems more reasonable when we see something accidental and spontaneous rather than something deliberately staged for our amusement.

7   That people do suffer on some reality TV shows is beyond question. The very existence of reality programming may be threatened by the increase in lawsuits by people who have been injured and/or traumatized by the stunts these shows have staged. One of the reasons such programming is attractive is that it can be much cheaper than traditional shows. That may change as insurance premiums for reality TV begin to reflect higher costs to insurers.

8   There is never any attempt to justify these shows as enriching or worthwhile in any way, though certainly not every program needs to be educational or highbrow. Nevertheless, it *does* raise the question as to why they are made. Perhaps a clue about what is going on lies in the aforementioned lawsuits. According to Barry B. Langberg, a Los Angeles lawyer who represents one couple:

9   "Something like this is done for no other reason than to embarrass people or humiliate them or scare them. The producers don't care about human feelings. They don't care about being decent. They only care about money."

10   Comments from various reality TV producers often fail to demonstrate much sympathy or concern with what their subjects experience. What we are seeing is a great callousness towards other human beings who are treated as means towards achieving financial and commercial success, regardless of the consequences for them. Injuries, humiliation, suffering, and higher insurance rates are all just the "cost of doing business" and a requirement for being edgier.

Where's the Reality?

11   One of the attractions of reality television is the supposed "reality" of it—unscripted and unplanned situations and reactions. One of the ethical problems of reality television is the fact that it isn't nearly as "real" as it pretends to be. At least in dramatic shows one can expect the audience to understand that what they see on the screen doesn't necessarily reflect the reality of the actors' lives. The same, however, cannot be said for heavily edited and contrived scenes one sees on reality shows.

12   There is now a growing concern about how reality television shows can help perpetuate racial stereotypes. In many shows a similar black female character has been featured. They are all different women, but share very similar character traits. It's gone so far that Africana.com has trademarked the expression The Evil Black Woman to describe this sort of individual: brazen, aggressive, pointing fingers, and always lecturing others on how to behave.

MSNBC 13
a television news
station

MSNBC has reported on the matter, noting that after so many "reality" programs, we can discern a pattern of "characters" that isn't very far different from the **stock characters** found in fictional programming. There's the sweet and naive person from a small town looking to make it big while still retaining small-town values. There's the party girl/guy who's always looking for a good time and who shocks those around him or her. There's the aforementioned Evil Black Woman with an Attitude, or sometimes Black Man with an Attitude. And the list goes on.

stock characters
types of
characters that
are common
in fiction (for
example,
the rugged
outdoorsman or
the genteel lady)

14 MSNBC quotes Todd Boyd, critical-studies professor at the University of Southern California's School of Cinema-Television. "We know all these shows are edited and manipulated to create images that look real and sort of exist in real time. But really what we have is a construction. . . . The whole enterprise of reality television relies on stereotypes. It relies on common stock, easily identifiable images."

15 Why do these stock characters exist, even in so-called "reality" television that is supposed to be unscripted and unplanned? Because that's the nature of entertainment. Drama is more readily propelled by the use of stock characters because the less you have to think about who a person really is, the more quickly the show can get to things like the plot (such as it may be). Sex and race are especially useful for stock characterizations because they can pull from a long and rich history of social stereotypes.

16 This is especially problematic when so few minorities appear in programming, whether reality or dramatic, because those few individuals end up being representatives of their entire group. A single angry white man is just an angry white man, while an angry black man is an indication of how all black men "really" are. MSNBC explains:

archetype
typical example

D.W. Griffith
an early American
filmmaker known
for his racist
attitudes who was
often attacked or
ridiculed in public

17 Indeed, the [Sista With an Attitude] feeds off preconceived notions of African American women. After all, she's an **archetype** as old as **D.W. Griffith**, first found in the earliest of movies where slave women were depicted as ornery and cantankerous, uppity Negresses who couldn't be trusted to remember their place. Think Hattie McDaniel in *Gone With the Wind*, bossing and fussing as she yanked and tugged on Miss Scarlett's corset strings. Or Sapphire Stevens on the much-pilloried *Amos N' Andy*, serving up confrontation on a platter, extra-spicy, don't hold the sass. Or Florence, the mouthy maid on *The Jeffersons*.

18 How do stock characters appear in "unscripted" reality shows? First, the people themselves contribute to the creation of these characters. They know, even if unconsciously, that certain behavior is more likely to get them air time. Second, the shows editors contribute mightily to the creation of these characters because they completely validate just that motivation. A black woman sitting around, smiling, isn't perceived to be as entertaining as a black woman pointing her finger at a white man and angrily telling him what to do.

19 An especially good (or egregious) example of this can be found in Manigault-Stallworth, a star of Donald Trump's *The Apprentice*. She has been called "the most hated woman on television" because of the behavior and attitude people see her with. But how much of

Courtesy of ZUMA Press, Inc./Alamy.

her on-screen persona is real and how much is a creation of the shows editors? Quite a lot of the latter, according to Manigault-Stallworth in an email quoted by MSNBC:

20   "What you see on the show is a gross misrepresentation of who I am. For instance, they never show me smiling, it's just not consistent with the negative portrayal of me that they want to present. Last week they portrayed me as lazy and pretending to be hurt to get out of working, when in fact I had a concussion due to my serious injury on the set and spent nearly . . .10 hours in the emergency room. It's all in the editing!"

21   Reality television shows are not documentaries. People are not put into situations simply to see how they react. The situations are heavily contrived, they are altered in order to make things interesting, and large amounts of footage are heavily edited into what the show's producers think will result in the best entertainment value for viewers. Entertainment, of course, often comes from conflict. So conflict will be created where none exists. If the show cannot incite conflict during the filming, it can be created in how pieces of footage are stitched together. It's all in what they choose to reveal to you—or not reveal, as the case may be.

Moral Responsibility

22   If a production company creates a show with the explicit intention of trying to make money from the humiliation and suffering which they themselves create for unsuspecting people, then that seems to me to be immoral and unconscionable. I simply cannot think of any excuse for such actions. Pointing out that others are willing to watch such events does not relieve them of the responsibility for having orchestrated the events and willed the reactions in the first place. The mere fact that they want others to experience humiliation, embarrassment, and/or suffering (and simply in order to increase earnings) is itself unethical. Actually going forward with it is even worse.

23   What of the responsibility of the reality TV advertisers? Their funding makes such programming possible, and therefore they must shoulder part of the blame as well. An ethical position would be to refuse to underwrite any programming, no matter how popular, if it is designed to deliberately cause others humiliation, embarrassment, or suffering. It's immoral to do such things for fun (especially on a regular basis), so it's certainly immoral to do it for money or to pay to have it done.

24   What of the responsibility of contestants? In shows which accost unsuspecting people on the street, there isn't really any. Many, however, have contestants who volunteer and sign releases. So aren't they getting what they deserve? Not necessarily. Releases don't necessarily explain everything that will happen and some are pressured to sign new releases part way through a show in order to have a chance at winning. If they don't, all they have endured up to that point is rendered useless. Regardless, the producers' desire to cause humiliation and suffering in others for profit remains immoral, even if someone volunteers to be the object of humiliation in exchange for money.

25   Finally, what about the reality TV viewers? If you watch such shows, why? If you find that you are entertained by the suffering and humiliation of others, that's a

problem. Perhaps an occasional instance wouldn't merit comment, but a weekly schedule of such pleasure is another matter entirely.

26   I suspect that people's ability and willingness to take pleasure in such things may stem from the increasing separation we experience from others around us. The more distant we are from each other as individuals, the more readily we can **objectify** each other and fail to experience sympathy and empathy when others around us suffer. The fact that we are witnessing events not in front of us but rather on television, where everything has an unreal and fictional air about it, probably aids in this process as well.

objectify
turn a person into
an object

27   I'm not saying that you shouldn't watch reality TV programming, but the motivations behind being a viewer are ethically suspect. Instead of passively accepting whatever media companies try to feed you, it would be better to take some time to reflect on why such programming is made and why you feel attracted to it. Perhaps you will find that your motivations themselves are not so attractive.

POST-READING

UNDERSTANDING AND ANALYZING THE READING

A. Building Vocabulary

Context

Using context and a dictionary if necessary, determine the meaning of each word as it is used in the selection.

_____ 1. prominence (paragraph 1)
     a. ethnicity
     b. importance
     c. adoration
     d. isolation

_____ 2. derive (paragraph 6)
     a. create
     b. extract
     c. replace
     d. conduct

_____ 3. spontaneous (paragraph 6)
     a. unplanned
     b. miraculous
     c. upsetting
     d. humorous

_____ 4. highbrow (paragraph 8)
     a. appealing to refined tastes
     b. wealthy
     c. low-priced
     d. related to higher education

_____ 5. callousness (paragraph 10)
     a. gentleness
     b. sensitivity
     c. hardness
     d. boldness

_____ 6. contrived (paragraph 11)
     a. cheap
     b. helpless
     c. artificial
     d. rude

_____ 7. brazen (paragraph 12)

    a. copper-colored

    b. boldly outspoken

    c. roasted

    d. sweet

_____ 8. discern (paragraph 13)

    a. prevent

    b. recognize

    c. create

    d. hide

_____ 9. egregious (paragraph 19)

    a. excellent

    b. shocking

    c. timely

    d. greedy

_____ 10. incite (paragraph 21)

    a. stir up

    b. settle

    c. hold back

    d. release

_____ 11. stem (paragraph 26)

    a. dominate

    b. react

    c. fluctuate

    d. originate

Word Parts

> ### A REVIEW OF PREFIXES AND SUFFIXES
>
> **UN-** means not.
> **MIS-** means wrongly.
> **-IBLE** refers to a state, condition, or quality
> **-IZE** means to make or become

Use your knowledge of word parts and the review above to fill in the blanks in the following sentences.

1. A _defensible_ (paragraph 4) reason is one that is capable of being _____.

2. A person who is _traumatized_ (paragraph 7) has _____ a victim of trauma (a deeply distressing experience or emotion).

3. A TV show that is _unscripted_ (paragraph 11) does _____ work with a script, but is rather improvised (that is, made up by the actors as they go along).

4. A _misrepresentation_ (paragraph 20) of a situation _____ states the facts or does not show reality correctly.

B. Understanding the Thesis and Other Main Ideas

Select the best answer.

_____ 1. Which of the following best states the thesis or central thought of the reading?

     a. While reality TV is undoubtedly popular, society should question the ethics and morality of the people who create reality TV programming as well as those who watch it.

     b. Reality TV is a type of television that is not only very commonplace but also a source of very large profits for the TV networks.

     c. It has been proven conclusively that reality TV is full of lies, fabrications, and outright deceit—all created for the sole purpose of gaining ratings and advertising revenue.

     d. Although several theories have been proposed, the most likely explanation for the popularity of reality TV is the pleasure people derive from seeing others humiliated.

_____ 2. The topic of paragraph 13 is

     a. the opinions of MSBNC executives.

     b. Evil Black Women with Attitudes.

     c. stock characters in fictional programming.

     d. the overall popularity of Black people as characters on reality TV.

_____ 3. The main idea of paragraph 21 is found in the

     a. first sentence.

     b. second sentence.

     c. fourth sentence.

     d. last sentence.

_____ 4. What is the implied main idea of paragraph 26?

     a. Television, by definition, lends itself to lies and the misrepresentation of reality.

     b. As various court cases have proved, eyewitness accounts of events are often unreliable.

     c. People may watch and enjoy reality TV because they feel isolated from other people and therefore unable to sympathize with them.

     d. The producers of reality TV should make more charitable donations to social-minded causes because they have the responsibility to "give back" to society.

C. Identifying Details

Select the best answer.

_____ 1. According to the author, the earliest example of reality TV is
   a. *I Love Lucy.*
   b. *The Price Is Right.*
   c. *Candid Camera.*
   d. *The Jeffersons.*

_____ 2. The selection discusses of all of the following common "stock characters" *except*
   a. the party guy.
   b. the nosy neighbor.
   c. the naïve small-town person.
   d. the Black man with an attitude.

_____ 3. According to the reading, the producers of reality TV use all of the following deceitful techniques *except*
   a. creating conflict among people when no conflict exists.
   b. encouraging bad behaviors that will get the characters more "air time."
   c. practicing active discrimination against people of certain races or ethnic backgrounds.
   d. editing film footage to create a false impression.

D. Recognizing Methods of Organization and Transitions

Select the best answer.

_____ 1. The pattern of organization used in paragraph 5 is
   a. classification.
   b. definition.
   c. comparison/contrast.
   d. process.

_____ 2. The organizational pattern used in paragraphs 6 and 15 is
   a. chronological order.
   b. listing.
   c. cause and effect.
   d. spatial order.

_____ 3. The transitional word or phrase that provides a clue to the organizational pattern used in paragraph 26 is

    a. may stem from.

    b. we experience.

    c. more readily.

    d. the fact that.

E. Reading and Thinking Visually

Select the best answer.

_____ 1. The author likely included the photo on page 382 in order to

    a. provide a suggestion for the best type of reality TV for readers to watch.

    b. offer a serious criticism of the questionable ethics exhibited by the producers of that particular TV show.

    c. illustrate the concept of The Evil Black Woman.

    d. illustrate the differences between reality TV and documentaries, which the author sees as much more "real" than reality TV.

F. Figuring Out Implied Meanings

Indicate whether each statement is true (T) or false (F).

_____ 1. The author believes that a long history of racial stereotypes forms the basis for many stock characterizations.

_____ 2. The author does not believe that game shows are a form of reality TV.

_____ 3. The author believes that just *thinking* about using people's suffering as a way of making money is unethical.

_____ 4. According to the author, a producer's ethics cannot be questioned if the star of a reality TV show signs a release that frees the producer from all responsibility.

_____ 5. The author thinks that the suffering experienced by the people portrayed on reality TV is not real.

_____ 6. The author implies that reality TV does not portray Black culture or Black people in a positive or realistic light.

G. Thinking Critically: Analyzing the Author's Technique

Select the best answer.

_____ 1. The author's primary purpose in "Ethics and Reality TV: Should We Really Watch?" is to

    a. confront readers with their own selfishness and force them to admit their immoral behaviors.

    b. examine how "real" reality TV is and examine the ethical responsibilities of the people who produce, participate in, and watch reality TV.

    c. offer a close analysis of the stereotypes that can be found on reality TV and address whether or not these stereotypes are based on truth.

    d. describe the negative experiences of those whose lives have been ruined by reality TV and who are now suing the producers.

_____ 2. Overall, the author's tone in this selection can best be described as

    a. enraged and bitter.

    b. amused and slightly shocked.

    c. critical and moral.

    d. offhand and irreverent.

_____ 3. Which of the following is a fact, not an opinion?

    a. "Turning away is as easy as hitting a button on the remote control." (paragraph 4)

    b. "A black woman sitting around, smiling, is not perceived to be as entertaining as a black woman pointing her finger at a white man and angrily telling him what to do." (paragraph 18)

    c. "An ethical position would be to refuse to underwrite any programming, no matter how popular, if it is designed to deliberately cause others humiliation, embarrassment, or suffering." (paragraph 23)

    d. "Many shows have contestants who volunteer and sign releases." (paragraph 24)

_____ 4. Which of the following is not a piece of evidence used by the author to support his thesis or central thought?

    a. a set of statistics showing how many people watch reality TV in any given week

    b. a quotation from a lawyer who is representing a couple who was mistreated on a reality TV show

        c. a professor from the University of Southern California's School of Cinema-Television

        d. the experiences of Manigault-Stallworth, who was once featured on a reality TV show

_____ 5. Throughout the reading, the author uses *rhetorical questions*—that is, questions addressed directly to readers. Rhetorical questions are used as starting-off points for a discussion or explanation. Which of the following is *not* a rhetorical question found in the reading?

        a. So what causes us to derive entertainment from the suffering of others?

        b. What of the responsibility of the reality TV advertisers?

        c. Why do these stock characters exist, even in so-called "reality" television that is supposed to be unscripted and unplanned?

        d. Why are reality TV shows so much more profitable than TV shows that have scripts and professional actors?

_____ 6. Which of the following statements is an example of irony?

        a. "These reality TV shows wouldn't be made if we didn't watch them." (paragraph 4)

        b. " But really what we have is construction. . . .The whole enterprise of reality television relies on stereotypes." (paragraph 14)

        c. "Reality television shows are not documentaries." (paragraph 21)

        d. "If you find that you are entertained by the suffering and humiliation of others, that's a problem." (paragraph 25)

_____ 7. Select the sentence that best explains the figurative expression "Or Sapphire Stevens . . . serving up confrontation on a platter, extra spicy, don't hold the sass." (paragraph 17)

        a. Everything Sapphire says is expressed eloquently.

        b. Sapphire delivers her confrontative words formally so as not to insult anyone.

        c. Sapphire uses her biting and sassy words to directly confront the recipient, and she doesn't hold back.

        d. Like a servant, Sapphire submissively delivers her confrontative words.

_____ 8. Which of the following sentences contains an example of **informal** language?

        a. "The first thing to keep in mind is that "Reality TV" is nothing new." (paragraph 2)

        b. "There is now a growing concern about how reality television shows can help perpetuate racial stereotypes." (paragraph 12)

c. "Sex and race are especially useful for stock characterizations because they can pull from a long and rich history of social stereotypes." (paragraph 15)

d. "Think Hattie McDaniel in *Gone With the Wind*, bossing and fussing as she yanked and tugged on Miss Scarlett's corset strings." (paragraph 17)

H. Thinking Critically: Analyzing the Author's Message

Select the best answer.

_____ 1. Which of the following would not be an example of *Schadenfreude*?

a. You have an enemy who goes bankrupt, and you enjoy watching his car get repossessed.

b. You feel a certain happiness when someone on the opposing baseball team strikes out.

c. You pass a homeless person lying on the sidewalk and wonder how he or she ended up so down and out.

d. You watch as a government social worker takes away a neighbor's child, and you think, "Serves her right."

_____ 2. In paragraph 14, Todd Boyd analyzes reality TV, saying "Really what we have is a construction." What does he mean?

a. New ideas for reality TV shows are constantly being formulated and developed.

b. The scenes shown on reality TV are just as planned as the scenes on traditional scripted TV.

c. If not for stereotypes, reality TV would not be nearly as popular.

d. The analysis of TV is best left to the academics and scholars who study it for a living, and who are therefore best qualified to judge it.

_____ 3. In paragraph 17, the reading mentions "ornery and cantankerous, uppity Negresses." Which of the following statements best describes Austin Cline's beliefs about the characterization of Black women?

a. He completely agrees with the depiction of Black women in early American film and television.

b. He believes that early depictions of Black women were exaggerated, but he thinks that Black women are now presented more realistically.

c. He thinks that historical presentations of Black women were accurate, but he believes that modern presentations are based mostly on stereotypes.

d. He feels that Black women have a long history of being portrayed inaccurately, and that those inaccurate portrayals continue to this day.

———— 4. In paragraph 19, what does the author mean by Maginault-Stallworth's "onscreen persona"?

    a. her overall personality as revealed by her behavior on *The Apprentice*

    b. the image she portrays on TV rather than the person she really is

    c. her racial and ethnic background

    d. her clothing, cosmetics, and other personal items

———— 5. "Ethics and Reality TV: Should We Really Watch?" can be interpreted as

    a. biased.

    b. propaganda.

    c. name calling.

    d. objective.

———— 6. The intended audience for this article is

    a. TV watchers in America.

    b. those who watch Reality TV and those who do not watch Reality TV.

    c. those who are entertained by the suffering of others.

    d. those who are experiencing separation from others around them.

WRITING IN RESPONSE TO THE READING

I. Writing a Summary

Write a summary of the reading (paragraphs 1–27) using the following guidelines:

- Be sure to use your own words, not those of the author.
- Write an opening statement that states the author's main point.
- Include the author's most important supporting ideas.
- Include key terms, important concepts and principles.
- Present the ideas in the order in which they appear in the reading.
- Indicate the source of the material you summarized (See Chapter 10 for information on documenting sources).

J. Analyzing the Issue

1. What contemporary issue is the author discussing in this reading? Phrase the issue as a question. Is the author arguing the "pro" side of this issue or the "con" side?

2. What is the author's background? Is he qualified to write about the topic? Why or why not?

3. Does the source from which this reading is taken help you determine the credibility of the information presented? Do you find any bias in the selection? Please explain both of your answers.

4. Evaluate the reading on the following criteria:

   a. Is the reading timely?

   b. Has the author provided sufficient evidence to support his main ideas? What other types of evidence might he provide to strengthen his claims?

   c. Does the author offer opposing viewpoints? Overall, how would you summarize the author's viewpoints on the issues discussed in the reading?

   d. What assumptions (either stated or implied) do you find in the reading?

   e. Does the article offer any emotional appeals? If so, identify them and evaluate their fairness.

5. Identify specific sentences and/or paragraphs in which the author states his value system.

K. Writing Paragraphs and Essays

*Write a **well-developed** paragraph or essay in response to one of the following writing prompts. As part of this assignment you will need to follow the writing process outlined below:*

- Use a prewriting strategy to generate ideas
- Complete a guided outline
- Write a rough draft
- Complete a peer revision guide
- Write a final draft using proper MLA format

1. Do you agree with the author's assertion that reality TV does not truly reflect reality? Why or why not? Write a paragraph or essay expressing your opinion.

2. Suppose the author wanted to include an image from a television show or film that is more beneficial to society than reality TV. Which TV show or film would you recommend? Explain your answer in a paragraph or essay.

3. In the reading, the author asks the important question, "Why do people watch reality TV?" and he suggests some possible answers. Write an essay in which you explore the appeal of reality TV. Why do you think reality TV is so popular with viewers?

4. The author talks a good deal about stock characters and stereotypes. Watch an episode of a reality TV show and write an essay in which you explore how

one or more characters fits (or does not fit) particular stereotypes of race, gender, ethnicity, age, or any other category.

5. Why do you think "everyday people" (who are not actors) agree to take part in a reality TV show? The author of this selection suggests TV executives' motives for producing reality TV, but he does not suggest why people agree to have their lives filmed and made public. Write an essay in which you explore people's possible motives for wanting to appear on reality TV. Would you ever appear in a reality TV show? Why or why not?

L. Working Collaboratively

1. **Thinking Deeply** After reading "Ethics and Reality TV: Should We Really Watch," break into groups and discuss the following questions:

   - What are the author's major objections to reality television?
   - What is the basis for each of the objections?
   - According to the author, how does watching reality television affect the viewer? Do you agree or disagree? Why?
   - Do you watch reality television? If so, why? If not, why?
   - Will reading this article make any difference in your attitude toward reality television?

   Select someone in your group to record the major points of your discussion so that you will be well prepared to report to the class.

2. **Thinking Visually** Working with a group, brainstorm a list of characters from a variety of reality television shows. Discuss how each character is portrayed and the stereotype he/she fits (race, gender, ethnicity, age, or any other stereotype). Using the chart paper provided to you by your instructor, create a chart that has three columns (see chart below). Use the information you have generated through brainstorming to fill in the chart. Be prepared to share and explain your chart to the class.

Name of Reality TV Show	Description of Character	Stock Character

3. **Thinking Concisely** Using the summary of "Ethics and Reality TV: Should We Really Watch" that you have already written, analyze the contents and consolidate your thoughts to **one word** that summarizes the article. After you have settled on one word, join a small group of your peers and share your word. You must be prepared to explain why you chose the word. Your group must ultimately settle on the best one word summary to share with the class.

4. **Thinking Critically** This activity will require you to experience media in a meaningful way. First you will select a reality television show to watch. You will then watch the show with a critical eye, asking yourself the following questions:

   ■ How does the show represent women?

   ■ How does the show represent racial groups?

   ■ How does the show portray life in America?

   ■ What moral issues are present in the show?

   ■ What ethical issues are present in the show?

   ■ Does anyone in the show suffer humiliation at the expense of entertainment?

   ■ To what group(s) of people would this reality television show appeal? Why?

   Be sure to take notes along the way. At the end of the show, you will synthesize your information and write a paragraph summarizing your findings. When you return to class, you will join a group of your peers and share your findings.

5. **Thinking Proactively** Working with a partner, write a letter to a local television station. In the letter, you will present compelling information that will persuade the general manager of the station to cancel a certain reality TV show. Remember: you must cite specific reasons and provide adequate support for each reason in order to have a chance at changing the manager's mind. If possible, get the name of the general manager and the address so that you can actually mail the letter to him/her.

SELECTION
6
Article Type

The Touch-Screen Generation

Hanna Rosin

DRE 098   PRE-READING

Source and Context

The following reading appeared in April of 2013 in *The Atlantic.com Magazine*. This publication features news and commentaries on a wide range of topics on both the national and international scene. Hanna Rosin, author of "The Touch-Screen Generation" is a national correspondent for *The Atlantic*.

A Note on the Reading

The topic of the effects of technology on young children is not a new one. When there was only television, parents were concerned about the amount of time their children were spending in front of the TV and the quality of the programming. Today, children have access to TV and a whole lot more; now, with the swipe of a finger, they can access an unlimited number of apps on a smart phone or an iPad. Read this selection to further your understanding of the issues and research that surround this phenomenon, and the growing concerns of parents.

Previewing the Reading

Using the steps listed on page 4, preview the reading selection. When you have finished, complete the following items.

1. The topic of the reading is _____

2. To whom is the author referring when she speaks of the touch-screen generation? _____

3. Indicate whether each statement is true (T) or false (F).
   - _____ a. The pictures on page 397 show children struggling to learn the swiping technique.
   - _____ b. Many developers of digital technology apps are parents themselves.
   - _____ c. Once the novelty wears off, young children use digital technology with the same frequency as they play with their other toys.
   - _____ d. Some digital technology apps do indeed have educational value.

Using Prior Knowledge

Based on your experience, how valuable to your entertainment and education is a smart phone or an iPad? Have these technological devices become a necessity in your life? Have you ever shared them with a young child and observed the ease with which they learn to use them?

DURING READING

Reading Tip

As you read, highlight and annotate the author's main points.

The Touch-Screen Generation
Hanna Rosin

Courtesy of Karin &
Uwe Annas/Fotolia.

Courtesy of Monkey Business
Images/Shutterstock.

Courtesy of mmphotographie
.de/Fotolia.

Courtesy of bloomua/Fotolia.

Young children—even toddlers—are spending more and more time with digital technology. *What will it mean for their development?*

1   On a chilly day last spring, a few dozen developers of children's apps for phones and tablets gathered at an old beach resort in Monterey, California, to show off their games. One developer, a self-described "visionary for puzzles" who looked like a skateboarder-recently-turned-dad, displayed a jacked-up, interactive game called Puzzingo, intended for toddlers and inspired by his own son's desire to build and smash. Two 30-something women were eagerly seeking feedback for an app called Knock Knock Family, aimed at 1-to-4-year-olds.

2   The gathering was organized by Warren Buckleitner, a longtime reviewer of interactive children's media who likes to bring together developers, researchers, and interest groups—and often plenty of kids, some still in diapers. It went by the Harry Potter–ish name Dust or Magic, and was held in a drafty old stone-and-wood hall barely a mile from the sea, the kind of place where Bathilda Bagshot might retire after packing up her wand.

Reprinted from *The Atlantic Monthly*, March 20, 2013.

3   Buckleitner spent the breaks testing whether his own remote-control helicopter could reach the hall's second story, while various children who had come with their parents looked up in awe and delight. But mostly they looked down, at the iPads and other tablets displayed around the hall like so many open boxes of candy. I walked around and talked with developers, and several paraphrased a famous saying of **Maria Montessori's**, a quote imported to ennoble a touch-screen age when very young kids, who once could be counted on only to chew on a square of aluminum, are now engaging with it in increasingly sophisticated ways: "The hands are the instruments of man's intelligence."

Maria Montessori the founder of the Montessori method of early childhood education

4   Not that long ago, there was only the television, which theoretically could be kept in the parents' bedroom or locked behind a cabinet; now there are smart phones and iPads with thousands of apps. To parents, childhood has undergone a somewhat alarming transformation in a very short time, but to children it has always been possible to do so many things with the swipe of a finger, to have hundreds of games packed into a gadget the same size as **Goodnight Moon**.

Goodnight Moon a popular bedtime storybook for young children

5   In 2011, the American Academy of Pediatrics updated its policy on very young children and media. In 1999, the group had discouraged television viewing for children younger than 2, citing research on brain development that showed this age group's critical need for "direct interactions with parents and other significant care givers." The updated report began by acknowledging that things had changed significantly since then. In 2006, 90 percent of parents said that their children younger than 2 consumed some form of electronic media. Nonetheless, the group took largely the same approach it did in 1999, uniformly discouraging passive media use, on any type of screen, for these kids. (For older children, the academy noted, "high-quality programs" could have "educational benefits.") The 2011 report mentioned "smart cell phone" and "new screen" technologies, but did not address interactive apps; nor did it broach the possibility that has likely occurred to those 90 percent of American parents, queasy though they might be: that some good might come from those little swiping fingers.

6   I had come to the developers' conference partly because I hoped that this particular set of parents, enthusiastic as they were about interactive media, might help me out of this conundrum, that they might offer some guiding principle for American parents who are clearly never going to meet the academy's ideals, and at some level do not want to. Perhaps this group would be able to articulate some benefits of the new technology that the more cautious pediatricians weren't ready to address. I nurtured this hope until about lunchtime, when the developers gathering in the dining hall ceased being visionaries and reverted to being ordinary parents, trying to settle their toddlers in high chairs and get them to eat something besides bread.

7   I fell into conversation with a woman who had helped develop Montessori Letter Sounds, an app that teaches preschoolers the Montessori methods of spelling. She was a former Montessori teacher and a mother of four. I myself have three children who are all fans of the touch screen. What games did her kids like to play? I asked, hoping for suggestions I could take home. She replied that they didn't play very much because their screen time was limited to half an hour on weekends.

8   Her answer so surprised me that I decided to ask some of the other developers who were also parents what their domestic ground rules for screen time were. One

said only on airplanes and long car rides; another said Wednesdays and weekends, for half an hour. The most permissive said half an hour a day, which was about my rule at home. At one point I sat with one of the biggest developers of e-book apps for kids, and his family. The toddler was starting to fuss in her high chair, so the mom did what many of us have done at that moment—stuck an iPad in front of her and played a short movie so everyone else could enjoy their lunch. When she saw me watching, she gave me the universal tense look of mothers who feel they are being judged. "At home," she assured me, "I only let her watch movies in Spanish."

9   By their pinched reactions, these parents illuminated for me the neurosis of our age: as technology becomes ubiquitous in our lives, American parents are becoming more, not less, wary of what it might be doing to their children. Technological competence and sophistication have not, for parents, translated into comfort and ease; instead, they have merely created yet another sphere that parents feel they have to navigate in exactly the right way. On the one hand, parents want their children to swim expertly in the digital stream that they will have to navigate all their lives; on the other hand, they fear that too much digital media, too early, will sink them. **Norman Rockwell** never painted *Boy Swiping Finger on Screen*, and our own vision of a perfect childhood has never adjusted to accommodate that now-common tableau. Add to that our modern fear that every parenting decision may have lasting consequences—that every minute of enrichment lost or mindless entertainment indulged will add up to some permanent handicap in the future—and you have deep guilt and confusion. To date, no body of research has definitively proved that the iPad will make your preschooler smarter. So what's a parent to do?

Norman Rockwell a 20th century American painter and illustrator who created scenes of typical American life

10   In 2001, the education and technology writer Marc Prensky popularized the term *digital natives* to describe the first generations of children growing up fluent in the language of computers, video games, and other technologies. (The rest of us are *digital immigrants*, struggling to understand.) This term took on a whole new significance in April 2010, when the iPad was released. iPhones had already been tempting young children, but the screens were a little small for pudgy toddler hands to navigate with ease and accuracy. Plus, parents tended to be more possessive of their phones, hiding them in pockets or purses. The iPad was big and bright, and a case could be made that it belonged to the family. Researchers who study children's media immediately recognized it as a game changer.

11   Previously, young children had to be shown by their parents how to use a mouse or a remote, and the connection between what they were doing with their hand and what was happening on the screen took some time to grasp. But with the iPad, the connection is obvious, even to toddlers. Touch technology follows the same logic as shaking a rattle or knocking down a pile of blocks: the child swipes, and something immediately happens, a "rattle on steroids," as Buckleitner calls it. To a toddler, this is less magic than intuition. At a very young age, children become capable of what the psychologist Jerome Bruner called "enactive representation"; they classify objects in the world not by using words or symbols but by making gestures, and their hands are a natural extension of their thoughts.

12   I have two older children who fit the early idea of a digital native—they learned how to use a mouse or a keyboard with some help from their parents and were well into school before they felt comfortable with a device in their lap. My youngest child

is a whole different story, because he was not yet 2 when the iPad was released. As soon as he got his hands on it, he located the Talking Baby Hippo app that one of my older children had downloaded. The little purple hippo repeats whatever you say in his own squeaky voice, and responds to other cues. My son said his name ("Giddy!"); Baby Hippo repeated it back. Gideon poked Baby Hippo; Baby Hippo laughed. Over and over, it was funny every time. Pretty soon he discovered other apps; Old MacDonald, by Duck Duck Moose, was a favorite. At first he would get frustrated trying to zoom between screens, or not knowing what to do when a message popped up, but after about two weeks, he figured all that out. I must admit, it was eerie to see a child still in diapers so competent and intent, as if he were forecasting his own adulthood. Technically I was the owner of the iPad, but in some ontological way it felt much more his than mine.

13   Without seeming to think much about it or resolve how they felt, parents began giving their devices over to their children to mollify, pacify, or otherwise entertain them. By 2010, two-thirds of children ages 4 to 7 had used an iPhone, according to the Joan Ganz Cooney Center, which studies children's media. The vast majority of those phones had been lent by a family member; the center's researchers labeled this the "pass-back effect," a name that captures well the reluctant zone between denying and giving.

14   The market immediately picked up on the pass-back effect, and the opportunities it presented. In 2008, when Apple opened up its App Store, the games started arriving at the rate of dozens a day, thousands a year. Now, by Buckleitner's loose count, more than 40,000 kids' games are available on iTunes, plus thousands more on Google Play. In the iTunes "Education" category, the majority of the top-selling apps target preschool or elementary-age children. As these delights and diversions for young children have proliferated, the pass-back has become more uncomfortable, even unsustainable, for many parents.

15   Ever since viewing screens entered the home, many observers have worried that they put our brains into a stupor. An early strain of research claimed that when we watch television, our brains mostly exhibit slow alpha waves—indicating a low level of arousal, similar to when we are daydreaming. These findings have been largely discarded by the scientific community, but the myth persists that watching television is the mental equivalent of, as one Web site put it, "staring at a blank wall." These common metaphors are misleading, argues Heather Kirkorian, who studies media and attention at the University of Wisconsin at Madison. A more accurate point of comparison for a TV viewer's physiological state would be that of someone deep in a book, says Kirkorian, because during both activities we are still, undistracted, and mentally active.

16   Because interactive media are so new, most of the existing research looks at children and television: "there is universal agreement that by at least age 2 and a half, children are very cognitively active when they are watching TV," says Dan Anderson, a children's-media expert at the University of Massachusetts at Amherst. Anderson's series of experiments on the zombie theory provided the first clue that even very young children can be discriminating viewers—that they are not in fact brain-dead, but rather work hard to make sense of what they see and turn it into a coherent narrative that reflects what they already know of the world. Now, 30 years later, we

understand that children "can make a lot of inferences and process the information," says Anderson. "And they can learn a lot, both positive and negative." Researchers never abandoned the idea that parental interaction is critical for the development of very young children, but they started to see TV watching in shades of gray. If a child never interacts with adults and always watches TV, well, that is a problem, but if a child is watching TV instead of, say, playing with toys, then that is a tougher comparison, because TV, in the right circumstances, has something to offer.

17   How do small children actually experience electronic media, and what does that experience do to their development? Since the '80s, researchers have spent more and more time consulting with television programmers to study and shape TV content. By tracking children's reactions, they have identified certain rules that promote engagement: stories have to be linear and easy to follow, cuts and time lapses have to be used very sparingly, and language has to be pared down and repeated.

18   A perfect example of a well-engineered show is Nick Jr.'s *Blue's Clues,* which aired from 1996 to 2006. Each episode features Steve (or Joe, in later seasons) and Blue, a cartoon puppy, solving a mystery. Steve talks slowly and simply; he repeats words and then writes them down in his handy-dandy notebook; there are almost no cuts or unexplained gaps in time. The great innovation of *Blue's Clues* is something called the "pause"—Steve asks a question and then pauses for about five seconds to let the viewer shout out an answer. Small children feel much more engaged and invested when they think they have a role to play, when they believe they are actually helping Steve and Blue piece together the clues. A longitudinal study of children older than 2 and a half showed that the ones who watched *Blue's Clues* made measurably larger gains in flexible thinking and problem solving over two years of watching the show.

19   For toddlers, however, the situation seems slightly different because children younger than 2 and a half exhibit what researchers call a "video deficit." This means that they have a much easier time processing information delivered by a real person than by a person on videotape. A natural assumption is that toddlers are not yet cognitively equipped to handle symbolic representation. (I remember my older son, when he was 3, asking me if he could go into the TV and pet Blue.) But there is another way to interpret this particular phase of development. Toddlers are skilled at seeking out what researchers call "socially relevant information": they tune in to people and situations that help them make a coherent narrative of the world around them. TV is static and lacks one of the most important things to toddlers, which is a "two-way exchange of information," argues Troseth, a developmental psychologist at Vanderbilt University.

20   *Blue's Clues* was on the right track. The pause could trick children into thinking that Steve was responsive to them, but the holy grail would be creating a scenario in which the guy on the screen did actually respond—in which the toddler did something and the character reliably jumped or laughed or started to dance or talk back. Like, for example, when Gideon said "Giddy" and Talking Baby Hippo said "Giddy" back, without fail, every time. That kind of contingent interaction (I do something, you respond) is what captivates a toddler and can be a significant source of learning for even very young children—learning that researchers hope the children can carry into the real world. It's not exactly the ideal social partner the American Academy of Pediatrics craves. It's certainly not a parent or caregiver, but it's as good an

approximation as we've ever come up with on a screen, and it's why children's-media researchers are so excited about the iPad's potential.

21   Sandra Calvert, the director of the Children's Media Center at Georgetown University, who conducted several studies on toddlers and iPads, takes a balanced view of technology: she works in an office surrounded by hardcover books, and she sometimes edits her drafts with pen and paper. But she is very interested in how the iPad can reach children even before they're old enough to access these traditional media. "People say we are experimenting with our children," she told me, "But from my perspective, it's already happened, and there's no way to turn it back. Children's lives are filled with media at younger and younger ages, and we need to take advantage of what these technologies have to offer. I'm not a Pollyanna; I'm pretty much a realist; I look at what kids are doing and try to figure out how to make the best of it."

22   Calvert's research is designed to answer a series of very responsible, high-minded questions: Can toddlers learn from iPads? Can they transfer what they learn to the real world? What effect does interactivity have on learning? What role do familiar characters play in children's learning from iPads? All worthy questions, and important, but also all considered entirely from an adult's point of view. The reason many kids' apps are grouped under "Education" in the iTunes store, I suspect, is to assuage parents' guilt (though I also suspect that in the long run, all those "educational" apps merely perpetuate our neurotic relationship with technology, by reinforcing the idea that they must be sorted vigilantly into "good" or "bad"). If small children had more input, many "Education" apps would logically fall under a category called "Kids" or "Kids' Games." And many more of the games would probably look something like the apps designed by a Swedish game studio named Toca Boca.

23   In 2011 the two developers, Emil Ovemar and Bjorn Jeffrey, launched Toca Tea Party. The game is not all that different from a real tea party. The iPad functions almost like a tea table without legs, and the kids have to invent the rest by, for example, seating their own plushies or dolls, one on each side, and then setting the theater in motion. First, choose one of three tablecloths, and then choose plates, cups, and treats. The treats are not what your mom would feed you, instead they are chocolate cakes, frosted doughnuts, cookies. It's very easy to spill the tea when you pour or take a sip, a feature added based on kids' suggestions during a test play (kids love spills, but spilling is something you can't do all that often at a real tea party, or you'll get yelled at). At the end, a sink filled with soapy suds appears, and you wash the dishes, which is also part of the fun, and then start again. That's it. The game is either very boring or terrifically exciting, depending on what you make of it. Ovemar and Jeffery knew that some parents wouldn't get it, but for kids, the game would be fun every time, because it's dependent entirely on imagination. Maybe today the stuffed bear will be naughty and do the spilling, while naked Barbie will pile her plate high with sweets. The child can take on the voice of a character or a scolding parent, or both. There's no winning, and there's no reward. Like a game of stuck-on-an-island, it can go on for five minutes or forever.

24   Soon after the release of Toca Tea Party, the pair introduced Toca Hair Salon, which is still to my mind the most fun game out there. The salon is no Fifth Avenue spa; it's a rundown-looking place with cracks in the wall. The aim is not beauty but subversion. Cutting off hair, like spilling, is on the list of things kids are not supposed

to do. You choose one of the odd-looking people or creatures and have your way with its hair, trimming it or dyeing it or growing it out. The blow-dryer is genius; it achieves the same effect as Tadao Cern's Blow Job portraits, which depict people's faces getting wildly distorted by high winds. In August 2011, Toca Boca gave away Hair Salon for free for nearly two weeks. It was downloaded more than 1 million times in the first week, and the company took off, and today, many Toca Boca games show up on lists of the most popular education apps.

25   Are they educational? "That's the perspective of the parents," Jeffery told me at the back of the grand hall in Monterey. "Is running around on the lawn educational? Every part of a child's life can't be held up to that standard." As we talked, two girls were playing Toca Tea Party on the floor nearby. One had her stuffed dragon at a plate, and he was being especially naughty, grabbing all the chocolate cake and spilling everything. Her friend had taken a little Lego construction man and made him the good guy who ate neatly and helped do the dishes. Should they have been outside at the beach? Maybe, but the day would be long, and they could go outside later.

26   The more I talked with the developers, the more elusive and unhelpful the "Education" category seemed. (Is *Where the Wild Things Are* educational? Would you make your child read a textbook at bedtime? Do you watch only educational television? And why don't children deserve high-quality fun?) Buckleitner calls his conference Dust or Magic to teach app developers a more subtle concept than pedagogy. By *magic*, Buckleitner has in mind an app that makes children's fingers move and their eyes light up. By *dust*, he means something that was obviously (and ploddingly) designed by an adult. Some educational apps, I wouldn't wish on the naughtiest toddler—take, for example, Counting With the Very Hungry Caterpillar, which turns a perfectly cute book into a tedious app that asks you to "please eat 1 piece of chocolate cake" so you can count to one.

27   During the course of reporting this story, I downloaded dozens of apps and let my children test them out. They didn't much care whether the apps were marketed as educational or not, as long as they were fun. Without my prompting, Gideon fixated on a game called LetterSchool, which teaches you how to write letters more effectively and with more imagination than any penmanship textbooks I've ever encountered. He loves the Toca Boca games, the Duck Duck Moose games, and random games like Bugs and Buttons. My older kids love The Numberlys, a dark fantasy creation of illustrators who have worked with Pixar that happens to teach the alphabet, and all my kids, including Gideon, play Cut the Rope a lot, which is not exclusively marketed as a kids' game. I could convince myself that the game is teaching them certain principles of physics—it's not easy to know the exact right place to slice the rope, but do I really need that extra convincing? I like playing the game; why shouldn't they?

28   Every new medium has, within a short time of its introduction, been condemned as a threat to young people. Pulp novels would destroy their morals, TV would wreck their eyesight, video games would make them violent. Each one has been accused of seducing kids into wasting time that would otherwise be spent learning about the presidents, playing with friends, or digging their toes into the sand. In our generation, the worries focus on kids' brainpower, about unused synapses withering

as children stare at the screen. People fret about television and ADHD, although that concern is largely based on a single study that has been roundly criticized and doesn't jibe with anything we know about the disorder.

29   There are legitimate broader questions about how American children spend their time, but all you can do is keep them in mind as you decide what rules to set down for your own child. The statement from the American Academy of Pediatrics assumes a zero-sum game: an hour spent watching TV is an hour not spent with a parent. But parents know this is not how life works. There are enough hours in a day to go to school, play a game, and spend time with a parent, and generally these are different hours. Some people can get so drawn into screens that they want to do nothing else but play games. Experts say excessive video gaming is a real problem, but they debate whether it can be called an addiction and, if so, whether the term can be used for anything but a small portion of the population. If your child shows signs of having an addictive personality, you will probably know it. One of my kids is like that; I set stricter limits for him than for the others, and he seems to understand why.

30   In her excellent book *Screen Time*, the journalist Lisa Guernsey lays out a useful framework—what she calls the three C's—for thinking about media consumption: content, context, and your child. She poses a series of questions—Do you think the content is appropriate? Is screen time a "relatively small part of your child's interaction with you and the real world?"—and suggests tailoring your rules to the answers, child by child. One of the most interesting points Guernsey makes is about the importance of parents' attitudes toward media. If they treat screen time like junk food, or "like a magazine at the hair salon"—good for passing the time in a frivolous way but nothing more—then the child will fully absorb that attitude, and the neurosis will be passed to the next generation.

31   "The war is over; the natives won." So says Marc Prensky, the education and technology writer, who has the most extreme parenting philosophy of anyone I encountered in my reporting. Prensky's 7-year-old son has access to books, TV, Legos, Wii—and Prensky treats them all the same. He does not limit access to any of them. "We live in a screen age, and to say to a kid, 'I'd love for you to look at a book but I hate it when you look at the screen' is just bizarre. It reflects our own prejudices and comfort zones; it's nothing but fear of change, of being left out."

32   Prensky's worldview really stuck with me. Are books always, in every situation, inherently better than screens? After I first interviewed Prensky, I decided to conduct an experiment. For six months, I would let my toddler live by the Prensky rules: I would put the iPad in the toy basket, along with the remote-control car and the Legos, and whenever he wanted to play with it, I would let him.

33   Gideon tested me the very first day. He saw the iPad in his space and asked if he could play. It was 8 a.m. and we had to get ready for school. I said yes, so for 45 minutes he sat on a chair and played as I got him dressed, got his backpack ready, and failed to feed him breakfast. This was extremely annoying and obviously untenable. The week went on like this—Gideon grabbing the iPad for two-hour stretches, in the morning, after school, at bedtime. Then, after about 10 days, the iPad fell out of his rotation, just like every other toy does. He dropped it under the bed and never looked for it, and it was completely forgotten for about six weeks.

34   Now he picks it up every once in a while, but not all that often. He has just started learning letters in school, so he's back to playing LetterSchool. A few weeks ago his older brother played with him, helping him get all the way through the uppercase and then lowercase letters. It did not seem beyond the range of possibility that if Norman Rockwell were alive, he would paint the two curly-haired boys bent over the screen, one small finger guiding a smaller one across, down, and across again to make, in their triumphant finale, the small *z*.

POST-READING

UNDERSTANDING AND ANALYZING THE READING

A. Building Vocabulary

Using context and a dictionary if necessary, determine the meaning of each word as it is used in the selection.

_____ 1. broach (paragraph 5)
   a. suggest for the first time
   b. fail to mention
   c. prove to be false
   d. dismiss

_____ 2. conundrum (paragraph 6)
   a. disturbing situation
   b. illegal activity
   c. anything that pleases
   d. anything that puzzles

_____ 3. articulate (paragraph 6)
   a. express clearly
   b. enlighten
   c. dispute
   d. deny

_____ 4. ubiquitous (paragraph 9)
   a. dangerous
   b. slow to respond
   c. absent from the body
   d. everywhere at once

_____ 5. proliferated (paragraph 14)
   a. spread rapidly
   b. failed
   c. changed quickly
   d. decreased

_____ 6. assuage (paragraph 22)
   a. improve
   b. intensify
   c. make less severe
   d. add to

_____ 7. elusive (paragraph 26)
   a. difficult to find
   b. numerous
   c. unexplored
   d. age-based

_____ 8. untenable (paragraph 33)
   a. unclear
   b. indefensible
   c. unimaginable
   d. improbable

Word Parts

> ### A REVIEW OF PREFIXES AND ROOTS
>
> **PER-** means through.
> **SPEC** means to see or look.
> **INTER-** means between

Use your knowledge of word parts and the review above to fill in the blanks in the following sentences.

1. A person who has a *perspective* (paragraph 25) on a situation is able to
   _____ it.

2. **Interaction** (paragraph 30) is action that occurs _____ two
   people, two groups, or two things.

B. Understanding the Thesis and Other Main Ideas

Select the best answer.

_____ 1. Which of the following is the best statement of the selection's thesis
        or central thought?

   a. Young children are affected more negatively by television than
      they are by more recent technological devices such as the smart
      phones and the iPad.

   b. Although parents are still concerned about issues surrounding
      the use of technology by young children, children of the touch-
      screen generation are embracing the technology and enjoying
      both the entertainment and educational aspects of it.

   c. Although most of the research has been done on children and
      television, the zombie theory seems to hold true for interactive
      media as well.

   d. Rather than fret about the effects of the latest technology on
      young children, parents need to become familiar with the tech-
      nology and encourage their children to use it appropriately.

_____ 2. Which of the following sentences states the main idea of
        paragraph 9?

   a. "By their pinched reactions, these parents illuminated for me
      the neurosis of our age: as technology becomes ubiquitous in
      our lives, American parents are becoming more, not less, wary of
      what it might be doing to their children."

b. "Technological competence and sophistication have not, for parents, translated into comfort and ease; instead they have merely created yet another sphere that parents feel they have to navigate in exactly the right way."

c. "Norman Rockwell never painted *Boy Swiping Finger on Screen*, and our own vision of a perfect childhood has never adjusted to accommodate that now-common tableau."

d. "Add to that our modern fear that every parenting decision may have lasting consequences—that every minute of enrichment lost or mindless entertainment indulged will add up to some permanent handicap in the future—and you have deep guilt and confusion."

_____ 3. The topic of paragraph 11 is
   a. the magic of touch technology.
   b. how parents teach toddlers to use a mouse.
   c. the connection between hand and screen.
   d. toddlers and touch technology.

C. Identifying Details

Select the best answer.

_____ 1. Who popularized the term *digital natives*?
   a. Maria Montessori
   b. Hanna Rosin
   c. Marc Prensky
   d. Sandra Calvert

_____ 2. Which one of the following effects of watching television was **NOT** cited in this article?
   a. childhood obesity
   b. damaged eyesight
   c. ADHD
   d. lack of direct interaction with parents and care givers

_____ 3. Young children are able to master touch technology because
   a. it does not require the use of small motor skills.
   b. because they spend most of their time holding or picking up objects.
   c. because their sense of touch is well developed.
   d. their hands are an extension of their thoughts.

_____ 4. The author states that Nick Jr.'s *Blues Clues'* great innovation was

a. slow and simple speech.

b. a cartoon puppy.

c. the pause.

d. no unexplained gaps in time.

D. Recognizing Methods of Organization and Transitions

Select the best answer.

_____ 1. The pattern of organization used in paragraph 6 is

a. classification.

b. definition.

c. cause and effect.

d. process.

_____ 2. The overall pattern of organization used for paragraphs 10–26 is

a. classification.

b. illustration

c. chronological order.

d. definition.

_____ 3. The organizational pattern used in paragraph 15 is

a. comparison.

b. contrast.

c. chronological order.

d. definition.

E. Reading and Thinking Visually

Select the best answer.

_____ 1. The author likely chose to include the photos on page 397 to

a. depict the intense concentration of children using technology.

b. illustrate how both genders enjoy touch-screen technology.

c. provide an example of children using technology.

d. demonstrate the natural ability of children to swipe.

_____ 2. The author of this article writes about the physiological state of a television viewer. The most accurate description of this state is

a. like someone deeply engrossed in a book.

b. like someone who is daydreaming.

    c. like someone who is totally zoned out and "zombiefied."

    d. like someone who is staring at a blank wall.

F. Figuring Out Implied Meanings

Indicate whether each statement is true (T) or false (F).

_____ 1. Parents are unsure of the best way to handle children's use of technology.

_____ 2. Designers of apps would be wise to market their products as educational apps in order to appeal to parents of young children.

_____ 3. Left on their own, children will discard all other toys and play only with a technological toy.

_____ 4. Researchers are finding that the responsible use of technology is not harmful to young children.

_____ 5. The problem with young children using technology is actually their parents and the attitude they have toward children using technology.

_____ 6. The author of the article concludes that parents must tightly monitor children's use of technology.

G. Thinking Critically: Analyzing the Author's Technique

Select the best answer.

_____ 1. The author begins the selection with information about the conference in order to

    a. illustrate the bizarre nature of game designers.

    b. highlight the appeal of apps to a toddler audience.

    c. provide an example of technological change.

    d. offer a solution for those who want to play computer games with their children.

_____ 2. The author's primary purpose in including information on *Blue's Clues* is to

    a. emphasize the importance of engagement or active viewing.

    b. recommend this show to parents as an alternative to allowing their children to play computer games.

    c. make readers aware of the rich resources that exist on public television stations.

    d. emphasize the dangers of children watching too much television.

_____ 3. The author's tone is best described as

    a. informative.

    b. irreverent.

    c. self-righteous.

    d. sarcastic.

_____ 4. Three of the following sentences from the reading are facts. One is an opinion. Which one is the opinion?

    a. "Soon after the release of Toca Tea Party, the pair introduced Toca Hair Salon, which is still to my mind the most fun game out there." (paragraph 24)

    b. "The child can take on the voice of a character or a scolding parent, or both." (paragraph 23)

    c. "In 2011, the American Academy of Pediatrics updated its policy on very young children and media." (paragraph 5)

    d. "Previously, young children had to be shown by their parents how to use a mouse or a remote, and the connection between what they were doing with their hand and what was happening on the screen took some time to grasp." (paragraph 11)

_____ 5. Which one of the following sentences contains a metaphor?

    a. ". . . some good might come from those little swiping fingers." (paragraph 5)

    b. ". . . they fear that too much digital media, too early, will sink them." (paragraph 9)

    c. "I nurtured this hope until about lunchtime . . ." (paragraph 6)

    d. "The hands are the instruments of man's intelligence." (paragraph 3)

_____ 6. To support her thesis, the author uses all of the following *except*

    a. research.

    b. direct quotations from people she has interviewed.

    c. personal experience.

    d. an interview with an Apple executive.

_____ 7. Which of the following sentences contains an example of *informal* language?

    a. "Her answer so surprised me that I decided to ask some of the other developers who were also parents what their domestic ground rules for screen time were." (paragraph 8)

    b. " But mostly they looked down, at the iPads and other tablets displayed around the hall like so many open boxes of candy." (paragraph 3)

c. "Ever since viewing screens entered the home, many observers have worried that they put our brains into a stupor."
(paragraph 15)

d. "One developer, a self-described 'visionary for puzzles' who
looked like a skateboarder-recently-turned-dad, displayed a
jacked-up, interactive game called Puzzingo, intended for toddlers and inspired by his own son's desire to build and smash."
(paragraph 1)

H. Thinking Critically: Analyzing the Author's Message

Select the best answer.

_____ 1. In which of the following paragraphs can you find the reason that
researchers think that the iPad holds such promise as a learning
tool?

a. paragraph 3

b. paragraph 11

c. paragraph 20

d. paragraph 27

_____ 2. What does the phrase "a rattle on steroids" mean in paragraph 11?

a. The iPad is like a very powerful rattle to toddlers; use of it is
intuitive.

b. The iPad makes the same noises as a rattle does, and so it appeals
to toddlers.

c. The iPad serves as a babysitter to toddlers just as a rattle pacifies
toddlers.

d. Both the iPad and a rattle are manipulated by the hands of
toddlers.

_____ 3. Why does the author mention Norman Rockwell in paragraph 9
and paragraph 34?

a. to emphasize the artistic nature of technology

b. to underscore the fact that the use of technology by young children has become a commonplace activity in our society

c. to illustrate the beauty of children artfully using technology

d. to emphasize the capabilities of technology to create beautiful
art

_____ 4. Why does the author put the word *education* in quotation marks in paragraph 22?

  a. She believes that many people are not aware of the existence of educational apps for the iPad.

  b. She wants to give emphasis to this term in an effort to convince the reader of the value of the iPad as a tool for learning.

  c. She wants to emphasize the educational value of apps in the iTunes store.

  d. She wants the audience to know that the apps labeled as educational may not really be educational.

WRITING IN RESPONSE TO THE READING

I. Writing a Summary

Write a summary of "The Touch-Screen Generation" (paragraphs 1–34).

J. Analyzing the Issue

1. Identify at least three objections that parents have to young children using technology. Then explain the research presented by the author to counter this objection.

2. Write a statement that briefly summarizes the author's position on young children using technology.

3. Identify at least one example of verbal or situational irony used by the author.

4. What is the author's background, and is she qualified to write about the topic? Why or why not? Do you find any bias in the selection?

K. Writing Paragraphs and Essays

Write a paragraph or essay in response to the following writing prompts. As part of this assignment you will need to follow the writing process outlined here:

- Use a prewriting strategy to generate ideas
- Complete a guided outline
- Write a rough draft
- Complete peer revision guide
- Write a final draft using proper MLA format

1. The author presents information on several apps that she finds either educational or entertaining to children. Write a paragraph or essay in which you discuss apps that you have found to be either helpful or entertaining. You must describe the app and also explain how/why these apps have value to you.

2. The author presents research in order to convince the reader of the value of the iPad to young children. Do you agree or disagree that the iPad can be of value to young children? Write a paragraph or essay in which you present your opinion and the reasons for your opinion.

3. Clearly, technology has changed our world in many ways. Write a paragraph or essay in which you compare technology that was present when you were a child with technology that is available to today's children. Be sure to provide examples to support your thesis.

4. Maria Montessori once stated that "the hands are the instruments of man's intelligence." Write a paragraph or essay in which you explain this statement. Be sure to provide examples to support your thesis.

5. Write a paragraph or essay about someone you know (you do not have to provide his or her real name) who is addicted to his/her smart phone or iPad. Why do you think this person is addicted? What addictive behaviors does he/she exhibit? How do you suggest that this person break the addiction?

L. Working Collaboratively

1. **Thinking Deeply** In a small group of your peers, discuss the following questions:

   - What technological tools do you own or use regularly?
   - How do these tools help you with your everyday life?
   - Try to imagine what life would be like without them? Are you living a better life through the use of these tools? How so?
   - How have these tools possibly created problems for you in life?

   Be prepared to share your findings with the class.

2. **Thinking Critically** Imagine that you are the author of an advice column of a local newspaper. One question that was submitted recently came from a parent who is unsure of how to responsibly handle the use of the iPad by her young child. What suggestions do you have for this parent? Working with a partner, draft a one-paragraph response to this parent in which you establish some clear guidelines for the parent to follow. Finally, be prepared to share your letter with the class.

3. **Thinking about Annotating** As you were reading "The Touch-Screen Generation," you annotated (made marginal notes) and highlighted the text. Now, working with a partner, review each other's highlighting and annotating, discuss the similarities and differences, and settle upon an acceptable version. To test the effectiveness of your highlighting, reread only the highlighted portions and ask yourself the following questions:

   - Does the highlighting tell what the passage is about?
   - Does it make sense?
   - Does it indicate the most important ideas in the passage?

4. **Thinking Personally** This activity will give you an opportunity to examine the amount of time you spend using technology during a specific period of time. For one four-hour period, log the time you spend watching television, talking on your phone, and using your computer or iPad. Be sure to record the time spent on each activity and a description of the activity. At the end of the four-hour period, analyze your use of technology. Has it made your life easier? Has it saved you time? Has it wasted your time? Has it entertained you? Has it enabled you to learn anything? Has it kept you from getting things done? Once you have analyzed your findings, write a short paragraph about what you have learned. Then, in class, join a group of your peers and share your findings.

ACTIVITIES: EXPLORING TECHNOLOGY

On your own or with a group of classmates, complete two of the following four activities.

1. It is likely that you own a smart phone and that you use it to send text messages and/or post to Facebook or some other type of social media. List at least three ways that using a smart phone or social media site has improved your life. Then list at least three ways in which you see smart phones and/or social media being misused (for example, people who send text messages while driving create extremely dangerous road conditions that can lead to people getting killed).

   _____

   _____

   _____

   _____

2. Conduct a Web search for an organization that is devoted to educating people about and preventing cyberbullying. (For example, you might try www. stopbullying.gov.) Read about the organization's mission, as well as a couple

of the articles on the organization's Web site. Summarize these articles in a paragraph, essay, or classroom presentation. Provide at least three tips for preventing or stomping out cyberbullying.

3. As we mentioned at the start of this chapter, technology has become pervasive in almost all areas of our lives. This chapter discussed just a few aspects of the topic. Other technological issues include:

   ■ The threat of identity theft through technological means

   ■ Brain research that suggests the addictive quality of technology

   ■ Serious privacy concerns as Web browsers track your movements online and then sell that information to companies who want to advertise their products to you

   ■ The effects of technology on the well-being of young children who spend a lot of time playing on computers

   ■ Technology's role in the theft of *intellectual property* such as music and books (if you have ever downloaded a book or a song from a "share" site, you have most likely stolen intellectual property).

   ■ The role technology plays in political campaigns and social unrest (for example, the Occupy Wall Street movement)

   Write an essay or prepare a class presentation about any of these topics, or any other technological topic in which you are interested.

4. Suppose you are the creator of reality TV programming and your boss gives you the following assignment: "Come up with a reality TV show that portrays people in a positive way, showing their innate goodness and generosity." Write an essay in which you explain the type of show you would create. What would the setting be? Who would the characters be? What sorts of events would drive the story and make TV viewers want to watch the show?

13 Relationships: Our Friends, Families, and Communities

How many people do you interact with daily?

If you're like most people, you don't keep track of the dozens, even hundreds, of people you see each day. Sociologists and psychologists often call humans "the social animal" because the vast majority of human beings seek the company of others. John Donne, the English poet, wrote a famous poem titled "No Man Is an Island," which begins:

> No man is an island,
> Entire of itself.
> Each is a piece of the continent,
> A part of the main.

But human relationships aren't necessarily easy. In fact, they often require a good deal of work, and they are at the center of many contemporary issues. Consider the following questions, which are often debated:

- Should gay people be allowed to marry? Is marriage a religious institution, or is it secular (non-religious)?

- Is marriage the ideal situation for most people, or should society embrace looser definitions of what constitutes a "couple"?

- When should a relationship end? How do divorces and break-ups affect not only the couple breaking up, but also their friends, family, and children?

The readings in this chapter look at just a few of the many issues surrounding interpersonal relationships today. Should two people have sex before they get married or even on the first date? Almost everyone finds it difficult to find the perfect romantic match—might dating Web sites help you find your "soul mate"? How has the Internet changed the way we look at and define communities, and are online communities as "real" as physical communities in which people interact face to face?

WHY ARE CONTEMPORARY ISSUES RELATED TO RELATIONSHIPS SO IMPORTANT?

Human beings are constantly redefining their relationships with other people, starting new relationships and sometimes ending other ones. Society's views of relationships affect people at the core of their being and influence their decisions. For example, it is often suggested that gay people tend to gather in liberal cities, where their relationships are more accepted. The legal system's laws regarding which relationships to recognize and which not to recognize can have major effects on spouses, ex-spouses, in-laws, and children.

How Do Relationships Relate to My College Experience?

The phrase "college experience" connotes much more than simply taking courses and studying for exams. Rather, it refers to an entire constellation of experiences you will encounter in college—from having a roommate, to developing relationships with your instructors, to managing your life, to planning your career. Relationships are involved in almost every aspect of the college experience and in many college courses. For example, business courses often require teamwork, which requires getting along with others in a group setting. In science labs, you will often have a lab partner with whom you share the work, and entire disciplines (such as sociology and communications) focus on human interactions and relationships.

Tips for Reading about Relationships

Here are some tips for reading not only the selections in this chapter, but any reading about relationships.

- **Apply the reading to your own experiences and life.** Students often find readings about relationships to be fairly "easy" and immediately applicable to their lives. As you read, think about how the selection applies to you or to other people you know. This is an excellent way to learn the concepts and ideas discussed in the reading.

- **Distinguish between the writer's opinions and research presented as evidence to support a thesis or main idea.** Much of what you read about relationships will be based on the writer's personal experiences. Such readings can be illuminating, but they may not be representative of the way most people feel. They are therefore mostly opinion pieces. In contrast, scientific research presented in a reading is more fact-based. Most writers give credit to the person who conducted the research, either directly (by giving the person's name and affiliation) or indirectly, by using a parenthetical research citation. For example, (Smith, 2009) refers to a research study conducted by someone named Smith, who published his or her results in 2009. Complete sources for parenthetical citations are usually found in footnotes or endnotes.

- **Keep an open mind.** Some readings about relationships may make you uncomfortable if they challenge your beliefs or expectations. Read carefully, keeping an open mind, and engage in critical thinking. Annotate the reading to record your reactions, and then analyze your reactions, asking yourself why you reacted the way you did.

Rubric for Writing Essays

In this chapter you will read articles about communication and technology and write essays in response to them. To be sure that you write clear and correct essays use the following rubric, a set of guidelines to follow in prewriting, writing, and revising an essay. Check the rubric often, especially as you begin each stage of the writing process.

I. Planning Use of prewriting strategy is evident

II. Organization Writing is unified and coherent
- Essay effectively accomplishes your purpose
- Essay is appropriate for your audience
- Thesis statement is clear and focused
- Sentences do not stray off topic
- Body paragraphs support the thesis statement
- Essay has an appealing introduction/conclusion
- Signal words and phrases are used appropriately

III. Content/Support
- Topic sentences are clear and focused
- Details are specific and adequate
- Details are logical and supportive of topic sentences
- Details are organized appropriately

IV. Grammar and Mechanics Use of language reflects Standard written English

V. Use of Technology MLA/APA format is used correctly

Comments/Suggestions for Improvement: _____

_____

_____

_____

_____

Revision and Proofreading Checklist

Revising, or editing, involves reviewing and often making major changes to every idea and sentence you have written. Proofreading is the part of the revision process that involves adding or deleting words and sentences, as well as correcting your grammar, spelling, and punctuation.

REVISION AND PROOFREADING LIST

Revision

- Does your essay accomplish your purpose?
- Is your essay appropriate for your audience?
- Is your thesis statement clearly expressed?
- Does each paragraph support your thesis?
- Is your essay logically organized?
- Have you used transitions to connect your ideas?
- Are your introduction, conclusion, and title effective?

Proofreading

- Each sentence ends with appropriate punctuation (period, question mark, exclamation point, and/or quotation mark)
- All punctuation within each sentence is correct (commas, colons, semicolons, apostrophes, dashes, and quotation marks)
- Every word is spelled correctly
- Capital letters are used where needed
- Numbers and abbreviations are used correctly
- No words have been omitted
- All typographical errors have been corrected
- All pages are numbered and in the correct order

Ending a Relationship

Joseph A. DeVito

DRE 096   PRE-READING

Source and Context

Joseph A. DeVito is the author of a textbook entitled *The Interpersonal Communication Book.* The selection that follows is an excerpt from a chapter in De-Vito's book.

A Note on the Reading

Read the selection to understand how to bring an end to a relationship and deal with the problems that arise from the ending.

Previewing the Reading

Using the steps listed on page 4, preview the reading selection. When you have finished, answer the following questions.

1. What word does the author use to indicate the ending of a relationship?

   _____

2. How many strategies for ending a relationship does the author present? ___

3. What are the six ways of dealing with a breakup?

   a. _____

   b. _____

   c. _____

   d. _____

   e. _____

   f. _____

Using Prior Knowledge

Ending a relationship can be very difficult. All of us, at some point in our lives, have ended or will end a relationship. The relationship may be with a friend, a family member, or a significant other. Think about a relationship that you have been in. Why did it end? How did it end? Was the ending painful? Were you and the other party able to move forward peacefully?

Reading Tip

Highlight key points of the article as you read. The headings will help you focus on the main ideas. Also, review the writing assignments at the end of the chapter before you begin reading. This information will help you with writing annotations that will be useful in responding to the various writing prompts.

Ending a Relationship

Joseph A. DeVito

1   Some relationships, of course, do end. Sometimes there is simply not enough to hold the couple together. Sometimes there are problems that cannot be resolved. Sometimes the costs are too high and the rewards too few, or the relationship is recognized as destructive and escape is the only alternative. As a relationship ends, you're confronted with two general issues: (1) how to end the relationship, and (2) how to deal with the inevitable problems that relationship endings cause.

The Strategies of Disengagement

2   When you wish to exit a relationship you need some way of explaining this—to yourself as well as to your partner. You develop a strategy for getting out of a relationship that you no longer find satisfying or profitable. The table (p. 422) identifies five major disengagement strategies. As you read down the table, note that the strategies depend on your goal. For example, you're more likely to remain friends if you use de-escalation than if you use justification or avoidance. You may find it interesting to identify the disengagement strategies you have heard of or used yourself, and see how they fit in with these five types.

Dealing with a Breakup

3   Regardless of the specific reason, relationship breakups are difficult to deal with; invariably they cause stress. You're likely to experience high levels of distress over the breakup of a relationship in which you were satisfied, were close to your partner, had dated your partner for a long time, and felt it would not be easy to replace the relationship with another one.

4   Given both the inevitability that some relationships will break up and the importance of such breakups, here are some suggestions to ease the difficulty that is sure to be experienced. These suggestions apply to the termination of any type of relationship—between friends or lovers, through death, separation, or breakup.

Break the Loneliness-Depression Cycle

5   The two most common feelings following the end of a relationship are loneliness and depression. These feelings are significant; treat them seriously. Realize that depression often leads to serious illness. In most cases, fortunately, loneliness and

depression are temporary. Depression, for example, usually does not last longer than three or four days. Similarly, the loneliness that follows a breakup is generally linked to this specific situation and will fade when the situation changes. When depression does last, is especially deep, or disturbs your normal functioning, it's time for professional help.

FIVE DISENGAGEMENT STRATEGIES

Think back to relationships that you have tried to dissolve or that your partner tried to dissolve. Did you or your partner use any of the strategies listed here?

Strategy	Function	Examples
Positive tone	To maintain a positive relationship; to express positive feelings for the other person	I really care for you a great deal but I'm not ready for such an intense relationship.
Negative identity management	To blame the other person for the breakup; to absolve oneself of the blame for the breakup	I can't stand your jealousy, your constant suspicions, your checking up on me. I need my freedom.
Justification	To give reasons for the breakup	I'm going away to college for four years; there's no point in not dating others.
Behavioral de-escalation	To reduce the intensity of the relationship	Avoidance; cut down on phone calls; reduce time spent together, especially time alone.
De-escalation	To reduce the exclusivity and hence the intensity of the relationship	I'm just not ready for so exclusive a relationship. I think we should see other people.

Take Time Out

6   Resist the temptation to jump into a new relationship while the old one is still warm or before a new one can be assessed with some objectivity. At the same time, resist swearing off all relationships. Neither extreme works well.

7   Take time out for yourself. Renew your relationship with yourself. If you were in a long-term relationship, you probably saw yourself as part of a team, as part of a couple. Now get to know yourself as a unique individual, standing alone at present but fully capable of entering a meaningful relationship in the near future.

Bolster Self-Esteem

8   When relationships fail, self-esteem often declines. This seems especially true for those who did not initiate the breakup. You may feel guilty for having caused

the breakup or inadequate for not holding on to the relationship. You may feel unwanted and unloved. Your task is to regain the positive self-image needed to function effectively.

9   Recognize, too, that having been in a relationship that failed—even if you view yourself as the main cause of the breakup—does not mean that you are a failure. Neither does it mean that you cannot succeed in a new and different relationship. It does mean that something went wrong with this one relationship. Ideally, it was a failure from which you have learned something important about yourself and about your relationship behavior.

Remove or Avoid Uncomfortable Symbols

10   After any breakup, there are a variety of reminders—photographs, gifts, and letters, for example. Resist the temptation to throw these out. Instead, remove them. Give them to a friend to hold or put them in a closet where you'll not see them. If possible, avoid places you frequented together. These symbols will bring back uncomfortable memories. After you have achieved some emotional distance, you can go back and enjoy these as reminders of a once pleasant relationship. Support for this suggestion comes from research showing that the more vivid your memory of a broken love affair—a memory greatly aided by these relationship symbols—the greater your depression is likely to be.

Seek Support

11   Many people feel they should bear their burdens alone. Men, in particular, have been taught that this is the only "manly" way to handle things. But seeking the support of others is one of the best antidotes to the unhappiness caused when a relationship ends. Tell your friends and family of your situation—in only general terms, if you prefer—and make it clear that you want support. Seek out people who are positive and nurturing. Avoid negative individuals who will paint the world in even darker tones. Make the distinction between seeking support and seeking advice. If you feel you need advice, seek out a professional.

Avoid Repeating Negative Patterns

12   Many people repeat their mistakes. They enter second and third relationships with the same blinders, faulty preconceptions, and unrealistic expectations with which they entered earlier ones. Instead, use the knowledge gained from your failed relationship to prevent repeating the same patterns.

13   At the same time, don't become a prophet of doom. Don't see in every relationship vestiges of the old. Don't jump at the first conflict and say, "Here it goes all over again." Treat the new relationship as the unique relationship it is. Don't evaluate it through past experiences. Use past relationships and experiences as guides, not filters.

—DeVito, *The Interpersonal Communication Book*, 9e, pp. 278–81

UNDERSTANDING AND ANALYZING THE READING

A. Building Vocabulary

Context

Using context and a dictionary if necessary, determine the meaning of each word as it is used in the selection.

_____ 1. inevitable (paragraph 1)

    a. undeniable

    b. believable

    c. unavoidable

    d. unending

_____ 2. absolve (table/column 2)

    a. set free

    b. cure

    c. remind

    d. deny

_____ 3. bolster (paragraph 8)

    a. to put aside

    b. to add to

    c. to examine

    d. to consider

_____ 4. antidotes (paragraph 11)

    a. remedies

    b. answers

    c. avenues

    d. sources

_____ 5. vestiges (paragraph 13)

    a. similarities

    b. warnings

    c. products

    d. evidence

Word Parts

> ## A REVIEW OF PREFIXES AND SUFFIXES
>
> **PRE-** means before.
> **-ION** means condition of.

Use your knowledge of word parts and review above to fill in the blanks in the following sentences.

1. **preconceptions** (paragraph 12) means opinions that were formed _____ the fact.

2. **depression** (paragraph 5) means _____ being depressed.

B. Understanding Main Ideas

Select the best answer.

_____ 1. Which of the following best states the main idea of the entire piece of writing?

    a. It is difficult to recover from a broken relationship.

    b. Ending a relationship can be difficult, but there are strategies that can help to ease the difficulty and move you forward.

    c. Some relationships are doomed to fail from the very beginning.

    d. The strategies of disengagement must be implemented one at a time in order to finalize the breakup completely and peaceably.

_____ 2. The topic of paragraph 5 is

    a. the need for individuals who suffer from loneliness and depression to seek professional counseling.

    b. the seriousness of loneliness and depression.

    c. the feelings of loneliness and depression that often come as the result of a breakup.

    d. the temporary nature of loneliness and depression.

_____ 3. The main idea of paragraph 10 is that reminders of the broken relationship should be

    a. removed from your life for awhile.

    b. destroyed.

    c. returned to the person who gave them to you.

    d. returned to the stores where they were bought, if possible, so that you can get money for them.

C. Identifying Details

Select the best answer.

_____ 1. In this selection, the term *disengagement* means

    a. breaking off an engagement.

    b. postponing an engagement.

    c. planning the way you will end a relationship.

    d. dissolving a relationship.

_____ 2. The strategy of Justification involves

    a. presenting the reasons for the breakup.

    b. ending the relationship just in time.

    c. giving each side of the relationship a chance to make the relationship work.

    d. proving that you were right all along.

_____ 3. Which of the following statements is an example of the Behavioral De-escalation strategy?

    a. "I think we should explore dating other people."

    b. "Maybe we should just call each other once a week for awhile."

    c. "I do not have time for a serious relationship."

    d. "I just need a little space."

_____ 4. Which of the following is **NOT** a good suggestion for dealing with a breakup?

    a. Ask others in your circle of friends to help you work through the breakup.

    b. Embrace yourself and accept the fact that you are not a failure.

    c. Take your time entering into a new relationship.

    d. Keep a picture of your partner in your room so that you can see it and be reminded of how much you now dislike the person.

D. Recognizing Methods of Organization and Signal Words

Select the best answer.

_____ 1. The overall organizational pattern of paragraphs 4–13 is

    a. chronological order.

    b. comparison and contrast.

    c. Illustration.

    d. order of importance.

_____ 2. A signal word or phrase that indicates the pattern of organization in paragraph 5 is

    a. these feelings

    b. for example

    c. similarly

    d. when

_____ 3. The organizational pattern of paragraph 8 is

    a. process.

    b. cause and effect.

    c. definition.

    d. illustration.

E. Making Inferences

Based on what is stated in the reading, indicate whether each statement is true (T) or false (F).

_____ 1. The author suggests that the ending of a relationship is common to mankind.

_____ 2. The author suggests that there really is no easy way to end a relationship.

_____ 3. The author believes that ending a relationship is easier than recovering from the end of a relationship.

_____ 4. The author believes that men handle disengagement better than women do.

_____ 5. The author believes that there can be some good to come out of a failed relationship.

F. Thinking Critically: Analyzing the Author's Technique

Select the best answer

_____ 1. When the author warns against a person becoming a "prophet of doom," he means

    a. a person can contribute to the greater good by using his/her failed relationship as an example from which others can learn.

    b. a person expects a new relationship to end in the same way as the former relationship.

    c. a person should not go around bad-mouthing the other person in the failed relationship.

    d. a person from a failed relationship should counsel others who are facing a failed relationship.

_____ 2. To support his points, the author uses primarily

    a. research about failed relationships.

    b. his own personal experience.

    c. quotations from those who have experienced a failed relationship.

    d. examples/illustrations.

_____ 3. The author's purpose in writing "Ending a Relationship" is to

a. provide the reader with ways to end a relationship and suggestions for dealing with a failed relationship.

b. discuss the effects of a failed relationship.

c. show how men and women differ in handling failed relationships.

d. warn against the pitfalls of a relationship in order to save relationships from failure.

_____ 4. The point of view of this article is

a. first person.

b. second person.

c. third person.

d. a combination of first person and third person.

_____ 5. Which of the following is an opinion, not a fact?

a. " Some relationships, of course, do end." (paragraph 1)

b. "Realize that depression often leads to serious illness." (paragraph 5)

c. ". . . research shows that the more vivid your memory of a broken love affair, the greater your depression is likely to be." (paragraph 10)

d. "Seeking the support of others is one of the best antidotes to the unhappiness caused when a relationship ends." (paragraph 11)

G. Thinking Critically: Analyzing the Author's Message

Select the best answer.

_____ 1. According to the author, the most negative disengagement strategy focuses on

a. justifying the breakup.

b. expressing caring feelings.

c. blame.

d. reducing the intensity.

_____ 2. When the author speaks of "individuals who will paint the world in even darker tones" (paragraph 11), he means that

a. some people tend to always look on the negative side of everything.

b. artists use dark colors to represent failed relationships.

c. those that are miserable tend to suck others into their misery.

d. some individuals seem to revel in the misfortune of others.

_____ 3. The author suggests that the most positive statement to be used in ending a relationship is

    a. "I need a little space."

    b. "I think that we need to spend more time apart from each other."

    c. "I know you won't understand, but I want to give you the reasons for the breakup."

    d. "I really like you, but I am not ready for a relationship right now."

WRITING IN RESPONSE TO THE READING

H. Writing a Summary

Complete the following summary of the selection by filling in the missing words. Remember that a summary should cover all of the author's main points.

Joseph A. DeVito wrote an article entitled _____.

In the article, he wrote about how to _____ and

how to _____. He listed __ disengagement

ment strategies. These include: _____

_____

The author also presented __ suggestions for dealing with a failed relationship. These suggestions include: _____

_____

_____.

I. Writing Paragraphs

Write a well-developed paragraph in response to one of the following writing prompts. As part of this assignment, you will need to follow the writing process outlined here:

- Use a prewriting strategy to generate ideas
- Complete a guided outline
- Write a rough draft
- Complete a peer revision guide
- Write a final draft using proper MLA format

1. Write a paragraph in which you discuss which disengagement strategy you think is the best one. Be sure to give reasons for your opinion.

2. There are many reasons for the breakup of a relationship. The author has suggested a few possible reasons. What are some other reasons? Write a

well-developed paragraph in which you discuss three possible reasons for the breakup of a relationship.

3. Can you think of a better way to break up than those the author has presented? If so, write a process paragraph in which you instruct the reader on exactly how to accomplish this task.

4. Sometimes a relationship ends through death or separation of some kind. This relationship may involve a friend or a family member. If this has happened to you, write a well-developed paragraph in which you discuss the ending of the relationship and your response to it.

5. Have you ever been the one to initiate a breakup? If so, write a well developed paragraph in which you discuss how you ended the relationship.

6. Have you ever had someone break up with you? If so, write a well-developed paragraph on what you learned from the experience.

J. Working Collaboratively

1. **Thinking Deeply** After reading the selection by Joseph A. DeVito, break into groups and discuss the following questions:

   - What are the different types of relationships that you might have?
   - What are some reasons for relationships to end?
   - How do the methods of breaking up vary depending on the type of relationship?
   - What are some other ways of ending a relationship?
   - Is there really a good way to end a relationship?
   - What are some other ways of moving on from a failed relationship?
   - What are some lessons that you have learned from a failed relationship?

   Select someone in your group to record the major points of your discussion so that you will be well prepared to report to the class.

2. **Thinking about Issues** Working with a partner, write a letter to an advice column describing a problem relationship that is on the brink of failure. Ask the author of the advice column for advice on how to end the relationship and move on. After writing the letter, change sides and assume the persona of the advice column author, and write a letter back advising the person on the best way to end the relationship and move on. Be creative and entertaining.

3. **Thinking Creatively** Pair up with a partner and create a dialogue. One of you will be ending the relationship, and the other will be receiving the news. The person who initiates the breakup should use one of the strategies suggested in the reading. The person receiving the news should react realistically. Be prepared to present your skit to the class. The members of the class should be able to determine the disengagement strategy being used.

SELECTION

8

Magazine Article

The High Art of Handling Problem People

Hara Estroff Marano

DRE 097 **PRE-READING**

Source and Context

Hara Estroff Marano is the Editor-at-Large of a magazine entitled *Psychology Today*. The selection that follows is an article from the May/June 2012 issue of the magazine.

A Note on the Reading

Read the selection to understand how difficult people present themselves and how you can develop the skills necessary to handle them artfully.

Previewing the Reading

Using the steps listed on page 4, preview the reading selection. When you have finished, answer the following questions.

1. What word does the author use to describe a difficult situation at home?

   _____

2. What four types of problem people does the author present?

   a. _____

   b. _____

   c. _____

   d. _____

3. How many ways to diffuse a difficult encounter does the author present?

   _____

4. Determine whether each statement is true or false.

   _____ a. It is a waste of time to try to talk a naysayer out of being negative.

   _____ b. Overpraised children do not present problems when they enter the work force.

Using Prior Knowledge

Difficult people are everywhere. Think of some people in your life who are difficult. How do they present themselves to you? What are your responses to their behavior? Do you wish you could respond to them in better ways?

DURING READING

Reading Tip

As you read, think about the people in your life who are problem people. Read carefully the author's explanations of the different types of problem people, what motivates their behaviors, and suggestions for handling these people. Be sure to highlight and annotate as you read.

The High Art of Handling Problem People

Hara Estroff Marano

Dealing with difficult people is a special skill—and an increasingly necessary one.

1   The walk-in medical clinic was about to close for the day when Susan Biali got a call from one of her longtime patients. Could the doctor please hang in a bit longer? The caller was feeling very ill and needed to see her immediately. An exhausted Biali extended her already burdensome day and waited for the patient to arrive. Some time later, the woman sauntered in; she was perfectly fine—she just needed a prescription refill.

2   "She totally lied to me," the Vancouver doctor recalls. "Afterwards, I was so upset that the degree of my reaction troubled me. I'm a general physician with some training in psychiatry, yet I couldn't put my finger on exactly why I was so bothered; I thought it was a flaw in myself."

3   Eventually, she identified what set her off: "You think you're in an innocuous situation—a typical doctor-patient encounter, but the woman took complete advantage of my compassion. Then, not only wouldn't she acknowledge the lie, but she looked at me blankly and demanded, 'Can't you just move on and give me my prescription?' She made me feel that I was the problem."

4   Ever wonder how an encounter goes so quickly awry; do you doubt your own perceptions; do you feel thrown totally off balance by another person; do you find yourself acting crazy when you're really a very nice person? Manipulation comes in many forms: There are whiners; there are bullies; here are the short-fused; not to forget the highly judgmental; or the out-and-out sociopath. But they often have one thing in common: Their MO is to provoke, then make you feel you have no reason to react—and it's all your fault to begin with! Feeling deeply discounted, even totally powerless, while having to jettison the original aim of an interaction is a distressing double whammy of social life—and a cardinal sign you're dealing with a difficult person. No, it's not you. It's them, and it's the emotional equivalent of being mowed down by a hit-and-run driver.

Reprinted by permission from *Psychology Today*, May/June 2012.

IN THE HOTHOUSE AT HOME VS. TOUGH AT WORK
In dealing with a difficult person, the setting is everything.

Handling difficult people at work is not quite the same as coping with problem people in family life. The goal is to get the work done, and that requires great caution and considerable strategizing. "It's not like a marriage, where the dailiness of living will allow you to repair a lot of interactions gone wrong," Lerner observes.

In a marriage, she says, it's often advisable to exit a conversation. Of course, there are a variety of ways to do that. A common one is to scream "I hate you" and slam a door behind you. Better, she advises, to say something like: "I love you, I want to be here for you, I want to hear your criticisms, but I cannot listen when you throw them at me rat-a-tat-tat. I need you to approach me with respect. So let's set up a 15-minute meeting after breakfast and start over." The difference is clarifying a loving position versus escalating things further.

5   It doesn't take a sociopath; anyone can be difficult in a heartbeat. "To a great extent, the problem is in the eye of the beholder," says Topeka, Kansas, psychologist Harriet Lerner, author of the now-classic *Dance of Anger* and the just-released *Relationship Rules*. "We all come into relationships with hot-button issues from our own past. For one person what's difficult might be dealing with someone who's judgmental. For another it might be a person who treats you as if you're invisible." That said, she adds that there are certain qualities that make people persistently hard to handle—hair-trigger defensiveness that obliterates the ability to listen, meanness, and a sense of worthlessness that leads people to bulk up self-esteem by putting down others, just to name a few.

6   Experience motivates most of us to avoid or minimize interacting with such people, but sometimes that problem person is a sibling, a boss, a coworker—even your mother—,and managing the relationship by distancing yourself or cutting it off altogether is impossible or undesirable. The goal, in such cases, is to prepare in advance for an encounter, knowing it will take a special effort to

It takes a great deal of emotional maturity to interact with someone very intense and angry.

Courtesy of Jeff Riedel.

hold onto your own sense of self, and to stay calm.

7   Although it is typically disturbing to be in the presence of such people, remaining composed in the face of unreasonableness helps you figure out exactly what species of difficulty you're dealing with. Therein lies your advantage: it allows you to predict the specific emotional trap being set for you, which is your passport to getting your own power back.

THE HOSTILE

Telltale signs: High, sometimes explosive, reactivity. Frequently disagreeable. Cynical. Mistrustful. Does not like to be wrong.

Where you'll find them: Corner offices. The Internet, often under the cloak of anonymity.

Call in the wild: "I am going to come and burn the f**king house down."

Notable sightings: Mel Gibson. Mike Tyson. Naomi Campbell. Chris Brown. Russell Crowe. Courtney Love.

8   People very low on the personality dimension of agreeableness typically express themselves with irritability, hostility, and noncooperativeness. They have a short fuse and are commonly cynical and mistrustful. They are not able to look at themselves, and they are hyperquick to

Courtesy of Jeff Riedel.

blame. Placating others is not a skill in their repertoire, nor do they endorse such a possibility. The trouble is their responses run to the intense side, and their reactivity and intensity breed more of the same in those who must deal with them, says Lerner. And so, not only are these people angry but you may be suddenly on the receiving end of criticism that feels extremely unfair. The hostile person will not be thinking clearly and is probably not taking in anything you say. "It takes a great deal of emotional maturity to deal with someone who is very intense and angry," she notes. "The reactivity is contagious and you are likely to get reactive yourself."

9   One common manifestation of hostility, especially in the workplace, is the bully

boss. Such people misuse power; they humiliate you in front of others; they are verbally abusive; they overcontrol and micromanage. They don't just differ with you, they do so contemptuously and lob unfair criticism at you. If bullies are technically competent at the jobs they do, they feel immune to punishment. As a result, there tend to be high rates of turnover among their underlings. In performance-oriented companies, getting rid of bullies may not be high on the agenda, no matter how much damage they do. Like bully kids, bully bosses do not see themselves accurately. They often view themselves as better than others, and they are not sensitive to the feelings of staffers. They misuse power to deliberately hurt those of lesser status.

10   It is possible, and often necessary, to confront a bully directly. But do so calmly and professionally, and never in public; this is an activity for behind closed doors. The bully will never back down in front of an audience; instead, you must declare the bully's behavior unacceptable, specify exactly what behaviors are at issue—"You may not demean me in front of my staff or others"—and instruct the bully, succinctly, on how you wish to be treated. "I need you to support me in the presence of others. Any issues you have

with my work we can discuss civilly in private."

11   An all-too-common variant of hostility is passive aggression, in which the hostility is covert, expressed in nonobvious, underhanded ways—dragging one's heels on a project, failing to respond to a meaningful request. It's often difficult to pin down the hostility, but the effects are usually clear—your goals and dreams are sabotaged. A colleague briefs you on events but leaves out critical information you need for getting your job done. Your spouse belittles you in front of others—and then insists he was "just kidding" as you seethe with rage and humiliation.

12   Sarcasm is a common tool of passive aggression, and frustration is a common response: You may find yourself getting upset and angry but can't be entirely sure it is justified. Over time, it becomes difficult if not impossible to trust anything offered by a passive-aggressive person.

THE REJECTION-SENSITIVE

Telltale signs: Constantly scanning for slights real and imagined. All slights deemed intentional. Becoming unglued at the hint of disapproval. In extremis, stalking (primarily by males).
Where you'll find them: Your inbox (most likely in an

email demanding to know why you failed to respond to a note, overture, etc.). Backstage. Poetry readings.
Call in the wild: "Are you annoyed with me for some reason?"
Notable sightings: Marilyn Monroe. Princess Diana. Michael Cartier. Liza Minnelli.

13   With a hair-trigger reaction to any indication that you don't like them or, in fact, disagree with them or didn't do what they asked, the rejection-sensitive walk around with what seems like a perpetual chip on their shoulder. They interpret everything through the lens "You somehow disrespect or dislike me." That's difficult, says Duke University psychologist Mark Leary, because you have to walk on eggshells around them and make sure that everything you say or do doesn't push the imaginary button where they feel they're being devalued by you.

14   Threats lurk everywhere for these people, who are constantly scanning their environment for signs of being excluded. You didn't call or send an email right away because you were bogged down in deadlines, and then your eldest was sent home sick from school? The resulting drop in self-esteem experienced by the rejection-sensitive begets an overwrought response to

slights real and imagined— all of which are presumed intentional.

15   They will dredge up evidence, citing lapses in your actions that defy memory. The irony is that, over time, the irritability, negativity, and self-doubt of the rejection-sensitive do in fact drive others to avoid them. And the rejection-sensitive don't act irrationally only in response to perceived slights; they expect rejection and anticipate it, and react automatically when reflective and strategic behavior would be in their better interests.

16   Rejection or the expectation of it makes them hostile. Their reactive aggression is more likely to manifest in passive rather than overt aggression, although stalking behavior is a form of aggression thought to result from rejection-sensitivity.

17   Unfortunately, the rejection-sensitive are present in increasing numbers. Many observers find that the psychological fragility that underlies rejection-sensitivity is on the rise. Common mood disorders such as depression are typically accompanied by hypersensitivity to rejection, and a whole generation of overpraised children, preoccupied with evaluation, has grown up and brought its overtuned rejection radar into the workplace as well as into personal relationships.

18   Fear of rejection tends to paralyze the afflicted. In the workplace, it can keep people from taking on new tasks or new assignments of any kind; instead they offer a host of irrational explanations for why each new project or new hire is a bad idea. Such a colleague may be unwilling to ask for needed help or direction for fear of rejection—and then fault you for not providing it. Competitive environments bring out the worst in them.

THE NEUROTIC

Telltale signs: Anxiety. Pessimism. Obstructionism. Naysaying. Shooting down the ideas of others.
Where you'll find them: Online medical chat rooms. Political blogs. Doctors' offices.
Call in the wild: "Yes, but . . ."
Notable sightings: Larry David. Woody Allen. Harold Camping. Chicken Little.

19   What you might experience as a minor frustration is, for the neurotic, a hopeless difficulty. Neuroticism is typically displayed as unhappiness, anxiety, and ease of emotional arousal. "These people don't realize they're being difficult," says Leary, "but they quickly get on other people's nerves. They are demanding, they worry about everything, and they think

they're only trying to be helpful and not creating problems. What makes them especially difficult in work environments, he explains, is that they tend to be obstructionists. "They're so worried about something going wrong that they disagree with others' ideas. They are naysayers," and in dredging up so much negativity, they stir up residual doubts in others and erode confidence in novel ideas and projects.

20   A hallmark of this type of difficult person is a pessimistic thinking style, a concern with "what's going to go wrong next in my life?" Although these people are innocently difficult, says Leary, it's still hard to deal with them because they are always going to say "Yes, but . . ." They'll find the cloud in any silver lining, discourage you from taking that solo cross-country trip or starting a new business.

21   It's futile to talk naysayers out of their misery. They are often immune to outside influence, so the best you can aim for is to understand their perspective without endorsing it: "My experience has been totally different," for example.

22   The basic challenge in dealing with difficult people of any stripe is to remain a calm presence in a highly charged emotional field. "You have to get your own reactivity down, even if it means deep-breathing to calm yourself," says Harriet Lerner. "That enables

you to listen well and understand what the other person is saying, and to respond with clarity, rather than participate in a downward-spiraling conversation." There's a temptation to write someone off as a difficult person. Resist it; "once you label someone as impossible, you are likely to miss all the good points the person might be making," Lerner observes.

THE EGOIST

Telltale signs: Own interests come first, last, and always. Takes everything personally. Unable to compromise, ever.

Insists on being seen as right by everyone.

Where you'll find them: Reality TV shows. Congress. Art school.

Call in the wild: "It's my way or the highway."

Notable sightings: Donald Trump. Kanye West. Chris Christie. Paris Hilton.

23   Our culture devalues stoicism and rewards overreacting to every little thing, especially on reality TV.

24   This is a group of people—Leary sees their numbers increasing—whose ego is far too involved in anything that happens. As a result they take everything personally. What makes them difficult is their fierce demands coupled with their inability to compromise. They frequently "lose it." Mention a problem to them and they immediately assume you are blaming them. "On top of the tangible problem, they add a layer of symbolism that makes everything about them," says Leary, "They live their life according to the symbolic meaning as opposed to solving the problem."

25   Leary argues that both egoic and egocentric individuals view the world through a self-centered lens, but the egoic are especially inclined to respond strongly when their desires are not satisfied. (Egotism, by contrast, refers to an inflated sense of one's positive qualities.)

---

7 WAYS TO DEFUSE A DIFFICULT ENCOUNTER

Having learned the hard way, Vancouver physician (and *PT* blogger) Susan Biali offers concrete steps for dealing with an unreasonable person.

- **Minimize time with problem people, and keep interactions as short as possible.**
- **Keep it logical.** Communications should be fact-based with minimal details, and don't try to connect and reason with difficult people; their response will often only make you more upset.
- **Focus on *them* in conversation.** One way to avoid being the target of demeaning comments, manipulation, or having your words twisted is to say as little as possible. They are a far safer subject of conversation than you are.
- **Give up the dream that they will one day be the person you wish them to be.** There are people in our lives who have moments when they seem to be the parent/partner/spouse/friend/whatever we've always wanted, yet they end up disappointing or hurting us. Accepting the person as is can be a remarkable relief.
- **Avoid topics that get you into trouble.** Before any interaction with a difficult person, mentally review the topics that invite attack and make an effort to avoid them. If your in-laws always demean your choice of career, change the topic immediately if they ask how your work is going.
- **Don't try to get them to see your point of view.** Don't try to explain yourself or get them to empathize with you—they won't, and you'll just feel worse for trying.
- **Create a distraction.** Play with a pet if there is one handy. Plan the interaction around some kind of recreational activity or entertainment, or get the other person to do something that absorbs their attention (taking it off you). Just don't use alcohol as your distraction of choice; it will only make you more likely to say or do something that will set you up as a target or make you feel bad later.

26 Leary, who has long identified problems of the self, says, "This type hit me when I saw Congress discussing the debt ceiling. There was so much posturing—'I have to show everybody I'm right'—rather than movement toward solving the problem." The egoic person is convinced his ideas are 100 percent right—and must be seen as right. Further, he feels entitled to have things happen his way. "A person who is convinced his perspectives, beliefs, and values are right cannot tolerate any conciliatory conversations. It's 'my way or no way.' " Politics is not the only home of the egoic; "these people wreck relationships, work, even societies," observes Leary.

27 There are times, he adds, when anyone can be egoic: "Something pushes a button and we get ego-involved and lose perspective." But with the truly egoic, such a response is independent of the stimulus.

28 With his Duke colleagues, Leary is currently investigating individual differences in how egoic and hyperegoic people tend to act. "The more egoic, the more difficult a person becomes."

29 It's thoroughly natural for people to put their own interests first, Leary observes. No animal can survive unless it does. "People have always been egoic about personal well-being," he explains. Today, however, he sees egoicism on the rise because many traditional restraints on behavior have been removed.

30 "It used to be that anger was viewed as a character defect. People now fly off the handle at the slightest provocation when others disagree with them. We no longer value the stoicism by which we tried to keep anger in check." Leary thinks reality TV shows of the past decade have helped breed egoicism "because they are based on people overreacting to things that have no or minor consequences for them."

POST-READING

UNDERSTANDING AND ANALYZING THE READING

A. Building Vocabulary

Context

Using context and a dictionary if necessary, determine the meaning of each word as it is used in the selection.

_____ 1. innocuous (paragraph 3)
   a. healthy
   b. dangerous
   c. risky
   d. harmless

_____ 2. obliterates (paragraph 5)
   a. blocks
   b. destroys
   c. replaces
   d. disturbs

_____ 3. cynical (paragraph 8)
   a. optimistic
   b. worried
   c. distrustful
   d. sad

_____ 4. placating (paragraph 8)
   a. loving
   b. serving
   c. appeasing
   d. denying

_____ 5. demean (paragraph 12)

    a. embarrass

    b. humiliate

    c. correct

    d. shame

_____ 6. succinctly (paragraph 12)

    a. politely

    b. rudely

    c. quickly

    d. concisely

_____ 7. futile (paragraph 18)

    a. useless

    b. helpless

    c. crazy

    d. difficult

_____ 8. stoicism (paragraph 26)

    a. honesty in all things

    b. indifference to pleasure or pain

    c. moderation in food and drink

    d. justice for all

_____ 9. conciliatory (paragraph 29)

    a. agreeable

    b. soothing

    c. opposing

    d. hostile

_____ 10. provocation (paragraph 33)

    a. suggestion

    b. situation

    c. annoyance

    d. difficulty

Word Parts

> ### A REVIEW OF PREFIXES AND SUFFIXES
>
> **IM-** means not.
> **INTER-** means between.
> **-NESS** means quality or state of.
> **-ITY** means state or condition of.

Use your knowledge of word parts and the review above to fill in the blanks in the following sentences.

1. An *impossible* (paragraph 6) task is one that is _____ possible to complete.

2. To minimize *interaction* (paragraph 6) with someone is to minimize the action _____ yourself and the other person.

3. People who lack *agreeableness* (paragraph 8) lack the quality of being _____, and they express themselves with *irritability* (paragraph 8) or the state of being _____.

B. Understanding the Thesis and Other Main Ideas

Select the best answer.

_____ 1. Which of the following best states the thesis or central thought of the reading?

    a. Difficult people are master manipulators.

    b. The key to dealing with difficult people is to avoid interacting with them if at all possible.

    c. Dealing with the different types of difficult people takes understanding and skill.

    d. People who create trouble for others, do so for one reason only: they want to build up their feeling of self-worth.

_____ 2. The topic of paragraph 12 is

    a. the hidden danger associated with confronting a bully.

    b. the triggers of bully behavior.

    c. the unacceptable behavior of a bully.

    d. how to confront a bully.

_____ 3. The main idea of paragraph 25 is found in the

    a. first sentence.　　　　c. fourth sentence.

    b. second sentence.　　　d. last sentence.

_____ 4. What is the implied main idea of paragraph 33?

    a. Flying off the handle is a natural outgrowth of egoicism.

    b. Expressing anger publicly has become commonplace and acceptable in our society.

    c. Reality TV is largely responsible for the ever-increasing number of problem people.

    d. In most cases, people generally fly off the handle over issues of great consequence.

C. Identifying Details

Select the best answer.

_____ 1. According to the author, there are certain qualities that make people hard to handle. The author cites all of the following *except*

    a. meanness.

    b. defensiveness.

    c. a sense of worthlessness.

    d. insecurity.

_____ 2. Which type of difficult person exhibits anxiety?

    a. the hostile

    b. the rejection-sensitive

    c. the neurotic

    d. the egoist

_____ 3. According to the reading, what question would the rejection-sensitive person be most likely to ask?

    a. "Have I done something to make you mad?"

    b. "Why can't we all just get along?"

    c. "Why are you being so sensitive?"

    d. "Why do you reject every idea I suggest?"

D. Recognizing Methods of Organization and Transitions

Select the best answer.

_____ 1. The pattern of organization used in paragraph 13 is

    a. classification.

    b. illustration.

    c. comparison/contrast.

    d. process.

_____ 2. The organizational pattern used in paragraph 33 is

    a. chronological order.

    b. listing.

    c. cause and effect.

    d. comparison/contrast.

_____ 3. The signal word or phrase that provides a clue to the organizational pattern used in paragraph 10 is

    a. one common manifestation.

    b. if bullies are technically competent.

    c. such people.

    d. they don't just differ.

E. Reading and Thinking Visually

Select the best answer.

_____ 1. The author likely included the photo on page 434 (woman with signs on her face) in order to

    a. stress the importance of being able to pick up on the often-subtle signs that naysayers present.

    b. show the effects the outside world has on the naysayer.

    c. help the reader understand the split personality of the naysayer.

    d. illustrate the difficulty of dealing with a neurotic person and the roadblocks he/she presents.

F. Figuring Out Implied Meanings

Indicate whether each statement is true (T) or false (F).

_____ 1. The author believes that the best way to deal with a problem person at home is to allow a person to calm down before addressing a problem.

_____ 2. The author believes that problem people are good at shifting the blame.

_____ 3. The author implies that schools share some of the blame for the increasing numbers of rejection-sensitive people.

_____ 4. According to the author, there is an art to handling difficult people.

_____ 5. The author thinks that all members of Congress are egoic persons.

_____ 6. The author implies that movie stars and important national figures all fall into one of the four categories of difficult people.

G. Thinking Critically: Analyzing the Author's Technique

Select the best answer.

_____ 1. The author's primary purpose in "The High Art of Handling Problem People" is to

    a. discuss the mental health concerns of problem people.

    b. educate people about the problems that Hollywood stars present to others who have to deal with them.

    c. help people to understand problem people so that they can better deal with them.

    d. expose difficult people so that others can avoid them.

_____ 2. Overall, the author's tone in this selection can best be described as

  a. sarcastic.   c. instructive.

  b. sympathetic.   d. persuasive.

_____ 3. Which of the following is a fact, not an opinion?

  a. "She made me feel that I was the problem." (paragraph 3)

  b. "With his Duke colleagues, Leary is currently investigating individual differences in how egoic and hyperegoic people tend to act." (paragraph 31)

  c. "Leary thinks reality TV shows of the past decade have helped breed egoicism . . ." (paragraph 33)

  d. "It's futile to talk naysayers out of their misery." (paragraph 18)

_____ 4. Which of the following is not a piece of evidence used by the author to support his thesis or central thought?

  a. statistics that explain the growth in number of difficult people

  b. examples of the behavior of each of the four types of difficult people

  c. quotes from psychologists

  d. a description of each of the four types of difficult people

_____ 5. Throughout the reading, the author uses _rhetorical questions_—that is, questions addressed directly to readers. Rhetorical questions are used as starting-off points for a discussion or explanation. Which of the following is _not_ a rhetorical question found in the reading?

  a. Find yourself acting crazy when you are really a nice person?

  b. Do bully bosses see themselves inaccurately?

  c. Feel thrown totally off balance by another person?

  d. Ever wonder how an encounter goes so quickly awry?

_____ 6. Which of the following statements is an example of irony?

  a. "It doesn't take a sociopath; anyone can be difficult in a heartbeat." (paragraph 5)

  b. "The reactivity is contagious and you are likely to get reactive yourself." (paragraph 9)

  c. "It is possible, and often necessary, to confront a bully directly." (paragraph 12)

  d. ". . . over time, the irritability, negativity, and self doubt of the rejection-sensitive do in fact drive others to avoid them." (paragraph 22)

_____ 7. Select the sentence that best explains the figurative expression "They'll (neurotic people) find the cloud in any silver lining . . ." (paragraph 17)

    a. Neurotic people walk around with a dark cloud hanging over them.

    b. Neurotic people will always find something negative even in something good.

    c. Even when silver is involved, neurotic people cannot be happy.

    d. Neurotic people often find a silver lining even in difficult situations.

_____ 8. Which of the following sentences contains an example of **informal** language?

    a. "Could the doctor please hang in a bit longer?" (paragraph 1)

    b. "The hostile person will not be thinking clearly and is probably not taking in anything you say." (paragraph 9)

    c. "What makes them difficult is their fierce demands coupled with their inability to compromise." (paragraph 27)

    d. "The more egoic, the more difficult a person becomes." (paragraph 31)

H. Thinking Critically: Analyzing the Author's Message

Select the best answer.

_____ 1. Which of the following is an accurate statement?

    a. The author believes that the risks involved with dealing with a difficult person at home are equal to the risks involved with dealing with a difficult person at work.

    b. The author believes that dealing with a difficult person at home is easier than dealing with a difficult person at work.

    c. The author believes that considerable strategizing is necessary in dealing with difficult people both at home and at work.

    d. The author believes that repairing a relationship at work is more important than repairing a relationship at home.

_____ 2. In paragraph 5, the author states that "we all come into relationships with hot-button issues from our own past." What does he mean?

    a. Old habits die hard. It is difficult to let go of a grudge.

    b. Some people are very good at reading others, and they delight in "pushing their button."

     c. We all have certain things that annoy us, and we carry a dislike for these annoyances into our relationships with others.

     d. The qualities that we most dislike in others are the very ones that we see in ourselves.

_____ 3. In paragraph 24, what does the author mean when he writes of a "generation of overpraised children, preoccupied with evaluation . . ."?

     a. Children will not do their best on any task unless they know they are being evaluated.

     b. The emphasis that schools put on evaluation has carried over to the home, and children now expect to be evaluated on their performance at home.

     c. Children have been praised even when they fail.

     d. Because children have been given exceptional praise for completing tasks that really deserve little praise at all, they expect praise for almost everything they do.

_____ 4. "The High Art of Handling Problem People" can be interpreted as

     a. biased.

     b. propaganda.

     c. name calling.

     d. objective.

_____ 5. The intended audience for this article is

     a. a general audience of all people.

     b. those who work with a difficult boss.

     c. those who are difficult people.

     d. counselors who work to help others deal with difficult people.

WRITING IN RESPONSE TO THE READING

I. Writing a Summary

Write a summary of the reading (paragraphs 1–27) using the following guidelines:

- Be sure to use your own words, not those of the author
- Write an opening statement that states the author's main point.
- Include the author's most important supporting ideas.
- Include key terms, important concepts, and principles.
- Present the ideas in the order in which they appear in the reading.
- Indicate the source of the material you summarized (See Chapter 10 for information on documenting sources)

J. Analyzing the Issue

1. What contemporary issue is the author discussing in this reading? Phrase the issue as a question. Is the author arguing the "pro" side of this issue or the "con" side?

2. What is the author's background? Is she qualified to write about the topic? Why or why not?

3. Does the source from which this reading is taken help you determine the credibility of the information presented? Do you find any bias in the selection? Please explain both of your answers.

4. Evaluate the reading on the following criteria:

   a. Is the reading timely?

   b. Has the author provided sufficient evidence to support her main ideas? What other types of evidence might she provide to strengthen her claims?

   c. Does the author offer opposing viewpoints? Overall, how would you summarize the author's viewpoints on the issues discussed in the reading?

   d. What assumptions (either stated or implied) do you find in the reading?

   e. Does the article offer any emotional appeals? If so, identify them and evaluate their fairness.

5. Identify specific sentences and/or paragraphs in which the author states her value system.

K. Writing Paragraphs and Essays

*Write a **well-developed** paragraph or essay in response to one of the following writing prompts. As part of this assignment you will need to follow the writing process outlined here:*

- Use a prewriting strategy to generate ideas
- Complete a guided outline
- Write a rough draft
- Complete a peer revision guide
- Write a final draft using proper MLA format

1. Do you agree with the author's assertion that "some types of troublemakers are on the rise"? Why or why not? Write a paragraph or essay expressing your opinion.

2. In many ways, television mirrors our society. Think of a TV character that you "know" well. Determine the type of troublemaker that he/she is, and

then write a paragraph or essay explaining how this person fits into one of the four categories of difficult people. Be sure to use specific examples to support your thesis.

3. Who is the most difficult person you know? Write a paragraph or essay analysis about this person's behavior. In your writing, you should focus on the reasons for the person's difficult behavior and use examples to support your reasons.

4. Difficult people tend to be difficult everywhere they go. Sometimes, the most outrageous behaviors we witness are in public places, like the doctor's office, the grocery store, the post office, etc. Think of some outrageous incidents that you have witnessed in public. To what category would you assign each of the difficult people? In a paragraph or essay, describe the incidents and analyze the behavior of the participants. To what category would you assign each of the difficult people?

5. "The High Art of Handling Problem People" presents information that should help you deal with the difficult people in your life. Choose one difficult person from either your public or your private life and write a paragraph or essay in which you explain how you will handle this person the next time a difficult situation arises.

L. Working Collaboratively

1. **Thinking Deeply** After reading "The High Art of Handling Problem People," break into groups and discuss the following questions:

   - How has the author categorized difficult people?
   - Can you think of other categories that should have been included?
   - Which one of the types of difficult people seems to be more prevalent in your life?
   - What seems to be the primary reason that "sets off" difficult people?
   - Does being difficult usually pay off? If so, how?
   - Will reading this article make any difference in your perception and handling of the difficult people in your life?

   Select someone in your group to record the major points of your discussion so that you will be well prepared to report out to the class.

2. **Thinking Visually** Working with a group, brainstorm a list of characters from a variety of television shows. Discuss how each character is portrayed and the type of difficult person he/she is. Using the chart paper provided to you by your instructor, create a chart that has three columns. (See the chart below.) Use the information you have generated through brainstorming to fill in the chart. Be prepared to share and explain your chart to the class.

Name of TV Show	Description of Character	Type of Difficult Person

3. **Thinking Concisely** Using the summary of "The High Art of Handling Problem People" that you have already written, analyze the contents and consolidate your thoughts to **one word** that summarizes the article. After you have settled on one word, join a small group of your peers and share your word. You must be prepared to explain why you chose the word. Your group must ultimately settle on the best one word summary to share with the class.

4. **Thinking Creatively** Pair up with a partner and create a dialogue. One of you will be "serving up" the difficulty, and the other will be receiving it. The dialogue should focus on both the difficulty and the proper response to the difficulty as suggested in the reading. Be prepared to present your skit to the class. The members of the class should be able to determine the type of difficult person by his/her actions and words.

SELECTION 9

Magazine Article

Is Facebook Making Us Lonely?

Stephen Marche

DRE 098   PRE-READING

Source and Context

The following reading appeared in April of 2012 in *The Atlantic.com Magazine*. This publication features news and commentaries on a wide range of topics on both the national and international scene. Stephen Marche, author of "Is Facebook Making Us Lonely?" is a contributor to *The Atlantic*.

A Note on the Reading

Social media have made it easier for people to connect with friends, family, and acquaintances, but this connection has not come without cost. In fact, as we have become more connected in the United States, we are spending more time on the computer than we do with our friends and family. We have been brought together, yet we have grown apart. Read this selection to further your understanding of the issues and research that surround this phenomenon, and how this phenomenon is affecting our society.

Previewing the Reading

Using the steps listed on page 4, preview the reading selection. When you have finished, complete the following items.

1. The topic of the reading is _____

   _____

2. The world's foremost expert on loneliness is _____.

3. Indicate whether each statement is true (T) or false (F).

   _____ a. The picture on the opening page shows a couple connected to the world but separated from each other.

   _____ b. The author suggests that having a chance to disconnect from ourselves is desirable.

   _____ c. Facebook is the only social medium that has made us more connected.

   _____ d. Social media is not making us lonely; we are making ourselves lonely by the way we are using social media.

Using Prior Knowledge

How connected do you feel to your family and friends? Has social media helped you to feel more connected? How often do you use Facebook or Twitter? Can you go a day without using one of them? Do you ignore your family and friends so that you can stay "plugged in?" Would you rather communicate with your friends online or face-to-face?

DURING READING

Reading Tip

As you read, highlight and annotate the author's main points.

Is Facebook Making Us Lonely?

Stephen Marche

Social media—from Facebook to Twitter—have made us more densely networked than ever. Yet for all this connectivity, new research suggests that we have never been lonelier (or more narcissistic)—and that this loneliness is making us mentally and physically ill. Following is a report on what the epidemic of loneliness is doing to our souls and our society.

Courtesy of Phillip Toledano.

Reprinted from *The Atlantic Monthly*, April 2012.

1   Yvette Vickers, a former *Playboy* playmate and B-movie star, best known for her role in *Attack of the 50 Foot Woman*, would have been 83 last August, but nobody knows exactly how old she was when she died. According to the Los Angeles coroner's report, she lay dead for the better part of a year before a neighbor and fellow actress, a woman named Susan Savage, noticed cobwebs and yellowing letters in her mailbox, reached through a broken window to unlock the door, and pushed her way through the piles of junk mail and mounds of clothing that barricaded the house. Upstairs, she found Vickers's body, mummified, near a heater that was still running. Her computer was on too, its glow permeating the empty space.

2   The *Los Angeles Times* posted a story headlined "Mummified Body of Former Playboy Playmate Yvette Vickers Found in Her Benedict Canyon Home," which quickly went viral. Within two weeks, by Technorati's count, Vickers's lonesome death was already the subject of 16,057 Facebook posts and 881 tweets. She had long been a horror-movie icon, a symbol of Hollywood's capacity to exploit our most basic fears in the silliest ways; now she was an icon of a new and different kind of horror: our growing fear of loneliness. Certainly she received much more attention in death than she did in the final years of her life. With no children, no religious group, and no immediate social circle of any kind, she had begun, as an elderly woman, to look elsewhere for companionship. Savage later told *Los Angeles* magazine that she had searched Vickers's phone bills for clues about the life that led to such an end. In the months before her grotesque death, Vickers had made calls not to friends or family but to distant fans who had found her through fan conventions and Internet sites.

3   Vickers's web of connections had grown broader but shallower, as has happened for many of us. We are living in an isolation that would have been unimaginable to our ancestors, and yet we have never been more accessible. Over the past three decades, technology has delivered to us a world in which we need not be out of contact for a fraction of a moment. In 2010, at a cost of $300 million, 800 miles of fiber-optic cable was laid between the Chicago Mercantile Exchange and the New York Stock Exchange to shave three milliseconds off trading times. Yet within this world of instant and absolute communication, unbounded by limits of time or space, we suffer from unprecedented alienation. We have never been more detached from one another, or lonelier. In a world consumed by ever more novel modes of socializing, we have less and less actual society. We live in an accelerating contradiction: the more connected we become, the lonelier we are. We were promised a global village; instead we inhabit the drab cul-de-sacs and endless freeways of a vast suburb of information.

4   At the forefront of all this unexpectedly lonely interactivity is Facebook, with 845 million users and $3.7 billion in revenue last year. The company hopes to raise $5 billion in an initial public offering later this spring, which will make it by far the largest Internet IPO in history. Some recent estimates put the company's potential value at $100 billion, which would make it larger than the global coffee industry— one addiction preparing to surpass the other. Facebook's scale and reach are hard to comprehend: last summer, Facebook became, by some counts, the first Web site to receive 1 trillion page views in a month. In the last three months of 2011, users generated an average of 2.7 billion "likes" and comments every day. On whatever

scale you care to judge Facebook—as a company, as a culture, as a country—it is vast beyond imagination.

5   Despite its immense popularity, or more likely because of it, Facebook has, from the beginning, been under something of a cloud of suspicion. The depiction of Mark Zuckerberg, in *The Social Network*, as a bastard with symptoms of Asperger's syndrome, was nonsense. But it felt true. It felt true to Facebook, if not to Zuckerberg. The film's most indelible scene, the one that may well have earned it an Oscar, was the final, silent shot of an anomic Zuckerberg sending out a friend request to his ex-girlfriend, then waiting and clicking and waiting and clicking—a moment of super-connected loneliness preserved in amber. We have all been in that scene: transfixed by the glare of a screen, hungering for response.

6   When you sign up for Google+ and set up your Friends circle, the program specifies that you should include only "your real friends, the ones you feel comfortable sharing private details with." That one little phrase, *Your real friends*—so quaint, so charmingly mothering—perfectly encapsulates the anxieties that social media have produced: the fears that Facebook is interfering with our real friendships, distancing us from each other, making us lonelier; and that social networking might be spreading the very isolation it seemed designed to conquer.

7   Facebook arrived in the middle of a dramatic increase in the quantity and intensity of human loneliness, a rise that initially made the site's promise of greater connection seem deeply attractive. Americans are more solitary than ever before. In 1950, less than 10 percent of American households contained only one person. By 2010, nearly 27 percent of households had just one person. Solitary living does not guarantee a life of unhappiness, of course. In his recent book about the trend toward living alone, Eric Klinenberg, a sociologist at NYU, writes: "Reams of published research show that it's the quality, not the quantity of social interaction, that best predicts loneliness." True. But before we begin the fantasies of happily eccentric singledom, of divorcées dropping by their knitting circles after work for glasses of Drew Barrymore pinot grigio, or recent college graduates with perfectly articulated, Steampunk-themed, 300-square-foot apartments organizing croquet matches with their book clubs, we should recognize that it is not just isolation that is rising sharply. It's loneliness, too. And loneliness makes us miserable.

8   We know intuitively that loneliness and being alone are not the same thing. Solitude can be lovely. Crowded parties can be agony. We also know, thanks to a growing body of research on the topic, that loneliness is not a matter of external conditions; it is a psychological state. A 2005 analysis of data from a longitudinal study of Dutch twins showed that the tendency toward loneliness has roughly the same genetic component as other psychological problems such as neuroticism or anxiety.

9   Still, loneliness is slippery, a difficult state to define or diagnose. The best tool yet developed for measuring the condition is the UCLA Loneliness Scale, a series of 20 questions that all begin with this formulation: "How often do you feel . . .?" As in: "How often do you feel that you are 'in tune' with the people around you?" And: "How often do you feel that you lack companionship?" Measuring the condition in these terms, various studies have shown loneliness rising drastically over a very short period of recent history. A 2010 AARP survey found that 35 percent of adults older than 45 were chronically lonely, as opposed to 20 percent of a similar group

only a decade earlier. According to a major study by a leading scholar of the subject, roughly 20 percent of Americans—about 60 million people—are unhappy with their lives because of loneliness. Across the Western world, physicians and nurses have begun to speak openly of an epidemic of loneliness.

10   The new studies on loneliness are beginning to yield some surprising preliminary findings about its mechanisms. Almost every factor that one might assume affects loneliness does so only some of the time, and only under certain circumstances. People who are married are less lonely than single people, one journal article suggests, but only if their spouses are confidants. If one's spouse is not a confidant, marriage may not decrease loneliness. A belief in God might help, or it might not, as a 1990 German study comparing levels of religious feeling and levels of loneliness discovered. Active believers who saw God as abstract and helpful rather than as a wrathful, immediate presence were less lonely. "The mere belief in God," the researchers concluded, "was relatively independent of loneliness."

11   But it is clear that social interaction matters. Loneliness and being alone are not the same thing, but both are on the rise. We meet fewer people. We gather less. And when we gather, our bonds are less meaningful and less easy. The decrease in confidants—that is, in quality social connections—has been dramatic over the past 25 years. In one survey, the mean size of networks of personal confidants decreased from 2.94 people in 1985 to 2.08 in 2004. Similarly, in 1985, only 10 percent of Americans said they had no one with whom to discuss important matters, and 15 percent said they had only one such good friend. By 2004, 25 percent had nobody to talk to, and 20 percent had only one confidant.

12   In the face of this social disintegration, we have essentially hired an army of replacement confidants, an entire class of professional carers. As Ronald Dworkin pointed out in a 2010 paper for the Hoover Institution, in the late '40s, the United States was home to 2,500 clinical psychologists, 30,000 social workers, and fewer than 500 marriage and family therapists. As of 2010, the country had 77,000 clinical psychologists, 192,000 clinical social workers, 400,000 nonclinical social workers, 50,000 marriage and family therapists, 105,000 mental-health counselors, 220,000 substance-abuse counselors, 17,000 nurse psychotherapists, and 30,000 life coaches. The majority of patients in therapy do not warrant a psychiatric diagnosis. This raft of psychic servants is helping us through what used to be called regular problems. We have outsourced the work of everyday caring.

13   We need professional carers more and more, because the threat of societal breakdown, once principally a matter of nostalgic lament, has morphed into an issue of public health. Being lonely is extremely bad for your health. If you're lonely, you're more likely to be put in a geriatric home at an earlier age than a similar person who isn't lonely. You're less likely to exercise. You're more likely to be obese. You're less likely to survive a serious operation and more likely to have hormonal imbalances. You are at greater risk of inflammation. Your memory may be worse. You are more likely to be depressed, to sleep badly, and to suffer dementia and general cognitive decline. Loneliness may not have killed Yvette Vickers, but it has been linked to a greater probability of having the kind of heart condition that did kill her.

14   And yet, despite its deleterious effect on health, loneliness is one of the first things ordinary Americans spend their money achieving. With money, you flee the cramped

city to a house in the suburbs or, if you can afford it, a McMansion in the exurbs, inevitably spending more time in your car. Loneliness is at the American core, a by-product of a long-standing national appetite for independence: The Pilgrims who left Europe willingly abandoned the bonds and strictures of a society that could not accept their right to be different. They did not seek out loneliness, but they accepted it as the price of their autonomy. The cowboys who set off to explore a seemingly endless frontier likewise traded away personal ties in favor of pride and self-respect. The ultimate American icon is the astronaut: Who is more heroic, or more alone? The price of self-determination and self-reliance has often been loneliness. But Americans have always been willing to pay that price.

15   Today, the one common feature in American secular culture is its celebration of the self that breaks away from the constrictions of the family and the state, and, in its greatest expressions, from all limits entirely. The great American poem is Whitman's "Song of Myself." The great American essay is Emerson's "Self-Reliance." The great American novel is Melville's *Moby-Dick*, the tale of a man on a quest so lonely that it is incomprehensible to those around him. American culture, high and low, is about self-expression and personal authenticity. Franklin Delano Roosevelt called individualism "the great watchword of American life."

16   Self-invention is only half of the American story, however. The drive for isolation has always been in tension with the impulse to cluster in communities that cling and suffocate. The Pilgrims, while fomenting spiritual rebellion, also enforced ferocious cohesion. The Salem witch trials, in hindsight, read like attempts to impose solidarity—as do the McCarthy hearings. The history of the United States is like the famous parable of the porcupines in the cold, from Schopenhauer's *Studies in Pessimism*—the ones who huddle together for warmth and shuffle away in pain, always separating and congregating.

17   We are now in the middle of a long period of shuffling away. In his 2000 book *Bowling Alone*, Robert D. Putnam attributed the dramatic post-war decline of social capital—the strength and value of interpersonal networks—to numerous interconnected trends in American life: suburban sprawl, television's dominance over culture, the self-absorption of the Baby Boomers, the disintegration of the traditional family. The trends he observed continued through the prosperity of the aughts, and have only become more pronounced with time: the rate of union membership declined in 2011, again; screen time rose; the Masons and the Elks continued their slide into irrelevance. We are lonely because we want to be lonely. We have made ourselves lonely.

18   The question of the future is this: Is Facebook part of the separating or part of the congregating; is it a huddling-together for warmth or a shuffling-away in pain?

19   Well before Facebook, digital technology was enabling our tendency for isolation, to an unprecedented degree. Back in the 1990s, scholars started calling the contradiction between an increased opportunity to connect and a lack of human contact the "Internet paradox." A prominent 1998 article on the phenomenon by a team of researchers at Carnegie Mellon showed that increased Internet usage was already coinciding with increased loneliness. Critics of the study pointed out that the two groups that participated in the study—high-school journalism students who were heading to university and socially active members of community-development

boards—were statistically likely to become lonelier over time. Which brings us to a more fundamental question: Does the Internet make people lonely, or are lonely people more attracted to the Internet?

20   The question has intensified in the Facebook era. A recent study out of Australia (where close to half the population is active on Facebook), titled "Who Uses Facebook?," found a complex and sometimes confounding relationship between loneliness and social networking. Facebook users had slightly lower levels of "social loneliness"—the sense of not feeling bonded with friends—but "significantly higher levels of family loneliness"—the sense of not feeling bonded with family. It may be that Facebook encourages more contact with people outside of our household, at the expense of our family relationships—or it may be that people who have unhappy family relationships in the first place seek companionship through other means, including Facebook. The researchers also found that lonely people are inclined to spend more time on Facebook: "One of the most noteworthy findings," they wrote, "was the tendency for neurotic and lonely individuals to spend greater amounts of time on Facebook per day than non-lonely individuals." And they found that neurotics are more likely to prefer to use the wall, while extroverts tend to use chat features in addition to the wall.

21   Moira Burke, until recently a graduate student at the Human-Computer Institute at Carnegie Mellon, used to run a longitudinal study of 1,200 Facebook users. That study, which is ongoing, is one of the first to step outside the realm of self-selected college students and examine the effects of Facebook on a broader population, over time. She concludes that the effect of Facebook depends on what you bring to it. Just as your mother said: you get out only what you put in. If you use Facebook to communicate directly with other individuals—by using the "like" button, commenting on friends' posts, and so on—it can increase your social capital. Personalized messages, or what Burke calls "composed communication," are more satisfying than "one-click communication"—the lazy click of a like. "People who received composed communication became less lonely, while people who received one-click communication experienced no change in loneliness," Burke tells me. So, you should inform your friend in writing how charming her son looks with Harry Potter cake smeared all over his face, and how interesting her sepia-toned photograph of that tree-framed bit of skyline is, and how cool it is that she's at whatever concert she happens to be at. That's what we all want to hear. Even better than sending a private Facebook message is the semi-public conversation, the kind of back-and-forth in which you half ignore the other people who may be listening in. "People whose friends write to them semi-publicly on Facebook experience decreases in loneliness," Burke says.

22   On the other hand, non-personalized use of Facebook—scanning your friends' status updates and updating the world on your own activities via your wall, or what Burke calls "passive consumption" and "broadcasting"—correlates to feelings of disconnectedness. It's a lonely business, wandering the labyrinths of our friends' and pseudo-friends' projected identities, trying to figure out what part of ourselves we ought to project, who will listen, and what they will hear. According to Burke, passive consumption of Facebook also correlates to a marginal increase in depression. "If two women each talk to their friends the same amount of time, but one of them spends more time reading about friends on Facebook as well, the one reading tends

to grow slightly more depressed," Burke says. Her conclusion suggests that my sometimes unhappy reactions to Facebook may be more universal than I had realized. When I scroll through page after page of my friends' descriptions of how accidentally eloquent their kids are, and how their husbands are endearingly bumbling, and how they're all about to eat a home-cooked meal prepared with fresh local organic produce bought at the farmers' market and then go for a jog and maybe check in at the office because they're so busy getting ready to hop on a plane for a week of luxury dogsledding in Lapland, I do grow slightly more miserable. A lot of other people doing the same thing feel a little bit worse, too.

23   Still, Burke's research does not support the assertion that Facebook creates loneliness. The people who experience loneliness on Facebook are lonely away from Facebook, too, she points out; on Facebook, as everywhere else, correlation is not causation. The popular kids are popular, and the lonely skulkers skulk alone. Perhaps it says something about me that I think Facebook is primarily a platform for lonely skulking. I mention to Burke the widely reported study, conducted by a Stanford graduate student, that showed how believing that others have strong social networks can lead to feelings of depression. What does Facebook communicate, if not the impression of social bounty? Everybody else looks so happy on Facebook, with so many friends, that our own social networks feel emptier than ever in comparison. Doesn't that *make* people feel lonely? "If people are reading about lives that are much better than theirs, two things can happen," Burke tells me. "They can feel worse about themselves, or they can feel motivated."

24   Burke will start working at Facebook as a data scientist this year.

25   John Cacioppo, the director of the Center for Cognitive and Social Neuroscience at the University of Chicago, is the world's leading expert on loneliness. In his landmark book, *Loneliness*, released in 2008, he revealed just how profoundly the epidemic of loneliness is affecting the basic functions of human physiology. He found higher levels of epinephrine, the stress hormone, in the morning urine of lonely people. Loneliness burrows deep: "When we drew blood from our older adults and analyzed their white cells," he writes, "we found that loneliness somehow penetrated the deepest recesses of the cell to alter the way genes were being expressed." Loneliness affects not only the brain, then, but the basic process of DNA transcription. When you are lonely, your whole body is lonely.

26   To Cacioppo, Internet communication allows only ersatz intimacy. "Forming connections with pets or online friends or even God is a noble attempt by an obligatorily gregarious creature to satisfy a compelling need," he writes. "But surrogates can never make up completely for the absence of the real thing." The "real thing" being actual people, in the flesh. When I speak to Cacioppo, he is refreshingly clear on what he sees as Facebook's effect on society. Yes, he allows, some research has suggested that the greater the number of Facebook friends a person has, the less lonely she is. But he argues that the impression this creates can be misleading. "For the most part," he says, "people are bringing their old friends, and feelings of loneliness or connectedness, to Facebook." The idea that a Web site could deliver a more friendly, interconnected world is bogus. The depth of one's social network outside Facebook is what determines the depth of one's social network within Facebook, not the other way around. Using social media doesn't create new social networks; it just

transfers established networks from one platform to another. For the most part, Facebook doesn't destroy friendships—but it doesn't create them, either.

27   In one experiment, Cacioppo looked for a connection between the loneliness of subjects and the relative frequency of their interactions via Facebook, chat rooms, online games, dating sites, and face-to-face contact. The results were unequivocal. "The greater the proportion of face-to-face interactions, the less lonely you are," he says. "The greater the proportion of online interactions, the lonelier you are." Surely, I suggest to Cacioppo, this means that Facebook and the like inevitably make people lonelier. He disagrees. Facebook is merely a tool, he says, and like any tool, its effectiveness will depend on its user. "If you use Facebook to increase face-to-face contact," he says, "it increases social capital." So if social media let you organize a game of football among your friends, that's healthy. If you turn to social media instead of playing football, however, that's unhealthy.

28   "Facebook can be terrific, if we use it properly," Cacioppo continues. "It's like a car. You can drive it to pick up your friends. Or you can drive alone." But hasn't the car increased loneliness? If cars created the suburbs, surely they also created isolation. "That's because of how we use cars," Cacioppo replies. "How we use these technologies can lead to more integration, rather than more isolation."

29   The problem, then, is that we invite loneliness, even though it makes us miserable. The history of our use of technology is a history of isolation desired and achieved. When the Great Atlantic and Pacific Tea Company opened its A&P stores, giving Americans self-service access to groceries, customers stopped having relationships with their grocers. When the telephone arrived, people stopped knocking on their neighbors' doors. Social media bring this process to a much wider set of relationships. Researchers at the HP Social Computing Lab who studied the nature of people's connections on Twitter came to a depressing, if not surprising, conclusion: "Most of the links declared within Twitter were meaningless from an interaction point of view." I have to wonder: What other point of view is meaningful?

30   Loneliness is certainly not something that Facebook or Twitter or any of the lesser forms of social media is doing to us. We are doing it to ourselves. Casting technology as some vague, impersonal spirit of history forcing our actions is a weak excuse. We make decisions about how we use our machines, not the other way around. Every time I shop at my local grocery store, I am faced with a choice. I can buy my groceries from a human being or from a machine. I always, without exception, choose the machine. It's faster and more efficient, I tell myself, but the truth is that I prefer not having to wait with the other customers who are lined up alongside the conveyor belt: the hipster mom who disapproves of my high-carbon-footprint pineapple; the lady who tenses to the point of tears while she waits to see if the gods of the credit-card machine will accept or decline; the old man whose clumsy feebleness requires a patience that I don't possess. Much better to bypass the whole circus and just ring up the groceries myself.

31   Our omnipresent new technologies lure us toward increasingly superficial connections at exactly the same moment that they make avoiding the mess of human interaction easy. The beauty of Facebook, the source of its power, is that it enables us to be social while sparing us the embarrassing reality of society—the accidental revelations we make at parties, the awkward pauses, the farting and the spilled

drinks and the general gaucherie of face-to-face contact. Instead, we have the lovely smoothness of a seemingly social machine. Everything's so simple: status updates, pictures, your wall.

32   But the price of this smooth sociability is a constant compulsion to assert one's own happiness, one's own fulfillment. Not only must we contend with the social bounty of others; we must foster the appearance of our own social bounty. Being happy all the time, pretending to be happy, actually attempting to be happy—it's exhausting. Last year a team of researchers led by Iris Mauss at the University of Denver published a study looking into "the paradoxical effects of valuing happiness." Most goals in life show a direct correlation between valuation and achievement. Studies have found, for example, that students who value good grades tend to have higher grades than those who don't value them. Happiness is an exception. The study came to a disturbing conclusion:

33   Valuing happiness is not necessarily linked to greater happiness. In fact, under certain conditions, the opposite is true. Under conditions of low (but not high) life stress, the more people valued happiness, the lower were their hedonic balance, psychological well-being, and life satisfaction, and the higher their depression symptoms.

34   The more you try to be happy, the less happy you are. Sophocles made roughly the same point.

35   Facebook, of course, puts the pursuit of happiness front and center in our digital life. Its capacity to redefine our very concepts of identity and personal fulfillment is much more worrisome than the data-mining and privacy practices that have aroused anxieties about the company. Two of the most compelling critics of Facebook— neither of them a Luddite—concentrate on exactly this point. Jaron Lanier, the author of *You Are Not a Gadget*, was one of the inventors of virtual-reality technology. His view of where social media are taking us reads like dystopian science fiction: "I fear that we are beginning to design ourselves to suit digital models of us, and I worry about a leaching of empathy and humanity in that process." Lanier argues that Facebook imprisons us in the business of self-presenting, and this, to his mind, is the site's crucial and fatally unacceptable downside.

36   Sherry Turkle, a professor of computer culture at MIT who in 1995 published the digital-positive analysis *Life on the Screen*, is much more skeptical about the effects of online society in her 2011 book, *Alone Together*: "These days, insecure in our relationships and anxious about intimacy, we look to technology for ways to be in relationships and protect ourselves from them at the same time." The problem with digital intimacy is that it is ultimately incomplete: "The ties we form through the Internet are not, in the end, the ties that bind. But they are the ties that preoccupy," she writes. "We don't want to intrude on each other, so instead we constantly intrude on each other, but not in 'real time.'"

37   Lanier and Turkle are right, at least in their diagnoses. Self-presentation on Facebook is continuous, intensely mediated, and possessed of a phony nonchalance that eliminates even the potential for spontaneity. ("Look how casually I threw up these three photos from the party at which I took 300 photos!") Curating the exhibition of

the self has become a 24/7 occupation. Perhaps not surprisingly, then, the Australian study "Who Uses Facebook?" found a significant correlation between Facebook use and narcissism: "Facebook users have higher levels of total narcissism, exhibitionism, and leadership than Facebook nonusers," the study's authors wrote. "In fact, it could be argued that Facebook specifically gratifies the narcissistic individual's need to engage in self-promoting and superficial behavior."

38   Rising narcissism isn't so much a trend as the trend behind all other trends. In preparation for the 2013 edition of its diagnostic manual, the psychiatric profession is currently struggling to update its definition of narcissistic personality disorder. Still, generally speaking, practitioners agree that narcissism manifests in patterns of fantastic grandiosity, craving for attention, and lack of empathy. In a 2008 survey, 35,000 American respondents were asked if they had ever had certain symptoms of narcissistic personality disorder. Among people older than 65, 3 percent reported symptoms. Among people in their 20s, the proportion was nearly 10 percent. Across all age groups, one in 16 Americans has experienced some symptoms of NPD. And loneliness and narcissism are intimately connected: a longitudinal study of Swedish women demonstrated a strong link between levels of narcissism in youth and levels of loneliness in old age. The connection is fundamental. Narcissism is the flip side of loneliness, and either condition is a fighting retreat from the messy reality of other people.

39   A considerable part of Facebook's appeal stems from its miraculous fusion of distance with intimacy, or the illusion of distance with the illusion of intimacy. Our online communities become engines of self-image, and self-image becomes the engine of community. The real danger with Facebook is not that it allows us to isolate ourselves, but that by mixing our appetite for isolation with our vanity, it threatens to alter the very nature of solitude. The new isolation is not of the kind that Americans once idealized, the lonesomeness of the proudly nonconformist, independent-minded, solitary stoic, or that of the astronaut who blasts into new worlds. Facebook's isolation is a grind. What's truly staggering about Facebook usage is not its volume—750 million photographs uploaded over a single weekend—but the constancy of the performance it demands. More than half its users—and one of every 13 people on Earth is a Facebook user—log on every day. Among 18-to-34-year-olds, nearly half check Facebook minutes after waking up, and 28 percent do so before getting out of bed. The relentlessness is what is so new, so potentially transformative. Facebook never takes a break. We never take a break. Human beings have always created elaborate acts of self-presentation. But not all the time, not every morning, before we even pour a cup of coffee. Yvette Vickers's computer was on when she died.

40   Nostalgia for the good old days of disconnection would not just be pointless, it would be hypocritical and ungrateful. But the very magic of the new machines, the efficiency and elegance with which they serve us, obscures what isn't being served: everything that matters. What Facebook has revealed about human nature—and this is not a minor revelation—is that a connection is not the same thing as a bond, and that instant and total connection is no salvation, no ticket to a happier, better world or a more liberated version of humanity. Solitude used to be good for self-reflection and self-reinvention. But now we are left thinking about who we are all the time,

without ever really thinking about who we are. Facebook denies us a pleasure whose profundity we had underestimated: the chance to forget about ourselves for a while, the chance to disconnect.

UNDERSTANDING AND ANALYZING THE READING

A. Building Vocabulary

Using context and a dictionary if necessary, determine the meaning of each word as it is used in the selection.

_____ 1. permeating (paragraph 1)
    a. failing to fill
    b. passing through every part
    c. brightening
    d. engulfing

_____ 2. deleterious (paragraph 14)
    a. harmful
    b. helpful
    c. pleasing
    d. questionable

_____ 3. ersatz (paragraph 26)
    a. artificial
    b. surface
    c. physical
    d. emotional

_____ 4. unequivocal (paragraph 27)
    a. unequal
    b. unimaginable
    c. impossible
    d. clear

_____ 5. leaching (paragraph 35)
    a. spreading
    b. lacking
    c. leaking
    d. decreasing

_____ 6. empathy (paragraph 35)
    a. the appearance of interest
    b. the intensity of feelings
    c. the lack of emotion
    d. the identification with the feelings of others

_____ 7. nonchalance (paragraph 37)
    a. abundance of interest
    b. lack of concern
    c. excitement
    d. craving for attention

_____ 8. narcissism (paragraph 37)
    a. excessive self-love
    b. lack of self-confidence
    c. well-developed social skills
    d. extreme loneliness

_____ 9. profundity (paragraph 40)
    a. shallowness
    b. impact
    c. depth
    d. value

Word Parts

> ### A REVIEW OF PREFIXES AND ROOTS
>
> **PRE-** means prior to.
> **DICT** means to say.
> **PSYCH-** means mind.

Use your knowledge of word parts and the review above to fill in the blanks in the following sentences.

1. Research that **predicts** an outcome (paragraph 7) _____ what will happen _____ the actual happening.

2. When the author of the reading states that loneliness is a psychological state (paragraph 8), he means that it is a condition of the _____.

B. Understanding the Thesis and Other Main Ideas

Select the best answer.

_____ 1. Which of the following is the best statement of the selection's thesis or central thought?

    a. The degree of loneliness experienced by Facebook users can be directly correlated to the number of close friends and family members they have.

    b. According to the latest research, the sudden increase in loneliness in our society can be directly linked to the excessive use of Facebook.

    c. Facebook and other social media are enabling people to stay more connected with others, while at the same time leading them to greater detachment from others and increased loneliness.

    d. Facebook, more than any other social media tool, has the potential to make people physically and emotionally ill.

_____ 2. Which of the following sentences states the main idea of paragraph 23?

    a. "Still, Burk's research does not support the assertion that Facebook creates loneliness."

    b. "The people who experience loneliness on Facebook are lonely away from Facebook, too, she points out."

    c. "Perhaps it says something about me that I think Facebook is primarily a platform for lonely skulking."

    d. "If people are reading about lives that are much better than theirs, two things can happen."

_____ 3. The topic of paragraph 14 is
   a. the effects of loneliness on one's physical health.
   b. man's quest for independence.
   c. paying for loneliness.
   d. the history of loneliness.

C. Identifying Details

Select the best answer.

_____ 1. Which author did **NOT** address the theme of self-invention in his writing?
   a. Walt Whitman
   b. Nathaniel Hawthorne
   c. Herman Melville
   d. Ralph Waldo Emerson

_____ 2. Which one of the following statements is **NOT** supported by the research of Moira Burke?
   a. "... the effect of Facebook depends on what you bring to it."
   b. "Personalized messages ... are more satisfying than "one-click communication ..."
   c. "The greater the proportion of face-to-face interactions, the less lonely you are."
   d. "Passive consumption of Facebook also correlates to a marginal increase in depression."

_____ 3. The author of the reading selection suggests that we are making ourselves lonely by the way we choose to use technology. Which one of the following uses of technology does he address?
   a. using the Internet for research rather than going to the library
   b. using Skype to visit with someone rather than visiting him/her in person
   c. using Facebook or email to send a message rather than using the telephone
   d. using the self-checkout at the grocery store rather than letting a cashier check out our groceries

_____ 4. The author writes about the "flipside of loneliness" as being
   a. congeniality.
   b. narcissism.
   c. intimacy.
   d. paranoia.

D. Recognizing Methods of Organization and Transitions

Select the best answer.

_____ 1. The pattern of organization used in paragraph 1 is
        a. classification.
        b. definition.
        c. narration.
        d. process.

_____ 2. The overall pattern of organization used for the reading selection is
        a. cause and effect.
        b. illustration.
        c. chronological order.
        d. definition.

_____ 3. The organizational pattern used in paragraph 10 is
        a. comparison.
        b. contrast.
        c. chronological order.
        d. illustration.

E. Reading and Thinking Visually

Select the best answer.

_____ 1. The author likely chose to include the photo on page 450 to
        a. illustrate how similar interests can bring people together.
        b. illustrate how both genders enjoy touch-screen technology.
        c. illustrate the intense concentration that the use of technology demands.
        d. illustrate the connection between technology and alienation.

F. Figuring Out Implied Meanings

Indicate whether each statement is true (T) or false (F).

_____ 1. The author suggests that while Facebook is a useful tool, the negatives about Facebook, far outweigh the positives.

_____ 2. Facebook cannot be blamed for making us lonely.

_____ 3. "Moderation in all things" is a good motto for people to keep in mind as they use Facebook or other social media tools.

_____ 4. No technological tool can produce the same benefits as face-to-face social interaction.

_____ 5. The inclusion of information about the glow of the computer in Yvette Vickers' house suggests that using the computer must have been the last thing that Yvette did before she died.

_____ 6. A healthy individual has a balance of solitude and social interaction in his/her life.

G. Thinking Critically: Analyzing the Author's Technique

Select the best answer.

_____ 1. The author begins the selection with information about Yvette Vickers in order to

a. illustrate how the effects of technology can extend far beyond one's natural lifetime.

b. underscore how those who live lives in the public eye are forgotten once their careers are over.

c. provide an example of the loneliness and solitude that characterized the final years of her life.

d. explain how Internet friends can often be more sympathetic and attentive than face-to-face friends.

_____ 2. The author uses the parable of the porcupines in the cold to illustrate

a. the tendency that the American people have had throughout history to come together and then move apart from each other.

b. how being together can be painful when some members of the group are "prickly."

c. the tendency that Americans have to criticize one another and drive people away.

d. emphasize the dangers of being together or apart for a long period of time.

_____ 3. The author's tone is best described as

a. self-righteous.

b. irreverent.

c. informative.

d. sarcastic.

_____ 4. Three of the following sentences from the reading are facts. One is an opinion. Which one is the opinion?

   a. "The *Los Angeles Times* posted a story headlined "Mummi-fied Body of Former Playboy Playmate Yvette Vickers Found in her Benedict Canyon Home," which quickly went viral." (paragraph 2)

   b. "Solitude can be lovely. Crowded parties can be agony." (paragraph 8)

   c. "Franklin Delano Roosevelt called individualism 'the great watchword of American life.' " (paragraph 15)

   d. "That study, which is ongoing, is one of the first to step out-side the realm of self-selected college students and examine the effects of Facebook on a broader population, over time." (para-graph 21)

_____ 5. Which one of the following sentences contains a simile?

   a. "Across the Western world, physicians and nurses have begun to speak openly of an epidemic of loneliness." (paragraph 9)

   b. "Rising narcissism isn't so much a trend as the trend behind all other trends." (paragraph 38)

   c. "Much better to bypass the whole circus and just ring up the gro-ceries myself." (paragraph 30)

   d. "Facebook can be terrific, if we use it properly. It's like a car." (paragraph 28)

_____ 6. To support her thesis, the author uses all of the following *except*

   a. research.

   b. quotations from lonely Facebook users.

   c. personal experience.

   d. information from newspaper and magazine stories.

_____ 7. Which of the following sentences contains an example of *informal* language?

   a. "The idea that a Web site could deliver a more friendly, intercon-nected world is bogus." (paragraph 26)

   b. "They did not seek out loneliness, but they accepted it as the price of their autonomy." (paragraph 14)

   c. "Burke will start working at Facebook as a data scientist this year." (paragraph 24)

   d. "The more you try to be happy, the less happy you are." (para-graph 34)

H. Thinking Critically: Analyzing the Author's Message

Select the best answer.

_____ 1. In which of the following paragraphs can you find the reason for the public's general suspicion of Facebook?

    a. paragraph 22

    b. paragraph 20

    c. paragraph 19

    d. paragraph 5

_____ 2. What does the author mean in paragraph 3 when he writes that "Vickers's web of connections had grown broader but shallower . . ."?

    a. She had many contacts but few real relationships.

    b. She had so many contacts that she could not keep up with them all.

    c. Her contacts were spread out broadly all over the world.

    d. The information she shared on the Internet with her many connections was shallow, surface information.

_____ 3. Why does the author mention in paragraph 24 that "Moira Burke will start working at Facebook as a data scientist this year"?

    a. to lend more credibility to her research

    b. to suggest that there could be some bias in her research

    c. to explain why she left the Human-Computer Institute at Carnegie Mellon.

    d. to reveal the depth of knowledge Burke has about Facebook

_____ 4. Why does the author put the words *Your real friends* in italics in paragraph 6?

    a. He wants to make sure the reader understands the quaintness of the words.

    b. He wants to send the message that Google+ is different from Facebook in that it encourages people to communicate with their real friends—the ones with whom they have a real relationship.

    c. He wants to persuade the reader to switch from Facebook to Google+.

    d. He wants to encourage Facebook users to take a closer look at the people they have friended in hopes that they will limit their friends to those with whom they have a relationship.

WRITING IN RESPONSE TO THE READING

I. Writing a Summary

Write a summary of "Is Facebook Making Us Lonely?" (paragraphs 1–40).

J. Analyzing the Issue

1. Identify at least three issues discussed in this reading. Then phrase each issue as a question that the author raises, discusses, or answers.

2. Write a statement that briefly summarizes the author's position on the use of Facebook.

3. Identify at least one example of verbal or situational irony used by the author.

4. What is the author's background, and is he qualified is to write about the topic? Why or why not? Do you find any bias in the selection?

K. Writing Paragraphs and Essays

Write a paragraph or essay in response to the following writing prompts. As part of this assignment you will need to follow the writing process:

- Use a prewriting strategy to generate ideas
- Complete a guided outline
- Write a rough draft
- Complete a peer revision guide
- Write a final draft using proper MLA format

1. The author states that "the more you try to be happy, the less happy you are." Write a paragraph or essay in which you explain what this statement means to you. Be sure to use examples/experiences to support your main thesis.

2. The author writes that "loneliness is slippery, a difficult state to define . . ." Write a paragraph or essay in which you define what loneliness means to you. Be sure to use examples/experiences to support your thesis.

3. John Cacioppo contends that "Facebook can be terrific, if we use it properly." Write a paragraph or essay in which you focus on the benefits of using Facebook. Be sure to provide examples to support your thesis.

4. Twitter and Facebook are both types of social media. Write a paragraph or essay in which you compare the two. Be sure to provide examples to support your thesis.

5. Write a paragraph or essay about someone you know (you do not have to provide his or her real name) who is addicted to Facebook. Why do you think this person is addicted? What addictive behaviors does he/she exhibit? How do you suggest that this person break the addiction?

L. Working Collaboratively

1. **Thinking Deeply** In a small group of your peers, discuss the following questions:

   - Why do you (or don't you) use Facebook?
   - How do you decide who to befriend on Facebook?
   - Why do you unfriend people on Facebook?
   - Has Facebook helped you to have better relationships with people? How so?
   - Has using Facebook ever created problems for you? How so?

   Be prepared to share your findings with the class.

2. **Thinking Critically** Imagine that you are the author of an advice column of a local newspaper. One question that was submitted recently came from a parent who is unsure of how to responsibly handle the use of Facebook by her teenage son/daughter. What suggestions do you have for this parent? Working with a partner, draft a paragraph length response to this parent in which you establish some clear guidelines for the parent to follow. Finally, be prepared to share your letter with the class.

3. **Thinking Locally** Imagine that you are on the staff of your college newspaper. Your editor has asked you to design a ten question survey about Facebook use by students on your campus. Working with a partner, create the survey. Be prepared to share your survey with the class. As an optional added activity, administer the survey to your friends on campus and report the findings to your class.

4. **Thinking Personally** This activity will give you an opportunity to examine yourself through someone else's eyes. Consider this question: If someone were to study your Facebook page and conversations, what would he/she conclude about your activities, your interests, your feelings, your likes/dislikes, your friends, and so on. Once you have analyzed the image you project on Facebook, write a short paragraph about what you have learned. You might also want to include what you think you should change about your Facebook persona. You will not be expected to share your writing with the class.

ACTIVITIES: EXPLORING RELATIONSHIPS

On your own or with a group of classmates, complete two of the following four activities.

1. As discussed at the start of this chapter, you interact with many people over the course of each day. To illustrate the truth of this statement, choose a day to track your interactions. Keep a list of every person with whom you interact. Don't forget about your Internet relationships. At the end of the day, try to categorize these people as to the type of relationship you have with them. Is it a casual or intimate relationship? Is it a family, friend, or romantic relationship? Feel free to generate your own categories. From this list, is there a relationship that needs to be ended? Is there one that is difficult? If so, you now have the tools to work through these relationships. Review the three readings in this chapter to see how the information in them can help to improve your relationships with others.

2. Conduct a Web search for an organization that is devoted to educating people about unhealthy or abusive relationships. Be sure to look within your own city to see what resources are available. Read about the organization's mission, as well as a couple of the articles on the organization's Web site. Summarize these articles in a paragraph, essay, or classroom presentation. Provide at least three tips for ending an abusive relationship.

3. Collect at least five magazine or newspaper articles that present a relationship issue. For each of the articles, answer the following questions: What is the relationship? What is the issue? How has the issue been handled? Be prepared to share your articles and the answers to the questions with your class.

4. As discussed at the start of this chapter, life is about relationships, and these relationships are often at the center of many controversial issues. This chapter discussed how to deal with difficult people, how to end a relationship, and the effects of technology on relationships. Other relationship issues include:

   - Gay marriages
   - Gay adoptions
   - Divorce
   - Child abuse
   - Internet romances
   - Teacher/Student romances
   - Workplace bullying

   Write an essay or prepare a class presentation about any of these topics, or any other relationship topic in which you are interested.

14 Conformity and Nonconformity: Following and Breaking the Rules

Do you follow the rules, or do you break them? Do you do what's expected of you, or do you do your own thing?

Every society is ruled by *norms*, which are spoken or unspoken rules of behavior. We grow up surrounded by these norms, and they become part of us. For example, even as a child, long before you have a driver's license, you learn that a red light means *stop*. Many social scientists believe that without norms, society would not be able to function. Those who follow the norms are said to *conform* to social expectations.

Here are some examples of the norms that influence our lives:

- Most children in the United States are required to attend school until they are 16.
- People are expected to behave properly in public and wear clothes that are appropriate for the situation.
- Mothers and fathers are expected to care for their children, and family members are expected to help take care of the elderly and sick.

But not everyone conforms to expected norms. For example, while many people who want to be successful follow the norm of attending college and then looking for a full-time job, others drop out of school and start their own businesses (Bill Gates of Microsoft is a famous example). While many people live a 9-to-5 life of work, family, and home, some people become musicians, living their lives mostly at night and traveling around the country (or the world) for much of the year.

In addition, norms are always undergoing change. In some areas, the "rules" are evolving or have not been defined yet. For instance, what types of etiquette do portable technologies require? Is it acceptable to talk on a cell phone on a crowded bus and in other public places? Should people be allowed to text while driving, or should laws be passed to prevent this?

This chapter offers three readings about conformity and how our personal decisions affect our lives, from the types of exercise we pursue, through the career choices we make, to the items we purchase. Throughout the readings you'll find examples of people who are following society's rules, as well as examples of people who are breaking the rules.

WHY IS CONFORMITY SUCH AN IMPORTANT CONTEMPORARY ISSUE?

American society has always been individualistic. The image of the tough, rugged American goes back to frontier days, when people built their own houses and farmed the land in order to survive. It's no surprise, then, that so many Americans struggle with the "rules" they feel are imposed on them. For example, feminism was a direct result of women's desire to have more choices in their lives, and the Civil Rights Movement was a direct result of people's desire to see all Americans treated equally and fairly. Many of these struggles are ongoing. To understand the options available to you and others, it is important to understand social expectations. Only then can you think critically about the pros and cons of conformity and decide which decisions are right for you.

How Do Conformity and Nonconformity Tie to My College Courses?

Understanding the norms of the major social institutions (such as family, education, and religion) is a key goal of most sociology courses. A subfield of psychology, *social psychology*, examines group behavior and expectations, the ways people behave in social settings. Literature courses are filled with tales of people who break the rules and do things their own way, while history and political science courses talk about larger-than-life figures (such as conquerors, generals, and presidents) whose unorthodox or individualistic beliefs and behaviors affected millions of people and changed society. And, of course, business courses teach the "rules" of business, from accounting through management, and talk about the consequences of breaking those rules (from getting fired through ending up in jail).

Tips for Reading about Conformity and Nonconformity

Here are some tips for reading not only the selections in this chapter, but any reading about conformity and nonconformity.

- **Consider context.** Different groups of people may be guided by very different sets of norms. For example, as a college student, you are expected to study and attend all your classes. At some colleges, however, student athletes follow a different set of "rules" from most other students. Their main focus may be the sport they play rather than their studies. As you read, ask yourself what specific *part* of society the author is writing about.

- **Pay close attention to the examples.** Readings about conformity and nonconformity often focus on individuals. What exactly are these people doing to follow or break society's rules? What are the consequences of their actions for themselves and others? What guides their behaviors?

- **Link the reading to your life, experiences, and opinions.** If you are reading a personal essay, put yourself in the author's position. Would you make the same choices or different choices? How would the opinions of others affect (or not affect) your choices?

SELECTION

10

Magazine Article

Extreme Health

Peter Martin

DRE 096   PRE-READING

Source and Context

This article originally appeared in *Esquire*, a men's magazine that was founded in 1932. Many highly regarded American writers have written for the magazine, including F. Scott Fitzgerald, Ernest Hemingway, and Norman Mailer. Articles in the magazine fall into several categories including politics, entertainment, style and grooming, and food and drink.

A Note on the Reading

While some health and fitness experts complain that Americans do not get enough exercise, some men go to the opposite extreme, taking part in brutal sporting competitions that test their endurance to its limit. Read "Extreme Health" to understand what motivates "extreme athletes."

Previewing the Reading

Using the steps listed on page 4, preview the reading selection. When you have finished, answer the following questions.

1. This reading is about _____.

2. The reason for increased participation in extreme sports may be the fact that people now live in _____.

3. Extreme sports provide men with something that is missing from their lives: _____.

Using Prior Knowledge

Do you play any sport(s), or have you ever participated in an athletic competition? What motivated you to do so?

DURING READING

Reading Tip

As you read, note the way the author uses the words nuts, extreme, lunatic, *and* abuse. *Does he use these words literally or figuratively? What is his attitude toward the athletes he profiles?*

Highlight and annotate key information as you read.

Extreme Health

Peter Martin

Too many American men are unhealthy and don't know it. So we found the most extreme fitness nuts in the world—men who train harder, push further, stay stronger—and asked for their help. The good news is, you don't have to be as extreme as they are. Just let some of their insanity rub off on you. A little bit of extreme goes a long way.

1   The man slaps the heavy basement door and turns around. His fingers leave a smear of perspiration that, when he returns in a few minutes, will be gone, evaporated by the thick, stagnant air of this interior stairwell. Wearing a forty-five-pound weighted vest, his shirt dark with sweat, Mark Merchant, forty-four, who co-owns the gym upstairs, has just run up and down twelve flights of stairs five times—with the vest—and he's starting back up. Next to the third-floor entrance, a bright yellow whistle hangs from the handrail, in case he becomes exhausted and needs medical assistance. Merchant passes it, breathing hard but solid. He has five more sets to go. Same as yesterday.

2   For some reason, men are doing stuff like this lately. They're running—far and hard, up stairwells, in marathons and ultra-marathons, over mountains, across nations, and occasionally under barbed wire. They are swimming and biking, too. Sometimes all three, and sometimes all in one day. Whatever it takes to prove they're alive. It's as if all men old enough to have watched **Bo Jackson** suddenly felt an innate responsibility to make him look like a wuss. A one-dimensional wuss even.

Bo Jackson
American athlete who participated in both football and baseball

Courtesy of Glynnis Jones/Shutterstock.

3   The statistics are pretty staggering, and not because they show that we're becoming a species of elite athletes. Everyday men running at their schlubby, everyday paces have raised the median overall marathon finish time over the last thirty years by almost forty-five minutes. And when marathons and similar events get boring, we invent new ones, like adventure racing—multi-sport events that combine athletics and navigation. The U.S. Adventure Racing Association, which didn't even exist until 1998, has gone from sanctioning thirteen races a year to more than four hundred—from a couple hundred participants to what USARA president Troy

Reprinted from *Esquire*.

Farrar vaguely, if unscientifically, estimates at "close to one million." Even if he's overestimating by half (and seriously, Troy), that's still a lot of working stiffs who are suddenly willing to spend their weekend running eight miles, rappelling down a cliff to a river, and then being told to build a raft and cross it.

4

Mount Kilimanjaro one of the highest mountains in the world, located in Tanzania, Africa

And then there are the real lunatics. Men like Rodney Cutler, a hair-salon entrepreneur and *Esquire's* grooming writer, who recently ran 159 miles in six days— that's more than a marathon a day, if you're counting—and then climbed **Mount Kilimanjaro**; like Todd Carmichael, who owns a coffee-roasting business and who in 2008 became the first American to reach the South Pole solo on foot, trekking seven hundred miles in thirty-nine days; and like Merchant, who for some reason has decided to enter something called the Death Race. Although smaller in number than the marathoners and adventure racers, they push not only the limits of their minds and bodies but the limits of what can be considered rational. Or even healthy.

5

singlet a sleeveless shirt

hunter-gatherer refers to early human societies; social scientists believe ancient societies focused on two major activities: hunting and gathering food

Why all the abuse? Because men want to find out if they can, for one thing—they all say that. And there's a bit of midlife crisis here, too—instead of buying convertibles and trying to look comfortable buying pot again, men are getting outside. But it also has to do with an urge that some of these guys say has always existed deep inside us. As Carmichael puts it, "The American dream started with exploration" —of our environment, our land, and our own personal limits. Life, liberty, and the pursuit of happiness, all in a numbered **singlet**. Jack Raglin, a sport psychologist at Indiana University who specializes in exercise and its connection to mental health, says this part is genetic. Extreme athletics, in some form or another, go back to the beginning. Raglin cites for-real scientific research that suggests that exercise is an exploration of an innate **hunter-gatherer** impulse. It seems that when athletics became about more than just running from dinosaurs, we crafted competitions around it, and that impulse led to crazy stuff like "the grind," a weeklong indoor-track endurance bike race from the late 1800s that put many contestants in the hospital. It later led to a market for body butter.

6

Blame the fact that we all live in cities. There are no farms to run, no bales of hay to toss, no sheep to round up or whatever. There are few physical requirements to being a man in an urban environment. So men are creating them. And with each mile they run, the greater their need becomes to huff out another. Once a man finishes one race, Raglin says, "It's like, What's the next milestone? For some people it becomes sort of like merit badges."

7

At some point, for some men, marathon merit badges stop being enough. So they run farther. Ultramarathons up to 150 miles. And they run crazier, entering obstacle-course-style races like the Tough Mudder, a ten-mile competition introduced in 2010 that has participants climbing walls, swimming through mud bogs, and jumping over fire. And if that's not enough, there's always the Death Race. Started in 2005 by a former securities trader, the race is designed to frustrate people, hurt people even, and make them quit. Although the Death Race covers only ten miles, it takes twenty-four hours to complete—and that's if you complete it at all. Of the five hundred people who have attempted the race, only forty-nine have finished.

8

Raglin says events like these provide men with something that's missing from their lives: motivation. Unlike humping it to the gym for an hour before work, when you focus on a race like one of these, your accomplishment is immediately quantifiable. You either finish or you don't. And after you do, hopefully you feel awful. Otherwise you wouldn't feel satisfied, the thinking goes. You follow?

9   I recently spent some time in this world of extremism to see what an average person could take from it. I worked out with Merchant, albeit with a much lighter vest—a vest that I was relieved of in my ninth run up the stairs after having been lapped. (Twice.) And while there's not a chance that I'll run the Death Race with him this summer, I did learn that I can get a much more effective workout in less time if I don't rest between sets or exercises. So there's a lesson. And late last year, although I didn't join Rodney Cutler for the six preclimb days of marathons (I had some meetings to attend, and also I'm, you know, sane), I did summit Kilimanjaro with him. My little affair with mountaineering may be over, but I discovered something that I'm sure will pop up in other parts of my life: how much better accomplishing something can feel when you've worked toward it—and hard—for many months. From all of these athletes, the lesson is simple: Find what you think are your limits. Then find new ones. Also, make sure you have a yellow whistle, just in case.

OUR EXTREME SPECIES

- In 2009, 478,590 men finished half marathons—a 53 percent increase since 2004.
- More than 275,000 men ran full marathons, a 26 percent increase over nine years.
- Overall, 59 percent of all marathon runners are now men.
- In 2000, 29,373 runners finished the New York City Marathon (the world's largest). In 2010, 45,103 finished.
- More than thirty new marathons were introduced in 2009 alone.
- In six years, the number of USA Triathlon-sanctioned events has more than doubled—from 1,541 to 3,500.
- When the U.S. Adventure Racing Association started in 1998, it sanctioned thirteen races. This year, there will be more than four hundred. Seventy percent of participants are men.
- The Death Race—an annual twenty-four-hour adventure race that aims to break athletes physically and mentally—started in 2005 in Vermont with eight participants. This summer, two hundred will attempt it. In the race's six-year history, only forty-nine people have completed the course—forty-five of them men.
- Tough Mudder, a ten-mile obstacle course designed by British Special Forces and held in locations across America, had 15,000 participants across the three events in its inaugural year, 2010.

POST-READING

UNDERSTANDING AND ANALYZING THE READING

A. Building Vocabulary

Context

Using context and a dictionary if necessary, determine the meaning of each word as it is used in the selection.

_____ 1. perspiration (paragraph 1)
    a. dirt
    b. sweat
    c. blood
    d. grease

_____ 2. stagnant (paragraph 1)
    a. fresh
    b. healthy
    c. unmoving
    d. humid

_____ 3. innate (paragraph 2)
    a. inborn
    b. extreme
    c. unavoidable
    d. challenging

_____ 4. staggering (paragraph 3)
    a. surprising
    b. walking awkwardly
    c. astonishing
    d. exaggerated

_____ 5. elite (paragraph 3)
    a. from a wealthy family
    b. in excellent physical condition
    c. best in a category
    d. devoted to participating in sports

_____ 6. paces (paragraph 3)
    a. steps in running or walking
    b. heartbeats
    c. struggles or challenges
    d. world records

_____ 7. sanctioning (paragraph 3)
    a. preventing
    b. punishing
    c. sinning
    d. approving

_____ 8. trekking (paragraph 4)
    a. participating
    b. fighting
    c. journeying
    d. flying

_____ 9. urge (paragraph 5)
    a. strong desire
    b. mental illness
    c. sense of adventure
    d. natural talent

_____ 10. albeit (paragraph 9)
    a. in spite of
    b. without
    c. although
    d. not

Word Parts

> ### A REVIEW OF PREFIXES
>
> **ULTRA-** means beyond or extreme.
> **MULTI-** means many.

Use your knowledge of word parts and the review above to fill in the blanks in the following sentences.

1. *Ultra-marathons* (paragraph 2) are marathons that push people _____ their usual physical boundaries or limits.

2. *Multi-sport* (paragraph 3) events combine _____ sports into a single event.

B. Understanding Main Ideas

Select the best answer.

_____ 1. The best statement of the thesis or central thought of "Extreme Health" is

   a. Both men and women are taking part in challenging marathons as a way of forgetting their problems and keeping themselves in good physical shape.

   b. While many people claim to be fitness enthusiasts and to exercise regularly, most of these people do not have the discipline or the desire to become true athletes who can participate and succeed in extreme sports.

   c. As a result of urban living and perhaps midlife crises, more and more men are taking part in extreme sports to expand their personal limits, while not necessarily realizing that intense athletic competitions may be as old as humanity itself.

   d. Of all the sporting competitions in the world, the two most difficult and punishing events are the Death Race and the Tough Mudder; in both of these events, people have died while trying to complete the competition.

_____ 2. The topic of paragraph 4 is

   a. Rodney Cutler.

   b. Mount Kilimanjaro.

   c. extreme athletes.

   d. the Death Race.

_____ 3. In which sentence of paragraph 5 does the main idea of paragraph 5 appear?

a. first

b. third

c. sixth

d. last

C. Identifying Details

Select the best answer.

_____ 1. In which state did the Death Race start?

a. Arizona

b. New York

c. Vermont

d. California

_____ 2. The first American man to reach the South Pole alone on foot was

a. Mark Merchant.

b. Todd Carmichael.

c. Rodney Cutler.

d. Jack Raglin.

_____ 3. The ten-mile obstacle course designed by British Special Forces is the

a. Tough Mudder.

b. Death Race.

c. U.S. Adventure Race.

d. Grind.

_____ 4. In which two activities did the author of this article, Peter Martin, take part?

a. the Death Race and the Tough Mudder

b. climbing Mount Kilimanjaro and running up and down a staircase wearing a weighted vest

c. fourteen ultramarathons across the world and two NASCAR-type car-racing events

d. "the grind" and the purchase of a Corvette as a result of his midlife crisis

D. Recognizing Methods of Organization and Transitions

Select the best answer.

_____ 1. The organizational pattern used in paragraph 4 and in the box titled "Our Extreme Species" (paragraph 10) is
   a. listing/enumeration.
   b. classification.
   c. process.
   d. order of importance.

_____ 2. What is the dominant organizational pattern of paragraph 5?
   a. comparison-contrast
   b. cause-effect
   c. spatial order
   d. definition

_____ 3. Which signal word or phrase is a clue to the dominant organizational pattern of paragraph 5?
   a. because
   b. instead of
   c. started with
   d. personal limits

E. Making Inferences

Based on what is stated in the reading, indicate whether each statement is true (T) or false (F).

_____ 1. Only about 10 percent of the people who have attempted the Death Race have finished it.

_____ 2. It is likely that a million people take part in U.S. Adventure Racing Association athletic events each year.

_____ 3. Over the past three decades, the average time for men completing marathons has steadily increased.

_____ 4. The author implies that extreme sports are partially a result of human beings' desire to keep pushing themselves to the next milestone of physical endurance.

_____ 5. The author sees Bo Jackson as an athlete whose achievements many amateurs are trying to emulate or exceed.

_____ 6. The author advises readers to test their limits, but also to have a back-up plan if they need help.

_____ 7. "The grind" began as a sporting event in the nineteenth century.

F. Thinking Critically: Analyzing the Author's Technique

Select the best answer.

_____ 1. The author's main purpose in "Extreme Health" is to

    a. motivate men of all ages to participate in extreme sporting events.

    b. explore the reasons why men take part in extreme sports while providing examples of some successful athletes and some particularly challenging sporting competitions.

    c. provide a detailed psychological explanation of what motivates three men (Rodney Cutler, Mark Merchant, and Todd Carmichael) to enter competitions like the Death Race.

    d. imply that most middle-aged men simply do not have the motivation it takes to exercise daily or push themselves physically.

_____ 2. The intended audience for "Extreme Health" is composed primarily of

    a. women.

    b. teenagers.

    c. the elderly.

    d. men.

_____ 3. The point of view of this article is

    a. first person.

    b. second person.

    c. third person.

    d. a combination of first and third person.

_____ 4. To support his thesis and main ideas, the author uses all of the following types of evidence **except**

    a. examples of female athletes.

    b. personal experience.

    c. scientific research.

    d. statistics and expert opinion.

_____ 5. Which one of the following sentences contains an example of **informal** language?

    a. Merchant passes it, breathing hard but solid.

    b. And then there are the real lunatics.

    c. Extreme athletes, in some form, go back to the beginning.

    d. For some reason, men are doing stuff like this lately.

_____ 6. Which of the following is a **fact**, not an opinion?

    a. It's as if all men old enough to have watched Bo Jackson suddenly felt an innate responsibility to make him look like a wuss. (paragraph 2)

    b. The U.S. Adventure Racing Association, which didn't even exist until 1998, has gone from sanctioning thirteen races a year to more than four hundred . . ." (paragraph 3)

    c. And there's a bit of a midlife crisis here, too—instead of buying convertibles and trying to look comfortable buying pot again, men are getting outside. (paragraph 5)

    d. And with each mile they run, the greater their need becomes to huff out another. (paragraph 6)

G. Thinking Critically: Analyzing the Author's Message

Select the best answer.

_____ 1. With which of the following statements would the author of "Extreme Health" be most likely to _disagree_?

    a. Taking part in extreme sports makes men feel more alive.

    b. Men seem to have an innate desire to push themselves to achieve the "next milestone."

    c. Extreme sports may be an extension of the American tradition of exploration.

    d. Men consistently outperform women in Olympic events.

_____ 2. What is the author implying when he says, "and seriously, Troy" in paragraph 3?

    a. He is suggesting that Troy Farrar is not really the president of the U.S. Adventure Racing Association.

    b. He is hinting that Troy Farrar does not take part in any extreme sporting events.

    c. He is suggesting that Troy Farrar is greatly exaggerating the number of people who take part in extreme sporting events.

    d. He is implying that The U.S. Adventure Racing Association does not sanction nearly as many events as Troy Farrar claims it does.

_____ 3. In paragraph 5, the author states that extreme athletics, in some form or another, "go back to the beginning." What does he mean?

    a. Athletes must take part in fairly easy competitions before they can take on more challenging competitions.

    b. Those who choose to participate in extreme competitions usually show an interest in athletics when they are young children.

    c. Extreme athletic competitions aren't a modern phenomenon; they actually go back to the beginning of humanity.

    d. People who participate in events like Death Race and Tough Mudder are born with genetic sequences that give them the endurance they need to take part in those events.

_____ 4. The author ends the article by saying "Also, make sure you have a yellow whistle, just in case" (paragraph 10). What is he suggesting?

    a. Blowing on a whistle can help an athlete control his or her breathing better.

    b. People who push themselves physically should make sure they have a way to call for help if they get into a situation they cannot handle.

    c. A yellow whistle means that the athlete should proceed with caution, while blowing a green whistle means the athlete is making good progress.

    d. Life is not all about athletic competitions; music is also important, as are other hobbies.

WRITING IN RESPONSE TO THE READING

H. Writing a Summary

Complete the following summary of the reading by filling in the missing words. Remember that a summary should cover all of the author's main points.

In "Extreme Health," the author Peter Martin begins by describing _____ _____, the co-owner of a gym who works out by climbing up and down a staircase with a _____-pound weight around his chest. Merchant is just one example of a trend in society: intense, extreme _____ _____. The number of these competitions, and the number of men participating in them, has grown substantially over the past few years. Some men, such as Rodney Cutler and _____, push themselves so hard that the author questions their _____. Martin provides several possible explanations for the major increase in extreme-sports participation. First, men just like to find out if they are physically capable of handling the sport. Second, some men are experiencing a _____ crisis and try to invigorate themselves by going outdoors. Third, extreme sports may be an extension of the American spirit of _____. Fourth, research has suggested that extreme

sporting competitions may be as old as humanity, an extension of the
_____ impulse. Fifth, men now live in
_____ and work in non-physical jobs, so they find ways
to be more physical. Finally, some men just want to push themselves to achieve
more and more, to get to the next _____ in their set of
physical goals, and to have a feeling of _____ when they
finish a very challenging physical contest. The author closes with some advice:
Find your _____, expand them, and make sure you have
a back-up plan in case of an emergency.

I. Writing Paragraphs

*Write a well-developed paragraph in response to one of the following writing
prompts. As part of this assignment you will need to follow the writing process
outlined here:*

- Use a prewriting strategy to generate ideas
- Complete a guided outline
- Write a rough draft
- Complete a peer revision guide
- Write a final draft using proper MLA format

1. Write a paragraph in which you summarize the likely reasons that men take
   part in extreme sporting events.

2. The men whose experiences are discussed in the reading—Mark Merchant,
   Rodney Cutler, Todd Carmichael—all like a challenge. What do you feel is
   the biggest challenge you face in your daily life? Write a paragraph answering this question.

3. In "Extreme Health," the author addresses the reasons why some men participate in extreme sports, but he fails to mention women. Some women
   also participate in extreme sports. Write a paragraph in which you address
   the reasons why some women participate in extreme sports.

4. Suppose someone offers you a million dollars if you are able to complete
   the Death Race. Do some online research to find out what the Death Race
   involves, and then write a paragraph in which you discuss what you would
   do to prepare for the competition.

5. The reading quotes Jack Raglin, a sports psychologist, who studies the connection between exercise and mental health. How do you think the two are connected? Write a paragraph in which you explore the connections between exercise and mental health. How and why does exercise make a person feel better?

6. Many extreme sports enthusiasts are daredevils. Do you know anyone like this? Write a paragraph describing this person and what he or she does to qualify himself or herself as a daredevil.

J. Working Collaboratively

1. **Thinking Personally** Create a list of the 5 greatest accomplishments of your life. Then pair up with a classmate. Share your lists of accomplishments, and ask your partner questions about the individual points on his or her list to get more information about him or her. Be prepared to introduce your partner to the class without reading his or her list.

2. **Thinking Deeply** After reading "Extreme Health," break into groups and discuss the following questions:

   Be prepared to report to the class on your discussion.

   - What is the author's attitude toward the extreme sports enthusiasts that he writes about? What is your attitude toward them?
   - Do you agree with the reasons the author gives for men taking part in extreme sporting events? What could be some other reasons?
   - Do you consider extreme spots enthusiasts to be non-conformists? Why or why not? What "rules" are they breaking?
   - Is the author qualified to write on the topic? Why or why not? How do his own experiences inform the article?
   - Why do you think the author failed to mention women in this article?

3. **Thinking "Extremely"** In a small group of your peers, brainstorm a list of extreme sports not mentioned in the article. Here are a few to get you started: abseiling, bungee jumping, hang gliding, parachuting, snowboarding. After brainstorming the list, each of you will choose an extreme sport to investigate further outside of class. You may use the Internet for this activity. When you return to class, you will bring with you a written paragraph about the sport. Be prepared to also share what you have learned with your group members.

4. **Thinking Visually** What characteristics do all extreme sports enthusiasts have in common? Working with a partner, create a graphic organizer (a web) that contains as many characteristics as you can think of. The design of your visual may be as creative as you want it to be.

5. **Thinking Creatively** Working with a partner, compose an interview with a make-believe extreme sports enthusiast (any sport you choose). You will want to include questions that address the sport itself, the reasons that the person participates in the sport, and the possible consequences of the sport. Once you have created the dialogue, you will then prepare to present this interview to the class. One of you will be the extreme sports enthusiast, and the other will be the interviewer.

The Mad Potter of Biloxi
Bruce Watson

DRE 097   PRE-READING

Source and Context

Bruce Watson is a writer, a historian, a journalist, and the author of three books on American History. The selection that follows is an article that he wrote for *Smithsonian* magazine. It was written to coincide with the opening of the Ohr Museum (called the Ohr-O'Keefe Museum of Art) in Biloxi, Mississippi.

A Note on the Reading

Read the selection to understand how an eccentric man who endured years of rejection and scorn became a famous American potter long after his death.

Previewing the Reading

Using the steps listed on page 4, preview the reading selection. When you have finished, answer the following questions.

1. In what city and state did the potter live? _____

2. What is the potter's name? _____

3. During what period of time did the potter create his pots? _____

4. After the potter achieved fame, he was referred to as _____
_____ and a _____.

Using Prior Knowledge

Think of some people in your life who are different from the norm. How are they different? Do they seem to enjoy being different? Are they confident in themselves or do they lack confidence? What do other people think of them?

DURING READING

Reading Tip

As you read, think about the people you know who just don't seem to fit in. Read carefully as the author presents a man who was misunderstood and characterized as both a genius and a madman. Follow along as the author traces the mad

potter's evolution from a local eccentric artist to "the Picasso of art p...
sure to highlight and annotate as you read. Also, review the writing assig...
at the end of the selection before you begin reading. This information will h...
with writing annotations that will be useful in responding to the various writing
prompts.

The Mad Potter of Biloxi

Bruce Watson

1   Riding the train south through the deep pine woods of Mississippi, tourists to the Gulf Coast came to Biloxi for sunshine and surf. Along with its beaches, the little town had its own opera house, white streets paved with crushed oyster shells, and fine seafood. Yet back in the 1880s, there were no casinos in Biloxi as there are now, and not much to do besides swim, stroll, and eat shrimp. Then the town added a new tourist attraction, one based on genius or madness, depending on your point of view.

2   Just a few blocks from shore, a five-story wooden pagoda labeled "BILOXI ART POTTERY" towered above the train tracks that ran along Delauney Street. Approaching it, a visitor saw hand-lettered signs; one read: "Get a Biloxi Souvenir Before the Potter Dies, or Gets a Reputation." Another proclaimed: "Unequaled, Unrivaled, Undisputed—Greatest Art Potter on Earth." Stepping inside, a curious tourist found a studio overflowing with pots, but not your ordinary garden variety. These pots featured rims that had been crumpled like the edges of a burlap bag. Alongside them were mugs and vases warped as if melted in the kiln. And colors! In contrast to the boring beiges of Victorian ceramics, these works exploded with color: livid red juxtaposed with gun metal grey, olive green splattered across bright orange, and royal blue mottled on a mustard yellow. The entire studio seemed like some mad potter's hallucination, and standing in the middle of it was the mad potter himself.

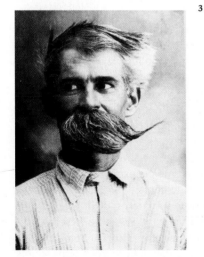

3   Viewed from across his cluttered shop, George Ohr didn't look mad. With his huge arms folded across his dirty apron, Ohr looked more like a blacksmith than a potter. But when he approached, the customer caught a glimpse of the 18-inch mustache wrapped around his cheeks and tied behind his head. And there was something in his eyes—dark, piercing, and wild—that suggested, at the very least, a highly refined eccentricity. If the pots weren't proof of the potter's lunacy, his prices were. This nut wanted $25 for a crumpled pot with wacky handles. "No two alike," he boasted, but to most customers each looked as weird as the next. And as the new century began, thousands of the colorful, misshapen works sat on shelves, leaving the potter mad at a world that didn't appreciate him. "I have a notion . . . that I am a mistake," Ohr wrote in 1901. Yet he predicted, "When I am gone, my work will be praised, honored, and cherished; it will come."

Reprinted from *Smithsonian Magazine*, September 2004, by permission of the author.

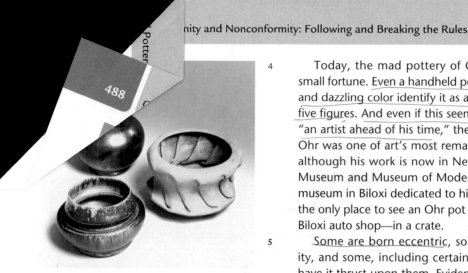

Courtesy of AAA Photostock/Alamy.

4   Today, the mad pottery of George Ohr sells for a small fortune. Even a handheld pot, if its eccentric shape and dazzling color identify it as an original Ohr, sells for five figures. And even if this seems just another story of "an artist ahead of his time," the resurgence of George Ohr was one of art's most remarkable comebacks. For although his work is now in New York's Metropolitan Museum and Museum of Modern Art and in an entire museum in Biloxi dedicated to his work, until the 1970s the only place to see an Ohr pot was in a barn behind a Biloxi auto shop—in a crate.

5   Some are born eccentric, some achieve eccentricity, and some, including certain rock stars and artists, have it thrust upon them. Evidence suggests that Ohr's "madness" was a combination of the three. Born in Biloxi just before the Civil War, he was the second of five children—"3 hens, 1 rooster and a duck," he remembered. Ohr considered himself the duck, a mischievous oddball who was "always in hot aqua." After elementary school, he spent a single season at a German academy in New Orleans before dropping out. He apprenticed as a file cutter, a tinker, and a blacksmith in his father's shop, then put out to sea—once. Finally, at 22, he found a career when a friend invited him to come to New Orleans and learn to be a potter. "When I found the potter's **wheel** I felt it all over like a wild duck in water," he remembered. After learning how to "boss a little piece of clay into a gallon jug," Ohr set out on his own to see what other potters were doing. In the early 1880s, he hitchhiked through 16 states, dropping in on ceramics studios, shows, and museums. When he came home, he had absorbed the essence of America's art pottery movement, which was beginning to do more with clay than make simple pots and vases. In Cincinnati's Rookwood studio and a few others, potters were decorating their wares based on Japanese or French ceramics, adding animals, birds, and bright floral designs. Ohr returned to Biloxi in 1883, determined to be not just a potter but an art potter.

6   While living with his parents, Ohr built his pottery shop, even crafting his own wheel and **kiln**, all for $26.80. Then he went looking for clay. Heading up the muddy Tchoutacabouffa River, Ohr spent days digging the red clay along its banks, loading it into his barge and floating it back home. To this day, potters suspect there was something special in that clay which enabled Ohr to **throw** wafer thin pots with a delicacy no one has ever equaled. Yet there was nothing special about Ohr's own pottery at first. Working in his small shop, he supported his family by churning out chimney flue pipes, planters, and ordinary pitchers. He amused some customers with clay "brothel tokens" imprinted with lewd rebuses; he shocked others with an occasional pot shaped like a vagina. Yet in his spare time, he experimented with the most shocking pots of all, the ones he called his "mud babies." Brooding over them "with the same tenderness a mortal child awakens in its parents," Ohr created fantastic shapes glazed with colors that seemed just plain crazy. When he took his mud babies to exhibitions in New Orleans and Chicago, they sold poorly, if at all, making Ohr feel even more like a mistake. But back home in Biloxi, humorous signs for his

wheel
a revolving disc on which the potter molds the clay

kiln
a furnace used to fire pottery

to throw
to shape on a potter's wheel

"Pot-Ohr-E" gave Ohr a reputation as an eccentric whose shop was worth a visit, if only for a laugh.

7   Potters say that fire adds devilish details to their work. No matter how carefully one throws a piece of ceramics, a kiln's inferno causes chemical glazes to erupt in surprising colors. For Ohr, fire was the catalyst to creativity. At 2 a.m. on October 12, 1894, Biloxi's Bijou Oyster Saloon caught fire, and the blaze spread quickly through downtown. It raged through the Opera House, several cottages, Ohr's mother's grocery and his father's blacksmith shop. Finally, it gutted the Pot-Ohr-E. The next day, Ohr picked through the ashes to dig out the charred remains of his "killed babies." He kept them for the rest of his life. When asked why, he responded, "Did you ever hear of a mother so inhuman that she would cast off her deformed child?" A loan enabled the potter to rebuild his shop, adding its telltale pagoda, and like a glaze that turns an astonishing magenta when fired, he emerged from the tragedy determined to make pottery as distinctive and original as George Edgar Ohr himself. "I am the apostle of individuality," he said, "the brother of the human race, but I must be myself, and I want every vase of mine to be itself."

8   In both museums and in private collections, nearly every Ohr pot is dated to the same short period—1895–1905. During this decade, Ohr labored at a feverish pace, turning out thousands of amazing, outrageous, and just plain wonderful pots, "no two alike." Even as **Cézanne** was breaking up the plane of the painter's canvas, Ohr was shattering the conventions of ceramics. He made pitchers whose open tops resembled yawning mouths; he threw slim, multi-tiered vases with serpentine handles; he lovingly shaped cups into symmetrical forms, then crumpled them as if to thumb his nose at the art world. He fired his works into kaleidoscopic colors that only a few years later would be called *fauve*, French for the "wild" hues of **Matisse** and other **Fauvists**. And almost a decade before the **Cubists** added print to their canvases, Ohr scrawled on his ceramics with a pin. On an umbrella stand he created for the Smithsonian in 1900, Ohr etched a long, rambling letter, adding a rambling salutation on its base that concluded:

> Mary had a little lamb
> "Pot-Ohr-E-George has (HAD) a
> little Pottery "Now" where is the Boy
> that stood in the Burning Deck.
> "This Pot is Here," and I am the
> Potter Who was
> G.E. Ohr.

9   Ohr also stepped up his self-promotion. Crafting his own image, he billed himself as Biloxi's "**Ohrmer Khayam**," and George E. Ohr, M.D.—the M.D., he explained, stood for "Mud Dauber." Signs outside his shop unabashedly proclaimed "Greatest Art Potter on Earth—You Prove the Contrary." As eccentric in private as in public, Ohr papered the parlor of his home in gaudy patchwork patterns. He and his wife, whom he called "my darling Josie," named their first two children Ella and Asa; each died in infancy. Then, noting that his own initials—G.E.O.—were the first three letters of his name, Ohr saddled his next seven kids with the same gimmick, naming

Cezanne
a famous 19th century French painter

Matisse
a famous 20th century French painter and sculptor

Fauvists
a group of artists who painted bold, distorted images

Cubists
a group of early 20th century artists who favored form more than color

Omar Khayyam
an ancient Persian poet

them Leo, Lio, Zio, Oto, Clo, Ojo, and Geo. He often stayed up late nights playing with rhymes, and in a local photography studio, he twisted his mustache and face to produce some of the wackiest portraits ever taken.

10   Locals were not amused, and many considered their native mud dauber certifiably insane. In promotion as in ceramics, however, Ohr was just ahead of his time. Decades before **Salvador Dalí** began his self-aggrandizing antics, Ohr asked a reporter, "You think I am crazy, don't you?" Assuming a sober demeanor, the "mad" potter confided, "I found out a long time ago that it paid me to act this way." It did not pay him well, however. Ohr was a notoriously bad businessman. He would never interrupt a discussion of his art pottery to sell his practical wares. He offered his favorite pots at shocking prices because he simply could not bear to part with them. Once or twice, when a customer actually bought one, Ohr chased him down Delauney Street, trying to talk him out of the purchase. Such whims kept Ohr's business in the red, yet he didn't seem to care. "Every genius is in debt," he said.

11   By the turn of the century, Ohr had earned a begrudging acceptance as an American original. A survey of ceramics in 1901 called his pottery "in some respects, one of the most interesting in the United States." Ohr exhibited his works around the country and in Paris, yet the prizes always went to more traditional pottery. Ohr's only medal, a silver, came at the 1904 Louisiana Purchase Centennial Exhibition in St. Louis. Still, he did not sell a single piece there. Even his few admirers misunderstood him. Praise came more often for his colors, which Ohr considered an accident enhanced by fire, than his shapes: "Colors or quality count nothing in my creations!," Ohr fumed, "God put no color or quality in souls." Determined to show his forte, he began making unglazed pots in even stranger contours.

12   Avant-garde critics might praise him, but far more common were the huffy dismissals. Staid critics said Ohr's "deliberately distorted" works displayed an utter lack "of good proportion, of grace, and of dignity." Looking to the future for acceptance, Ohr announced he would no longer sell his works piece by piece but would "dispose of the whole collection to one creature or one country." If few were interested in single pots, however, no one was interested in thousands. Ohr remained determined to get his due. When a New Orleans museum accepted just a dozen of 50 pieces he sent them, he told the curator to "send it all back immediately!" Once in a fit of rage he gathered a shovel, lantern, and bag of pots, then rowed deep into Biloxi's Back Bay to bury his treasure like some pirate. If he left a map, it was probably burned by his son Lio who, one evening after his father's death, torched all his papers, including the secret recipes to his lovely glazes. Ohr's buried treasure is still in the Back Bay—somewhere.

13   In 1907, claiming he hadn't sold one of his mud babies in more than 20 years, Ohr closed his shop. Though just 50, he never threw another pot. Having inherited a comfortable sum when his parents died, he devoted the rest of his life to enhancing his reputation as a local loon. He let his beard grow long and white, then posed as Moses. During Biloxi's Mardi Gras, he roamed the streets robed as Father Time. In his final years, he could be seen racing his motorcycle along the beach, his white hair and beard flying. He often spoke in a disjointed stream of consciousness: "We are living in an age of wheels—more wheels, and wheels within wheels—and machine art works—is a fake and fraud of the deepest die." Rejected yet confident that his time would come, Ohr died of throat cancer in 1918. His pottery, some 7,000 pieces in

Salvador Dalí
a famous
eccentric 20th
century Spanish
painter

crates, remained in the attic above his sons' auto repair shop. Every now and then, a few kids carrying BB guns would sneak into the shop, steal a few pots and take them out for target practice, but the rest just sat there gathering a coating of dust and oil.

14   A half-century later, James Carpenter, an antiques dealer from New Jersey, was making his annual winter tour of the Gulf Coast. Carpenter wasn't looking for pottery; he was shopping for old car parts. One sweltering summer afternoon in 1968, he stopped at Ohr Boys Auto Repair in Biloxi. While he was browsing, Ojo Ohr, then in his 70s, approached Carpenter's wife, who sat in the car reading. In his slow Mississippi drawl, Ojo asked, "Would y'all like to see some of my Daddy's pottery?" Carpenter rolled his eyes as if to suggest they had to be going, but his wife said, "Sure." Soon the Carpenters were trudging behind Ojo, past the rusted fenders and discarded hubcaps, to a back barn. Ohr's son opened the doors to reveal the most amazing collection of pottery in the history of American ceramics. Several pieces were set out on tables but the rest filled crates stacked to the 12-foot ceiling. A few had been cleaned of their greasy film; catching the sunlight, they sparkled like the day Ohr gave them life.

15   Carpenter had never heard of Ohr—few outside Biloxi had. Yet he recognized the beauty of the work, and so did Ohr's son. When Carpenter reached for a pot to pick it up, "Ojo chewed me all out," he recalled: "Nobody handles my Daddy's pottery!' Ojo said." But with care and permission, Carpenter examined a few pots, wondering if he might be able to sell them, and finally, he decided to take a gamble. He offered $15,000—about two bucks a pot—for the entire lot. Ojo left to consult with his brother and came back shaking his head; he wanted $50,000. Carpenter departed, promising to contact the Ohr brothers later. When he returned the following summer with $50,000, Ojo had upped the price to $1.5 million. After three more summers of negotiations, for a price rumored to be closer to the lower figure, Carpenter took Ohr's treasures back to New Jersey where they began trickling into the marketplace.

16   The art world had since caught up to Ohr. During the 1950s, a school of Abstract Expressionist ceramics had flowered, creating free-form works that looked more like sculpture than pottery. Still, Ohr's reputation grew slowly. Artists, including Jasper Johns and Andy Warhol, bought his pots, as did several collectors, but Smithsonian's curator of ceramics protested Ohr's inclusion in a major show claiming he was "just plain hokey." Only in 1984, when Ohr pots appeared in paintings by Johns at the Castelli Gallery in New York did the praise and honor begin to flow. One-man shows followed. Hollywood collectors, including Steven Spielberg and Jack Nicholson, entered the market. Today, the same pots scorned a century ago sell for a few thousand to $100,000. Back when such prices sounded insane, Ohr had often exasperated exhibition curators who asked him for an exact value of his pots. "Worth their weight in gold," he answered. Now, it seems he was right.

Pablo Picasso 17   No longer dismissed as mad, Ohr has been hailed as "the **Picasso** of art pottery"
a famous 20th   and a "clay prophet." His resurrection proves that madness, like beauty, is in the eye of
century Spanish   the beholder. But then, he always knew that, and so did any visitors to his shop who
painter and   were paying strict attention. On their way out of the cluttered, crowded studio, they
sculptor   passed one final hand-lettered sign. It suggested neither madness nor genius but the self-confidence that helped a mad potter endure decades of rejection. Translated for its Latin, the sign read: "A Masterpiece, second to none, The Best; Therefore, I am!"

UNDERSTANDING AND ANALYZING THE READING

A. Building Vocabulary

Context

Using context and a dictionary if necessary, determine the meaning of each word as it is used in the selection.

_____ 1. juxtaposed (paragraph 2)
    a. hidden under
    b. placed next to
    c. blended with
    d. tinted with

_____ 2. eccentricity (paragraph 3)
    a. peculiarity
    b. upbringing
    c. sensitivity
    d. appreciation

_____ 3. lunacy (paragraph 3)
    a. insanity
    b. talent
    c. originality
    d. individuality

_____ 4. resurgence (paragraph 4)
    a. rising again
    b. story
    c. emergence
    d. success

_____ 5. rebuses (paragraph 6)
    a. colors
    b. metals
    c. sayings
    d. symbols

_____ 6. lewd (paragraph 6)
    a. polite
    b. colorful
    c. obscene
    d. concise

_____ 7. serpentine (paragraph 8)
    a. short
    b. matching
    c. curvy
    d. multiple

_____ 8. forte (paragraph 11)
    a. stubborn side
    b. strong point
    c. true genius
    d. individuality

_____ 9. staid (paragraph 12)
    a. solemn
    b. soothing
    c. opposing
    d. hostile

_____ 10. exasperated (paragraph 16)
    a. confused
    b. confronted
    c. ignored
    d. annoyed

Word Parts

> ### A REVIEW OF PREFIXES AND SUFFIXES
>
> **RE-** means action done over again.
> **MIS-** means wrong or incorrectly.
> **-ION** means action or condition.
> **-ANCE** is used to form a noun from an adjective or a verb.

Use your knowledge of word parts and the review above to fill in the blanks in the following sentences.

1. The *resurgence* (paragraph 4) of a career means that it has become successful _____.

2. To say that George Ohr was *misunderstood* (paragraph 11) by many people indicates that many people understood Ohr _____.

3. By the beginning of the twentieth century, some people began to accept Ohr. Their _____ (the noun form of accept) was not whole-hearted. (paragraph 11)

4. The mad potter endured years of *rejection* (paragraph 17). This means that he was _____. (the verb form of rejection)

B. Understanding the Thesis and Other Main Ideas

Select the best answer.

_____ 1. Which of the following best states the thesis or central thought of the reading?
   a. Oftentimes, fame does not come to a person until after he/she is dead.
   b. People who choose to live an eccentric life are often misunderstood.
   c. Success cannot be achieved without persistence.
   d. The life of an artist is a lonely one.

_____ 2. The topic of paragraph 5 is
   a. Ohr's early life.
   b. 3 hens, 1 rooster, and a duck.
   c. where Ohr got the inspiration for his pottery.
   d. Ohr's formal schooling.

_____ 3. The main idea of paragraph 7 is found in the

    a. first sentence.

    b. third sentence.

    c. fourth sentence.

    d. last sentence.

_____ 4. What is the implied main idea of paragraph 2?

    a. Ohr was well respected in spite of his madness.

    b. Ohr was a non-conformist.

    c. The vision for Ohr's pottery and studio came to him in a dream.

    d. Ohr did not have the money to produce fine pottery.

C. Identifying Details

Select the best answer.

_____ 1. According to the author, there are several ways to explain a person's eccentricity. The author cites all of the following *except*

    a. being born eccentric

    b. achieving eccentricity

    c. denying eccentricity

    d. having eccentricity thrust upon oneself

_____ 2. To this day, what do potters think was the secret to the delicacy of Ohr's pots?

    a. the clay he used

    b. the water from the Tchoutacabouffa River

    c. the size of Ohr's hands

    d. the hand-crafted wheel and kiln that he used

_____ 3. Ohr referred to himself in all but one of the following ways. Which description of himself did Ohr **not** use?

    a. "Unequaled, Unrivaled, Undisputed—Greatest potter on Earth."

    b. "I have a notion . . . that I am a mistake."

    c. ". . . I felt . . . like a wild duck in water."

    d. "There is nothing special about my pottery."

D. Recognizing Methods of Organization and Transitions

Select the best answer.

_____ 1. The pattern of organization used in paragraph 3 is
   a. classification.
   b. illustration.
   c. comparison/contrast.
   d. process.

_____ 2. The organizational pattern used in paragraph 5 is
   a. chronological order.
   b. listing.
   c. cause and effect.
   d. comparison/contrast.

_____ 3. The signal word or phrase that provides a clue to the organizational pattern used in paragraph 14 is
   a. in his slow Mississippi drawl.
   b. several pieces were set out.
   c. then in his 70s.
   d. while he was browsing.

E. Reading and Thinking Visually

Select the best answer.

_____ 1. The author likely included the photo on page 487 in order to
   a. show the resemblance Ohr bore to Moses.
   b. show the effects of living a life of rejection.
   c. underscore Ohr's eccentricity.
   d. prove Ohr's lunacy.

F. Figuring Out Implied Meanings

Indicate whether each statement is true (T) or false (F).

_____ 1. The author believes that Ohr's pottery is highly overrated and overpriced.

_____ 2. The author believes that Ohr's eccentricity contributed to his success.

_____ 3. The author implies that lack of self-confidence led Ohr to stray from the norm.

_____ 4. According to the author, Ohr's sons were protective of their deceased father's pottery.

_____ 5. The author suggests that Ohr worked hard at appearing to be crazy.

_____ 6. The author implies that Ohr's pieces of pottery were as unique and eccentric as he was.

G. Thinking Critically: Analyzing the Author's Technique

Select the best answer.

_____ 1. The author's primary purpose in "The Mad Potter of Biloxi" is to

a. show the relationship between genius and insanity.

b. show the consequences that come when one chooses to live life outside the norms of society.

c. help people to better understand artists.

d. document the life of George Ohr, an eccentric yet great American art potter.

_____ 2. Overall, the author's tone in this selection can best be described as

a. sarcastic.

b. sympathetic.

c. matter of fact.

d. persuasive.

_____ 3. Which of the following is a fact, not an opinion?

a. "Viewed from across his cluttered shop, George Ohr didn't look mad." (paragraph 3)

b. "While living with his parents, Ohr built his pottery shop, even crafting his own wheel and kiln, all for $26.80." (paragraph 6)

c. "Now, it seems he was right." (paragraph 16)

d. "His resurrection proves that madness, like beauty, is in the eye of the beholder." (paragraph 17)

_____ 4. Which of the following is not a piece of evidence used by the author to support his thesis or central thought?

a. quotes from George Ohr

b. examples of the behavior of George Ohr

c. appraisals conducted by art experts

d. descriptions of Ohr's art pottery

_____ 5. Which of the following phrases is an example of a metaphor?

     a. "The entire studio seemed like some mad potter's hallucination . . ." (paragraph 2)

     b. ". . . I am a mistake." (paragraph 3)

     c. "He apprenticed as a file cutter . . ." (paragraph 5)

     d. ". . . I felt it all over like a wild duck in water." (paragraph 5)

_____ 6. Which of the following statements is an example of irony?

     a. "Once in a fit of rage he gathered a shovel, lantern, and bag of pots, then rowed deep into Biloxi's Back Bay to bury his treasure like some pirate." (paragraph 12)

     b. "His pottery, some 7,000 pieces in crates, remained in the attic above his sons' auto repair shop." (paragraph 13)

     c. "Locals were not amused, and many considered their native mud dauber certifiably insane." (paragraph 10)

     d. "This nut wanted $25 for a crumpled pot with wacky handles." (paragraph 3)

_____ 7. Select the sentence that best explains the figurative expression "mud babies." (paragraph 6)

     a. Ohrs "mud babies" were small pots that resembled the color of mud.

     b. The clay that Ohr used was the consistency and color of mud.

     c. The care that Ohr took in creating pots out of clay was like that of a parent caring for a child.

     d. Ohr's creative process gave rise to a new generation of potters called "mud babies."

_____ 8. Which of the following sentences contains an example of **informal** language?

     a. "He let his beard grow long and white, then posed as Moses." (paragraph 13)

     b. ". . . but Smithsonian's curator of ceramics protested Ohr's inclusion in a major show claiming he was just plain hokey." (paragraph 16)

     c. ". . . Back when prices sounded insane, Ohr had often exasperated exhibition curators who asked him for an exact value of his pots." (paragraph 16)

     d. "It suggested neither madness nor genius but the self-confidence that helped a mad potter endure decades of rejection." (paragraph 17)

H. Thinking Critically: Analyzing the Author's Message

Select the best answer.

_____ 1. Which of the following is an accurate statement?

    a. The author believes that Ohr's feelings of being odd originated with his birth order; he was the second of five children.

    b. The author believes that George Ohr's madness at the beginning of his life was an act, but as Ohr grew older, his pretend madness became true insanity.

    c. The author believes that George Ohr's success was at least partially due to his courage and self-confidence.

    d. The author believes that Ohr was motivated by money and fame.

_____ 2. In paragraph 17, the author states that "... Ohr has been hailed as a clay prophet." Which of the following Ohr quotes most closely resembles a prophetic statement?

    a. "When I am gone, my work will be praised, honored, and cherished; it will come."

    b. "I am the apostle of individuality."

    c. "I found out a long time ago that it paid me to act this way."

    d. "God put no color or quality in souls."

_____ 3. In paragraph 2, what does the author mean when he writes "The entire studio seemed like some mad potter's hallucination ..."?

    a. No two pieces of pottery in the studio were the same.

    b. The observer's senses were bombarded with bizarre colors and shapes.

    c. The vision for the design of the studio came to Ohr in a dream.

    d. There was so much clutter in the studio that the observer had a hard time focusing.

_____ 4. "The Mad Potter of Biloxi" can be interpreted as

    a. biased.

    b. propaganda.

    c. name calling.

    d. objective.

_____ 5. The intended audience for this article is

    a. potters and sculptors.

    b. art critics.

    c. a general audience.

    d. people from Mississippi.

WRITING IN RESPONSE TO THE READING

I. Writing a Summary

Write a summary of the reading (paragraphs 1–17) using the following guidelines:

- Be sure to use your own words, not those of the author
- Write an opening statement that states the author's main point.
- Include the author's most important supporting ideas.
- Include key terms, important concepts and principles.
- Present the ideas in the order in which they appear in the reading.

J. Analyzing the Issue

1. What contemporary issue is the author discussing in this reading? Phrase the issue as a question.

2. What is the author's background? Is he qualified to write about the topic? Why or why not?

3. Does the source from which this reading is taken help you determine the credibility of the information presented? Do you find any bias in the selection? Please explain both of your answers.

4. Evaluate the reading on the following criteria:

   a. Is the reading timely?

   b. Has the author provided sufficient evidence to support his main ideas? What other types of evidence might he provide to strengthen his claims?

   c. Does the author offer opposing viewpoints? Overall, how would you summarize the author's viewpoints on the issues discussed in the reading?

   d. What assumptions (either stated or implied) do you find in the reading?

   e. Does the article offer any emotional appeals? If so, identify them and evaluate their fairness.

5. Identify specific sentences and/or paragraphs in which the author states his value system.

K. Writing Paragraphs and Essays

*Write a **well-developed** paragraph or essay in response to one of the following writing prompts. As part of this assignment you will need to follow the writing process outlined here:*

- Use a prewriting strategy to generate ideas
- Complete a guided outline
- Write a rough draft
- Complete a peer revision guide
- Write a final draft using proper MLA format

1. The author implies that George Ohr's self-confidence was his secret weapon; it helped him to endure a lifetime of ridicule. What character trait is your secret weapon, and how has it helped you thus far in your life? Write a paragraph or essay in which you define your secret weapon and explain how it has helped you.

2. George Ohr predicted, "When I am gone, my work will be praised, honored, and cherished; it will come." How do you want to be remembered when you are gone? What legacy will you leave to your family and the world? Write a paragraph or essay in which you answer the question and provide details to support your answer.

3. Do you consider yourself to be a conformist or a nonconformist? Write a paragraph or essay in which you explain your position and give examples to support it.

4. Author Mignon McLaughlin once said that "Every society honors its live conformists and its dead troublemakers." Do you agree or disagree with this statement? Write a paragraph or essay in which you state your position and support it with examples.

5. George Ohr was misunderstood by both his admirers and his critics. Can you relate to this aspect of his life? How have you been misunderstood in life, and how has it affected you? Write a paragraph or essay in which you discuss either the causes or the effects of being misunderstood.

L. Working Collaboratively

1. **Thinking Deeply** After reading "The Mad Potter of Biloxi," break into groups and discuss the following questions:

- What societal rules did George Ohr break?
- What were the consequences of his actions for himself and his family?
- What guided his behavior?
- Was he happy with himself?
- What do you think was the source of his self-confidence?

- Was he a genius or a madman or both?
- What type of relationship do you think he had with his wife and his children?
- What do you think George Ohr wanted more than anything else in the world?
- What can you take away from this reading selection? How will it make a difference in your life? How will it make a difference in the way you view other people?

Select someone in your group to record the major points of your discussion so that you will be well prepared to report to the class.

2. **Thinking Visually** Working with a partner, create a bumper sticker that summarizes a lesson you have learned from this article. Your creation should feature both a graphic and a slogan. You may design it by hand, or you may use the computer. After you have designed the bumper sticker, write a paragraph explaining it.

3. **Thinking about Conformity** Think of a song, a movie, a book, a television show, or a quote that addresses the topic of conformity or nonconformity. You may use the Internet to search this topic if you need to. Bring your example to class and share it with a group of your peers. Be prepared to explain how your example addresses the topic.

4. **Thinking Creatively** Pair up with a partner and create an interview with George Ohr. One of you will be Ohr and the other will be the interviewer. You do not necessarily have to include only material from the reading selection. You also may include questions that the reading prompted. Your answers must be realistic and in keeping with Ohr's personality and beliefs. Be prepared to present your skit to the class.

SELECTION

12

Textbook Selection

Groups and Conformity

Michael R. Solomon

DRE 098   PRE-READING

Source and Context

The following reading is taken from a business textbook, *Consumer Behavior: Buying, Having, and Being*. Consumer behavior is often considered a subfield of psychology, and it is the study of how, when, and why people buy (or do not buy) products and services. The author, Michael R. Solomon, is Professor of Marketing and Director of the Center for Consumer Research at Saint Joseph's University.

A Note on the Reading

How do other people influence your decisions regarding what to buy? Read "Groups and Conformity" for some insight into this question.

Previewing the Reading

Using the steps listed on page 4, preview the reading selection. When you have finished, complete the following items.

1. This reading is about _____.

2. Indicate whether each statement is true (T) or false (F).

    _____ a. The term *reference group* is generally used to describe any external influence that provides social cues.

    _____ b. We are acquainted with the people in aspirational reference groups.

    _____ c. We tend to get away with less in a group setting.

Making Connections

How do you go about making decisions regarding what to buy? Does your process differ if you are buying something cheap (for example, gum) versus something more expensive (for example, a car)? If so, how?

Reading Tip

As you read, pay attention to the boldface terms, which indicate important concepts in the field of consumer behavior. Annotate while you read and note how each of these terms relates to your own life and experiences.

Groups and Conformity

Michael R. Solomon

1   Zachary leads a secret life. During the week, he is a straitlaced stock analyst for a major investment firm. He spends a big chunk of the week worrying about whether he'll have a job, so work is pretty stressful these days. However, his day job only pays the bills to finance his real passion: cruising on his Harley-Davidson Road Glide Custom. His Facebook posts are filled with lunchtime laments about how much he'd rather be out on the road (hopefully his boss won't try to friend him). Actually, Zach feels it's worth the risk: He's participating in Harley's free country social media promotion that encourages riders to post their stories ("freedom statements") on Facebook and Twitter to see if they'll include one of his posts on a Harley **banner ad**. His girlfriend worries a bit about his getting totaled in an accident, but Zach knows if he stays alert the only way that will probably happen is if he can't kick his habit of texting her while he's driving the bike.

banner ad
an Internet advertisement that appears across the top or bottom of a Web site

2   Come Friday evening, it's off with the Brooks Brothers suit and on with the black leather, as he trades in his Lexus for his treasured Harley. A dedicated member of HOG (Harley Owners Group), Zachary belongs to the "RUBs" (rich urban bikers) faction of Harley riders. Everyone in his group wears expensive leather vests with Harley insignias and owns customized "low riders." Just this week, Zach finally got his new Harley perforated black leather jacket at the company's Motorclothes Merchandise web page. As one of the Harley web pages observed, "it's one thing to have people buy your products. It's another thing to have them tattoo your name on their bodies." Zach had to restrain himself from buying more Harley stuff; there were vests, eyewear, belts, buckles, scarves, watches, jewelry, even housewares ("home is the road") for sale. He settled for

Courtesy of Ljupco Smokovski/Shutterstock.

a set of Harley salt-and-pepper shakers that would be perfect for his buddy Dan's new crib.

3   Zachary's experiences on social media platforms make him realize the lengths to which some of his fellow enthusiasts go to make sure others know they are hog riders. Two of his riding buddies are in a lively competition to be "mayor" of the local Harley dealership on **foursquare**, while many others tweet to inform people about a group ride that will occur later in the day—kind of a **flashmob** on wheels.

4   Zach spends a lot of money to outfit himself to be like the rest of the group, but it's worth it. He feels a real sense of brotherhood with his fellow RUBs. The group rides together in two-column formation to bike rallies that sometimes attract up to 300,000 cycle enthusiasts. What a sense of power he feels when they all cruise together—it's them against the world!

5   Of course, an added benefit is the business networking he's accomplished during his jaunts with his fellow professionals who also wait for the weekend to "ride on the wild side—these days it would be professional suicide to let your contacts get cold, and you can't just count on LinkedIn to stay in the loop."

foursquare
a social media Web site

flashmob
a large group of people who gather together spontaneously as a result of reading something on the Web

Reference Groups

6   Humans are social animals. We belong to groups, try to please others, and look to others' behavior for clues about what we should do in public settings. In fact, our desire to "fit in" or to identify with desirable individuals or groups is the primary motivation for many of our consumption behaviors. We may go to great lengths to please the members of a group whose acceptance we covet.

7   Zachary's biker group is an important part of his identity, and this membership influences many of his buying decisions. He has spent many thousands of dollars on parts and accessories since he became a RUB. His fellow riders bond via their consumption choices, so total strangers feel an immediate connection with one another when they meet. The publisher of *American Iron*, an industry magazine, observed, "You don't buy a Harley because it's a superior bike, you buy a Harley to be a part of a family."

8   Zachary doesn't model himself after just *any* biker—only the people with whom he really identifies can exert that kind of influence on him. For example, Zachary's group doesn't have much to do with outlaw clubs whose blue-collar riders sport big Harley tattoos. The members of his group also have only polite contact with "Ma and Pa" bikers, whose rides are the epitome of comfort and feature such niceties as radios, heated handgrips, and floorboards. Essentially, only the RUBs comprise Zachary's *reference group*.

9   A **reference group** is "an actual or imaginary individual or group conceived of [as] having significant relevance upon an individual's evaluations, aspirations, or behavior." Reference groups influence us in three ways: *informational, utilitarian,* and *value-expressive.* Table 1 describes these influences. In this chapter we'll focus on how other people, whether fellow bikers, coworkers, friends, family, or simply casual acquaintances, influence our purchase decisions. We'll consider how our group memberships shape our preferences because we want others to accept us or even because we mimic the actions of famous people we've never met. We'll also explore

TABLE 1 THREE FORMS OF REFERENCE GROUP INFLUENCE

Informational Influence	· The individual seeks information about various brands from an association of professionals or independent group of experts.
	· The individual seeks information from those who work with the product as a profession.
	· The individual seeks brand-related knowledge and experience (such as how Brand A's performance compares to Brand B's) from those friends, neighbors, relatives, or work associates who have reliable information about the brands.
	· The brand the individual selects is influenced by observing a seal of approval of an independent testing agency (such as Good Housekeeping).
	· The individual's observation of what experts do (such as observing the type of car that police drive or the brand of television that repairmen buy) influences his or her choice of a brand.
Utilitarian Influence	· So that he or she satisfies the expectations of fellow work associates, the individual's decision to purchase a particular brand is influenced by their preferences.
	· The individual's decision to purchase a particular brand is influenced by the preferences of people with whom he or she has social interaction.
	· The individual's decision to purchase a particular brand is influenced by the preferences of family members.
	· The desire to satisfy the expectations that others have of him or her has an impact on the individual's brand choice.
Value-Expressive Influence	· The individual feels that the purchase or use of a particular brand will enhance the image others have of him or her.
	· The individual feels that those who purchase or use a particular brand possess the characteristics that he or she would like to have.
	· The individual sometimes feels that it would be nice to be like the type of person that advertisements show using a particular brand.
	· The individual feels that the people who purchase a particular brand are admired or respected by others.
	· The individual feels that the purchase of a particular brand would help show others what he or she is or would like to be (such as an athlete, successful business person, good parent, etc.).

Source: Adapted from C. Whan Park and V. Parker Lessig, "Students and Housewives: Differences in Susceptibility to Reference Group Influence," *Journal of Consumer Research* 4 September 1977): 102. Copyright © 1977 JCR, Inc. Reprinted with permission of The University of Chicago Press.

why some people in particular affect our product preferences and how marketers find those people and enlist their support to persuade consumers to jump on the bandwagon.

When Are Reference Groups Important?

10   Recent research on smoking cessation programs powerfully illustrates the impact of reference groups. The study found that smokers tend to quit in groups: When one person quits, this creates a ripple effect that motivates others in his social network to give up the death sticks also. The researchers followed thousands of smokers and nonsmokers for more than 30 years, and they also tracked their networks of relatives, coworkers, and friends. They discovered that over the years, the smokers tended to cluster together (on average in groups of three). As the overall U.S. smoking rate declined dramatically during this period, the number of clusters in the sample decreased, but the remaining clusters stayed the same size; this indicated that people quit in groups rather than as individuals. Not surprisingly, some social connections were more powerful than others. A spouse who quit had a bigger impact than did a friend, whereas friends had more influence than siblings. Coworkers had an influence only in small firms where everyone knew one another.

11   Reference group influences don't work the same way for all types of products and consumption activities. For example, we're not as likely to take others' preferences into account when we choose products that are not very complex, that are low in perceived risk, or that we can try before we buy. In addition, knowing what others prefer may influence us at a general level (e.g., owning or not owning a computer, eating junk food versus health food), whereas at other times this knowledge guides the specific brands we desire within a product category (e.g., if we wear Levi's jeans versus Diesel jeans, or smoke Marlboro cigarettes rather than Virginia Slims).

12   Why are reference groups so persuasive? The answer lies in the potential power they wield over us. **Social power** is "the capacity to alter the actions of others." To the degree to which you are able to make someone else do something, regardless of whether they do it willingly, you have power over that person. The following classification of power bases helps us to distinguish among the reasons a person exerts power over another, the degree to which the influence is voluntary, and whether this influence will continue to have an effect even when the source of the power isn't around.

- **Referent power**—If a person admires the qualities of a person or a group, he tries to copy the referent's behaviors (e.g., choice of clothing, cars, leisure activities), just as Zack's fellow bikers affected his preferences. Prominent people in all walks of life affect our consumption behaviors by virtue of product endorsements (e.g., Lady Gaga for Polaroid), distinctive fashion statements (e.g., Kim Kardashian's displays of high-end designer clothing), or championing causes (e.g., Brad Pitt for UNICEF). **Referent power** is important to many marketing strategies because consumers voluntarily modify what they do and buy in order to identify with a referent.

Marketing Opportunity

A recent real-life experiment demonstrates the potential social value of harnessing reference group power. For years the Sacramento, California, Municipal Utility District tried various tactics to goad people into using less energy, such as awarding rebates to residents who buy energy-saving appliances. These efforts weren't working too well, so the district tried something new: It told people how their energy consumption compared to their neighbors' energy consumption. Thirty-five thousand randomly selected customers received statements that rated their energy use compared to 100 of their neighbors who lived in homes of a similar size. The relatively energy-efficient customers earned two smiley faces on their statements, and those whose usage was higher than average opened their envelopes to see frowns (they had to delete the frown part after customers got too upset with this criticism). After six months, the utility found that customers who had gotten the "frown" report cards reduced energy use by 2 percent compared to the rest of the district.

Some colleges employ a similar technique when they create a competition among dormitories to identify which residence hall does the best job of conserving resources. At Central College in Pella, Iowa, students who live in a "green dorm" can access a Web site that tells them how much power their specific suite uses compared to the other suites in the building. Peer pressure is powerful.

• • • • • • • • • • • • • • • • • •

- **Information power**—A person possesses **information power** simply because she knows something others would like to know. Editors of trade publications such as *Women's Wear Daily* often possess tremendous power because of their ability to compile and disseminate information that can make or break individual designers or companies. People with information power are able to influence consumer opinion by virtue of their (assumed) access to the "truth."

- **Legitimate power**—Sometimes we grant power by virtue of social agreements, such as the authority we give to police officers, soldiers, and yes, sometimes even professors. The **legitimate power** a uniform confers wields authority in consumer contexts, including teaching hospitals where medical students don white coats to enhance their standing with patients. Marketers "borrow" this form of power to influence consumers. For example, an ad that shows a model who wears a white doctor's coat adds an aura of legitimacy or authority to the presentation of the product ("I'm not a doctor, but I play one on TV").

- **Expert power**—To attract the casual Internet user, U.S. Robotics signed up British physicist Stephen Hawking to endorse its modems. A company executive commented, "We wanted to generate trust. So we found visionaries who use U.S. Robotics technology, and we let them tell the consumer how it makes their lives more productive." Hawking, who has Lou Gehrig's disease and speaks via a synthesizer, said in one TV spot, "My body may be stuck in this chair, but with the Internet my mind can go to the end of the universe." Hawking's **expert power** derives from the knowledge he possesses about a content area. This helps to explain the weight many of us assign to professional critics' reviews of restaurants, books, movies, and cars—even though, with the advent of blogs and open-source references such as Wikipedia, it's getting a lot harder to tell just who is really an expert!

- **Reward power**—A person or group with the means to provide positive reinforcement has **reward power**. The reward may be the tangible kind, such as the contestants on Survivor experience when their comrades vote them off the island. Or it can be more intangible, such as the approval the judges on *American Idol* deliver to contestants.

- **Coercive power**—We exert **coercive power** when we influence someone because of social or physical intimidation. A threat is often effective in the short term, but it doesn't tend to stick because we revert to our original behavior as soon as the bully leaves the scene. Fortunately, marketers rarely try to use

A physician has expert power, and a white coat reinforces this expertise by conferring legitimate power.

Courtesy of Jupiterimages/Thinkstock.

this type of power (unless you count those annoying calls from telemarketers!). However, we can see elements of this power base in intimidating salespeople who try to succeed with a "hard sell."

Types of Reference Groups

13   Although two or more people normally form a group, we often use the term *reference group* a bit more loosely to describe any external influence that provides social cues. The referent may be a cultural figure who has an impact on many people (e.g., Michelle Obama) or a person or group whose influence operates only in the consumer's immediate environment (e.g., Zachary's biker club). Reference groups that affect consumption can include parents, fellow motorcycle enthusiasts, the Tea Party, or even the Chicago Bears, the Dave Matthews Band, or Spike Lee.

14   Some people influence us simply because we feel similar to them. Have you ever experienced a warm feeling when you pull up at a light next to someone who drives the exact car as yours? One reason that we feel a bond with fellow brand users may be that many of us are a bit narcissistic (not you, of course); we feel an attraction to people and products that remind us of ourselves. That may explain why we feel a connection to others who happen to share our name. Research on the **name-letter effect** finds that, all things equal, we like others who share our names or even ini-

tials better than those who don't. When researchers look at large databases like Internet phone directories or Social Security records, they find that Johnsons are more likely to wed Johnsons, women named Virginia are more likely to live in (and move to) Virginia, and people whose surname is Lane tend to have addresses that include the word *lane*, not *street*. During the 2000 presidential campaign, people whose surnames began with B were more likely to contribute to George Bush, whereas those whose surnames began with G were more likely to contribute to Al Gore.

15   Obviously, some groups and individuals are more powerful than others and affect a broader range of our consumption decisions. For example, our parents may play a pivotal role as we form our values on many important issues, such as attitudes about marriage or where to go to college. We call this **normative influence**—that is, the reference group helps to set and enforce fundamental standards of conduct. In contrast, a Harley-Davidson club exerts **comparative influence** because it affects members' decisions about specific motorcycle purchases.

Brand Communities and Consumer Tribes

16   Before it released the popular Xbox game *Halo 2*, Bungie Studios put up a Web site to explain the story line. However, there was a catch: The story was written from the point of view of the Covenant (the aliens who are preparing to attack Earth in the game)—and in *their* language. Within 48 hours, avid gamers around the world shared information in gaming chat rooms to crack the code and translate the text. More than 1.5 million people preordered the game before its release. This cooperative effort illustrates a major trend in consumer behavior.

17   A **brand community** is a group of consumers who share a set of social relationships based on usage of or interest in a product. Unlike other kinds of communities, these members typically don't live near each other—except when they may meet for brief periods at organized events or **brandfests** that community-oriented companies such as Jeep or Harley-Davidson sponsor. These events help owners to "bond" with fellow enthusiasts and strengthen their identification with the product as well as with others they meet who share their passion. In virtually any category, you'll find passionate brand communities (in some cases devoted to brands that don't even exist anymore); examples include the 3Com Ergo Audrey (discontinued Internet appliance), Apple Newton (discontinued personal digital assistant), BMW MINI (car), Garmin (GPS device), Jones Soda (carbonated beverage), Lomo and Holga (cameras), Tom Petty and the Heartbreakers (musical group), StriVectin (cosmeceutical), and Xena: *Warrior Princess* (TV program).

18   Researchers find that people who participate in these events feel more positive about the products as a result, and this enhances brand loyalty. They tend to forgive product failures or lapses in service quality, and they're less likely to switch brands even if they learn that competing products are as good or better. Furthermore, these community members become emotionally involved in the company's welfare, and they often serve as brand missionaries as they carry its marketing message to others. Researchers find that brand community members do more than help the product build buzz; their inputs actually create added value for themselves and other members as they develop better ways to use and customize products. For example,

it's common for experienced users to coach "newbies" in ways to maximize their enjoyment of the product so that more and more people benefit from a network of satisfied participants. In other cases members benefit because their communities empower them to learn; for example, a study that looked at people who suffered from thyroid problems and who indicated they were uninformed and ill prepared to make decisions about their treatment later exhibited more active involvement and informed decision making after they participated in an online community with others who shared their health issues. Figure 1 demonstrates this process of **collective value creation**.

19   The notion of a **consumer tribe** is similar to the idea of a brand community; it is a group of people who share a lifestyle and can identify with each other because of a shared allegiance to an activity or a product. Although these tribes are often unstable and short-lived, at least for a time members identify with others through shared emotions, moral beliefs, styles of life, and of course the products they jointly consume as part of their tribal affiliation.

20   Some companies, especially those that are more youth-oriented, use a **tribal marketing strategy** that links their product to, say, a group of shredders.

FIGURE 1 THE PROCESS OF COLLECTIVE VALUE CREATION IN BRAND COMMUNITIES

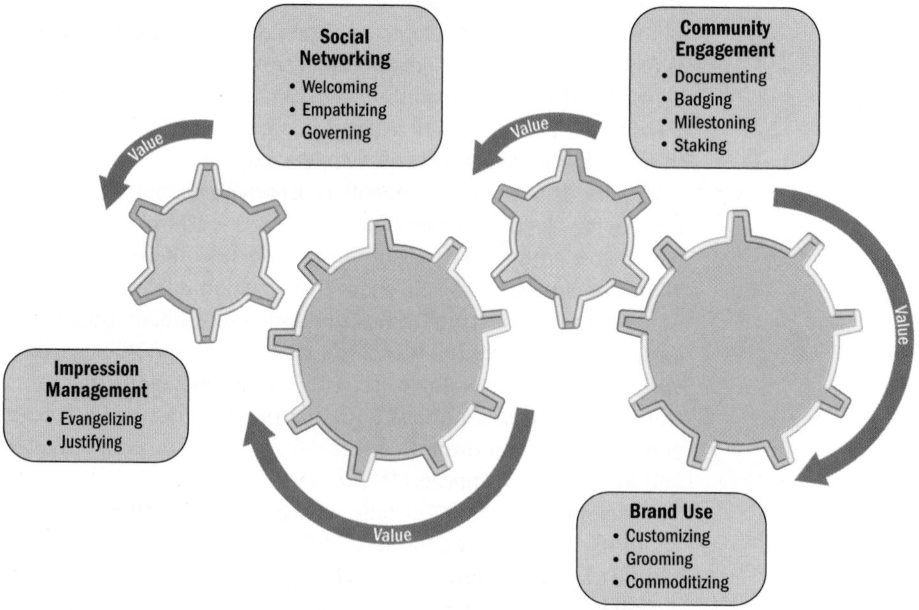

Reprinted with permission from *Journal of Marketing*, published by the American Marketing Association, Schau, Hope Jensen, Albert M. Muñiz, and Eric J. Arnould, September 2009, 73, 30–51.

CB AS I SEE IT

Professor John Schouten, *University of Portland*

There is no such thing as purely personal significance. To the extent that we create individual meaning at all, we do so from a shared language of objects, words, feelings, and experiences whose meanings have already been constructed by social groups. Similarly, there is no such thing as an individual consumer decision. We make our choices from assortments that society has provided, based on values and expectations that we have learned, questioned, embraced, or rejected as members of social groups.

Some groups or communities we choose. Others choose us. Ultimately, the character of our membership in any group is a matter of constant negotiation. Communities of any kind often coincide with or create markets. In response to shared needs and desires, humans come together, harness creativity and labor, and produce new goods and services. In the best cases, the creative power of community can accomplish tremendous good through cultural change. The LOHAS (Lifestyles of Health and Sustainability) community is one such social group, made up of both consumers and businesses. See lohas .com for more about the community's goals and impact.

Our biggest challenge today, in my view, is the collision between escalating human consumption and the rapidly declining capacity of the earth's natural systems to support it. I believe the best real hope for a tolerable human future lies in the ability of communities to redefine acceptable modes of consumer behavior and to participate actively and creatively in making them not only possible but also preferable to those practices that currently undermine the foundation of our existence.

For me, the most exciting aspects of communities are their dynamism and their power to effect change at levels ranging from individual purchases to global movements for social and environmental justice. Recently my studies have turned to such "communities of purpose." For example, for more than three years now Diane Martin and I have been engaged with groups of people determined to make Walmart more environmentally sustainable. Self-selecting community members include Walmart executives and associates, key members of its supply chain, environmental activists, academics, and others. Uniting these diverse participants are shared goals of carbon neutrality, zero waste, and products that support the sustainable use of the earth's finite resources. So far these groups have achieved impressive results, helping Walmart to divert millions of tons of waste from landfills, radically reduce its use of fossil fuels, develop more sustainable products, and (true to Walmart's mission) continue to profit, even in times of economic recession, with low prices to its customers. Explore walmartstores.com/ sustainability and its link to Sustainable Value Networks for more about the results of these ongoing efforts.

However, there also are plenty of tribes with older members, such as car enthusiasts who gather to celebrate such cult products (see Chapter 4) as the Citroën in Europe and the Ford Mustang in the United States, or "foodies" who share their passion for cooking with other Wolfgang Puck wannabes around the world.

Membership versus Aspirational Reference Groups

21   A **membership reference group** consists of people we actually know, whereas we don't know those in an **aspirational reference group**, but we admire them anyway. These people are likely to be successful businesspeople, athletes, performers, or whoever rocks our world. Not surprisingly, many marketing efforts that specifically adopt a reference group appeal concentrate on highly visible, widely admired figures (such as well-known athletes or performers); they link these people to brands so that the products they use or endorse also take on this aspirational quality. For example, an amateur basketball player who idolizes Miami Heat star Dwyane Wade might drool over a pair of Air Jordan 12 Dwyane Wade PE shoes. One study of business students who aspired to the "executive" role found a strong relationship between products they associated with their *ideal selves* and those they assumed that real executives own. Of course, it's worth noting that as social media usage increases, the line between those we "know" and those we "friend" gets blurrier. Still, whether offline or online, we tend to seek out others who are similar. Indeed, one study even found that people on Twitter tend to follow others who share their mood: People who are happy tend to re-tweet or reply to others who are happy, while those who are sad or lonely tend to do the same with others who also post negative sentiments.

22   Because we tend to compare ourselves to similar others, many promotional strategies include "ordinary" people whose consumption activities provide informational social influence. How can we predict which people you know will be part of your membership reference group? Several factors make it more likely:

- **Propinquity**—As physical distance between people decreases and opportunities for interaction increase, they are more likely to form relationships. We call this physical nearness **propinquity**. An early study on friendship patterns in a housing complex showed the strong effects of this factor: All things equal, residents were much more likely to be friends with the people next door than with those who lived only two doors away. Furthermore, people who lived next to a staircase had more friends than those at the ends of a hall (presumably, they were more likely to "bump into" people as they used the stairs).

- **Mere exposure**—We come to like persons or things if we see them more often. Social scientists call this tendency the **mere exposure phenomenon**. Greater frequency of contact, even if unintentional, may help to determine one's set of local referents. The same effect holds when we evaluate works of art or even political candidates. One study predicted 83 percent of the winners of political primaries solely by the amount of media exposure each candidate received.

- **Group cohesiveness**—**Cohesiveness** refers to the degree to which members of a group are attracted to each other and how much each values his

Marketing Opportunity

Most consumers only admire their aspirational reference groups from afar, but more and more of them shell out big bucks to get up close and personal with their heroes. Fantasy camps today are a $1 billion industry as people pay for the chance to hang out—and play with—their idols. Baseball camps mix retired players with fans have been around for many years, but now other types let people mingle with their favorite hockey players, poker players, even members of the U.S. women's national soccer team. At one camp, 80 people each paid about $8,000 to jam with rock stars including Nils Lofgren, Dickey Betts, and Roger Daltrey. One enthusiastic novice gushed afterward, "We all grow up with heroes and never get to share a moment with them. But I got to live out my fantasy."

• • • • • • • • • • • • • • • •

or her membership in this group. As the value of the group to the individual increases, so too does the likelihood that the group will influence that individual's consumption decisions. Smaller groups tend to be more cohesive because in larger groups the contributions of each member are usually less important or noticeable. By the same token, groups often try to restrict membership to a select few, which increases the value of membership to those who do get in.

Positive versus Negative Reference Groups

23   Reference groups impact our buying decisions both positively and negatively. In most cases, we model our behavior to be in line with what we think the group expects us to do. Sometimes, however, we also deliberately do the *opposite* if we want to distance ourselves from **avoidance groups**. You may carefully study the dress or mannerisms of a group you dislike (e.g., "nerds," "druggies," or "preppies") and scrupulously avoid buying anything that might identify you with that group. For example, rebellious adolescents do the opposite of what their parents desire to make a statement about their independence. In one study, college freshman reported consuming less alcohol and restaurant patrons selected less fattening food when drinking alcohol and eating junk food linked to members of avoidance groups.

24   Your motivation to distance yourself from a negative reference group can be as powerful or more powerful than your desire to please a positive group. That's why advertisements occasionally show an undesirable person who uses a competitor's product. This kind of execution subtly makes the point that you can avoid winding up like *that* kind of person if you just stay away from the products he buys. As a once-popular book reminded us, "Real men *don't* eat quiche!"

We Like to Do It in Groups

25   We get away with more when we do it in a group. One simple reason: The more people who are together, the less likely it is that any one member will get singled out for attention. That helps to explain why people in larger groups have fewer restraints on their behavior. For example, we sometimes behave more wildly at costume parties or on Halloween than we do when others can easily identify us. We call this phenomenon **deindividuation**—a process whereby individual identities become submerged within a group.

26   **Social loafing** is a similar effect; it happens when we don't devote as much to a task because our contribution is part of a larger group effort. You may have experienced this if you've worked on a group project for a class! Waitpersons are painfully aware of social loafing: People who eat in groups tend to tip less per person

The Tangled Web

The Web encourages the rise of a new kind of avoidance group: **antibrand communities.** These groups also coalesce around a celebrity, store, or brand—but in this case they're united by their disdain for it. The Rachael Ray Sucks Community on the blogging and social-networking site LiveJournal claims more than 1,000 members who don't hesitate to post their latest thoughts about the various short-comings, flaws, and disagreeable traits of the (otherwise popular) television food person-ality. They criticize Ray's overuse of chicken stock, her kitchen hygiene, her smile (posters like to compare it to The Joker's of Batman fame), her penchant for saying "Yum-o!" and so on. The community has a basic rule for membership: "You must be anti-Rachael!"

One team of researchers that studies these communities observes that they tend to attract social idealists who advocate non-materialistic lifestyles. After they interviewed members of online communities who oppose Walmart, Starbucks, and McDonald's, they concluded that these antibrand communities provide a meeting place for those who share a moral stance; a support network to achieve common goals; a way to cope with workplace frustrations (many members actually work for the companies they bash!); and a hub for in-formation, activities, and related resources. Another study chronicles the level of oppo-sition the Hummer inspires. For example, whereas brand enthusiasts celebrate the Hummer's road safety because of its size and weight, antibranders who drive smaller cars slam the vehicle's bulk. One driver posted this message: "The H2 is a death machine. You'd better hope that you don't collide with an H2 in your economy car. You can kiss your ass goodbye thanks to the H2's massive weight and raised bumpers. Too bad you couldn't af-ford an urban assault vehicle of your own."

• • • • • • • • • • • • • • •

than when they eat alone. For this reason, many restaurants automatically tack on a fixed gratuity for groups of six or more.

27   Furthermore, the decisions we make as part of a group tend to differ from those each of us would choose on our own. The **risky shift effect** refers to the observation that group members tend to consider riskier alternatives after the group discusses an issue than they would if each mem-ber made his or her own decision without talking about it with others. Psychologists propose several explanations for this increased riskiness. One possibility is that something similar to social loafing occurs. As more people are involved in a decision, each individual is less accountable for the out-come, so this results in *diffusion of responsibility*. The practice of placing blanks in at least one of the rifles a firing squad uses diffuses each soldier's responsibility for the death of a prisoner, because it's never certain who actually shot him. Another explanation is the *value hypothesis*, which states that our culture values risky behavior, so when people make decisions in groups they conform to this expectation.

28   Research evidence for the risky shift is mixed. A more general finding is that group discussion tends to increase **decision polarization**. This means that the direction the group members leaned before discussion began (whether a risky choice or a conservative choice) becomes even more extreme in that direction after the group talks about it. Group discussions regarding product purchases tend to cre-ate a risky shift for low-risk items, but they yield even more conservative group decisions for high-risk products.

29   Even shopping behavior changes when people do it in groups. For example, people who shop with at least one other person tend to make more unplanned purchases, buy more, and cover more areas of a store than do those who browse solo. Both normative and informational social influ-ence explains this. A group member may buy something to gain the approval of the others, or the group may simply expose her to more products and stores. Either way, retail-ers are well advised to encourage group-shopping activities.

30   The famous Tupperware party is a successful example of a **home shopping party** that capitalizes on group pressures to boost sales. In this format a company repre-sentative makes a sales presentation to a group of people who gather at the home of a friend or acquaintance. The shopping party works due to informational social influence:

Costumes hide our true identities and encourage deindividuation.

Courtesy of Sergei Bachlakov/Shutterstock.

Participants model the behavior of others who provide them with information about how to use certain products, especially because a relatively homogeneous group (e.g., neighborhood homemakers) attends the party. Normative social influence also operates because others can easily observe our actions. Pressures to conform may be particularly intense and may escalate as more and more group members "cave in" (we call this process the *bandwagon effect*).

31 In addition, these parties may activate deindividuation or the risky shift. As consumers get caught up in the group, they may agree to try new products they would not normally consider. These same dynamics underlie the latest wrinkle on the Tupperware home-selling technique: the Botox party. The craze for Botox injections that paralyze facial nerves to reduce wrinkles (for 3 to 6 months, anyway) is fueled by gatherings where dermatologists or plastic surgeons redefine the definition of house calls. For patients, mixing cocktail hour with cosmetic injections takes some of the anxiety out of the procedure. Egged on by the others at the party, a doctor can dewrinkle as many as 10 patients in an hour. An advertising executive who worked on the Botox marketing strategy explained that the membership reference group appeal is more effective than the traditional route that uses a celebrity spokesperson to tout the injections in advertising: "We think it's more persuasive to think of your next-door neighbor using it." The only hitch is that after you get the injections, your face is so rigid your friends can't tell if you're smiling!

Conformity

32   The early Bohemians who lived in Paris around 1830 made a point of behaving, well, differently from others. One flamboyant figure of the time earned notoriety because he walked a lobster on a leash through the gardens of the Royal Palace. His friends drank wine from human skulls, cut their beards in strange shapes, and slept in tents on the floors of their garrets. Sounds a bit like some frats we've visited.

33   Although in every age there certainly are those who "march to their own drummers," most people tend to follow society's expectations regarding how they should act and look (with a little improvisation here and there, of course). **Conformity** is a change in beliefs or actions as a reaction to real or imagined group pressure. In order for a society to function, its members develop **norms**, or informal rules that govern behavior. Without these rules, we would have chaos. Imagine the confusion if a simple norm such as stopping for a red traffic light did not exist.

34   We conform in many small ways every day, even though we don't always realize it. Unspoken rules govern many aspects of consumption. In addition to norms regarding appropriate use of clothing and other personal items, we conform to rules that include gift-giving (we expect birthday presents from loved ones and get upset if they don't materialize), sex roles (men often pick up the check on a first date), and personal hygiene (our friends expect us to shower regularly). We also observe conformity in the online world; research supports the idea that consumers are more likely to show interest in a product if they see that it is already very popular.

35   One study analyzed how millions of Facebook users adopted apps to personalize their pages. Researchers tracked, on an hourly basis, the rate at which 2,700 apps were installed by 50 million Facebook users. They discovered that once an app had reached a rate of about 55 installations a day, its popularity started to soar. Facebook friends were notified when one of their online buddies adopted a new app, and they could also see a list of the most popular ones. Apparently this popularity feedback was the key driver that determined whether still more users would download the software.

36   Still, we don't mimic others' behaviors all the time, so what makes it more likely that we'll conform? These are some common culprits:

- **Cultural pressures**—Different cultures encourage conformity to a greater or lesser degree. The American slogan "Do your own thing" in the 1960s reflected a movement away from conformity and toward individualism. In contrast, Japanese society emphasizes collective well-being and group loyalty over individuals' needs.

- **Fear of deviance**—The individual may have reason to believe that the group will apply *sanctions* to punish nonconforming behaviors. It's not unusual to observe adolescents shunning a peer who is "different" or a corporation or university passing over a person for promotion because she is not a "team player."

- **Commitment**—The more people are dedicated to a group and value their membership in it, the greater their motivation to conform to the group's wishes. Rock groupies and followers of TV evangelists may do anything their idols ask of them, and terrorists willingly die for their cause. According to the

principle of least interest, the person who is *least* committed to staying in a relationship has the most power because that party doesn't care as much if the other person rejects him. Remember that on your next date.

- **Group unanimity, size, and expertise**—As groups gain in power, compliance increases. It is often harder to resist the demands of a large number of people than only a few, especially when a "mob mentality" rules.

- **Susceptibility to interpersonal influence**—This trait refers to an individual's need to have others think highly of him or her. Consumers who don't possess this trait are *role-relaxed*; they tend to be older, affluent, and to have high self-confidence. Subaru created a communications strategy to reach role-relaxed consumers. In one of its commercials, a man proclaims, "I want a car. . . . Don't tell me about wood paneling, about winning the respect of my neighbors. They're my neighbors. They're not my heroes."

POST-READING

UNDERSTANDING AND ANALYZING THE READING

A. Building Vocabulary

Context

Using context and a dictionary if necessary, determine the meaning of each word as it is used in the selection.

_____ 1. straitlaced (paragraph 1)
   a. well-dressed
   b. wealthy
   c. successful
   d. conservative

_____ 2. faction (paragraph 2)
   a. percentage
   b. role model
   c. group within a larger group
   d. extreme enthusiast

_____ 3. jaunts (paragraph 5)
   a. concerts
   b. conversations
   c. trips
   d. company meetings

_____ 4. covet (paragraph 6)
   a. desire
   b. dislike
   c. need
   d. refuse

_____ 5. niceties (paragraph 8)
   a. stolen goods
   b. accessories
   c. attachments
   d. unnecessary items

_____ 6. epitome (paragraph 8)
   a. symbol
   b. metaphor
   c. center
   d. embodiment

_____ 7. narcissistic (paragraph 14)

    a. self-conscious

    b. impatient

    c. vain

    d. aging

_____ 8. pivotal (paragraph 15)

    a. central

    b. secondary

    c. unimportant

    d. parental

_____ 9. flamboyant (paragraph 32)

    a. modest

    b. animated

    c. flammable

    d. floating

_____ 10. notoriety (paragraph 32)

    a. income

    b. jail

    c. admiration

    d. recognition

Word Parts

> ### A REVIEW OF PREFIXES AND SUFFIXES
>
> **HOMO-** means same.
> **-TION** means the act of.

Use your knowledge of word parts and the review above to fill in the blanks in the following sentences.

1. In a relatively *homogeneous* (paragraph 20) group, many of the people are

    _____.

2. *Improvisation* (paragraph 22) is the _____ improvising, or responding without preparation.

B. Understanding the Thesis and Other Main Ideas

Select the best answer.

_____ 1. The thesis or central thought of "Groups and Conformity" is best stated as:

    a. Conformity is the result of several factors including cultural pressures, fear of deviance, commitment, group unanimity, and susceptibility to interpersonal influence.

    b. Because human beings are inherently social, they often look to different types of reference groups as they make purchase decisions; and in many of these decisions, the desire to conform to social norms plays an important role.

c. While most reference groups are based on membership or aspiration, a completely different type of reference group, called an avoidance group, reflects an individual's desire not to be like the members of a group that the individual dislikes or disdains.

d. While groups are an important determinant of consumer behavior in the United States, the influence of social groups (such as friends and coworkers) is much smaller in other countries where the dominant culture focuses more on individuality than on group conformity.

_____ 2. The main idea of paragraph 14 is found in the

    a. first sentence.

    b. second sentence.

    c. sixth sentence.

    d. last sentence.

_____ 3. The topic of paragraph 20 is

    a. the bandwagon effect.

    b. group pressures.

    c. Tupperware.

    d. home shopping parties.

For questions 4–8, match the term in column A with the definition in column B.

Column A: Term	Column B: Definition
_____ 4. aspirational reference group	a. A change in actions or beliefs in reaction to imagined or real group pressures.
_____ 5. deindividuation	b. The idea that the person who is least committed to being in a relationship holds the most power in that relationship.
_____ 6. principle of least interest	c. A process by which individual people, and their identities and personalities, become submerged within a group identity.
_____ 7. normative influence	d. A group of people, usually composed of highly visible, widely admired athletes or performers, whose success people wish to associate themselves with (or whose behaviors they seek to emulate).
_____ 8. conformity	e. The process by which a reference group helps establish and enforce basic standards of conduct for its group members.

C. Identifying Details

Select the best answer.

_____ 1. To which group do wealthy Harley-Davidson owners often belong?

  a. WYSIWIGs

  b. RUBs

  c. DOAs

  d. HOGs

_____ 2. The motorcycle group most likely to have extremely comfortable motorcycles are

  a. Ma and Pa bikers.

  b. wealthy bikers.

  c. RUBs.

  d. subscribers to *American Iron*.

_____ 3. The average number of smokers in a "smoking cluster" is

  a. 3.

  b. 5.

  c. 6.

  d. 8.

_____ 4. According to the reading, what is the most likely address for a man named Brian Court?

  a. 14 Main Street

  b. 2605 Adriana Road

  c. 173 Phoenix Court

  d. 42689 Palisade Avenue

_____ 5. Suppose you have an aversion to punk rockers. For you, punk rockers are a(n)

  a. aspirational reference group.

  b. utilitarian reference group.

  c. normative group.

  d. avoidance group.

D. Recognizing Methods of Organization and Signal Words

For questions 1–4, match the paragraph in column A with its organizational pattern in column B.

Column A: Term	Column B: Organizational Pattern
_____ 1. Paragraph 9	a. generalization and example
_____ 2. Paragraph 11	b. addition
_____ 3. Paragraph 35	c. definition
_____ 4. Paragraph 37	d. listing/enumeration

Select the best answer.

_____ 5. The signal word or phrase that points to the cause-effect pattern in paragraph 36 is

    a. analyzed.

    b. personalize.

    c. popularity.

    d. driver.

E. Reading and Thinking Visually

Based on Table 1 on page 505, indicate whether each item is a type of informational influence, utilitarian influence, or value-expressive influence.

_____ 1. An aspiring young athlete purchases basketball shoes that are advertised by a professional basketball player such as Michael Jordan or Kobe Bryant.

_____ 2. A female employee at a local flower shop decides to wear the same brand of perfume favored by the shop's other female employees.

_____ 3. A recent college graduate buys a car that is recommended as a "Best Buy" by *Consumer Reports*, an unbiased consumer-advocacy magazine.

F. Figuring Out Implied Meanings

Indicate whether each statement is true (T) or false (F).

_____ 1. In both the real world and the online world, we tend to seek people who are similar to us.

_____ 2. In Japan, people are more likely to focus on individualistic efforts rather than group needs.

_____ 3. In the decision to quit smoking, spouses have a stronger influence than friends.

_____ 4. Consumers are more likely to take other people's preferences into account when they are buying products with a low perceived value.

_____ 5. A role-relaxed woman does not care much about what people think of her.

_____ 6. Parents are more likely to exert comparative influence than normative influence.

_____ 7. In general, people in larger groups have fewer restraints on their behavior.

_____ 8. A person named Sara Thompson is more likely to like someone named Sally Tremont than someone named Barbara Michaels.

_____ 9. The early Bohemians were known for their strict adherence to social norms.

G. Thinking Critically: Analyzing the Author's Techniques

Select the best answer.

_____ 1. The author's purpose in "Groups and Conformity" is to

    a. provide an overview of the influence of reference groups and conformity on consumers' buying decisions, while providing key definitions, examples, and research findings.

    b. make students aware of the unseen forces at work in advertising, on the Internet, and in public gathering places like malls and coffeehouses.

    c. explain the differences between specific reference groups and specific conformist groups, while showing readers how to make better purchasing decisions.

    d. expose the unethical practices of companies like Harley-Davidson and Tupperware, which take advantage of people's desires to be part of a group or community.

_____ 2. In "Groups and Conformity," the author often uses informal language. Which of the following is *not* an example of informal language?

    a. "perfect for his buddy Dan's new crib" (paragraph 2)

    b. "they link these people to brands" (paragraph 21)

    c. "sounds a bit like some frats we've visited" (paragraph 33)

    d. "remember that on your next date" (paragraph 37)

_____ 3. In paragraph 10, "death sticks" is figurative language whose literal meaning is

    a. baseball bats.

    b. falling branches.

    c. swords.

    d. cigarettes.

_____ 4. The type of evidence used to support the main ideas in paragraphs 10 and 36 is

    a. the author's personal experience.

    b. quotes from experts.

    c. research studies.

    d. analogies.

_____ 5. The author's tone is best described as

    a. informative.

    b. irreverent.

    c. self-righteous.

    d. abstract.

H. Thinking Critically: Analyzing the Author's Message

Select the best answer.

_____ 1. What is the connotation of the phrase "freedom statements" that is used on Harley-Davidson's social media? (paragraph 1)

    a. important business documents, such as spreadsheets and corporate mission statements

    b. historical records of freed slaves, such as Harriet Tubman

    c. sense of freedom from responsibilities and the demands of one's job

    d. Twitter updates by political prisoners in countries like Russia and China

_____ 2. According to the reading, what is the best definition of a "ripple effect" (paragraph 10)?

    a. a pattern that is not easily explained

    b. the likelihood that people will give up smoking in groups instead of individually

    c. the overall decrease in sales of a particular product (such as cigars and cigarettes)

    d. the continuing and spreading results of an event or action

_____ 3. Paragraph 36 uses the term "popularity feedback." Which of the following is the best example of popularity feedback?

    a. A singer's CD is #1 on the charts, so more people buy a copy of that CD.

    b. The most attractive people tend to be the most popular in social situations.

    c. A college freshman from out of state attempts to make as many friends as possible during his first year on campus.

    d. A young woman who works for a political action committee avoids buying goods in stores that make use of underpaid overseas child labor.

_____ 4. The term "mob mentality" in paragraph 37 refers to

    a. people who see the Mafia as an aspirational reference group.

    b. the tendency for large groups of people to exert powerful influence over the individuals in that group.

    c. the belief that most people prefer the company of others rather than being alone.

    d. the large number of psychological or mental disorders in urban areas with large populations.

I. Reviewing and Organizing Ideas

Complete the following outline of the reading by filling in the missing words or phrases.

I. Introduction: Story of _____, proud owner of a Harley-Davidson motorcycle

II. Reference Group: actual or imaginary person or group with an influence on an individual's evaluations, aspirations, and behavior

    A. When Are Reference Groups Important?

        1. Recent research on smoking _____: Powerful impact of reference groups

        2. Not all reference group influences work the same way

B. Types of Reference Groups

1. Name-letter effect: We like others who share our names or initials more than we like those who don't

2. _____: Reference group helps set and enforce standards of conduct

3. _____: Affects group members' decisions through comparison with other members of the group

C. Membership vs. Aspirational Reference Groups

1. Membership reference group: Consists of people we already know

2. Aspirational reference group: _____

_____

D. _____

1. Avoidance groups: People we want to distance ourselves from

E. We Like to Do It in Groups

1. _____ : Process whereby individual identities become submerged within a group

2. Group shopping behavior and _____ parties: People more likely to buy more when shopping in a group, where pressure to conform may be intense (bandwagon effect)

III. Conformity

A. _____: change in beliefs or actions as a reaction to real or imagined group pressure

B. Norms: informal rules that govern behavior

C. Factors that influence conformity

1. Cultural pressures

2. Fear of _____

3. _____

4. Group unanimity, size, and expertise

5. Susceptibility to interpersonal influence

J. Analyzing the Issue and Argument

1. List at least three arguments the author makes in "Groups and Conformity."

2. Is the author qualified to write on the topic? Why or why not? How does the source of the reading provide a hint regarding its overall reliability?

3. Does the author provide sufficient evidence to support his main ideas? What other types of evidence might he provide to strengthen his arguments?

4. Which terms does the author define clearly and directly? Which terms are defined indirectly or not at all? What are the definitions of the latter terms?

5. What assumptions does the author make about his readers?

6. Evaluate the reading on the following criteria:

    a. Is the reading timely?

    b. Do you find any evidence of bias in the reading? Explain.

    c. Does the author offer any opposing viewpoints? If so, does he refute them, and how? If not, what might some opposing viewpoints be?

    d. Does the reading offer any emotional appeals? If so, identify them and evaluate their fairness.

K. Writing Paragraphs and Essays

Write a paragraph or essay in response to the following prompts.

1. The reading begins with the example of Zachary, who uses his motorcycle as a way of getting away from his everyday life. What hobby do you engage in when you want to forget about your problems or have a sense of freedom? (For example, do you surf the Web or rent movies?) Write a paragraph or essay about your favorite get-away-from-it-all pastime.

2. The reading discusses the way people can influence one another to quit smoking. Write a paragraph or essay in which you explore some of the ways people can help friends or family members achieve a goal (for instance, getting more exercise, losing weight, or getting a good grade on an exam).

3. Write a one-paragraph summary of the information included in Table 1 on page 505.

4. Write an essay in which you explore three groups to which you aspire (that is, three groups you would like to belong to). Be sure to explain why you would like to belong to the three groups.

5. What are the norms for behavior in the college classroom and on campus? Write an essay in which you explore these norms. What are the sanctions for deviating from these norms?

L. Working Collaboratively

1. **Thinking Deeply** In a small group of your peers, discuss the following questions:

   - What does it mean to be a conformist? In what ways are you a conformist?

   - What does it mean to be a non-conformist? In what ways are you a non-conformist?

   - Are you the same person in both public and private settings? If not, how and why are you different in these two settings?

   - How are your buying habits influenced by others? What things do you buy in order to fit in?

   Be prepared to share your findings with the class.

2. **Thinking Critically** Imagine that you are the author of an advice column of a local newspaper. Working with a partner, develop a question that deals with an issue presented in the reading. For example, you might have a person write in about her shopping behavior when she is with a friend. Her question might be, "Why do I always buy more when I shop with my friend?" (Don't use this question; develop one of your own.)Working with a partner, draft a paragraph length response to the person in which you explain her behavior and suggest ways for her to change the behavior. Finally, be prepared to share your letter with the class.

3. **Thinking Visually** Bring to class a magazine ad or information about a television ad that features a celebrity who endorses a particular product. Working with a group of your peers, discuss the following questions:

   - Who is featured in your ad, and what product is he or she endorsing?

   - Why do you think the company chose that spokesperson?

   - To whom is the company trying to appeal? Do you think that celebrity endorsements help sell products? Do such techniques work on you? Why or why not?

   Be prepared to share the key points of your group discussion with the class.

ACTIVITIES: EXPLORING CONFORMITY AND NONCONFORMITY

On your own or with a group of classmates, complete two of the following activities.

1. Celebrity magazines (like *Us* and *People*) are filled with photos of glamorous Hollywood stars and musicians. What norms are dominant in Hollywood? How do you think the lives of celebrities are fundamentally different from those of the typical American? Provide at least three examples of the ways in which celebrities' lives differ from that of the "average" person. For instance,

some celebrities have hundreds of thousands of followers on their Twitter accounts. Does the average person have that many followers? Why would so many people choose to follow a celebrity's "tweets"?

2. The readings in this chapter discussed just a few aspects of conformity and nonconformity. Other issues related to this topic include:

- **Dress codes:** What is appropriate to wear in different situations? Do men's dress codes differ from women's? If so, how and why? How have dress codes changed over the years?

- **Hairstyles:** If you are going for a job interview, what are the expectations for how you should wear your hair? What are the "do's" and the "don'ts" for both women and men?

- **Body adornment:** How does society view piercings, tattoos, and other body adornments? How have these perceptions changed over the years? For example, what did a tattoo signal in 1950, and what does it signal today?

- **Political protest:** The United States protects freedoms of speech and demonstration. How is political protest a form of nonconformity, and what types of new tools for political protest or political change are now available (that were not available 20 years ago)?

- **Life on and off the grid:** "The grid" refers to the system by which companies and the government track you and your activities: your Social Security number, your address, your place of employment, and so forth. Some people, the ultimate nonconformists, choose to live "off the grid." What motivates these people, and why?

Write an essay or prepare a class presentation about any of these topics, or any other topic regarding conformity or nonconformity.

3. As mentioned in the introduction to this chapter, different sets of norms apply to different groups of people. Write an essay or prepare a presentation in which you compare and contrast two sets of norms. Choose from the list below, or choose two other groups you find particularly interesting.

- Team athletes (for example, baseball and football players) vs. individual athletes (for example, gymnasts and ice skaters)

- Upperclassmen (juniors and seniors) vs. underclassmen (freshmen and sophomores)

- Students in introductory courses (for example, introduction to psychology) vs. students in a discipline's upper-level courses (for example, psychological statistics or abnormal psychology)

- Adolescents/teenagers vs. senior citizens

4. Television sitcoms often have characters who "march to the beat of a different drummer." They are different from the norm; they are nonconformists. Choose a character that you "know" well and explain in a paragraph or an essay why you consider this character to be a nonconformist. How does he or she behave? What do others think of his or her behavior? How is he or she affected by the opinions of others? What do viewers think of this character?

Casebook for Critical Thinking: Global Warming

EXAMINING ONE ISSUE IN DEPTH

Throughout this book, you've read many selections that look at various aspects of contemporary issues. As you pursue your college studies, you will often be asked to study one topic in more depth, consulting multiple sources to gain a deeper understanding of it. In term papers and on written exams, you will need to synthesize all of these sources to demonstrate your mastery of the topic.

In this section, we take a closer look at a contemporary issue—global warming and climate change. Because the issue is so important, it is studied across different academic disciplines. You may think that students who take courses in the Earth Science department study weather and climate, and you would be correct. But the topic is also a part of many other college courses. For example:

- **Sociology** courses may examine how climate change impacts society.
- **Geography** courses may look at the impact of climate change in different countries.
- **Environmental science** courses may examine the pollution and global warming caused by extracting and burning fossil fuels.
- **Business** courses may look at the effects of environmental laws on businesses.
- **Political science** courses may study the success of political parties that run on a platform of environmental awareness.

To give you a taste of how different disciplines approach the same topic, the readings in this section will present different aspects of global warming and climate change. These readings come from different types of sources, including textbooks, Web sites, government agencies, and blogs.

Tips for Reading about Global Warming and Climate Change

Here are some tips for reading not only the selections in this section, but any reading about global warming and climate change.

- **Know the difference between climate and weather.** Time is the key difference between weather and climate. **Weather** refers to atmospheric conditions over a relatively short period of time (such as a year or a decade). **Climate** refers to patterns in the atmosphere over relatively long periods of time, such as centuries, millennia, or longer. (A century is a period of 100 years, and a millennium is a period of 1000 years.)
- **Understand the role of computer modeling in weather and climate studies.** It is impossible to predict weather and climate perfectly. The further into the future the prediction is, the more it must rely on computer simulations that use past history, as well as scientific observations, to predict what will happen in the future. But some people argue that these computer models can be wrong or unreliable.

■ **Be aware of underlying concerns about financial considerations and lifestyle.** Resistance to laws that seek to limit global warming and climate change is often based on financial considerations. Many argue that it will be extremely expensive to change current methods of energy production, and many fear that such massive expenses will cause high levels of unemployment. Others believe that people should not change their traditions or lifestyles over an issue whose importance they believe is being exaggerated. And still others fear that the eventual costs will be overwhelming if climate change is not aggressively addressed now.

As you read any selection on the topic of global warming and climate change, it is essential that you examine the credibility of the source and look for indications of bias.

Tips for Synthesizing Sources

As you consult many sources to learn more about a specific topic, you will need to *synthesize* this information into a coherent, useful whole. Here are some tips to help you work with and synthesize multiple sources.

1. **Choose sources that are trustworthy and reliable.** Carefully examine the results of your initial search for information. For example, suppose you conduct a Google search on the topic. Do not assume that the first ten "hits" are the best sources of information. Always examine the "About Us" section of the Web site for more information about the sponsor. Do not assume that nonprofit organizations (denoted by .org in their Web addresses) are unbiased.

2. **Read for the "big picture": Identify the thesis or central thought and main ideas.** As you set out to learn more about a particular topic, you should first establish a broad base of knowledge. The first time you read each source, look for the key ideas. What argument is the author making? What are the author's main points? You can go back and learn the details later.

3. **Use electronic search tools if you are working with electronic documents.** Suppose you are working with ten documents and you are researching the topic of extinction. Conduct a search for the word "extinction" to help you find information about that topic within the document. In printed books, consult the index.

4. **Look for areas of common agreement.** As you read multiple sources, you may encounter the same information several times. Make note of the facts on which most reliable, credible people agree. Having a solid understanding of these facts can help you evaluate an author's claims and determine if the author is biased.

5. **Be suspicious of highly emotional language.** As you read multiple sources, you may find yourself favoring readings that are colorful and intense while paying less attention to sources that seem more "dry" or dull. Avoid this tendency and seek objective sources as you begin your research. As you learn

more about the topic, you will be better able to evaluate and synthesize sources in which the author offers strong opinions or exhibits strong bias.

Previewing

An important part of working with multiple sources is the ability to find the information you are looking for. Previewing can be extremely helpful in this regard.

EXERCISE 1: WORKING COLLABORATIVELY TO ACTIVATE BACKGROUND KNOWLEDGE

Directions: Before you preview the following readings, work with a small group of your peers to activate your background knowledge by discussing the following questions and relating them to your own experiences. At the conclusion of your group discussion, you should be prepared to actively participate in a whole class discussion of the questions.

1. What do you already know about global warming and climate change?

2. Do you think summers have felt hotter in recent years?

3. Have you, a friend, or a family member been affected by a weather-related natural disaster, such as a hurricane, cyclone, or wildfire?

4. How much do you know about the reasons dinosaurs went extinct?

5. Do you have friends or family in other countries? What are their opinions about global warming and climate change?

6. Does the company you work for have any "green" (environmentally friendly) policies or programs?

7. Why are some people so skeptical of climate change? Why are others so convinced it is a reality?

EXERCISE 2: LOCATING INFORMATION

Directions: Preview each of the eight readings on pages 534–557. Indicate the reading(s) in which you can find the type of information listed below.

INFORMATION ON GLOBAL WARMING AND CLIMATE CHANGE	SOURCE 1	SOURCE 2	SOURCE 3	SOURCE 4	SOURCE 5	SOURCE 6	SOURCE 7	SOURCE 8
1. Rising temperatures in the United States								
2. An overview of the ways climate change may affect Earth								

INFORMATION ON GLOBAL WARMING AND CLIMATE CHANGE	SOURCE 1	SOURCE 2	SOURCE 3	SOURCE 4	SOURCE 5	SOURCE 6	SOURCE 7	SOURCE 8
3. The geologic time scale								
4. The effects of climate change on countries around the world								
5. Effects of climate change on weather, sea level, and people								
6. The opinions of climate change skeptics								
7. The government's role in managing the effects of climate change								
8. Details of Hurricane Sandy								
9. Corporate citizenship and the role of businesses in protecting the environment								
10. An argument for retreating from the ocean's edge in terms of human population and development								
11. The extinction of plants and animals								

READING AND EVALUATING SOURCES

The following eight sources present a variety of perspectives on the issue of global warming and climate change. Your instructor may assign all of the readings or select among and assign specific sources. Each reading is followed by critical thinking questions specific to the reading. At the end of the casebook you will find Synthesis and Integration Questions and Activities that draw upon two or more of the sources contained here.

As you read the sources, use the tips provided above for reading about global warming and synthesizing sources. You might also want to highlight as you read and/or write a brief summary of each.

SOURCE 1: NASA WEB SITE

How Will Global Warming Change Earth?

This reading is taken from the Web site of the National Aeronautics and Space Administration (NASA), the U.S. government agency responsible for the space program and space exploration. NASA satellites take images of the globe, and NASA makes these images available free on the Web.

1   The impact of increased surface temperatures is significant in itself. But global warming will have additional, far-reaching effects on the planet. Warming modifies rainfall patterns, amplifies coastal erosion, lengthens the growing season in some regions, melts ice caps and glaciers, and alters the ranges of some infectious diseases. Some of these changes are already occurring.

Global warming will shift major climate patterns, possibly prolonging and intensifying the current drought in the U.S. Southwest. The white ring of bleached rock on the once-red cliffs that hold Lake Powell indicate the drop in water level over the past decade—the result of repeated winters with low snowfall. Courtesy of Alysta/Fotolia.

Changing Weather

2   For most places, global warming will result in more frequent hot days and fewer cool days, with the greatest warming occurring over land. Longer, more intense heat waves will become more common. Storms, floods, and droughts will generally be

more severe as precipitation patterns change. Hurricanes may increase in intensity due to warmer ocean surface temperatures.

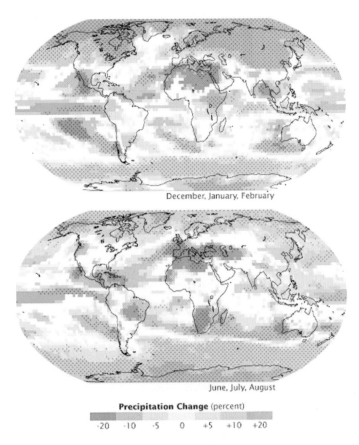

December, January, February

June, July, August

Precipitation Change (percent)

-20   -10   -5   0   +5   +10   +20

Apart from driving temperatures up, global warming is likely to cause bigger, more destructive storms, leading to an overall increase in precipitation. With some exceptions, the tropics will likely receive less rain (orange) as the planet warms, while the polar regions will receive more precipitation (green). White areas indicate that fewer than two-thirds of the climate models agreed on how precipitation will change. **Stippled** areas reveal where more than 90 percent of the models agreed. (©2007 IPCC WG1 AR-4.)

stippled
dotted

3   It is impossible to pin any single unusual weather event on global warming, but emerging evidence suggests that global warming is already influencing the weather. **Heat waves, droughts, and intense rain events have increased in frequency** during the last 50 years, and human-induced global warming more likely than not contributed to the trend.

Rising Sea Levels

4   The weather isn't the only thing global warming will impact: rising sea levels will erode coasts and cause more frequent coastal flooding. Some island nations will

disappear. The problem is serious because up to 10 percent of the world's population lives in vulnerable areas less than 10 meters (about 30 feet) above sea level.

5   Between 1870 and 2000, the sea level increased by 1.7 millimeters per year on average, for a total sea level rise of 221 millimeters (0.7 feet or 8.7 inches). **And the rate of sea level rise is accelerating.** Since 1993, NASA satellites have shown that sea levels are rising more quickly, about 3 millimeters per year, for a total sea level rise of 48 millimeters (0.16 feet or 1.89 inches) between 1993 and 2009.

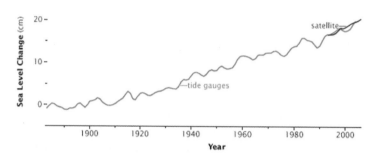

Sea levels crept up about 20 centimeters (7.9 inches) during the twentieth century. Sea levels are predicted to go up between 18 and 59 cm (7.1 and 23 inches) over the next century, though the increase could be greater if ice sheets in Greenland and Antarctica melt more quickly than predicted. Higher sea levels will erode coastlines and cause more frequent flooding. (Graph ©2007 Robert Rohde.)

6   The Intergovernmental Panel on Climate Change (IPCC) estimates that sea levels will rise between 0.18 and 0.59 meters (0.59 to 1.9 feet) by 2099 as warming sea water expands, and mountain and polar glaciers melt. These sea level change predictions may be underestimates, however, because they do not account for any increases in the rate at which the world's major ice sheets are melting. As temperatures rise, ice will melt more quickly. Satellite measurements reveal that the Greenland and West Antarctic ice sheets are shedding about 125 billion tons of ice per year—enough to raise sea levels by 0.35 millimeters (0.01 inches) per year. If the melting accelerates, the increase in sea level could be significantly higher.

Impacting Ecosystems

7   More importantly, perhaps, global warming is already putting pressure on ecosystems, the plants and animals that co-exist in a particular climate zone, both on land and in the ocean. Warmer temperatures have already shifted the growing season in many parts of the globe. The growing season in parts of the Northern Hemisphere became two weeks longer in the second half of the 20th century. Spring is coming earlier in both hemispheres.

8   This change in the growing season affects the broader ecosystem. Migrating animals have to start seeking food sources earlier. The shift in seasons may already be causing the lifecycles of pollinators, like bees, to be out of synch with flowering plants and trees. This mismatch can limit the ability of both pollinators and plants to survive and reproduce, which would reduce food availability throughout the food chain.

9   Warmer temperatures also extend the growing season. This means that plants need more water to keep growing throughout the season or they will dry out, increasing the risk of failed crops and wildfires. Once the growing season ends, shorter, milder winters fail to kill **dormant** insects, increasing the risk of large, damaging infestations in subsequent seasons.

dormant
in a state of
rest or sleep

10   In some ecosystems, maximum daily temperatures might climb beyond the tolerance of **indigenous** plants or animals. To survive the extreme temperatures, both marine and land-based plants and animals have started to migrate towards the poles. Those species, and in some cases, entire ecosystems, that cannot quickly migrate or adapt, face extinction. The IPCC estimates that 20-30 percent of plant and animal species will be at risk of extinction if temperatures climb more than 1.5° to 2.5°C.

indigenous
native

Impacting People

11   The changes to weather and ecosystems will also affect people more directly. Hardest hit will be those living in low-lying coastal areas, and residents of poorer countries who do not have the resources to adapt to changes in temperature extremes and water resources. As tropical temperature zones expand, the reach of some infectious diseases, such as malaria, will change. More intense rains and hurricanes and rising sea levels will lead to more severe flooding and potential loss of property and life.

One inevitable consequence of global warming is sea-level rise. In the face of higher sea levels and more intense storms, coastal communities face greater risk of rapid beach erosion from destructive storms. This aerial photograph shows people walking on the beach in front of some of the homes destroyed by Hurricane Sandy, in Mantoloking, New Jersey, USA, on April 27, 2013. Courtesy of epa european pressphoto agency by b.v./Alamy.

12   Hotter summers and more frequent fires will lead to more cases of heat stroke and deaths, and to higher levels of near-surface ozone and smoke, which would cause more "code red" air quality days. Intense droughts can lead to an increase

in malnutrition. On a longer time scale, fresh water will become scarcer, especially during the summer, as mountain glaciers disappear, particularly in Asia and parts of North America.

13   On the flip side, there could be "winners" in a few places. For example, as long as the rise in global average temperature stays below 3 degrees Celsius, some models predict that global food production could increase because of the longer growing season at mid-to-high latitudes, provided adequate water resources are available. The same small change in temperature, however, would reduce food production at lower latitudes, where many countries already face food shortages. On balance, most research suggests that the negative impacts of a changing climate far outweigh the positive impacts. Current civilization—agriculture and population distribution—has developed based on the current climate. The more the climate changes, and the more rapidly it changes, the greater the cost of adaptation.

14   Ultimately, global warming will impact life on Earth in many ways, but the extent of the change is largely up to us. Scientists have shown that human emissions of greenhouse gases are pushing global temperatures up, and many aspects of climate are responding to the warming in the way that scientists predicted they would. This offers hope. Since people are causing global warming, people can mitigate global warming, if they act in time. Greenhouse gases are long-lived, so the planet will continue to warm and changes will continue to happen far into the future, but the degree to which global warming changes life on Earth depends on our decisions now.

Critical Thinking Questions

1. What are some possible effects of longer, more intense heat waves? Think about the effects on individuals, on agriculture, and on energy usage.

2. Does this reading state conclusively that humans are responsible for creating the more intense weather events of the past fifty years?

3. All of the measurements in this reading are given first in the metric system, followed by a conversion into the U.S. system—for example, "0.18 and 0.59 meters (0.59 to 1.9 feet)." Why do the authors use metric measurements first? What does this tell you about the intended audience for the article?

4. Identify at least three statements of fact and three statements of opinion in the reading.

5. What do the authors mean by the following phrase in paragraph 8? "This mismatch can limit the ability of both pollinators and plants to survive and reproduce, which would reduce food availability throughout the food chain."

6. Do you perceive bias in this selection, or does the selection represent an attempt to present multiple sides of the issue? Explain.

7. Explain the meaning of the following sentence in paragraph 13. "The more the climate changes, and the more rapidly it changes, the greater the cost of adaptation."

8. Provide three words to describe the tone of this reading.

Directions: After answering the critical thinking questions on your own, pair up with a classmate and share your answers. As you discuss the questions, add to your answers the information you learn from your partner.

SOURCE 2: COASTALCARE.ORG WEB SITE

We Need to Retreat from the Beach
Orrin Pilkey

CoastalCare.org is an environmental organization. According to its Web site, two of its goals are to "raise awareness of the many unsustainable practices that are harming the world's beaches and coasts" and to "advocate for sensible, science-based policies and regulations that will protect and preserve coastlines and beaches around the world." The author, Orrin H. Pilkey, is James B. Duke Professor Emeritus of Geology at Duke University.

Aerial pictures of North Carolina's coast, after superstorm Sandy devastated the area. Courtesy of the Program for the Study of Developed Shorelines.

1   As ocean waters warm, the Northeast is likely to face more Sandy-like storms. [Hurricane Sandy affected a large section of the East coast in November 2012.] And as sea levels continue to rise, the surges of these future storms will be higher and even more deadly. We can't stop these powerful storms. But we can reduce the deaths and damage they cause.

Reprinted from *CoastalCare.org*, November 15, 2012.

barrier islands
narrow strips of
land near the
coast

2

Hurricane Sandy's immense power, which destroyed or damaged thousands of homes, actually pushed the footprints of the **barrier islands** along the South Shore of Long Island and the Jersey Shore landward as the storm carried precious beach sand out to deep waters or swept it across the islands. This process of barrier-island migration toward the mainland has gone on for 10,000 years.

3

Yet there is already a push to rebuild homes close to the beach and bring back the shorelines to where they were. The federal government encourages this: there will be billions available to replace roads, pipelines and other **infrastructure** and to clean up storm debris and provide security and emergency housing. Claims to the National Flood Insurance Program could reach $7 billion. And the Army Corps of Engineers will be ready to mobilize its sand-pumping dredges, dump trucks, and bulldozers to rebuild beaches washed away time and again.

infrastructure
system of
buildings and
transportation
that helps society
function

4

But this "let's come back stronger and better" attitude, though empowering, is the wrong approach to the increasing hazard of living close to the rising sea. Disaster will strike again. We should not simply replace all lost property and infrastructure. Instead, we need to take account of rising sea levels, intensifying storms and continuing shoreline erosion.

5

I understand the temptation to rebuild. My parents' retirement home, built at 13 feet above sea level, five blocks from the shoreline in Waveland, Miss., was flooded to the ceiling during Hurricane Camille in 1969. They rebuilt it, but the house was completely destroyed by Hurricane Katrina in 2005. (They had died by then.) Even so, rebuilding continued in Waveland. A year after Katrina, one empty Waveland beachfront lot, on which successive houses had been wiped away by Hurricanes Camille and Katrina, was for sale for $800,000.

6

That is madness. We should strongly discourage the reconstruction of destroyed or badly damaged beachfront homes in New Jersey and New York. Some very valuable property will have to be abandoned to make the community less vulnerable to storm surges. This is tough medicine, to be sure, and taxpayers may be forced to compensate homeowners. But it should save taxpayers money in the long run by ending this cycle of repairing or rebuilding properties in the path of future storms. Surviving buildings and new construction should be elevated on pilings at least two feet above the 100-year flood level to allow future storm overwash to flow underneath. Some buildings should be moved back from the beach.

7

Respecting the power of these storms is not new. American Indians who occupied barrier islands during the warm months moved to the mainland during the winter storm season. In the early days of European settlement in North America, some communities restricted building to the bay sides of barrier islands to minimize damage. In Colombia and Nigeria, where some people choose to live next to beaches to reduce exposure to **malarial** mosquitoes, houses are routinely built to be easily moved.

malarial
carrying
malaria

8

We should also understand that armoring the shoreline with sea walls will not be successful in holding back major storm surges. As experience in New Jersey and elsewhere has shown, sea walls eventually cause the loss of protective beaches. These beaches can be replaced, but only at enormous cost to taxpayers. The 21-mile stretch of beach between Sandy Hook and Barnegat Inlet in New Jersey was replenished between 1999 and 2001 at a cost of $273 million (in 2011 dollars). Future replenishment will depend on finding suitable sand on the **continental shelf**, where it is hard to find.

continental shelf
the borders of a
continent

9   And as sea levels rise, replenishment will be required more often. In Wrightsville Beach, N.C., the beach already has been replenished more than 20 times since 1965, at a cost of nearly $54.3 million (in 2011 dollars). Taxpayers in at least three North Carolina communities—Carteret and Dare Counties and North Topsail Beach—have voted down tax increases to pay for these projects in the last dozen years. The attitude was: we shouldn't have to pay for the beach. We weren't the ones irresponsible enough to build next to an eroding shoreline.

10   This is not the time for a solution based purely on engineering. The Army Corps undoubtedly will be heavily involved. But as New Jersey and New York move forward, officials should seek advice from oceanographers, coastal geologists, coastal and construction engineers and others who understand the future of rising seas and their impact on barrier islands.

11   We need more resilient development, to be sure. But we also need to begin to retreat from the ocean's edge.

Critical Thinking Questions

1. What is the thesis or central thought of this selection? What course of action is the author arguing for or against?

2. What does the author imply about the cost of waterfront property in the United States?

3. What evidence does the author provide to support his assertion that previous generations were more successful in protecting themselves (and their homes) from storm damage than current generations?

4. Identify at least three ways coastal communities could minimize damage from future storms.

5. What does the author imply about engineers' approach to controlling the effects of hurricanes and other extreme weather events that affect coastal areas?

6. This article does not specifically mention climate change or global warming. How is this article's content related to the topics of climate change and global warming?

EXERCISE 4: WORKING COLLABORATIVELY

Directions: After answering the critical thinking questions on your own, pair up with a classmate and share your answers. As you discuss the questions, add to your answers the information you learn from your partner.

SOURCE 3: HUMAN EVENTS WEB SITE

The Debunking of Global Warming Continues

John Hayward

The Human Events Web site offers what it calls "powerful conservative voices." According to the organization's mission statement, Human Events aims for accurate presentation of the facts but admits that its coverage is not unbiased. The About Us section of their Web site states, "We look at events through eyes that favor limited constitutional govern-ment, local self-government, private enterprise, and individual freedom. These were the principles that inspired the Founding Fathers. We believe that today the same principles will preserve freedom in America."

1   The Cult of Global Warming still has a huge amount of money and political influ-ence, so no landmark on the steady unraveling of their con job should go unre-marked. A big one arrived in the form of a study conducted by Anthony Watts and an army of volunteer assistants: the data assembled by the National Oceanic and Atmospheric Administration, and commonly cited for years in support of the global warming scare, is wildly inaccurate. It literally doubled the amount of actual warm-ing that took place over the past half-century.

2   This occurred because most of the climate stations in the United States are located within the **heat envelopes** of major cities. They weren't detecting any "global warming." They were, in essence, detecting engine heat. The readings from accu-rate weather stations were actually adjusted upwards to agree with the inaccurate readings.

heat envelopes areas of higher temperatures within cities produced by buildings and humans

3   Global-warming skeptics couldn't be any more vindicated if the entire climate change establishment cried "Never mind!" in unison, then scurried back to their labs to conjure up a new apocalyptic man-made threat they could blame on capitalist success.

4   "Is this a case of deliberate fraud by Warmist scientists hell bent on keeping their funding gravy train rolling?" asks highly vindicated skeptic James Delingpole. "Well, after what we saw in **Climategate** anything is possible. (I mean it's not like NOAA is run by hard-left eco activists, is it?) But I think more likely it is a case of confirmation bias. The Warmists who comprise the climate scientist establishment spend so much time communicating with other warmists and so little time paying attention to the views of dissenting scientists such as Henrik Svensmark—or Fred Singer or Richard Lindzen or indeed Anthony Watts—that it simply hasn't occurred to them that their temperature records need adjusting downwards, not upwards."

Climategate refers to a situation in which several scientists were found to have falsified data about global warming

5   This is not an arbitrary point of contention between academics. Billions of dol-lars in wealth has been destroyed in the name of global warming. Americans still live under the dominion of laws passed on the basis of junk science. A generation of children has been aggressively indoctrinated in this garbage throughout their school years. The indoctrination remains useful to the Left, because it has taught kids to view the human race as a kind of cancer, which can be controlled only

Reprinted from *Human Events*, July 30, 2012.

by a synchronized effort between politically correct scientists and government agencies.

6   Delingpole facetiously cautions against triumphalism in the wake of this NOAA analysis, because it would be "plain wrong" to dance on global warming's grave. He's kidding, of course. In truth, it is critical to make the shame and fraud of global warming part of our common knowledge. We must carefully document how this scam was perpetrated, and remember the techniques it employed—from corrupt "hockey stick graphs" to mountains of wildly inaccurate data—so that we never fall for anything like it again. Politicized pseudoscience comes at the expense of real science, and that is an expense we can never afford.

Critical Thinking Questions

1. Identify at least four examples of biased and/or emotional language in this selection.

2. Which single piece of evidence does the author use to argue that global warming is a hoax? Is enough evidence offered to support the thesis? Why or why not?

3. The author uses the terms "junk science" (paragraph 5) and "pseudoscience" (paragraph 6). What do these terms mean?

4. "Many people who argue in favor of global warming are actually pursuing a personal agenda against the wealthy and against businesses." Would the author agree or disagree with this statement? Why or why not? Cite direct support (or direct contradiction) of this statement within the reading.

5. Suppose a scientist believes that children who have only one parent grow up to have more emotional problems than children with two parents. The scientist communicates with other scientists who believe the same thing and may therefore be likely to dismiss evidence that refutes their belief. According to this article, what type of bias is affecting these scientists?

6. Provide three words that describe the tone of this selection.

7. How does the author's use of the word "critical" in paragraph 6 differ from the meaning of the word in the phrase "critical thinking"?

8. Overall, what was the author's purpose for writing "The Debunking of Global Warming Continues"?

EXERCISE 5: WORKING COLLABORATIVELY

Directions: After answering the critical thinking questions on your own, pair up with a classmate and share your answers. As you discuss the questions, add to your answers the information you learn from your partner.

SOURCE 4: ENVIRONMENT: THE SCIENCE BEHIND THE STORIES

Climate Change and Extinction
Jay Withgott and Scott Brennan

The following selection is taken from an introductory environmental science textbook. Both authors have taught environmental science to college students. In a letter to students, the authors write, "Within your lifetime, our global society must chart a promising course for a sustainable future—or it will risk peril. The stakes could not be higher, and the path we take will depend largely on how we choose to interact with our environment."

Some Species Are More Vulnerable to Extinction than Others

1   In general, extinction occurs when environmental conditions change rapidly or severely enough that a species cannot adapt genetically to the change; the slow process of **natural selection** simply does not have enough time to work. All manner of events can cause extinction—climate change, the rise and fall of sea level, the arrival of new species, severe weather events, and more. In general, small populations are vulnerable to extinction because fluctuations in their size could easily, by chance, bring the population size to zero. Species narrowly specialized to some particular resource or way of life are also vulnerable, because environmental changes that make that resource or way of life unavailable can doom them.

natural selection natural process by which stronger individuals survive and pass their genes on to their offspring

2   The golden toad was a prime example of a vulnerable species. It was endemic to the Monteverde **cloud forest**, meaning that it occurred nowhere else on the planet. Endemic species face relatively high risks of extinction because all their members belong to a single and sometimes small population. At the time of its discovery, the golden toad was known from only a 4-km² (988-acre) area of Monteverde. It also required very specific conditions to breed successfully. During the spring at Monteverde, water collects in shallow pools within the network of roots that span the cloud forest's floor. The golden toad gathered to breed in these root-bound reservoirs, and it was here that Jay Savage and his companions collected their specimens in 1964. Monteverde provided ideal habitat for the golden toad, but the extent of that habitat was minuscule—any environmental stresses that deprived the toad of the resources it needed to survive might doom the entire world population of the species.

cloud forest a type of tropical or subtropical forest characterized by persistent cloud cover

3   In the United States, a number of **amphibians** are limited to very small ranges and thus are vulnerable to extinction. The Yosemite toad is restricted to a small region of the Sierra Nevada in California, the Houston toad occupies just a few areas of Texas woodland, and the Florida bog frog lives in a tiny region of Florida wetland. Fully 40 salamander species in the United States are restricted to areas the size of a typical county, and some of these live atop single mountains (Figure 4-1).

amphibian family of animals that includes frogs, toads, newts, and salamanders

Earth Has Seen Several Episodes of Mass Extinction

4   Most extinction occurs gradually, one species at a time. The rate at which this type of extinction occurs is referred to as the *background extinction rate*. However, Earth has seen five events of staggering proportions that killed off massive numbers

FIGURE 4-1

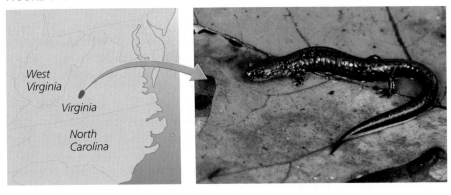

The Peaks of Otter salamander (*Plethodon hubricht*) lives on only a few peaks in Virginia's Blue Ridge Mountains. About 40 other salamander species in the United States are restricted to similarly small ranges. Small range sizes leave these creatures vulnerable to extinction if severe changes occur in their local environment. Courtesy of Lynda Richardson/Corbis.

of species at once. These episodes, called **mass extinction events**, have occurred at widely spaced intervals in Earth history and have wiped out 50–95% of our planet's species each time.

5   The best-known mass extinction occurred 65 million years ago and brought an end to the dinosaurs (although birds are modern representatives of dinosaurs). Evidence suggests that the impact of a gigantic asteroid caused this event, called the Cretaceous-Tertiary, or K-T, event. As massive as this extinction event was, however, it was moderate compared to the mass extinction at the end of the Permian period 250 million years ago. **Paleontologists** estimate that 75–95% of all species may have perished during this event, described by one researcher as the "mother of all mass extinctions." Scientists do not yet know what caused the end-Permian extinction event, although **hypotheses** include an asteroid impact, massive volcanism, **methane** releases and global warming, or some combination of factors.

paleontologist
one who studies fossilized animals and plants

hypotheses
scientific guesses

methane
a colorless, odorless flammable gas

habitat
natural home of a plant or animal

biodiversity
the variety of life in the world

The Sixth Mass Extinction Is Upon Us

6   Many biologists have concluded that Earth is currently entering its sixth mass extinction event—and that we are the cause. Indeed, the Millennium Ecosystem Assessment estimated that today's extinction rate is 100–1,000 times higher than the background rate, and rising. Changes to Earth's natural systems set in motion by human population growth, development, and resource depletion have driven many species extinct and are threatening countless more. The alteration and outright destruction of natural **habitats**, the hunting and harvesting of species, and the introduction of species from one place to another where they can harm native species—these processes and more have combined to threaten Earth's **biodiversity**.

7   Amphibians such as the golden toad are disappearing faster than just about any other type of organism. According to the most recent scientific assessments, 40% of frog, toad, and salamander species are in decline, 30% are in danger of extinction, and nearly 170 species have vanished just within the last few years or decades. Some species are disappearing in remote and pristine areas, suggesting that chytrid fungus could be responsible. But researchers think a variety of causes are affecting amphibians in a "perfect storm" of impacts.

geologic
relating to the study of Earth

speciation
the evolution of a new species

8   When we look around us, it may not appear as though a human version of an asteroid impact is taking place, but we cannot judge such things on our own time-scale. On the **geologic** timescale, extinction over 100 years or even 10,000 years appears instantaneous. Moreover, **speciation** is a slow enough process that it will take life millions of years to recover—by which time our own species will most likely not be around.

—Withgott and Brennan, *Environment: The Science Behind the Stories*, pp. 58–61.

Critical Thinking Questions

1. How much did you know about extinction before you read this selection? How has the reading changed your ideas about extinction (if at all)?

2. What role does climate change play in extinction? Does the author provide sufficient evidence to support his position?

3. Suppose higher temperatures cause entire plant species to die. How might the extinction of plant species be related to the extinction of animal species?

4. The reading discusses the golden toad of Monteverde. Can you think of other examples of endemic species—that is, plants or animals that are found in only one place on Earth? (Hint: Think about Australia.)

5. In which mass extinction may global warming have played a role, the Cretaceous-Tertiary event or the extinction at the end of the Permian period? What was the likely cause of the other mass extinction event?

6. In paragraph 8, which specific species do the authors imply will be extinct millions of years from now?

EXERCISE 6: WORKING COLLABORATIVELY

Directions: After answering the critical thinking questions on your own, pair up with a classmate and share your answers. As you discuss the questions, add to your answers the information you learn from your partner.

SOURCE 5: ENVIRONMENTAL DEFENSE FUND BLOG

Hot Topic: Climate Change and Our Extreme Weather
Steven Hamburg

This reading is taken from the Web site of the Environmental Defense Fund, an organiza-tion whose stated mission is to "preserve the natural systems on which all life depends, focusing on the most critical environmental problems." Steven Hamburg, the author of this selection, writes and speaks about the organization's commitment to science-based advocacy and, according to the Web site, "is responsible for the scientific integrity of EDF's positions and programs."

1   Americans have been griping all summer about the weather. It feels hotter than usual this year (2012).

2   Turns out, that's because—it is.

3   The National Oceanic and Atmospheric Administration (NOAA) just confirmed that America is enduring the hottest weather in our recorded history.

4   In fact, the past 12 months have been **the warmest 12 months in the conti-nental U.S. since record-keeping began back in 1895**.

5   It's not a coincidence either. NOAA says the odds of our record heat being a random event—rather than part of a global warming trend—are about **1 in 1.6 million**.

6   How hot is it, really? Consider these facts from NOAA:
- From June 1st through July 10th of this year, the U.S. broke **147 all-time high-temperature records**.
- In June of 2012, communities across the U.S. **broke 2,284 daily maximum temperature records**. In the week of July 1st through July 9th of this year, they **broke another 2,071**.
- The average temperature in the contiguous United States was 71.2 degrees Fahrenheit this June—**two full degrees** above the 20th-century average.

7   Those scary statistics are just for the past six weeks. But our miserable June fol-lowed the blistering heat from *last* year.

8   Take a look at this partial list of cities that broke records from June of 2011 through May of 2012:
- **Detroit—101 degrees** (daily record)
- **Syracuse—101 degrees** (daily record)
- **Mitchell, SD—102 degrees** (daily record)
- **Minneapolis—103 degrees** (daily record)
- **Bridgeport, CT—103 degrees** (all-time record)
- **Denver—105 degrees** (all-time record)

Reprinted from *Climate 411*, July 13, 2012, Environmental Defense Fund.

- **Newark—108 degrees** (all-time record)
- **Houston—109 degrees** (all-time record)
- **Miles City, MT—111 degrees** (all-time record)
- **Wichita—111 degrees** (daily record)
- **Little Rock—114 degrees** (all-time record)
- **Childress, TX—117 degrees** (all-time record)

9   We've included some of those temperatures in our newest EDF public service announcement, which is running on the jumbo screen in Times Square. The blazing temperatures have led to other problems as well:

- The U.S. Drought Monitor says more than **56 percent of the contiguous United States is now under drought conditions**—the highest level since record-keeping began in 2000.
- Wildfires destroyed 1.3 million acres in Colorado and across the U.S. last month.
- Wyoming recorded its driest June ever this year; Colorado and Utah recorded their second-driest Junes.

10   At the same time:

- **Florida recorded its wettest June ever**—thanks in part to Tropical Storm Debby, which dumped more than two feet of rain on some towns, and spawned flash floods and almost two dozen tornadoes.
- **Duluth, Minnesota also had record floods** last month.
- Large parts of the East Coast got hit by a killer **Derecho storm** that killed more than two dozen people; more than three million lost electricity, some for more than a week.
- Washington, D.C. broke its record for worst heat wave ever, according to the *Washington Post*.

Derecho storm
a type of
windstorm

11   Unfortunately, these bad weather trends are not unexpected. For a long time now, the world's top climate researchers have told us about the strong evidence of links between dangerous weather and climate change.

12   Here at EDF, we've been talking—and blogging—about the issue for a long time. It was barely more than six months ago that we posted about the **IPCC** report on climate change and extreme weather. Sadly, looking back at the last round of weather disasters gives our current sweltering summer a sense of déjà vu.

IPCC
Intergovern-
mental Panel on
Climate Change;
created by the
United Nations
to study climate
change
worldwide

13   Greenhouse gas pollution traps heat in our atmosphere, which interferes with normal weather patterns. That means we can expect more—and probably worse— weird weather in the future.

14   Climate change doesn't just mean higher heat. It means more severe and damaging weather events across the country—including more frequent and heavier rains in some areas, increased drought in others, a potential increase in the intensity of hurricanes, and more coastal erosion because of rising sea levels.

15   Changing weather patterns changes will affect our agriculture, water supplies, health and economy. They'll affect every American community and, ultimately, every American.

16   That's why EDF is dedicated to reducing carbon pollution.

17   After all the reports, and all the statistics, and all the bad weather—there's no excuse for not fighting climate change.

Critical Thinking Questions

1. What does the author see as the main cause of climate change? Do you think the author provides adequate evidence to support this position?

2. Which type of graphic or visual aid would best express the information found in paragraphs 8 and 10?

3. How has the author chosen to use boldface type in this reading? What purpose does it serve?

4. The author's biographical note discusses EDF's commitment to "science-based advocacy." What does this term mean, and what does it imply about the reading's possible level of bias?

5. The biographical note explains that the author, Steven Hamburg, is responsible for the "scientific integrity" of EDF's positions and programs. What does this mean?

6. This article refers to all temperatures in the Fahrenheit scale (which is used in the United States), not in the Celsius scale (which is used in many other parts of the world). What does this imply about the author's audience?

EXERCISE 7: WORKING COLLABORATIVELY

Directions: After answering the critical thinking questions on your own, pair up with a classmate and share your answers. As you discuss the questions, add to your answers the information you learn from your partner.

SOURCE 6: THE BUSINESS ETHICS BLOG

Storms, Global Warming, and Corporate Citizenship
Chris MacDonald

Chris MacDonald, Ph.D., teaches at Ryerson University in Toronto, Canada, where he is Director of the Jim Pattison Ethical Leadership Education & Research Program. This selection is taken from his personal blog about business ethics.

Reprinted from the *Business Ethics Blog*, November 2, 2012, by permission of Chris MacDonald.

Frankenstorm
refers to
Hurricane Sandy,
which did billions
of dollars of
damage to the
U.S. east coast
in 2012

CFL
compact
fluorescent light
bulb

B2B
business-to-
business

externalities
side effects

1   Humans are (very likely) changing the earth's climate. And changes in climate are (very likely) making storms worse. And worse storms are (definitely) a bad thing. Granted, it's hard—in fact, foolish—to try to draw a straight line between any individual's or even any corporation's behavior and the **Frankenstorm** that just slammed New York and surrounding areas, but the fact remains that the devastation that storm wrought was not the effect of a mere freak of nature. As *Business Week* bluntly put it, "it's global warming, stupid."

2   But what matters more than the cause of global warming is what we can do about it. In particular, what can business do about it?

3   Large-scale problems tend to require large-scale solutions, and so there's a natural tendency to leave such issues to government. This is so for two reasons. First is simple scope: you driving a hybrid car or switching to **CFL** bulbs just isn't going to accomplish much. Second is the nature of collective action problems: each of us benefits from a wasteful, energy-intensive lifestyle, and it seems narrowly rational to let other people (or other companies) bear the costs of doing things differently. But the fact that it's tempting, or even narrowly rational, to let others bear the burden, or to wait for government to act, doesn't make it the right thing, or even the minimally decent thing, to do.

4   So what can businesses do—what is it possible for them to do—in response to a trend in global warming that is clearly posing increased risks?

5   To begin, of course, they can work to avoid making things worse, by avoiding burning carbon and adding to the load of carbon dioxide in the atmosphere. This means looking at relatively small, obvious stuff like seeking energy efficiencies in their operations, promoting telecommuting, reducing air travel, and so on. Luckily, most such efforts are relatively painless, since they tend to reduce costs at the same time. Sometimes mere laziness or a focus on "how we've always done things" gets in the way of making such win-win changes. Don't be lazy. Innovate. Share best practices with your suppliers, with other companies in your sector, and if you're a **B2B** company, with your customers.

6   The second thing that businesses can do is to work with, rather than against, government efforts at making things better. In particular, it is a fundamental obligation of corporate citizenship not to block government action aimed at effective action at slowing climate change, and in particular action aimed at dealing effectively with the effects of climate change. If, for example, a government wants to pass rules forcing businesses to pay the full cost of their energy usage, or rules that impose industry-wide energy efficiency rules, business should welcome rather than oppose such changes. Energy inefficiencies impose costs on other people, and hence count as the kind of **externalities** that go against the fundamental principles of a market economy.

7   It's also worth noting that asking what business can do is not quite the same as asking what your business, or any particular business, can do. Business organizations and trade associations abound, and there's plenty they can do to a) help members share best practices and b) foster industry-wide standards that can help businesses live up to their social obligations while at the same time maintaining a level playing field.

8

human capital
the talents
and training of
individuals

Finally, business can do the things that business is supposed to be good at: efficient management, synergistic use of a range of kinds of **human capital**, and innovation. That stuff isn't just a good recipe for commercial success. It's an absolute obligation. And innovation is clearly the key among those three aptitudes. Efficiency—tightening our belts—will only get us so far. We desperately need a whole slew of truly brilliant new ideas for products, services, and productive processes over the next decade if we are to meet the collective challenge posed by changes in our environment. And it's foolish to expect government to provide those ideas. It's time for business to step up to the plate. There can be no better way to manifest a commitment to corporate citizenship than to be the kind of corporate citizen that sees a business model in trying to help us all cope with global warming.

Critical Thinking Questions

1. The author uses the phrase "(very likely)" twice in the first paragraph. Why has he used parentheses to enclose this phrase?

2. Why are the solutions to large-scale problems (such as global warming) often left to governments rather than individuals?

3. What is the overall thesis or central idea of this article? What is the author arguing for or against? What types of evidence does the author offer to support this thesis?

4. What does the author mean by the phrase "win-win changes" in paragraph 5?

5. The author states that businesses should work to protect the environment because that is the right thing to do. But what other benefits do such practices have for businesses?

6. Based on paragraph 7, who is the intended audience for this blog post?

7. According to the author, which is the most important of a business's "three aptitudes"? What role can this aptitude play in fighting global warming?

EXERCISE 8: WORKING COLLABORATIVELY

Directions: After answering the critical thinking questions on your own, pair up with a classmate and share your answers. As you discuss the questions, add to your answers the information you learn from your partner.

SOURCE 7: *THE HUFFINGTON POST* (ONLINE NEWSPAPER)

Climate Change: Countries That May Be Hit Hardest
Jeremy Hsu

This selection is taken from a widely read online newspaper, The Huffington Post. *It was originally published in* InnovationNewsDaily, *which, according to its Web site, "reports on futuristic technologies, innovations, disruptive ideas, and cool gadgets that will shape the future, and explain why it all matters and how it will affect your life."*

1   Rising seas threaten to drown island countries such as the Maldives and Kiribati in the era of global warming—a dire scenario that has forced leaders to plan for floating cities or consider moving their entire populations to neighboring countries. Most countries won't need to take such drastic steps to simply survive, but many more will similarly experience the uglier side of climate change.

2   The countries potentially facing the worst fates may not necessarily experience the greatest climate change, but instead lack the resources to cushion their people against climate-related disasters such as hurricanes, floods, heat waves and droughts. That has historically made a huge difference in rates of death or displacement from such events—Hurricane Jeanne killed just three people in the U.S. in 2004, but resulted in the deaths of more than 1,500 people in Haiti and displaced about 200,000 Haitians.

3   "This of course is different than future likelihood to suffer, but I believe that those who suffered most in the past are probably most vulnerable to future disasters, because they are unable to prepare for, cope with, and recover from these kinds of disasters," said J. Timmons Roberts, a professor of environmental studies and sociology at Brown University.

4   The most fortunate countries could fortify themselves against the worst of climate change and possibly take in climate change refugees from other parts of the world. Both historical data and climate model predictions have given some idea of what to expect.

Climate Change Hotspots

5   North America, Europe, and Asia can generally expect more severe heat waves and droughts alongside more intense storms related to flooding, said Michael Wehner, a climate scientist at Lawrence Berkeley National Laboratory in California. On the other hand, cold snaps could become less severe.

6   Other regions could see even more radical changes in their normal climates.

7   "Central America, the Caribbean, and the Mediterranean are projected to experience what is now considered drought as a new normal condition," Wehner told *InnovationNewsDaily*. "The impacts on agriculture could be severe, especially on impoverished nations."

8   The melting Arctic is experiencing some of the greatest warming—often with devastating consequences for local wildlife and people—but climate change's great-

Reprinted from the *Huffington Post*, August 14, 2012, Innovation News Daily.

est impact may take place in more densely populated regions. Jason Samson, a former Ph.D. candidate at McGill University in Canada, highlighted the relationship between climate conditions and population density in a 2011 paper published in the journal *Global Ecology and **Biogeography***.

"Strongly negative impacts of climate change are predicted in Central America, central South America, the Arabian Peninsula, Southeast Asia, and much of Africa," wrote Samson and his colleagues.

That paper's findings echo the vulnerable regions identified by the Intergovernmental Panel on Climate Change (IPCC)—the Arctic, Africa, small islands (such as the Maldives and Kiribati), and the Asian and African **megadeltas** where huge cities filled with millions of people face rising seas, **storm surges**, and flooding rivers.

Countries in the Danger Zone

So what countries face the greatest danger from climate change? Maplecroft, a British consultancy, has created a "Climate Change and Environment Risk Atlas," a list of 193 countries ranked by those most vulnerable to climate change because of factors such as population density or state of development.

The 2012 edition of the risk atlas identified 30 countries as being at extreme risk. The top 10 most at risk include: Haiti, Bangladesh, Sierra Leone, Zimbabwe, Madagascar, Cambodia, Mozambique, Democratic Republic of Congo, Malawi, and the Philippines.

Some countries with lower risk ratings still have danger zones that face "extreme risk" from climate change. Maplecroft pointed to the southwest of Brazil and China's coastal regions as examples, even though both countries rate as "medium risk" overall. Six of the world's fastest-growing cities also received "extreme risk" ratings: Calcutta in India, Manila in the Philippines, Jakarta in Indonesia, Dhaka and Chittagong in Bangladesh, and Addis Ababa in Ethiopia.

The countries in the best position to adapt to climate change's challenges mostly include those in Northern Europe, such as Finland, Ireland, Sweden, and Norway, CNN reported. Iceland topped the list, but the United States also had a relatively low risk rating.

Living with Climate Change

The climate risk assessments emphasized the wealth difference between the most and least vulnerable countries. That has proven historically true as well, Roberts said. He and a colleague, Bradley Parks, looked at 4,040 climate-related disasters from 1980 to 2003 in their book *A Climate of Injustice* (MIT Press, 2006).

"The rates [of people killed or made homeless], when adjusted for population, were 100 times higher in some African and Pacific islands than in the USA," Roberts explained.

But even developed countries such as the U.S. face risks when it comes to climate-related disasters—regardless of whatever future climate change may bring. Wehner suggested that climate change during his lifetime would be "manageable" as far as living in the U.S., but added that his grandchildren would face tougher choices.

Roberts, who lives in Rhode Island on top of a hill near Narragansett Bay, took an even more cautious approach about buying beachfront property even in the U.S.

---

biogeography
the study of the distribution of plants and animals across the world

megadelta
a delta is the fertile region at the end of a river; a *megadelta* is a very large delta

storm surges
higher levels of water at coastlines following heavy rains or winds

9
10
11
12
13
14
15
16
17
18

19 "While I would love to look out over the water, I would think twice before buying land or property, and especially before putting my family right at sea level, in a place that may suffer storm surge," Roberts said.

Critical Thinking Questions

1. What does the phrase "projected to experience" in paragraph 7 mean?

2. What is a "new normal condition" (paragraph 7), and how does this phrase relate to global warming and climate change?

3. What are some possible benefits of global warming?

4. Which type of visual or graphic aid would best represent the information presented in paragraphs 12–14?

5. What is the overall relationship between a country's level of wealth and its ability to adapt to climate change?

6. What does the term "developed country" (paragraph 17) mean? Provide examples of three developed countries.

7. Is climate change more likely to affect highly populated areas or lightly populated areas? Explain your answer.

EXERCISE 9: WORKING COLLABORATIVELY

Directions: After answering the critical thinking questions on your own, pair up with a classmate and share your answers. As you discuss the questions, add to your answers the information you learn from your partner.

SOURCE 8: GLOBAL WARNING? (INFOGRAPHIC)

Global Warning?

This infographic originally appeared on the Web site of Reusethisbag.com, a company that sells reusable shopping bags. On the "About Us" page of its Web site, the company quotes its president, Doug Lober: "We started the company as a way to give back and help the environment! We all grew up here in California and have seen plastic bags on the beach and in the water for years! Recently I was running on the beach and found 6 plastic bags during my mile and a half trip. Other than that, there isn't much one person alone can do to make a significant impact on this crazy world. But . . . if we spread the word about the importance of reusing our grocery bags, work together, and somehow this movement catches on, the resulting benefit is going to be huge!"

Global Warning?

Or a global-sized myth? We'll explore the two sides of the ever-growing debate on global warming and who's causing it.

phytoplankton
microscopic plants floating in water

The U.S.A. is home to 5.7% of the population and 25% of the Earth's CO₂ pollution.

70% of the Earth's oxygen is produced by ocean **phytoplankton.**

Ocean waters have warmed by a full degree Fahrenheit since 1970.

Scientific Consensus

The Climate Skeptics

I'm melting!

Arctic ice is rapidly disappearing, and the region may have its first completely ice-free summer by 2040 or earlier. Polar bears and indigenous cultures are already suffering from the sea-ice loss.

"Most climate science is based on computer modeling. **The climate is too complex and unpredictable for us to model accurately.**"

Courtesy of ReuseThisBag.com.

↑ **70%**
Coral Bleaching

Coral reefs, which are highly sensitive to small changes in water temperature, suffered the worst bleaching—or die-off in response to stress—ever recorded in 1998, with some areas seeing bleach rates of 70 percent.

Hottest in 400 years

The rate of warming is increasing. The 20th century's last two decades were the hottest in 400 years and possibly the warmest for several millennia.

2,500 Scientists   From   **130** Countries

Have concluded that **humans have caused** all or most of the current **planetary warming.**

"Climate change assumes a man-made cause so most research is conducted under that assumption. **We need more studies to examine possible natural causes.**"

"Climate sensitivity to CO_2 is relatively unknown and based on many assumptions. Further research is needed before we take drastic steps that might hurt us economically."

"Climate change skepticism among US citizens has risen 14% from 1997."

The Solution?

The future is still unclear. The amount by which the temperature will continue to rise depends at least in part on what actions are taken (or not taken) to limit the amount of **greenhouse gas** emissions globally.

↓ **50%**
↓ **80%**

(Greenhouse Gases)

Stabilizing GHG concentrations around 450-550 parts per million (ppm), or about twice pre-industrial levels. This is the point at which many believe the most damaging impacts of climate change can be avoided.

Is the change worth it? Is focusing on short term economic gain too risky in light of the state of Earth's precious **ecosystems**?

How much do we have to change? How much of a reduction in greenhouse gas emissions would be enough to have a significant effect?

ANSWER?

Depending on our choices, scientists predict that the Earth could eventually warm by as little as 2.5 degrees or as much as 10 degrees Fahrenheit.

2.5°   Or   **10°**
(By reacting)   (By not reacting)

greenhouse gas
the most common gases in "greenhouse gas" are carbon dioxide, methane, nitrous oxide, and fluorinated gases

ecosystem
a biological community of organisms that interact

Sources

http://news.nationalgeographic.com/news/2004/12/1206_041206_global_warming.html
http://science.howstuffworks.com/environmental/green-science/climate-skeptic1.htm
http://www.acoolerclimate.com/making-sense-of-global-warming-debate/http://www.website.com
http://www.drroyspencer.com/global-warming-natural-or-manmade/

Designed by Shawn Murdock

Critical Thinking Questions

1. List three points with regard to global warming on which most scientists agree.

2. List three arguments made by people who are skeptical of the claim that climate change is a serious issue.

3. Why are the numbers cited in this infographic—"2500 scientists from 130 countries"—possibly misleading?

4. What does the infographic mean when it refers to "pre-industrial levels" of greenhouse gas (GHG) emissions?

5. Does this infographic imply that global warming is inevitable, or does it imply that global warming can be stopped?

6. According to this source, what is the single best way to combat global warming?

EXERCISE 10: WORKING COLLABORATIVELY

Directions: After answering the critical thinking questions on your own, pair up with a classmate and share your answers. As you discuss the questions, add to your answers the information you learn from your partner.

SYNTHESIS AND INTEGRATION QUESTIONS AND ACTIVITIES

The following questions and activities ask you to synthesize information from two or more sources.

1. **Comparing Tone and Author's Purpose**. Compare the tone of Source 1 and Source 2. How does the writer's purpose in Source 1 differ from the writer's purpose in Source 2?

2. **Summarizing Sources**. Summarize what you have learned about the role of global warming in the extinction of species. Use information from Source 1 (especially paragraph 10) and Source 4.

3. **Examining Authors' Viewpoints**. Compare and contrast the author's view of time in Source 4 and Source 5. Why is the study of time so essential to an understanding of global warming and climate change?

4. **Comparing Sources.** How and why are some of the conclusions of Source 5 incompatible with the information provided in Source 1?

5. **Determining Agreement and Disagreement Between Sources**. Would Professor J. Timmons Roberts, who is quoted in Source 7, agree with the author's thesis in Source 2? Why or why not?

6. **Creating a Visual Summary**. Create a graphic or visual aid to summarize, in one place, the place-specific information found in Sources 5 and 7.

7. **Finding Agreement Among Sources**. Based on your reading of three or more of these sources, including Source 8, what facts do most people agree on with regard to climate change?

8. **Finding Disagreement Among Sources**. Based on your reading of three or more of these source, including Source 8, what are the major areas of disagreement?

9. **Identifying Statements of Opinion**. Using three or more sources, underline at least five statements of opinion.

10. **Assessing Reliability.** Place the sources in order from most reliable/ most unbiased to least reliable/most biased. Be prepared to explain your ranking.

11. **Preparing a Fact Sheet**. Prepare a list of ten facts regarding global warming and climate change that would be useful in writing a response paper on the issue of global warming.

Index